PEARSON
my World GEOGRAPHY

Europe and Russia

PEARSON

Boston, Massachusetts • Chandler, Arizona • Glenview, Illinois • Upper Saddle River, New Jersey

D1088958

ISBN-13 978-0-13-369592-2
ISBN-10 0-13-369592-1

16 16

Master Teachers and Contributing Authors

George Sabato
Past President, California Council
    for the Social Studies
Placerville Union School District
Placerville, California

Michael Yell
Past President, National Council
    for the Social Studies
Hudson Middle School
Hudson, Wisconsin

Program Authors

Gregory H. Chu
Professor and Chair of Department
    of Geography
University of Wisconsin-La Crosse
La Crosse, Wisconsin

Don Holtgrieve
Department of Planning, Public
    Policy, and Management
University of Oregon
Eugene, Oregon

Susan Hardwick
Department of Geography
University of Oregon
Eugene, Oregon

Program Consultant

Grant Wiggins
President of Authentic Education
Hopewell, New Jersey

Teacher Consultants

James F. Dowd IV
Pasadena, California

Susan M. Keane
Rochester Memorial School
Rochester, Massachusetts

Timothy T. Sprain
Lincoln Middle School
La Crosse, Wisconsin

Marilyn Weiser
North Dakota Geographic
    Alliance Coordinator
Minot State University
Minot, North Dakota

CONTENTS

Europe and Russia

Serhiy, from Ukraine
in Eastern Europe
◀

Yasmin, who lives
in Sweden, in
Western Europe
▼

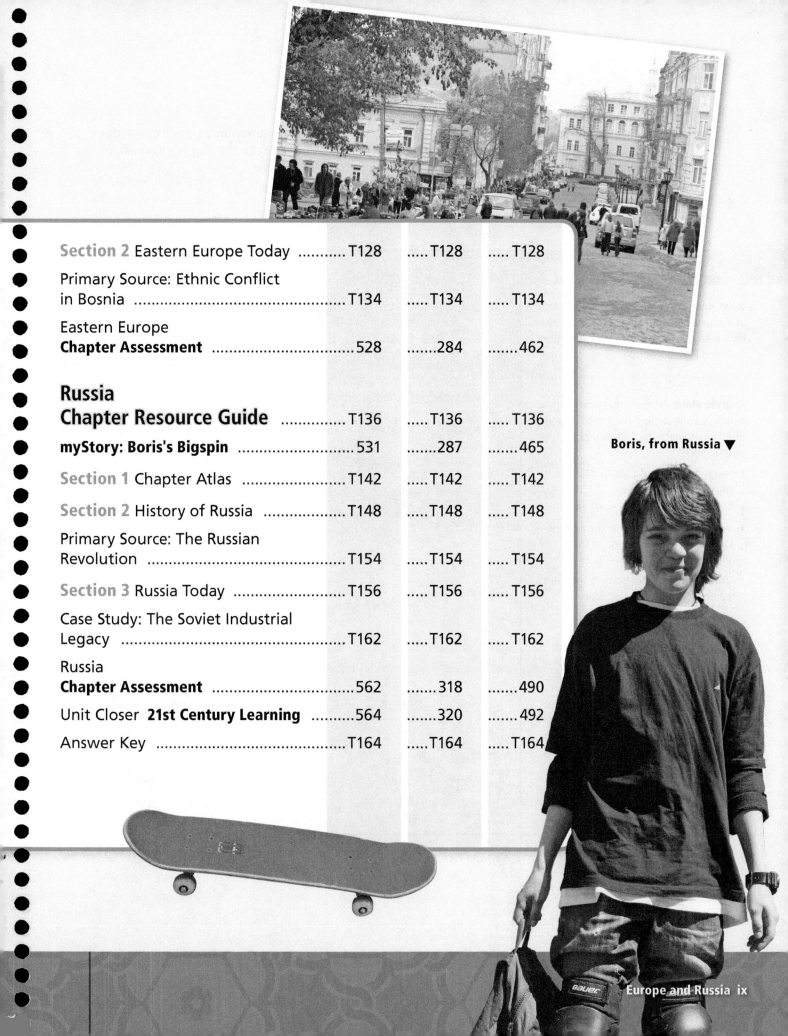

Boris, from Russia ▼

Europe and Russia

- Prepare students to learn about Europe and Russia and activate prior knowledge by creating KWL (Know, Want to know, Learned) tables and filling out only the K and W columns. Correct any misconceptions or misinformation in the tables.

- Have students preview maps, photos, and other visuals, and predict what they will learn about Europe and Russia.

GUIDE ON THE SIDE

What time is it there? Have students look at the time zone display to determine by how many hours the times in Washington, D.C. and Paris differ. (six)

Analyze Maps Point out the political map and time zone display. Ask the following questions to help students gather information.

- What is the largest country in this region? (Russia)
- What is the capital of Spain? (Madrid)
- What island nations lie in the Atlantic Ocean? (Iceland, Ireland, United Kingdom)
- What body of water borders Southern Europe? (Mediterranean Sea)

Regional Overview

Europe and Russia

The many countries of Europe plus Russia reach from the Atlantic Ocean to the Pacific Ocean. Russia spreads over two continents, Europe and Asia. More than 590 million people live in Europe with another 140 million in Russia. Most live in urban areas. More than 230 languages are spoken here, such as English, French, Spanish, Basque, Greek, Finnish, and Russian.

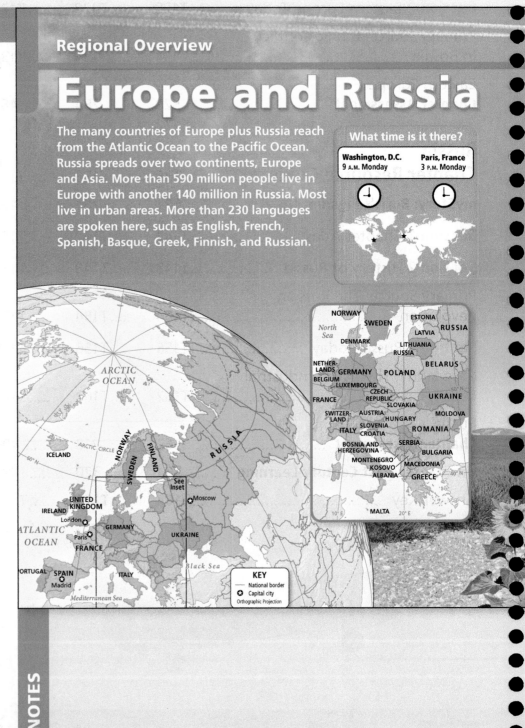

What time is it there?

Washington, D.C.	Paris, France
9 A.M. Monday	3 P.M. Monday

KEY
— National border
⊙ Capital city
Orthographic Projection

NOTES

THE UNIT AHEAD

In this unit students will

- study the geography of Europe and Russia.
- get to know three teenagers from Sweden, Ukraine, and Russia.
- go On Assignment in Europe and Russia.

- make connections among the physical geography, history, politics, economics, and culture of Europe and Russia.

The Unit Ahead

→ **Chapter 8**   Ancient and Medieval Europe

→ **Chapter 9**   Europe in Modern Times

→ **Chapter 10**   Western Europe

→ **Chapter 11**   Eastern Europe

→ **Chapter 12**   Russia

my worldgeography.com

Plan your trip online by doing a Data Discovery Activity and watching the myStory Videos of the region's teens.

my Story

Yasmin
Age: 18
Home: Bjärred, Sweden
Chapter 10

my Story

Serhiy
Age: 16
Home: Bezpalche, Ukraine
Chapter 11

my Story

Boris
Age: 15
Home: Moscow, Russia
Chapter 12

A field of sunflowers and lavender in France

GUIDE ON THE SIDE

my Story

Make Predictions Make predictions about the teens whom students will get to know in this unit.

- Yasmin lives in Sweden but frequently visits relatives in Spain. In what way might she benefit from drawing on more than one culture? (Sample: She might enjoy the music, art, or food of several different cultures.)

- Serhiy lives on his family's farm in a small village in Ukraine. How might his life be different from yours? (Samples: hard physical work, no malls or entertainment)

- Boris enjoys riding his skateboard around Moscow. What other interests do you think he might have? (Sample: other extreme sports like snowboarding)

NOTES

GEOGRAPHY

Scandinavian Peninsula The two nations of Norway and Sweden share the Scandinavian Peninsula, which is approximately 1,150 miles long. Each country extends the length of the peninsula, with Norway taking up the western side and Sweden taking up the eastern side. The northern reaches of the peninsula stretch into the Arctic Circle. A mountainous mass extends the entire length of the peninsula, but its character is quite different within the borders of each of the two countries. In Norway, the mountains are steeply rugged and stretch to the coast, where fjords cut sharply into them. In Sweden, the mountains have more gentle slopes, which build in a gradual incline from the coast along the Baltic Sea.

GUIDE ON THE SIDE

Analyze Visuals Ask students to look at the labeled satellite photo, which shows key physical patterns in the region.

- What type of landforms dominate the Scandinavian Peninsula? (hills, mountains, and plains)

- In which direction do the Alps extend? (east–west)

- What part of Europe might be best for farming? Explain. (the plains in the north because they are level)

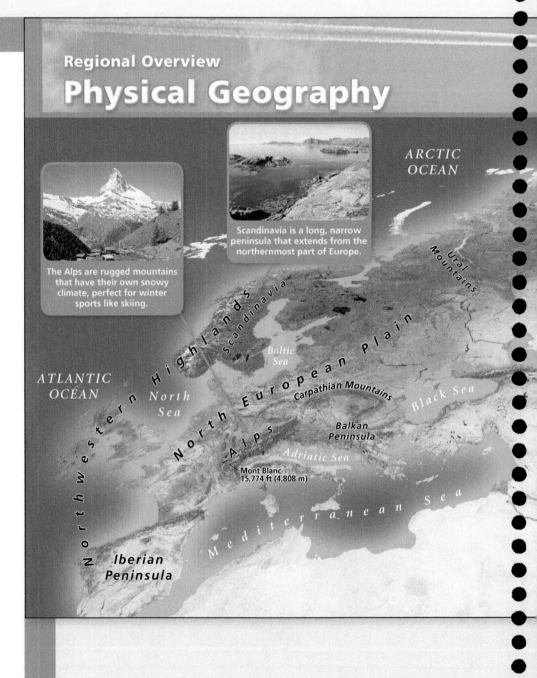

Regional Overview
Physical Geography

The Alps are rugged mountains that have their own snowy climate, perfect for winter sports like skiing.

Scandinavia is a long, narrow peninsula that extends from the northernmost part of Europe.

ARCTIC OCEAN

Ural Mountains

Scandinavia

Northwestern Highlands

Baltic Sea

North European Plain

Carpathian Mountains

Black Sea

ATLANTIC OCEAN

North Sea

Alps

Balkan Peninsula

Adriatic Sea

Mont Blanc
15,774 ft (4,808 m)

Mediterranean Sea

Iberian Peninsula

NOTES

QUICK FACTS

The Highest Alps The Alps, a mountain chain known for its rugged, scenic beauty, have dozens of peaks that rise higher than 4,000 meters (13,123 feet). The five mountains with the highest elevations are as follows:

- Mont Blanc, France, 15,771 feet
- Dufourspitze, Switzerland, 15,203 feet
- Nordend, Switzerland, 15,121 feet
- Zumsteinspitze, Switzerland, 14,970 feet
- Signalkuppe, Switzerland, 14,947 feet

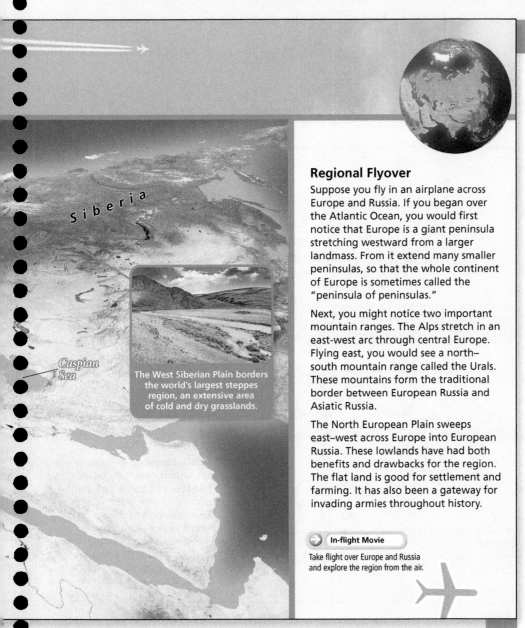

Siberia

Caspian Sea

The West Siberian Plain borders the world's largest steppes region, an extensive area of cold and dry grasslands.

GUIDE ON THE SIDE

Regional Flyover

Suppose you fly in an airplane across Europe and Russia. If you began over the Atlantic Ocean, you would first notice that Europe is a giant peninsula stretching westward from a larger landmass. From it extend many smaller peninsulas, so that the whole continent of Europe is sometimes called the "peninsula of peninsulas."

Next, you might notice two important mountain ranges. The Alps stretch in an east-west arc through central Europe. Flying east, you would see a north–south mountain range called the Urals. These mountains form the traditional border between European Russia and Asiatic Russia.

The North European Plain sweeps east–west across Europe into European Russia. These lowlands have had both benefits and drawbacks for the region. The flat land is good for settlement and farming. It has also been a gateway for invading armies throughout history.

▶ **In-flight Movie**

Take flight over Europe and Russia and explore the region from the air.

Analyze Visuals Read Regional Flyover and ask the following questions about the labeled satellite photo.

- What part of Europe appears to have sparse vegetation? (Southern Europe)

- Why do you think the Urals were chosen as the traditional border between Europe and Asia? (Sample: They extend north and south for a long way and make an obvious division.)

- Which is larger in area, the continent of Europe or the country of Russia? (Russia)

▶ **In-flight Movie**

Before playing the In-flight movie, ask
- What have you seen or would you expect to see while looking out the window of a plane?
- What can you find out about a place by flying overhead?
- How is this information important to understanding the geography of a place?

NOTES

GEOGRAPHY

The Sami Although the far northern regions are among the least densely populated lands in Europe, a group of people called the Sami live there. The Sami are descended from nomadic peoples; their traditional way of life was based on reindeer herding. Today, the Sami live in the northernmost parts of Norway, Sweden, Finland, and European Russia. Very few are still nomads; most live permanently in modern housing.

Some work in farming or fishing. Others are employed in commercial jobs.

For a long time, the national governments of the four countries tried to force the Sami to assimilate. As a result, most Sami speak the language of the country in which they live, and many no longer speak Sami at all. The Sami languages are part of the Finno-Ugric language family.

GUIDE ON THE SIDE

Where People Live

Analyze Maps Point out the maps of Europe About 1890 and Europe Today. Have students use these maps with the text to better understand the human geography of Europe and Russia.

- In 1890, what nations and empires bordered Russia? (Sweden-Norway, Germany, Austria-Hungary, Romania, and Ottoman empire)

- Compare the two maps. During which time period did Europe have more countries? (today)

Regional Overview
Human Geography

Europe About 1890
Europe was composed of large empires at the end of the 1800s.

London about 1890

Europe Today
In the 1900s, large empires fell, leading to the creation of many smaller countries.

London today

Where People Live

Throughout history, the population density of Europe has been high because of its temperate climate, miles of coastline and rivers, and acres of good farmland.

Russia, on the other hand, is the largest nation on Earth, but about 80 percent of the population live in the smaller, European part of the country. This is because only about 7 percent of Russia's land is good for farming, and its harbors are blocked by ice for months. Russia is a land of extremes—harsh climate, rugged terrain, and great distances.

HISTORY

The Slavs and Their Languages Europe has three major language families: Germanic, Romance, and Slavic. More Europeans speak Slavic languages than languages from the other two groups. The Slavic languages are found mostly in Southern and Eastern Europe. They include Belarusian, Bulgarian, Czech, Macedonian, Polish, Russian, Serbo-Croatian, Slovak, Slovene, and Ukrainian. The Slavic peoples had their origins in Asia. They migrated west and south into Europe beginning about A.D. 400 or 500. Historically, the Slavs have remained divided into smaller ethnic groups. Movements to unite all the Slavs under the leadership of a dominant group such as Serbians or Russians have ultimately failed and have often sparked conflicts.

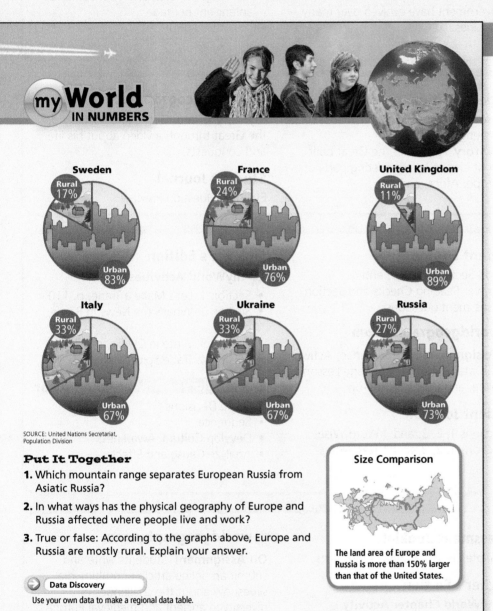

myWorld IN NUMBERS

Sweden
Rural 17%
Urban 83%

France
Rural 24%
Urban 76%

United Kingdom
Rural 11%
Urban 89%

Italy
Rural 33%
Urban 67%

Ukraine
Rural 33%
Urban 67%

Russia
Rural 27%
Urban 73%

SOURCE: United Nations Secretariat, Population Division

Put It Together

1. Which mountain range separates European Russia from Asiatic Russia?

2. In what ways has the physical geography of Europe and Russia affected where people live and work?

3. True or false: According to the graphs above, Europe and Russia are mostly rural. Explain your answer.

Data Discovery

Use your own data to make a regional data table.

Size Comparison

The land area of Europe and Russia is more than 150% larger than that of the United States.

myWorld in Numbers

Analyze Charts Point out the graphs and use the questions below to help students analyze the data and draw conclusions.

- Which country or countries shown here are most urbanized? (United Kingdom)

- Which country or countries are least urbanized? (Italy and Ukraine)

Data Discovery

Students can practice chart and graph skills online with the Data Discovery features on Europe and Russia. Students can use their trackers to save data for their On Assignment stories later in the unit.

PUT IT TOGETHER 1. the Ural Mountains **2.** Europeans tend to live where the climate is milder, the land is good for farming, and bodies of water are near. **3.** False—every graph shows the rural population as much less than 50 percent.

ANSWERS

Plan With Understanding by Design*

Chapter Objectives
Begin With the End in Mind

Students will demonstrate the following enduring understandings:
- Democracy and representative government have evolved over many centuries.
- Political power involves a complex set of relationships.
- Our religions, arts, and sciences have an ancient heritage.

Connect
Make Learning Meaningful

Student Edition
- **Essential Question** What are the challenges of diversity?
- **myStory** Alexander the Great built a vast empire by conquering parts of Europe, Africa, and Asia.

my worldgeography.com
myStory Video Get to know Alexander the Great through a video about his life and conquests.

Student Journal
Essential Question Preview

Experience
Teach Knowledge and Skills

Student Edition
- Read Sections 1, 2, 3, and 4.
- Answer Reading Checks and Section Assessment questions.

my worldgeography.com

On Assignment myStory Video, Active Atlas, Data Discovery, Language Lesson, Timeline, and Culture Close-up

Student Journal
- Sections 1, 2, 3, and 4 Word Wise
- Sections 1, 2, 3, and 4 Take Notes

Teacher's Edition
myWorld Activities
- Section 1: Let's Make a Trade, p. T10
- Section 2: What's the News in Rome, p. T18
- Section 3: Write in Cyrillic, p. T26
- Section 4: Trade Spices Up Life, p. T34

21st Century Learning Online Tutor
- Make Decisions
- Sequence
- Develop Cultural Awareness
- Analyze Cause and Effect

Understand
Assess Understanding

Assessment Booklet
- Chapter Tests
- Benchmark Tests

Teacher's Edition
myWorld Chapter Activity
Students examine photographs of artifacts, fill out field reports, and make a timeline of artifacts.

Student Journal
Essential Question Writer's Workshop

my worldgeography.com

On Assignment Students write and submit an online article or multimedia slideshow about the challenges of diversity in ancient and medieval Europe.

Success Tracker™
Online at myworldgeography.com
Administer chapter tests and remediate understanding.

Student Edition
Chapter Assessment

Connect to the Essential Question

 Essential Question

What are the challenges of diversity?

Use the Essential Question poster and follow these steps to help students understand the Essential Question.

Connect to Their Lives

1. Ask students to define *diversity*. (If students have already studied this Essential Question, encourage them to note changes in the way they define or think about diversity.) Point out that this term refers to a wide range of differences that may exist among a group of people. Focusing on tastes and interests, encourage students to identify the different tastes among friends, students, or members of their community. Invite them to describe how people express these different tastes.

2. Have students list the ways people express differences in taste. Post the following chart for them to complete, or have students turn to the *Essential Question Preview* page in their **Student Journals.**

Categories	Clothing	Food	Music	Interests
Expressions of Different Tastes				

3. Discuss students' responses. Ask, Do some differences in taste encourage or discourage interaction with other groups?

Connect to the Content

4. Now have students brainstorm types of diversity within a country or region. Examples might include the religious or ethnic differences within the population.

5. Ask students to identify the challenges of such diversity. Post the following chart for them to complete. (Help them to understand what might be included in each category. For example, one of the challenges of language diversity might be the inability to communicate with others.)

Type of Diversity	Ethnic	Religous	Political	Linguistic
Challenges				

6. After previewing the chapter, have students make chapter-related predictions on the *Essential Question Preview* page in the **Student Journal.**

7. Remind students that they will answer a prompt related to the Essential Question on each section's *Take Notes* page in the **Student Journal.**

Explore  my worldgeography.com

Welcome to myWorldGeography

http://www.myworldgeography.com

ON ASSIGNMENT: Ancient and Medieval Europe

For this chapter's assignment, students will
- take a digital trip to Europe during ancient and medieval times.
- take on the role of a journalist.
- gather notes, images, and data for their story throughout their journey.
- write a compelling news article or create a multimedia slideshow on this chapter's Essential Question: *What are the challenges of diversity?*

ITINERARY

During their trip, students will make the following stops:

 myStory Video

Learn more about the life of Alexander the Great.

 Active Atlas

Read physical, political, and special purpose maps.

 Data Discovery

Study charts about life in ancient and medieval Europe.

 Timeline

Learn about invasions of the Roman Empire.

 Culture Close-up

Explore life on a medieval manor.

While on their trip, students will practice the following skills:
- **Interpret** graphic representations of data.
- **Synthesize** information into an interesting article.
- **Evaluate** the challenges of diversity.

TakingITGlobal for Educators

Extend the reach of every lesson by helping students connect to a global community of young people with common interests and concerns. Visit myworldgeography.com to
- explore Country Pages relating to Europe.
- delve deeper into this chapter's Essential Question, *What are the challenges of diversity?*
- find online alternatives to and solutions for the Unit Closer Activity.

  my worldgeography.com

TEACHER CENTER

Preview and assign student materials, enrich your teaching, and track student progress with the following resources:
- Online Lesson Planning and Resource Library
- Presentations for Projection
- Online Teacher's Edition and Ancillaries
- Google Earth Links™

Assess Enduring Understandings

 myWorld Chapter Activity   **Step-by-Step Instructions**   **2 hr**

Piecing Together the Past

Teach this activity at the end of the chapter to assess enduring understandings.

OBJECTIVES

Students will demonstrate the following enduring understandings:

- Democracy and representative government have evolved over many centuries.
- Political power involves a complex set of relationships.
- Our religions, arts, and sciences have an ancient heritage.

Students will provide the following evidence of understanding:

- Field Report
- Timeline of Artifacts

LEARNING STYLES

- Visual
- Logical

MATERIALS

- Activity Support: Student Instructions and Rubric, p. T6
- Activity Support: Field Report, p. T7
- Activity Cards: #43–48
  43. Archaeological Site A
  44. Archaeological Site B
  45. Archaeological Site C
  46. Archaeological Site D
  47. Archaeological Site E
  48. Archaeological Site F

Activity Steps

1. **Set Expectations** Explain that groups will visit six archaeological sites. At each one, an Activity Card will show artifacts from a culture of Europe. Groups will describe the artifacts, infer how they were used, and identify the culture. Tell students to fill out *Activity Support: Field Report* for each site.

2. **Field Report**
   - Place the Activity Cards at different stations in the room. Refer to the stations as archaeological sites.
   - Divide the class into small groups. Each group will visit all six sites in the order you designate. Explain that the sites are not in chronological order.
   - Give each student a copy of *Activity Support: Student Instructions and Rubric* and *Activity Support: Field Report*. Every student is to record data about each site, so they will need to re-create the *Field Report* in their notebooks.

   ELL **Intermediate** Provide these definitions: **archaeologist**—a person who studies the past by examining the things people left behind; **artifact**—an object, such as a tool, made by a human.

3. **Class Discussion** For the first site, ask a student from each group to share what the group wrote on the field report. If groups drew different conclusions, ask them to give their reasons. Use the same discussion process for each site.

   L1 **Special Needs** To help students who have trouble with aural processing, write on the board an outline of what to share: 1. What the artifact was and how it was used; 2. The artifact's date; 3. What culture they think lived at the site.

4. **Timelines** After the class discussion, students should return to their groups. Each group should work together to make an illustrated timeline.

   ELL **Intermediate/Early Advanced** Tell what the abbreviations B.C. and A.D. stand for. Explain that the designation goes after the date when it is B.C. but before the date when it is A.D. Give examples.

KEY **Time**   **Individual**   **Pairs**   **Small Group**    **Whole Class**

Name_____ Class_____ Date_____

myWorld Chapter Activity Support   **Student Instructions and Rubric**

Piecing Together the Past

Activity Instructions Read the following summary of your myWorld Chapter Activity. Follow your teacher's directions for more information.

1. Your group will visit six archaeological sites in Europe and study the artifacts at each one. Decide whether the culture that lived at each one was ancient Greece, ancient Rome, early Christian, the Byzantine Empire, or medieval Western Europe. (Some cultures have more than one site.)

2. Each member of your group should record information about all six sites. Your teacher will tell you which site to visit first. Study the Activity Card you find there. Identify the artifacts, and as a group complete *Activity Support: Field Report.* Some sites may have fewer than three artifacts.

3. Go to all six sites as directed by your teacher. At each site, study the card and fill out a copy of *Activity Support: Field Report* or a copy of the page in your notebook.

4. After you have visited all the sites, share your conclusions with the class. If the other groups drew different conclusions, listen to them and then decide which seems right.

5. After the discussion, return to your group. Together you will make a timeline. Place the artifacts listed in the *Field Report* at appropriate places. Share your completed timeline in class.

myWorld Chapter Activity Rubric	3 Exceeds Understanding	2 Reaches Understanding	1 Approaches Understanding
Group Participation	Participates fully in analyzing the data, listens to others, contributes to the group's conclusion, encourages group to make a detailed timeline	Helps analyze the data and participates in the discussion; discusses the timeline and does an equal share of work to complete the timeline	Able to describe the general opinion of the group; expresses some ideas about the timeline but does not help complete it
Field Report	Fully completes the chart and answers the questions on the Field Report with great detail	Completes the chart and questions on the Field Report	Completes less than half the chart and questions on the Field Report
Discussion	Offers opinions about two or more sites and supports those opinions with reasons	Offers an opinion about one or two sites but rarely supports opinions with sufficient reasons	Does not offer opinions about any sites, or does not give any reasons

Name_____ Class_____ Date _____

Piecing Together the Past

Directions You will fill out the form below for each of the six archaeological sites that your group visits. To do this, you will need to copy the report on five additional sheets of paper or pages in your notebook. You will use this information later to take part in a discussion and to make a group timeline.

Field Report

Archaeological site _____

	Artifact	Artifact	Artifact
Describe the artifact.			
What is the artifact's date?			
What was it made of?			
What was its purpose?			

What culture do you think lived here? Why?

_____

_____

Timeline Copy this timeline on your own paper, making it larger. You can use colors or patterns to represent each culture. Then write the name of each artifact at the appropriate places on the timeline. You may add drawings of some of the artifacts if you want.

| Greek |
| Roman/Early Christian |
| Byzantine |
| Medieval |

| 800 B.C. | 400 B.C. | 0 | A.D. 400 | A.D. 800 | A.D. 1200 |

T7

Ancient and Medieval Europe

- Introduce the Essential Question so that students will be able to understand the big ideas of this chapter (see earlier page, Connect to the Essential Question).
- Help students prepare to learn about Ancient and Medieval Europe by looking at the chapter's maps, charts, and photos.

- Have students make and record chapter predictions with the *Essential Question Preview* in the **Student Journal.**
- Ask them to analyze the maps on this page.

GUIDE ON THE SIDE

 Explore the Essential Question . . .

Have students complete the Essential Question Writer's Workshop in their **Student Journal** to demonstrate in-depth understanding of the question in the context of this chapter.

Analyze Maps Point out that the map shows where ethnic groups lived in ancient times.

- What ethnic group lived in Macedonia? (Balkan peoples)
- What ethnic group lived north of the Black Sea? (the Scythians)
- Where did the Celtic peoples live? (Gaul and Britain)

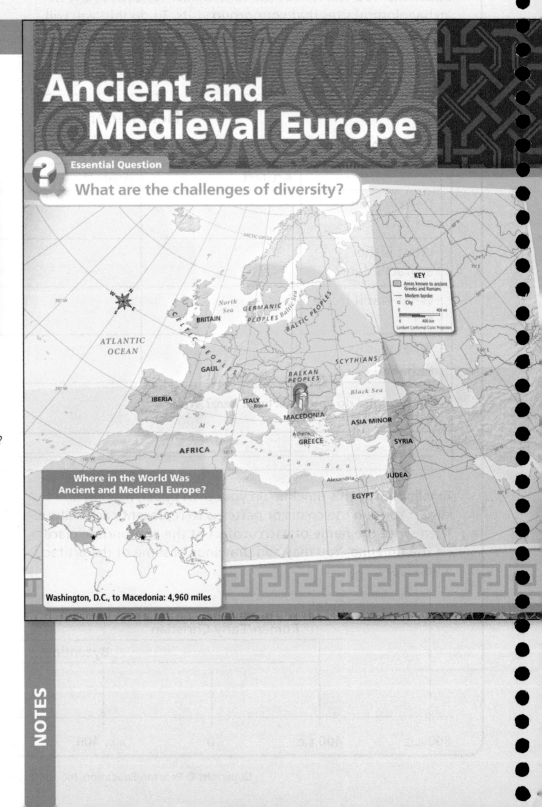

Ancient and Medieval Europe

? Essential Question

What are the challenges of diversity?

KEY
- Areas known to ancient Greeks and Romans
- Modern border
- City

0   400 mi
0   400 km
Lambert Conformal Conic Projection

ARCTIC CIRCLE

North Sea   GERMANIC PEOPLES   Baltic Sea   BALTIC PEOPLES

CELTIC PEOPLES

BRITAIN

ATLANTIC OCEAN

GAUL

IBERIA

ITALY
Rome

BALKAN PEOPLES

SCYTHIANS

Black Sea

MACEDONIA

Athens GREECE

ASIA MINOR

SYRIA

AFRICA

Mediterranean Sea

Alexandria

JUDEA

EGYPT

Where in the World Was Ancient and Medieval Europe?

Washington, D.C., to Macedonia: 4,960 miles

INTRODUCE my Story

Get students excited to learn about Ancient and Medieval Europe by first experiencing the region through the eyes of Alexander the Great, who conquered a vast empire.

• Read myStory and watch the myStory Video about his life.

• Have students complete *A Prophecy Fulfilled* in the **Student Journal** to prepare to learn what was prophesied and how Alexander the Great made the prophecy come true.

my Story

A Prophecy Fulfilled

In this section, you'll read about Alexander the Great, a Macedonian warrior who conquered much of the world known to the ancient Greeks. *What does Alexander's story tell you about life in the ancient Greek world?*

Explore the Essential Question
• at my worldgeography.com
• using the myWorld Chapter Activity
• with the Student Journal

Story by Michael Chatlien for myWorld Online

In 334 B.C., Alexander the Great led his army from Europe into Asia. His troops came from Macedonia and Greece. Alexander wanted to defeat the Persian forces led by Darius III. The two armies met at the Granicus River in present-day Turkey. With 75,000 troops, Darius III seemed to have the advantage. Alexander had only 35,000 soldiers. Even so, he felt that he was destined to defeat Darius and conquer Asia. Indeed, his upbringing prepared him to become a great ruler.

Alexander's father was Philip II, the king of Macedonia. His mother was Olympias, a princess from western Greece. Olympias taught Alexander that he was descended from the great warrior Achilles. And Philip convinced his son that Macedonian kings were descended from the god Hercules.

At age 12, Alexander tamed Bucephalus. The name means "ox's head" and refers to the wild horse's massive head.

GUIDE ON THE SIDE

A Prophecy Fulfilled

• **Cause and Effect** Why did Alexander lead his army into Asia? (He wanted to defeat the Persians led by Darius.)

• **Identify Evidence** What evidence shows that it was going to be difficult for Alexander to defeat Darius? (Alexander had only 35,000 troops, while Darius had 75,000.)

• **Identify Main Ideas** What type of family was Alexander born into? (His father was a king; his mother was a princess; his family believed it was descended from a great warrior named Achilles and from the god Hercules.)

→ On Assignment

Have students go to myworldgeography.com to receive their assignments from a virtual newspaper editor. Students will explore Europe and beyond in order to better understand the story of Alexander the Great and the Key Ideas of the chapter.

NOTES

HISTORY

Philip of Macedon (382 to 336 B.C.) Alexander's father was King Philip II of Macedonia, a country to the north of Greece. After Philip's father died, Philip's two older brothers each ruled in turn. During their reigns, Macedonia experienced much conflict. Philip came to the throne in 359 B.C. For the first year of his rule, he made concessions and paid off enemies to buy time as he developed a disciplined, innovative army. Then he expanded Macedonia through a series of marriages, alliances, and conquests. Athens declared war in 340 B.C., and Philip and his troops invaded Greece the next year. He won the war through skillful use of his cavalry. As the conqueror of Greece, Philip was much hated. He also had a falling out with his queen. An assassin stabbed him to death as he attended his daughter's wedding in 336 B.C.

GUIDE ON THE SIDE

- **Predict** How well prepared do you think Alexander was to rule? Explain. (Sample: He was very well prepared because he had studied science, the arts, politics, sports, and combat.)

- **Analyze Text** Read the quotation that accompanies the picture of Alexander speaking to his troops. How do you think that declaration made the troops feel? (Sample: It inspired them to be as courageous as Alexander.)

- **Infer** Why do you think Alexander had his warriors and horses move in a phalanx, or a wedge-shaped formation? (Sample: to force an opening in the enemy line)

The Greeks perfected the phalanx, a wedge-shaped battle formation.

The Persian king Darius faced Alexander in battle three times.

"There is no part of my body remaining free of wounds. I have been wounded with the sword, shot with arrows, and hit with stones for the sake of your lives, your glory, and your wealth."

The respected philosopher Aristotle taught the young Alexander. From him, Alexander learned about science, the arts, and politics. While he studied, he also trained in sports and combat. When Alexander's father Philip conquered Greece, Alexander commanded a division in his father's army.

Philip then wanted to invade Asia, but his plans were cut short when a bodyguard murdered him. So at the age of 20, Alexander became king of Macedonia and Greece. Two years later, he invaded the Persian Empire, seeking to be ruler of Asia as well.

At the shores of the Granicus River, Alexander readied his troops for combat. It would be the first of three battles against the Persians. The Greek historian Arrian described how both armies waited at the edge of the river ready to attack. Alexander shouted for his men to show courage:

66 Alexander leaped upon his steed, ordering those about him to follow, and exhorting [urging] them to show themselves valiant men. 99

The cavalry attacked first, with warriors and horses moving in a phalanx formation. Archers and spear throwers then joined in to support the assault.

CULTURE

The Gordian Knot According to legend, the Gordian knot was found in the city of Gordium. In one version of the legend, the knot fastened the yoke of a chariot that had belonged to King Gordius, ancient founder of the city, to a pole. The reason the knot was impossible to undo was that the ends of the rope were hidden inside the knot. In some legends, Alexander figured out how to untie the knot by taking out the pole and finding the rope ends. However, the legend in which he cut the knot is the one that is best known, perhaps because it shows Alexander's bold, impulsive character. "Cutting the Gordian knot" is still used as a saying to mean finding a quick and unexpected solution to a complex problem.

Alexander raises his sword to cut apart the Gordian knot.

Alexander is said to have wept when he looked out over his empire, sad because there were no more worlds to conquer.

Next the foot soldiers joined in and dealt the crushing blow. The modern historian Robin Lane Fox describes Alexander's army in combat:

> 66 Nobody who faced them ever forgot the sight; they kept time to their roaring of the Greeks' ancient war cry, Alalalalai; their scarlet cloaks billowed, and the measured swishing of their sarissas [long pikes], up and down, left and right, seemed to frightened observers like the quills of a metal porcupine. 99

The Greeks crushed the Persians. Darius and his troops retreated eastward. Alexander needed more troops, so he set off to find new recruits to join his army. On his march, Alexander came upon the legendary Gordian knot. This knot was tied to an ox cart. An ancient prophecy stated that the person who untied the knot would rule Asia. Alexander first tried to undo the huge knot and could not. Frustrated, he drew his sword and cut it with one stroke. This may not be a true story, but Alexander did go on to fulfill the prophecy.

Later, at the battle of Issus, the Greeks were again victorious. Darius escaped, but he offered Alexander a peace treaty. He said he would give Alexander a large sum of money and the Persian lands west of the Euphrates River. Alexander's general Parmenio advised his commander to accept the terms—but Alexander had greater ambitions.

He faced Darius again at Gaugamela. With a third victory here, Alexander took control of much of Southwest Asia. It was still not enough—Alexander wanted India.

After eight long years of marching and fighting, the army reached the western border of India. Alexander's troops had become homesick and wanted to turn back. Coenus, an old commander, gathered his courage as he spoke for his fellow soldiers,

> 66 Do not lead us now against our will. . . .But, rather, return of your own accord to your own land. . .and carry to the home of your fathers these victories great and small. 99

Alexander reluctantly agreed to return to Macedonia, but he would not make it home. He died of a mysterious illness at Babylon in 323 B.C.

Alexander's empire stretched from Macedonia and Greece in the west to the borders of India in the east. This region included much of the world that was known to the ancient Greeks. Indeed, the prophecy of the Gordian knot had come true.

 myStory Video

Join Alexander the Great as he conquers a vast empire.

GUIDE ON THE SIDE

- **Express an Opinion** What do you think of Alexander's solution to the problem of the Gordian knot? Explain. (Samples: He cheated by cutting the knot. He was smart not to waste time trying to untie it.)

- **Compare Viewpoints** Reread the advice Parmenio gave Alexander and notice whether Alexander followed it. Restate their views of the situation in your own words. (Sample: Parmenio was saying, "Take this deal. It's as good as it's going to get." Alexander was saying, "No, I know I can win.")

- **Compare and Contrast** How was Alexander different from his troops? (The troops wanted to go home once they reached India; Alexander wanted to keep building an empire.)

 myStory Video

Have students watch the video at myworldgeography.com about Alexander's life as the conqueror of a vast empire. Tell students to use their trackers to take notes on how Alexander won victories.

SECTION 1 LESSON PLAN

Ancient Greece

OBJECTIVES

Students will know

- Greek contributions to philosophy, learning, and the arts.
- forms of government that developed in ancient Greece, especially direct democracy.

Students will be able to

- label an outline map of Greece.
- compare and contrast Sparta and Athens.

SET EXPECTATIONS

In this section, students will

- read Ancient Greece.
- plan a trading voyage.
- go On Assignment in ancient Europe and explore maps of ancient Greece.

CORE CONCEPTS

You may wish to teach or reteach the following lessons from the Core Concepts Handbook:

- The Arts, pp. 94–95
- Cultural Diffusion and Change, pp. 96–97
- Foundations of Government, pp. 104–105

KEY

Differentiated Instruction	English Language Instruction
L1 Special Needs **L2** Extra Support	**ELL** Beginner **ELL** Early Intermediate **ELL** Intermediate
L3 On-Level **L4** Challenge	**ELL** Early Advanced **ELL** Advanced

1 Connect
Make learning meaningful

Make Connections Ask students to name the type of government the United States has. Then ask them to name situations in which they have been able to vote. Did they vote directly on rules or for representatives to make the rules? Finally, tell students that in this section they will learn about the earliest democracy.

ELL **Intermediate** Define the word *democracy* as "government by the people" and *representative* as "a person who votes or speaks for someone else."

Activate Prior Knowledge Remind students that in Core Concept 8.2: Political Systems, they learned that types of states include city-states and empires. In this chapter, they will learn how Greece, a land of city-states, became part of a vast empire ruled by Alexander the Great. Ask why they think countries build empires.

L3 **On-Level** To connect with students' lives, ask if any of them have played video games about empire building or world conquest. What are the goals of such games?

Prepare Follow the steps in the section **Preview.** Preteach the Key Terms. Then have students complete *Word Wise* in their journals using in-text clues and the glossary for help.

2 Experience
Teach knowledge and skills

Read Use **Background** notes and **Guide on the Side** questions to model active reading. Have students use *Take Notes* in their **Student Journal** to record important places to know in ancient Greece on an outline map. Students should use the maps in the Active Atlas at myworldgeography.com for assistance.

L2 **Extra Support** Remind students that once temperatures drop below zero, they are expressed in negative numbers that get larger as they move further below zero. Something similar happens with dates in the B.C. range. The larger the date, the further back it is in time.

ELL **Early Intermediate** For Spanish speakers, explain that the Greek word for city-state, *polis*, is the root of *policía* and *política*. Ask them to translate those words into English and predict what *pol* means.

L4 **Challenge** Have students choose one of the deities from *Enrichment: Greek Gods and Goddesses*, do research, and make a cartoon retelling a myth about that deity.

 **Practice: myWorld Activity** Students will plan a Greek trade expedition and draw an trade map showing the imports and exports they chose. **Step-by-Step Instructions** and **More Activities** follow on p. T10.

SECTION 1 RESOURCE GUIDE

FOR THE STUDENT

my worldgeography.com Student Center
- Active Atlas
- myStory Video

Student Edition (print and online)
- Ancient Greece

Student Journal (print and online)
- Section 1 Word Wise
- Section 1 Take Notes

21st Century Learning Online Tutor
- Read Political Maps
- Make Decisions

FOR THE TEACHER

my worldgeography.com Teacher Center
- Online Lesson Planner
- Presentations for Projection
- SuccessTracker

ProGuide: Europe and Russia
- Section 1 Lesson Plan, pp. T8–T9
- myWorld Activity Step-by-Step Instructions, p. T10
- Activity Support: Planning Table, p. T11
- myWorld Geography Enrichment, p. T12
- Section Quiz, p. T13

Accelerating the Progress of ELLs
- Peer Learning Strategies, p. 46

---

3 Understand
Assess understanding

Review Review *Word Wise* and *Take Notes* in the **Student Journal.**

Assess Knowledge and Skills Use the Section Assessment and Section Quiz to check students' progress.

Assess Understanding Review students' responses to the Section Assessment Essential Question prompt.

Remediate Use these strategies to review and remediate.

If students struggle to . . .	Try these strategies.
Name democratic reforms in ancient Greece	Suggest that they explain how specific actions by Solon and Pericles helped democracy.
Describe how Athens and Sparta were alike and different	Have students work in pairs. One should become an expert on Athens and the other on Sparta.
Make decisions	Assign additional practice with the **21st Century Online Tutor.**

ELL Support

ELL Objective Students will be able to use English to make comparisons.

Cultural Connections To give students practice comparing societies, let them use their native languages to name similarities and differences between the shopping areas of their families' home countries and the communities where they live now. Then have them practice comparisons in English by completing this sentence: "The two places are alike because they both _____."

ELL Early Advanced/Advanced Content Tip Give students the following list of words: *Greek, warlike, democracy, city-state, philosophy, kings, learning.* Have them draw a Venn diagram with the ovals labeled Athens and Sparta and place the terms in the correct places on the diagram.

ELL Activity On the board, list the prefixes *im-* and *in-*, which mean "in," and *ex-*, which means "out." Teach the terms *interior* and *exterior.* Have students draw a house with stick people inside and out, and label them appropriately. **(Verbal/Visual)**

myWorld Activity   Step-by-Step Instructions

 20 min

Let's Make a Trade

OBJECTIVES

Students will
- plan a trade expedition.
- draw an illustrated trade map.

LEARNING STYLE

- Logical
- Visual

21st Century Learning

- Make Decisions

MATERIALS

- Activity Support: Planning Table, p. T11
- Colored pencils or markers
- Old magazines

Activity Steps

1. Divide the class into groups. Each group is the crew of an ancient Greek trading ship. Tell students they are going to plan a trade expedition by deciding what products to export and what products to import. Then they will draw an illustrated trade map to show their decisions. Suggest that groups assign their members the roles of researcher, note taker, artist, labeler, and presenter. Give each group a copy of *Activity Support: Planning Table*.

    ELL Early Intermediate/Intermediate Write these definitions on the board: **export**—a product one country sells to another; **import**—a product one country buys from another; **trade partners**—countries that sell products to each other.

2. Groups should begin by having the researcher find information in the textbook about Greek trade. The note taker should record on the *Planning Table* the

resources that Greeks had, those they lacked, and Greece's trade partners. Next, the groups should decide what to export, what to import, and which trade partner is most likely to have the goods they need. They may check other chapters of their book to find information about trade partners' resources.

3. The artist and labeler should use the directions on *Activity Support: Planning Table* to make the illustrated trade map.

    L2 Extra Support Provide a stack of old magazines so that students who lack artistic ability or confidence can cut out photographs to represent trade goods.

4. One student from each group should present and explain their maps to the class. If space allows, display all the group maps in the classroom.

More Activities From myWorld Teachers

 Local Connection Have students work in pairs to make a list of buildings in your community that were influenced by Greek architecture. As an extension, students could take photographs of several buildings and make a poster. **(Visual)**

Persuasive Speech Students should imagine they are citizens of an ancient Greek city-state that is ruled by a harsh tyrant. Have them write a speech that tries to

persuade their fellow citizens to overthrow the tyrant and set up a democracy. **(Verbal)**

Olympic Committee Have groups plan an athletic competition for their fellow students. The games should simulate actual games from the Greek Olympics—for example, throwing a Frisbee to simulate the discus toss. **(Kinesthetic)**

my worldgeography.com (Teacher Center) Find additional resources in the online Teacher Center.

Name _____ Class _____ Date _____

myWorld Activity Support   **Planning Table**

Let's Make a Trade

Directions Use the table below to plan your trade expedition. Then follow the directions below the table to draw an illustrated trade map.

Planning Table			
1. What resources did Greece lack?		**2.** Which of these resources do you want to import?	
3. What resources did Greece have in abundance?		**4.** Which of these resources are you willing to export?	
5. Who were Greece's trade partners?		**6.** Which trade partner do you want to trade with?	

Draw an Illustrated Trade Map

1. Turn to the maps in Section 1. Use them as models. On your own paper, draw an outline map that shows Greece, the trade partner you chose, and the lands and seas between the two. Label the map.

2. Draw an arrow going from Greece to the country you chose as a trade partner and another arrow going back to Greece.

3. Next to the arrow moving away from Greece, draw symbols for the goods you are exporting. Next to the arrow moving toward Greece, draw symbols for the goods you are importing.

4. Make a key to show what each symbol stands for.

5. Share your map with the class.

Name _____ Class _____ Date _____

Enrichment: Greek Gods and Goddesses

Directions Study the table below. Answer the questions that follow and complete the activity.

The Chief Greek Gods and Goddesses

Name	Role in Greek Mythology
Zeus	Ruler of the gods; lord of the sky; more powerful than all the gods combined; weapon was the thunderbolt
Hera	Goddess of marriage, married women, and childbirth; Zeus's wife; jealous of Zeus's relationships with other women
Poseidon	God of oceans, seas, and earthquakes; brother of Zeus; carried a three-pronged spear called a trident
Hades	God of the underworld; king of the dead; brother of Zeus; rarely left the underworld to visit Earth
Athena	Goddess of wisdom, arts and crafts, and war; Zeus's favorite child; sprang full-grown from his forehead; wore armor
Apollo	God of music, medicine, poetry, truth, and light; son of Zeus and Leto; twin brother of Artemis; associated with the sun
Artemis	Goddess of hunting; daughter of Zeus and Leto; twin sister of Apollo; carried bow and arrows; associated with the moon
Ares	God of war; son of Zeus and Hera; full of murder and fury; not widely worshiped or the subject of many myths
Hephaestus	God of fire; blacksmith of the gods; husband of Aphrodite; only god who was ugly and lame
Aphrodite	Goddess of love and beauty; wife of Hephaestus; full of laughter and trickery; sprang to life from sea foam
Hermes	Messenger of the gods; son of Zeus and Maia; wore winged sandals and winged hat; protector of traders, travelers, and thieves

1. Which of the gods or goddesses would sailors worship? Why?

_____

_____

2. Which of the gods do you think were most frightening to the ancient Greeks? Why?

_____

_____

3. Activity Make a family tree showing how the other gods and goddesses were related to Zeus.

Name _____ Class _____ Date _____

Section Quiz

Directions Answer the following questions using what you learned
in Section 1.

1. ____ What was the Peloponnesian War?
   a. a conflict between Greece and Persia
   b. a conflict between Athens and Sparta
   c. a conflict between Greece and
   Macedonia
   d. a conflict between Macedonia and
   Athens

2. ____ What is the name for a government
   ruled by a small group of people?
   a. democracy
   b. monarchy
   c. oligarchy
   d. tyranny

3. ____ What was a city-state?
   a. a fortified city and surrounding
   farmlands
   b. the marketplace of ancient Greek cities
   c. the temple of the goddess Athena
   d. the part of a Greek city located on a hill

4. ____ What institution did Athenian
   democracy introduce to the legal system,
   which many countries use today?
   a. banishment
   b. juries
   c. representatives
   d. tyrants

5. ____ Why was Solon important?
   a. He was the Macedonian king who
   united Greece.
   b. He set up salaries for officials so poor
   people could serve.
   c. He was the general who defeated the
   Persian invaders.
   d. He ended slavery for people who fell
   into debt.

6. Complete the Venn diagram below with details about how
   Athens and Sparta were similar and different.

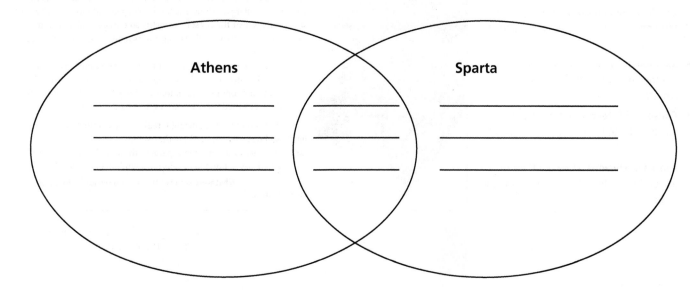

Athens   Sparta

Ancient Greece

- Model preparing to read by previewing the Key Ideas, Key Terms, headings, visuals, and captions. Have students make predictions about what they will learn. For ELL support, post the prompt, "I predict I will read about . . ."

- Preview and practice the skill, Read Political Maps, by looking at the map *The Aegean World*. Ask,

Where was Athens located in relation to Sparta? (It was northeast of Sparta.)

- Preteach this section's high-use Academic Vocabulary and Key Terms using the chart on the next page and in-text definitions. Have students practice Key Terms by completing the *Word Wise* page in their journals.

GUIDE ON THE SIDE

Reading Skill

Label an Outline Map Have students identify the Places to Know! on the outline map of the region in the **Student Journal** while they read.

The Aegean World

- **Identify Details** Into what sea does Greece jut? (the Mediterranean Sea)

- **Cause and Effect** Why did the ancient Greeks depend more on fishing than farming? (Their land was rocky, and the surrounding seas held many fish.)

- **Summarize** What kinds of resources did they use for building? (marble and limestone)

- **Cause and Effect** What geographic reason affected where Greeks settled? (the availability of fertile soil)

- **Draw Conclusions** How did the terrain affect the ability of Greek communities to unite? (It prevented unity.)

Section 1

Ancient Greece

Key Ideas
- Geography played a part in shaping Greek civilization.
- Through trade, conquest, and cultural exchange, ancient Greece prospered.
- Ancient Greece left a rich heritage in learning, philosophy, and the arts.
- Democratic government developed in ancient Greece.

Key Terms • city-state • oligarchy • cultural hearth • direct democracy • philosophy

 Visual Glossary

 Reading Skill: Label an Outline Map Take notes using the outline map in your journal.

A Minoan ceremonial object in the shape of a bull's head ▼

The civilization of ancient Greece has had a great effect on today's world. Democratic government traces its roots back to this civilization. Modern science began with the ancient Greek thinkers. In the arts and architecture, ancient Greek ideas remain strong today.

The Aegean World
Greece is a peninsula and a group of islands that jut out from southern Europe into the Mediterranean Sea. The Aegean World also included the islands of Crete and Rhodes, and the lands of Ionia.

Physical Geography The Greek peninsula is a mountainous area with an irregular coastline. The land is rugged and mostly rocky. Only small valleys near the coast have fertile soil. In general, the climate in this region is warm and dry. Summers tend to be hot and dry and winters mild.

The seas around Greece are full of fish. Because they had so little farmland, the ancient Greeks depended on the sea for their food. The mountains contain large amounts of marble and limestone. The ancient Greeks used these resources to construct buildings.

Greek Settlements The ancient Greeks mostly settled in valleys with fertile soil near the coast. There they set up farms and fished. Mountains or bodies of water often separated these settled areas. As a result, each settled area tended to develop its own independent spirit.

Reading Check What were some of the natural resources found in ancient Greece?

READING CHECK some fertile soil, fish, marble, and limestone

ACADEMIC VOCABULARY

High-Use Word	Definition and Sample Sentence
fortified	*adj.* strengthened by walls *The castle was fortified with stone walls.*
livestock	*n.* farm animals raised for food and profit *The farmer kept his livestock in pens.*

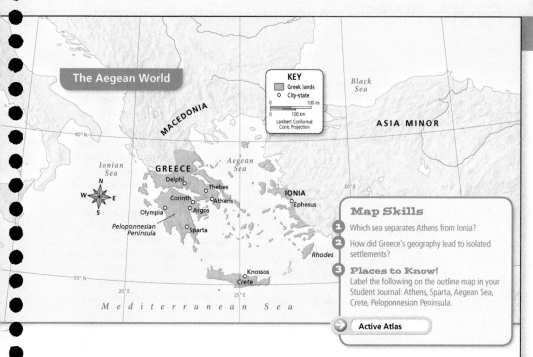

The Aegean World

KEY
Greek lands
○ City-state

0   100 mi
0   100 km
Lambert Conformal
Conic Projection

Black Sea
MACEDONIA
40° N
ASIA MINOR
Ionian Sea
GREECE
Delphi
Aegean Sea
Thebes
Corinth   Athens
IONIA
Ephesus
30° E
Olympia   Argos
Peloponnesian Peninsula   Sparta
Rhodes
35° N
Knossos
Crete
20° E   25° E
M e d i t e r r a n e a n   S e a

Map Skills

1. Which sea separates Athens from Ionia?
2. How did Greece's geography lead to isolated settlements?
3. **Places to Know!** Label the following on the outline map in your Student Journal: Athens, Sparta, Aegean Sea, Crete, Peloponnesian Peninsula.

 Active Atlas

The Rise of City-States

In prehistoric times, two civilizations developed in the Aegean region. The people called the Minoans lived on Crete and many other islands. The Mycenaeans (my suh nee uns) lived on the Greek mainland.

Minoans and Mycenaeans Around 3000 B.C., the Minoan civilization emerged on the island of Crete. The Minoans were skilled sailors who developed a writing system. They traded with mainland Greece, Egypt, and Sicily.

Around 1400 B.C., Mycenaeans from the mainland conquered the Minoans. They borrowed the Minoan system of writing and built <u>fortified</u> towns. Around 1200 B.C., the Mycenaean civilization collapsed for unknown reasons.

City-States Form The many fortified towns in Greece gradually developed into city-states. A **city-state** is a city or town that controls surrounding villages and farmland nearby.

Each city-state was independent and often fought frequently with other city-states. Many city-states were aristocracies run by wealthy landowners. The word *aristocracy* means "rule by the best people." Laws were based on tradition.

In many city-states, farmers and merchants rebelled against the aristocrats. To restore order, tyrants took control. A tyrant is a leader who gains total power by force. In some areas, the tyrants were replaced by an **oligarchy,** or government in which a small group of people rule.

fortified, *adj.,* strengthened by walls

MAP SKILLS 1. Aegean Sea **2.** It had many mountains. **3.** Places should be labeled accurately.

The Rise of City-States

- **Cause and Effect** What did Mycenaean civilization borrow from Minoan civilization? (its writing system)

- **Categorize** What is the difference between a town and a city-state? (A city-state is larger; it controls surrounding villages and lands.)

- **Problem Solve** How was the rise of tyrants an answer to a problem? (Farmers and merchants rebelled, and strong rulers took over to restore order.)

Map Skills Have students look at the map of the Aegean world.

- In what region was Ionia located? (Asia Minor)

- What type of landform is Rhodes? (an island)

Active Atlas

Have students go online to learn more about the physical geography of Greece.

CULTURE

Mycenae and the Trojan War According to legend, King Agamemnon was the ruler of Mycenae. When the Trojan prince Paris carried off Helen, the wife of Agamemnon's brother, Agamemnon decided to go to war. He called on the other rulers of Greek city-states to unite with him, sail across the Aegean Sea, and attack the city of Troy. Mycenae contributed 100 ships. Agamemnon was the commander in chief of all the Greek forces. The war lasted ten years before trickery ended it: the Greeks used the gift of the Trojan horse to smuggle their troops into Troy.

- **Identify Main Ideas** How did Greece become a cultural hearth? (Trade brought cultural influences to Greece and spread Greek culture throughout the Mediterranean region.)

Athenian Democracy

- **Sequence** Which came first in Athens, democracy or oligarchy? (oligarchy)

Closer Look

Rulers of the Seas

- **Identify Details** Why was the ship shown here called a trireme? (It had three levels of oarsmen.)
- **Cause and Effect** How were trade ships powered? (by a single square sail)
- **Categorize** What products did the Greeks trade? (wine, olive oil, almonds)

Trade Networks Expand Sea trade gave the Greeks a vital link to the outside world. Trade goods included olive oil, gold, silver, and iron. Greek merchants traded with people from Asia Minor, Egypt, and Mesopotamia. As trade expanded, so did the power of the city-states.

Trade also spread Greek culture throughout the Mediterranean region. It brought cultural influences to Greece. In this way, ancient Greece became a **cultural hearth,** or a center of new practices and ideas that spread.

Trade also led to colonization. By the 500s B.C., Greek colonies had spread to modern day Italy, France, Spain, Libya, Egypt, and Turkey.

Reading Check **How did city-states develop?**

Athenian Democracy

As Greek power and wealth spread, its largest city-state, Athens, began to encourage political freedom at home.

First Stirrings of Democracy In Athens, reformers wanted to stop the abuse of power. These reformers looked to replace the oligarchy with a democracy.

One of these reformers was Solon. He ended the practice of enslaving people who were unable to repay their debts. Solon granted all citizens the right to vote for government officials. However, citizens only included adult males who had Athenian parents. Women citizens could not participate in politics. Foreign residents were denied citizenship.

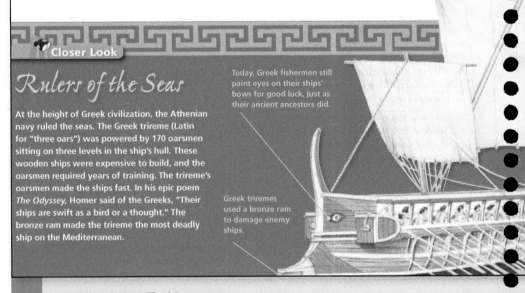

Closer Look

Rulers of the Seas

At the height of Greek civilization, the Athenian navy ruled the seas. The Greek trireme (Latin for "three oars") was powered by 170 oarsmen sitting on three levels in the ship's hull. These wooden ships were expensive to build, and the oarsmen required years of training. The trireme's oarsmen made the ships fast. In his epic poem *The Odyssey*, Homer said of the Greeks, "Their ships are swift as a bird or a thought." The bronze ram made the trireme the most deadly ship on the Mediterranean.

Today, Greek fishermen still paint eyes on their ships' bows for good luck, just as their ancient ancestors did.

Greek triremes used a bronze ram to damage enemy ships.

READING CHECK The Mycenaeans set up fortified towns. These towns developed into city-states that controlled surrounding villages and farmlands.

ECONOMICS

The First Coins Many ancient people used precious metals as a means of exchange, but the first people to mint coins were the Lydians of southwest Asia. Sometime shortly after 650 B.C., they began to make coins of electrum, an alloy of gold and silver. During the reign of King Croesus (560–546 B.C.), Lydia adopted a bimetallic system that used coins of pure gold and coins of pure silver. Greek city-states began minting silver coins sometime around the reign of Croesus. The coins of Corinth had the winged horse Pegasus on one side, while the coins of Athens showed an owl, which was a symbol of Athena.

In the mid-400s B.C., the statesman Pericles made more democratic reforms in Athens. For example, he set up salaries for public officials so that poor people could serve in government. Pericles famously said,

66 Here each individual is interested not only in his own affairs but in the affairs of the state as well. 99

Athenian Direct Democracy Under Pericles, Athens became the world's first **direct democracy.** In direct democracy, citizens take part directly in the day-to-day affairs of government. Today, in most democratic countries, such as the United States, people instead participate in government through elected representatives.

However, there are some examples of direct democracy-style governments in the modern world. One of these is in Switzerland, where citizens have the ability to vote on federal laws. Another is the town hall style of city government used in many communities in the New England region of the United States.

Reading Check **What reforms did Solon propose?**

Life in Ancient Greece

The period between the end of the Persian Wars and the death of Alexander (about 500 B.C.–323 B.C.) is called the classical period. It was a time of great advances in learning and art. Athens, named for the goddess of wisdom, was the most important cultural center of classical Greece.

The Greeks were also skilled sea traders. Trade ships were usually powered by a single square sail. The wooden ships were durable, and some lasted as long as 80 years. Pirates and shipwrecks were constant threats. The Greeks most commonly traded olive oil, wine, and almonds.

THINK CRITICALLY **How was slavery connected to Greek naval power?**

The Greeks have cultivated olives for thousands of years. The ancient Greeks exported olive oil in clay vessels like the one below.

myWorldActivity
Let's Make a Trade

READING CHECK He granted all citizens the right to vote and he ended the practice of enslaving people for debt.

THINK CRITICALLY Sample: The Greeks used slaves to row their warships.

PRIMARY SOURCE

The First Democracy "Our constitution does not copy the laws of neighboring states; we are rather a pattern to others than imitators ourselves. Its administration favors the many instead of the few; this is why it is called a democracy. If we look to the laws, they afford equal justice to all in their private differences; if no social standing, advancement in public life falls to reputation for capacity, class considerations not being allowed to interfere with merit; nor again does poverty bar the way, if a man is able to serve the state, he is not hindered by the obscurity of his condition."

—Pericles, "Funeral Oration"

GUIDE ON THE SIDE

Closer Look

A New Form of Government and Justice

- **Connect** What word do we get from the Greek word *demokratia*? (democracy)

- **Identify Main Ideas** Who ran the government in ancient Athens? (all citizens)

- **Compare and Contrast** How were the Magistrates, the Boule, and the People's Court chosen? (Both the Boule and the People's Court were chosen at random; the Magistrates were elected.)

- **Summarize** Who was a citizen in Athens? (men who were at least 18 and sons of Athenians)

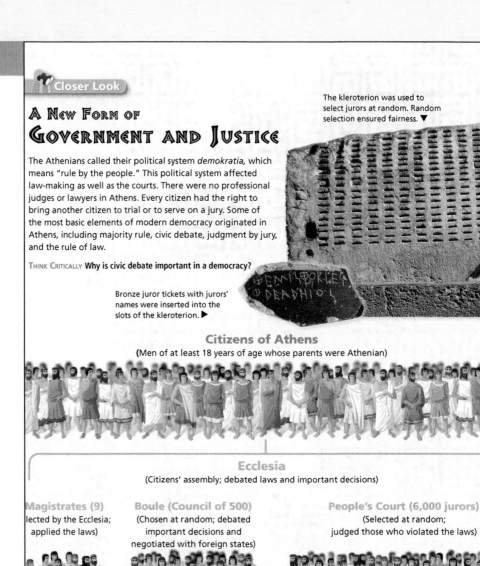

Closer Look

A New Form of GOVERNMENT AND JUSTICE

The Athenians called their political system *demokratia*, which means "rule by the people." This political system affected law-making as well as the courts. There were no professional judges or lawyers in Athens. Every citizen had the right to bring another citizen to trial or to serve on a jury. Some of the most basic elements of modern democracy originated in Athens, including majority rule, civic debate, judgment by jury, and the rule of law.

THINK CRITICALLY **Why is civic debate important in a democracy?**

The kleroterion was used to select jurors at random. Random selection ensured fairness. ▼

Bronze juror tickets with jurors' names were inserted into the slots of the kleroterion. ▶

Citizens of Athens
(Men of at least 18 years of age whose parents were Athenian)

Ecclesia
(Citizens' assembly; debated laws and important decisions)

Magistrates (9)
elected by the Ecclesia; applied the laws)

Boule (Council of 500)
(Chosen at random; debated important decisions and negotiated with foreign states)

People's Court (6,000 jurors)
(Selected at random; judged those who violated the laws)

THINK CRITICALLY Sample: Civic debate is important because it helps people examine various sides of an issue before casting a vote or passing a law.

GOVERNMENT

Governments of Ancient Greece Most city-states of ancient Greece did not have democratic forms of government.

- Corinth was ruled by oligarchy for most of its history, with a period of rule by tyrants from about 657 to 550 B.C.

- Thebes was ruled by a king and was the legendary home of Oedipus.
- Argos was also ruled by a king.
- Sparta was ruled by an oligarchy and two kings.

Greek Religion The Greeks believed in many deities, or beings with supernatural powers. These gods and goddesses ruled over different areas of human life and the natural world. The chief god was Zeus, who ruled from his home on Mount Olympus. He was lord of the sky and rain.

The Greeks had no book or manuscripts to explain their religion. Rather, they used mythology, or a collection of stories told about history or gods. To honor the gods, the Greeks made beautiful statues in marble and built magnificent temples.

Love of Wisdom The Greeks also studied **philosophy,** or "love of wisdom." Greek scholars applied logic, or reason, to a study of knowledge and the world.

The Greek philosopher Plato wrote about government, ethics, and religion. Other important philosophers were Plato's teacher, Socrates, and Aristotle, Plato's student. In *Poetics,* Aristotle said,

> 66 Poetry, therefore, is a more philosophical and a higher thing than history: for poetry tends to express the universal, history the particular. 99

The ancient Greeks also investigated science and mathematics. People used to believe that the sun circled Earth. Using mathematics and careful observation, the astronomer Aristarchus (a ris TAHR kus) concluded that Earth circled the sun. Almost 2,000 years passed before scientists widely accepted this idea.

The Greeks also studied the past, but they did more than simply record events. The historian Herodotus is known as the father of history because he was the first

to note events and analyze them. Two of ancient Greece's most important historians were also soldiers. Thucydides wrote the history of the Peloponnesian Wars, while Xenophon recorded Greek history as well as the sayings of Socrates.

Arts and Leisure The ancient Greeks developed a rich literary tradition, especially in poetry and drama. The playwrights Aeschylus, Sophocles, and Euripides wrote great tragedies, or serious works that have flawed heroes. Aristophanes' plays were comedies that often poked fun at Greek society.

The ancient Greeks made many advances in architecture. The most impressive type of public building in classical Greece was the temple. It consisted of a long chamber that housed a statue of a god or goddess. Columns surrounded the chamber. The most famous Greek temple is the Parthenon in Athens.

Greeks held public festivals to honor their gods. One such festival at Olympia was held every four years to honor Zeus. City-states would send their best athletes to compete in these festivals, which were known as the Olympic Games. Athletes from all over Greece competed in running, wrestling, and jumping.

Public and Private Life Though the public buildings in ancient Greece were impressive, most people lived in simple homes of mud bricks. They ate simple meals of bread, cheese, olives, and fish. Very few people ate meat since there was little space in which to raise <u>livestock</u>.

▲ On this ancient Greek vase, harvesters use sticks to knock olives from the trees.

livestock, *n.,* farm animals raised for food and profit

- **Categorize** Who was Plato, and what did he do? (He was an important Greek philosopher. He wrote about government, ethics, and religion.)
- **Cause and Effect** How did the Greeks affect scientific knowledge? (Aristarchus proposed that Earth orbited the sun, but this idea did not become widely accepted for 2,000 years.)
- **Connect** How did the ancient Greeks influence modern sports? (They began the Olympic Games.)

Analyze Visuals Have students look at the photograph of the vase.

- What were the main colors of Greek pottery? (red and black)
- How does Greek pottery help us learn about Greek life? (It is decorated with scenes of daily activities.)

HISTORY

The Battle of Thermopylae During the Persian Wars, an enormous Persian army invaded Greece in 480 B.C. They were going to have to march through a narrow pass of Thermopylae, which is located in central Greece. One of Sparta's two monarchs, King Leonidas I, led a small force of 6,000 to 7,000 soldiers (including 300 Spartans) to hold the pass. Their purpose was to delay the Persian army even though they knew they would almost certainly die. The Persians did eventually win the battle and go on to destroy Athens. However, the deaths of Leonidas and his army have symbolized a noble sacrifice ever since.

GUIDE ON THE SIDE

- **Identify Details** What was at the agora? (council house, religious shrines, marketplace)
- **Summarize** What did Greek women do? (ran the home, served as priestesses)
- **Compare and Contrast** How were slaves different from free people? (They did not have the same rights, and they were owned by someone.)

Conflict and Decline

- **Identify Main Ideas** What city-state was the great rival of Athens? (Sparta)

Map Skills Have students look at the map *The Empire of Alexander the Great.*

- What country in Africa was part of Alexander's empire? (Egypt)
- Why do you think there were many cities called Alexandria? (Sample: Alexander named cities after himself to show his power.)

 Active Atlas

Have students go online to learn more about the empire of Alexander the Great.

At the heart of the Greek city lay the agora, a public space that included the council-house, religious shrines, and the marketplace. Most of those who gathered in the agora were freemen, discussing politics or bargaining for goods and services.

These freemen were generally upper-class leaders of social and political life. The upper class included aristocrats, wealthy landowners, and, later, successful merchants. As free residents and citizens, they possessed more rights than anyone else.

For the most part, women ran the home. Women had few rights. They could not vote or own property. Some women served as priestesses in temples.

Slavery One third of the population of Athens were slaves. These people were owned by someone else and did not have the same rights as free people. Many slaves were captured during wartime or were children whose parents had been enslaved. Slaves did most of the hard labor in ancient Greece. A slave might be able to buy his or her freedom or obtain it from a grateful master.

Reading Check How did the Greeks influence the study of history?

Conflict and Decline

At sea, Athens' navy was superior. On land, Sparta's army challenged Athens.

Soldiers Rule Sparta The Spartans devoted themselves to military might from an early age. As adults, Spartan warriors were expected to put their military careers before wives and families.

A gold coin on which Alexander is portrayed as Ares, the god of war. ▼

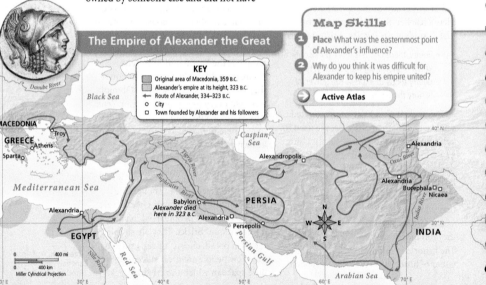

Map Skills
1. Place What was the easternmost point of Alexander's influence?
2. Why do you think it was difficult for Alexander to keep his empire united?
Active Atlas

MAP SKILLS 1. Indus River **2.** Sample: It was so vast that traveling from one end to the other took months.

READING CHECK They were the first to note and analyze historic events.
READING CHECK the Persians

SECTION 1 ASSESSMENT 1. Samples: Athens was a city-state known for learning. Greece influenced other cultures, so it was a cultural hearth. In direct democracy, citizens help make laws. The study of wisdom and knowledge is philosophy. **2.** They settled in valleys with fertile soil near coasts. **3.** Average citizens could take part in

CORE CONCEPTS: CULTURAL DIFFUSION AND CHANGE

Review Core Concept 7.6 before having students read about Alexander the Great and the legacy of his empire. Review cultural diffusion, cultural change over time, and acculturation. Explain that the empire of Alexander the Great brought about the blending of Greek and Asian cultures. This cultural blending led to a period called the Hellenistic Age.

Spartan women enjoyed more freedom than the women of Athens. They could own land and take part in business.

The city-state of Sparta was governed by an oligarchy led by the army. At the top of Spartan society were aristocrats who were also professional military men. Unlike the citizens of Athens, the people of Sparta played a much smaller part in government.

The Persian Wars War was frequent among the Greeks, but an outside threat united the city-states. That threat was the invading Persian army led by Darius, the king of Persia.

The Greek army met the Persians first at the Battle of Marathon. The Greeks surrounded the Persians, and the enemy fled to their ships in the Aegean Sea.

Darius's son Xerxes commanded the Persians in the second war with the Greeks. As allies, the Spartans joined the Greeks to stop the Persians at Thermopylae. Finally, Xerxes sailed for home after losing thousands of men and more than 200 ships in the Battle of Salamis.

Decline of the City-States In spite of their alliance, these two city-states remained enemies. War broke out between Athens and Sparta in 431 B.C. It was called the Peloponnesian War and continued off and on for 27 years. Athens was at last defeated, ending the golden age of this once-great city-state. The war also hurt other city-states around Greece, toppling governments and damaging trade. Greek culture did not end, but ongoing conflict kept it from reaching the unity or stability that had made it strong.

Spread of Greek Culture As you read at the beginning of this chapter, Alexander conquered most of the world known to the ancient Greeks. Greek culture eventually spread across southwest Asia, southern Europe, and North Africa. Today, the impact of Greek culture remains strong in democratic forms of government as well as in art and architecture.

Reading Check **Which common enemy united Athens and Sparta?**

As king, Alexander was popular and much loved. He died of an unknown illness at age 32. ▼

GUIDE ON THE SIDE

- **Compare and Contrast** How was Sparta different from Athens? (Sparta was devoted to a military life, not learning. Also, Sparta was ruled by an oligarchy.)

- **Identify Details** In what war did Athens and Sparta fight each other? (the Peloponnesian War)

- **Cause and Effect** What was the outcome of the Peloponnesian War? (Sparta defeated Athens and ended its golden age.)

Section 1 Assessment

Key Terms
1. Use each of the following terms in a sentence: city-state, cultural hearth, direct democracy, philosophy.

Key Ideas
2. Where did most of the ancient Greeks settle?
3. Name some of the democratic reforms made during the golden age of Athens.
4. How did the Greeks defeat the Persians?

Think Critically
5. **Draw Conclusions** How were Sparta and Athens similar and different?
6. **Draw Inferences** Do you think Aristotle was influenced by Plato and Socrates? Explain why or why not.

? Essential Question
What are the challenges of diversity?
7. How did the diversity of Alexander the Great's Empire affect Greek culture? Go to your Student Journal to record your answer.

government; public officials were paid salaries. **4.** Sparta with its strong army and Athens with its strong navy united to defeat Persia. **5.** Similarities: Sparta and Athens were both powerful city-states. Differences: Sparta stressed the military. Athens stressed the arts and learning. Sparta had an oligarchy. Athens had a democracy. Sparta had a strong army. Athens had a strong navy. **6.** Sample: Plato taught Socrates, who was Aristotle's teacher, so both men influenced Aristotle. **7.** Sample: Diversity probably changed Greek culture by introducing foreign influences.

ANSWERS

 myStory Video

Have students go online to learn more about the life of Alexander the Great.

Ancient Greek Literature

OBJECTIVES

Students will

- learn the characteristics of fables and epic poetry in ancient Greek literature.
- **21st Century Learning** be able to synthesize information from two documents to form a generalization.
- **ELL** learn multiple meanings for the word *siren*.

SET EXPECTATIONS

In this lesson, students will

- read and analyze two documents from ancient Greek literature.
- make up a fable and recount it in a narrative essay.

---

1 Connect

Post the word *odyssey* on the board, and ask if anyone knows what it means. Define it as a long journey with a series of adventures. Explain that it comes from the name of the Greek hero Odysseus. Ask students to think of stories and movies about heroes who are taking a journey and who must overcome obstacles along the way. Create a concept web centered on the word *odyssey* by listing the adventures, such as fighting monsters or overcoming natural obstacles, typically featured in such a story.

---

2 Experience

Preview Have students preview the two pages and study the images. Read the Key Idea, glossary terms, and definitions. Clarify any questions about the meaning of these words by providing examples.

Read Slowly read aloud the excerpt from *Aesop's Fables* without stopping. Read the document again, this time stopping to read the questions at the left, and prompt students to analyze the meaning of words. Have students answer the questions using the location of the letters to give clues. Do the same for the excerpt from *The Odyssey*. Lead a discussion starting with students' responses to the questions. Ask, What do you think is the purpose of each piece of literature? How do the purposes compare?

ELL **Intermediate** Ask students if they know what a siren is. Define it as a loud, wailing sound that gives a warning. Play a sound clip to demonstrate. Then explain that the word comes from Greek mythology; a Siren was a creature that was half woman, half bird.

myWorld Activity: Planning an Odyssey Have students use *Activity Support: Itinerary* to plot their own epic adventure modeled on *The Odyssey*. Students will imagine three different adventures that present challenges and decide how the hero will overcome each challenge. Encourage students to use their imaginations. Point out that the Siren is an example of how Homer mixed fantasy with reality to make his epic exciting and unique. **(Verbal)**

L1 **Special Needs** Require each student to invent one adventure, as opposed to three, and incorporate the whole class's adventures into a giant oral epic, giving each student a turn to tell his or her part of the tale.

L4 **Challenge** Encourage students to write a story or long poem based on their outlines. For student poets, provide an example of meter for them to follow.

20 min

---

3 Understand

Review Go back to the Key Idea. Remind students that each writer told a story that has lasted for centuries. Ask what they think the enduring appeal of each story is.

Assess Have students complete **Analyze the Documents.** Review their answers to determine if students have met the lesson objectives.

Remediate If students struggle to identify similarities between the dog in the manger and the Sirens, have them fill out a two-column table with the headings *Actions* and *Effect on Others*.

Name _____ Class _____ Date _____

myWorld Activity Support   Itinerary

Planning an Odyssey

Directions A plan for a trip is called an *itinerary.* Use this worksheet to plan the itinerary of an adventure like the one in the *Odyssey*. Include places you would like to explore and conflicts you would likely have. The problems could be mythical, such as encounters with monsters, or realistic, such as a storm.

I. Introduction

    A. Who the hero is (Give the character that represents you a name.) _____

    B. Where the hero is going _____

    C. Why the hero wants to get there _____

    _____

II. Where the first adventure is _____

    A. What the problem is _____

    B. How the hero overcomes it _____

    _____

III. Where the second adventure is _____

    A. What the problem is _____

    B. How the hero overcomes it _____

    _____

IV. Where the third adventure is _____

    A. What the problem is _____

    B. How the hero overcomes it _____

    _____

V. Conclusion

    A. Reaching the destination _____

    B. What happens there _____

    _____

CULTURE

Homer Almost nothing is known of Homer, the great poet of the ancient Greek world. As far back as the mid-600s B.C., the Greeks attributed the *Iliad* and the *Odyssey* to his authorship. The poems were composed in the Ionic dialect of Greek, so scholars generally believe that Homer was a native of Ionia, the western coast of Asia Minor. By analyzing the language, scholars have also narrowed down the period in which the poems were composed. It was probably the late 700s B.C. Homer was most likely trained as an oral poet. Legend says that he was blind, but that claim cannot be proven.

GUIDE ON THE SIDE

Synthesize Use the lettered prompts to help students analyze the documents and synthesize information from both of them.

ANSWERS

A He is keeping the oxen from getting to their food.

B The dog cannot eat or sleep in the hay that he is keeping from the oxen.

C Sample: The moral points out that the dog is acting selfishly and hurting others for no gain of his own.

Primary Source

Ancient Greek Literature

Key Idea
- The ancient Greeks left a legacy of many great works of literature, including moral fables and epic poems.

Ancient Greece produced a wealth of literature that influenced later cultures. Greek plays and works of philosophy are still read today. Storytelling also played a large role in Greek literature. *Aesop's Fables* is a collection of short tales that teach a moral by telling a story, usually about animals. Perhaps the most famous pieces of all Greek literature are the two epic poems by Homer—*The Iliad* and *The Odyssey*. An epic poem is a long poem that tells a story about heroes. In *The Odyssey*, the warrior Odysseus encounters many dangers as he tries to return home after the Trojan War.

▲ A portrait believed to be of the ancient Greek poet Sappho

Stop at each circled letter on the right to think about the text. Then answer the question with the same letter on the left.

A **Solve Problems** What problem is the dog making for the oxen?

B **Identify Evidence** What detail shows that the dog is being cruel, rather than trying to protect something he needs?

C **Synthesize** How does the moral at the end relate to the fable?

manger, *n.*, a box that holds food for cattle or horses

begrudge, *v.*, to give reluctantly

The Dog in the Manger

66 A Dog lay in a <u>manger</u>, and by his growling and snapping prevented **A** the oxen from eating the hay which had been placed for them. 'What a selfish Dog!' said one of them to his **B** companions; 'he cannot eat or sleep in the hay himself, and yet refuses to allow those to eat who can.' People often <u>begrudge</u> others what **C** they cannot enjoy themselves. 99

—Aesop, *Aesop's Fables*, translated by George Fyler Townsend

Diego Velázquez's 1640 portrait of Aesop shows the ancient Greek author as a modest man holding a book of his fables. ▶

21st Century Learning · SYNTHESIZE

Explain to students that synthesizing means putting together different things to make something new. For example, they could take something they learn from each excerpt to say something new about Greek literature. To synthesize, they have to both express the main ideas of each excerpt and make connections between the two.

To assist your students in synthesizing information from two sources, use the scaffolded questions at the left of each excerpt. Encourage students to identify the main ideas and supporting details in each excerpt. Then, have them look for similarities and differences among the ideas. Model how to do this with a Venn diagram. Finally, ask students to write a statement that explains what the two pieces have in common and what this similarity teaches us about ancient Greek literature. For additional help, refer students to the **21st Century Online Tutor** *Synthesize*.

Stop at each circled letter on the right to think about the text. Then answer the question with the same letter on the left.

D **Categorize** Is the speaker giving Odysseus a warning or a recommendation? How do you know?

E **Draw Conclusions** What happens to men when they first hear the cry of the Sirens?

F **Identify Evidence** What happens to the men the Sirens bewitch? What evidence proves this?

Siren, *n.,* a mythical creature, part bird and part woman, who lures sailors to their death on the rocks

bewitch, *v.,* to cast a spell over

loll, *v.,* to relax in a leaning position

flay, *v.,* to strip off or to skin

The Sirens' Song

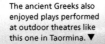

66 **Listen with care**
D **to this, now, and a god will arm**
   your mind.
   Square in your ships' path are <u>Sirens</u>,
   crying
   beauty to <u>bewitch</u> men coasting by;
   woe to the innocent who hears that
   sound!
   He will not see his lady nor his children
   in joy, crowding about him, home from
   sea;
E **the Sirens will sing his mind away**
   on their sweet meadow <u>lolling</u>.
F **There are bones**
   of dead men rotting in a pile
   beside them
   and <u>flayed</u> skins shrivel around
   the spot. 99

—Homer, *The Odyssey,*
translated by Robert Fitzgerald

An ancient Greek vase showing Odysseus resisting the call of the Sirens ▼

Analyze the Documents

1. **Synthesize** What do the dog in the fable and the Sirens have in common?
2. **Writing Task** Write your own fable to teach a lesson.

The ancient Greeks also enjoyed plays performed at outdoor theatres like this one in Taormina. ▼

ANSWERS

D It is a warning. The person says, "Listen with care to this."

E The men stop traveling, lose their minds, and relax in a meadow.

F They die. The evidence is the pile of bones and the shriveled skins.

ANALYZE THE DOCUMENTS

1. They interfere with others and prevent them from living their lives.

2. Sample opening paragraph of fable: My best friend and I went to the convenience store. While we were there, we saw a strange boy pocket a candy bar without paying. "What should we do?" I whispered to my friend. "Should we tell the owner?" Sample moral: Honesty is the best policy.

Ancient Rome

OBJECTIVES

Students will know

- the factors that led to the decline of the Roman empire.
- the origins and spread of Christianity.

Students will be able to

- sequence historical events.
- write the introductory paragraph of a news article.

SET EXPECTATIONS

In this section, students will

- read Ancient Rome.
- write a news article about a historical event.
- go On Assignment in ancient Europe and explore maps of the Roman empire.

CORE CONCEPTS

You may wish to teach or reteach the following lessons from the Core Concepts Handbook:

- Families and Societies, pp. 88–89
- Religion, pp. 92–93
- Political Systems, pp. 106–107

KEY

Differentiated Instruction	English Language Instruction
L1 Special Needs **L2** Extra Support	**ELL** Beginner **ELL** Early Intermediate **ELL** Intermediate
L3 On-Level **L4** Challenge	**ELL** Early Advanced **ELL** Advanced

1 Connect
Make learning meaningful

Make Connections Ask the class to name your state's U.S. senators or any other senators they know. Ask them what senators do. Then explain that the term *Senate* comes from ancient Rome. Have students predict what kind of government Rome had.

ELL Advanced Have students work in pairs to list words they might expect to use if they were writing a paragraph about the Senate.

Activate Prior Knowledge Remind students that in the previous section they learned about Alexander the Great. Ask them to summarize what Alexander did. Then tell them that in this section, they will read about the next world empire.

L2 Extra Support Draw students' attention to the visuals in the **myStory** about Alexander the Great. Ask them to describe what is happening in each one and use the pictures to predict events in the lives of Roman leaders that might be similar to or different from events in Alexander's story.

Prepare Follow the steps in the section **Preview.** Preteach the Key Terms. Then have students complete *Word Wise* in their journals using in-text clues and the glossary for help.

2 Experience
Teach knowledge and skills

Read Use **Background** notes and **Guide on the Side** questions to model active reading. Have students use *Take Notes* in their **Student Journal** to place important events from Roman history in chronological order. Have students complete **21st Century Online Tutor** *Sequence*, and apply this skill to reading the section.

L3 On-Level Have students read *Enrichment: Biography of Julius Caesar* to learn more about this important figure in Roman history.

ELL Intermediate/Early Advanced Give students a list of transitional words and phrases that signal time sequence, such as *later, after, before*, and *the next year*.

L4 Challenge Give students a choice of short speeches from Shakespeare's play *Julius Caesar* to deliver to the class.

 Practice: myWorld Activity Students will write the introduction to a news article about an event in Roman history. **Step-by-Step Instructions** and **More Activities** follow on p. T18.

SECTION 2 RESOURCE GUIDE

FOR THE STUDENT

worldgeography.com Student Center

- Data Discovery
- Active Atlas
- Timeline

Student Edition (print and online)

- Ancient Rome

Student Journal (print and online)

- Section 2 Word Wise
- Section 2 Take Notes

21st Century Learning Online Tutor

- Sequence
- Summarize

FOR THE TEACHER

worldgeography.com Teacher Center

- Online Lesson Planner
- Presentations for Projection
- SuccessTracker

ProGuide: Europe and Russia

- Section 2 Lesson Plan, pp. T16–T17
- myWorld Activity Step-by-Step Instructions, p. T18
- Activity Support: Fact Gathering, p. T19
- myWorld Geography Enrichment, p. T20
- Section Quiz, p. T21

Accelerating the Progress of ELLs

- Organizing Information Strategies, p. 48

---

3 Understand
Assess understanding

Review Review *Word Wise* and *Take Notes* in the **Student Journal**.

Assess Knowledge and Skills Use the Section Assessment and Section Quiz to check students' progress.

Assess Understanding Review students' responses to the Section Assessment Essential Question prompt.

Remediate Use these strategies to review and remediate.

If students struggle to . . .	Try these strategies.
Explain what led to the fall of the Roman empire	Give students a cause-and-effect graphic organizer on which to record details from the section.
Sequence	Assign additional practice with the **21st Century Online Tutor.**
Write introductions to news articles	Give them photocopied news articles and have them look for details about *who, what, where, when, why,* and *how.*

ELL Support

ELL Objective Students will be able to use English to express events in chronological order.

Cultural Connections Have students think of a story from their own lives in which events occurred over a period of time. Let them use their native languages to tell the story. Ask them to identify signal words they used to indicate time. Then have students translate those sequencing words into English.

ELL Early Intermediate Content Tip Introduce terms of architecture. Use photos or drawings to teach students the terms *concrete, arch,* and *aqueduct.*

ELL Activity Have students work in pairs to list causes of the fall of the Roman Empire. Then each student should choose one of those causes and depict it in a drawing. **(Visual)**

myWorld Activity   **Step-by-Step Instructions**

 30 min

What's the News in Rome

OBJECTIVES

Students will

- gather facts about an event in Roman history.
- write the first paragraph of a news article.

LEARNING STYLE

- Verbal

21st Century Learning

- Summarize

MATERIALS

- Activity Support: Fact Gathering, p. T19
- Books on Roman history
- Sample newspaper articles

Activity Steps

1. Tell students to choose a partner. Explain that they are going to write the introduction to a news article about an event in Roman history. Their first step is to review the section and choose an event.

   ELL Intermediate Provide students a list of story ideas to choose from. Topics include the conquests of Julius Caesar, Caesar's assassination, or the capture of Rome in 476.

2. Explain that the structure of a news article is like an upside-down pyramid. The most important details are put at the top, and less important details follow. The introductory paragraph should answer the questions *who, what, where, when, why*, and *how*.

   L3 On-Level Make a transparency of a news article. Display it to the class and use different-colored markers to underline the details that tell who, what, where, when, why, and how.

3. Distribute copies of the Activity Support. Students should find details about the event from their textbooks and from history books that you provide. They should record those details on *Activity Support: Fact Gathering*.

   ELL Beginner Have students translate the six question words into their native language for reference.

4. When students have gathered enough facts, they should work together to write an introductory paragraph of a news story that summarizes their event. Urge them to check it carefully to make sure it includes all the most important information.

5. Finally, have pairs of students exchange and read each other's paragraphs. Readers should be able to answer all six questions just from reading the introduction.

 More Activities From myWorld Teachers

Local Connection On the board, draw a concept web centered on the words *local government*. Have the class name not just town councils but also clubs, student council, condominium associations, etc. **(Verbal)**

Jury Duty Divide the class into groups. Each group is a jury that must decide whether the Roman government should arrest Julius Caesar's assassins as murderers or honor them as patriots. Then have the groups share their verdicts and the reasons for them with the class. **(Logical/Verbal)**

Pompeii Have students use books that you provide to research Pompeii and then make a mosaic or mural that shows some aspect of daily life there. **(Visual)**

my worldgeography.com (Teacher Center) → Find additional resources in the online Teacher Center.

Name _____ Class _____ Date _____

myWorld Activity Support **Fact Gathering**

What's the News in Rome

Directions You and your partner will gather facts about an event
in Roman history and write a news article about it. In a news article,
the most important details are in the introductory paragraph. That
paragraph should answer the questions *Who, What, Where, When,
Why,* and *How.* Later paragraphs give less important information.
Choose an event to write about and use this worksheet to answer the
six questions. Then write the first paragraph for the news article on
your own paper by summarizing the answers.

Event From Roman History _____

Who _____

_____

What _____

_____

Where _____

_____

When _____

_____

Why _____

_____

How _____

_____

Extra, Extra! If you have time, finish writing your news article.
Each new paragraph should have less important information than
the paragraph before it.

T19

Name _____ Class _____ Date _____

Enrichment: Biography of Julius Caesar

Directions Read the story below. Answer the questions that follow.

Julius Caesar was born in about 100 B.C. to one of Rome's most noble families. In 65 B.C., Caesar was elected to public office. He provided many public games, which made him popular. After three years, he gained the office of *praetor*, which was second only to the consuls. He allied himself with two other powerful Roman men, Pompey and Crassus. By 59 B.C., Caesar had become one of the ruling consuls. He made reforms that helped poor people, which turned conservative leaders against him.

Starting in 58 B.C., Caesar led an army to conquer Gaul (modern France) and won many victories there. When Caesar returned to Rome, Pompey suspected that Caesar wanted to rule Rome by himself. Taking sides with the conservatives, Pompey opposed Caesar. Civil war broke out, and Caesar defeated his enemies in Italy. Pompey fled to Egypt. When Caesar followed him there, he learned that the Egyptians had killed Pompey. While in Egypt, Caesar met the Egyptian queen Cleopatra. Caesar supported Cleopatra in a civil war and made her sole ruler of Egypt.

Caesar defeated Pompey's sons and returned to Rome. Instead of punishing his enemies from the war, he pardoned them. The Roman people made him a dictator—first for ten years and later for life. At a public festival, an ally of Caesar's named Mark Antony offered him a crown. Caesar refused to accept it. Even so, many people suspected that Caesar was plotting to become king. Because of this, several aristocrats assassinated Caesar on March 15, 44 B.C.

Civil war broke out again. In the end, Caesar's grandnephew Octavian became the emperor of Rome, and the republic ended.

1. Why was Caesar popular with the common people of Rome?

_____

2. What is your opinion of Caesar as a ruler? Explain your answer using details from the biography.

_____

_____

_____

Name _____ Class _____ Date _____

Section Quiz

Directions Answer the following questions using what you learned
in Section 2.

1. ____ What were the wealthy aristocrats of
ancient Rome called?
   a. Etruscans
   b. Patricians
   c. Plebeians
   d. Tribunes

2. ____ Why did aristocrats assassinate Julius
Caesar?
   a. They wanted to set up a different
   dictator.
   b. They thought he was too soft on
   plebeians.
   c. They discovered that he had poisoned
   the emperor.
   d. They wanted to bring back the Roman
   Republic.

3. ____ What spread the new religion of
Christianity?
   a. the decrees of Emperor Nero
   b. believers in the Roman army
   c. the conversion of Constantine I
   d. Jewish merchants and teachers

4. ____ Who became the first Roman
emperor?
   a. Augustus
   b. Cicero
   c. Crassus
   d. Pompey

5. ____ What invaders attacked the Roman
Empire and weakened it?
   a. Byzantines, Etruscans, and Goths
   b. Carthaginians, Jews, and Visigoths
   c. Huns, Vandals, and Visigoths
   d. Jews, Etruscans, and Vandals

6. What were the achievements of Rome in the areas of literature,
building, and art?

_____

_____

_____

_____

_____

_____

_____

Ancient Rome

- Model preparing to read by previewing the Key Ideas, Key Terms, headings, visuals, and captions. Have students make predictions about what they will learn. For ELL support, post the prompt, "I predict I will read about . . ."

- Preview and practice the reading skill, Sequence, by using examples from a previous chapter.

- Preteach this section's high-use Academic Vocabulary and Key Terms using the chart on the next page and in-text definitions. Have students practice Key Terms by completing the *Word Wise* page in their journals.

GUIDE ON THE SIDE

Reading Skill

Sequence Have students practice this skill while they read by completing the *Take Notes* graphic organizer in the **Student Journal**.

The Roman Republic

- **Identify Details** What geographic advantages did Rome have? (a river that led to the sea, fertile soil, stone for building, and hills that provided protection)

- **Summarize** What did the Romans learn from the Etruscans? (a writing system, the phalanx, paved streets, the arch)

Section 2

Ancient Rome

Key Ideas
- The Roman empire expanded through trade and conquest.
- Roman ideas about law and government remain important today.
- Christianity arose during the Roman empire and spread throughout Europe.

Key Terms • patrician • plebeian • representative democracy • Pax Romana • aqueduct

○ **Visual Glossary**

 Reading Skill: Sequence Take notes using the graphic organizer in your journal.

◄ Livia, wife of the Roman emperor Augustus, shown as Ceres, the goddess of grains.

Historians are not sure about the origins of ancient Rome. One legend says it was founded by Aeneas, the Greek hero of Virgil's poem *The Aeneid*. Aeneas is said to have escaped after the Trojan War and traveled to Latium. There, he married a princess and founded the town that would become Rome.

We do know that by the 700s B.C., a shepherd people called the Latins lived in central Italy. From their simple villages came a great empire.

The Roman Republic

Around 1000 B.C., the Latins settled near the Tiber River in central Italy. This river gave them access to the sea. The region also had fertile soil and marble and limestone for building. The surrounding hills protected the settlement. The Latins named the village Rome.

Etruscan Influence To the north lived the Etruscans, an advanced group of artists, builders, and sailors. In their sea travels, the Etruscans had learned things from many other cultures, including the Greeks.

The Etruscans expanded into Latium, ruling with the consent of the Romans. The presence of the Etruscans added much to Roman society and its government. The Etruscans introduced a writing system that they adapted from the Greeks. This formed the basis of the Latin alphabet that we use today. In addition, the Etruscans brought a strong military tradition to Rome, including the use of the Greek phalanx formation. Roman cities were improved through Etruscan methods of paving streets and using stone arches to support heavy structures such as bridges.

ACADEMIC VOCABULARY

High-Use Word	Definition and Sample Sentence
diplomacy	*n.* the art and practice of conducting negotiations between nations *The ambassador used diplomacy to prevent a war.*
province	*n.* a country or region under control of a larger government *The empire collected taxes from the province.*

From Kingdom to Republic In 509 B.C., the Romans overthrew the Etruscan kings and established a republic. A republic is a government without king or emperors.

The republic had a Senate and a citizens' assembly, which it adopted from the Etruscans. The assembly was divided into two groups: the **patricians** and the **plebeians.** The patricians were wealthy aristocrats. The plebeians were all the remaining citizens. A patrician's vote counted for more than a plebeian's vote. The assembly elected two consuls, who led the government. A group of 300 wealthy citizens were appointed to serve in the Senate, which passed the laws.

In the early 400s B.C., after many protests, the plebeians gained the right to have representatives called tribunes. A tribune could overturn the act of any public official that was unjust to any citizen. Then the plebeians were given their own assembly. Eventually, the plebeians' votes counted as much as the patricians' votes.

During a crisis, the power of government was given to a dictator. The Roman statesman Cicero describes the role of dictator.

> 66 [W]hen a serious war or civil [disagreements] arise, one man shall hold, for not longer than six months, the power which ordinarily belongs to the two consuls . . . he shall be 'master of the people.' 99

Roman Law The Romans wrote down their laws, the Twelve Tables, around 450 B.C. With written laws, people would know their rights and duties rather than rely on customs that could be ignored.

The Roman government was considered a **representative democracy,** meaning that elected representatives made the political decisions. This system prevented any one individual from gaining too much power. It differed from Athenian direct democracy. The republic of Rome influenced representative governments throughout the world, including, centuries later, that of the United States.

Roman Checks and Balances

Some modern democracies still use the system of checks and balances devised in ancient Rome. This system ensures that no one branch of the government becomes too powerful.

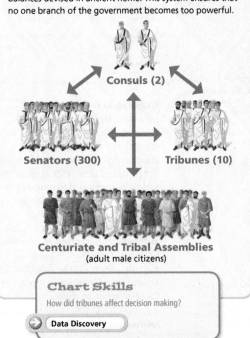

Consuls (2)

Senators (300)   Tribunes (10)

Centuriate and Tribal Assemblies
(adult male citizens)

Chart Skills

How did tribunes affect decision making?

 Data Discovery

CHART SKILLS They could overturn any public act and so reverse decisions.

COMMON MISCONCEPTIONS

All Romans Wore Togas The toga was a loosely draped garment that is famous as the traditional dress of ancient Rome. It was a large oval piece of fabric that was draped around the body in a complicated way with many folds. During the early time of the Republic, almost everyone wore togas, but gradually different classes of people stopped wearing them. First women and then laboring people gave up wearing the toga. In time, patricians wore them only on formal occasions. The toga did remain the state dress of the emperor and other high officials.

- **Cause and Effect** How did Rome become the strongest Mediterranean power? (by defeating Carthage)

Rome Becomes an Empire

- **Summarize** Why did Rome turn to the rule of a dictator in about 100 B.C.? (Several revolts occurred.)

- **Draw Conclusions** Did Caesar's death have the effect the aristocrats wanted? Explain. (Sample: No, it led to chaos and the end of the republic.)

Map Skills Point students to the map of the Roman empire.

- What African city was nearest to Italy? (Carthage)

- What geographic pattern did the Roman empire follow in Africa and Southwest Asia? (It extended along coastlines and rivers.)

→ **Active Atlas**

Have students go online to learn more about the Roman empire.

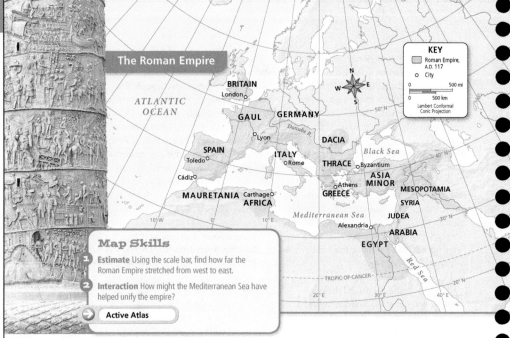

The Roman Empire

KEY
Roman Empire, A.D. 117
○ City
0 ___ 500 mi
0 ___ 500 km
Lambert Conformal Conic Projection

Map Skills

1 **Estimate** Using the scale bar, find how far the Roman Empire stretched from west to east.

2 **Interaction** How might the Mediterranean Sea have helped unify the empire?

→ **Active Atlas**

▲ This column commemorates the emperor Trajan's victories in the Dacian Wars (A.D. 100–106).

diplomacy, *n.,* the art and practice of conducting negotiations between nations

Rome Expands Rome set about expanding through alliances and conquests. The Romans used military strength and <u>diplomacy</u> to turn conquered people into allies. Defeated people signed treaties, or agreements, in which they promised to provide troops to Rome. In this way, the Roman army grew to be the largest force in Italy.

During the 200s and 100s B.C., the mighty Roman army fought its main rival, Carthage, in the Punic Wars. Rome won each war, destroying Carthage. The defeat secured Rome's position of superiority in the Mediterranean region.

Reading Check What were some of the reforms gained by the plebeians?

Rome Becomes an Empire

By 100 B.C., the republic was becoming unstable. After several revolts, the republic came under the control of dictators and military leaders.

Beginnings of Empire In the 50s B.C., Julius Caesar conquered Gaul, land that is much of present-day France and Belgium. He then invaded Italy and made himself the sole ruler of Rome and its territories. Hoping to restore the republic, aristocrats assassinated Caesar.

The result was chaos and the end of the republic. Caesar's nephew Octavian eventually emerged as the victor. He took the name Augustus and became the first Roman emperor in 27 B.C.

READING CHECK representation by tribunes, their own assembly, equal voting power with the patricians

MAP SKILLS 1. about 4,500 miles **2.** The Mediterranean Sea was a great avenue for trade. This trade helped unify the empire.

QUICK FACTS

The Colosseum The giant amphitheater known as the Colosseum was built approximately between A.D. 70 and 82. It measures 620 by 513 feet. About 50,000 spectators could sit within the Colosseum. It was the scene of battles between gladiators and contests between men and animals. At times, it was even flooded so mock naval battles could take place. Over the centuries, the Colosseum has been damaged by lightning, earthquakes, and vandals. However, it remains a popular tourist attraction and a symbol of ancient Rome.

The Empire Unifies The rule of Augustus started a period of stability known as the **Pax Romana** (Roman Peace). This period lasted for about 200 years.

Rome set up colonies in conquered areas. Many Roman citizens migrated to these colonies. Some of the people conquered by the Romans became citizens. The spread of Roman law helped to unify the empire. The empire was also united by a network of roads that helped soldiers move and keep order.

Trade along Roman roads and across the seas also stabilized the empire. The use of coins made trade easier. The empire gained wealth from trade and tributes paid by <u>provinces</u>. Tributes were a type of taxation.

Gradually, wealthy Romans came to admire Greek culture. Greek books were copied and sold widely. Learned Romans read both Latin and Greek. Greco-Roman culture was spread throughout the empire with colonies in Gaul, Spain, and North Africa. In addition to cultural influences, Roman colonists received Roman citizenship and lived under Roman law.

Reading Check What was the result of Caesar's assassination?

Life in Ancient Rome

The basic social unit in ancient Rome was the family. The father had complete control over the family and the home.

Roman women worked in the home. They could not vote or participate in politics. Gradually, Roman women did gain more rights. Emperors' wives, such as Livia and Julia Agrippina, also influenced politics in Rome.

Slavery in Ancient Rome About one third of the people in Rome were slaves. The economy depended on their work.

Sometimes, a slave could buy his or her freedom. Freed slaves were allowed to become citizens. Household slaves sometimes became trusted companions. Other slaves led short, brutal lives. Some worked in copper or tin mines. Gladiator slaves faced death in arena matches in the Colosseum. Slaves also worked as farmers or as rowers on Roman warships.

myWorldActivity
What's the News in Rome?

province, *n.*, country or region under control of a larger government

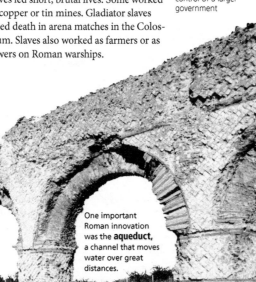

One important Roman innovation was the **aqueduct**, a channel that moves water over great distances.

READING CHECK Caesar's assassination caused chaos that led to the end of the republic and to the first emperor.

ANSWERS

PRIMARY SOURCE

Acts of the Apostles The book of Acts in the New Testament describes how some of the earliest missionary journeys spread Christianity: "As [Paul and Timothy] went from town to town, they delivered to them for observance the decisions that had been reached by the apostles and elders who were in Jerusalem. So the churches were strengthened in the faith and increased in numbers daily. They went through the region of Phrygia and Galatia, having been forbidden by the Holy Spirit to speak the word in Asia. When they had come opposite Mysia, they attempted to go into Bithynia, but the Spirit of Jesus did not allow them; so, passing by Mysia, they went down to Troas."
—Acts 16:4–8 (New Revised Standard Version)

GUIDE ON THE SIDE

- **Identify Details** What type of literature did Virgil and Horace write? (poetry)

- **Categorize** In what scientific fields did Romans make discoveries? (astronomy and anatomy)

Judaism and Christianity

- **Compare and Contrast** How did Jewish belief and Roman belief differ? (The Jews believed in one God; the Romans believed in many.)

- **Summarize** Why did the Jews rebel? (They resented Roman rule.)

Map Skills Point out the map on the spread of Christianity.

- Why do the arrows lead away from Jerusalem? (Christianity began there.)

- Why do you think Christianity spread first to areas near large cities? (Sample: because many people traveled there for trade)

Active Atlas

Have students go online to learn more about the spread of Christianity.

Roman Religion Romans worshiped many deities, some of whom were adopted from the Greeks and the Etruscans. In Rome, religion was tied closely to political life and emperors were sometimes worshiped as gods.

Roman Achievements Like the Greeks, Romans made statues in marble. Roman literature includes poetry by Virgil and Horace, and essays by Cicero. Architects perfected the arch and invented concrete to build temples and public buildings.

In Roman Egypt, Ptolemy (TAH luh mee) calculated the size and distance of the sun and the paths of the stars and planets across the sky. The Greek Galen discovered how parts of the body worked.

Reading Check What elements helped to unify the Roman empire?

Judaism and Christianity

The Jews of Judea lived in an area that came under direct Roman rule in A.D. 63. In the centuries before the Roman empire, the Jews had spread to Egypt and to other parts of southwest Asia. The Jews believed in one God. This belief is called monotheism. The Romans, who believed in many gods, did not force them to change their practices.

Jews Flee Harsh Rule Some Jews, however, resented foreign rule and rebelled against the Romans. The Romans struck back harshly and destroyed the Jewish Temple in Jerusalem in A.D. 70.

The Romans killed many thousands of Jews. Other Jews left the ruined province for other parts of the empire. Many moved to Italy and other parts of Europe.

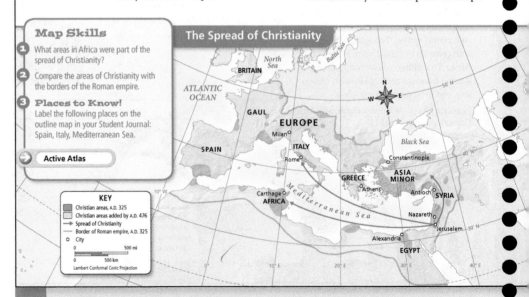

Map Skills

1. What areas in Africa were part of the spread of Christianity?
2. Compare the areas of Christianity with the borders of the Roman empire.
3. **Places to Know!** Label the following places on the outline map in your Student Journal: Spain, Italy, Mediterranean Sea.

Active Atlas

The Spread of Christianity

KEY
- Christian areas, A.D. 325
- Christian areas added by A.D. 476
- → Spread of Christianity
- — Border of Roman empire, A.D. 325
- ○ City

0   500 mi
0 500 km
Lambert Conformal Conic Projection

MAP SKILLS 1. Carthage and Egypt **2.** The areas were similar, but Christianity spread farther east. **3.** Places should be accurately labeled.

READING CHECK citizenship, religion, trade, family structures

READING CHECK Rome harshly punished Jews who rebelled.

ECONOMICS

Inflation in Ancient Rome During the period A.D. 235 to A.D. 284, the Roman empire went through a period of extreme instability, including numerous invasions and civil wars. Dozens of emperors ruled, most for very short reigns. Because of the wars, the emperors had high expenses. To make their treasuries stretch further, they reduced the percentage of precious metal in coins. In time, people began to lose faith in coins, so they hurried to spend what money they had on goods they thought would retain value. The increased spending sparked a period of high inflation that lasted for decades.

Birth and Spread of Christianity Around 4 B.C., a Jew named Jesus was born in Judea. He grew up in Nazareth and learned to be a carpenter.

When he was 30 years old, he became a religious teacher. Jesus preached that there was only one God. However, many of his followers believed that Jesus was the Messiah. Jews believed that a leader called the Messiah would bring them freedom. The name Christ comes from the Greek word for messiah. Jesus's followers later came to be known as Christians. Jesus's teachings formed the basis for a new religion, Christianity.

Christianity gradually spread across the Roman empire and into neighboring lands. For more than 200 years, Christians faced harsh treatment from the Roman government. Then, in A.D. 312, Roman emperor Constantine I became a Christian. Over the next 100 years, Christianity spread across much of Europe, and most Romans became Christians.

Reading Check Why did the Jews want to flee Roman rule?

The Western Empire Falls

Historians are not sure what caused the fall of the Roman empire. One theory proposes that the Romans used so many everyday objects made of lead that people may have sickened and died from lead poisoning. Most likely the collapse came from several factors.

Instability and Division From A.D. 235 to A.D. 284, there were 60 men who declared themselves emperor. Prices increased, taxes rose, and disease reduced the population. The Roman army weakened as it came to depend more on mercenaries, or soldiers who fought for money rather than for loyalty to a leader or nation.

Diocletian eventually divided the empire into eastern and western lands to make it easier to govern. Constantine moved the capital east, renaming it Constantinople. The Eastern Roman empire went on to thrive as the Byzantine empire, while the west fell to Germanic invaders.

Reading Check Identify one factor that led to the fall of the Roman empire.

Invaders!

▶ **378** Visigoths defeat the Roman army.
▶ **406** Vandals attack Gaul.
▶ **410** Visigoths sack Rome.
▶ **441** Attila (above) and the Huns begin to invade the empire.
▶ **450** Angles, Saxons, Jutes invade Britain (traditional date).
▶ **476** Rome falls to the Germanic leader Odoacer.

Timeline

Section 2 Assessment

Key Terms
1. Define each of these key terms with a complete sentence: patrician, plebeian, representative democracy, Pax Romana, aqueduct.

Key Ideas
2. Why was Julius Caesar assassinated?
3. How did the conversion of Constantine I affect religion in Europe?
4. Name three elements that led to the fall of the Roman empire.

Think Critically
5. **Compare and Contrast** How did Roman democracy differ from ancient Greek democracy?
6. **Problem Solving** If you were in charge of the Roman empire, how would you prevent it from collapsing? List at least three ways.

Essential Question
What are the challenges of diversity?
7. How did the Romans use citizenship to unify a diverse empire? Go to your Student Journal to record your answer.

ANSWERS

GUIDE ON THE SIDE

• **Identify Main Ideas** Whose teachings became the basis for Christianity? (Jesus)
• **Summarize** What did Jews believe the Messiah would do for them? (They believed he would bring freedom to the Jews.)

The Western Empire Falls

• **Draw Conclusions** What effect would it have on an empire to have 60 different rulers in less than 50 years? (Sample: It would cause constant change, uncertainty, and perhaps anxiety among people.)
• **Problem Solve** Why did Diocletian divide the empire in two? (to make each section easier to govern)

 Timeline

Have students go online to learn more about invasions of the Roman empire.

The Fall of the Roman Empire

OBJECTIVES

Students will

- identify various theories about the fall of the Roman empire.
- **21st Century Learning** categorize information from primary sources.
- **ELL** learn the differences between the synonyms *decay* and *decline*.

SET EXPECTATIONS

In this lesson, students will

- read and analyze two documents on the fall of the Roman empire.
- write an outline for a persuasive essay urging the ancient Romans to protect themselves.

1 Connect

Ask students to think of a situation in which they realized that a sports team was going to fail to have a successful season. Ask, What were some of the reasons for the failure? List their answers on the board. Encourage them to think of both internal reasons, such as a decline in talent or injuries on the team, and external reasons, such as the strength of the team's opponents. Then ask, How might an empire's problems be similar to a sports team's problems? What factors might challenge an empire's power?

2 Experience

Preview Have students preview the two pages and the images. Read the Key Idea, glossary terms, and definitions. Clarify any questions about the meaning of these words by providing examples.

Read Slowly read aloud the excerpt "Numerous Enemies" without stopping. Read the document again, this time stopping to read the questions at the left and prompting students to rethink and analyze the meaning of the words. Have students answer the questions using the location of the letters to provide clues. Do the same for the excerpt "Lead Poisoning." Lead a discussion starting with students' responses to the questions. Ask, Which of these theories sounds most likely to you? Could they both be true? Explain.

ELL **Early Advanced/Advanced** Help students to understand the difference between the similar words *decay* and *decline*. Both words mean "a loss of quality," but they have different connotations. The original meaning of *decay* is rotting, so it hints at death. The original meaning of *decline* is a downward slope, so it hints at a worsening trend but one that could be changed.

myWorld Activity: Act Before It's Too Late! Have students work together to develop warnings about the fall of Rome. Give each student a copy of *Activity Support: Mural Planning*. Working in small groups, have them reread the excerpts on the fall of the Roman empire, choose a danger faced by Rome, and make a sketch for a mural to warn about it.

30 min

3 Understand

Review Go back to the Key Idea. Discuss with students how each writer offers theories about why the Roman empire weakened and declined. Discuss how the causes fit in the following categories: cultural, political, economic, and military. Explain how some causes might fit into more than one category.

Assess Have students complete **Analyze the Documents.** Review their answers to determine if students have met the lesson objectives.

Remediate If students struggle to differentiate internal and external issues, have them ask themselves, *Does this problem come from outside or inside the empire's borders?*

Name _____ Class _____ Date _____

myWorld Activity Support **Mural Planning**

Act Before It's Too Late!

Directions Working in a small group, design a mural (wall painting) to warn the ancient Romans of one of the dangers they face. First reread both of the excerpts about the fall of the Roman empire. You may also review Section 2. Then as a group choose the danger that you want to warn about and make a sketch of a mural to alert the people of Rome. Use the worksheet below to plan your mural. Then sketch the mural on your own paper.

Name the danger. _____

Category (political, economic, military, cultural) _____

_____

What will happen if Romans ignore the danger _____

_____

What Romans can do to end the danger _____

_____

What visual image you want to use _____

A quotation from one of the excerpts to use on the mural _____

_____

_____

HISTORY

Edward Gibbon The historian Edward Gibbon caused a controversy by suggesting in *The Decline and Fall of the Roman Empire* that Christianity was one of the reasons the empire weakened. Gibbon himself was a skeptic who did not believe in the supernatural or in God's intervention in human life. In his history of Rome, he treated Christianity with irony. He blamed the religion for teaching pacifism and emphasizing life after death, and he claimed those teachings weakened the desire of Romans to defend their empire. Although more recent historians still respect Gibbon's book, most have placed more emphasis on political and economic causes of the empire's decline.

GUIDE ON THE SIDE

Categorize Use the lettered prompts to help students analyze the documents in order to sort the information.

ANSWERS

A Sample: Gibbon believed the Romans were not aware of the number of their enemies. He might be correct because they did not seem to take steps to protect themselves.

B Sample: He thought they were uncivilized and probably looked down on them; he called them voracious, turbulent, and barbarians.

C The fruits of industry were products of the Roman economy, grown by farmers and made by artisans. The tribes did not have such wealth.

Primary Source

The Fall of the Roman Empire

Key Idea
- Many different problems contributed to the fall of the Roman empire. Historians have investigated its causes for centuries.

For centuries, scholars have wondered why the powerful Roman empire collapsed. In its final years, the Roman empire was weakened by economic, military, political, and social problems. In the 1700s, the English historian Edward Gibbon wrote that Rome fell to stronger Germanic invaders. For generations, his ideas were unquestioned. Today, most historians agree that many factors led to the collapse of the empire. The topic remains popular with researchers and historians who continue to propose new ideas about what weakened the once-mighty empire.

▲ This Roman coin depicts Mars, the god of war.

Stop at each circled letter on the right to think about the text. Answer the question with the same letter on the left.

A **Draw Conlusions** How does Gibbon believe the Romans viewed their situation? Might he have been correct? Explain.

B **Identify Bias** What was Gibbon's view of the northern tribes? How can you tell?

C **Draw Inferences** What were the "fruits of industry," and why would the northern tribes want them?

voracious, *adj.,* extremely hungry
ravish, *v.,* to seize and carry away by force
barbarian, *adj.,* those considered uncivilized by the ancient Greeks and Romans

Numerous Enemies

In this marble relief, a Germanic swordsman defends himself against a Roman warrior. ▼

66 **The Romans were ignorant of the**
A **extent of their danger, and**
the number of their enemies. Beyond the Rhine and Danube, the northern countries of Europe and Asia were filled with [a great many] tribes of hunters
B and shepherds, poor, <u>voracious</u>, and turbulent [agitated]; bold in arms, and impatient to <u>ravish</u> the
C fruits of industry. The <u>Barbarian</u> world was agitated by the rapid impulse of war. 99

—Edward Gibbon,
The History of the Decline and Fall of the Roman Empire, 1776–1788

ANALYZE THE DOCUMENTS **1.** The danger within the empire was lead poisoning and the danger outside was enemy barbarians. **2.** Sample outline:

I. Introduction: Problems Faced by Romans
  A. Not enough defenses against "barbarians"
  B. Lead poisoning

II. What to do about lack of defenses
  A. Why Germanic tribes pose a danger
  B. How to strengthen defenses

III. What to do about lead poisoning

21st Century Learning CATEGORIZE

To assist your students in categorizing information, practice the skill by writing the following categories on the board: Cultural, Political, Economic, and Military. Give the class the following examples and ask them to name the correct category for each one: rapidly rising prices, a period when many emperors ruled for short times, an army of foreigners with little loyalty to Rome, and conflict over whether patricians or plebeians would have the most power.

Point out word clues, such as *prices*, that indicate what category to choose. Then have students use the scaffolded questions at the left of each excerpt to identify theories about why Rome declined. Have them look for verbal clues to tell them which causes were external and which were internal. For example, a cause that was related to daily life would be internal. For additional help, refer students to the **21st Century Online Tutor** *Categorize*.

Stop at each circled letter on the right to think about the text. Then answer the question with the same letter on the left.

D Draw Conclusions What does "the decay of their bodies and health" mean?

E Draw Inferences Why did the Romans use so much lead?

F Synthesize If most people in an empire accidentally ingested something that damaged their health, how might this have affected the empire as a whole?

chronic, *adj.*, occurring often and lasting a long time

metallurgist, *n.*, a person who works with metals

ingest, *v.*, to take food or chemicals into the body

Lead Poisoning

66 In 1983, Jerome O. Nriagu, an environmental scientist . . . theorized that the decline of the empire had its roots not in the decay of Roman ideals and morality, but in the **D** decay of their bodies and health. The cause of this decay, Nriagu wrote, was <u>chronic</u> lead poisoning. A soft gray metal that is **E** plentiful in nature, lead was used by the Romans to make many household items. Roman <u>metallurgists</u> blended lead with tin to make a silver-gray metal known as pewter. Craftsmen used the handsome metal to make cups, plates, spoons, cooking pots, **F** and wine vessels. . . . What the Romans did not know is that lead is one of the most poisonous metals a person can <u>ingest</u>. 99

—Bradley Steffens,
The Fall of the Roman Empire, 1994

ANSWERS

D They were sick.

E It was plentiful, soft enough to mold, and could be made into the handsome metal pewter.

F The empire would be weakened because of widespread sickness and death.

Analyze the Documents

1. **Categorize** According to these documents, what was a danger within the empire and what was a danger outside the empire?
2. **Writing Task** Make an outline for a persuasive essay in which you try to convince people in the Roman empire to make changes to save themselves.

▲ Lead keys from ancient Rome

A. Why lead poses a danger
B. How to decrease use of lead in daily life

IV. Conclusion
   A. Summary of two dangers
   B. Restatement of recommended actions
   C. Emotional appeal to take action

Early Middle Ages

OBJECTIVES

Students will know

- that the legacy of the Byzantine empire included a law code, Orthodox Christianity, and the Cyrillic alphabet.
- how European feudalism functioned.

Students will be able to

- summarize the social roles that existed during feudalism.
- demonstrate awareness of other writing systems.

SET EXPECTATIONS

In this section, students will

- read Early Middle Ages.
- convert words from the Latin to the Cyrillic alphabet.
- go On Assignment in medieval Europe and learn about manor life.

CORE CONCEPTS

You may wish to teach or reteach the following lessons from the Core Concepts Handbook:

- Land Use, pp. 50–51
- Political Systems, pp. 106–107
- Historical Maps, pp. 124–125

KEY

Differentiated Instruction	English Language Instruction	
L1 Special Needs **L2** Extra Support	**ELL** Beginner **ELL** Early Intermediate	**ELL** Intermediate
L3 On-Level **L4** Challenge	**ELL** Early Advanced **ELL** Advanced	

1 Connect
Make learning meaningful

Make Connections Ask students to think about the difference between renting and owning property. Do renters have as much control over property as owners? Why might some people want to buy a home rather than rent one?

ELL Early Advanced/Advanced The term *landlord* is a compound word that goes back to feudalism when *lords* owned the *land* and allowed peasants to live there in exchange for work.

Activate Prior Knowledge In the previous chapter, students learned that invasions by Germanic tribes caused the western half of the Roman empire to collapse. Ask them to predict what Europeans did to protect themselves when they no longer had the Roman army to defend them.

L2 Extra Support Guide students by asking the following questions: What do you do to protect yourself? (lock house doors; stay home after dark) How do relationships with people increase your safety? (less likely to be bullied when in a group)

Prepare Follow the steps in the section **Preview.** Preteach the Key Terms. Then have students complete *Word Wise* in their journals using in-text clues and the glossary for help.

2 Experience
Teach knowledge and skills

Read Use **Background** notes and **Guide on the Side** questions to model active reading. Have students use *Take Notes* in their **Student Journal** to summarize how feudalism worked. Have students complete **21st Century Online Tutor** *Summarize,* and apply this skill to reading the section.

L1 Special Needs Have students with reading difficulties work with a partner to learn how feudal society was structured by studying *Enrichment: Feudalism Social Pyramid.*

ELL Early Intermediate/Intermediate Give students cards with the following names: Anna Comnena, Charles Martel, Charlemagne, Clovis, Justinian, and Theodora. Have them divide the cards into two piles, according to whether the person was linked to the Byzantine empire or to the Frankish kingdoms and Holy Roman Empire.

L4 Challenge Students can read about King Arthur and then draw a comic strip about one of the adventures of Arthur or his knights.

Practice: my World Activity Students will practice using the Cyrillic alphabet by converting English words from Latin letters to Cyrillic letters. **Step-by-Step Instructions** and **More Activities** follow on p. T26.

SECTION 3 RESOURCE GUIDE

FOR THE STUDENT

my worldgeography.com Student Center
- Active Atlas
- Culture Close-up

Student Edition (print and online)
- Early Middle Ages

Student Journal (print and online)
- Section 3 Word Wise
- Section 3 Take Notes

21st Century Learning Online Tutor
- Summarize
- Develop cultural awareness

FOR THE TEACHER

my worldgeography.com Teacher Center
- Online Lesson Planner
- Presentations for Projection
- SuccessTracker

ProGuide: Europe and Russia
- Section 3 Lesson Plan, pp. T24–T25
- 🏃 myWorld Activity Step-by-Step Instructions, p. T26
- Activity Support: Alphabet Table, p. T27
- myWorld Geography Enrichment, p. T28
- Section Quiz, p. T29

Accelerating the Progress of ELLs
- Reading Support Strategies, p. 42

---

3 Understand
Assess understanding

Review Review *Word Wise* and *Take Notes* in the **Student Journal.**

Assess Knowledge and Skills Use the Section Assessment and Section Quiz to check students' progress.

Assess Understanding Review students' responses to the Section Assessment Essential Question prompt.

Remediate Use these strategies to review and remediate.

If students struggle to . . .	Try these strategies.
Understand the feudal economic exchange of military service for land	Remind students that today people often do military service for free college tuition.
Summarize	Assign additional practice with the **21st Century Online Tutor.**
Show cultural awareness of other writing systems	Display samples of writing in Arabic, Hebrew, Korean, Chinese, and Japanese.

ELL Support

ELL Objective Students will be able to use English to express a summary of the important characteristics of feudalism.

Cultural Connections To connect to the idea of knights, have students use English or their native languages to share songs or stories about legendary warriors in their culture.

ELL Beginner Content Tip Find and copy pictures of a knight, a manor, a king, a castle, and other aspects of medieval life. Give students the pictures and a list of terms. Have them match the terms to the images.

ELL Activity If students' first language uses non-Latin characters, ask them to write a few names in that language on the board before the class does the Cyrillic alphabet activity. They might write *Europe* and the name of their family's homeland. If students' first language uses the Latin alphabet, ask them to describe other ways it differs from English, such as accents or sounds that English lacks. **(Verbal)**

myWorld Activity   **Step-by-Step Instructions**

 20 min

Write in Cyrillic

OBJECTIVES

Students will
- convert words from one alphabet to another.
- compare similarities between alphabets.

LEARNING STYLE
- Visual
- Verbal

21st Century Learning
- Develop cultural awareness

MATERIALS
- Activity Support: Alphabet Table, p. T27

Activity Steps

1. Review with students the information in Section 3 about the Cyrillic alphabet. Pass out copies of *Activity Support: Alphabet Table* to each student. Go over the chart, drawing special attention to characters that represent sounds not used in English and combinations of sounds.

2. Have students choose partners. Each pair should take a few minutes to practice using the Cyrillic alphabet by using its letters to write their names.

   ELL **Intermediate** If students' first language is one that uses non-Latin characters, encourage them to demonstrate how to write their name in that language as well.

3. Tell students to work individually to choose one sentence from Section 3 of their textbook and rewrite it on the lines provided using Cyrillic letters. When they finish, they should exchange papers

with their partners and try to convert each other's sentences back to English.

   L2 **Extra Support** To make this step more manageable, provide students with a page that lists several short sentences from the section and tell them to choose one.

4. Conclude the activity by using the following questions to lead a class discussion: What is the relationship between writing and knowledge? (Writing allows people to record their history and learning.) How did the invention of the Cyrillic alphabet spread literacy and learning in Eastern Europe? (It made it possible for Eastern Europeans to read and write their language using their own writing system.) How was the invention of the Cyrillic alphabet similar to the actions of monks who copied ancient manuscripts? (Both actions helped preserve learning.)

 More Activities From myWorld Teachers

Local Connection Have pairs of students look in the Yellow Pages to see if there are any Orthodox churches in your area. They should list them and note whether the churches identify themselves with a particular country (for example, Greek Orthodox or Russian Orthodox). **(Verbal)**

Design a Castle Students should research castles of the Middle Ages using books you provide and

then draw a plan for one. Each castle should provide for food, water, shelter, defense, and spiritual needs. Drawings should show the castle's location. **(Visual)**

Be a Troubadour Write a song or a rap about the adventures of a medieval knight. Perform your song for class as if it were a music video, with group members acting out the adventure. **(Verbal/Rhythmic)**

 my worldgeography.com **Teacher Center** ➔ Find additional resources in the online Teacher Center.

Name _____   Class _____ Date _____

myWorld Activity Support   **Alphabet Table**

Write in Cyrillic

Directions Study the alphabet table below and answer the
questions. Practice using the Cyrillic alphabet by writing your name
on the space provided. Then, on the blank lines, choose a sentence
from the textbook and rewrite it in Cyrillic letters. Exchange pages
with a partner. See if you can correctly change each others' sentences
back to English.

1. Which letters are the same in both alphabets?

_____

2. Which letters in the Cyrillic alphabet are confusing because they
   look like a different letter of the Latin alphabet?

_____

The Cyrillic Alphabet			
Cyrillic	**Latin**	**Cyrillic**	**Latin**
А а	(A)	П п	(P)
Б б	(B)	Р р	(R)
В в	(V)	С с	(S)
Г г	(G)	Т т	(T)
Д д	(D)	У у	(U)
Е е	(E)	Ф ф	(F)
Ё ё	(YO)	Х х	(KH)
Ж ж	(ZH)	Ц ц	(TS)
З з	(Z)	Ч ч	(CH)
И и	(I)	Ш ш	(SH)
Й й	(Y)	Щ щ	(SHCH)
К к	(K)	ъ	(-)
Л л	(L)	ы	(Y)
М м	(M)	Ю ю	(YU or IU)
Н н	(N)	Я я	(YA or IA)
О о	(O)		

My first name: _____

Sentence: _____

_____

_____

_____

Name _____ Class _____ Date _____

Enrichment: Feudalism Social Pyramid

Directions Study the diagram below. Answer the questions
that follow.

1. Who had the most power in feudal society?

_____

_____

2. Explain how nobles could be both lords and vassals.

_____

_____

3. Who do you think did the most hard labor in feudal society?
   Explain.

_____

_____

Name _____ Class _____ Date _____

Section Quiz

Directions Answer the following questions using what you learned
in Section 3.

1. ____ Why is the medieval period also called
   the Middle Ages?
   a. because the most important events took
      place in central Europe
   b. because nobles lived in castles in the
      center of circular walls
   c. because it came between the ancient
      and modern periods
   d. because the church taught people to live
      between heaven and earth

2. ____ How did monks preserve ancient
   culture?
   a. by hiding statues in their monasteries
   b. by teaching classical law in universities
   c. by copying Greek and Roman works
   d. by building churches modeled after
      temples

3. ____ What legacy did Emperor Justinian
   leave for modern Europe?
   a. a legal code that organized Roman laws
   b. a treaty with the Roman Catholic Church
   c. a method of absolute rule
   d. an ancient sports stadium

4. ____ What was the Great Schism of 1054?
   a. a split between eastern and western
      churches
   b. a war between Slavic and Byzantine
      empires
   c. a deadly earthquake that struck
      Constantinople
   d. a ban on using icons in Christian worship

5. ____ Who expanded the Frankish kingdom
   and established a Western European
   empire?
   a. Clovis
   b. Charlemagne
   c. Justinian
   d. Theodora

6.

Feudal Duties	
A lord owed his vassals	**A vassal owed his lord**

Early Middle Ages

SECTION PREVIEW

- Model preparing to read by previewing the Key Ideas, Key Terms, headings, visuals, and captions. Have students make predictions about what they will learn. For ELL support, post the prompt, "I predict I will read about . . ."

- Preview and practice the reading skill, Summarize, by using examples from movies or television shows.

- Preteach this section's high-use Academic Vocabulary and Key Terms using the chart on the next page and in-text definitions. Have students practice Key Terms by completing the *Word Wise* page in their journals.

GUIDE ON THE SIDE

Reading Skill

Summarize Have students practice this skill while they read by completing the *Take Notes* graphic organizer in the **Student Journal.**

The Byzantine Empire

- **Identify Main Ideas** Where did the center of power move after Rome fell? (east to Constantinople)

- **Infer** How did Justinian's law code help rulers unify power? (Sample: It helped them keep order by clearly defining laws.)

Section 3
Early Middle Ages

Key Ideas
- The Byzantine empire influenced the religion and writing systems of Eastern Europe.
- Charlemagne united most of Western Europe.
- Feudalism and manorialism shaped relations among medieval Europeans.

Key Terms • schism • lord • vassal • feudalism • manorialism

○ Visual Glossary

Reading Skill: Summarize Take notes using the graphic organizer in your journal.

The emperor Justinian ruled the Byzantine empire from 527 to 565.

After the fall of the Roman empire, a new age dawned in Europe. This age is often called the medieval period or Middle Ages. The word *medieval* comes from the Latin words for "middle" and "age." Historians use this term because the medieval period is beween the ancient and modern periods of European history.

The Byzantine Empire
As the Western Roman empire declined, power shifted east. The Eastern Roman empire remained strong. Its capital, Constantinople, grew rich on trade. Historians refer to the surviving eastern empire as the Byzantine empire.

Emperor Justinian's Rule Justinian ruled as an autocrat, or a single ruler with absolute power. He ruled both the empire and the Christian Church. Under Justinian, the empire expanded through conquest and trade. Justinian's wife Theodora served as his close advisor and, in effect, co-ruler. One of Justinian's greatest acts as emperor was to organize Roman laws into one code, called Justinian's Code. By the 1100s, these laws had reached Western Europe and helped monarchs unify their power. These laws remain part of many countries' laws.

Byzantine Christianity Since early Christian times, leaders called patriarchs had led the Christian churches in different regions. In the west, the head of the Church was the patriarch of Rome, known as the pope. The pope claimed the power to lead all Christians.

ANSWERS

ACADEMIC VOCABULARY

High-Use Word	Definition and Sample Sentence
legacy	*n.* something transmitted or received from a predecessor *The new king inherited a legacy of political stability from his father.*
manuscript	*n.* a document written by hand *In the desk, Jenny found the manuscript of a novel her mother had written.*

In the east, the highest official was the patriarch of Constantinople. This patriarch obeyed the Byzantine emperor. Unlike Christian priests in Western Europe, the Byzantine clergy had the right to marry. Greek, not Latin, was the language of the eastern Church.

A New Alphabet During Roman times, a people called the Slavs lived in what is now Poland, Belarus, and Ukraine. The Slavs had been farmers and traders for centuries. This commerce brought them in contact with the Byzantine empire.

In about 863, two Byzantine Greeks, the brothers Cyril and Methodius, traveled to Eastern Europe to bring Christianity to the Slavs. While there, they translated the Greek Bible into a Slavic language. This translation let people learn about Christianity in a language they understood. The brothers invented the Cyrillic alphabet. This alphabet combined Greek and Latin letters to express the sounds in the Slavic languages. In this way, writing and Christianity spread among the Slavic peoples. Today, people in Eastern Europe—as well as some in Russia and Mongolia—write in the Cyrillic alphabet.

Christianity Splits Gradually, the two branches of Christianity grew more divided. The Eastern church rejected the pope as leader of all Christians. Finally, the church went through an official **schism** (SIZ um), or split, called the Great Schism of 1054. The Byzantine church became the Eastern, or Greek, Orthodox church. The Western church became the Roman Catholic Church. These churches remain divided today.

The Byzantine Empire Falls By the time of the Great Schism, the Byzantine empire had begun to weaken. The emperors lost their lands to invaders such as the Arabs. Arabs conquered most of the Byzantine lands in North Africa and southwest Asia during the 600s. The Arabs were Muslims, or followers of Islam, a new religion. Like Judaism and Christianity, Islam was based on the worship of one god.

In addition, powerful merchants from the Italian city-state of Venice took control of important Byzantine trade routes. Then,

myWorldActivity
Write in Cyrillic

Cyril and Methodius, whom Christians revere as saints, hold religious documents writtten in Cyrillic. How did this alphabet get its name? ▼

CAPTION The alphabet was named after Cyril.

CORE CONCEPTS: POLITICAL SYSTEMS

Review Core Concept 8.2 before having students read about Clovis and Charlemagne and their empires. Review monarchies and empires, and explain to students that after the Western Roman empire fell, Frankish kings tried to establish strong governments. Also explain that the people in the Germanic tribes ruled by Clovis and Charlemagne did not have a history of centralized governments. Ask, What problems might be encountered by a ruler who tried to unite independent, local tribes?

GUIDE ON THE SIDE

- **Cause and Effect** How did rule by the Ottomans affect life in Constantinople? (They changed the name of the city to Istanbul and made it a center of Muslim culture.)

- **Identify Main Ideas** How did the Byzantine empire leave a lasting legacy for the world? (by preserving ancient learning)

New Kingdoms in Europe

- **Compare Viewpoints** How do you think Germanic and Roman ideas of government differed? (Sample: The Germanic tribes were loyal to a local leader rather than to a central government.)

Analyze Maps Have students look at the map of the Byzantine empire.

- What were the two large regions that the Byzantine empire controlled? (the Balkan Peninsula, Asia Minor)

→ **Active Atlas**

Have students go online to learn more about the Byzantine empire.

in 1453, the Ottoman Turks captured Constantinople. This meant the end of the Byzantine empire. The Turks changed the city's name to Istanbul. They also introduced Islam and made Istanbul a center of Muslim culture.

Byzantine Achievements Building on Greco-Roman culture, the Byzantine empire lasted for almost 1,000 years. Its artists advanced art and architecture. Its scholars preserved ancient learning. One such scholar was Anna Comnena, the first important female historian in the west. The Byzantine <u>legacy</u> led to Europe's later cultural flowering, the Renaissance.

legacy, *n.,* something transmitted or received from a predecessor

Reading Check **What did Cyril and Methodius achieve?**

The Byzantine Empire

KEY
Byzantine Empire, about 1020

0   400 mi
0   400 km
Miller Cylindrical Projection

Map Skills

1 **Interaction** What cultures might have influenced Constantinople?

2 **Places to Know!** Label the following places on the outline map in your Student Journal: Asia Minor, Balkan Peninsula, Constantinople.

→ **Active Atlas**

New Kingdoms in Europe

By around A.D. 450, Germanic tribes had taken control of most of the Western Roman empire.

Germanic Tribes Take Control Different tribes controlled the various parts of the region. A Germanic tribe called the Visigoths settled in Spain. The Angles, Jutes, and Saxons—later known as the Anglo-Saxons—took over most of Britain. And the Franks set up a kingdom in Gaul, in present-day France and Belgium.

Within each of these kingdoms, people were loyal only to their local leader. As a result, the idea of a central government disappeared.

Rise of the Franks A king of the Franks named Clovis defeated the last Roman commander in 486. He then established a kingdom that stretched from the Rhine region in the east to the Pyrenees Mountains in the west. Later, this area was named France after the Franks.

After Clovis's death, his kingdom was divided into smaller kingdoms. In the early 700s, however, the Frankish ruler Charles Martel united these kingdoms.

Charlemagne During the 770s, Charles Martel's grandson, Charlemagne (742–814), became king of the Franks. He conquered much of Western Europe and expanded the Frankish empire.

Charlemagne strongly supported the Catholic Church. He believed that by converting people to Christianity all across his growing empire, he could unite and strengthen it. Pope Leo III crowned Charlemagne Holy Roman Emperor in 800.

MAP SKILLS **1.** Asian and European **2.** Places should be labeled accurately.

READING CHECK They translated the Bible into the Slavic language and invented the Cyrillic alphabet.

CULTURE

Illuminated Manuscripts One of the main art forms of medieval Europe was illuminated manuscripts—handwritten books decorated with gold or silver, brilliant colors, miniature pictures, or decorative designs. Many such books have survived because they were made of tough, animal-skin pages protected by wooden covers. The term *illuminated* came from the use of gold, which made the pages look as though they had light shining on them. Commonly, pages had elaborate initial letters, intricate decorative designs, portraits of saints, and pictures of beasts, which were often symbolic. One reason illuminated manuscripts were produced in large numbers is that most people were illiterate, so the illustrations helped to pass on church teachings.

This was important because a Christian pope had crowned a Germanic ruler as a successor to Roman emperors.

Charlemagne reestablished the rule of law, which had weakened after the fall of Rome. For example, he declared that judges should base their decisions on accepted laws. He also set up a school at his palace, though he himself could not write. This school attracted scholars from all of Europe.

After Charlemagne's death, the empire was divided among his sons. Some of these lands later became the modern countries of France and Germany.

Vikings and Magyars During the 800s and 900s, Viking invaders made terrifying raids along the coasts and rivers of Europe. The Vikings came from Scandinavia in northern Europe. They conquered parts of what are now England, Scotland, Ireland, France, and Ukraine. The Vikings who settled in France were called Normans. The Normans later conquered England.

Viking and Norman invaders also helped shape powerful kingdoms in England and in Ukraine. The kingdom in Ukraine, called Kievan Rus, adopted Eastern Christianity. The modern nations of Ukraine, Belarus, and Russia grew out of Kievan Rus.

During the 900s, a people called the Magyars conquered what is now Hungary. They made fearsome raids into Germany, Italy, and other parts of Western Europe. Around 1000, the Magyars converted to Christianity. The Magyars formed the kingdom of Hungary.

Christian Life The Christian church and its teachings were the center of medieval life. The church sent people across Europe to spread Christianity and gain new members. Gradually, most pagans in Europe converted to the Christian religion. A pagan was someone who worshiped more than one god. Although Western Europeans were divided politically, the Catholic Church united them through religion. Eastern Europeans were united through the Eastern Orthodox Church. *Orthodox* means following traditional or established beliefs.

Statue of Charlemagne ▼

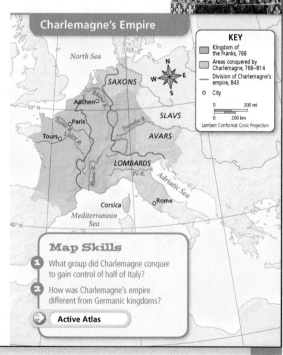

Charlemagne's Empire

KEY
- Kingdom of the Franks, 768
- Areas conquered by Charlemagne, 768–814
- Division of Charlemagne's empire, 843
- City

0   200 mi
0   200 km
Lambert Conformal Conic Projection

North Sea

SAXONS

Aachen

Paris

Tours

SLAVS

AVARS

LOMBARDS
Po R.

Adriatic Sea

Corsica

Rome

Mediterranean Sea

Map Skills

1. What group did Charlemagne conquer to gain control of half of Italy?

2. How was Charlemagne's empire different from Germanic kingdoms?

 Active Atlas

MAP SKILLS 1. Lombards **2.** It was much larger than the Germanic kingdoms.

- **Infer** Why do you think Charlemagne set up a school, even though he could not write? (Sample: He believed educated people made better public officials.)

- **Express an Opinion** Why do you think Charlemagne's empire did not last? (Sample: because the Germanic peoples were used to having smaller states)

- **Summarize** How did the Roman Catholic Church take the place of the old empire? (It unified Europe religiously instead of poltically.)

Map Skills Have students study the map of Charlemagne's empire.

- What ethnic group lived to the east of the empire? (the Slavs)

- What Mediterranean island was part of the empire? (Corsica)

 Active Atlas

Have students go online to learn more about Charlemagne's empire.

ANSWERS

GEOGRAPHY

Castle Defenses Castle builders used knowledge of geography to make castles safer. From ancient times, people knew that defenders had an advantage if they could hold a high place, especially if the enemy had to attack across open ground. Medieval castle building made use of this principle. The earliest castles were strongholds built atop high mounds circled by a ditch. Later, baileys (open grounds between encircling walls) were added to the defenses. Having to cross water or walls slowed attackers and made them vulnerable. By the 1200s, many castles were being built backed up against a cliff to limit the lines of approach. The invention of artillery that could topple castle walls caused the practice of castle building to decline in the 1500s and 1600s.

- **Identify Main Ideas** Who were monks and nuns? (They were men and women who lived in religious communities.)

- **Cause and Effect** What inspired Hildegard of Bingen's work? (her visions of God)

Feudalism and Manorialism

- **Identify Details** What were nobles who received lands in exchange for service called? (vassals)

Chart Skills Have students look at the chart *Feudalism: The Medieval Way of Life.*

- Who had the job of handling territory? (lords)

- Who were the warriors? (knights)

- Who had to obey all the other classes? (peasants)

Data Discovery

Have students go online to learn more about feudalism.

Male Christian religious people called monks lived in monasteries, secluded communities focused on prayer and service. These monks made copies of the Bible and Greek and Roman works. They helped to preserve valuable <u>manuscripts</u>, many of which contained ancient learning.

manuscript, *n.,* a document written by hand

Women joined religious orders as nuns. Some nuns became abbesses, or heads of female religious communities. The German abbess Hildegard of Bingen wrote poems and music inspired by her visions of God.

Reading Check What were some of Charlemagne's reforms?

Feudalism: The Medieval Way of Life

King
Provides money, recruits army on demand, grants land to his many lords

Lords
Protect the king and manage territory

Knights
Protect both the lords and the king

Peasants
Work the land

Chart Skills
Describe the relationship between the king and the peasants in feudalism.

Data Discovery

Feudalism and Manorialism

As you have read, during the late Roman empire, people began to accept the protection and control of landowners from the nobility. In the Middle Ages, barbarians and other warriors took control of most of the land. They offered protection to the peasants, or small farmers, living on the land in return for service. Each landowning warrior pledged loyalty to a tribal leader called a **lord,** or to the king. A lord was a man who controlled large areas of land. In return for the warrior's service, the lord or king offered protection.

How Feudalism Worked As time went by, kings granted land to lords in return for service. Lords, in turn, granted land to noble soldiers called knights in return for military service. A noble who received the land was called a **vassal.** The system of rights and duties connecting lords and vassals was called **feudalism.**

The lord promised to protect his vassals. In return, the vassals provided military support and money or food for their lord. The peasants were subject to both lords and vassals. Lords and vassals also had trained warriors called knights to serve them.

Lords sometimes quarreled over territory. In these conflicts, a vassal and his knights would help their lord in battle.

CHART SKILLS The king and the peasants are separated by two other classes: lords and knights.

READING CHECK He revised the legal system and started a school in the palace.

READING CHECK The knight's role was to help his lord in battle.

SECTION ASSESSMENT 1. Lords were nobles who received lands from monarchs. Vassals received land from lords and gave them military service. Feudalism was the system that united them. **2.** It was a code that organized Roman laws.

PRIMARY SOURCE

King Arthur's Coronation "And at the feast of Pentecost all manner of men assayed to pull at the sword that would assay; but none might prevail but Arthur, and pulled it out afore all the lords and commons that were there, wherefore all the commons cried at once, We will have Arthur unto our king, we will put him no more in delay, for we all see that it is God's will that he shall be our king, and who that holdeth against it, we will slay him. . . . And so anon was the coronation made. And there was he sworn unto his lords and the commons for to be a true king, to stand with true justice from thenceforth the days of this life."

—Thomas Malory, *Le Morte D'Arthur,* translated by William Caxton

By the end of the early Middle Ages, feudalism had spread across both Western and Eastern Europe. Feudalism was supported by an economic system called manorialism.

How Manorialism Worked The economic relationship that existed between lords or knights and peasants was called **manorialism.** The center of the system was the manor, a huge estate that included the lord's house or castle, farmland, pastures, peasants, and possibly a village. Many of the peasants who lived on the manor were serfs, or people who belonged to the estate as laborers. They were not slaves, but they were not free to move, marry, or buy land without the lord's permission.

Each manor was self-sufficient, supplying all the food, clothing, and shelter needed by both the lord and peasants. Peasants and their lords were thus dependent on one another.

The wife of the lord was called a lady. She attended to domestic chores and managed the servants. Literacy was not common even among noblewomen. Ladies had few rights. Some lords chose a wife for her dowry, or a payment of money and land provided at the time of marriage. In most parts of Europe, women could own land. When a woman's parents died, however, their land passed to the oldest brother in many countries.

Peasants led hard lives working from sunup to sundown. Their diets seldom varied and disease was common.

Reading Check **What was the knight's role in feudalism?**

Culture Close-up

▲ Peasants farmed their own plots of land as well as those of the lord.

- **Develop Cultural Awareness** What was a manor? (It was a large estate owned by a feudal lord and worked by peasants.)

- **Draw Conclusions** In what way was marriage an economic arrangement? (Lords gained lands and money from the women they married.)

Section 3 Assessment

Key Terms

1. Write a short paragraph showing how these key terms are related: lord, vassal, feudalism.

Key Ideas

2. What was Justinian's Code?

3. How did medieval monks preserve ancient learning?

4. What was feudalism?

Think Critically

5. **Categorize** Draw a table of three rulers who tried to unify Western Europe after the fall of the Roman empire. Under each ruler, list his ethnic group, time of rule, and accomplishments.

6. **Draw Inferences** Do you think peasants often traveled far from the manor? Explain why or why not.

Essential Question

What are the challenges of diversity?

7. How did cultural differences between the East and the West affect the Christian church? Go to your Student Journal to record your answer.

Culture Close-up

Have students go online to learn more about medieval manors.

Learned Women of the Middle Ages

OBJECTIVES

Students will

- describe the roles and experiences of medieval women.
- **21st Century Learning** compare viewpoints expressed in separate documents.
- **ELL** learn terms associated with women in religious communities.

SET EXPECTATIONS

In this lesson, students will

- read and analyze two documents on the lives of medieval women.
- compare religious teaching about women with the advice given by a secular writer.

1 Connect

Bring in a few copies of women's magazines and hold them up for the class to see. Ask students if they or any of their relatives read women's magazines. Note that men read the magazines, too. Ask, Do you think these magazines cover all the topics that women might want to read about? What kinds of advice do those magazines offer? List answers on the board. Encourage the class to name broad categories such as cooking, decorating, clothes, makeup, health, relationships, and work life. Ask, In which of these types of advice do you think women in the Middle Ages would have been interested? What choices do women have today that they might not have had in the Middle Ages? Why are the changes in women's opportunities and roles important?

2 Experience

Preview Have students preview the two pages and the images of Hildegard of Bingen and Christine de Pisan. Read the Key Idea, glossary terms, and definitions. Clarify any questions about the meaning of these words by providing examples.

Read Slowly read aloud the excerpt "A Feather on the Breath of God" without stopping. Read the document again, this time stopping to read the questions at the left. Prompt students to rethink and analyze the meaning of the words. Have students answer the questions using the location of the letters to provide clues. Do the same for the excerpt "The Wise Housewife." Lead a discussion starting with students' responses to the questions. Ask, What responsibilities did medieval women have? In what ways were they independent? In what ways were they dependent on others?

ELL **Intermediate/Early Advanced** Give students the following terms associated with female religious life: *nun*—an unmarried woman who has given her life to the church; *convent*—a building where nuns live; *abbey*—a church used by a group of nuns; *abbess*—the head of a convent. Ask students to use each word in a sentence.

myWorld Activity: A Capable Wife Have students read a passage from the Bible that provides insight into teachings during the Middle Ages about social expectations of women. Students will read this source and compare it with a source by Christine de Pisan. Give each student a copy of *Activity Support: Source Analysis*. Working in pairs, have them read the passage and answer the questions below.

15 min

3 Understand

Review Go back to the Key Idea. Discuss with students how each writer portrayed women's lives.

Assess Have students complete **Analyze the Documents.** Review their answers to determine if students have met the lesson objectives.

Remediate If students struggle to compare viewpoints, have them first paraphrase each writer's main point by completing the following sentences:
"Hildegard of Bingen wrote _____."
"Christine de Pisan wrote _____."

Name _____ Class _____ Date _____

myWorld Activity Support   **Source Analysis**

A Capable Wife

Directions In the Middle Ages, the Catholic Church was the center of European life. Priests gave sermons to teach people how the church wanted them to live. As learned women, Hildegard of Bingen and Christine de Pisan were probably familiar with Bible passages about women's roles, such as the verses below. With a partner, read the passage. Then use the questions to analyze the passage and compare it to the excerpt by Christine de Pisan.

> A capable wife who can find? She is far more precious than jewels.
> The heart of her husband trusts in her, and he will have no lack of gain.
> She does him good, and not harm, all the days of her life.
> She seeks wool and flax, and works with willing hands.
> She is like the ships of the merchant, she brings her food from far away.
> She rises while it is still night and provides food for her household and tasks for her servant-girls.
> She considers a field and buys it; with the fruit of her hands she plants a vineyard.

> —Proverbs 31:10–16, *New Revised Standard Version*

1. According to this passage, what are some of the specific actions that a capable, or skilled, wife does?

   _____

   _____

2. How would you describe the character of such a woman?

   _____

3. How does the woman described in this passage compare with Christine de Pisan and the wife she described?

   _____

   _____

HISTORY

Hildegard of Bingen Born to a noble family in 1098, Hildegard received her education at a cloister in what is now Germany. As a child, she claimed to receive mystic visions. In her forties, Hildegard had another vision that she believed instructed her to write down and publicize her visions. Some modern scholars believe the visions were the product of migraines, but Hildegard's contemporaries believed that they were from God. After a committee of theologians investigated the matter, they declared her visions to be authentic. With the assistance of a monk, she recorded 26 of the visions. Hildegard is also well known for her songs, which she wrote to be used during worship services. Some of these songs are still performed today. Hildegard died in 1179. She has never been officially canonized as a saint, but her feast day is honored in parts of Germany.

GUIDE ON THE SIDE

Compare Viewpoints Use the lettered prompts to help students analyze the documents for the viewpoints of each writer before comparing them.

ANSWERS

A Sample: It sounds like a fairy tale because it says, "Listen now: a king sat on his throne."

B The air affects the movement of the feather, which has no control over its fate.

C The feather is Hildegard, and the air is God. She feels that God directs her life completely.

Learned Women of the Middle Ages

Key Idea
- Most medieval women were expected to be obedient wives, mothers, and daughters, but a few women were educated, and some left fascinating written records of their lives and thoughts.

▲ A medieval woman uses scissors to cut cloth.

Most medieval women had limited roles. Peasant women worked in the fields or as servants. Noble women tended their husbands' manors. Women were not expected to become writers or teachers, but some did so anyway. Hildegard of Bingen was an educated noblewoman who became the abbess of a religious order. She had visions that she said were from God, and she wrote essays, poems, and songs. Christine de Pisan was a Venetian woman who lived in Paris. After her husband died, she made a living by copying manuscripts and by writing poems and books on women's behavior.

This medieval image shows Hildegard receiving divine visions in the form of flames. ▼

Stop at each circled letter on the right to think about the text. Then answer the question with the same letter on the left.

A Categorize What kind of story does the first sentence make you anticipate? Explain.

B Draw Conclusions Who or what affects the motion of the feather?

C Draw Inferences Who is the air and who is the feather? Explain what this reveals about Hildegard of Bingen.

adorn, *v.,* decorate
vestment, *n.,* ceremonial clothing
of its own accord, *adv. phrase,* on its own
borne, *v.,* carried

A Feather on the Breath of God

66 Listen now: a king sat on his **A** throne, high pillars before him splendidly <u>adorned</u> . . . . They showed the king's <u>vestments</u> in great honor everywhere. Then the king chose to lift a small **B** feather from the ground, and he commanded it to fly just as the king himself wished. But a feather does not fly <u>of its own accord</u>; it is <u>borne</u> up by the air. So too I am. . . . I depend entirely **C** on God's help. 99

—Hildegard of Bingen, letter written in 1148

21st Century Learning COMPARE VIEWPOINTS

To assist your students in comparing the viewpoints expressed by two writers, use the scaffolded questions at the left of each excerpt. Encourage students to identify the main ideas in each excerpt. Repeated readings and paraphrasing sentences in their own words will help students to pull out the main ideas. Then have them look for similarities and differences among the ideas. Suggest that students ask themselves, *What does each writer think* *about women's roles? How would each writer define duty?* Then have students write a sentence summarizing what they have concluded. When students analyze the passage from Proverbs, have them compare the viewpoint of its author with contemporary viewpoints, including their own, on women's roles. For additional help, refer students to the **21st Century Online Tutor** *Compare Viewpoints*.

GUIDE ON THE SIDE

Stop at each circled letter on the right to think about the text. Then answer the question with the same letter on the left.

D **Solve Problems** What should a housewife do if she has more food than her family can eat?

E **Draw Conclusions** Why is it important not to give away anything that is stale or damaged?

F **Synthesize** According to Christine de Pisan, what is the best kind of charity?

indigent, *n.,* poor people

charity, *n.,* the giving of money or help to those in need

alms, *n.,* money and goods given to the poor

childbed, *n.,* the bed of a woman who is giving birth to a child

The Wise Housewife

66 This wise woman will take great care that no food goes bad around her house, that **D** nothing goes to waste that might help the poor and <u>indigent</u>. If she gives them to the **E** poor, she will ensure that the leftovers are not stale and that the clothes are not moth-eaten. [I]f she loves the welfare of her soul **F** and the virtue of <u>charity</u>, she will not give her <u>alms</u> only in this way, but with the wine from her own cellar and the meat from her table, to poor women in <u>childbed</u>, to the sick, and often to her poor neighbors. 99

—Christine de Pisan,
The Treasure of the City of Ladies,
translated by Sarah Lawson

◄ Christine de Pisan instructing a young man ►

ANSWERS

D She should give the extra to the poor.

E Sample: Such damaged items don't really help people and will make them feel mistreated.

F to give away the best you have

Analyze the Documents

1. **Compare Viewpoints** Which of these writers was more concerned with practical matters and which was more concerned with spiritual matters?

2. **Writing Task** Decide what kind of an essay you would write about these two learned women. Then write the thesis statement you would use in the essay.

ANALYZE THE DOCUMENTS
1. Christine de Pisan was more practical and Hildegard of Bingen was more spiritual. **2.** Sample thesis statement: The lives of Christine de Pisan and Hildegard of Bingen show that some medieval women gained learning and made lasting achievements.

High and Late Middle Ages

OBJECTIVES

Students will know

- the causes and effects of the Crusades.
- the reasons that trade and cities grew.
- how limits placed on the English monarchy were the first steps toward democracy.

Students will be able to

- explain why feudalism declined.
- draw conclusions about what led to the rise of nations in Western Europe.

SET EXPECTATIONS

In this section, students will

- read High and Late Middle Ages.
- simulate taking part in the spice trade.
- go On Assignment in medieval Europe and gather data from maps.

CORE CONCEPTS

You may wish to teach or reteach the following lessons from the Core Concepts Handbook:

- Trade, pp. 66–67
- Money Management, pp. 68–69
- Urbanization, pp. 80–81

KEY

Differentiated Instruction		English Language Instruction		
L1 Special Needs	**L2** Extra Support	**ELL** Beginner	**ELL** Early Intermediate	**ELL** Intermediate
L3 On-Level	**L4** Challenge	**ELL** Early Advanced	**ELL** Advanced	

1 Connect
Make learning meaningful

Make Connections Ask the class to list what attracts people to cities. If you live in a rural area, focus on visits to cities, and if you live in a city, focus on the attractions of the downtown area. Ask, Do you think you want to live in a city when you are older? Why or why not?

L1 Special Needs Bring in photographs of city attractions and vibrant city life for students to respond to as they take part in the discussion.

Activate Prior Knowledge Have students review the relationship between peasants and landowners in feudal society. Ask students to predict what would happen if peasants heard about jobs that paid wages. Ask, What would the peasants do? How might the landowners respond?

ELL Early Intermediate Define *wages* as "money paid for work." Define *artisan* as "a person who is skilled at a craft." Show examples of things made by artisans, such as pottery, jewelry, wooden bowls, or leather bags.

Prepare Follow the steps in the section **Preview.** Preteach the Key Terms. Then have students complete *Word Wise* in their journals using in-text clues and the glossary for help.

2 Experience
Teach knowledge and skills

Read Use **Background** notes and **Guide on the Side** questions to model active reading. Have students use *Take Notes* in their **Student Journal** to list causes and effects of major events. Have students use **21st Century Online Tutor** *Analyze Cause and Effect*, and apply this skill to reading the section.

L2 Extra Support Give students cards with these statements: *Crusaders went to the Middle East. Trade increased. Cities grew. Feudalism declined.* The cards should be mixed up. Students should put the cards in order, and then state how each event helped cause the next event.

ELL Advanced Explain that the word *crusade* often means "a campaign to support a cause." Give this example: "Leo is on a crusade to stop climate change." Ask students to write other examples.

L4 Challenge Have students read *Enrichment: Descriptions of the Black Death*. Then have them write and deliver a public service announcement telling people what to do if someone they know catches the plague.

Practice: myWorld Activity Students will learn about the spice trade by taking part in a trade simulation. **Step-by-Step Instructions** and **More Activities** follow on p. T34

SECTION 4 RESOURCE GUIDE

FOR THE STUDENT

my worldgeography.com Student Center

- Active Atlas
- Data Discovery
- Language Lesson

Student Edition (print and online)
- High and Late Middle Ages

Student Journal (print and online)
- Section 4 Word Wise
- Section 4 Take Notes

21st Century Learning Online Tutor

- Analyze cause and effect
- Draw conclusions

FOR THE TEACHER

my worldgeography.com Teacher Center

- Online Lesson Planner
- Presentations for Projection
- SuccessTracker

ProGuide: Europe and Russia

- Section 4 Lesson Plan, pp. T32–T33
- myWorld Activity Step-by-Step Instructions, p. T34
- Activity Support: Trade Good Cards, p. T35
- myWorld Geography Enrichment, p. T36
- Section Quiz, p. T37

Accelerating the Progress of ELLs

- Comprehension Check Strategies, p. 53

---

3 Understand
Assess understanding

Review Review *Word Wise* and *Take Notes* in the Student Journal.

Assess Knowledge and Skills Use the Section Assessment and Section Quiz to check students' progress.

Assess Understanding Review students' responses to the Section Assessment Essential Question prompt.

Remediate Use these strategies to review and remediate.

If students struggle to . . .	Try these strategies.
Explain the effects of the Crusades	Help students to categorize the effects in terms of economy and culture.
Analyze causes of the decline of feudalism	Have students make flowcharts showing changes in population, warfare, and power.
Ask questions	Assign additional practice with the **21st Century Online Tutor.**

ELL Support

ELL Objective Students will be able to acquire new vocabulary using flashcards.

Cultural Connections To give students practice with explaining cause and effect, ask these questions: *Why did your family move here? How has the move changed your family's life?* Allow students to give their answer in English or their native languages.

ELL Intermediate/Early Advanced Content Tip Point out two different ways that the word *trade* is used in the section. In "Returning crusaders increased trade," it means "buying and selling goods." In "Women were also active in the silk and wool trades," it means "a kind of work that uses a skill."

ELL Activity Give students the following terms and tell them to make flashcards: harness, clock, eyeglasses, windmill, guild, and cannon. On the back, they should write a definition and a list of related words. **(Verbal)**

my worldgeography.com Lesson Planner

myWorld Activity **Step-by-Step Instructions**

 15 min

Trade Spices Up Life

OBJECTIVES

Students will

- negotiate the exchange of trade goods.
- draw conclusions about the effects of trade.

LEARNING STYLE

- Kinesthetic
- Verbal

21st Century Learning

- Draw Conclusions

MATERIALS

- Activity Support: Trade Good Cards, p. T35
- Scissors

Activity Steps

1. Divide the class into groups of three. Tell the groups to divide up the roles of Chinese, Arab, and Italian traders. Give each group a copy of *Activity Support: Trade Good Cards.* Have students cut apart the trade good cards and give them to the right traders.

2. Define a middleman as a trader who buys goods from one person and sells them to another. Explain that Italian merchants and Chinese merchants never traded directly. They traded their goods through middlemen in places like Arabia.

   L4 **Challenge** Ask students to think of middle-men in our economy. Give an example, such as a car dealer who buys from the factory and sells to consumers. Ask students to list others.

3. Have students do one round of trade. First the Arab trader must go to China and negotiate to exchange one or more trade good cards with the Chinese

trader. Then the Italian trader goes to Arabia and negotiates with the Arab trader. Suggest that traders use questions to learn what the others want. Caution students not to trade everything they have in a single round.

   ELL **Beginner/Early Intermediate** Give students this model to use as they trade: "I want _____ because _____. What do you want for it?"

4. Students should conduct two more rounds of trade using the same two steps.

5. Have groups make a chart listing which goods each trader has at the end of trading. The groups should share their final results with the class. As a class, discuss how the availability of desirable trade goods in each region stimulated trade. Then ask, How would the trade in Asian goods affect the economy of Italian cities? (They would grow wealthy.)

More Activities From myWorld Teachers

 Local Connection Have students interview local union members to find out the protections offered by unions. Then groups of students should work to make posters comparing modern unions with medieval guilds. **(Visual)**

Obituary Have students write an obituary for Joan of Arc. Summarize how she became a leader of the French army and why the English executed her. **(Verbal)**

 Petition Tell students to suppose that they are medieval lords. Have them work with a partner to decide which of the following statements they support: *The Crusades must stop* or *The Crusades must continue.* Then they should write a petition to the pope, stating their position and giving three reasons in support of it. **(Logical/Verbal)**

my worldgeography.com **Teacher Center** → Find additional resources in the online Teacher Center.

Name _____ Class _____ Date _____

myWorld Activity Support **Trade Good Cards**

Trade Spices Up Life

Directions Working in a group of three, divide up the roles of Chinese trader, Arab trader, and Italian trader. Cut out the trade good cards below and give them to the correct trader. Following your teacher's directions, conduct three rounds of trade. Remember that the Chinese and Italian traders cannot trade with each other. They can trade only with the Arab trader. At the end of three rounds, share your results with the class.

CHINA	**CHINA**	**CHINA**
100 bolts of silk (a beautiful fabric that only the Chinese knew how to make)	2 tons of cinnamon (a sharp-flavored spice that the Chinese got from Southeast Asia)	500 porcelain dishes (more beautiful and fragile than pottery; only made in China)

ARABIA	**ARABIA**	**ARABIA**
450 bolts of cotton (from Egypt; a lighter fabric than wool; did not grow in Europe)	4 tons of coffee (a bean that didn't grow in Europe; brewed a drink that gave energy)	300 pounds of pepper (from India; most valued spice; it masked the taste of rotten meat)

ITALY	**ITALY**	**ITALY**
500 wooden logs (a plentiful resource in Europe but a scarce one in the Middle East)	6 tons of wheat (used for bread and other basics; grown plentifully in Europe)	400 casks of wine (made from grapes grown in France and Italy)

T35

Name _____ Class _____ Date _____

Enrichment: Descriptions of the Black Death

Directions Read the two quotations below. Answer the questions that follow and complete the activity.

Document A

The infection spread to everyone who had any contact with the diseased. Those infected felt themselves penetrated by a pain throughout their whole bodies and, so to say, undermined. Then there developed on the thighs or upper arms a boil about the size of a lentil, which the people called "burn boil." This infected the whole body, and penetrated it so that the patient violently vomited blood. This vomiting of blood continued without intermission for three days, there being no means of healing it, and then the patient expired.

—Michael Platiensis, who wrote about the arrival of the plague in Messina in 1347 from *The Black Death: A Chronicle of the Plague* by Johannes Nohl, translated by C.H. Clarke

Document B

The victims died almost immediately. They would swell beneath the armpits and in the groin, and fall over while talking. Father abandoned child, wife husband, one brother another; for this illness seemed to strike through breath and sight. And so they died. None could be found to bury the dead for money or friendship.

—Agnolo di Tura, who wrote about life in Siena during the period 1300–1351 from *The Black Death* by William Bowsky

1. Why were people so frightened of the disease?

_____

_____

2. How did people react when they found out someone they knew was ill?

_____

_____

3. Activity Use the information above to write a newspaper story or a public service announcement about the Black Death.

Name _____ Class _____ Date _____

Section Quiz

Directions Answer the following questions using what you learned
in Section 4.

1. _____ Why did Pope Urban II call for
Christians to go on a Crusade?
 a. to win back the Roman Empire
 b. to win back the Holy Land
 c. to conquer the Byzantines
 d. to conquer the Muslims in Spain

2. _____ Where were there many ports that
traded with the East?
 a. Germany
 b. England
 c. Italy
 d. Spain

3. _____ In what areas of culture and learning
did Muslims make great advances?
 a. history and philosophy
 b. history and portrait painting
 c. mathematics and medicine
 d. medicine and portrait painting

4. _____ What led to increased trade between
Europe and Asia?
 a. the Black Death
 b. the Crusades
 c. the Hundred Years' War
 d. the Reconquista

5. _____ What was the long-term effect of
the Magna Carta?
 a. a weakening of the power of feudal
lords
 b. the surrender of French territory to
English rule
 c. the rise of strong trading cities
 d. the development of more democratic
government

6. Use details from the section to fill out the following chart with the
cause and effects of the Black Death.

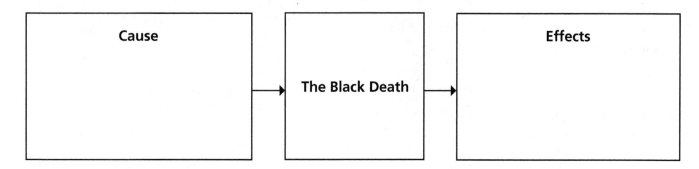

High and Late Middle Ages

- Model preparing to read by previewing the Key Ideas, Key Terms, headings, visuals, and captions. Have students make predictions about what they will learn. For ELL support, post the prompt, "I predict I will read about . . ."

- Preview and practice the reading skill, Analyze Cause and Effect, by using examples from current events.

- Preteach this section's high-use Academic Vocabulary and Key Terms using the chart on the next page and in-text definitions. Have students practice Key Terms by completing the *Word Wise* page in their journals.

GUIDE ON THE SIDE

Reading Skill

Analyze Cause and Effect
Have students practice this skill while they read by completing the *Take Notes* graphic organizer in the **Student Journal.**

The Crusades and the Wider World

- **Summarize** What changes took place during the High Middle Ages? (Universities formed, merchants gained power, and farming improved.)

- **Cause and Effect** Why did Christians and Muslims both want to control the Holy Land? (Both thought it was sacred ground.)

- **Infer** How did the pope try to motivate people to fight in the First Crusade? (Sample: He made it sound like the Crusade was a holy war.)

Section 4
High and Late Middle Ages

Key Ideas
- The Crusades opened up medieval Europe to trade and new ideas.
- In the High Middle Ages, growth in trade routes led to the rise of cities.
- The Magna Carta limited the king's power and led to more democratic government.
- With the growth of cities, nation-building began in Europe.

Key Terms • Crusades • Reconquista • guild • Magna Carta

 Visual Glossary

Reading Skill: Analyze Cause and Effect Take notes using the graphic organizer in your journal.

By 1000, feudalism had stabilized Europe and the population was growing. Universities formed, merchants gained power, and farming techniques improved. This period is called the High Middle Ages. It lasted until the early 1300s. During the Late Middle Ages, however, wars, disease, and famine hit Europe hard. As a result, the the feudal system weakened and collapsed.

The Crusades and the Wider World
By 1081, the Seljuk Turks had overrun much of the Byzantine empire. These people had migrated from Central Asia, and when they reached the Middle East, they converted to Islam. As they conquered new lands, they converted the defeated peoples to Islam.

The Turks also took control of Palestine. This region was sacred to Jews, Christians, and Muslims. It was known to Christians as the Holy Land. Many Christians in Europe objected to Muslim control of the Holy Land.

The Holy Wars Begin In 1095, Pope Urban II urged church leaders to organize the **Crusades,** a series of military expeditions to free the Holy Land from Muslim rule. At the Council of Clermont, named for the town in France where it was held, Pope Urban II urged people of all classes to unite to take back Jerusalem in a holy war,

◄ Knights wore suits of armor such as this one during the Middle Ages.

❝ You common people who have been miserable sinners, become soldiers of Christ! You nobles, do not [quarrel] with one another. Use your arms in a just war! Labor for an everlasting reward. ❞

ANSWERS

ACADEMIC VOCABULARY

High-Use Word	Definition and Sample Sentence
expel	*v.* to force someone to leave a place *The landlord wanted to expel the people who did not pay rent.*
subdue	*v.* to bring under control *The wrestler from our school managed to subdue all opponents in the tournament.*

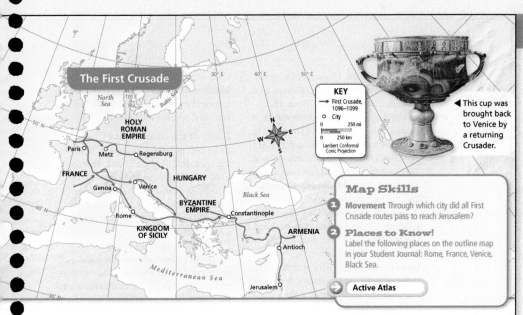

The First Crusade

KEY
→ First Crusade, 1096–1099
○ City

0   250 mi
0   250 km
Lambert Conformal Conic Projection

◀ This cup was brought back to Venice by a returning Crusader.

Map Skills

1. **Movement** Through which city did all First Crusade routes pass to reach Jerusalem?

2. **Places to Know!** Label the following places on the outline map in your Student Journal: Rome, France, Venice, Black Sea.

Active Atlas

Europeans responded to the pope's call for different reasons. Some went to war for religious reasons. They believed that God wanted the Holy Land to be Christian. Others had more worldly reasons. Some knights wanted to win new possessions in the Holy Land. Others wanted the status that came from military success. Of course, Muslims in the Holy Land wanted it to remain Muslim. They did not want foreign Christian rulers.

By the summer of 1096, a large European army had formed and headed for the Holy Land. This force captured Jerusalem, and Christian leaders divided Palestine into four states. Many Muslims in the region faced brutal treatment. Then European leaders sent a second Crusade to the Holy Land. Internal quarrels weakened this force, and Muslims defeated them.

In 1187, the Muslim leader Saladin recaptured Jerusalem. Further Crusades were attempted but failed. These conflicts led to bitter feelings between Christians and Muslims that have lasted to this day.

Muslims in Spain By 718, Muslims had conquered most of Spain. Spanish Christians controlled only a small area in northern Spain. During Muslim rule, many Spanish people converted to Islam. Muslim leaders also tolerated the practice of Judaism and Christianity.

Muslims made important advances in mathematics and medicine. They studied the learning of the ancient Greeks and Romans. In addition, they built beautiful mosques and palaces. During the 900s, Córdoba became a center of Muslim culture. Muslim influence helped shape art and literature in Christian Spain.

MAP SKILLS **1.** Constantinople
2. Places should be accurately labeled.

GUIDE ON THE SIDE

- **Cause and Effect** Why did people go on Crusades? (for religious reasons, for material gain, or for military status)

- **Connect** How did the Crusades leave a legacy that still affects us today? (It caused bitter feelings between Christians and Muslims.)

- **Identify Details** In what areas of learning did Muslims make advances? (mathematics and medicine)

Map Skills Point out the map *The First Crusade.*

- Did the crusaders travel by land or by sea? (by land)

- What city on the crusaders' route was farthest from Jerusalem? (Paris)

 Active Atlas

Have students go online to learn more about the Crusades.

CORE CONCEPTS: URBANIZATION

Review Core Concept 6.4 before having students read about the growth of cities during the Middle Ages. Review the reasons for the growth of cities, and ask students to note why people began to move to towns. Ask, Did people in the Middle Ages move to cities for the same reasons that people make that move today? Also, tell students to pay attention to the role trade played in the growth of medieval cities. Ask, Why do cities make good centers for trade?

GUIDE ON THE SIDE

- **Compare and Contrast** How were the Crusades and the Reconquista alike? (Both were Christian campaigns to win lands from Muslims.)

- **Cause and Effect** What long-term negative effect did the Inquisition have on Spain? (Many skilled and educated people left the country.)

- **Synthesize** How did the Crusades affect the economy of Europe? (The Crusades made people aware of Asian goods and stimulated trade.)

Map Skills Point out the map *Medieval Trade Routes*.

- What Italian trade city was closest to France? (Genoa)

- What body or bodies of water would a trader cross while going from Constantinople to China? (Black Sea, possibly the Caspian Sea)

- Were English merchants more likely to travel to Spain by sea or land? (sea)

⊙ **Active Atlas**

Have students go online to learn more about medieval trade routes.

expel, *v,* to force someone to leave a place

The Reconquista Christians living in northern Spain began to take back land from the Muslims in the 1000s. This was the beginning of the **Reconquista,** or reconquering of Spain by Christians. In 1469, the marriage of Ferdinand of Aragon and Isabella of Castile united Spain. Together, they attacked Granada, the last Muslim stronghold, in 1492. Granada fell and the Reconquista was complete.

Under Ferdinand and Isabella, the religious tolerance that had existed under the Muslims came to an end. A Church court called the Inquisition was set up to try to punish people who practiced religions other than Christianity. Some Jews and Muslims were burned at the stake.

Over time, more than 150,000 Jews and Muslims fled or were <u>expelled</u> from Spain, among them some of the most skilled and educated people in the nation.

Effects of the Crusades The Crusades had a lasting impact on society. Returning crusaders increased trade, bringing back exotic spices and fabrics from the Middle East (Southwest Asia and North Africa). Much of this trade used money rather than barter, or the exchange of one good for another.

People also gained a broader view of the world and discovered new ideas. Sailors learned to use the magnetic compass and the astrolabe, a device that measured the position of the sun, moon, and stars.

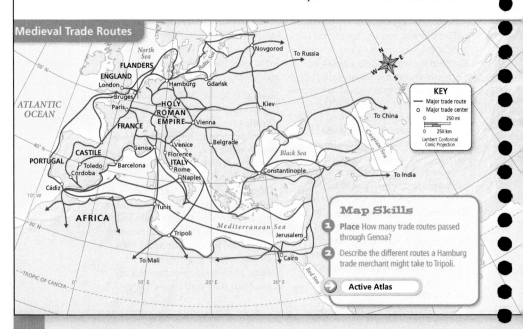

Medieval Trade Routes

KEY
— Major trade route
○ Major trade center
0   250 mi
0   250 km
Lambert Conformal
Conic Projection

Map Skills
1. **Place** How many trade routes passed through Genoa?
2. Describe the different routes a Hamburg trade merchant might take to Tripoli.

⊙ **Active Atlas**

MAP SKILLS 1. Four routes led to Genoa. **2.** A merchant would most likely travel from Hamburg overland to Venice and then by sea to Tripoli. Another route would be overland to Genoa, by sea to Tunis, and overland to Tripoli.

ECONOMY

Medieval Fairs A fair is a temporary market where buyers and sellers can meet to do business. Fairs usually occur at set locations at the same time each year. The Romans introduced the idea of fairs to Northern Europe. After the Western Roman empire fell apart, the economy declined and the practice of holding fairs died away. Under Charlemagne, trade began to prosper again, and fairs appeared once more. Most were located at places where trade routes crossed. Important fairs were held near Paris and in the Champagne region of France. People gathered to trade furs from Russia, spices from East Asia, dyes and precious objects from the Mediterranean, and cloth from Germany and Flanders.

In this way, sailors could know their position on Earth's surface out of sight of land.

The compass and astrolabe were among the new ideas or technologies that Europe gained from contact with the Muslim world. Europeans also learned to make gunpowder and paper from Muslims, although these technologies first developed in China.

Muslims had preserved much of the learning of the ancient Greeks and Romans. Muslims also studied ancient Indian learning. Muslims drew on this ancient learning to make advances in science and mathematics. They passed this knowledge on to medieval Europeans.

Reading Check How did the Crusades increase trade?

The Rise of Cities

During the 1000s, more and more people moved from manors to cities. Many factors led to this migration.

Farming Improves During the Middle Ages, farmers found ways to improve agriculture. They gained more cropland by draining swamps and clearing forests. They also developed the horse collar and harness so horses instead of oxen could be used to plow fields. Horses plowed faster than oxen. In this way, they could plant more, harvest more, and even have surplus, or extra, crops.

As the food supply increased, people became healthier. Peasants were able to earn extra money by selling surplus crops. Some used this money to buy their freedom from their lord. Freed peasants sometimes moved to cities and towns.

Technology Develops While Europeans learned new technologies from the Muslims, they also developed new skills and products of their own. Among these were clocks, eyeglasses, and upright windmills. Military technologies like plate armor and cannons made the armies strong. Engineering advances let Europeans build soaring cathedral towers.

Commerce Begins In towns, many peasants learned special skills as craft workers. They specialized in leather goods or gold objects and sold these goods in their shops or at local markets or trade fairs.

Some merchants sold these goods along trade routes throughout Europe and Asia. They exchanged both goods and ideas. Some expanded commerce by setting up banks and issuing loans.

myWorldActivity
Trade Spices Up Life

The winged lion on top of the column is the symbol of the city of Venice. *What evidence do you see of the city's history in this modern photograph?* ▼

READING CHECK Returning crusaders brought back spices and fabrics from the Middle East, thereby spurring trade with this region.

CAPTION Sample: The buildings look historic. The pillar with the winged lion might date from the Renaissance.

GOVERNMENT

The Model Parliament The first truly representative parliament met in 1295 during the reign of King Edward I. Earlier in Edward's reign, he had often called meetings of the Great Council, which included church and lay magnates, and the King's Court, a small group of semiprofessional advisers. In 1295, he added the following to Parliament: lower-ranking clergy, two knights from each county, two burgesses from each borough, and two citizens from each city. That parliament came to be called the Model Parliament.

- **Identify Main Ideas** What major economic and social change occurred because of the growth of trade? (The middle class developed.)
- **Cause and Effect** Why did people build tall houses? (Cities had limited space, so people built upward.)
- **Connect** How were medieval cities different from modern cities? (Sample: There were no sewers.)

Limiting the King's Power

- **Compare Viewpoints** Why did William the Conqueror believe he had the right to invade England? (He believed he was heir to the English throne.)

Analyze Visuals Have students look at the picture of the Magna Carta.

- What groups from medieval society are shown? (clergy, nobles, king)

(→) **Language Lesson**

Have students go online to learn more about the Magna Carta.

The Italian Trade Centers The port of Venice was a busy place. Ships from Constantinople arrived loaded with gold, silks, and spices. Traders loaded these goods onto mules and began the trek to markets in Northern Europe.

The city-state of Venice was only one of the new commerce centers in present-day Italy. Cities such as Florence, Genoa, and Naples also served as hubs for goods coming into Europe.

The New Merchant Class As people moved to towns, many towns grew into cities. In urban areas, a person could earn a good living by working as a merchant, an artisan, or a craftsperson. As a result, the group of people who earned more than peasants grew.

This group became known as the middle class since they still ranked below the nobles. As their numbers increased, so did their political and economic power.

For protection, merchants and craftspeople formed **guilds.** A guild is an association of people who have a common livelihood. Guilds protected members from unfair business practices. They also set prices and wages. Women could sometimes become guild members. They often specialized in needlecraft and papermaking. Women were also active in the silk and wool trades.

City Life Develops As cities grew, they spread outward—and upward. People needed more living space and built homes with two or three stories. In the largest cities, a church called a cathedral formed the center of the city. These cathedrals became centers of learning and city life.

Weekly market stalls were replaced by permanent shops, though hawkers still rolled through the streets with their carts. There were no sewers or garbage collection, so medieval streets could be dirty as well as noisy and crowded.

Reading Check Why were medieval city craftsmen known as a middle class?

Limiting the King's Power

During the High Middle Ages, the power of kings was put to the test.

Normans Conquer England During the 1000s, England was fairly prosperous with good agricultural land. William, duke of Normandy in northern France, believed himself to be heir to the English throne.

(→) **Language Lesson**

King John signs the Magna Carta. A copy of the original document is above.

READING CHECK They became known as a middle class because they ranked below nobles but above peasants.

PRIMARY SOURCE

Magna Carta Present the following excerpts from the Magna Carta to students to have them determine how the barons wanted to limit King John's power:

28. No constable or other bailiff of ours shall take corn or other provisions from any one without immediately tendering money there for, unless he can have postponement thereof by permission of the seller.

30. No sheriff or bailiff of ours, or other person, shall take the horses or carts of any freeman for transport duty, against the will of the said freeman.

31. Neither we nor our bailiffs shall take, for our castles or for any other work of ours, wood which is not ours, against the will of the owner of that wood.

When it was given to an Anglo-Saxon noble named Harold, William invaded England with a huge army. He defeated Harold at the Battle of Hastings in 1066. William was crowned king of England and became known as William the Conqueror.

At the time, most of the people in England were Anglo-Saxon. The Normans treated them as inferiors. Many Anglo-Saxon lords tried to revolt, but after several years, William <u>subdued</u> them. Over time, the Normans and Anglo-Saxons intermarried, becoming one people.

Magna Carta After William's death, kings often struggled with lords for control of England. During the early 1200s, King John demanded large amounts of money without consulting the lords. He also set severe penalties for minor crimes.

Lords and church leaders rebelled. Soon, they forced King John to sign a charter called the **Magna Carta.** This was a document that limited the English king's power. The Magna Carta helped lead to more democratic government in England.

By the late 1200s, King Edward I expanded his meetings with lords and church leaders to include town representatives. These meetings came to be called the Model Parliament. They were the beginning of England's Parliament, its legislative or lawmaking assembly. Royal courts made rulings based on earlier cases. The courts created a body of common law, which was applied equally in any part of a country.

Hundred Years' War In the 1330s, the French attempted to take over an English-held province in southwest

France. This conflict started a series of wars between France and England known as the Hundred Years' War (1337–1453).

By 1428, the English had taken over northern France. In Orleans, a peasant girl named Joan of Arc appeared. She claimed that she had been told by God to lead the French army into battle. In desperation, the French king agreed. The 17-year-old Joan led the army to victory. However, the next year, the English captured Joan and she was burned at the stake as a witch.

New weapons developed at this time changed warfare. The English longbow launched arrows that pierced the armor of French knights. In addition, gunpowder and cannons became common. Cannons could destroy castle walls. In this way, two of the major defenses of feudal lords—knights and castles—became much less effective.

subdue, *v*, to bring under control

At the right, the English soldiers use longbows, while the French at the left use crossbows. *How might cannons be used in this scene?* ▼

CAPTION to knock down castle walls

- **Identify Bias** How did Normans view Anglo-Saxons? (They thought they were inferior.)
- **Analyze Cause and Effect** How did King John anger the nobles? (He demanded large amounts of money, and he imposed severe penalties.)
- **Build Cultural Awareness** Who was Joan of Arc? (a French girl who claimed God told her to lead an army against the English)

Analyze Visuals Have students look at the painting of a medieval battle.

- Do you think the longbowmen are shown as having an advantage over the crossbowmen? Explain. (Sample: Yes, there are more longbowmen and they all seem ready to fire.)
- Will the armor of the French protect them? Explain. (No, the longbow can penetrate armor.)

ANSWERS

HISTORY

The Longbow Commonly the longbow was six feet in length and made of yew, a hard, fine-grained wood. It shot arrows that were about 37 inches long. The range varied from 450 to 1,000 feet, depending on the weight of the arrow being shot.

The advantage of the longbow over the crossbow was that the longbow could be fired much more quickly. The disadvantage was that it required a great deal of strength. To draw back the string and shoot an arrow required a force of 150 to 180 pounds.

- **Compare and Contrast** How was the impact of the Hundred Years' War different for England and France? (France developed a strong monarchy, while England developed a stronger legislature.)

Medieval Society Weakens

- **Cause and Effect** What caused famine in the 1300s? (bad weather and poor harvests)

- **Synthesize** How did famine contribute to the spread of the Black Death? (Hunger weakened people, so they caught disease more easily.)

Closer Look

The Black Death

- **Identify Main Ideas** What spread the disease? (flea-covered rats)

- **Cause and Effect** What did many people believe caused the disease? (Many people thought the plague was a punishment from God for their sins.)

Flea-ridden rats from ships reached land and transmitted the plague germs. ▼

Closer Look

The Black Death

Europe's busy ports unloaded more than trade goods or returning Crusaders. They also brought rats covered with the fleas that carried germs for the deadly bubonic plague. Flea-covered rats thrived in filthy medieval cities, and the plague spread quickly to the countryside. People knew very little about how disease was spread. Physicians were powerless to treat the victims. Gravediggers could not keep up with the number of dead. Many people believed that the plague was a punishment from God for their sins.

THINK CRITICALLY Why do you think the Black Death caused such fear?

Doctors wore masks to protect against the "evil air" that they thought caused disease. The beak held spices that did little to disguise the smell of sickness and death. ▶

This medieval image shows the fear that people felt during the time of the plague— death might claim a person at any time. ▼

The French finally won the Hundred Years' War. The war led England and France down two different paths. The French increased the power of the monarchy. The English increased Parliament's "power of the purse," or its financial role in government.

Reading Check **What did the Magna Carta do?**

Medieval Society Weakens

Improvements in farming during the High Middle Ages caused Europe's population to grow. By the 1300s, the population had outgrown the food supply. When harvests, or crops gathered for food, were low, people experienced famines. Famines are times of hunger and starvation. Famines were just one of the hardships that increasingly weakened medieval society.

Famine Strikes In 1315, bad weather caused poor harvests in Europe. These conditions continued for two more years. By that time, many Europeans were starving. Historians estimate that about ten to fifteen percent of the population died during the winter of 1317.

The Black Death Arrives As the famines continued in later years, the constant hunger made people sickly. In 1347, Europe faced a terrible epidemic, or a widespread outbreak of disease. Because people were already weakened from poor nutrition, the epidemic was disastrous. The disease was bubonic plague, or the Black Death. Victims suffered swelling and extreme pain. Death came quickly, usually in a matter of days.

THINK CRITICALLY People did not understand the cause or cure.

READING CHECK The Magna Carta used law to limit royal power.

SECTION 4 ASSESSMENT **1.** The Crusades were a campaign to take the Holy Land. The Reconquista was a campaign to expel Muslims from Spain. A guild is an

READING CHECK The Black Death caused a labor shortage and the decline of manorialism.

COMMON MISCONCEPTIONS

No More Black Death Most people associate bubonic plague with the Middle Ages, but the disease still exists. Epidemics have occurred periodically around the world. The last great pandemic took place in 1922 when more than 10 million people died globally. The reason the disease cannot be eradicated is that wild rodents carry infected fleas. Wherever large populations of wild rodents live, pockets of the disease remain. The World Health Organization reports 1,000 to 3,000 cases every year. They have occurred in the United States and parts of South America; Africa; and Central, South and Southeast Asia. In the 2000s, government officials began to fear that terrorists might try to develop the plague into a biological weapon. Such fears were heightened by the report that a camp of 40 suspected terrorists all died of the disease in January 2009.

Michael Platiensis, an eyewitness, described the disease,

> 66 Those infected felt themselves penetrated by a pain . . . Then there developed on the thighs or upper arms a boil. . . . This infected the whole body, . . . [three days later], there being no means of healing it, and then the patient expired. 99

Physicians had many theories about what caused the plague, all of them wrong. They tried several cures, but nothing worked. Some people falsely blamed the plague on Jews or beggars. These accusations spread, and, in some cites, thousands of Jews were tortured and killed.

By the time the Black Death ended in the early 1400s, the medieval world had begun to change. About 25 million Europeans died from the plague—from one quarter to one third of the population. The dead came from all levels of society, rich and poor. Suddenly, Europe faced a labor shortage. The disease also caused religious turmoil as many of the faithful began to have doubts.

Decline of Medieval Europe War, famine, and the Black Death changed medieval Europe profoundly. With millions of workers dead, production declined and food shortages were common. Economic uncertainty led to social upheaval. Important social structures such as manorialism and feudalism began to break down.

In manorialism, the labor of the peasant was vital. Following the plague, however, peasants began to leave the manors. In order to convince them to stay, lords offered for the first time to pay them wages. Some lords converted cropland to pastures for raising sheep. Some peasants still left the manors seeking higher wages or moving to cities.

Feudal lords found it harder to defend themselves against new weapons such as guns and cannons. In the cities, feudal influence weakened against wealthy merchants and powerful guilds. However, spurred by fresh ideas, a new age called the Renaissance was about to begin.

Reading Check **How did the Black Death change Europe?**

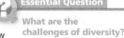

my World IN NUMBERS

The Black Death killed **50,000** of **180,000** people in Paris.

Section 4 Assessment

Key Terms

1. Use each of the following terms in a sentence: Crusades, Reconquista, guild, Magna Carta.

Key Ideas

2. Why did the middle class grow during the High Middle Ages?

3. What were some of the main results of the Crusades?

4. How did the Great Famine and the Black Death lead to the decline of feudalism?

Think Critically

5. **Draw Inferences** How do you think feudal lords felt about the growth of cities? Explain.

6. **Draw Conclusions** How might the Hundred Years' War affect nation-building in France and England?

? Essential Question

What are the challenges of diversity?

7. How did diversity have both positive and negative effects on Spain? Go to your Student Journal to record your answer.

- **Identify Details** What is another name for the Black Death? (bubonic plague)

- **Distinguish Fact From Opinion** Does the following statement express a fact or an opinion? "Then there developed on the thighs or upper arms a boil." Explain. (It is a fact because it describes observed symptoms of the disease.)

- **Cause and Effect** How did the plague affect religious belief? (It caused religious turmoil because some people began to have doubts.)

- **Sequence** How did the plague help end manorialism? Describe the series of events that brought about the change. (The plague killed many people. There were not enough workers for all the work that had to be done. To obtain workers, people had to offer wages. Peasants began to work for money instead of on their lords' manors.)

ANSWERS

organization of artisans. The Magna Carta limited the power of English rulers.
2. People had new opportunities to work as a merchant or artisan. The number of people who earned more than peasants grew. **3.** The Crusades increased trade and spread knowledge. They caused bitterness between Christians and Muslims that, for some, still persists. **4.** They greatly reduced the population, so many lords had to pay wages to workers to farm their lands. **5.** Sample: They felt angry that guilds challenged their power. **6.** Sample: Each country probably became unified against its enemy. **7.** Muslims influenced culture, but Christians and Muslims fought.

KEY TERMS AND IDEAS

1. With an oligarchy, a small group of people rule. With a direct democracy, citizens vote directly on political issues.

2. A tribune could overturn any unjust act of any public official.

3. Similarities—Both Athens and the Roman Republic had governments in which citizens helped rule. Differences—Athens had a direct democracy in which all citizens could take part in making laws; Rome had a representative government in which a group of elected people made laws.

4. No; Manorialism was a self-contained system. On manors, people grew food, made clothes, and built shelters. So a lot of trade was not needed.

5. Christianity spread mainly through missionaries traveling throughout Europe and teaching their beliefs. Also, some kings declared Christianity the official religion of their kingdoms.

6. He invaded England and defeated Harold at the Battle of Hastings.

7. After the Reconquista, the Spanish rulers considered any Jews or Muslims remaining in Spain to be a threat. So they started the Spanish Inquisition, a court that imprisoned Muslims and Jews and often killed them if they didn't convert to Christianity.

THINK CRITICALLY

8. Sample: Because the Romans had a time of peace and prosperity, they could focus on government and culture.

9. Spartan life centered on the military. Also, Spartans were trained to endure pain. As a result, they had a very strong military that was able to conquer Peloponnesus and Athens.

10. The Black Death was a very deadly disease. Cities were very dirty, which helped the disease spread. Back then, no one knew what caused the Black Death. So they couldn't prevent it. Also, no one knew how to cure the Black Death.

11. Peasants were able to earn more money by growing more food. So many of them were able to buy their freedom from their lord. In addition, increasing trade made more money available. So more people were able to earn a living as a merchant or craft person. These professions formed guilds that challenged the authority of feudal lords.

Ancient and Medieval Europe

Chapter Assessment

Key Terms and Ideas

1. **Compare and Contrast** How is an **oligarchy** different from a **direct democracy**?

2. **Recall** What was the job of a tribune in the ancient Roman Republic?

3. **Compare and Contrast** What are some similarities and differences between the government of ancient Athens and that of the Roman Republic?

4. **Discuss** Did **manorialism** encourage trade? Why or why not?

5. **Describe** How did Christianity spread during the early Middle Ages?

6. **Recall** How did William the Conqueror gain the English crown?

7. **Explain** How was the **Reconquista** connected to the Spanish Inquisition?

Think Critically

8. **Determine Relevance** How did the Pax Romana lead to stability across the Roman empire?

9. **Test Conclusions** Why do you think Sparta was able to take control of the Peloponnesian Peninsula and defeat Athens? Support your answer with evidence from the chapter.

10. **Analyze Information** About 25 million Europeans died from the Black Death. Name three factors that contributed to this huge death toll.

11. **Core Concepts: Economics** How did economics contribute to the decline of feudalism?

Places to Know

For each place, write the letter from the map that show its location.

12. Athens
13. Constantinople
14. Spain
15. Venice
16. Rome
17. Sparta
18. **Estimate** Using the scale, estimate how far Constantinople was from Rome.

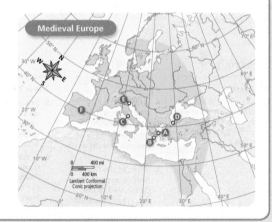

Medieval Europe

PLACES TO KNOW

12. A
13. D
14. F
15. E
16. C
17. B
18. roughly 800 miles

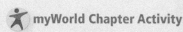 **myWorld Chapter Activity**

Piecing Together the Past Find Step-by-Step Instructions, Student Instructions and Rubric, and an Activity Support on pp. T5–T7. **(Visual/Logical)**

 21st Century Learning

Generate New Ideas Students' dialogues should be written in standard dialogue format with boldface names followed by colons. Dialogue should be creative in terms of the student's ability to imagine the speakers but also show a clear understanding of the king and Joan of Arc's actions and beliefs.

→ **Online Assessment**

Tailor review and assessment to each student's needs with an array of online assessments.
• Self-Test
• On Assignment Article or Slideshow
• Success Tracker

Ancient and Medieval Europe   Chapter Assessment

? Essential Question
myWorld Chapter Activity

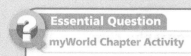 **Piecing Together the Past** Choose one image from the chapter activity cards. Follow your teacher's instructions and do your own field research to find similar objects in other European cultures. Then write a caption for each object you find, summarizing how it reflects diversity in European culture.

21st Century Learning
Generate New Ideas

Write Dialogue Write a scene in which Joan of Arc tries to convince the king to let her lead the French army into battle. Include:
• Joan's visions
• the king's desperation
• the city of Orleans
• the English army
• the French army

WRITING TASK TIP

IDENTIFY DETAILS Suggest that students notice how many craft workers are mentioned. Ask, What kind of economy could support such a variety of workers?

Document-Based Questions

Success Tracker — Online at myworldgeography.com

Use your knowledge of the Middle Ages and Documents A and B to answer Questions 1–3.

Document A

London Population
(Population (thousands) vs Year)
Years: 60, 200, 1100, 1200, 1340
SOURCE: www.demographia.com

Document B

" Each trade occupied its own quarter—butchers and tanners around the Châtelet, money-changers, goldsmiths, and drapers on the Grand Pont, scribes, illuminators, and parchment- and ink-sellers on the left bank around the University [of Paris]."

— Historian Barbara Tuchman describing Paris during the High Middle Ages

1. Which of the following might explain the drop in London's population from A.D. 200 to A.D. 1100?
   A decline of Greece, rise of feudalism
   B decline of Greece, rise of trade
   C decline of Rome, rise of feudalism
   D decline of Rome, rise of trade

2. Based on Document B, which of the following best describes Paris during the High Middle Ages?
   A an economically busy city with few craft workers
   B an economically busy city with many craft workers
   C an economically quiet city with few craft workers
   D an economically quiet city with many craft workers

3. **Writing Task** Describe details in Document B that show prosperity in medieval Paris.

DOCUMENT-BASED QUESTIONS

1. C

2. B

3. The description shows a city that is very economically active. The presence of so many craft workers indicate that most of them are probably earning good wages. This type of activity probably helped the economic growth of Paris. Also, the presence of goldsmiths shows that many people must have had money to buy luxuries.

Plan With Understanding by Design*

Chapter Objectives
Begin With the End in Mind

Students will demonstrate the following enduring understandings:
- Innovations in science and technology affect politics, economics, and everyday life.

- The quest for knowledge and the emphasis on reason have improved life and brought about modern culture.
- Democratic ideals form the basis for governments that are accountable to citizens and promote prosperity.

Connect
Make Learning Meaningful

Student Edition
- **Essential Question** What makes a nation?
- **myStory** Queen Elizabeth I inspires her navy to save England by defeating the Spanish Armada.

my worldgeography.com
myStory Video Get to know Queen Elizabeth I through a video about her life.

Student Journal
Essential Question Preview

Experience
Teach Knowledge and Skills

Student Edition
- Read Sections 1, 2, 3, 4, and 5.
- Answer Reading Checks and Section Assessment questions.

my worldgeography.com
On Assignment myStory Video, Active Atlas, Data Discovery, Timeline, and Culture Close-up

Student Journal
- Sections 1, 2, 3, 4, and 5 Word Wise
- Sections 1, 2, 3, 4, and 5 Take Notes

Teacher's Edition
myWorld Activities
- Section 1: A Life-Changing Product, p. T46
- Section 2: Sailing for Riches, p. T54
- Section 3: Long Live the Revolution, p. T60
- Section 4: Runaway Prices, p. T66
- Section 5: Tear Down This Wall, p. T74

21st Century Learning Online Tutor
- Identify Trends
- Give an Effective Presentation
- Analyze Cause and Effect
- Publish Your Work

Understand
Assess Understanding

Assessment Booklet
- Chapter Tests
- Benchmark Tests

Teacher's Edition
myWorld Chapter Activity Students analyze images of inventions from the Renaissance through the early 1900s, discuss how they led to modern life, and make a poster on technological progress.

Student Journal
Essential Question Writer's Workshop

my worldgeography.com
On Assignment Students write and submit an online article or multimedia slideshow about what makes a nation.

Success ☆ Tracker™
Online at myworldgeography.com
Administer chapter tests and remediate understanding.

Student Edition
Chapter Assessment

---

* "Understanding by Design" is registered as a trademark with the Patent and Trademark Office by the Association for Supervision of Curriculum Development (ASCD). ASCD has not authorized, approved or sponsored this work and is in no way affiliated with Pearson or its products.

Connect to the Essential Question

Essential Question

What makes a nation?

Follow these steps to help students understand the Essential Question.

Connect to Their Lives

1. Ask students to think about foreign nations that they have visited, read about, or seen in TV shows and movies. What makes those nations different from the United States? As students share their answers with the class, list them on the board.

2. Then ask students to sort the different answers by the following categories: institutions, geography, culture, other. Post the following table for them to complete or have students turn to the *Essential Question Preview* page in their **Student Journal.**

Things That Make Nations Different From Each Other			
Institutions	**Geography**	**Culture**	**Other**

Connect to the Content

3. Now ask students to suppose that they are going to found a new nation. Ask, What are the most important, most essential things that your nation would need?

4. Post the following web on the board. Have students use it to record their ideas about what makes a nation.

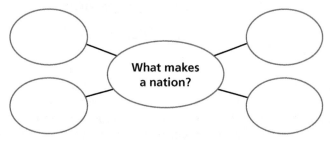

5. After previewing the chapter, have students make chapter-related predictions on the *Essential Question Preview* page in the **Student Journal.**

6. Remind students that they will answer a prompt related to the Essential Question on each section's *Take Notes* page in the **Student Journal.**

Explore my worldgeography.com

Welcome to myWorldGeography

http://www.myworldgeography.com

ON ASSIGNMENT: Europe in Modern Times

For this chapter's assignment, students will
- take a digital trip to Europe during the past three centuries.
- take on the role of a journalist.
- gather notes, images, and data for their story throughout their journey.
- create a news article or multimedia slideshow on this chapter's Essential Question: What makes a nation?

ITINERARY

During their trip, students will make the following stops:

myStory Video

Learn more about the life of Queen Elizabeth I.

Active Atlas

Read physical, political, and special purpose maps.

Data Discovery

Study charts about life in early modern Europe.

Timeline

Learn about World War I and World War II.

Culture Close-up

Explore Paris, France, during the French Revolution.

While on their trip, students will practice the following skills:

- **Interpret** graphic representations of data.
- **Synthesize** information into an interesting article.
- **Evaluate** the characteristics of nations.

TIGed
TakingITGlobal for Educators

Extend the reach of every lesson by helping students connect to a global community of young people with common interests and concerns. Visit myworldgeography.com to
- explore Country Pages relating to Europe in Modern Times
- delve deeper into this chapter's Essential Question, *What makes a nation?*
- find online alternatives to and solutions for the Unit Closer 21st Century Learning Activity.

 worldgeography.com
TEACHER CENTER

Preview and assign student materials, enrich your teaching, and track student progress with the following resources:
- Online Lesson Planning and Resource Library
- Presentations for Projection
- Online Teacher's Edition and Ancillaries

Assess Enduring Understandings

 **myWorld Chapter Activity**   **Step-by-Step Instructions**   **2 hr**

Technology: Then and Now

Teach this activity at the end of the chapter to assess enduring understandings.

OBJECTIVES

Students will demonstrate the following enduring understandings:

- Innovations in science and technology affect politics, economics, and everyday life.
- The quest for knowledge and the emphasis on reason have improved life and brought about modern culture.
- Democratic ideals form the basis for governments that are accountable to citizens and promote prosperity.

Students will provide the following evidence of understanding:

- Inventions Analysis Table
- Technology: Then and Now Poster

LEARNING STYLES

- Logical
- Visual

MATERIALS

- Activity Support: Student Instructions and Rubric, p. T42
- Activity Support: Analysis Table, p. T43
- Activity Cards: #49–54
  49. Navigation
  50. Printing
  51. Science
  52. Industry
  53. Warfare
  54. Transport

Activity Steps

1. **Set Expectations** Tell students they will use six Activity Cards to study inventions that changed life in Europe and led to modernization. They will study inventions related to one field, then hear from other students about other inventions. They will complete *Activity Support: Analysis Table* and make a poster linking past and recent inventions. Review the activity instructions and rubric on the next page.

   ELL **Advanced** Use these definitions to teach the difference between synonyms: **modern** *adj.* relating to recent times (often used as the opposite of ancient); **contemporary** *adj.* belonging to the current time. To test understanding, ask, Was World War II a modern or contemporary event?

2. **Analysis Table Jigsaw**
   - Organize six groups to analyze inventions related to navigation, printing, science, industry, warfare, and transport. Distribute one Activity Card to each group and distribute copies of *Activity Support: Analysis Table* to each student.
   - Have groups study images of inventions, discuss how each changed everyday life, and record their

   ideas on *Analysis Table.* Tell students to leave the last column blank.
   - Rearrange students in jigsaw groups to exchange findings. Each student then completes the remaining rows on *Analysis Table.*

3. **Make Modern Connections** After completing all six rows, groups should think of related recent inventions for the historical inventions listed on the table, and record these in the last column.

   L2 **Extra Support** Explain that changing an old invention or combining inventions can create a new invention. Give examples, such as a camera phone.

4. **Make an Illustrated Poster** Have groups make an illustrated poster to show how inventions, past and present, contribute to modern life. Groups may organize their information in any way that fits the theme "Technology: Then and Now," and may use found or drawn images.

   L1 **Special Needs** Provide stencils for large lettering, technology magazines, and flyers from home and technology stores.

KEY **Time**   **Individual**   **Pairs**   **Small Group**   **Whole Class**

Name _____ Class _____ Date _____

 myWorld Chapter Activity Support **Student Instructions and Rubric**

Technology: Then and Now

Activity Instructions Read the following summary of your myWorld Chapter Activity. Follow your teacher's directions for more information.

1. Your group is going to study how technology changed life in Europe and led to modernization. You will be given a card with images of inventions related to one of six fields: navigation, printing, science, industry, warfare, or transport. Some cards show one invention; some cards show more.

2. In your group, study the card and answer the questions on it. Enter information related to your card on *Activity Support: Analysis Table*. Leave the column about recent inventions blank.

3. The teacher will then rearrange the groups, and you will hear about the inventions discussed in other groups. Then fill out the remaining lines on *Analysis Table* as you did in Step 2.

4. As a group, complete the last column by thinking of a recent invention related to each of the six fields. (The first one has been done for you.)

5. Make an illustrated poster on the theme of "Technology: Then and Now." On the poster, link past inventions to recent ones, and use captions to explain how the inventions changed life to make it more modern. Group members should divide up the tasks of organizing, researching, illustrating, and writing.

myWorld Chapter Activity Rubric	3 Exceeds Understanding	2 Reaches Understanding	1 Approaches Understanding
Group Participation	Leads discussion of the images, encourages others, and helps others complete the table.	Participates in discussion of the images, listens to others, and contributes equally to the table.	Listens to others and contributes unequally to the table.
Teaching	Shares main points and details of first group's findings with second group.	Shares main points of first group's findings with second group.	Shares some points of first group's findings with second group.
Poster	Takes responsibility for and completes more than one task for the poster.	Takes responsibility for and completes one task for the poster.	Helps to complete one task for the poster.

Name _____ Class _____ Date _____

 myWorld Chapter Activity Support   Analysis Table

Technology: Then and Now

Directions Study the Activity Cards and discuss how the inventions changed life in Europe. (Some cards have one invention; some have more.) In your first group, fill out the row related to your group's Activity Card but leave the final column blank. In your second group, fill out the remaining rows. Then complete the final column with recent inventions related to the inventions in each row. One has been done for you.

Inventions	Who Used Them	Positive Effects	Negative Effects		Recent Invention
49. Navigation 1. _____ 2. _____					GPS device
50. Printing 1. _____ 2. _____					
51. Science 1. _____ 2. _____					
52. Industry 1. _____ 2. _____					
53. Warfare 1. _____ 2. _____					
54. Transport 1. _____ 2. _____					

Share Your Work Work with your group to make an illustrated poster on the subject of "Technology: Then and Now." Present your poster to the class.

   T43

Europe in Modern Times

- Introduce the Essential Question so that students will be able to understand the big ideas of this chapter (see earlier page, Connect to the Essential Question).

- Help students prepare to learn about modern Europe by looking at the chapter's maps, charts, and photos.

- Have students make and record chapter predictions with the *Essential Question Preview* in the **Student Journal.**

- Ask them to analyze the maps on this page.

GUIDE ON THE SIDE

Explore the Essential Question . . .

Have students complete the Essential Question Writer's Workshop in their **Student Journal** to demonstrate in-depth understanding of the question in the context of this chapter.

Analyze Maps Point out the political map.

- What two countries are located directly to the west of the North Sea? (England and Scotland)

- Which country is larger, Spain or England? (Spain)

- In what direction did the Spanish Armada have to sail from Spain to reach England? (north)

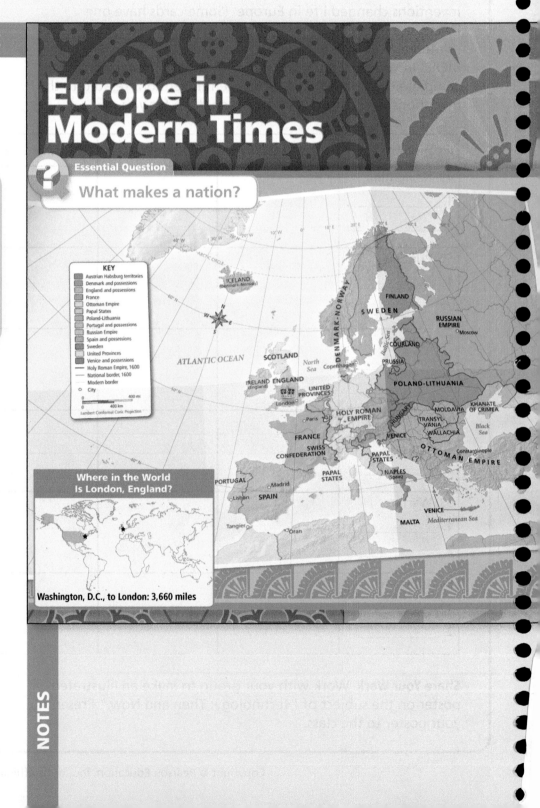

Europe in Modern Times

? Essential Question

What makes a nation?

KEY

- Austrian Habsburg territories
- Denmark and possessions
- England and possessions
- France
- Ottoman Empire
- Papal States
- Poland-Lithuania
- Portugal and possessions
- Russian Empire
- Spain and possessions
- Sweden
- United Provinces
- Venice and possessions
- Holy Roman Empire, 1600
- National border, 1600
- Modern border
- ○ City

0   400 mi
0   400 km
Lambert Conformal Conic Projection

Where in the World Is London, England?

Washington, D.C., to London: 3,660 miles

INTRODUCE my **Story**

Get students excited to learn about modern Europe by first experiencing the region through the eyes of Queen Elizabeth I of England.

- Read myStory and watch the myStory Video about her life.
- Have students complete *The Battle of the Spanish Armada* in the **Student Journal** to prepare to learn about the rivalries among European nations.

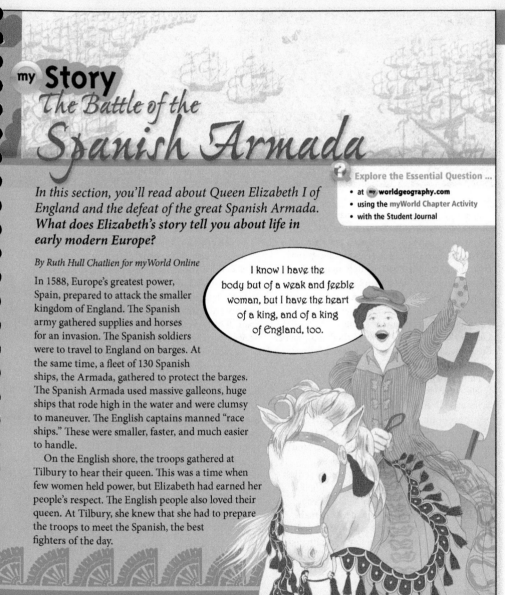

my **Story**
The Battle of the Spanish Armada

In this section, you'll read about Queen Elizabeth I of England and the defeat of the great Spanish Armada. What does Elizabeth's story tell you about life in early modern Europe?

Explore the Essential Question ...
- at my **worldgeography.com**
- using the **myWorld Chapter Activity**
- with the **Student Journal**

By Ruth Hull Chatlien for myWorld Online

In 1588, Europe's greatest power, Spain, prepared to attack the smaller kingdom of England. The Spanish army gathered supplies and horses for an invasion. The Spanish soldiers were to travel to England on barges. At the same time, a fleet of 130 Spanish ships, the Armada, gathered to protect the barges. The Spanish Armada used massive galleons, huge ships that rode high in the water and were clumsy to maneuver. The English captains manned "race ships." These were smaller, faster, and much easier to handle.

On the English shore, the troops gathered at Tilbury to hear their queen. This was a time when few women held power, but Elizabeth had earned her people's respect. The English people also loved their queen. At Tilbury, she knew that she had to prepare the troops to meet the Spanish, the best fighters of the day.

I know I have the body but of a weak and feeble woman, but I have the heart of a king, and of a king of England, too.

GUIDE ON THE SIDE

my **Story**

The Battle of the Spanish Armada

- **Compare and Contrast** How were the English and Spanish ships different? (The English ships sailed faster and were easier to handle than the Spanish ships.)

- **Draw Conclusions** How did the difference between the fleets give the English an advantage in battle? (They could move more quickly into the most advantageous positions.)

- **Identify Main Ideas** Why was Elizabeth unusual for her time period? (Few women held positions of power at the time.)

➔ On Assignment

Have students go to myworldgeography.com to receive their assignments from a virtual newspaper editor. Students will explore Europe in modern times in order to better understand Queen Elizabeth's experiences and the key ideas of the chapter.

NOTES

HISTORY

Philip and Elizabeth Many criss-crossing ties complicated the relationship between Philip II of Spain and Elizabeth I of England. Catherine of Aragon, whom King Henry VIII divorced to marry Elizabeth's mother, was Philip's great-aunt. Those who supported Catherine and her daughter Mary refused to accept Henry's marriage to Anne Boleyn; in their view, Elizabeth was an illegitimate child with no right to the English throne. To add further complexity to the relationship, Philip had been married to Elizabeth's older half-sister Mary and ruled jointly with her while she was queen of England. If Mary had been able to have a child, Philip's son or daughter would have inherited the throne and Elizabeth never would have become queen.

GUIDE ON THE SIDE

- **Compare and Contrast** What religious difference existed between the rulers of Spain and England? (Philip was Catholic and Elizabeth was Protestant.)

- **Analyze Sources** How would you paraphrase the sentence *I have no desire to make windows into men's souls?* (Sample: Elizabeth didn't want to try to read anyone's mind.)

- **Identify Details** What disadvantages did the Spanish have? (They had no maps, they were less skillful with cannons, and their supplies of food and water were low.)

In 1587, Elizabeth's advisors convinced her to order the death of her cousin, Mary, Queen of Scotland. They saw Mary, a Catholic, as a threat to Elizabeth, a Protestant.

Elizabeth and trusted court advisors planned the strategy for the battle with the Spanish navy.

Spain's attack against England happened in a time of religious conflict between Catholics and Protestants. Catholicism had been the main religion of Western Europe until the early 1500s. At that time, some Christians left the Roman Catholic Church and started their own Protestant churches.

Spain's king, Philip II, was a very religious man who wanted to restore Catholicism to all of Europe. Elizabeth, who was a Protestant, urged Philip to let Protestants in the Netherlands practice their religion. At that time, the Netherlands was a Spanish possession.

Philip also believed that he should be king of England because he had been married to Mary I. Mary was Elizabeth's half-sister who ruled England before her death in 1558. Religious strife had shaken England ever since Henry VIII, father of Elizabeth and Mary, broke with the Catholic Church and started the Protestant Church of England.

As queen, one of Protestant Elizabeth's earliest acts was to order a compromise with Catholics. Unlike Philip, she did not want to force people to share her religion. "I have no desire to make windows into men's souls," she said. Her wise actions prevented civil war in England, although tension remained throughout her reign.

Spain and England were also rival empire-builders. England wanted an empire and colonies like those of Spain. Those colonies had brought fabulous wealth, such as gold and silver, to Spain. English ships had attacked Spanish ships and taken their gold and silver.

As the Spanish Armada set sail, the huge fleet appeared to be invincible, or unbeatable. Yet, the Spanish had several weaknesses. Besides sailing heavier ships, the Spanish captains had no maps of the coasts of Scotland or Ireland. The Spanish soldiers were brave fighters, but in the use of cannon, they lagged behind their rivals. In addition, food stores had been loaded too early and were rotting. Water barrels leaked, and cannon balls were poorly made or the wrong size. In addition, there were discipline problems on board the Spanish ships.

The Spanish were sure that they would win and saw the battle as a holy war. Philip even had the ships' sails painted with the cross of St. George, the symbol of the medieval Crusaders. In spite of the seeming advantage of the Spanish, Elizabeth predicted,

❝ Let tyrants fear. . . .We shall shortly have a famous victory over these enemies of my God, of my kingdom, and of my people. ❞

NOTES

PRIMARY SOURCE

Elizabeth's Speech at Tilbury "I have always so behaved myself, that under God, I have placed my chiefest strength and safeguard in the loyal hearts and goodwill of my subjects, and therefore I am come amongst you, as you see, at this time, not for my recreation, but being resolved, in the midst and heat of the battle, to live or die amongst you all, to lay down for my God, and for my Kingdom, and for my People, my honour, and my blood, even in the dust."
—Queen Elizabeth I, "Speech to Her Troops"

The Spanish navy had helped make Spain a wealthy global empire. But the Spanish sailed old-fashioned, slower ships. Their loss to England changed sea warfare and the fortunes of Spain.

As the Spanish Armada neared the coast of England, the English fleet moved into position. For several days, the English managed to keep the Spanish ships at a distance.

At midnight, the English sent fireships loaded with explosives into the midst of the Spanish fleet. The Spanish commanders were forced to cut the ships' anchor cables and sail out to sea to avoid catching fire. The Spanish formation became disorganized, and the English took advantage of the confusion to attack at dawn. A decisive battle took place, and the losses to Spain far outweighed those of England. Spanish domination of the seas had ended.

The English felt this victory proved that God was on their side. English admirals received a medal that said, "God blew and they were scattered." This victory at sea was one of the greatest triumphs of Elizabeth's reign.

myStory Online

Join Elizabeth and her advisors as they plan the battle against the Spanish Armada.

GUIDE ON THE SIDE

- **Identify Main Ideas** What was one strategy the English used against the Spanish? (The English sent fireships loaded with explosives into the midst of the Armada.)

- **Identify Evidence** What action shows how desperate the Spanish were to escape the English attack? (They cut the cables holding their anchors.)

 myStory Video

Have students watch the video about Elizabeth I and the Spanish Armada. Tell students to take notes on the causes of the conflict between Spain and England and the reasons for the English victory.

New Ways of Thinking

OBJECTIVES

Students will know

- how the Renaissance changed European art and learning.
- the causes and effects of the Reformation.

Students will be able to

- label an outline map.
- identify economic and cultural trends caused by Italy's trade with Asia.

SET EXPECTATIONS

In this section, students will

- read New Ways of Thinking.
- make an advertisement for Asian trade goods that changed European life.
- go On Assignment in Europe and examine maps and charts about the Reformation.

CORE CONCEPTS

You may wish to teach or reteach the following lessons from the Core Concepts Handbook:

- Trade, pp. 66–67
- Religion, pp. 92–93
- The Arts, pp. 94–95

KEY

Differentiated Instruction

- **L1** Special Needs
- **L2** Extra Support
- **L3** On-Level
- **L4** Challenge

English Language Instruction

- **ELL** Beginner
- **ELL** Early Intermediate
- **ELL** Intermediate
- **ELL** Early Advanced
- **ELL** Advanced

1 Connect
Make learning meaningful

Make Connections Ask students what paintings and statues they have seen in museums, public places, offices, or homes. Did they think the art was realistic? Explain that in this section, they will learn about the Renaissance, a cultural movement in Europe that produced great realism in art.

ELL **Intermediate** Clarify terms for discussing art. *Realistic* means "looks like real life." *Perspective* describes an artistic technique that gives a three-dimensional appearance. Distinguish this meaning from the common one, "point of view."

Activate Prior Knowledge Remind students that the Crusades started two major trends. Desire for Asian goods stimulated trade, and contact with other cultures brought new knowledge to Europe. Have students list products from Asia that became popular and new knowledge that was gained. Ask how they think cultures respond to new trends and ideas.

L3 **On-Level** To guide the discussion, ask, Why might people want to stop cultural change? Why might people welcome new knowledge?

Prepare Follow the steps in the section **Preview.** Preteach the Key Terms. Then have students complete *Word Wise* in their journals using in-text clues and the glossary for help.

2 Experience
Teach knowledge and skills

Read Use **Background** notes and **Guide on the Side** questions to model active reading. Have students use *Take Notes* in their **Student Journal** to record important places to know in Renaissance Europe on an outline map. Students should use the maps in the Chapter Atlas and the Active Atlas at myworldgeography.com for assistance.

L2 **Extra Support** Give students a flowchart labeled *Italian Renaissance; Northern Renaissance; Protestant Reformation; Catholic Reformation* to track the cause-and-effect relationships as they read. Offer the **Online Student Edition** as a reading option.

ELL **Advanced** In the word *Renaissance*, which means "rebirth," the prefix *re-* means again. This prefix also appears in *reform* and *Reformation*. Have students predict what *reform* means, check the definition in a dictionary, and use it in a sentence.

L4 **Challenge** Have students read *Enrichment: Biography of Leonardo da Vinci*. Urge them to write Leonardo's reply as part of the activity.

 Practice: myWorld Activity Students will make an advertisement to persuade Europeans to buy Asian goods. **Step-by-Step Instructions** and **More Activities** follow on p. T46.

SECTION 1 RESOURCE GUIDE

FOR THE STUDENT

my worldgeography.com Student Center

- myStory Video
- Active Atlas
- Data Discovery

Student Edition (print and online)
- New Ways of Thinking

Student Journal (print and online)
- Section 1 Word Wise
- Section 1 Take Notes

21st Century Learning Online Tutor

- Read Special-Purpose Maps
- Identify Trends

FOR THE TEACHER

my worldgeography.com Teacher Center

- Online Lesson Planner
- Presentations for Projection
- SuccessTracker

ProGuide: Europe and Russia

- Section 1 Lesson Plan, pp. T44–T45
- myWorld Activity Step-by-Step Instructions, p. T46
- Activity Support: Write Slogans, p. T47
- myWorld Geography Enrichment, p. T48
- Section Quiz, p. T49

Accelerating the Progress of ELLs

- Peer Learning Strategies, p. 46

---

3 Understand
Assess understanding

Review Review *Word Wise* and *Take Notes* in the **Student Journal.**

Assess Knowledge and Skills Use the Section Assessment and Section Quiz to check students' progress.

Assess Understanding Review students' responses to the Section Assessment Essential Question prompt.

Remediate Use these strategies to review and remediate.

If students struggle to . . .	Try these strategies.
Describe how the Renaissance changed art	Show images of medieval and Renaissance art and ask students to describe the differences.
Explain how the Renaissance helped cause the Reformation	Give students a cause-effect flowchart and direct them to look for effects of humanism and the printing press.
Identify trends	Assign additional practice with the **21st Century Online Tutor.**

ELL Support

ELL Objective Students will use English to describe art and architecture.

Cultural Connections Let students use their home languages to describe a statue or painting that they have seen. Have them share information such as subject, color, material, and location. Then have them use English to share one detail about the work of art with the class.

ELL Intermediate Content Tip Have students use drawings or magazine photos to make flash cards for the following terms: *painting, statue, mural, dome, column,* and *arch.* When the flash cards are finished, have students label each one either "art" or "architecture."

ELL Activity Give students this list of terms to write on separate slips of paper with symbols you post to help with word meaning: *magnetic compass, silk cloth, porcelain, gunpowder, spices, tea.* Have them divide the terms into two categories: *Improved Daily Life* or *Improved Sailing and Warfare.* **(Verbal/Kinesthetic)**

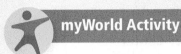

  30 min

myWorld Activity **Step-by-Step Instructions**

A Life-Changing Product

OBJECTIVES

Students will

- describe the impact of Asian trade goods on European life.
- make a persuasive advertisement.

LEARNING STYLE

- Verbal
- Visual

21st Century Learning

- Identify Trends

MATERIALS

- Activity Support: Write Slogans, p. T47
- Poster board or paper
- Colored markers or pencils
- Magazine ads

Activity Steps

1. Give each student a copy of *Activity Support: Write Slogans*. Then lead a class discussion on how the following Asian trade goods changed European life: magnetic compass, porcelain, silk cloth, gunpowder, spices, and tea. Have students record the information in the middle column of their tables.

   L1 Special Needs If students have difficulty with aural processing, record the discussion answers on the board or a transparency so students may copy them.

2. Organize the class in small groups. Tell students that each group is an association of merchants and that several of their ships have just brought cargos of Asian goods to Venice. The merchants want to advertise the goods to the Venetian people.

   ELL Intermediate/Early Advanced Explain that when the noun *Venice* is changed to an adjective,

the c changes to a *t,* so the adjective is *Venetian.* Similarly, the adjective for *Florence* is *Florentine.*

3. The groups should make catchy advertising slogans for each item and record them on the table. Suggest that the slogans stress how the goods will improve European life.

   L2 Extra Support Bring in magazine ads with catchy slogans. Suggest that students list the persuasive words used in such slogans.

4. Groups should cooperate to make an advertisement showing the goods that will be sold at the market. They should display the completed ads to the class.

5. Finally, hold a class discussion about the impact of trade. Ask, What economic and social trends did the trade in Asian goods cause? (more wealth in cities, increased trade) How did social classes change? (A middle class arose.)

More Activities From myWorld Teachers

 Local Connection Have students look through the churches section of the yellow pages, count different denominations, and share the findings in class the next day. Ask students to use what they learned about the Reformation to form a theory about why so many denominations exist. **(Logical)**

Northern Renaissance Art Use an art book or fine art transparencies to show one or more

paintings by Northern Renaissance artists like Peter Breugel. Ask the class to point out details that show evidence of a growing middle class. **(Visual/Logical)**

 A Matter of Perspective Have pairs of students study the feature on perspective in their textbook. Then they should work together to make a simple sketch of a building using the principle of perspective. **(Visual)**

my worldgeography.com **Teacher Center** Find additional resources in the online Teacher Center.

Name _____ Class _____ Date _____

myWorld Activity Support   Write Slogans

A Life-Changing Product

Directions You and your classmates are Venetian merchants who have just received several shiploads of goods from the East. You want to make an advertisement that will tell the people of Venice that the market has new and exciting goods for sale. Use the table below to decide what to say about each item. In the middle column, list the ways that the item changed European life. Then in the right-hand column, write a catchy and persuasive advertising slogan for each item. Finally, make an ad with pictures of the trade items, slogans, and any other information you think is important.

WRITE SLOGANS		
Trade Item	**How It Changed Life in Europe**	**Advertising Slogan**
magnetic compass		
porcelain		
silk cloth		
gunpowder		
spices (pepper, cinnamon, cloves, ginger)		
tea		

Name _____ Class _____ Date _____

Enrichment: Biography of Leonardo da Vinci

Directions Read the biography below. Answer the questions that follow and complete the activity.

Leonardo da Vinci was one of the most brilliant thinkers of the Renaissance. He painted and drew, studied science, designed buildings, worked as an engineer, and proposed inventions. He was born in 1452 near the town of Vinci in the republic of Florence. His mother was a peasant, and his father was a landlord. As a child, Leonardo received only a basic education in reading, writing, and arithmetic. Later, he studied Latin and advanced mathematics. At the age of 15, he was apprenticed to an artist in Florence, where he learned to paint and sculpt.

When he was 30, Leonardo moved to Milan to work as a painter and engineer for a duke. While there, he finished one of his most famous paintings, a wall mural called *The Last Supper.* It shows Jesus eating with his 12 disciples shortly before his death.

In 1499, a French army invaded Milan, so Leonardo left. He eventually returned to Florence. For the rest of his life, Leonardo worked as an artist, engineer, and architect for powerful men of the Renaissance. He spent his last years in France at the court of King Francis I.

In addition to *The Last Supper,* Leonardo painted the *Mona Lisa,* possibly the most famous painting in the world. He left many sketches of ideas for inventions, including one that looks like a helicopter.

1. Why do you think rulers wanted Leonardo to work for them?

_____

_____

2. The phrase *Renaissance man* means an educated, well-rounded person who does well in many areas. Do you consider Leonardo such a person? Explain.

_____

_____

3. **Activity** Imagine that you are a Renaissance ruler. Write a letter to Leonardo to persuade him to come work at your court.

Name _____ Class _____ Date _____

Section Quiz

Directions Answer the following questions using what you learned
in Section 1.

1. _____ Which of the following cities was an
important coastal trade center in Italy?
a. Antwerp
b. Florence
c. Paris
d. Venice

2. _____ What style of art did Renaissance
artists copy?
a. Classical art
b. French art
c. German art
d. Muslim art

3. _____ Humanist scholars changed learning
by studying
a. secular subjects.
b. Christian theology.
c. Germanic mythology.
d. the history of printing.

4. Which of the following was a belief of the
Protestant reformers?
a. Only the clergy can interpret the Bible.
b. Buying an indulgence can earn pardon
for sin.
c. A Christian's salvation comes by faith
alone.
d. Church tradition is as important as the
Bible.

5. Which of the following people
was a Christian Humanist?
a. Desiderius Erasmus
b. Jan Hus
c. Martin Luther
d. Leonardo da Vinci

6. How did the printing press help to spread learning?

_____

_____

_____

New Ways of Thinking

- Model preparing to read by previewing the Key Ideas, Key Terms, headings, visuals, and captions. Have students make predictions about what they will learn. For ELL support, post the prompt, "I predict I will read about . . ."

- Preview and practice reading special-purpose maps by looking at the map *Protestant and Catholic Europe*. Ask, What general pattern describes how Europe was divided between Catholics and Protestants?

- Preteach this section's high-use Academic Vocabulary and Key Terms using the table on the next page and in-text definitions. Have students practice Key Terms by completing the *Word Wise* page in their journals.

GUIDE ON THE SIDE

Reading Skill

Label an Outline Map While they read, have students identify the Places to Know! on the outline map of the region in the **Student Journal.**

The Italian Renaissance

- **Cause and Effect** What influence from Italy's past helped to start the Renaissance? (Italy had been the center of the Roman Empire and its classical culture.)

- **Connect** What new practices became the basis of modern banking? (depositing money and writing checks)

- **Compare and Contrast** How did Italy differ from kingdoms in other parts of Europe? (It was divided into city-states.)

Section 1
New Ways of Thinking

Key Ideas
- European Renaissance thinkers and artists took a new interest in humanity and the world around them.
- Critical thinking in Renaissance Europe led to the Reformation.

Key Terms • Renaissance • humanism • perspective • Reformation • Catholic Reformation

 Visual Glossary

 Reading Skill: Label an Outline Map Take notes using the graphic organizer in your journal.

Leon Battista Alberti drew on ancient models for his Renaissance church, Santa Maria Novella, in Florence, Italy.▼

The Late Middle Ages brought many changes to Europe. Feudalism came to an end. Farmers began producing more agricultural goods than they needed. Trade increased. These changes led to a new age in European history called the **Renaissance,** or "rebirth," a time of a renewed interest in art and learning.

The Italian Renaissance
Italy is a peninsula in southern Europe. Italy had been the center of the Roman Empire. This classical influence contributed to the Renaissance.

Trade Grows and Cities Compete Italian traders brought silks and spices back from Asia. They sold these in Italian cities such as Genoa, Venice, and Florence. These cities were major trade centers. In the markets, people exchanged coins of different lands. Merchants adopted a system to deposit money and write checks. These practices became the basis of modern banking.

Unlike the kingdoms of other parts of Europe, Italy was divided into city-states. These city-states were often ruled by one powerful family. In addition to ruling families, city-states were dominated by a wealthy merchant class. City-states fought often. They invented taxes on property and income and other ways to finance their wars.

ACADEMIC VOCABULARY

High-Use Word	Definition and Sample Sentence
rapid	*adj.* fast *A period of rapid change can make people feel confused.*
doctrine	*n.* a teaching or principle *The pope explained the new doctrine in a letter to all Catholics.*

Old and New Ideas Inspire Trade brought Europeans into contact with the learning of Asia and the Muslim world. For example, Muslim mathematician Al-Khwarizmi (al KWAHR iz mee) had used Hindu-Arabic numerals and developed algebra in the 700s. Muslim scholars had copied and preserved works from ancient Greece and Rome. Many of these had been lost in Europe. Europeans also learned Chinese techniques such as block printing and papermaking.

During the Renaissance, European scholars took an interest in ancient Greek and Roman ideas. This was the beginning of **humanism,** or the study of secular, or nonreligious, subjects such as history and philosophy. Humanists emphasized individual accomplishment and serving the people of this world instead of focusing on religion.

Art Copies Nature Medieval artists had focused on teaching spiritual lessons. As a result, their art was symbolic, not realistic. In contrast, the Greeks and Romans had honored nature and tried to make their art lifelike. Renaissance artists imitated the realism of classical art.

Art changed in two major ways during the Renaissance. First, artists studied the human body so that they could create lifelike statues and paintings. Second, Renaissance painters used **perspective,** a technique that allows artists to portray a three-dimensional space on a flat surface.

Artists Michelangelo and Leonardo da Vinci both created Renaissance masterpieces. Michelangelo carved sculptures, such as the statue *David.* He also painted scenes from the Bible on the ceiling of the Sistine Chapel in Rome. Leonardo painted the famous portrait *Mona Lisa.* He also drew thousands of diagrams of ideas for inventions. Architect Filippo Brunelleschi (fee LEEP po broo nel LES kee) used classical features such as domes, columns, and arches in his buildings.

Reading Check What did humanists emphasize?

A New Perspective

For *The Last Supper* **(1495–1497), Leonardo used perspective to make the painting as realistic as possible.** *How did Leonardo use perspective to focus on the figure of Jesus?*

- **Build Cultural Awareness** What cultures contributed to Renaissance art and learning? (Chinese, Greek, Roman, and Muslim)

- **Connect** Do you think modern education is more like medieval or Renaissance education? Explain. (Sample: Renaissance education; people today study history and philosophy, not just religion.)

- **Identify Details** Who were some important artists of the Italian Renaissance? (Michelangelo and Leonardo da Vinci)

READING CHECK They emphasized studying secular subjects and serving people of the world.

CAPTION Jesus is at the center and all the lines in the painting lead to him.

ANSWERS

QUICK FACTS

Venetian Vocabulary Venice had more than just an artistic effect on northern Europe; its language was influential too. Venetian differs significantly from standard Italian because it evolved directly from Latin at an earlier period. After scholars such as Dante and Petrarch developed vernacular Italian from their native Tuscan, that language gradually came to supersede Venetian in national importance. However, most residents of Venice still speak Venetian and take care to keep it separate from the Italian they must use to deal with outsiders.

English has borrowed many words from Venetian, including *artichoke, arsenal, ballot, casino, ghetto, gondola, lagoon, lotto, pistachio, quarantine, scampi, sequin,* and *zany.* The international greeting *ciao* comes from a Venetian phrase that means your humble servant: *vostro schiavo.*

GUIDE ON THE SIDE

The Northern Renaissance

- **Identify Details** What lands in Northern Europe did Mediterranean traders sail to? (England, Flanders, and Germany)

- **Compare and Contrast** What did Germany and Flanders have in common with Italy? (They were all divided into small competitive states.)

- **Summarize** What was the Hanseatic League? (a trade association of over 60 towns in Germany and other lands.)

Analyze Visuals Have students examine the pictures of the Gutenberg press and the book pages.

- Which method used smaller print, thus allowing for more words on a page? (the printing press)

myWorld Activity

A Life-Changing Product Find Step-by-Step Instructions and an Activity Support on pp. T46–T47. (Verbal/Visual)

Gutenberg's Press

Gutenberg and his pressmen examine a newly printed page (above). The page at the left was copied out by hand. The page at the right was printed using movable type. *How did Gutenberg's printing press change books?*

The Northern Renaissance

A network of land and sea trade routes linked the city-states of Italy with the kingdoms and small states of Northern Europe. These northern lands included England, Germany, and Flanders (a region now divided between France and Belgium). Like Italy, Germany and Flanders were divided into small, competitive states.

Northern Cities Grow Improved ships made traveling by sea faster than traveling overland. As a result of <u>rapid</u> sea travel, trade between northern and southern Europe increased. Trade also increased within northern Europe. Some northern towns decided to form trade associations so they could have more influence over trade. For example, the Hanseatic (han see AT ik) League was a group of more than 60 towns in Germany and other lands. They worked together to improve trade among members.

rapid, *adj.,* fast

myWorld Activity
A Life-Changing Product

Cities and countries began to specialize in the production of certain goods. The countries of England, France, and Flanders produced cloth. Northeastern Europe produced grain. Germany, Hungary, and Austria mined copper, iron, gold, and silver. Trade helped northern cities such as London, Paris, Brugge (BROOG uh), and Lyon grow. A middle class of traders and craftsmen developed. Middle-class people were wealthier than peasants and could buy more goods. This encouraged trade.

Renaissance Ideas Spread Renaissance ideas spread to northern Europe in several ways. First, traders brought the new ideas with them. Second, rulers such as King Francis I of France invited Renaissance scholars and artists to visit their courts. Third, many northern nobles and wealthy members of the middle class traveled to Italy for their education. While in Italy, they learned about Renaissance ideas.

CAPTION The printing press made it easier to produce books so there were more of them.

CULTURE

Who Was Shakespeare? In the 1800s, Delia Bacon proposed that the plays credited to Shakespeare were written by a secret group of aristocrats led by her ancestor, Sir Francis Bacon. She claimed that few facts are known about Shakespeare and doubted his qualifications because he did not attend university. Yet, more is known about Shakespeare's life than about most writers of his period, and a university education in the late 1500s focused on theology, not the humanist subjects Bacon assumed. Since then, people have proposed other names as the real author of the works, among them Christopher Marlowe, and Edward de Vere, the earl of Oxford. However, both Marlowe and Oxford died before many of the plays were written. Shakespeare's contemporaries did not question his authorship; the writer Ben Jonson knew him well. Most scholars today accept that William Shakespeare, in fact, penned the plays.

New technology helped spread knowledge. In the 1400s, German craftsman Johannes Gutenberg invented the printing press. Gutenberg made movable type, or pieces of metal formed into letters of the alphabet. He then printed pages by using a machine to squeeze paper against inked type. Before the printing press, the only way to reproduce writing was by hand. The press made it possible to create copies of books much faster than ever before. As more books became available, more people learned to read.

Renaissance ideas began to influence northern artists and writers. Flemish artist Pieter Bruegel (PEA tur BROO gel) the Elder painted lively scenes of peasant life. German artist Albrecht Dürer (AHL brekt DYOOR ur) used Italian techniques of realism and perspective to create lifelike paintings.

The English playwright William Shakespeare wrote brilliant plays seen as key works of Renaissance humanism. In his play *Hamlet*, he expressed the Renaissance view of human potential:

> 66 What a piece of work is a man, how noble in reason, how infinite in faculties, in form and moving, how express and admirable in action, how like an angel in apprehension, how like a god! 99

Shakespeare's work remains popular today, both on stage and in movies.

Some northern writers, known as Christian humanists, combined classical and religious studies. The Dutch scholar Erasmus (ih RAZ mus) studied the New Testament in its original Greek language. He suggested the Catholic Church make

changes, such as teaching in modern languages instead of Latin. The English humanist Thomas More wrote about an ideal society in his book *Utopia*. Today, we use the word *utopia* to mean a place of perfection in laws and society.

Reading Check **Who spread Renaissance ideas to Northern Europe?**

Above, a diagram shows the structure of the Globe Theatre.

At the right, modern actors perform a play by Shakespeare in London's Globe Theatre, an authentic replica of the theater where these plays were first performed.

READING CHECK traders, nobles who were educated in Italy, and artists and scholars who went to work in Northern Europe

GUIDE ON THE SIDE

- **Cause and Effect** What technology helped to spread Renaissance ideas? (The printing press made it possible to produce many more copies of books, thus spreading knowledge.)
- **Build Cultural Awareness** Who was William Shakespeare? (He was an English playwright who is still studied today.)
- **Identify Main Ideas** Who were Christian humanists? (They were writers who combined classical and religious studies.)

Analyze Visuals Have students examine the images of the Globe Theatre.

- In Shakespeare's time, the seats on the ground were very cheap. Why do you think that was so? (Sample: They did not have as good a view of the stage.)

ANSWERS

CORE CONCEPTS: RELIGION

Review Core Concept 7.4 before reading about the Reformation. Remind students of the origins of Christianity and its core beliefs. Review how the church split into the Roman Catholic Church and the Eastern Orthodox Church. One of the issues that prompted the Great Schism was disagreement over the authority of the pope. Explain to students that questions about the pope's authority would resurface during the Reformation. Also remind students that the Roman Catholic Church's power increased greatly during the Middle Ages. Ask, What are some possible problems associated with strong central authority?

GUIDE ON THE SIDE

The Protestant Reformation

- **Identify Evidence** What evidence shows that the Catholic Church had serious problems? *(Leaders were corrupt or had rich lifestyles, and the Inquisition took wealth from the people it put on trial.)*

- **Identify Details** What reformers were killed for criticizing the church? *(Jan Hus and Girolamo Savonarola)*

Chart Skills Have students examine the table comparing Catholicism and Lutheranism.

- Which set of beliefs put more emphasis on the Bible? *(Lutheranism)*

- Which set of beliefs seems more compatible with democracy? Explain. *(Sample: Lutheranism; it lets people decide for themselves.)*

 Data Discovery

Have students go to myworldgeography.com to learn more about religious conflicts in Europe.

The Protestant Reformation

During the Renaissance, humanism led Europeans like Erasmus to think critically about the Catholic Church. Some learned Europeans began to read the Bible and interpret it for themselves instead of simply following the Church's interpretation.

Criticisms of the Church Some Europeans began to believe that the Church did not uphold the Bible's teachings. Some felt that Church leaders were corrupt. Others thought that the Church had become too rich, or that it was too involved in politics.

The Inquisition also led to criticism. The Inquisition was a church court set up to try people accused of heresy, or religious belief contrary to established Church teachings. The Church gained wealth by taking property from people accused of heresy.

Early critics of the Church, such as John Wycliffe, Jan Hus (yahn hous), and Girolamo Savonarola (jee ROH lah moh sah voh nuh ROH lah), risked their lives by speaking out. Church leaders executed both Hus and Savonarola, yet the calls for reform did not end.

The printing press helped spread the desire for change. As books grew more common, more people were able to read the Bible and scholarly works. People formed their own ideas about religion. More people questioned Church teachings.

Luther Calls for Reform The Church made money by selling indulgences, or pardons for sin. A German monk named Martin Luther studied the Bible and came to believe that people could neither buy nor earn pardon for sin. In 1517, Luther drafted the 95 Theses, a list of arguments against indulgences. He sent the list to to a church official who called for an investigation of Luther's beliefs. Luther's call for reform started the **Reformation,** a religious movement in which calls for reform led to the emergence of non-Catholic, or Protestant, churches.

Comparing Catholicism and Lutheranism		
	Catholicism	**Lutheranism**
Salvation	Faith and good works bring salvation.	Faith alone brings salvation.
Sacraments	Priests perform the seven sacraments, or rituals.	Accepts some sacraments, but rejects others because they lack Biblical grounding.
Head of the Church	The pope, together with the bishops	Elected councils
Importance of the Bible	Bible is one source of truth; Church tradition is another.	Bible alone is the source of truth.
Interpretation	Bible is interpreted by priests according to tradition and Church leadership.	People read and interpret the Bible for themselves.

Chart Skills

Note the differences in the heads of the two churches. Why was this difference important?

Data Discovery

CHART SKILLS The Catholic Church had a single head; Lutherans had a council. This is important because the Catholic structure puts more emphasis on authority and less on individual freedom.

PRIMARY SOURCE

The 95 Theses These statements come from Martin Luther's *95 Theses*, which sparked the Reformation:

1. Our Lord and Master Jesus Christ, when He said, "Repent," willed that the whole life of believers should be repentance.

6. The pope cannot remit any guilt, except by declaring that it has been remitted by God . . .

32. They will be condemned eternally [those] who believe themselves sure of their salvation because they have letters of pardon.

37. Every true Christian, whether living or dead, has part in all the blessings of Christ and the Church; and this is granted him by God, even without letters of pardon.

Luther believed that religious salvation came only from faith. He also believed that the Bible—not the Church—was the only true authority for Christian life. He encouraged ordinary people to study the Bible. People began Lutheran churches based on Luther's teachings.

Other Protestants took the movement even further. In his book *Institutes of the Christian Religion*, John Calvin offered an explanation of Protestant beliefs. His main theme is the belief that God has complete control over the universe. Calvin also stressed morality and hard work.

The Reformation began a series of events in which churches continued to split up over various disagreements. One new group of Protestants, the Anabap-

tists, baptized only adults. Other new churches included the Baptists, the Mennonites, and the Quakers. In the 1700s, English clergyman John Wesley founded the Methodist Church.

The Reformation and Government
During this time period, many European rulers forced their people to follow the ruler's religion. Catholics and Protestants felt certain that their own beliefs were the only correct <u>doctrines.</u> Many people did not think other views should be allowed. Sometimes, state churches punished people of other faiths. Such abuses of religious power later led the authors of the U.S. Constitution to call for separation of church and state.

doctrine, *n.*, teaching or principle

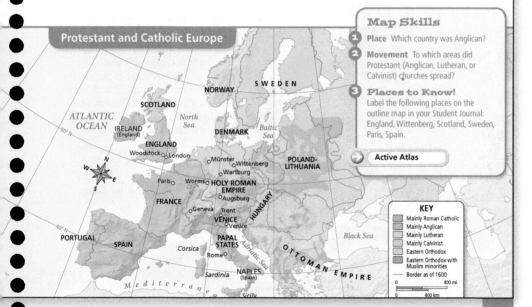

Protestant and Catholic Europe

Map Skills

1 **Place** Which country was Anglican?

2 **Movement** To which areas did Protestant (Anglican, Lutheran, or Calvinist) churches spread?

3 **Places to Know!** Label the following places on the outline map in your Student Journal: England, Wittenberg, Scotland, Sweden, Paris, Spain.

Active Atlas

KEY
- Mainly Roman Catholic
- Mainly Anglican
- Mainly Lutheran
- Mainly Calvinist
- Eastern Orthodox
- Eastern Orthodox with Muslim minorities
- Border as of 1600

0   400 mi
0   400 km

MAP SKILLS 1. England **2.** England, parts of Ireland, Scotland, Norway, Sweden, Denmark, parts of the Holy Roman Empire, Poland-Lithuania, Hungary, Switzerland **3.** Students should correctly label each place on the outline map in their **Student Journal.**

- **Summarize** Why did Luther object to the sale of indulgences? (He believed that salvation came by faith alone, not by something a person could buy.)

- **Identify Details** What did John Calvin teach? (God's complete control, hard work, strict morality)

- **Connect** Why did the authors of the U.S. Constitution decide to separate church and state? (They wanted to prevent religious persecution by the state.)

Map Skills Discuss the map of Protestant and Catholic Europe.

- What religions were in Ireland? (Catholicism and Anglicanism)

- Why do you think Italy remained Catholic? (The Papal States were there.)

21st Century Learning

Read Special-Purpose Maps Have students develop this skill with the interactive online tutorial and activities.

Active Atlas

Have students go to myworldgeography.com to learn more about how Europe was divided religiously.

HISTORY

Seizing Monastic Lands After Henry VIII split with the Catholic Church, he remained very suspicious of monasteries and feared that they retained their loyalty to Rome. At first he dissolved almost 400 religious institutions that had less than £200 by claiming that they were too small to function effectively. After a Catholic rebellion in 1536, he proceeded to dissolve all the remaining monasteries in England and seize their lands. By these confiscations, the English crown gained property that equaled roughly one-eighth of the lands in England and Wales. Henry VIII later sold most of the land to aristocrats to help pay for his wars and foreign policy. These transactions had an added political benefit. Nobles who gained confiscated church lands had no interest in seeing Catholicism return to England.

• **Infer** Why do you think Henry wanted a son to rule after him rather than a daughter? (Women were not considered men's equals in the 1500s in Europe, and he probably thought a daughter would not be strong enough to keep the country safe.)

• **Draw Conclusions** How do you think England was affected by having its rulers change the religion of the country from Catholic to Protestant to Catholic and finally back to Protestant? (There was probably a lot of turmoil and conflict and perhaps some persecution.)

The Catholic Reformation

• **Build Cultural Awareness** In which countries did Catholicism remain especially strong? (Spain and Italy)

Analyze Visuals Have students look at the portraits of Henry VIII and Catherine of Aragon.

• What symbols of power do you see in these portraits? (the jewels worn by both monarchs and Henry's sword)

• What signs of wealth appear in these portraits? (clothes made from deep colors and soft fabrics, jewels)

Each of the small states in Germany followed the religion of its ruler. Some German princes remained Catholic, while others became Lutheran. Religious conflict in Germany was a cause of the Thirty Years' War. The war raged in central Europe from 1618 to 1648. The fighting left Germany in ruins.

Religion in England Religion also played a major role in English politics. King Henry VIII wanted to have sons to rule after him, but he and his wife Catherine of Aragon had only one child who survived infancy—a daughter. Henry, who was Catholic, asked the pope to allow him to end his marriage. The pope refused. In response, Henry declared that England was no longer under the authority of the pope. Instead, Henry formed a new church, the Church of England. This church is also called the Anglican church. As head of the Church of England, Henry ended his marriage.

Henry went on to have five more wives, one more daughter, and one son. Each of his three children later ruled England in turn. When power changed hands, England went from Protestant to Catholic, and finally, under the rule of Elizabeth I, to Protestant again.

Reading Check How did Martin Luther begin the Reformation?

A New Church

CATHERINE of ARRAGON

Henry VIII broke with the pope to divorce Catherine of Aragon (above). Even though he was head of the Church of England, he never abandoned the Catholic faith.

The Catholic Reformation

Even after the Protestant Reformation, millions of Europeans remained Catholic. The Catholic Church was especially strong in Italy and Spain. In response to reformers' criticisms, the Church began to make changes. These changes, which helped keep Catholicism strong, are called the **Catholic Reformation**.

The Catholic Church Responds When Luther posted his 95 Theses, Pope Leo X did not take the event very seriously. He believed that the calls for change would soon end. However, the pope did excommunicate Luther—that is, he banned Luther from the Catholic Church.

In 1545, Pope Paul III took action against the Reformation. He called Church leaders to the Council of Trent where they rejected several key Protestant beliefs.

READING CHECK Luther wrote his 95 Theses, criticizing the Catholic Church.

READING CHECK Loyola's writings became the basis for the Jesuit Order, whose members spread Catholicism as teachers and missionaries.

SECTION 1 ASSESSMENT 1. The Renaissance was a rebirth of learning. The Reformation led to new Protestant churches. The Catholic Reformation clarified Catholic beliefs and cleaned up abuses. **2.** Greek, Roman, Muslim, Chinese

HISTORY

The Jesuits After several years of study, Ignatius of Loyola and several companions formed a new religious order in 1534—the Society of Jesus, or Jesuits. The Jesuit Order played a significant role in modernizing the Catholic Church. Loyola did away with some medieval practices, such as regular penances and fasts, and emphasized that Jesuits must be flexible, ready to move and serve in a variety of ministries around the world. The order was very disciplined, had a centralized authority, and required of its members a special vow of obedience to the pope. Loyola also stressed scholarship, making the Jesuits a highly educated order. Toward the end of his life, Loyola helped to create a system of schools, and the Jesuits became known as an order of teachers. The Jesuits also sent out missionaries to such far-flung regions as India and the Congo.

First, it decided that only the Catholic Church and its leaders could interpret the Bible. Second, the council declared that Church tradition was just as important a guide for Christian life as the Bible. Third, the council decided that both faith and good deeds were needed for salvation.

The Church Renews Itself Over time, the Catholic Church ended many of the abuses that Protestants had criticized. This helped Catholics remain loyal to the faith. Also, Catholic mystics such as John of the Cross and Teresa of Avila wrote inspiring works about their faith. Mystics are people who aim to experience the presence of God. Many mystics have written about their experiences.

In addition, Ignatius (ig NAY shus) of Loyola helped the Church gain new strength. He was a Spanish soldier who became religious while recovering from war injuries. Loyola wrote a set of spiritual exercises that became the basis for the Jesuit order of priests. The Jesuits were disciplined and well trained. They became educators in Catholic schools. Many became missionaries. The Catholic Reformation and the work of Jesuits helped to spread Catholicism to European colonies around the world.

Reading Check How did Ignatius of Loyola help strengthen Catholicism?

▶ **myStory Online**

Queen Elizabeth rallies the troops at Tilbury.

Essential Question

Section 1 Assessment

Key Terms

1. Explain how the following terms affected European life in the period covered in this section: Renaissance, Reformation, Catholic Reformation.

Key Ideas

2. What cultures helped to shape the Renaissance?

3. How did the Renaissance help cause the Reformation?

4. What were two Catholic responses to the Reformation?

Think Critically

5. **Compare and Contrast** How were Italy and Germany alike and different?

6. **Synthesize** How did the printing press affect the spread of Protestantism?

7. **Analyze Cause and Effect** How did trade expand knowledge?

What makes a nation?

8. How might a desire to build a stronger nation affect a ruler's decision to become a Protestant or a Catholic? Go to your Student Journal to record your answer.

- **Infer** Why do you think the leaders of the Catholic Church rejected the new Protestant beliefs? (Samples: They really believed the beliefs were false. They did not want to admit Protestants were right because then people might leave the church.)

- **Cause and Effect** How did mystics help strengthen the Catholic Church? (They wrote about their faith and inspired people.)

- **Summarize** What great change did Ignatius of Loyola experience? (He went from being a soldier to being a religious scholar.)

▶ **myStory Video**

Have students watch the video about Elizabeth I and the Spanish Armada. Tell students to note how the Reformation related to the conflict between England and Spain.

ANSWERS

3. Humanists encouraged secular ideas; the printing press spread ideas. 4. The Council of Trent rejected Protestant beliefs; the Jesuit order formed. 5. Both relied on trade; both were divided into small states. Unlike Italian city-states, German towns formed an alliance. Italy remained Catholic, while Germany was split religiously. 6. It made it easier to make copies of reformers' writings. 7. Trade exposed Europeans to other cultures' ideas. 8. Samples: Some rulers wanted to end the pope's influence. Some felt the Catholic Church's support strengthened them.

Renaissance Views of Rulers

OBJECTIVES

Students will

- use documents to form opinions about what makes a good ruler.
- **21st Century Learning** compare the different viewpoints on leadership expressed by Renaissance writers.
- **ELL** understand the terms *love, fear,* and *honor* as applied to rulers.

SET EXPECTATIONS

In this lesson, students will

- read and analyze documents on ruling in the Renaissance.
- write a letter recommending a text that contemporary government officials should study.

1 Connect

Post the question *What makes a good president?* inside a circle. Make a web with students' responses, e.g. *good communicator* or *wisdom.* Then ask the class to provide examples of each quality in action. For example, for good communicator, they might mention the ability to explain government programs clearly in the State of the Union address. Explain that students are going to read the opinions of two different Renaissance writers about what qualities make a good ruler. Tell them to recall their own opinions as they read.

2 Learn

Preview Have students preview the two pages and identify the images of Niccolò Machiavelli and Thomas More. Read the Key Idea, glossary terms, and definitions. Clarify any questions about the meaning of these words by providing examples.

Read Slowly read aloud the excerpt from *The Prince* without stopping. Read the document again, this time stopping to read the questions at the left and prompting students to rethink and analyze the meaning of the words. Have students answer the questions using the location of the letters to provide clues. Do the same for the excerpt from *Utopia.* Lead a discussion starting with students' responses to the questions. Ask, How does each writer describe a good ruler?

ELL **Intermediate** Provide illustrations of *love, fear,* and *honor* as ways that people can respond to rulers. Show how the responses differ in terms of warmth—love being the warmest feeling about the ruler, then honor, then fear. Ask students to name other people in their lives whom they love, honor, or fear.

 myWorld Activity: A Queen's Opinion Distribute the *Activity Support: Compare Viewpoints.* Have pairs of students analyze an excerpt from Queen Elizabeth I's "Farewell Speech" and compare her views on ruling to those of Machiavelli and More. **(Verbal/Logical)**

20 min

3 Understand

Review Go back to the Key Idea. Make 2-column tables listing More's and Machiavelli's main points.

Assess Have students complete **Analyze the Documents.** Review their answers to determine if students have met the lesson objectives.

Remediate If students struggle to identify personal qualities of the rulers described in the excerpts, have them make two concept webs. One should be centered on the question *What kind of person makes other people afraid?* and the other centered on the question *What kind of person receives honor from others?*

Name _____ Class _____ Date _____

myWorld Activity Support   Compare Viewpoints

A Queen's Opinion

Directions Read the excerpt below from Queen Elizabeth I's last speech to Parliament. Use the definitions of the bold words for help. Underline or highlight phrases that describe how she felt about being a ruler. Then complete the activities below.

Queen Elizabeth I, from "The Farewell Speech," 1601

To be a king and wear a crown is a thing more **glorious** to them that see it than it is pleasant to them that bear it. For myself I was never so much **enticed** with the . . . royal authority of a Queen as delighted that God hath made me his **instrument** to maintain his truth and glory and to defend his kingdom. . . . It is my desire to live nor reign no longer than my life and reign shall be for your good.

glorious: splendid or magnificent
enticed: tempted or drawn to
instrument: a person used by another to do something

Analyze Sources

1. According to Queen Elizabeth, is it more glorious to see a crown or to wear one? What do you think she meant?

_____

_____

2. What did Elizabeth think God wanted her to do as a ruler?

_____

3. What do you learn about Elizabeth from the last sentence?

_____

Compare Viewpoints

4. Were Queen Elizabeth's ideas about rulers more like the ideas of Machiavelli or More? Explain.

_____

_____

HISTORY

Machiavelli's Life Niccolò Machiavelli (1469–1527) was born to a wealthy family in Florence. The ruler Piero Soderini appointed Machiavelli to high office when he was 29. Machiavelli was in charge of the republic's foreign affairs in subject territories for 14 years. During that time, he observed how rulers dealt with rebels. In 1512, Soderini was overthrown and the Medici family returned to rule Florence. They imprisoned and tortured Machiavelli. Afterward, Machiavelli was exiled. While he was away, he wrote *The Prince*, which he dedicated to Lorenzo di Piero de' Medici to gain favor. Several years later, Machiavelli returned to Florence. In the 1520s, he wrote a history of the republic.

Compare Viewpoints Use the lettered prompts to help students identify the viewpoint of each writer, so they can compare the two after reading both excerpts.

ANSWERS

Ⓐ either fear or love

Ⓑ Sample: It is better to be feared because love might not last.

Ⓒ Sample: He has a very negative view of human nature, which causes him to want to control people through negative emotions.

Renaissance Views of Rulers

Key Idea
● With a new focus on social issues, Renaissance thinkers considered the use of power and the character of a good ruler.

The Renaissance brought an increased emphasis on secular, or non-religious matters, such as how to govern. Before the Renaissance, most thinkers had focused on religious matters. The Renaissance princes who ruled Italian city-states sought advice on the practical aspects of government. Niccolò Machiavelli's *The Prince* provided just such a guide for Renaissance rulers, though it had little say about what was good for society. In England, Thomas More wrote *Utopia* to express his ideas about the perfect society. These two Renaissance writers offered very different portraits of the ideal ruler.

▲ A medal with a portrait of Queen Elizabeth I

Portrait of Machiavelli ▼

Stop at each letter on the right to think about the text. Then answer the question with the same letter on the left.

Ⓐ **Categorize** According to Machiavelli, what are the two possible ways for subjects to feel about their ruler?

Ⓑ **Analyze Primary Sources** What emotion does Machiavelli think rulers should inspire, and why?

Ⓒ **Identify Bias** How does Machiavelli's view of human nature shape his view of how to rule? Explain.

dispense with, *v.,* to get rid of
assert, *v.,* to argue, claim
fickle, *adj.,* not reliable or loyal
covetous, *adj.,* greedy

Feared Rulers

❝ . . . [A] question arises:

Ⓐ whether it be better to be loved than feared or feared than loved? It may be answered that one should wish to be both, but, because it is difficult to unite them in one person, it is much

Ⓑ safer to be feared than loved, when, of the two, either must be <u>dispensed with</u>. Because this is

Ⓒ to be <u>asserted</u> in general of men, that they are ungrateful, <u>fickle</u>, false, cowardly, <u>covetous</u>. . . . ❞

—Niccolò Machiavelli,
The Prince, 1513,
translated by W. K. Marriott

To assist your students in comparing viewpoints, use the scaffolded questions at the left of each excerpt. Urge students to break the task into two steps. First, they should restate each writer's viewpoint. For support, provide and have students complete this sentence frame for each writer: "Machiavelli/More believes that rulers should be _____ because _____." Second, students should look for ways that the two views are similar or different. Give them useful phrases to express differences between the two viewpoints, such as *In contrast* or *On the other hand*. For additional help, refer students to the **21st Century Online Tutor** *Compare Viewpoints*.

GUIDE ON THE SIDE

Stop at each letter on the right to think about the text. Then answer the question with the same letter on the left.

D Draw Conclusions In More's ideal world, what kind of character do magistrates have?

E Analyze Cause and Effect How do the people respond to the rule of the magistrates?

F Draw Inferences What do you think the sheaf of grain stands for? Explain what it says about the role of the prince.

zealously, *adv.,* eagerly

magistracy, *n.,* the position of a magistrate, a powerful legal official

exact, *v.,* to get by force

diadem, *n.,* crown

sheaf, *n.,* bunch

Ideal Rulers

" Any man who campaigns too <u>zealously</u> for a <u>magistracy</u> is sure to fail. They live together harmoniously **D** and the magistrates are never proud or cruel. Instead they are called fathers, and deservedly. Because the magistrates do not <u>exact</u> honor from people against their will, the **E** people honor them willingly, as they should. Not even the prince has the distinction of robe or <u>diadem</u>; he **F** is known only by a <u>sheaf</u> of grain carried before him. In the same way the priest is known by a wax candle. "

—Thomas More, *Utopia*, 1516,
translated by H.V.S. Ogden

▲ Portrait of Thomas More by Hans Holbein

ANSWERS

D Sample: They should be humble, kind, and not ambitious.

E Sample: They honor the magistrates willingly.

F Sample: The grain indicates that the prince provides for his people's needs, such as food.

This statue of Grand Duke Ferdinando I de' Medici portrays the kind of Renaissance ruler that Machiavelli described. ▶

Analyze the Documents

1. **Compare Viewpoints** How are Machiavelli's and More's ideas about rulers similar and different?
2. **Writing Task** Write a letter to the U.S. president. Recommend that government officials be required to study either *The Prince* or *Utopia*, and explain why. Include a sentence stating why you decided against the other work.

ANALYZE THE DOCUMENTS 1. Both accept that people should be ruled by a prince. They differ in that Machiavelli thinks that princes should be feared, while More depicts them as humble providers for their people. **2.** Samples: Dear President: Your officials should read *The Prince* because people don't obey the law unless they are forced into it by fear. Dear President: I think officials should read *Utopia* because the officials there don't abuse their power.

Europe Expands

OBJECTIVES

Students will know

- the technological, political, and economic causes of the Age of Exploration.
- why European countries wanted colonies in Africa, Asia, and the Americas.

Students will be able to

- sequence events in the Age of Exploration.
- give a persuasive presentation about the benefits of exploration.

SET EXPECTATIONS

In this section, students will

- read Europe Expands.
- try to persuade a king to sponsor a voyage to the Americas by using a cost-benefit analysis.
- go On Assignment in Europe and explore a map about absolutism and data on the Columbian Exchange.

CORE CONCEPTS

You may wish to teach or reteach the following lessons from the Core Concepts Handbook:

- Migration, pp. 78–79
- Cultural Diffusion and Change, pp. 96–97
- Political Systems, pp. 106–107

KEY

Differentiated Instruction

L1 Special Needs **L2** Extra Support
L3 On-Level **L4** Challenge

English Language Instruction

ELL Beginner **ELL** Early Intermediate **ELL** Intermediate
ELL Early Advanced **ELL** Advanced

1 Connect
Make learning meaningful

Make Connections Ask if students have ever played a game in which the goal was "Winner take all." Ask, How does it feel to win such a game? How does it feel to lose? Tell students that this section explains how European nations competed for power.

ELL Advanced Give students this definition: **compete** *v.* to do a thing with the goal of winning over others. Ask students to suggest meanings for the related words *competition* and *competitor*.

Activate Prior Knowledge Remind students that during the Crusades, Italy became the European point of entry for Asian goods. Controlling such trade made Italy rich. Ask students to predict how other European countries responded to Italy's new status.

L2 Extra Support Present this example: Local stores have agreed to sell pens to only one student in your class. The whole class must now buy pens from the one student, who charges more for a pen than the store. Ask, Is it fair for the only supplier to charge more? What might you do to change the situation?

Prepare Follow the steps in the section **Preview.** Preteach the Key Terms. Then have students complete Word Wise in their journals using in-text clues and the glossary for help.

2 Experience
Teach knowledge and skills

Read Use **Background** notes and **Guide on the Side** questions to model active reading. Have students use *Take Notes* in their **Student Journal** to record events of the Age of Exploration in order. Have students complete **21st Century Online Tutor** *Sequence*, and apply this skill to reading the section.

L2 Extra Support Explain that Section 2 is mostly written in sequence, but a few events are out of order because they are grouped thematically. For example, the Portuguese voyages of 1488 and 1497 are discussed together before Columbus's voyage of 1492 from Spain. Tell students to pay close attention to dates.

ELL Intermediate To help students express time relationships, teach this colloquial usage: To talk about a single year, say, "*In* 1492," but to talk about a longer period of time, say, "*During* the 1700s."

L3 On-Level Have students study *Enrichment: Columbian Exchange*, answer the questions, and complete the activity.

 Practice: myWorld Activity Students will do a cost-benefits analysis and then make a presentation asking a king to sponsor a voyage of exploration. **Step-by-Step Instructions** and **More Activities** follow on p. T54.

SECTION 2 RESOURCE GUIDE

FOR THE STUDENT

my worldgeography.com Student Center
- Active Atlas
- Data Discovery

Student Edition (print and online)
- Europe Expands

Student Journal (print and online)
- Section 2 Word Wise
- Section 2 Take Notes

21st Century Learning Online Tutor
- Sequence
- Give an Effective Presentation

FOR THE TEACHER

my worldgeography.com Teacher Center
- Online Lesson Planner
- Presentations for Projection
- SuccessTracker

ProGuide: Europe and Russia
- Section 2 Lesson Plan, pp. T52–T53
- myWorld Activity Step-by-Step Instructions, p. T54
- Activity Support: Cost-Benefit Analysis, p. T55
- myWorld Geography Enrichment, p. T56
- Section Quiz, p. T57

Accelerating the Progress of ELLs
- Reading Support Strategies, p. 42

---

3 Understand
Assess understanding

Review Review *Word Wise* and *Take Notes* in the Student Journal.

Assess Knowledge and Skills Use the Section Assessment and Section Quiz to check students' progress.

Assess Understanding Review students' responses to the Section Assessment Essential Question prompt.

Remediate Use these strategies to review and remediate.

If students struggle to . . .	Try these strategies.
Sequence events	Provide a timeline running from 1400 to 1800 on which to record events.
Describe the technology of the Age of Exploration	Have them review the illustrations of the ships and navigation tools in their textbook.
Give an effective presentation	Assign additional practice with the **21st Century Online Tutor.**

ELL Support

ELL Objective Students will be able to use persuasive language in English.

Cultural Connections To give students practice in using persuasive techniques, ask them to share words from their home languages that mean "unusually high in quality." Then ask them to work with a partner to translate some of those terms into English.

ELL Intermediate Content Tip Give a group of students cards with the following verbs: *trade, sail, sponsor, explore,* and *conquer.* Students should look up definitions of the words, and then act out the meaning of each verb in pairs.

ELL Activity Give pairs of students a list of adjectives such as *wise, rich, healthy, famous, powerful, popular,* and *handsome.* They should plug each adjective into the sentence "This voyage will make you more _____." Then they should decide which of those statements make sense to use in their presentation to the king. **(Verbal/Logical)**

 30 min

Sailing for Riches

OBJECTIVES
Students will
- analyze the costs and benefits of exploration.
- deliver a persuasive presentation.

LEARNING STYLE
- Logical
- Verbal

21st Century Learning
- Give an Effective Presentation

MATERIALS
- Activity Support: Cost-Benefit Analysis, p. T55

Activity Steps

1. Organize students in pairs and tell them that they are explorers who must persuade a king to pay for a voyage to the Americas. Give each pair a copy of *Activity Support: Cost-Benefit Analysis*. Explain that their first task is to demonstrate that such a voyage will be profitable. The *Cost-Benefit Analysis* will help them list specific details they can use to persuade the king that he will gain from the voyage.

> **L2 Extra Support** Give students a contemporary example of costs and benefits. For example, the cost of a downloaded song might be a dollar. The benefit is the hours of enjoyment the student gains from listening to the song. In a cost-benefit analysis, a person decides if the benefit is worth more than the cost.

2. Students should use information in their texts and their own knowledge to fill in the flowchart. It isn't necessary to attach monetary values to their entries.

3. Have students think of reasons why the benefits would outweigh the costs. Suggest that they use general comparisons, such as "We might find gold, which is more valuable than the cost of supplies."

> **ELL Early Intermediate/Intermediate** Give students these models to use when making comparisons: "The cost of _____ is less than the value of _____" or "The cost of _____ is more than the value of _____."

4. After completing the *Cost-Benefit Analysis*, students should prepare their presentation to the king. Each partner should deliver part of the presentation.

> **L3 On-Level** If students have difficulty dividing up their presentation, suggest these ways to organize: One student might explain the costs while the other explains the benefits. Or one might write an introduction and conclusion, while the other writes the body text.

More Activities From myWorld Teachers

 Local Connection Display a map of your state or county. Have students point out names that are Native American, Spanish, French, or English in origin. Ask the class to draw conclusions about the colonial past of your region. **(Verbal/Logical)**

Triangular Trade Have groups of students use their textbooks and history books that you provide to research the triangular trade. Then they should make an illustrated map showing the three legs of the trading triangle, with labels indicating what was carried on each leg. **(Kinesthetic/Visual)**

 Opinion Page Have students write an editorial on one of two topics: advocating the need for trans-Atlantic voyages to break into the spice trade or telling the Spanish king how to spend the silver and gold brought back from the Americas. **(Verbal)**

my worldgeography.com   Teacher Center → Find additional resources in the online Teacher Center.

Name _____ Class _____ Date _____

myWorld Activity Support   Cost-Benefit Analysis

Sailing for Riches

Directions You and your partner are explorers who want to
persuade a European king to pay for a voyage to the Americas. To do
so, you must convince the king that the benefits of the voyage will
be worth more than the costs. Use the flowchart below to prepare
a cost-benefit analysis of a voyage to the Americas. Then use the
information to write and deliver a short presentation to persuade the
king to sponsor your voyage. Each of you should take part in making
the presentation, so divide up which points you will make. Add drama
to your plea to convince the king that he truly should support you.

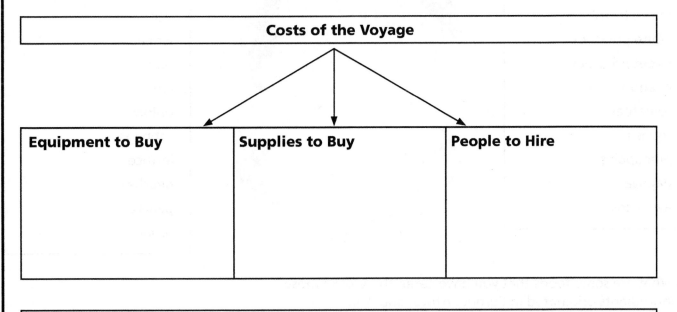

Costs of the Voyage		
Equipment to Buy	**Supplies to Buy**	**People to Hire**

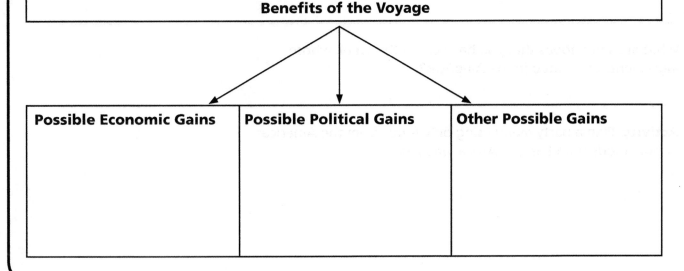

Benefits of the Voyage		
Possible Economic Gains	**Possible Political Gains**	**Other Possible Gains**

Name _____ Class _____ Date _____

Enrichment: The Columbian Exchange

Directions Read the introduction and then study the chart below. Answer the questions that follow and complete the activity.

Introduction Before Columbus reached the Americas, Native Americans grew many crops that were unknown in Europe. Similarly, Europeans grew many crops that were unknown in the Americas. Once Europeans reached the Americas, they carried plants back and forth between the two hemispheres. This transfer of crops is called the Columbian Exchange.

Crops of the Americas		**Crops of Europe, Africa, Asia**
maize (corn)		rice
white potatoes		wheat
sweet potatoes		oats
peanuts		rye
tomatoes		onions
squash		cabbage
pineapples		lettuce
papaya		peaches
avocados		pears
		sugar

1. What are some foods that you have eaten this week whose ingredients originated in Europe, Africa, and Asia?

_____

2. What are some foods that you have eaten this week whose ingredients originated in the Americas?

_____

3. **Activity** Plan a party menu using only foods from the Americas or only foods from Europe, Africa, and Asia.

Name _____ Class _____ Date _____

Section Quiz

Directions Answer the following questions using what you learned in Section 2.

1. _____ Which Portuguese prince sponsored voyages of exploration?
   a. Ferdinand of Castile
   b. Henry the Navigator
   c. Henry VIII
   d. Amerigo Vespucci

2. _____ Whose book increased European interest in Asia?
   a. Christopher Columbus
   b. Vasco da Gama
   c. Kublai Khan
   d. Marco Polo

3. _____ What was the triangular trade?
   a. trade among three city-states in Italy
   b. a trans-Atlantic trade pattern with three stages
   c. trade from England to Spain to the Netherlands
   d. trade among three empires in the New World

4. _____ What American products became the basis for Spain's wealth?
   a. diamonds and rubies
   b. gold and silver
   c. fish and lumber
   d. sugar and tobacco

5. _____ What was a caravel?
   a. a type of navigation instrument
   b. a type of spice from Asia
   c. a type of small, light ship
   d. a crop found in the Americas

6. On the table below, record where each country had colonies.

Location of Colonies	
England	
France	
Netherlands	
Portugal	
Spain	

Europe Expands

- Model preparing to read by previewing the Key Ideas, Key Terms, headings, visuals, and captions. Have students make predictions about what they will learn. For ELL support, post the prompt, "I predict I will read about . . ."
- Preview and practice sequencing using examples from your community's early modern history.

- Preteach this section's high-use Academic Vocabulary and Key Terms using the table on the next page and in-text definitions. Have students practice Key Terms by completing the *Word Wise* page in their journals.

GUIDE ON THE SIDE

 Reading Skill

Sequence While they read, have students practice this skill by completing the *Take Notes* graphic organizer in the **Student Journal.**

The Age of Exploration

- **Draw Conclusions** How would accurate maps help sailors? (Sample: They would help them to recognize strange coastlines.)

- **Infer** What effect do you think Marco Polo's book had on exploration? (Sample: It increased the number of people who wanted to explore.)

- **Synthesize** Why do you think Henry the Navigator was interested in helping to find a route to China? (He wanted his country to prosper from trade with Asia.)

Section 2

Europe Expands

Key Ideas
- Renaissance ideals, competition among rulers, and the expansion of trade led to an age of exploration.
- Exploration and a search for wealth led European states to create colonial empires.

Key Terms • cartography • caravel • plantation • northwest passage • triangular trade • absolutism

(→) **Visual Glossary**

→ **Reading Skill: Sequence** Take notes using the graphic organizer in your journal.

A modern replica of English explorer Sir Francis Drake's ship *Golden Hind*

By 1300, innovations such as navigational charts, triangular sails, and magnetic compasses had made sailing easier. These new technologies also helped Renaissance mapmakers develop **cartography,** the science of making accurate maps and globes. A new age of exploration was about to begin.

The Age of Exploration

During the 1300s, Italian merchant Marco Polo published a book about his travels in China and India. His descriptions of the wealth and wonders of Asia increased European interest in the continent.

Portugal Sets Sail Portugal led the search for a sea route to Asia. The Portuguese sailed **caravels,** small, triangular-sailed oceangoing ships. Henry the Navigator, a Portuguese prince, paid for voyages to Asia and helped train explorers in navigation.

Throughout the 1400s, Portuguese ships explored the west coast of Africa by sailing farther and farther south. In 1488, Bartolomeu Dias became the first explorer to travel around the southern tip of Africa. In 1497, Vasco da Gama reached India. During the first half of the 1500s, the Portuguese established trading centers in India, Southeast Asia, and China. They enabled Portugal to end Italy's control over trade with Asia.

ACADEMIC VOCABULARY

High-Use Word	Definition and Sample Sentence
finance	*v.* to raise or provide funds *The rich man agreed to finance the student director's movie.*
convict	*v.* to find or prove guilty *The lawyer urged the jury to convict the accused murderer.*

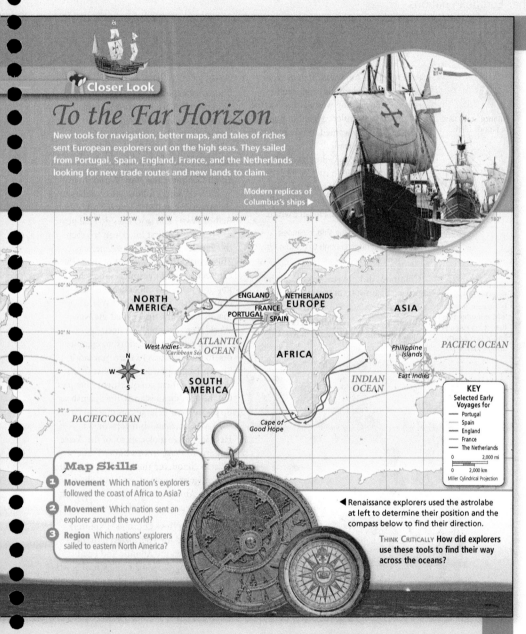

Closer Look

To the Far Horizon

New tools for navigation, better maps, and tales of riches sent European explorers out on the high seas. They sailed from Portugal, Spain, England, France, and the Netherlands looking for new trade routes and new lands to claim.

Modern replicas of Columbus's ships ▶

KEY
Selected Early Voyages for
— Portugal
— Spain
— England
— France
— The Netherlands

0   2,000 mi
0   2,000 km
Miller Cylindrical Projection

◀ Renaissance explorers used the astrolabe at left to determine their position and the compass below to find their direction.

THINK CRITICALLY **How did explorers use these tools to find their way across the oceans?**

Map Skills

1. **Movement** Which nation's explorers followed the coast of Africa to Asia?
2. **Movement** Which nation sent an explorer around the world?
3. **Region** Which nations' explorers sailed to eastern North America?

GUIDE ON THE SIDE

Closer Look

To the Far Horizon

- **Draw Conclusions** Why would sailors need to calculate their ship's position? (Sample: On the ocean, there are no visible landmarks to steer by.)

Map Skills Point out and discuss the map of European exploration.

- According to this map, which nations reached Asia? (Spain and Portugal)

MAP SKILLS 1. Portugal **2.** Spain **3.** Spain, England, France, Netherlands

THINK CRITICALLY Explorers used these instruments to find their direction and position.

ANSWERS

GEOGRAPHY

Treaty of Tordesillas After Columbus claimed the lands that he explored for Spain, the Spanish monarchs wanted to ensure that they would be able to keep rival countries out of the Americas. They appealed to Pope Alexander VI, who happened to be a Spaniard, for help. He set up a line of demarcation that ran from the North Pole to the South Pole along a line that lay roughly 700 miles west of the coast of Africa. Other European nations were forbidden to explore to the west of that line. Portugal was upset by the exclusion, so Spanish and Portuguese ambassadors negotiated a treaty to move the line of demarcation nearly 500 miles farther west. This change allowed Portugal to claim Brazil in South America. Neither England, France, nor the Netherlands ever accepted the line of demarcation. They each established colonies in the Americas.

GUIDE ON THE SIDE

- **Identify Evidence** What evidence shows that Columbus thought he had sailed to Asia? (He believed he had landed in the Indies, so he named the people Indians.)

An Age of Empires

- **Cause and Effect** Why did European nations want colonies? (to gain wealth in the form of gold, land, and raw materials)

- **Identify Evidence** How did Balboa prove that he was not in Asia? (Western Asia connects to Europe, yet Balboa saw another ocean west of where he was standing.)

- **Identify Details** What were some of the kinds of wealth Spain gained from its colonies? (crops, huge amounts of silver and gold)

finance, *v.,* to raise or provide funds

Reaching the Americas Italian explorer Christopher Columbus promised to reach Asia by sailing westward across the Atlantic. Spain's rulers agreed to <u>finance</u> his voyage. They wanted to take part in the rich Asian spice trade.

In October 1492, Columbus and his crew made landfall in the Caribbean. He believed he had reached the Indies—islands in Southeast Asia—so he called the native people Indians. He later wrote:

66 They came to the ship in canoes, … some of them large enough to contain forty or forty-five men. 99

Columbus did not reach Asia, but he helped Spain start an empire in the Americas.

Reading Check Why did Portugal and Spain look for water routes to Asia?

This painting from India shows Europeans (bottom left) bringing gifts to the Indian ruler. *Why might Europeans bring gifts?* ▼

An Age of Empires

The age of exploration was also an age of imperialism, or empire-building. European countries expanded their empires by taking over other lands as colonies. These colonies made European nations wealthy and powerful.

Spain Conquers the New World Many Spanish explorers followed Columbus to the Americas. In 1513, Vasco Nuñez de Balboa (VAHS koh NOO nyes deh bal BOH uh) became the first European to reach the Pacific Ocean from the Americas. This proved that he was not in Asia. The explorer Amerigo Vespucci (ah meh REE goh ves POOH chee) believed that explorers had found a "New World." A mapmaker at the time called the New World *America* after Vespucci.

Spain sent conquistadors, or conquerors, to the Americas to seize new lands. They used gunpowder, a Chinese invention, to help them conquer native peoples. On the Caribbean islands, the Spanish set up **plantations,** or large commercial farms.

In Mexico, Spanish troops under Hernán Cortés took control of the Aztec Empire. In Peru, troops under Francisco Pizarro conquered the Inca Empire. Spain took huge amounts of gold and silver from its American colonies. The Spanish empire covered much of the Americas.

Establishing New Colonies Explorers also searched for a **northwest passage,** a route between the Atlantic and Pacific Oceans along the northern coast of North America. They hoped to increase trade with Asia by finding a faster sea route.

CAPTION Sample: They might bring gifts to show their friendly intentions.

READING CHECK They wanted to take part in the profitable trade with Asia.

ECONOMICS

Mercantilism The European monarchs who sought American colonies were following the economic theory of mercantilism. Mercantilist theory proposed that nations must have large reserves of precious metals and a favorable trade balance. Acquiring more wealth than rival nations was the primary goal of mercantilism. To make this happen, nations sought colonies that would provide raw materials and serve as markets for goods manufactured in the mother country. Colonies were forbidden to engage in manufacturing or to trade with rival nations. Eventually, economists realized that restrictions could hinder economic growth and that all types of trade and production could be beneficial. Mercantilism gave way to laissez-faire economics, which believed that the market corrected itself without regulation.

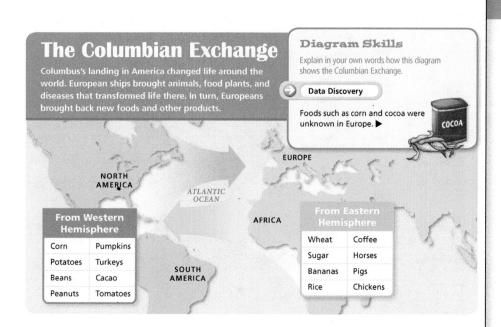

The Columbian Exchange

Columbus's landing in America changed life around the world. European ships brought animals, food plants, and diseases that transformed life there. In turn, Europeans brought back new foods and other products.

Diagram Skills

Explain in your own words how this diagram shows the Columbian Exchange.

 Data Discovery

Foods such as corn and cocoa were unknown in Europe. ▶

COCOA

From Western Hemisphere

Corn	Pumpkins
Potatoes	Turkeys
Beans	Cacao
Peanuts	Tomatoes

From Eastern Hemisphere

Wheat	Coffee
Sugar	Horses
Bananas	Pigs
Rice	Chickens

NORTH AMERICA

ATLANTIC OCEAN

EUROPE

AFRICA

SOUTH AMERICA

Explorers never found a northwest passage, but others established new colonies in North America. Both England and France claimed lands in eastern North America. They also traded with Native Americans for furs to take back to Europe.

By the mid-1700s, England had a group of colonies stretching down the Atlantic coast of North America. Early settlements included Jamestown in Virginia and Plymouth Colony in New England. The Netherlands had also founded North American colonies, but the English took them over.

The Dutch, English, and French had colonies in other regions. The Dutch controlled land in the East Indies. England and France had additional colonies in India.

England also founded colonies in Australia during the early 1800s. Most of these colonies began as places to send people <u>convicted</u> of crimes. By the late 1800s, though, most colonists in Australia were not criminals. Those colonists went to Australia to make a living in agriculture, mining, or in Australia's growing cities.

Plantation Agriculture Plantations in the Caribbean and southeastern North America produced crops such as sugar and tobacco. Plantation agriculture required huge numbers of workers. At first, landowners used Native Americans, but they fell ill from European diseases. Europeans began to bring enslaved Africans to do this work.

convict, *v.,* to find or prove guilty

 myWorld Activity Sailing for Riches

GUIDE ON THE SIDE

- **Infer** Why did France and England concentrate on the northern part of North America? (Spain had already claimed many of the lands to the south.)

- **Summarize** Why did European colonizers decide to enslave Africans? (They needed huge numbers of workers, and the Indians died from European diseases in great numbers.)

Diagram Skills Discuss the diagram and tables.

- Where did potatoes originate? (the Americas)

 myWorld Activity

Sailing for Riches Find Step-by-Step Instructions and an Activity Support on pp. T54–T55. **(Logical/Verbal)**

Data Discovery

Have students go to myworldgeography.com to learn more about the Columbian Exchange.

ANSWERS

GOVERNMENT

Divine Right of Kings The theory of the divine right of kings was used in Europe to support absolutism. According to this belief, God granted kings their authority, so they ruled as his representatives on Earth. As such, they were not answerable to legislative bodies or other earthly institutions. In some cases, monarchs used the doctrine to assert their authority over the church itself. A French bishop named Jacques-Bénigne Bossuet was one of the theorists of the divine right of kings. He believed that the king's person and authority were sacred. Bossuet also claimed that the king's power was similar to that of a father's. The political revolutions that took place in England, America, and France during the late 1600s and 1700s effectively ended European belief in the divine right of kings.

GUIDE ON THE SIDE

- **Draw Conclusions** Which leg of the triangular trade was helped by currents and winds? (the leg that went from the Americas to Europe.)

An Age of Absolutism

- **Identify Main Ideas** What limits were placed on the power of absolute rulers? (none)

- **Categorize** Who reigned as an absolute ruler in Spain? (Philip II)

Map Skills Point out and discuss the map of European absolutism.

- In what empire were Vienna and Prague located? (Austria-Hungary)

- Which was more unified, France or Germany? (France)

Map Skills

1. **Location** Which large country separated Spain's possessions?

2. **Place** Why might Spain have had trouble controlling its European empire?

3. **Places to Know!** Label the following places on the outline map in your Student Journal: Paris, Constantinople, London, Poland.

> Active Atlas

> Active Atlas

Have students go to myworldgeography.com to learn more about absolutist rule.

▲ A china vase made in the 1700s for King Augustus II the Strong, Elector of Saxony and King of Poland

In time, a system known as the triangular trade developed. The **triangular trade** was a three-stage pattern of Atlantic trade that carried goods and enslaved people between Europe, Africa, and the Americas. In the first stage, Europeans shipped manufactured goods from Europe to Africa. These goods were traded for slaves and gold. In the second stage, ships carried enslaved Africans to the Americas. In the third stage, ships carried sugar and other agricultural products back to Europe. Trade winds and ocean currents helped ships along this trade route.

Reading Check Why did European nations compete for colonies?

An Age of Absolutism

During this time, European nations grew in size and power to become nation-states. A nation-state is a region that shares a government and is independent from other states. Monarchs during this time felt that God had chosen them to rule, a belief called the divine right of kings. They also believed in absolutism. **Absolutism** is a political system of centralized and unlimited government power.

Absolute Power in Spain Perhaps the most powerful monarch in Europe was Spain's Philip II. Philip kept firm control over the Spanish empire. As he once said, "It is best to keep an eye on everything."

MAP SKILLS 1. France **2.** Its provinces were distant and separated. **3.** Places should be labeled correctly.

READING CHECK They each wanted to increase their wealth and power.

READING CHECK live richly, make wars

SECTION ASSESSMENT 1. Cartography is the science of making maps. A plantation was a huge agricultural estate. Europeans looked for a route through North America to Asia, called the northwest passage. The triangular trade had three

---

HISTORY

The Sun King Born in 1638, Louis XIV became king at the age of four years, eight months. When he was nine, nobles who opposed the powerful prime minister, Cardinal Mazarin, began a civil war. Mazarin won the five-year conflict, but the years of poverty, hunger, and terror that Louis endured emotionally scarred him for life. When Mazarin died in 1661, Louis assumed absolute control over France. He retained a distrust of the nobles and controlled them by compelling them to live at Versailles, where he corrupted them with gambling and dissipated living. He showed his favor by granting nobles the privilege of handing him articles of clothing as he dressed. Other monarchs throughout Europe began to imitate Louis's grand way of living. However, his luxuries and his wars placed a terrible financial burden on his country. Louis died in 1715.

Philip was a Catholic, and he used his power to back Catholicism throughout Europe. Conflict between Catholics and Protestants led to fighting in the Spanish Netherlands.

Spain also came into conflict with England. King Philip wanted to end English attacks on Spanish ships carrying gold and silver from the Americas. He also wanted to force England, a Protestant country, to return to the Catholic Church. But, as you have read, in 1588, the English navy defeated a Spanish navy fleet, called the Armada.

The Sun King Just as the sun is the center of the solar system, Louis XIV was the center of the French government. Known as the Sun King, he centralized power around the throne. In fact, Louis believed he was so important that he said "L'état, c'est moi," meaning "I am the state."

Louis wanted to make France the greatest nation in Europe. He spent years building the biggest palace in Europe at Versailles. He encouraged the growth of industry and built canals and roads. He sent the French army to build colonies in Asia and the Americas. Under Louis, France was at war almost constantly.

Prussia and Austria In 1740, Prussia seized Austrian territory in what is now Poland. That same year, Austrian Empress Maria Theresa began her 40-year rule, making Vienna a cultural center.

Although both Austrian and Prussian rulers were absolutists, Prussia practiced religious tolerance. Both struggled for years to control Central Europe.

Reading Check How did European rulers use their power?

King Louis XIV wears robes decorated with golden fleurs-de-lis, a symbol of France.
▼

- **Predict** What long-term effects do you think the reign of Louis XIV had on France? Support your prediction with details. (Samples: Louis's reign probably made many enemies for France. Heavy spending probably hurt France's economy but support of industry probably helped it.)

- **Identify Main Ideas** What European country was Prussia's great rival? (Austria)

Analyze Visuals Have students examine the portrait of Louis XIV.

- What symbols of wealth and power do you see in this portrait? (furs, a crown, a scepter, a sword, a medal)

- How does this portrait compare to the portrait of Henry VIII in the previous section? (Sample: Both rulers look proud. Louis XIV is wearing a fancy wig and seems to be more concerned with fashion.)

Section 2 Assessment

Key Terms

1. Write complete sentences to define each of the following terms: cartography, plantation, northwest passage, triangular trade, absolutism

Key Ideas

2. Why did Spain support Columbus's voyages of exploration?

3. Which three European nations established colonies in eastern North America?

4. Why did European powers create colonies in the Americas?

Think Critically

5. **Identify Bias** What did the actions of Europeans reveal about their attitudes toward non-Europeans?

6. **Draw Inferences** How would Spain's discovery of huge quantities of silver and gold in the Americas affect relations with other European nations?

7. **Identify Evidence** How did absolutism help monarchs build power at home and abroad?

? Essential Question

What makes a nation?

8. How might wars among European powers have helped build loyalty to the new nation-states? Go to your Student Journal to record your answer.

legs that linked Europe, Africa, and the Americas. Absolutism was the theory that kings should have total power. **2.** It wanted to find a route to Asia. **3.** France, England, Netherlands **4.** They wanted to gain wealth from precious metals and agriculture. **5.** The actions show that Europeans looked down on non-Europeans. For example, they took Indians' lands and enslaved Africans. **6.** The wealth helped it build more ships and armies than its rivals. **7.** They had unlimited power to gain wealth, enact policies, and fight wars. **8.** People wanted to defend their nation when it was attacked.

An Age of Revolutions

OBJECTIVES

Students will know

- how the Scientific Revolution advanced technology and knowledge.
- how the Enlightenment led to revolutions.
- the effects of the Industrial Revolution.

Students will be able to

- analyze causes and effects of political and technological revolutions.
- publish work about the French Revolution.

SET EXPECTATIONS

In this section, students will

- read An Age of Revolutions.
- design and write a blog about the French Revolution.
- go On Assignment in Europe and explore key moments of the French Revolution.

CORE CONCEPTS

You may wish to teach or reteach the following lessons from the Core Concepts Handbook:

- Science and Technology, pp. 98–99
- Urbanization, pp. 80–81
- Political Structures, pp. 108–109

KEY

Differentiated Instruction

L1 Special Needs   **L2** Extra Support
L3 On-Level   **L4** Challenge

English Language Instruction

ELL Beginner   **ELL** Early Intermediate   **ELL** Intermediate
ELL Early Advanced   **ELL** Advanced

1 Connect
Make learning meaningful

Make Connections Define labor-saving devices and give an example, such as a vacuum cleaner. Ask, What is your favorite labor-saving device that you have at home? After students have shared answers, tell them that Section 3 is about a period in which many labor-saving devices were invented.

ELL **Early Intermediate/Intermediate** Give students these definitions: **invent** v. to produce something new; **invention** n. a new thing or process that someone has devised. Have them think of examples.

Activate Prior Knowledge Remind students that in previous sections, they read that Europeans learned about Muslim mathematical advances and that Europeans traveled to new lands. Ask students to predict how these events might affect science.

L2 **Extra Support** Define *revolution* as "a period of dramatic change." Explain that political revolutions involve overthrowing a government while a technological revolution involves changing the way tasks are done.

Prepare Follow the steps in the section **Preview.** Preteach the Key Terms. Then have students complete *Word Wise* in their journals using in-text clues and the glossary for help.

2 Experience
Teach knowledge and skills

Read Use **Background** notes and **Guide on the Side** questions to model active reading. Have students use *Take Notes* in their **Student Journal** to record causes and effects of the Scientific, French, and Industrial revolutions. Have students complete **21st Century Online Tutor** *Analyze Cause and Effect* and apply this skill to reading the section.

L3 **On-Level** Have students read *Enrichment: Important Inventions* and answer the questions below the table.

ELL **Beginner** Bring in pictures of items connected to the Industrial Revolution, such as coal, factory, machine, steamboat, and locomotive. Label and post the pictures on your word wall during the unit.

L4 **Challenge** Have students research the French and American revolutions and plan a documentary or multimedia presentation comparing them. Students should focus on the question of why the two revolutions turned out differently.

 Practice: myWorld Activity Students will work with partners to plan a blog and publish posts about the French Revolution. **Step-by-Step Instructions** and **More Activities** follow on p. T60.

SECTION 3 RESOURCE GUIDE

FOR THE STUDENT

my worldgeography.com Student Center
- Culture Close-up

Student Edition (print and online)
- An Age of Revolutions

Student Journal (print and online)
- Section 3 Word Wise
- Section 3 Take Notes

21st Century Learning Online Tutor
- Analyze Cause and Effect
- Publish Your Work

FOR THE TEACHER

my worldgeography.com Teacher Center
- Online Lesson Planner
- Presentations for Projection
- SuccessTracker

ProGuide: Europe and Russia
- Section 3 Lesson Plan, pp. T58–T59
- myWorld Activity Step-by-Step Instructions, p. T60
- Activity Support: Blog Planner, p. T61
- myWorld Geography Enrichment, p. T62
- Section Quiz, p. T63

Accelerating the Progress of ELLs
- Comprehension Check Strategies, p. 53

---

3 Understand
Assess understanding

Review Review *Word Wise* and *Take Notes* in the **Student Journal.**

Assess Knowledge and Skills Use the Section Assessment and Section Quiz to check students' progress.

Assess Understanding Review students' responses to the Section Assessment Essential Question prompt.

Remediate Use these strategies to review and remediate.

If students struggle to . . .	Try these strategies.
Analyze causes	Assign additional practice with the **21st Century Online Tutor.**
Describe the effects of the different revolutions	Give them a table with two columns: *Name of Revolution, What Changed?*
Publish their work	Provide a proofreading checklist.

ELL Support

ELL Objective Students will be able to use English to explain causes.

Cultural Connections To give students practice in explaining causes, ask them to translate the noun *reason* into their home languages. Let them use their home languages to describe a change they made recently and to explain why by listing reasons.

ELL Advanced Content Tip In the section *Philosophers Study Society*, point out the quotation by Thomas Hobbes. Explain that the word *brutish* comes from the noun *brute*, which means "an animal" or "a person who does not think or have sensitive feelings." Ask students to explain what they think a *brutish* society would be like.

ELL Activity Allow students to act out a skit of a real or imagined event during the French Revolution. Then they can write their blog post about the event in the skit. **(Kinesthetic/Verbal)**

 myWorld Activity   **Step-by-Step Instructions**

 20 min

Long Live the Revolution

OBJECTIVES

Students will
- plan a blog about the French Revolution.
- write a blog post.

LEARNING STYLE

- Visual
- Verbal

21st Century Learning

- Publish Your Work

MATERIALS

- Activity Support: Blog Planner, p. T61
- Colored markers
- Glue or tape
- Books on the revolution
- Printouts of sample blogs

Activity Steps

1. Tell students that they are going to work in pairs to plan a blog about the French Revolution. Either assign or allow students to choose partners. Then give each pair a copy of *Activity Support: Blog Planner*.

   ELL **Intermediate** Give students this vocabulary list: **blog** a journal published on the Internet (short for web log); **post** a short article or diary entry on a blog; **banner** a rectangular box that displays a headline at the top of a page.

2. Have partners work together to complete the *Blog Planner*. Provide books about the French Revolution to give students ideas for pictures and banner art.

   L3 **On-Level** Give students color copies of sample blog pages so that they can see a variety of blog designs.

3. Once students have completed their planning, each partner should write a blog post. Partners may discuss ideas and help each other revise their posts.

   L2 **Extra Support** On the board, draw a template to help students write their posts. At the top, put blanks labeled Headline and Author. Then have several blank writing lines for the body. Below that, have two blanks labeled Date and Subject Tags.

4. When students are satisfied with their work, they can copy the blog banner at the top of a piece of blank paper and then glue or tape their posts sequentially below it so it looks like a blog page. Publish their blogs by displaying them in the classroom or on your school's class blogging site.

More Activities From myWorld Teachers

Local Connection As a class, list activities that take place in your community on Independence Day. Then ask individual students to design a float for a July 4th parade to remind people of the revolutionary origin of the holiday. **(Visual)**

Majority Rule Have groups identify various American institutions (such as schools, sports, businesses, religion). Students should categorize which have democratic forms of governance and which have non-democratic forms. **(Logical)**

Do It Yourself Make a class list of hobbies based on jobs common before industrialization: gardening, sewing, carpentry, etc. Ask, Why do people still do these activities instead of buying mass-produced goods? Have students write a public service ad praising "do-it-yourself" in modern times. **(Verbal/Logical)**

my worldgeography.com (**Teacher Center**) Find additional resources in the online Teacher Center.

Name _____ Class _____ Date _____

myWorld Activity Support   **Blog Planner**

Long Live the Revolution

Directions Working with a partner, plan a blog about the French Revolution. Then each of you should write a post to publish on the blog. Use steps 1 through 6 below to plan your blog.

1. First decide whether your blog will sound as though it were written during the French Revolution or whether it will be a modern blog about the history of the revolution.

_____

2. Some blogs feature political discussions, some publish humorous essays, and some are diaries. What focus will your blog have?

_____

3. A blog needs a catchy title that people will remember. What will you call your blog?

_____

4. Using color will convey messages about your blog. For example, a blog about the environment might use a green background.
   • What will your background color be? _____
   • What color will you use for headlines? _____

5. Most blogs have a banner across the top with the blog's title and a picture. Banners also sometimes list the blog authors. Draw your blog banner in the box below.

6. After you plan your blog, each of you should type or write a blog post on lined paper. Be sure your post fits the focus of the blog. Each post should have a title, a date, your name, and subject tags to help people find it when searching the Internet.

Name _____ Class _____ Date _____

Enrichment: Important Inventions

Directions Study the table below. Answer the questions that follow.

Instruments Invented During the Scientific Revolution		
Inventor	**Invention**	**Use**
Galileo (early model); Fahrenheit (more accurate model)	thermometer	Measures temperature; used in weather forecasting, science, and medicine
Galileo (improved earlier instruments)	telescope	Allows people to view distant objects; used in astronomy, warfare, and other fields
Hans Jansen, Zacharias Jansen, Hans Lippershey (first model); Antony Von Leeuwenhoek (improved model)	microscope	Produces enlarged images of very small objects; used in scientific experiments
Evangelista Torricelli	barometer	Measures atmospheric pressure; used in weather forecasting

1. Which of the instruments do scientists use for measuring?

_____

2. Which of the instruments do scientists use for observation?

_____

3. Think about the scientific method. Why are the tasks of measuring and observation important to scientists following the scientific method?

_____

_____

Name _____ Class _____ Date _____

Section Quiz

Directions Answer the following questions using what you
learned in Section 3.

1. _____ Which Enlightenment thinker taught
   that life is "brutish," and societies need
   strong rulers?
   a. Thomas Hobbes
   b. John Locke
   c. Jean-Jacques Rousseau
   d. Voltaire

2. _____ Which Renaissance scientist first
   proposed the heliocentric theory?
   a. Francis Bacon
   b. Nicolaus Copernicus
   c. Galileo Galilei
   d. Isaac Newton

3. _____ In what industry did the Industrial
   Revolution begin?
   a. coal mining
   b. electrical production
   c. steel manufacturing
   d. textile manufacturing

4. _____ What belief helped support the
   development of absolutism?
   a. the divine right of kings
   b. the heliocentric view of the universe
   c. the human right to liberty
   d. Newton's laws of motion

5. _____ Which of the following statements
   is true?
   a. The Industrial Revolution inspired the
   American Revolution.
   b. The Enlightenment inspired the French
   Revolution.
   c. The English Civil War inspired the
   Dutch rebellion.
   d. The Scientific Revolution inspired the
   English Civil War.

6. What Enlightenment ideas became part of the United States
   government?

   _____

   _____

   _____

T63

An Age of Revolutions

- Model preparing to read by previewing the Key Ideas, Key Terms, headings, visuals, and captions. Have students make predictions about what they will learn. For ELL support, post the prompt, "I predict I will read about . . ."

- Preview and practice analyzing cause and effect with examples of past or recent changes in your community.

- Preteach this section's high-use Academic Vocabulary and Key Terms using the table on the next page and in-text definitions. Have students practice Key Terms by completing the *Word Wise* page in their journals.

GUIDE ON THE SIDE

Reading Skill

Analyze Cause and Effect
While they read, have students practice this skill by completing the *Take Notes* graphic organizer in the **Student Journal.**

A Scientific Revolution

- **Compare and Contrast** How did medieval and Renaissance views of science differ? (Medieval scholars used religion to explain the world; Renaissance thinkers used logic and reason in scientific study.)

- **Summarize** Who suggested new ways to approach science? (Francis Bacon, René Descartes, Isaac Newton)

- **Identify Main Ideas** What did medieval scientists think was at the center of the universe? (Earth)

Section 3
An Age of Revolutions

Key Ideas
- The Scientific Revolution brought advances in knowledge and technology.
- The Enlightenment applied reason to human affairs and led to political revolutions in England, France, and other European countries.
- The Industrial Revolution transformed Europe's economy and landscape.

Key Terms • Scientific Revolution • Enlightenment • English Bill of Rights • French Revolution • Industrial Revolution

 Visual Glossary

Reading Skill: Analyze Cause and Effect Take notes using the graphic organizer in your journal.

London's Royal Greenwich Observatory was established in the 1600s to study the stars and navigation. ▼

Medieval scholars had relied on religion and ancient writings to explain the world. But Renaissance thinkers questioned these old beliefs. Instead, they relied on logic, reason, and observation. Their ideas would transform science, government, and the economy.

A Scientific Revolution
During the Renaissance, scholars began studying the world around them. This led to the **Scientific Revolution,** a series of major advances in science during the 1500s and 1600s.

Science Changes Over time, scholars developed new ways to approach science. Francis Bacon taught that scientists should observe and interpret facts. René Descartes (ruh NAY day KAHRT) stressed the use of logic, or reason, to form scientific theories. Isaac Newton believed in testing theories using the scientific method, or controlled experiments.

Scientists Make Discoveries Medieval scientists believed that the sun, planets, and stars orbited, or circled, Earth. This theory was part of Catholic teachings. But in 1543, Polish astronomer Nicolaus Copernicus argued that the planets orbit the sun.

Italian astronomer Galileo Galilei (gal uh LAY oh gal uh LAY ee) agreed with Copernicus. Galileo published evidence that Earth circled the sun. In 1633, the Catholic Church put Galileo on trial for contradicting Church teaching. To save his life, Galileo signed a confession stating that his books were wrong.

ANSWERS

ACADEMIC VOCABULARY

High-Use Word	Definition and Sample Sentence
greedy	*adj.* having a strong desire for wealth and possessions *Greedy people do not like to give money to others.*
consent	*n.* agreement or approval *Democratic governments rely on the consent of their citizens.*

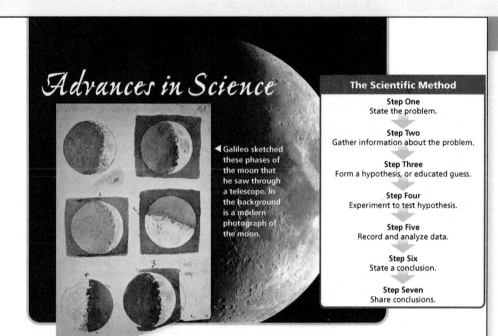

Advances in Science

◄ Galileo sketched these phases of the moon that he saw through a telescope. In the background is a modern photograph of the moon.

The Scientific Method

Step One
State the problem.

Step Two
Gather information about the problem.

Step Three
Form a hypothesis, or educated guess.

Step Four
Experiment to test hypothesis.

Step Five
Record and analyze data.

Step Six
State a conclusion.

Step Seven
Share conclusions.

The English scientist Isaac Newton studied how the physical world worked. He described gravity and explained how objects moved in space.

Results of Discovery Scientific and technological advances improved life. Agricultural advances led to larger harvests. Inventors built instruments to measure longitude, latitude, and speed. The work of astronomers resulted in a more accurate calendar.

Thomas Newcomen and James Watt invented steam engines. Alessandro Volta and Michael Faraday conducted electrical experiments. Electricity and steam later became important energy sources.

Reading Check **How did the scientific method change science?**

The Enlightenment

The **Enlightenment** was a movement during the 1600s and 1700s to apply observation and reason to human affairs. The movement drew on the success of the Scientific Revolution.

Philosophers Study Society Enlightenment thinkers believed that nothing was beyond the human mind. Some studied the nature of reality. Many wrote about society and government. Thomas Hobbes believed that people were selfish and greedy and needed a strong ruler. Hobbes painted this picture of life without a strong ruler in his book *Leviathan*:

greedy, *adj.,* having a strong desire for wealth and possessions

❝ There is … continual fear and danger of violent death, and the life of man [is] solitary, poor, nasty, brutish, and short. ❞

READING CHECK The scientific method changed science so that it became based on observation, reason, and experimentation.

GUIDE ON THE SIDE

- **Predict** What types of changes would electricity and steam engines make possible?
  (Samples: factories, appliances, better transportation, lights)

The Enlightenment

- **Connect** How did the Scientific Revolution lead to the Enlightenment? (Philosophers used the scientific techniques of applying observation and reason to explain human behavior.)

- **Express an Opinion** Do you consider Thomas Hobbes an optimist or a pessimist? Explain. (Sample: He was a pessimist; he expected the worst from people unless a strong ruler controlled them.)

Analyze Visuals Have students examine the photograph, drawings, and flowchart.

- Which invention helped Galileo make these drawings? (the telescope)

- In the scientific method, what do scientists use to create a hypothesis? (information that they have gathered)

PRIMARY SOURCE

Reasons for American Independence The Enlightenment ideas that led to uprisings in Britain and France also contributed to the American Revolution. In this excerpt, Thomas Paine uses reason and logic to justify American independence: "I have heard it asserted by some, that as America has flourished under her former connection with Great Britain, the same connection is necessary towards her future happiness, and will always have the same effect. Nothing can be more fallacious than this kind of argument. . . . I answer roundly that America would have flourished as much, and probably much more, had no European power taken any notice of her. The commerce by which she hath enriched herself are the necessaries of life, and will always have a market."

—Thomas Paine, *Common Sense*

GUIDE ON THE SIDE

- **Categorize** What Enlightenment thinkers contributed to the development of modern democracy? (Locke, Montesquieu, Rousseau)

- **Compare Viewpoints** How did the ideas of enlightened rulers differ from the views of Enlightenment philosophers? (The enlightened rulers believed in some reform but they continued to rule absolutely.)

Democratic Revolutions

- **Express an Opinion** Why do you think the English went back to having a monarchy after a period of having a republic? (Sample: They were used to monarchy.)

Analyze Charts Point out the flowchart on the development of democracy.

- What government body limited the English monarchy? (Parliament)

- Which two documents placed limits on the monarchy? (the Magna Carta and the English Bill of Rights)

myWorld Activity

Long Live the Revolution Find Step-by-Step Instructions and an Activity Support on pp. T60–T61. **(Visual/Verbal)**

myWorld Activity
Long Live the Revolution

consent, *n.,* agreement or approval

Other philosophers had political views that shaped modern democracy. John Locke wrote that people are born with the right to life, liberty, and property. Charles-Louis Montesquieu (MAHN tus kyoo) believed that the powers of government should be separated into branches. Jean-Jacques Rousseau (roo SOH) said that government depends on the people's consent. These ideas later shaped Americans' views of government.

Enlightened Rulers A few European rulers were influenced by Enlightenment ideas about government. Frederick II of Prussia improved education and outlawed torture. Joseph II of Austria ended serfdom, a system in which peasants were forced to work for a noble.

These reforms were limited. For example, Frederick II promoted religious tolerance but allowed discrimination against Jews. Frederick and other absolute monarchs kept firm control over their people. This would soon begin to change.

Reading Check How did Enlightenment thinkers shape democracy?

Democratic Revolutions

The political ideas of the Enlightenment helped shape modern government. They also led to a period of violent change.

Changes in England During the 1600s, the English Parliament gradually took power away from the monarchy. In 1628, Parliament forced King Charles I to sign the Petition of Right. This document ended illegal taxation and imprisonment.

Conflict between Parliament and the monarchy continued. A civil war began in 1642. In 1649, Parliamentary forces executed the king. England became a commonwealth, or a republic.

The English government went through many changes over the next 40 years. Charles I's sons regained the throne but had renewed conflicts with Parliament. Parliament then gave the throne to William and Mary in 1689, under the condition that they sign the English Bill of Rights. The **English Bill of Rights** was an act that limited the power of the monarch and listed the rights of Parliament and the English people. England's absolute monarchy had come to an end.

The Magna Carta Paves the Way

Magna Carta (1215)
The king and nobles must respect the law.

A Struggle for Democracy (1295–1641)
Representatives of the English people struggle with kings for power.

English Revolution and Restoration (1641–1688)
The monarchy is abolished and Parliament rules England as a republic. The monarchy is restored in 1660. Conflicts between the king and Parliament resume.

English Bill of Rights (1689)
King William and Queen Mary agree to the English Bill of Rights. The Bill of Rights ensures the superiority of Parliament over the monarchy.

American Declaration of Independence (1776)
The monarchy is abolished and replaced with a democratic government in the United States.

How does this flowchart show the changing relationship of government and the people?

CAPTION The flowchart shows that the people gradually gained more political power and influence over government.

READING CHECK They proposed the ideas that led to democracy, such as separation of powers, human rights, and the consent of the governed.

COMMON MISCONCEPTIONS

End of the French Monarchy Some students might think that revolution in France led to the founding of a democracy, as it did in the United States. Explain that the French Revolution did not permanently end monarchy. Napoleon Bonaparte ruled as emperor from 1799 to 1815. After his defeat, the Bourbon family was restored to the throne. Two brothers of Louis XVI ruled France in succession. A second revolution in July 1830 ended the older line of Bourbon rulers and made their cousin Louis-Philippe a "citizen king." He was overthrown in 1848 when the Second Republic was established with Napoleon's nephew Louis Napoleon as president. This republic also proved short-lived as Louis Napoleon declared himself emperor in 1852. He ruled for nearly 20 years, but the disastrous Franco-Prussian War proved his undoing. France has had a republican government since 1871 except during World War II.

Revolution in France In France, society was divided into three groups called estates: clergy (the First Estate), nobles (the Second Estate), and common people (the Third Estate). Most French people were in the Third Estate. They paid heavy taxes and had few rights.

Enlightenment ideas inspired some French people to demand a voice in government. However, King Louis XVI refused to give up any of his powers. On July 14, 1789, a mob stormed the Bastille, a Paris prison. This marked the start of the **French Revolution,** a political movement that removed the French king from power and formed a republic.

The Revolution took a brutal turn. During the Reign of Terror in 1793 and 1794, the republic's government killed thousands of its opponents.

Napoleon Takes Power Meanwhile, Napoleon Bonaparte rose quickly in the French army. In 1799, he took power in France as a dictator.

Napoleon wanted to create a mighty French empire. In the Napoleonic Wars, he conquered much of Europe. His invasion of Russia proved disastrous, however. The French army was weakened, and Napoleon was defeated in 1815.

Revolution Spreads French domination led to growing nationalism, or devotion to one's country. Many Europeans also wanted greater democracy. In 1848, revolutions broke out across Europe. By 1871, both Germany and Italy had become unified nations.

Reading Check **What caused the French Revolution?**

The Reign of Terror
The promise of the French Revolution quickly soured. What had been a revolution calling for brotherhood and liberty turned into a civil war. Respected leaders such as Robespierre became feared tyrants.

A French mob storms the Bastille. ▼

Robespierre, who sentenced hundreds to the guillotine, was executed himself in 1794. ▼

The French Republic's government used the falling blade of the guillotine (right) to silence opponents. ▶

Culture Close-up

ANSWERS

- **Infer** Why did the revolutionaries in France kill so many people? (Samples: to gain total power; to prevent the monarchy from being restored)

- **Cause and Effect** What unexpected effect did Napoleon's conquests have on Europe? (They spread nationalism.)

- **Categorize** What two countries became unified nations in the 1870s because of nationalism? (Germany and Italy)

myWorld Activity

Long Live the Revolution Find Step-by-Step Instructions and an Activity Support on pp. T60–T61. **(Visual/Verbal)**

Culture Close-up

Have students go to myworldgeography.com to explore key events of the French Revolution.

CORE CONCEPTS: SCIENCE AND TECHNOLOGY

Review Core Concept 7.7 before reading about the Industrial Revolution. Discuss how technology and scientific advances can change culture and daily life. Also review how technology can change the way humans interact with their environment. Remind students of ancient technologies that improved agriculture, such as irrigation and the plow. Ask, What might happen if technology improved other areas, such as manufacturing and transportation? How might life change?

GUIDE ON THE SIDE

The Industrial Revolution

- **Identify Main Ideas** Where did the Industrial Revolution begin? (in Great Britain)

- **Cause and Effect** What transformed the textile industry? (larger, faster machines for spinning and weaving)

- **Summarize** What problems did industrialism cause? (overly rapid urban growth, pollution, child labor, and the spread of disease)

Analyze Visuals Have students look at the images of industrialization.

- What negative effects of industrialization are shown on this page? (pollution and child labor)

Life in the Industrial Age

The Industrial Revolution has been chronicled in art, literature, and photography. It transformed life and society across Europe. Industrialization had both positive and negative aspects. Its innovations remain part of modern life.

- Widespread pollution from factories
- Long work hours, child labor common
- Overcrowded living conditions

The Industrial Revolution

Alongside these political revolutions, a different kind of revolution began. The **Industrial Revolution** was a shift from hand tools driven by animal or human power to large-scale machinery powered by fuels or natural forces. It led to a growth of cities and large organizations and to rapid changes in technology. The Industrial Revolution began in Britain but soon spread to the rest of Europe.

Technology Changes Industry Before the Industrial Revolution, most people were farmers. Others worked at home. There, they used hand tools to make cloth, leather goods, and other items.

In England in the mid-1700s, this process began to change. Fast, new machines in factories began to do much of the work once done by people in their homes. The textile industry was the first to change. Inventors developed machines for spinning thread and weaving cloth.

Transportation also changed. Coal and steampower made steamboats and locomotives possible. These ships and trains carried raw materials to factories. They brought finished goods to distant markets.

Industry Changes Landscapes Entrepreneurs, or people who start businesses, built factories in areas that had a labor supply, resources such as coal, and good transportation. Towns without access to coal and iron or to transportation often did not industrialize.

Industrial towns grew quickly as workers moved there for jobs in factories. This rapid growth caused problems such as housing shortages. People had to live in crowded apartment buildings. Many people had no access to clean water.

Cities could not dispose adequately of waste, and coal-burning factories polluted the air. Diseases spread rapidly in these crowded, dirty conditions. Working conditions in factories were difficult. Factories and mines often hired young children to work dangerous jobs.

Trade Grows Workers in factories produced far more goods than individual workers ever had. Industrialized nations needed new places to sell these products. Many of the new markets were in European colonies in Africa and Asia. Colonies also provided raw materials for European manufacturers.

my World
IN NUMBERS

From 1770 to 1821, the British population grew from **8.3** million to **14.2** million.

READING CHECK During the Industrial Age, jobs, pollution, urban growth, disease, and medical research all grew. Standards of living rose and education became widespread.

SECTION 3 ASSESSMENT 1. The Scientific Revolution changed scientific study. The Enlightenment changed political ideas. The English Bill of Rights limited monarchs' power. The French Revolution overthrew the monarchy. The Industrial Revolution transformed manufacturing. **2.** Goods began to be made by factory

CULTURE

Charles Dickens The Victorian novelist Charles Dickens wrote several books that touched on the impact of the Industrial Revolution. In *David Copperfield*, he portrayed the terrible conditions under which children often had to work, something he knew first-hand. When he was only 12, his family was in such bad straits financially that Charles had to leave school and do manual work in a factory. The novel *Hard Times* is set in a fictionalized industrial city called Coketown. It portrays the squalor in which textile workers lived and the hardships of their work life. It criticizes utilitarianism, a philosophy that focused on producing the greatest general good for society—in Dickens's view—at the expense of individuals. The novel also satirizes education that focuses only on practicality and facts, and ignores imagination and creativity.

- Better public education and social reforms
- Improvements in healthcare, public hygiene
- Advances in arts and sciences

GUIDE ON THE SIDE

Positive Effects The Industrial Age also brought improvements. During this period, doctors and scientists made advances in research and medicine. Louis Pasteur and Robert Koch discovered that germs caused disease. Researchers found ways to cure or prevent illness. Cities built sewer systems to dispose of waste and prevent disease. Inventors developed ways to use electric power.

Because production was more efficient, the cost of goods went down. With the number of jobs increasing and the price of products decreasing, people could afford to buy more goods. For example, people began to wear clothing made in factories instead of at home. Middle-class families purchased new labor-saving devices, such as sewing machines. As a result, the standard of living—or the level of comfort—rose for millions of people.

Another positive change was greater access to primary school education. Where once only some boys had attended school, now girls too could receive an education.

Reading Check How did life change during the Industrial Age?

- **Identify Details** What developments improved public health? (medical research, sewers in cities)

- **Cause and Effect** What social improvements did the Industrial Revolution bring about? (rising standards of living, spread of education)

Analyze Visuals Have students look at the images of improvements brought about by industrialization.

- What advances do the images on this page show? (education and improvements in medicine)

Section 3 Assessment

Key Terms

1. Using full sentences, describe how each of the following terms relates to social and political change: Scientific Revolution, Enlightenment, English Bill of Rights, French Revolution, Industrial Revolution.

Key Ideas

2. How did the Industrial Revolution transform methods of manufacturing goods?

3. What did Isaac Newton contribute to the Scientific Revolution?

4. How did the Scientific Revolution influence Enlightenment thought?

5. How did the Enlightenment affect rulers' ideas?

Think Critically

6. **Categorize** Which of the events discussed in this section would you call political revolutions and which would you call cultural revolutions?

7. **Synthesize** How did the Enlightenment change governments in Europe?

Essential Question

What makes a nation?

8. How did the Napoleonic Wars encourage nationalistic feelings in Europe? Go to your Student Journal to record your answer.

machines rather than by workers at home. **3.** Newton contributed to the scientific method and defined gravity and how objects moved. **4.** Philosophers applied reason to the study of human behavior. **5.** The Enlightment inspired some rulers to make reforms. **6.** Political: English Civil War, French Revolution; Cultural: Scientific and Industrial revolutions **7.** The Enlightenment led to reforms but also to revolutions that overthrew monarchs. **8.** Conquered peoples learned about nationalism from the French and wanted their own nations.

ANSWERS

Wars and Hardship

OBJECTIVES

Students will know

- the causes and effects of World War I and World War II.
- how the Great Depression brought about hardship and unrest in Europe.

Students will be able to

- compare and contrast the two world wars.
- draw conclusions about the impact of hyperinflation on Germany in the 1920s.

SET EXPECTATIONS

In this section, students will

- read Wars and Hardship.
- go shopping during a simulation of spiraling inflation.
- go On Assignment in Europe and explore a map, table, diagram, and timeline about the two world wars.

CORE CONCEPTS

You may wish to teach or reteach the following lessons from the Core Concepts Handbook:

- Economic Process, pp. 60–61
- Economic Systems, pp. 62–63
- Historical Sources, pp. 120–121

KEY

Differentiated Instruction	English Language Instruction
L1 Special Needs **L2** Extra Support	**ELL** Beginner **ELL** Early Intermediate **ELL** Intermediate
L3 On-Level **L4** Challenge	**ELL** Early Advanced **ELL** Advanced

1 Connect
Make learning meaningful

Make Connections Ask students to suppose that they are running for student government. Have them discuss why it would be important to have a network of supporters. Then tell them that they are going to read about what happened when European countries formed elaborate military alliances.

L2 Extra Support Make sure students understand the basic agreement that underlies alliances: "If you go to war, I will help you fight. If I go to war, you will help me fight."

Activate Prior Knowledge Remind students that national rivalries fueled the Age of Exploration, and industrialization caused European nations to compete for colonies. Have students predict how those events might have affected relationships among countries in Europe.

ELL Early Advanced/Advanced Explain that *depression* usually means sadness or low spirits. In Section 4, students will use its economic meaning: "a period of low economic production." During depressions, businesses fail and people lose jobs.

Prepare Follow the steps in the section **Preview.** Preteach the Key Terms. Then have students complete *Word Wise* in their journals using in-text clues and the glossary for help.

2 Experience
Teach knowledge and skills

Read Use **Background** notes and **Guide on the Side** questions to model active reading. Have students use *Take Notes* in their **Student Journal** to record how World War I and World War II were similar and different. Have students complete **21st Century Online Tutor** *Compare and Contrast,* and apply this skill to reading the section.

L1 Special Needs Have students read the **Online Student Edition**, pausing to write down a question about the material under each heading. Gather questions and answer as a group.

ELL Intermediate Post this model for writing cause and effect sentences: _____ caused _____ because _____. The effect of _____ was _____.

L4 Challenge Have students analyze the graph on *Enrichment: Deaths of World War II.* Have them use their knowledge of the war to prepare a speech that explains why some countries had a much higher death toll than others.

Practice: myWorld Activity Students will experience hyperinflation by trying to purchase groceries whose prices are increasing much faster than student incomes. **Step-by-Step Instructions** and **More Activities** follow on p. T66.

SECTION 4 RESOURCE GUIDE

FOR THE STUDENT

my worldgeography.com **Student Center**
- Active Atlas
- Data Discovery
- Timeline

Student Edition (print and online)
- Wars and Hardship

Student Journal (print and online)
- Section 4 Word Wise
- Section 4 Take Notes

21st Century Learning **Online Tutor**
- Compare and Contrast
- Draw Conclusions

FOR THE TEACHER

my worldgeography.com **Teacher Center**
- Online Lesson Planner
- Presentations for Projection
- SuccessTracker

ProGuide: Europe and Russia
- Section 4 Lesson Plan, pp. T64–T65
- 🏃 myWorld Activity Step-by-Step Instructions, p. T66
- Activity Support: German Marks, p. T67
- myWorld Geography Enrichment, p. T68
- Section Quiz, p. T69

Accelerating the Progress of ELLs
- Organizing Information Strategies, p. 48

3 Understand
Assess understanding

Review Review *Word Wise* and *Take Notes* in the **Student Journal.**

Assess Knowledge and Skills Use the Section Assessment and Section Quiz to check students' progress.

Assess Understanding Review students' responses to the Section Assessment Essential Question prompt.

Remediate Use these strategies to review and remediate.

If students struggle to . . .	Try these strategies.
Compare and contrast the wars	Suggest students compare weapons, alliances, and outcomes.
Understand how hardship caused political change	Give them a three-column table with the heads *Problems, Emotions, Actions*. Have them complete the table with details from the section.
Draw conclusions	Assign additional practice with the **21st Century Online Tutor.**

ELL Support

ELL Objective Students will be able to say large numbers in English.

Cultural Connections To give students practice in discussing prices, ask them to think of a product that sells for different prices in different stores, such as jeans sold in high-end department stores and discount stores. Let them use their home languages to describe the different prices.

ELL Beginning Content Tip Use a map to locate World War II battles in Europe, North Africa, East Asia, Southeast Asia, and the Pacific islands.

ELL Activity Post the number 1,600 twice. Explain that many numbers over a thousand can be said two ways. On the first number, circle the *16* and then the *00* as you say "sixteen hundred." On the second number, circle the *1*, and then the *600* as you say "one thousand, six hundred." Post *2,400, 3,800,* and *6,400.* Have partners practice saying each number two different ways. **(Verbal/Logical)**

my worldgeography.com **Lesson Planner**

myWorld Activity   **Step-by-Step Instructions**

⏱ **20 min** 👥

Runaway Prices

OBJECTIVES

Students will

- simulate shopping for food with money that is rapidly losing value.
- discuss the impact of hyperinflation on society.

LEARNING STYLE

- Kinesthetic
- Logical

21st Century Learning

- Draw Conclusions

MATERIALS

- Activity Support: German Marks, p. T67
- Scissors
- Copies of a grocery price list

Activity Steps

1. Organize groups of five students. Tell the groups to appoint a banker and a grocer. The other students are consumers. Give every student a copy of *Activity Support: German Marks.* Groups should cut apart the money and deposit it with their banker.

   ELL **Beginner/Early Intermediate** Ask students to name the currency of their family's home country.

2. Give each grocer a copy of a price list with the data below. Tell them to keep the list secret.

   Round 1, Jan. 1922 400 marks
   Round 2, Apr. 1922 600 marks
   Round 3, July 1922 1,000 marks
   Round 4, Oct. 1922 6,400 marks
   Round 5, Jan. 1923 36,000 marks

   L1 **Special Needs** Create one-mark notes and use smaller values in the price list (Round 1:

   2 marks, Round 2: 3 marks, etc.) to lessen the difficulty of the math in the exercise.

3. To start Round 1, the bankers give each consumer 1,200 marks. Tell the consumers to buy milk, bread, and meat from the grocer and save leftover money. The grocer will tell them the total price of food.

4. For Rounds 2, 3, and 4, the bankers will give each consumer 1,400, 1,600, and 1,800 marks, and the grocers will tell them the new food prices. By Round 4, consumers should run out of money.

   L4 **Challenge** Have students write a diary entry from the perspective of a German person dealing with hyperinflation.

5. Have a grocer read out the price for Round 5. Ask, When prices rise so quickly, what choices do people have to make? How might people respond to a leader who promises to restore the economy?

More Activities From myWorld Teachers

Local Connection Have students list five non-technological things they buy and what those items cost. Then have them ask their parents how much the items cost when they were young. Have the class discuss their findings the next day. **(Verbal)**

Please Enlist Have pairs of students work together to make a recruitment poster for either World War I or World War II. Tell them that the poster must clearly

show reasons for fighting in that particular war and for a particular alliance or country. **(Visual)**

Redrawing the Map Have students role play a foreign minister and write an argument for or against breaking the great European empires into separate nations after World War I. **(Verbal/Logical)**

 my worldgeography.com   **Teacher Center** →   Find additional resources in the online Teacher Center.

Name _____ Class _____ Date _____

myWorld Activity Support   **German Marks**

Runaway Prices

Directions Cut apart the German marks below and give all of your group's money to the banker. In each round, the banker will give you an income that you can use to buy food.

✂ -

200 Marks	**200 Marks**	**200 Marks**
200 Marks	**200 Marks**	**200 Marks**
200 Marks	**200 Marks**	**200 Marks**
200 Marks	**200 Marks**	**200 Marks**
200 Marks	**200 Marks**	**200 Marks**
200 Marks	**200 Marks**	**200 Marks**

Name _____ Class _____ Date _____

Enrichment: Deaths of World War II

Directions Study the graph below. Answer the questions that follow.

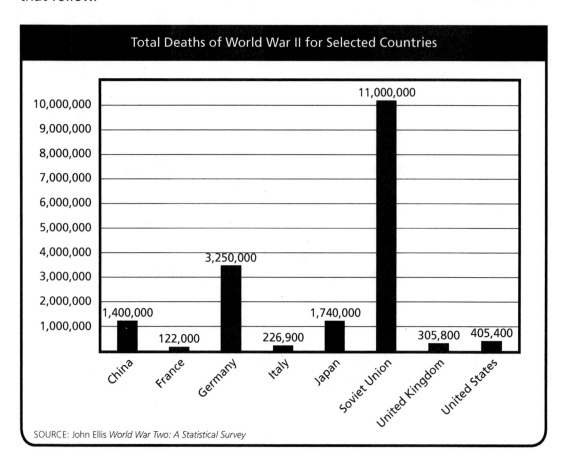

Total Deaths of World War II for Selected Countries

SOURCE: John Ellis *World War Two: A Statistical Survey*

1. How many combined deaths did the three Axis Powers have?

_____

2. Which Axis Power had the most deaths?

_____

3. Which country had the most deaths? How many deaths were there?

_____

4. Which country's death toll was closest in number to that of the United States?

_____

Name _____ Class _____ Date _____

Section Quiz

Directions Answer the following questions using what you learned
in Section 4.

1. _____ How did World War I change
warfare?
   a. by introducing the atomic bomb
   b. by showing the effectiveness of trench
   warfare
   c. by being the first truly modern, global
   conflict
   d. by demonstrating the success of the
   blitzkrieg

2. _____ Which of the following was a result
of World War I?
   a. the humiliation of Germany
   b. U.S. membership in the League of
   Nations
   c. Russian prosperity
   d. growth of the Ottoman Empire

3. _____ What event began World War II in
Europe?
   a. Germany's invasion of France
   b. Germany's invasion of Poland
   c. Germany's occupation of Austria
   d. Germany's alliance with the Soviet
   Union

4. _____ What was one reason for the global
spread of the Great Depression?
   a. The United States demanded that
   Germany repay its war debt.
   b. Inflation in Germany spread to the
   United States.
   c. The governments of France and
   Germany increased workers' wages.
   d. Loans linked banks around the world.

5. _____ What happened on June 6, 1944,
that changed the course of World War II?
   a. The Allies crossed the English Channel
   and invaded France.
   b. The Soviet Union invaded Germany
   from the east.
   c. Japan carried out a surprise attack on
   Pearl Harbor.
   d. Nazi Germany surrendered after Adolf
   Hitler killed himself.

6. What were the characteristics of fascism?

_____

_____

_____

_____

Wars and Hardship

- Model preparing to read by previewing the Key Ideas, Key Terms, headings, visuals, and captions. Have students make predictions about what they will learn. For ELL support, post the prompt, "I predict I will read about . . ."

- Preview and practice comparing and contrasting, by looking at similar and different views on an important issue in your community.

- Preteach this section's high-use Academic Vocabulary and Key Terms using the table on the next page and in-text definitions. Have students practice Key Terms by completing the *Word Wise* page in their journals.

GUIDE ON THE SIDE

Reading Skill

Compare and Contrast While they read, have students practice this skill by completing the *Take Notes* graphic organizer in the **Student Journal.**

The Great War: World War I

- **Compare and Contrast** How was World War I different from previous conflicts? (It was the first modern, global conflict.)

- **Cause and Effect** How did nationalism affect relationships between countries? (It caused some nations to feel hostile toward rival nations.)

Section 4

Wars and Hardship

Key Ideas	

Key Ideas
- World War I resulted in defeat for Europe's multinational empires and their division into new nations.
- The Great Depression brought hardship and political unrest to Europe.
- World War II brought catastrophe for Jews and other Europeans and led to the defeat of Germany and Italy by the Allied powers.

Key Terms • World War I • Great Depression • communism • fascism • World War II • Holocaust

 Visual Glossary

 Reading Skill: Compare and Contrast Take notes using the graphic organizer in your journal.

When the 1900s began, large multinational empires controlled central Europe. A series of alliances linked Europe's great powers into competing blocs.

The Great War: World War I

World War I (1914–1918), or the Great War, was the first modern global conflict. It involved most of Europe, the United States, Canada, and many parts of Africa and Asia.

Causes of War World War I had four main causes: nationalism, imperialism, militarism, and alliances.

- **Nationalism**—Nationalism, or devotion to one's nation or people, sometimes led to hostility toward other nations.
- **Imperialism**—European imperial powers competed to extend their empires by seizing territory to add to their colonies in Africa and Asia.
- **Militarism**—For decades, European countries had been building up military power and adopting warlike attitudes.
- **Alliances**—In a complex system of alliances, many European countries had agreed to defend one another from attack. These alliances pulled nations into the war.

Fighter pilots engage in a dramatic dogfight during World War I.

ACADEMIC VOCABULARY

High-Use Word	Definition and Sample Sentence
humiliate	v. to embarrass or to reduce a person's feeling of self-worth
	Jeannie was afraid that wearing the old coat would humiliate her.
slump	n. a marked decline
	When the economy went into a slump, many people lost jobs.

War Breaks Out In June 1914, a Serbian nationalist killed the Austrian archduke. Austria-Hungary declared war on Serbia. One by one, the major European powers entered the war to support their allies. The fighting later spread overseas.

In Europe, armies fought on two fronts. On the Western Front, Germany battled the Allied Powers—France and Britain. Soldiers lived in a network of trenches dug into the earth. For years, they gained little ground. On the Eastern Front, Germany and Austria-Hungary fought Russia. But when the Russian Revolution began in 1917, Russia pulled out of the war.

In 1917, the United States entered the war on the side of the Allies. U.S. troops helped force the Germans out of France. Exhausted, Germany sought a truce, and the war ended on November 11, 1918.

Consequences of War The Allies forced Germany to sign the Treaty of Versailles. The treaty humiliated Germany. It made Germany give up territory and pay huge reparations, or sums for war damage.

Other treaties carved up Austria-Hungary into several new nations, ended the Ottoman Empire, and created new countries. For example, Yugoslavia was a federation of Slavic republics, including Serbia. Poland was shaped from parts of Germany, Austria-Hungary, and Russia. The maps below show these changes.

Reading Check What were the four main causes of World War I?

humiliate, v., to embarrass or to reduce a person's feeling of self-worth

- **Cause and Effect** How did the alliance system cause the war to spread? (Even though the war started between two nations, their allies soon joined the fight.)
- **Summarize** In general, how did the number of countries in Europe change because of World War I? Why? (It increased because several empires broke apart.)

Map Skills Have students examine the map of Europe before and after the Great War.
- What happened to Serbia after World War I? (It became part of Yugoslavia.)

Map Skills
1. **Region** How did Europe change after World War I?
2. **Place** What areas of Europe changed the most? Why do you think this happened?

Active Atlas

Europe Before and After World War I

Active Atlas
Have students go to myworldgeography.com to explore effects of World War I on political geography in Europe.

READING CHECK nationalism, militarism, imperialism, and a system of alliances

MAP SKILLS 1. Empires fell apart; new nations were formed. **2.** Eastern Europe changed the most because that was where the empires were.

ECONOMICS

Smoot-Hawley Tariff After World War I, American business owners feared that the prosperity gained from wartime production would decline. Specifically, they were afraid European imports might cut into their profits. In 1922, the United States imposed a tariff of nearly 40 percent on imports. However, farmers soon began to feel the effects of competition from European farm products, so they lobbied for an agricultural tariff. After the stock market crash of 1929, support for U.S. protectionism grew. In 1930, the United States passed the Smoot-Hawley Act, which further raised tariff rates. This made it much harder for foreign countries to export to the United States and deepened the financial crisis overseas. Other countries retaliated with their own tariffs and world trade declined, deepening the Great Depression.

The Great Depression

- **Infer** How did Germany's economy affect its ability to pay reparations? (Its economic problems made it hard for Germany to make payments.)

- **Cause and Effect** What triggered the stock market crash? (Stock prices declined, lenders demanded repayment of loans, and stockholders sold too many stocks too quickly.)

- **Problem Solve** What could countries have done differently to lessen the economic crisis? (not passed tariffs)

- **Cause and Effect** What other conditions worsened the Great Depression? (loans between banks; problems left from the war)

Chart Skills Have students examine the unemployment graph.

- Which country had the lowest unemployment rate? (Great Britain)

Data Discovery

Have students go to myworldgeography.com to learn about Europe during the Great Depression.

myWorld Activity

Runaway Prices Find Step-by-Step Instructions and an Activity Support on pp. T66–T67. **(Kinesthetic/Logical)**

---

myWorld Activity
Runaway Prices

The Great Depression

Germany had lost land, people, and resources. At the same time, Germany owed billions of dollars in reparations. The government printed money to try to make these payments. As a result, German money lost value. The price of goods increased rapidly during a period of inflation. Many Germans lost their savings. This caused unrest and political instability in Germany.

A Global Financial Crisis Develops
During the 1920s, the American economy had grown dramatically. At same time, prices on the U.S. stock market rose.

slump, *n.*, a marked decline

A man uses German money as wallpaper. Inflation had made the money worthless. ▼

Many Americans bought stocks, some with borrowed money, hoping to make a profit as the prices of stocks increased.

At first, stock prices soared. Then stocks leveled off and fell. Nervous lenders demanded repayment. Investors sold stocks to repay the loans. Heavy selling drove prices down quickly. In October 1929, the U.S. stock market collapsed.

Many investors lost fortunes selling their stocks for much less than they had paid. People and businesses who had borrowed money could not repay their debts. Soon, banks failed and businesses closed. As a result, millions of people were out of work. This was the beginning of the **Great Depression,** a deep, worldwide economic slump that lasted through the 1930s. It caused hardship around the world.

Europe Suffers Hard Times To protect its farmers, the United States put tariffs, or taxes, on imported farm products. These tariffs hurt European economies, so European countries imposed their own tariffs. Global trade slowed. The French and German governments lowered wages, hoping to help reduce the costs of goods. Instead, this only angered workers and increased hardship.

Banks around the world were linked by loans. As a result, U.S. banking problems spread to other nations. Some European banks failed. Most European countries had not yet recovered from World War I. These new financial troubles made hard times even harder.

Reading Check How did the Great Depression spread from the United States to Europe?

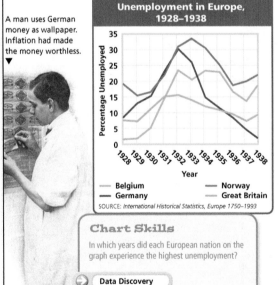

Unemployment in Europe, 1928–1938

Percentage Unemployed vs. Year

— Belgium
— Germany
— Norway
— Great Britain

SOURCE: *International Historical Statistics, Europe 1750–1993*

Chart Skills

In which years did each European nation on the graph experience the highest unemployment?

Data Discovery

CHART SKILLS Belgium: 1932; Germany: 1932; Britain: 1932; Norway: 1933

READING CHECK Banks were linked through loans; also, the U.S. tariffs hurt the European economy.

QUICK FACTS

Timeline of Hitler's Life

1889: Born in Austria-Hungary.

1907: Moves to Vienna to study art but is not accepted into art school.

1914–1918: Fights for Germany in World War I.

1919: Joins a worker's party; renames it National Socialist German Worker's (Nazi) Party in 1920.

1923: Is convicted of treason for attempted coup; in prison, writes *Mein Kampf.*

1925: Reestablishes the Nazi Party.

1933: Becomes chancellor of Germany.

1939: Orders German troops to invade Poland, starting World War II.

1944: Survives an assassination attempt.

1945: Facing certain defeat, commits suicide.

A War of Ideas

After World War I, antidemocratic leaders took power in Italy, Germany, and other European countries. Those governments took control of daily life.

The Rise of Communism The 1917 Russian Revolution led to the formation of the communist government of the Soviet Union. **Communism** is an economic and political system in which the state, run by a Communist Party, takes over industry and farmland and controls most organizations.

Communism promised to share wealth among all workers. During the Great Depression, workers across Europe found this promise very appealing.

Fascism in Italy and Spain In Italy, nationalist pride led to fascism. **Fascism** is a political system that stresses national strength, military might, and the belief that the state is more important than individuals. Fascists use propaganda and violence to achieve goals and believe that a dictator—a leader with unlimited powers—should rule. In the 1920s, fascist Benito Mussolini took power in Italy. He promised to build a strong Italian empire. During the 1930s, fascists under Francisco Franco took control of Spain.

Nazis Take Power in Germany Many Germans resented the Treaty of Versailles and blamed it for their hardships. Some blamed Germany's democratic government for obeying the treaty.

Adolf Hitler had served in the German army during World War I. Like many other Germans, he felt that Germany had been treated unfairly after the war.

Hitler came to lead a small, fascist German political party, the Nazi Party. Hitler's ideas included extreme nationalism, racism, and anti-Semitism, or prejudice against Jews. Hitler unfairly blamed Jews for Germany's economic problems.

In 1923, the Nazis tried and failed to overthrow the government. Hitler was jailed, but worked after his release to rebuild the Nazi Party. Amid the Great Depression, the Nazis gained strength in the early 1930s. In 1932, the Nazis won more votes than any other party, but less than a majority of votes. Nonetheless, in 1933, Hitler became head of Germany's government.

Understanding Political Systems

	Democracy	Communism	Fascism
Individuals and the State	Individuals' rights are more important than government interests.	Government interests are more important than individuals' rights.	Government interests are more important than individuals' rights.
Values	Freedom, individuals' rights, justice	Obedience, discipline, economic security	Obedience, discipline, national pride, military power
Government	The people and their elected representatives make decisions; control of people's lives is minimal.	Communist party makes all decisions; extreme control of all aspects of life.	Fascist party controls all aspects of life; government is permanent and necessary for national progress.

Chart Skills

Compare the values associated with fascism to those of democracy and communism.

→ Data Discovery

▲ Flag of Italy under fascism

CHART SKILLS The values of fascism were more like those of communism than democracy; for example, both fascism and communism stressed discipline and obedience.

GUIDE ON THE SIDE

A War of Ideas

- **Summarize** Why did communism appeal to many workers? (It promised to share wealth.)

- **Problem Solve** Which cause of World War I continued to cause problems, such as fascism, after the war? (nationalism)

- **Compare Viewpoints** How did Mussolini appeal to Italian nationalism? (He promised to build a strong empire.)

- **Identify Bias** What is anti-Semitism? (prejudice against Jews)

Chart Skills Have students read the table on political systems.

- How did the three systems view individuals? (Communism and fascism distrusted individuals; democracy valued them.)

→ Data Discovery

Have students go online to learn more about European governments.

COMMON MISCONCEPTIONS

The First World War Many people believe that World War I and World War II were the first global conflicts in history. In fact, the Seven Years' War, called the French and Indian War in North America, was fought on four different continents. It began as a skirmish in North America in 1754, in which the French ousted a Virginia force under George Washington from a post on the Ohio River. The European phase of the war began in 1756 as Austria and Prussia battled over the resource-rich province of Silesia. Austria's ally France and Prussia's ally Britain spread the war worldwide as they fought over overseas colonial holdings. Outside Europe, battles took place in Africa, India, and the West Indies in addition to the lengthy war in North America. Britain ultimately won and acquired France's North American and Indian colonies.

▲ The Nazis forced Jewish people to wear yellow stars for identification.

- **Infer** How did the Nazis make it difficult for Jews to protect themselves? (The Nazis took away their rights as citizens.)

World War II

- **Categorize** What were the Axis nations? (Germany, Italy, and Japan)

- **Summarize** What were the main events of the first two years of the war? (Germany invaded Poland; Germany occupied much of Europe; and Britain fought on against Germany alone.)

Map Skills Direct students to examine the map of wartime opponents.

- What Allied nation remained unconquered in 1942? (Great Britain)

- What country in the center of Europe was neutral? (Switzerland)

 **Active Atlas**

Have students go to myworldgeography.com to learn more about World War II in Europe.

Once in power, Hitler ruled as a dictator. He controlled every aspect of German life, using secret police to spy on people. Hitler imprisoned or killed his opponents. Because Germany's economy improved under the Nazis, many Germans accepted Nazi rule.

The Nazi government passed a number of laws against Jews, eliminating their rights as citizens. In 1938, Nazis led anti-Jewish riots in Germany and Austria. For 48 hours, Nazis systematically destroyed Jewish synagogues and Jewish businesses. Nazi hatred toward Jews later led to the Nazi "Final Solution," or the attempted killing off of all Jews.

Reading Check Why were the German people attracted to the Nazi Party?

Wartime Opponents, 1942

KEY
Allied territory, 1942
Axis territory, 1942
Neutral territory, 1942
Borders as of 1938
0   400 mi
0   400 km
Lambert Conformal Conic Projection

North Sea

Baltic Sea

Black Sea

Mediterr

World War II

Under Adolf Hitler, Germany built a powerful army and formed an alliance with Italy and Japan. These countries were called the Axis Powers. Britain and France formed the Allied Powers, later joined by the United States and Soviet Union.

War Begins Hitler wanted to build a mighty German empire across Europe. In 1938, German troops occupied Austria and seized part of Czechoslovakia. Germany and the Soviet Union then secretly agreed to divide Poland between them. On September 1, 1939, Germany invaded Poland. Two days later, Britain and France declared war on Germany. **World War II,** the second major global conflict of the 1900s, had begun.

War in Europe By the end of 1940, Germany's powerful armies had conquered much of Europe. Italy attacked North Africa. At first, Britain fought on alone, with the help of some military aid from the United States.

The German air force repeatedly bombed British military targets and civilian areas, but the British did not give up.

Map Skills

Place Who controlled more of Europe in 1942, the Allies or the Axis Powers?

Active Atlas

READING CHECK The Nazis stressed national strength, and the economy improved under their rule.

MAP SKILLS the Axis Powers

READING CHECK Allied forces invaded Germany from two sides.

SECTION 4 ASSESSMENT 1. World War I lasted from 1914 to 1918. The Great Depression was a severe economic slump. Communism is a system in which the state outlaws private property and controls society. Fascism is a system that stresses the importance of the state and rule by dictators. World War II lasted from 1939

HISTORY

Fire Bombing of Dresden Many European cities suffered devastating damage during World War II. One city that almost didn't survive was Dresden, Germany. Before the war, it was known as the "Florence on the Elbe" because it was home to many beautiful buildings, including a palace, Germany's largest Protestant church, and several museums. On February 13 and 14, 1945, a force of about 800 British and American aircraft bombed the city heavily and nearly obliterated its center section. Additional raids took place until April 17, 1945. Historians estimate that the raids killed between 35,000 and 135,000 people. U.S. author Kurt Vonnegut was a prisoner in the city and survived only because the Germans had him working in an underground meat locker. The raids accomplished little of military value but destroyed many priceless works of art.

British Prime Minister Winston Churchill inspired the people with stirring speeches:

❝ We have before us many, many long months of struggle and of suffering. You ask, what is our policy? I will say: It is to wage war, by sea, land and air, with all our might and with all the strength that God can give us. ❞

In June 1941, Germany broke its earlier agreement and invaded the Soviet Union. The Soviet Union joined the Allied Powers. Soviet resistance, brutal winter weather, and a lack of supplies finally forced Germany to retreat in 1943.

America Enters the War In late 1941, Japan bombed Pearl Harbor, a U.S. naval base in Hawaii. This pushed the United States into the war. American forces helped the Allies defeat Italy.

With U.S. help, the Allies pushed back into western Europe. On June 6, 1944, D-Day, more than 150,000 Allied troops invaded German-occupied France. The Allies slowly forced German troops back across France into Germany. At the same time, Soviet troops invaded Germany from the east. Germany surrendered on May 7, 1945. World War II ended later that year with Japan's surrender to the United States.

Effects of the War Approximately 17 million European soldiers died in World War II. Millions of civilians died as well. Many civilian deaths occurred in the **Holocaust,** the mass murder of Jews by the Nazis during World War II. The Nazis murdered 6 million Jews and another 5 million people from other groups.

After the war, Europe's cities, roads, and farms lay in ruins. Much of the continent needed to be rebuilt.

Reading Check How were the Allied forces able to win World War II?

World at War

▸ 1914 World War I begins.
▸ 1918 World War I ends.
▸ 1919 The Treaty of Versailles
▸ 1939 Germany invades Poland; France and Britain declare war on Germany. World War II begins.
▸ 1941 The United States enters the war.
▸ 1945 Germany and Japan surrender. World War II ends.

   Timeline

- **Analyze Sources** Why do you think the British people found Churchill's speech so inspiring? (Sample: He promises not to give up but to use every resource Britain has.)

- **Build Cultural Awareness** How many people were killed in the Holocaust? (About six million Jews and five million other people were killed.)

Analyze Visuals Have students examine the timeline showing events from World War I and World War II.

- Which of the two wars lasted longer? (World War II)

Section 4 Assessment

Key Terms

1. Define each of the following terms using a complete sentence: World War I, Great Depression, communism, fascism, World War II, Holocaust.

Key Ideas

2. Whom did the Nazis kill during the Holocaust?

3. How did competition among nations contribute to World War I?

4. How did the Great Depression affect Europe?

5. Which nations defeated the Axis Powers in World War II?

Think Critically

6. **Problem Solving** How did Germany's situation after World War I help cause the next world war?

7. **Compare Viewpoints** How might French citizens have felt about the Treaty of Versailles? Compare their viewpoint to that of German citizens.

Essential Question

What makes a nation?

8. Why did so many nations gain independence after World War I? Go to your Student Journal to record your answer.

   Timeline

Have students go to myworldgeography.com to explore key events of World War I and World War II.

to 1945. The Holocaust was the Nazi program to kill Jews. **2.** The Nazis killed Jews and other people they judged inferior. **3.** European nations saw each other as rivals to be defeated. **4.** Tariffs hurt the economy and trade slowed. **5.** The Allies defeated the Axis Powers. **6.** The damages imposed after World War I hurt Germany's economy, and Germans resented their former enemies. **7.** The French probably approved of punishing Germany. Germans hated the treaty. **8.** Ethnic groups who had been ruled by empires got their own nations.

ANSWERS

The World Wars in Art

OBJECTIVES

Students will

- make connections between important documents and the experience of living through World War I and World War II.
- **21st Century Learning** compare and contrast the experience of the two wars.
- **ELL** understand how to use the prefix *un-*.

SET EXPECTATIONS

In this lesson, students will

- read and analyze two documents on World War I and World War II.
- write a poem responding to wartime documents.

1 Connect

Post the word *war* with two arrows pointing down from it. At the end of one arrow write the word *military*. At the end of the other arrow, write the word *civilians*. Make sure students are familiar with the meaning of both words. Ask, Have any of your family members served in the military during a war? What did you learn from them about war? How are the civilians who stay home affected by wars? Allow the class to brainstorm answers to those questions and post them for all to see.

2 Learn

Preview Explain to students that they are going to read a poem written about World War I and an account of the Holocaust in World War II. Have students preview the two pages and identify the images of the poppy and pile of shoes. Have them study the image of marching soldiers. Read the Key Idea, glossary terms, and definitions. Clarify any questions about the meaning of these words by providing examples.

Read Slowly read aloud the poem "In Flanders Fields" without stopping. Read the document again, this time stopping to read the questions at the left and prompt students to rethink and analyze the meaning of the words. Have students answer the questions using the location of the letters to provide clues. Do the same for the excerpt from *Survival in Auschwitz*. Lead a discussion starting with students' responses to the questions. Ask, How are the situations described in these two documents different?

ELL **Intermediate** Remind students that the prefix *un-* means "not." Point out that the narrator is worried that the shoes swept in the heap have become "unmatched." Have students paraphrase what this means; make sure they understand that shoes that belong in a pair have become separated.

myWorld Activity: Vivid Writing Distribute the *Activity Support: Sensory Details*. Have students work on their own to analyze how they are affected emotionally by the sensory details in "In Flanders Fields" and the excerpt from *Survival in Auschwitz*.

15 min

3 Understand

Review Go back to the Key Idea. Ask, Judging from these documents, which war caused more suffering for civilians? Compare the soldier speaking in the poem "In Flanders Fields" to the civilian narrator of *Survival in Auschwitz*. Which one do you admire more? Why?

Assess Have students complete **Analyze the Documents.** Review their answers to determine if students have met the lesson objectives.

Remediate If students struggle to identify sensory details, list the five senses. Ask the class to give examples of descriptive words that would appeal to each sense. For example, *sour* would appeal to taste.

Name _____ Class _____ Date _____

myWorld Activity Support **Sensory Details**

Vivid Writing

Directions Reread the poem "In Flanders Fields" and the excerpt from *Survival in Auschwitz*. Both pieces use **sensory** language, or words and phrases that appeal to the five senses: sight, sound, smell, touch, and taste. These sensory details help readers imagine what war is like. Use the table below to record sensory details from the two pieces. There may not be an entry for every sense or box.

Sensory Details		
	From "In Flanders Fields"	**From *Survival in Auschwitz***
Sight		
Sound		
Smell		
Taste		
Touch		

Draw Conclusions

1. What do you feel when you read "In Flanders Fields"?

_____

2. Which words in the poem are related to that feeling, or mood?

_____

3. What do you feel when you read the excerpt from *Survival in Auschwitz*?

_____

4. Which words in the poem are related to that feeling, or mood?

_____

CULTURE

Poppies for Veterans Flanders is a region in Belgium where a lot of the fighting in World War I took place. John McCrae, who wrote "In Flanders Fields," was a military surgeon who witnessed the war's high casualties. He died of pneumonia and meningitis during the war. His poem became very popular and widely associated with World War I. Because of the poem, veterans' groups began to sell cloth poppies to raise money to support those who have fought in wars overseas. They still do so today.

GUIDE ON THE SIDE

Compare and Contrast Use the lettered prompts to help students identify details to use while comparing the experiences of World Wars I and II.

ANSWERS

A They represent rows of graves in a cemetery.

B The narrator is a soldier who has died in battle and is buried there.

C Just as a relay race takes many runners to win, a war takes many soldiers to win.

Primary Source

The World Wars in Art

Key Idea
- Historical accounts of wars give us important information about conflicts and those involved in them.

▲ A poppy worn in remembrance of war veterans

Eyewitness accounts make the experience of battle frighteningly real. Ancient historians like Herodotus recorded the heroism of the Greeks against the Persians. In 1812, Philippe Paul de Ségur remembered Napoleon's "skeletons of soldiers" as the French army returned in defeat from Russia. But few accounts of war have been as powerful as those left by the poets, novelists, and artists who experienced World War I and World War II. Not only did they write about fighting the enemy on the battlefield, but these artists also recorded the horrors of the Holocaust.

Stop at each letter on the right to think about the text. Then answer the question with the same letter on the left.

A *Identify Evidence* What do the crosses indicate?

B *Synthesize* Who is the narrator and how did he come to be in Flanders?

C *Draw Inferences* Why does the poet use the image of a relay race here?

scarce, *adv.,* hardly or barely
quarrel, *n.,* disagreement, dispute
foe, *n.,* enemy

In Flanders Fields

❝ In Flanders fields the poppies blow
A Between the crosses row on row,
That mark our place; and in the sky
The larks, still bravely singing, fly
<u>Scarce</u> heard amid the guns below.

B We are the Dead. Short days ago
We lived, felt dawn, saw sunset glow,
Loved and were loved, and now we lie
In Flanders fields.

Take up our <u>quarrel</u> with the <u>foe</u>:
C To you from failing hands we throw
The torch; be yours to hold it high.
If ye break faith with us who die
We shall not sleep, though poppies grow
In Flanders fields. ❞
—Lieutenant Colonel John McCrae, M.D., after the Battle of Ypres, Belgium, 1915

British soldiers walk across the battlefield near Ypres during World War I.

21st Century Learning COMPARE AND CONTRAST

To assist your students in comparing and contrasting the two documents, suggest that they focus on specific elements such as the time, the place, the narrator's civilian or military status, and the events being described. Which of these are similar and which are different? After students have considered specific aspects of the two documents, suggest that they create a Venn diagram on which to record the similarities and differences between the two. Finally, they should summarize those similarities and differences either verbally or in writing. For additional help, refer students to the **21st Century Online Tutor** *Compare and Contrast*.

Stop at each letter on the right to think about the text. Then answer the question with the same letter on the left.

D Synthesize How many times does the word "and" appear in the first sentence? How does this affect the way you read it?

E Summarize Why does mixing up the shoes seem so "crazy" to the narrator?

F Draw Conclusions Why does the German watch "with interest" how the men react to the cold?

heap, *n.,* pile
writhe, *v.,* to twist and turn

Heaps of Shoes

66 Now another German comes and tells us to put the shoes in a certain corner,
D and we put them there, because now it is all over and we feel outside this world and the only thing is to obey.

Someone comes with a broom and sweeps away all the shoes, outside
E the door in a <u>heap</u>. He is crazy, he is mixing them all together, ninety-six pairs, they will be all unmatched.

The outside door opens, a freezing wind enters and we are naked and cover ourselves up with our arms. The wind blows and slams the door; the German reopens it and stands
F watching with interest how we <u>writhe</u> to hide from the wind, one behind the other.

Then he leaves and closes it. 99
—Primo Levi, *Survival in Auschwitz,* 1958

Piles of shoes taken from prisoners sent to the concentration camp at Auschwitz ▼

ANSWERS

D Sample: The word *and* appears four times. Readers may have to pause for breath as they read the long, repetitious sentence.

E The narrator does not understand that the shoes will not be returned.

F Sample: The German soldier likes to watch the men suffer because he believes they are inferior to him.

Analyze the Documents

1. **Compare and Contrast** Both the poem and the text above show courage and bravery. Compare and contrast how each source does this.
2. **Writing Task** Write a short poem in reaction to either "In Flanders Fields" or to the excerpt from *Survival in Auschwitz.*

ANALYZE THE DOCUMENTS 1. The poem first establishes the idea of bravery with the larks singing above the cemetery; the passing of the torch conveys the idea of honor and passing the task on from one group of brave soldiers to the next. The prose text shows how prisoners endure harsh treatment. **2.** Student poems may rhyme or use free verse; they should be divided into lines and possibly stanzas; they should contain sensory language and include details from the two primary sources.

SECTION 5 LESSON PLAN

Rebuilding and New Challenges

OBJECTIVES

Students will know
- how the Cold War divided Europe.
- why the European Union was formed.
- how democracy spread through Eastern Europe.

Students will be able to
- describe main events related to the democratization and unification of Europe.
- use symbols and mottos to express protest.

SET EXPECTATIONS

In this section, students will
- read Rebuilding and New Challenges.
- make a protest poster about the Berlin Wall or communist rule of East Germany.
- go On Assignment in Europe and explore a map of the European Union.

CORE CONCEPTS

You may wish to teach or reteach the following lessons from the Core Concepts Handbook:
- Economic Development, pp. 64–65
- Migration, pp. 78–79
- Conflict and Cooperation, pp. 110–111

KEY

Differentiated Instruction
- **L1** Special Needs
- **L2** Extra Support
- **L3** On-Level
- **L4** Challenge

English Language Instruction
- **ELL** Beginner
- **ELL** Early Intermediate
- **ELL** Intermediate
- **ELL** Early Advanced
- **ELL** Advanced

---

1 Connect
Make learning meaningful

Make Connections Discuss what it is like when two friends argue and refuse to speak to each other. Ask students, Do the friends try to make others take sides? Does their hostility cause further conflicts? Then explain that after World War II, Europe experienced a *Cold War*, in which the region was divided between two political systems that were hostile to each other.

ELL Intermediate Explain that the term *Cold War* is used in contrast to a *hot war*, or shooting war. The United States and the Soviet Union were rivals for more than 40 years but never fought directly. Also explain the use of *cold* to describe someone who is unfriendly.

Activate Prior Knowledge Review that World War II ended in Europe when U.S. troops invaded Germany from the west and Soviet troops invaded from the east. Ask, What type of government do you think each side wanted postwar Germany to have?

L2 Extra Support Remind students that the United States is a democracy, and the Soviet Union was communist. Review the systems.

Prepare Follow the steps in the section **Preview.** Preteach the Key Terms. Then have students complete *Word Wise* in their journals using in-text clues and the glossary for help.

2 Experience
Teach knowledge and skills

Read Use **Background** notes and **Guide on the Side** questions to model active reading. Have students use *Take Notes* in their **Student Journal** to record details about democratization and unification. Have students complete **21st Century Online Tutor** *Identify Main Ideas and Details*, and apply this skill to reading the section.

L2 Extra Support Ask students to summarize Germany's postwar history through drawings to indicate when it was unified and when it was divided.

ELL Intermediate/Early Advanced Tell students that the prefix *uni-* means "single or one." Have them make a word web with *uni-* in the middle and related words from the section and their own knowledge surrounding it. They should add a definition next to each related word.

L4 Challenge Have students read *Enrichment: The Berlin Wall* to learn more about the effect of the Berlin Wall on Germany.

 Practice: myWorld Activity Students will exercise free speech by creating a protest poster to display on the Berlin Wall. **Step-by-Step Instructions** and **More Activities** follow on p. T74.

SECTION 5 RESOURCE GUIDE

FOR THE STUDENT

my worldgeography.com Student Center

- Active Atlas

Student Edition (print and online)
- Rebuilding and New Challenges

Student Journal (print and online)
- Section 5 Word Wise
- Section 5 Take Notes

21st Century Learning Online Tutor

- Identify Main Ideas and Details
- Generate New Ideas

FOR THE TEACHER

my worldgeography.com Teacher Center

- Online Lesson Planner
- Presentations for Projection
- SuccessTracker

ProGuide: Europe and Russia
- Section 5 Lesson Plan, pp. T72–T73
- 🏃 myWorld Activity Step-by-Step Instructions, p. T74
- Activity Support: Mottos and Symbols, p. T75
- myWorld Geography Enrichment, p. T76
- Section Quiz, p. T77

Accelerating the Progress of ELLs
- Reading Support Strategies, p. 42

---

3 Understand
Assess understanding

Review Review *Word Wise* and *Take Notes* in the Student Journal.

Assess Knowledge and Skills Use the Section Assessment and Section Quiz to check students' progress.

Assess Understanding Review students' responses to the Section Assessment Essential Question prompt.

Remediate Use these strategies to review and remediate.

If students struggle to . . .	Try these strategies.
Explain how Germany came to be reunified	Guide students in creating a cause-and-effect diagram or timeline showing steps to reunification.
Understand the relationship between the European Union and its member nations	Use the analogy of its being like a "United States of Europe," also explaining key differences.
Generate new ideas while designing their poster	Assign additional practice with the **21st Century Online Tutor.**

ELL Support

ELL Objective Students will be able to use the terms *eastern* and *western* to discuss patterns of European history.

Cultural Connections Ask students to think of an important event from U.S. history or the history of their family's homeland. Let them use their home languages to tell what happened. If the event has a special name, such as "Fall of the Berlin Wall," ask them to translate it into English and share it with the class.

ELL Beginner Content Tip Give pairs of students notecards with the names of countries mentioned in this section. Have the pairs divide the cards into two piles: Eastern Europe and Western Europe.

ELL Activity Give students the following models to use in writing mottos for their Berlin Wall posters. Suggest that partners try different words from the table on *Activity Support: Mottos and Symbols* until they think the sentences make sense: *We want _____! Down with _____! _____ must be stopped!* **(Verbal)**

myWorld Activity   **Step-by-Step Instructions**   ⏱ **20 min**

Tear Down This Wall

OBJECTIVES

Students will

- generate new ideas to design a protest poster for the Berlin Wall.
- explain the significance of their design to the class.

LEARNING STYLE

- Visual
- Verbal

21st Century Learning

- Generate New Ideas

MATERIALS

- Activity Support: Mottos and Symbols, p. T75
- Colored markers or pencils
- Glue or tape
- Blank paper or white cardboard

Activity Steps

1. Explain to students that while the Berlin Wall remained standing, it was a symbol of the Cold War. In democratic West Berlin, people had free speech, so they were able to write and speak out against communism and the division of their country. The people of East Berlin could not do so without risking arrest.

   ELL **Advanced** The word *protest* is made of the prefix *pro-*, which means "forth" and *-test*, which comes from a Latin root meaning "to declare something as true." Have students look up the related words *attest* and *testimony*.

2. Tell students that they have the chance to design a protest poster to display on the Berlin Wall. First they should use the questions on *Activity Support:*

Mottos and Symbols to plan their poster. Then they can draw their design on their own paper. Remind students that on an effective poster, drawings and mottos should be large enough to be read from a distance. Using too many words or pictures will make the poster too busy.

L1 **Special Needs** Using mural paper, make one large banner as a class. Let each student write slogan words and draw symbols to create a class collage of protest.

3. After students have completed their designs, have them show the drawings to the class. Ask, Why did you choose those mottos and symbols? How does the design relate to the situation in Berlin during the Cold War?

More Activities From myWorld Teachers

Local Connection Tell students that a wall has divided your community, and identify a street that it runs along. Make a class list of businesses, public facilities, and landmarks in the forbidden zone. Ask students to write letters to officials explaining how the wall affects them based on where they live. **(Verbal)**

Assessing Gorbachev Have pairs of students design a political cartoon that expresses an opinion

about Mikhail Gorbachev's long-term impact on the Soviet Union. **(Logical/Visual)**

Big Business Have groups of students form a multinational corporation that will purchase both U.S. and European businesses. Students should decide what types of businesses they want to buy. Then they should design a brochure trying to persuade investors to buy stock in the corporation. **(Logical/Verbal)**

my worldgeography.com   **Teacher Center**   →   Find additional resources in the online Teacher Center.

Name _____ Class _____ Date _____

myWorld Activity Support   **Mottos and Symbols**

Tear Down This Wall

Directions One difference that existed between East Germany and West Germany was freedom of speech. West Germans could take part in protests. If East Germans protested government actions, they were arrested. West Germans used their freedom to cover the west side of the Berlin Wall with protests. Work with your partner to design a protest poster that could have been displayed on the Berlin Wall.

1. What will your poster say? Will it criticize communist rule or the division of Germany? Will it urge East Germans to fight for freedom?

_____

_____

2. Write a motto—a short, powerful phrase—to express your message.

_____

_____

3. What visual symbols could you use to express your message? Use your own ideas or symbols from the table below.

_____

_____

4. Draw the poster on your own paper or posterboard. Write the motto neatly, and use correct spelling and grammar.

IDEA	SYMBOL
Peace	dove, peace sign
Power	guns, fists, soldiers
Oppression	tank, stomping boot, chains
Separation	barbed wire, fence
Unity	clasped hands, bridge
Hope	rainbow, rising sun
Freedom	flying bird, broken chain
Germany	map, flag, eagle

Name _____ Class _____ Date _____

Enrichment: The Berlin Wall

Directions Read the article below. Answer the questions that follow.

After World War II, Germany was divided into two countries. East Germany was communist, while West Germany was democratic. The division caused many Germans to be separated from family members. The city of Berlin was located deep inside East Germany. Berlin was divided into two zones. East Berlin belonged to East Germany, and West Berlin belonged to West Germany. People from West Berlin could travel freely to the West.

Between 1949 and 1961, about 2.5 million people left East Germany by going to West Berlin. Among those who escaped were skilled workers, professionals, and educated people. As a result, East Germany lost skills and knowledge. That hurt the economy. To stop further escapes, the East German government built a temporary wall between the two halves of the city. The wall went up on the night of August 12–13, 1961.

Over time, the government replaced the temporary wall with a permanent wall. It stood 15 feet high in places. The wall between the two parts of the city was 28 miles long. The government also built a 75-mile wall all around the outside border of West Berlin. In spite of the wall, about 5,000 people managed to cross to freedom. However, guards arrested another 5,000 and killed 191 people trying to escape.

Democratic revolutions swept Europe in 1989. In response to protests, the East German government announced it would open borders with West Germany. Germans rushed to the wall and began to tear it down with pickaxes. The government sent bulldozers to knock part of the wall down. For the first time in 28 years, Germans from both sides of the border could cross freely. Soon afterward, the countries reunited.

1. Why did the East German government want to stop people from migrating to West Germany?

   _____

2. What does the high number of people who left East Germany tell you about the quality of life there?

   _____

3. Why do you think Germans were so eager to tear down the wall that they started to dismantle it themselves?

   _____

Name _____ Class _____ Date _____

Section Quiz

Directions Answer the following questions using what you learned
in Section 5.

1. _____ The U.S. program to help European
countries rebuild after the war was called
  a. the Berlin airlift.
  b. the Marshall Plan.
  c. the North Atlantic Treaty Organization.
  d. the Warsaw Pact.

2. _____ Which city was divided into
two zones, one communist and one
noncommunist?
  a. Berlin
  b. Moscow
  c. Prague
  d. Warsaw

3. _____ Which two countries did the Soviet
Union invade to crush anticommunist
rebellions?
  a. Czechoslovakia and Austria
  b. Czechoslovakia and Hungary
  c. Hungary and Poland
  d. Poland and Romania

4. Why did France and West Germany start
to build a political and economic union
in Europe?
  a. They wanted a strong alliance to attack
the Soviet Union.
  b. They wanted to protect themselves
from another Great Depression.
  c. They wanted to prevent their two
countries from starting another war.
  d. They wanted to make an alliance that
would rival NATO.

5. What was the Maastricht Treaty?
  a. the agreement that reunified Germany
  b. the agreement that made the
European Union
  c. the agreement that founded the
Warsaw Pact
  d. the agreement that established NATO

6. Use the graphic organizer below to record events that led to the
reunification of Germany.

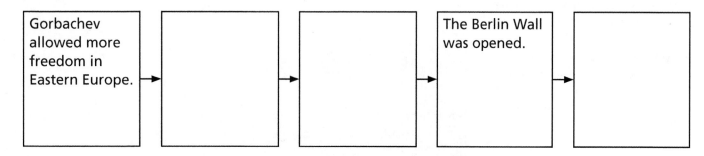

Gorbachev allowed more freedom in Eastern Europe.	→		→		→	The Berlin Wall was opened.	→	

   T77

SECTION PREVIEW

- Model preparing to read by previewing the Key Ideas, Key Terms, headings, visuals, and captions. Have students make predictions about what they will learn. For ELL support, post the prompt, "I predict I will read about . . ."

- Preview and practice identifying main ideas and details by using the examples of main roads and side streets in your community.

- Preteach this section's high-use Academic Vocabulary and Key Terms using the table on the next page and in-text definitions. Have students practice Key Terms by completing the *Word Wise* page in their journals.

GUIDE ON THE SIDE

Reading Skill

Identify Main Ideas and Details While they read, have students practice this skill by completing the *Take Notes* graphic organizer in the **Student Journal.**

Cold War and Division

- **Categorize** Where did the Soviet Union install communist governments? (in Eastern Europe)

- **Identify Main Ideas** Why did the United States and Britain distrust the Soviet Union? (They did not want the Soviet Union to spread communism.)

- **Synthesize** Judging from the photograph and what you read in Section 4, what did European nations use Marshall Plan funds for? (Samples: rebuilding, food, medical help)

Section 5

Rebuilding and New Challenges

Key Ideas
- After World War II, the Cold War divided Europe between the democratic West and the communist East.
- Western European nations joined together in the late 1900s to promote free trade and peaceful interaction.
- When communism collapsed in the Soviet Union, Eastern Europe adopted democracy and Germany reunified.

Key Terms • Cold War • Marshall Plan • Berlin Wall • European Union (EU)

 Visual Glossary

Reading Skill: Identify Main Ideas and Details Take notes using the graphic organizer in your journal.

When World War II ended, Soviet troops occupied most of Eastern Europe. The Soviet Union set up communist governments there. U.S. troops backed democratic governments in Western Europe.

Cold War and Division

The United States and Britain wanted to stop the Soviet Union from spreading communism. The result was the **Cold War,** a long period of hostility between the Soviet Union and the democratic West.

To encourage democracy and oppose communism, the United States created the **Marshall Plan,** a U.S. recovery plan that offered money to help European countries recover from the war. This money helped Western Europe rebuild.

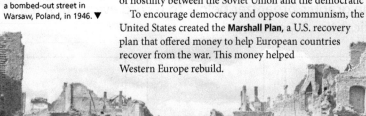

A woman walks down a bombed-out street in Warsaw, Poland, in 1946. ▼

ANSWERS

High-Use Word	Definition and Sample Sentence
symbolize	*v.* to represent or express something *To many people, the bald eagle symbolizes the United States.*
transfer	*n.* a carrying over of something from one situation to another *Whenever a new president is elected, the government goes through a transfer of power.*

International Cooperation After World War II, many nations joined together to form the United Nations (UN). The UN's main task was to safeguard world peace. The UN later went on to help people cope with disasters and poverty.

The Berlin Wall Goes Up The Cold War divided Europe between Soviet-controlled, communist Eastern Europe and democratic Western Europe, mostly allied with the United States. This split ran roughly along the line where the troops of the Western Allies met the Soviet troops at the end of World War II.

This dividing line ran right through the center of Germany. The Soviets occupied East Germany, which became communist. West Germany, occupied by the Western Allies, became a democracy.

The Soviets and Western Allies also divided Germany's capital, Berlin, located within East Germany. In 1948, the Soviets blocked land and sea access to West Berlin. The United States and Britain flew supplies into Berlin for 11 months until the Soviets lifted the blockade.

About 2.5 million East Germans fled to the West by crossing into West Berlin. In 1961, East Germany built a wall around West Berlin to prevent escapes. The **Berlin Wall** <u>symbolized</u> Cold War divisions.

The Democratic West Unites Helped by American aid, Western Europe's economy recovered quickly. By 1951, factories were producing more than ever. Nations such as Italy adopted democracy. Meanwhile, European nations were forced to give up their colonies. For example, Britain made India and other colonies independent.

▲ This 1962 nuclear explosion at a U.S. testing site was part of a Cold War arms race with the Soviet Union.

In 1949, the United States and Western European countries formed a military alliance called the North Atlantic Treaty Organization (NATO). The United States was NATO's strongest member. After the war, the United States and the Soviet Union became the world's dominant nations, or superpowers.

Communists Control the East The Soviet Union viewed Eastern European countries as satellites, or dependent countries. In response to NATO, the Soviet Union and its satellites formed a military alliance called the Warsaw Pact in 1955. Eastern Europe had weak, state-controlled economies.

The Soviets often used force to control Eastern Europe. In 1956, Soviet forces invaded Hungary and blocked democratic change. In 1968, Soviet troops crushed a reform movement in Czechoslovakia.

symbolize, *v.,* to represent or express something

Reading Check **How did the Soviet Union gain and keep control of Eastern Europe?**

- **Draw Conclusions** How did its location make West Berlin vulnerable? (It was surrounded by communist East Germany.)

- **Identify Main Ideas** What were the two competing alliances in Europe? (NATO, which included the United States and Western Europe, and the Warsaw Pact, which included the Soviet Union and Eastern Europe)

- **Cause and Effect** How did the Soviet Union prevent democratic reform in Eastern Europe? (by using armed force)

READING CHECK It gained control during World War II when it moved from the east to invade Germany. It kept control by setting up communist governments and using force.

PRIMARY SOURCE

The Iron Curtain "From Stettin in the Baltic to Trieste in the Adriatic an iron curtain has descended across the Continent. Behind that line lie all the capitals of the ancient states of Central and Eastern Europe. Warsaw, Berlin, Prague, Vienna, Budapest, Belgrade, Bucharest and Sofia; all these famous cities and the populations around them lie in what I must call the Soviet sphere, and all are subject, in one form or another, not only to Soviet influence but to a very high and in some cases increasing measure of control from Moscow."

—Winston Churchill, "Iron Curtain Speech," March 5, 1946

GUIDE ON THE SIDE

Closer Look

Divided Europe

Analyze Sources What do you think Churchill wanted to convey with the phrase *an iron curtain*? (Sample: a barrier that people could not pass through)

Map Skills Discuss the map.

- How did Norway differ from its Scandinavian neighbors? (It joined NATO.)

⊙ **Active Atlas**

Have students go to myworldgeography.com to learn more about divided Europe.

Closer Look

In 1946, Winston Churchill, former British prime minister, said "[A]n iron curtain has descended across the Continent." During the Cold War, the Iron Curtain was a fortified set of defenses between the democratic west and the communist east. East of the Iron Curtain, West Berlin was surrounded by the Berlin Wall, a concrete barrier that prevented East Germans from moving to democratic West Berlin.

THINK CRITICALLY **How might Germans have felt about the Iron Curtain?**

Map Skills

1. **Location** What nation was divided by the Iron Curtain?

2. **Places to Know!** Label these places on the outline map in your Student Journal: Romania, Belgium, Greece, Portugal, Italy.

Divided Europe

KEY
- NATO, 1957
- Warsaw Pact, 1957
- Iron Curtain

0 ____ 400 mi
0 ____ 400 km
Lambert Conformal Conic projection

ICELAND
FINLAND
SWEDEN
NORWAY
SOVIET UNION
North Sea
UNITED KINGDOM
DENMARK
IRELAND
NETHERLANDS
POLAND
BELGIUM
EAST GERMANY
ATLANTIC OCEAN
LUXEMBOURG
WEST GERMANY
CZECHOSLOVAKIA
FRANCE
AUSTRIA
HUNGARY
SWITZERLAND
ROMANIA
Black Sea
YUGOSLAVIA
ITALY
BULGARIA
PORTUGAL
SPAIN
ALBANIA
TURKEY
GREECE
Mediterranean Sea

Below, Greek children receive food supplied by the Marshall Plan. At right, construction of the Berlin Wall begins in 1961.

THINK CRITICALLY Samples: They may have been angry that their country was divided. They may have feared that the communists would cross the "Iron Curtain" and take over West Germany too.

MAP SKILLS 1. Germany **2.** Students should correctly label places on the outline map in their **Student Journal.**

CORE CONCEPTS: CONFLICT AND COOPERATION

Review Core Concept 8.4 before reading about the European Union. Remind students that the purpose of treaties is sometimes to end wars and sometimes to form alliances or to forge international agreements. Review different international organizations that students are familiar with, such as the United Nations.

Ask, What is the purpose of such organizations? Then remind students that conflict between Germany and France contributed to the two world wars that were fought in the twentieth century. Ask, What might Germany and France do to promote cooperation rather than conflict between their two countries?

GUIDE ON THE SIDE

The European Union

Long-standing hostility between Germany and France played a role in fueling Europe's wars. After World War II, West German and French leaders searched for a way to exist in peace.

Forming a Community In 1951, France and West Germany agreed to coordinate their coal and steel production. This would tie the countries economically and help to prevent future wars. Italy, Belgium, Luxembourg, and the Netherlands also signed the agreement.

In 1957, those six countries formed the European Economic Community, or Common Market. This was a free trade zone. It let manufactured goods and services move freely among the countries. Trade increased dramatically.

Toward a Unified Europe Six more countries had joined the Common Market by 1986. The Common Market nations signed the Maastricht Treaty in 1992. This treaty created the **European Union (EU)**, an economic and political partnership. Starting in 1995, an open-borders policy allowed people to move freely among many EU nations.

In 2002, most EU nations adopted a single currency called the euro. A currency is a unit of money, like the dollar. Sharing a common currency made trade easier. However, some countries rejected the euro so that they could keep control of their money. In 2003, a treaty let Eastern European countries join the EU. By 2008, the EU had grown to include 27 nations.

Reading Check **Why did West Germany and France form a common market?**

Democracy Spreads East

By the 1980s, communism was failing. Weak Soviet and Eastern European economies could not compete with Western market economies.

Communism Fails In Eastern Europe, government officials planned what farms should grow and what factories should produce. Officials made decisions based on the state's wishes rather than people's needs. For example, they made tanks instead of home appliances. Second, people had no motive to work hard because the government limited their pay. As a result of these two problems, communist countries often had shortages of food and consumer goods.

European Economic Community

NETHERLANDS

BELGIUM WEST GERMANY

LUXEMBOURG

FRANCE

ITALY

KEY
European Economic Community, 1957
National border, 1957

0   200 mi
0   200 km
Lambert Conformal Conic Projection

The European Union

- **Infer** How would a free trade zone help prevent wars? (Each member country would depend economically on the others.)

- **Identify Main Ideas** What group joined the EU, causing it to grow rapidly after 2003? (Eastern European countries)

Democracy Spreads East

- **Cause and Effect** Why did the Soviet Union often have shortages of food and consumer goods? (inefficient central planning and poorly motivated workers)

Analyze Maps Have students examine the map of the European economic community.

- Which founding country was the smallest? (Luxembourg)

READING CHECK Hostility between the two countries had fueled the two world wars, so they thought becoming economically dependent on each other would help keep the peace.

ANSWERS

GOVERNMENT

A New EU Constitution As the EU expanded, its leaders realized that the alliance's original structures were inadequate to unite more than 20 nations. In 2002, a group headed by former French president Valéry Giscard d'Estaing began to draft a new constitution. The process sparked controversies, such as how to distribute power among large and small nations and whether to include mention of Europe's Christian heritage. The draft constitution was finished in 2004 and submitted to member states for ratification. In 2005, voters in the Netherlands and France rejected the constitution. All members had to accept the constitution for it to go into effect. In 2007, a reform treaty, which was intended to replace the failed constitution, was signed and submitted to member states. In June 2008, Irish voters rejected it, halting the process once again.

GUIDE ON THE SIDE

- **Identify Details** What reforms did Mikhail Gorbachev introduce? (He loosened government control in the Soviet Union and allowed Eastern Europe more democracy and freedom.)

- **Summarize** How did Poland become an example of democratic reform to the rest of Eastern Europe? (A Polish union demanded free elections, which led to the end of communist rule in Poland. This example inspired other nations to overthrow their communist governments.)

- **Categorize** What other countries besides Poland threw off communist rule? (Czechoslovakia, Romania, Hungary, Bulgaria, East Germany)

Analyze Visuals Have students examine the paired photographs.

- Why do you think the Hungarians toppled Stalin's statue? (He represented Soviet oppression.)

 myWorld Activity

Tear Down This Wall Find Step-by-Step Instructions and an Activity Support on pp. T74–T75. **(Visual/Verbal)**

---

transfer, *n.,* a carrying over of something from one situation to another

myWorld Activity
Tear Down This Wall

Left, people pass the head of a Soviet ruler broken from a statue during the 1956 uprising in Hungary; at right, a volunteer collects money for the Polish Solidarity party.

In 1985, Mikhail Gorbachev became the new leader of the Soviet Union. Gorbachev was younger than other leaders and more open to change. In the late 1980s, Gorbachev began to loosen government control within the Soviet Union. He supported greater democracy, particularly in the Soviet satellites of Eastern Europe. Gorbachev also gave Eastern European countries more freedom to choose their own way.

A Democratic Revolution Spreads In 1980, a Polish shipyard workers' union called Solidarity went on strike. The Polish government granted some union demands and the union head, Lech Walesa (lek vah WEN suh), became a hero. Solidarity went on strike again in 1988. In response to the strike, the government agreed to hold free elections. Voters courageously chose Solidarity candidates over communist candidates, ending communist rule in Poland.

Poland's example inspired other countries. In Czechoslovakia, thousands of people protested the communist government in 1989. In response to the protests, the government agreed to give up power. This peaceful transfer of power is known as the Velvet Revolution. In free elections later that year, Czechoslovakians elected writer Vaclav Havel (VAHTS lahv HAH vul) president. Havel described his people's experience.

> 66 People have passed through a very dark tunnel at the end of which there was a light of freedom. 99
> —Vaclav Havel, 1990

Romania overthrew its communist government in 1989, but its communist dictator killed many protesters before giving up power. Hungary's Communist Party went out of existence, and in 1990 the country elected a non-communist government. Bulgaria also held its first free elections in 1990.

Germany Reunifies During 1989, East Germans began protesting for democratic change. East Germany's communist government at first refused to make changes. The government then began to respond to some protester demands.

Finally, on November 9, 1989, East German border guards opened the gates of the Berlin Wall. East and West Germans rushed to greet each other.

Demands for reform led to free elections, which removed the communist government from power in 1989. A year later, on October 3, 1990, the two halves of Germany were reunified.

PRIMARY SOURCE

The Fall of the Berlin Wall "After a while, we walked to Potsdammer Platz. This used to be the center of Berlin. All traffic once passed through the Potsdammer Platz. Now it was a large empty field, bisected by the wall. . . . It was still very dark and cold at 5 A.M. Perhaps 7,000 people were pressed together, shouting, cheering, clapping. We pushed through the crowd. From the East German side we could hear the sound of heavy machines. With a giant drill, they were punching holes in the wall. Every time a drill poked through, everyone cheered. The banks of klieg lights would come on. People shot off fireworks and emergency flares and rescue rockets. Many were using hammers to chip away at the wall. There were countless holes."

—Andreas Ramos, an American eyewitness, in the personal essay "The Fall of the Berlin Wall"

GUIDE ON THE SIDE

The Soviet Union Falls Nationalism and the desire for reform rocked the Soviet Union. In 1990, the Soviet republic of Lithuania demanded independence. The Soviet army invaded Lithuania.

Soviet citizens took to the streets to protest the invasion. The army refused to fight the people. In 1991, the Soviet Union broke apart into 15 new nations, including Moldova, Ukraine, Belarus, Lithuania, Latvia, and Estonia in Eastern Europe. The largest post-Soviet nation was Russia.

Reading Check How did Eastern Europe gain freedom from communism?

▲ In this 1990 political cartoon, Soviet leader Mikhail Gorbachev is pictured as Humpty Dumpty sitting on a crumbling wall with the symbol of the Soviet Union. *What does this cartoon mean?*

THE WALL COMES DOWN

During the late 1980s, communist governments across Eastern Europe followed the lead of the Soviet Union. They began to allow their opponents to speak more freely. Some scheduled free elections. East Germany's government resisted these changes. In the fall of 1989, however, East German people began to hold peaceful protests. The protesters said they wanted democracy. East German leaders knew that the Soviet Union was no longer willing to put down peaceful protests. When border guards opened the Berlin Wall on November 9, 1989, Germans on both sides began to knock it down.

❝ **We are the people!** ❞
—Chant of East German democracy protesters, 1989

- **Identify Main Ideas** What role did nationalism play in the fall of the Soviet Union? (The Soviet republic of Lithuania demanded independence, and eventually the Soviet Union broke apart into 15 nations.)
- **Compare and Contrast** In what way did the calls for reform bring about opposite results in Germany and the Soviet Union? (Germany reunified; the Soviet Union disbanded.)

Analyze Visuals Have students examine the Gorbachev cartoon and the photograph of the Berlin Wall.

- What is happening to the wall in the cartoon? (It is cracking apart.)
- In the photograph, is the man hammering the wall a civilian or a soldier? (a civilian)

READING CHECK Soviet leader Gorbachev encouraged more democracy and freedom. Protests led to elections in which the people voted out communist governments.

CAPTION Sample: During Gorbachev's term in office, the Soviet Union began to crack apart.

HISTORY

Basque Separatists Al-Qaeda has not been the only terrorist group to attack Madrid. The ETA, a group fighting for an independent Basque state, has also claimed responsibility for bombings. About 850,000 Basques live in Spain with another 130,000 in southern France. They speak a non-Indo-European language that is a remnant of the languages spoken in southwest Europe before Roman conquest. In 1895, the Basque

Nationalist political party formed. In 1959, some young people broke away and formed the ETA because the Basque Nationalists refused to take up armed struggle. In the decade since, the ETA has committed many acts of sabotage, assassination, kidnapping, robbery, and extortion. One of its most recent terrorist acts was a bombing of the Madrid international airport in 2006.

GUIDE ON THE SIDE

▲ In 2004, terrorists bombed this train in Spain. In the inset, a London man reads about the 2005 terrorist bombings in that city.

Europe Faces Challenges

- **Categorize** What qualifications did Eastern European nations need to join the EU? (democratic governments and strong market economies)

- **Problem Solve** What leftover problems from communism made it difficult to develop democracy? (corruption and lack of trust for leaders)

- **Summarize** What gave Eastern Europeans the new right to move to Western Europe for work? (EU membership)

Analyze Visuals Have students examine the photograph of the Madrid bombings.

- Why do you think terrorists would choose a commuter train as target? (It can carry a lot of people.)

Europe Faces Challenges

After reunifying, Germany struggled economically. East German factories were outdated and inefficent, and many went out of business. Unemployment soared in eastern Germany. Some citizens failed to adapt to the market economy, which required initiative and hard work.

Integrating the East After the collapse of communism, Europe worked to rebuild ties between East and West. The EU opened membership to Eastern European nations who could show that they had democratic governments and strong market economies. Most eastern nations had to make reforms before joining the EU. Even so, their economies often remained weak due to problems similar to those in eastern Germany.

Communist rule had not prepared people for democracy either. Many people in formerly communist lands did not trust their leaders. Government corruption had been widespread under communist rule and remained a problem.

International Issues In the late 1900s, a global economy developed as foreign trade and multinational corporations grew. The EU began to consider issues such as free trade with nonmember nations.

Incidents of international terrorism also scarred Europe. In 2004, the terrorist group al-Qaeda exploded bombs on commuter trains in Madrid, Spain, killing nearly 200. Afterward, European countries worked together to fight terrorism.

Immigration was another challenge. When Eastern European countries joined the EU, thousands of Eastern Europeans moved to western European countries for work. Many Western Europeans resented the newcomers. In addition, immigrants from Africa and Asia, some of them illegal, poured into Europe. Some Europeans began to fear that immigrants would take their jobs. Europeans and their leaders had to find ways to accommodate growing populations with customs and languages from outside of Europe.

READING CHECK Communist states used inefficient central planning and had outdated equipment. People who lived in formerly communist states have had a hard time adapting to the market economy.

SECTION 5 ASSESSMENT **1.** The Cold War grew from the wartime Soviet occupation of Eastern Europe. The Marshall Plan gave aid to war-torn countries. The Berlin Wall divided postwar Berlin. The EU was founded to prevent another war. **2.** The EU is an economic and political partnership. **3.** It wanted to spread

GEOGRAPHY

The Immigration Debate Many geographic factors influence the debate over immigration in Europe. One factor is the ease with which illegal immigrants enter Southern Europe. For example, only eight miles separate Spain from Africa at the closest point. As a result, hundreds of Africans try to make the crossing in secret each year, and many die because they travel in unsafe boats. Estimates of illegal immigrants in the EU range from 4.5 to 8 million. On the other hand, Europe may soon feel the need for immigrants as laborers. Countries such as Germany, Italy, Poland, and Spain have low birth rates and may face a labor shortage as their population ages and leaves the workforce.

Wind farms such as this one off the coast of Denmark make Europe a world leader in alternative energy sources.

Energy and the Environment Because of its industry, Europe has long fought pollution. For example, it has tried to reduce the air pollution that causes acid rain, which kills forests. The EU also signed the Kyoto Protocol, an agreement to reduce the emission of greenhouse gases that contribute to climate change.

Europe also aims to reduce its dependence on foreign oil. The EU is trying to reduce energy consumption, switch to cleaner forms of transportation, and use renewable energy such as wind and bio-fuels.

Reading Check What economic challenges did Eastern Europe face after the collapse of communism?

Section 5 Assessment

Key Terms

1. Using complete sentences, describe how each of the following terms relates to consequences from World War II: Cold War, Marshall Plan, Berlin Wall, European Union.

Key Ideas

2. What kind of partnership is the European Union?

3. Why did the Soviet Union set up communist states in Eastern Europe?

4. Which two countries began the movement to create a European Union and why?

5. How did change in the Soviet Union clear the way for democracy in Eastern Europe?

Think Critically

6. **Draw Conclusions** Why did Western Europe develop stronger economies than Eastern Europe?

7. **Make Decisions** What decisions do you think the German government could make to improve the economy of the former East Germany?

? Essential Question

What makes a nation?

8. Why do you think East and West Germans still felt that they belonged to a single nation even after more than 40 years apart? Go to your Student Journal to record your answer.

Democracy in Eastern Europe

OBJECTIVES
Students will

- make connections between important documents and the development of democracy in Eastern Europe.
- **21st Century Learning** synthesize information from the speeches of two European leaders.
- **ELL** be able to understand and write similes.

SET EXPECTATIONS
In this lesson, students will

- read and analyze two documents on Eastern Europe's struggle for democracy.
- write an introductory paragraph for an essay on democracy in Eastern Europe.

1 Connect

Provide the following examples: 1. a large school with many separate classrooms under the direction of one principal and 2. a small club that a young person starts with his or her friends. Ask, Which of these is more likely to be run as a democracy? (club) Which of these is more like an empire? (school) Discuss reasons why large empires are more likely to have autocratic rule than democratic rule. Then explain to students that they are going to read about two Eastern European nations that were once small regions within vast empires. In each case, they fought to gain independence and democratic government.

2 Learn

Preview Have students preview the two pages and identify the two speakers and their respective countries. Read the Key Idea, glossary terms, and definitions. Clarify any questions about the meaning of these words by providing examples.

Read Slowly read aloud the excerpt from "Speech at the Pittsburg Banquet" without stopping. Read the document again, this time stopping to read the questions at the left and prompt students to rethink and analyze the meaning of the words. Have students answer the questions using the location of the letters to provide clues. Do the same for the excerpt from "New Year's Address to the Nation." Lead a discussion starting with students' responses to the questions. Ask, When were these two speeches given, and who was the audience for each one?

ELL **Advanced** Explain that in the first speech, they will read a simile, which is a comparison between two different things. Give them an example—*Her hair is like black silk*—and ask what hair and silk have in common. Let them practice writing similes with this model: "A _____ is like a _____."

 myWorld Activity: Outline an **Introductory Paragraph** Distribute the *Activity Support: Outline Form* to students and have them choose a partner. Tell them to use information from the primary sources to create an outline for their response to **Analyze the Documents:** Write Introductions.

20 min

3 Understand

Review Go back to the Key Idea. Discuss with students how each writer presented the struggle of Eastern European nations to throw off the empires that ruled them and establish democracy.

Assess Have students complete **Analyze the Documents.** Review their answers to determine if students have met the lesson objectives.

Remediate If students struggle to synthesize the two speeches, have them use details from the speeches to complete a flowchart that has three boxes: Obstacles to Democracy; Price Paid for Democracy; and What the Speakers Want Listeners to Do.

Name _____ Class _____ Date _____

myWorld Activity Support   Outline Form

Outline an Introductory Paragraph

Directions Use information from the speeches by Lajos Kossuth and Vaclav Havel to answer the questions below. Then use the form beneath the questions to plan your introductory paragraph for Analyze the Documents: Write Introductions. Choose details from each of the excerpts to include in your paragraph.

Draw Conclusions

1. What was similar about the forces that tried to prevent Hungary and Czechoslovakia from becoming democratic?

_____

2. Judging from the dates of these speeches, how long did Eastern Europe struggle to gain democracy?

_____

Outline Your Paragraph

A. First, capture the reader's attention with a hook. Choose a quotation or an interesting fact from one of the excerpts.

Hook _____

_____

B. Decide on a main idea for your essay about Eastern Europe. For example, you might want to focus on the difficulty of achieving democracy. Write a thesis statement that expresses the main idea of your essay.

Thesis Statement _____

_____

C. Think of three supporting points that will help to prove your main idea. Each point will become the topic of a body paragraph. Use information from the two excerpts to help you decide on supporting points.

1. _____

2. _____

3. _____

QUICK FACTS

A Unique Country Hungary has several cultural and historical reasons for feeling separate from its Eastern European neighbors. The people of Hungary speak a language that is unrelated to the Germanic, Romance, and Slavic languages that dominate Europe. Hungary was an independent nation for more than six centuries (892 to 1526)—the only nation in its region to maintain independence so long. Even after Hungary became part of the Ottoman and later Hapsburg empires, Hungarians retained a sense of their own unique identity. That sense of uniqueness persisted under communist rule.

GUIDE ON THE SIDE

Synthesize Use the lettered prompts to help students identify the most important ideas from each excerpt. Then ask what the ideas have in common.

ANSWERS

Ⓐ gaining independence from the Austrian Empire

Ⓑ Some people thought it wasn't worth worrying about because it was only one country; Kossuth's view was exactly the opposite.

Ⓒ Eating a salad is like conquering an empire. You can't do either one all at once. You have to do it piece by piece. "Leaf by leaf" refers to conquering one country at a time.

Primary Source

Democracy in Eastern Europe

Key Idea
- The people of Eastern Europe made great sacrifices to win independence and achieve freedom and democracy.

Democracy developed more slowly in Eastern Europe than in Western Europe. Large empires such as Russia and Austria controlled much of the region for centuries. The rulers of these empires did not allow the region's different peoples to form their own independent countries. In Hungary, the nationalist Lajos Kossuth (LAH yohsh KAW shoot) fought unsuccessfully to free his country from Austrian control during the revolutions of 1848. Vaclav Havel became president after Czechoslovakia threw off communist rule in 1989.

▲ Hungarian composer Béla Bartók fled the Nazi regime in 1940 to live in the United States.

Hungarian revolutionary Lajos Kossuth ▼

Stop at each letter on the right to think about the text. Then answer the question with the same letter on the left.

Ⓐ **Draw Conclusions** What was the Hungarian cause that Kossuth mentioned here?

Ⓑ **Compare Viewpoints** How did some other people view Hungary's cause? Explain how that compared to Kossuth's view.

Ⓒ **Identify Main Ideas and Details** What did Kossuth compare a salad to? Explain how the detail "leaf by leaf" relates to this idea.

consideration, *n.,* careful thought

despotism, *n.,* government by a ruler with absolute power

The Cause Of One Country

❝ I first heard my humble claims contradicted, by telling me that the **Ⓐ** cause of Hungary was not worthy of much <u>consideration</u>—because, **Ⓑ** after all, it is only the cause of one country. . . . Let me tell those who don't care about the violation of the law of nations in Hungary . . . let me tell them that the freedom and independence of the world is **Ⓒ** like the salad—not even the jaws of <u>despotism</u> can swallow at once— but only leaf by leaf. ❞

—Lajos Kossuth, "Speech at the Pittsburgh Banquet," 1852

To assist your students in synthesizing ideas from two different documents, use the scaffolded questions at the left of each excerpt. Urge students to notice similarities in the information and ideas in the two speeches. For example, both countries wanted to break free of domination by autocratic empires. Suggest that once students identify a common idea in the two speeches, they explore that idea's universal meaning. For example, students might identify the following universal idea: *Harsh autocratic rule cannot wipe out the human desire for self-rule.* For additional help, refer students to the **21st Century Online Tutor** *Synthesize.*

GUIDE ON THE SIDE

Stop at each letter on the right to think about the text. Then answer the question with the same letter on the left.

D **Categorize** What were some of the sacrifices people made to gain freedom?

E **Analyze Cause and Effect** Why did the government persecute some people?

F **Solve Problems** What do you think Czechs and Slovaks today can do to make sure past sacrifices are not forgotten?

perish, v., to die, especially a violent or early death

totalitarian, adj., describing a government in which a dictator or one political party has complete control of the country

persecute, v., to harass or subject to unfair treatment because of race, religion, ethnic origin, or political beliefs

The Price Of Freedom

❝ We had to pay, however, for our present freedom. Many citizens **D** perished in jails in the 1950s, many were executed, thousands of human lives were destroyed, hundreds of thousands of talented people were forced to leave the country. Those who defended the honor of our nations during the Second **E** World War, those who rebelled against totalitarian rule and those who simply managed to remain themselves and think freely, were **F** all persecuted. We should not forget any of those who paid for our present freedom in one way or another. ❞

—Vaclav Havel,
"New Year's Address to the Nation,"
January 1, 1990

ANSWERS

D imprisonment, death, having to leave their country

E The government persecuted those who rebelled against it.

F Samples: Write books about them, erect statues, and prosecute those who abused power.

Above, Czechoslovak president Vaclav Havel; below, demonstrators carry Czechoslovak flags in Prague during the Velvet Revolution in 1989.

Analyze the Documents

1. Synthesize According to Kossuth and Havel, what forces made it difficult to establish democracy in Eastern Europe?

2. Writing Task Write an opening paragraph on the topic *Eastern Europe's Fight for Democracy.* Include details from the two speeches in your paragraph. If you use a direct quote, be sure to format it correctly.

ANALYZE THE DOCUMENTS

1. despotism, totalitarianism

2. Answers will vary. Paragraphs should contain a topic sentence—such as "Eastern Europeans fought for more than a century to gain democracy"— supported by details from each speech. If students use direct quotations, the quotations should be in quotation marks and the authors should be cited.

1. Humanists encouraged secular study and stressed the importance of the individual. They encouraged people to think for themselves. This led to a questioning of church authority that paved the way for the Reformation.

2. Painting and sculpture became more realistic in appearance.

9. Italy had been the seat of the Roman Empire, so classical culture remained an influence. Italy's location made it good for trade, which helped it prosper and exposed it to many cultural influences.

10. It is an opinion because it expresses his belief, not something that can be proved.

11. The fighting spread from Europe overseas to other continents.

12. The two countries were hostile to each other and armed themselves to be able to destroy each other. They each tried to gain the most allies.

13. Sample: Intergrating the East is most important in order to prevent future conflicts between wealthy regions and those that are less prosperous.

3. Portugal sailed south, around the tip of Africa, and then northeast to India. Spain sailed west looking for Asia, but landed in the Americas instead.

4. The emphasis on studying nature and the willingness to question authority helped bring about the Scientific Revolution.

5. Workers began to move to cities for factory jobs, so cities grew rapidly.

6. Both led to the overthrow of monarchies and the establishment of new types of government that did not last long.

7. Empires broke apart and new nations were formed.

8. They were overjoyed. They rushed to greet each other.

Europe in Modern Times

Chapter Assessment

Key Terms and Ideas

1. **Discuss** How did **humanism** help lead to the Reformation?

2. **Summarize** In what ways did art change during the **Renaissance**?

3. **Compare and Contrast** What different routes did Portugal and Spain take when trying to find a way to reach Asia during the Age of Exploration?

4. **Recall** What Renaissance attitudes helped bring about the Scientific Revolution?

5. **Explain** How did the **Industrial Revolution** change where people lived?

6. **Compare and Contrast** What did the English Civil War and the **French Revolution** have in common?

7. **Explain** How did **World War I** change the map of central and eastern Europe?

8. **Describe** What emotions did East Germans and West Germans experience when the **Berlin Wall** was opened? How do you know?

Think Critically

9. **Draw Conclusions** How did geography contribute to Italy's role in beginning the Renaissance?

10. **Distinguish Between Fact and Opinion** Thomas Hobbes described life without strong government as "poor, nasty, brutish, and short." Is that a fact or an opinion? Explain.

11. **Identify Evidence** Use evidence from the text to describe how World War I was a global war.

12. **Drawing Inferences** How was the Cold War like a war even though the United States and the Soviet Union never engaged in battle?

13. **Problem Solving** Turn again to the last red heading in Section 5. Which of the problems described in the blue headings should be Europe's first priority? Support your answer with examples from the text.

Places to Know

For each place, write the letter from the map that shows its location.

14. **Berlin**
15. **London**
16. **Rome**
17. **Romania**
18. **Belgium**
19. **Constantinople**
20. **Portugal**
21. **Estimate** Using the scale bar, estimate how far fighter pilots flew between Berlin and London during World War II.

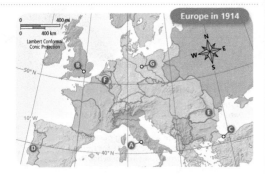

Europe in 1914

PLACES TO KNOW

14. G
15. B
16. A
17. E

18. F
19. C
20. D
21. about 580 miles

myWorld Chapter Activity

Technology: Then and Now Find Step-by-Step Instructions, Student Instructions and Rubric, and an Activity Support on T41–T43. **(Logical/Visual).**

Summarize Students' essays should state an opinion and support it with evidence such as data and quotations. To be effective, essays should also acknowledge opposing opinions and make an effort to refute them. If students need help with this skill, direct them to the online tutorial *Summarize*.

→ Online Assessment

Tailor review and assessment to each student's needs with an array of online assessments.
• Self-Test
• On Assignment Article or Slideshow
• Success Tracker

? Essential Question
myWorld Chapter Activity

Technology Then and Now Follow your teacher's instructions to examine different kinds of technology that developed in early modern Europe. This technology may be related to advances in science or medicine, warfare, industry, or transportation. At the time, these inventions were cutting-edge technology. Make an illustrated poster linking these examples of past technology to current examples of technology.

21st Century Learning
Communication

Summarize Write an essay arguing for or against adding new Eastern European members to the European Union. Include
• the benefits of adding these members
• the drawbacks of adding these members
• the economic and political impact of adding these members
• your opinion
• two reasons in support of your opinion

Document-Based Questions

Success ★ Tracker™
Online at myworldgeography.com

Use your knowledge of early modern Europe and Documents A and B to answer Questions 1–3.

Document A

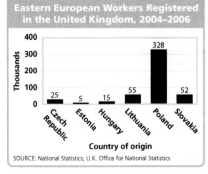

Eastern European Workers Registered in the United Kingdom, 2004–2006

Thousands (y-axis): 0, 100, 200, 300, 400

Czech Republic: 25
Estonia: 5
Hungary: 15
Lithuania: 55
Poland: 328
Slovakia: 52

Country of origin

SOURCE: National Statistics; U.K. Office for National Statistics

1. Which country shown here had the most workers registered in the United Kingdom?
A Estonia
B Latvia
C Poland
D Slovakia

Document B

" It's my dream to return to Poland, but not for 30 percent of my salary. So many have gone west [that] to return, they might not have to receive equal pay, but certainly more than now."

—Jacek Cukrowski,
"Where have all our migrants gone? Eastern Europe wants them back,"
Christian Science Monitor

2. What would convince Cukrowski to return to Poland?
A more salary than he earns in the West
B a better salary than Polish workers earn now
C exactly the same salary that Polish workers earn
D 30 percent of the salary that he earns in the West

3. Writing Task If Eastern Europeans keep moving to Western Europe for jobs, how might Eastern Europe's economy be affected? Explain.

WRITING TASK TIP

Analyze Cause and Effect Model how to give a balanced assessment by giving one positive and one negative effect. Show students how to do this for Western Europe. For example, a positive effect might be that irrigation of new people into Western Europe will increase sales of consumer goods, but a negative effect might be conflict between Easterners and Westerners over jobs. Direct students to describe how the economy of Eastern Europe might be similarly affected.

DOCUMENT-BASED QUESTIONS

1. C

2. B

3. Students should use data from Document A and the opinions expressed in Document B to draw the conclusion that many workers are leaving Eastern Europe. Then they should infer the impacts on Eastern Europe of that migration, such as money sent back to relatives in Eastern Europe and the loss of skills and knowledge as laborers flee west.

Plan With Understanding by Design*

Chapter Objectives
Begin With the End in Mind

Students will demonstrate the following enduring understandings:
- Joining international alliances can have advantages and disadvantages for member nations.
- Migration and trade often lead to cultural diffusion and cultural borrowing.
- Service industries and global trade are transforming modern economies.

Connect
Make Learning Meaningful

Student Edition
- **Essential Question** Is it better to be independent or interdependent?
- **myStory** Yasmin's life is shaped by her diverse Spanish, Pakistani, and Scandinavian heritages.

my worldgeography.com
myStory Online Get to know Yasmin through a video of her life and home.

Student Journal
Essential Question Preview

Experience
Teach Knowledge and Skills

Student Edition
- Read Sections 1, 2, 3, and 4.
- Answer Reading Checks and Section Assessment questions.

my worldgeography.com

On Assignment Active Atlas, Data Discovery, and Culture Close-up

Student Journal
- Sections 1, 2, 3, and 4 Word Wise
- Sections 1, 2, 3, and 4 Take Notes

Teacher's Edition
✗ myWorld Activities
- Section 1: Danube Cleanup, p. T88
- Section 2: Cradle to Grave?, p. T96
- Section 3: Make a Travel Poster, p. T102
- Section 4: Southern Europe's Neighbors, p. T110

21st Century Learning Online Tutor
- Read Physical Maps
- Work in Teams
- Compare and Contrast
- Analyze Cause and Effect

Understand
Assess Understanding

Assessment Booklet
- Chapter Tests   • Benchmark Tests

Teacher's Edition
✗ myWorld Chapter Activity Students analyze data about Norway, vote on Norway's membership in the European Union, and write a short essay explaining their position.

Student Journal
Essential Question Writer's Workshop

my worldgeography.com

On Assignment Students write and submit an article or a multimedia slideshow about independence and interdependence among Western European countries.

Success ☆ Tracker™
Online at myworldgeography.com
Administer chapter tests and remediate understanding.

Student Edition
Chapter Assessment

*"Understanding by Design" is registered as a trademark with the Patent and Trademark Office by the Association for Supervision of Curriculum Development (ASCD). ASCD has not authorized, approved or sponsored this work and is in no way affiliated with Pearson or its products.

Connect to the Essential Question

 Essential Question

Is it better to be independent or interdependent?

Use the Essential Question poster and follow these steps to help students understand the Essential Question.

Connect to Their Lives

1. Have students think of an area in their lives in which they are able to act on their own. (If students have already studied this Essential Question, encourage them to think of new examples.) What do they like about being independent? What do they dislike about it?

2. Have students think of an area in their lives in which they must depend on others. What do they like about being interdependent, and what do they dislike about it?

3. Post the following table for them to complete or have students turn to the Essential Question Preview page in their **Student Journal.**

	Advantages	Disadvantages
Independence		
Interdependence		

Connect to the Content

4. Now have students name areas in which countries act independently and areas in which countries act interdependently. Point out that some areas, such as fighting a war, can be done either independently or interdependently, depending on the circumstances.

5. Post the following Venn diagram on the board. Have students use it to record their ideas about areas of national independence and interdependence.

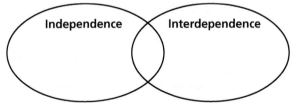
Independence   Interdependence

6. After previewing the chapter, have students make chapter-related predictions on the *Essential Question Preview* page in the **Student Journal.**

7. Remind students that they will answer a prompt related to the Essential Question on each section's *Take Notes* page in the **Student Journal.**

Explore my worldgeography.com

Welcome to myWorldGeography

http://www.myworldgeography.com

ON ASSIGNMENT: Western Europe

For this chapter's online mission, students will
- take a digital trip to Western Europe.
- take on the role of a journalist.
- gather notes, images, and data for their story throughout their journey.
- write an article or multimedia slideshow connecting the information and images gathered during their trip and this chapter's Essential Question: *Is it better to be independent or interdependent?*

ITINERARY

During their trip, students will make the following stops:

 myStory Video

Learn more from Yasmin about her family and her hobbies.

 Active Atlas

Read physical, political, and special purpose maps.

 Data Discovery

Gather data from charts and graphs about Western Europe.

 Culture Close-up

Explore a Gothic cathedral in Chartres, France.

While on their trip, students will practice the following skills:

- **Interpret** graphic representations of data.
- **Evaluate** the benefits of both independence and interdependence.
- **Synthesize** information into an interesting article.

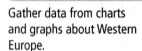
TakingITGlobal for Educators

Extend the reach of every lesson by helping students connect to a global community of young people with common interests and concerns. Visit myworldgeography.com to
- explore Country Pages relating to Western Europe.
- delve deeper into this chapter's Essential Question, *Is it better to be independent or interdependent?*
- find online alternatives to and solutions for the Unit Closer 21st Century Learning Activity.

my worldgeography.com

TEACHER CENTER

Preview and assign student materials, enrich your teaching, and track student progress with the following resources:
- Online Lesson Planning and Resource Library
- Presentations for Projection
- Online Teacher's Edition and Ancillaries
- Google Earth Links

Assess Enduring Understandings

 myWorld Chapter Activity   **Step-by-Step Instructions**   2 hr

Norway and the European Union

Teach this activity at the end of the chapter to assess enduring understandings.

OBJECTIVES

Students will demonstrate the following enduring understandings:

- Joining international alliances can have advantages and disadvantages for member nations.
- Migration and trade often lead to cultural diffusion and cultural borrowing.
- Service industries and global trade are transforming modern economies.

Students will provide the following evidence of understanding:

- Analysis Table about EU membership
- Position essay on EU Membership

LEARNING STYLES

- Visual
- Verbal
- Interpersonal

MATERIALS

- Activity Support: Student Instructions and Rubric, p. T84
- Activity Support: Analysis Table, p. T85
- Activity Cards: #55–60
    - 55. Control of Revenue
    - 56. Cultural Identity
    - 57. Sovereignty
    - 58. Protectionism
    - 59. Sustainable Resources
    - 60. Independence

Activity Steps

1. Set Expectations Explain that students will use six Activity Cards to determine advantages and disadvantages of EU membership for Norway. They will first study one source of data, then hear from other students about other data. They will complete an *Analysis Table Jigsaw* and write a short essay stating their position on membership. Review the activity rubric on the following page.

2. Analysis Table Jigsaw

- Divide the class into six groups to analyze specific data about control of revenue, cultural identity, sovereignty, protectionism, sustainable resources, or independence. Distribute one Activity Card to each group and give each student a copy of *Activity Support: Analysis Table*.

- In their first group, students discuss the data on the card and record their findings on the *Analysis Table* line for their topic. Each student should vote based on the data they have discussed so far.

- Rearrange students using a jigsaw. In this new group, students hear about the findings of other groups and fill out the rest of the *Analysis Table*.

L2 Extra Support Students might be confused by the rating scale and think that five is positive, or an advantage. Explain that the scale refers to the *strength* of both advantages and disadvantages. Give an example to make this clear.

3. Tally the Data Each student tallies scores for advantages and disadvantages. Tell students that even though their scores may indicate a certain trend, they may choose to disagree with the trend when they vote for or against EU membership. Each student should write his or her final individual vote on the Activity Support. Using a show of hands, then tally the votes of the entire class.

ELL Beginner/Early Intermediate Paraphrase the quotations on the Activity Cards into simpler language that students will understand.

4. Essay Each student writes a short essay about whether Norway should join the EU and why.

ELL Intermediate Students may opt to give a short speech stating their position instead of writing an essay.

Name _____ Class _____ Date _____

myWorld Chapter Activity Support   **Student Instructions and Rubric**

Norway and the European Union

Activity Instructions Read the following summary of your myWorld Chapter Activity. Follow your teacher's directions for more information.

1. Your group represents a particular interest group in Norway. You will be given a card with specialized data. Use the data to decide whether to support joining the European Union.

2. With your group, study the card and answer the questions on it. On your worksheet, write down one advantage and one disadvantage for membership as shown by the data. Score each one on a scale of 1 to 5. If the advantage or disadvantage is very strong, give it a 5. If it is weak, give it a 1.

3. The teacher will then rearrange the groups and you will hear about the data discussed in other groups. After this discussion, fill out the remaining lines on your worksheet as you did in Step 2. Complete each line with a group vote based on the new data.

4. At the bottom of the table, tally the scores for advantages and disadvantages. Check the box at the lower right with your vote.

5. Write a short essay describing your group's findings and vote. State whether you agree with the vote and why.

myWorld Chapter Activity Rubric	3 Exceeds Understanding	2 Reaches Understanding	1 Approaches Understanding
Group participation: Analyzing, contributing, listening, forming consensus	Participates fully in analyzing the data, listens to others, contributes to the group conclusion	Helps analyze the data and participates in the discussion	Able to describe the general opinion of the group
Individual essay or speech stating position on EU members	Presents a clear position on membership; states reasoned support of or dissent from group findings	States position on membership but not in a forceful way; states good support of or dissent from group findings	Vague about position on membership; presents some of the reasons
Grammar, spelling	Advocates position with correct grammar and no spelling errors	Advocates position with few grammar and spelling errors	States position with several spelling and grammar errors

Name _____ Class _____ Date _____

 myWorld Chapter Activity Support Analysis Table

Norway and the European Union

Directions Fill out the Analysis Table using data from the Activity Cards. In your first group, write your scores only on the line related to your data, then vote. If you score the advantage higher than the disadvantage, the trend is generally in favor of membership. In your second group, complete the remaining lines and take a group vote for each line. At the end of the discussion, cast your final individual vote at the lower right.

Interest Group Card	One Advantage	Score 1 to 5	One Disadvantage	Score 1 to 5	Should Norway join the EU?
Control of Revenue					Group Vote □ Yes □ No
Cultural Identity					Group Vote □ Yes □ No
Sovereignty					Group Vote □ Yes □ No
Protectionism					Group Vote □ Yes □ No
Sustainable Resources					Group Vote □ Yes □ No
Independence					Group Vote □ Yes □ No
		Total Score		Total Score	My Final Vote □ Yes □ No

State Your Position On your own paper, write a short essay describing your group's findings and vote. State whether you agree with the vote and why.

Western Europe

- Introduce the Essential Question so that students will be able to understand the big ideas of this chapter (see earlier page, Connect to the Essential Question).
- Help students prepare to learn about Western Europe by looking at the chapter's maps, charts, and photos.

- Have students make and record chapter predictions with the *Essential Question Preview* in the **Student Journal.**
- Ask them to analyze the maps on this page.

GUIDE ON THE SIDE

Explore the Essential Question . . .

Have students complete the Essential Question Writer's Workshop in their **Student Journal** to demonstrate in-depth understanding of the question in the context of this chapter.

Analyze Maps Point out the political map of Western Europe.

- What bodies of water surround Spain? (Atlantic Ocean, Mediterranean Sea)
- What country is on the same peninsula as Spain? (Portugal)
- What country is on the same peninsula as Sweden? (Norway)
- Which of the two countries is larger? (Sweden)
- What island country is located to the northwest of France? (United Kingdom)

Western Europe

Essential Question

Is it better to be independent or interdependent?

KEY
- National border
- ⊛ Capital city
- ○ Other city

0 ——— 400 mi
0 ——— 400 km
Lambert Conformal Conic Projection

Where in the World Is Western Europe?

Washington, D.C., to Lund: 4,060 miles

INTRODUCE my Story

Get students excited to learn about Western Europe by first experiencing the region through the eyes of Yasmin, a young woman who lives in Sweden but travels often to Spain to visit relatives.

- Read myStory and watch the myStory Video about Yasmin's life.

- Have students complete *Europe at Her Doorstep* in the **Student Journal** to prepare to learn about diversity in Europe and the impact of the European Union on citizens.

my Story

Europe at Her Doorstep

In this section, you'll read about Yasmin, a young woman living in Sweden who has family in Spain and Pakistan. What does Yasmin's story tell you about life in Western Europe today?

Explore the Essential Question
- at my **worldgeography.com**
- using the myWorld Chapter Activity
- with the **Student Journal**

By Jake Johnson for myWorld Online

Yasmin straps on her dancing shoes. She glances in the mirror, adjusts her dress, and taps her way into the dance studio. With a rose in her hair and a colorful shawl stretched between her hands, Yasmin practices flamenco, a traditional Spanish dance. Inside the studio, the music makes Yasmin think of the warm Mediterranean while Sweden's winter winds blow outside.

Yasmin was born in Madrid, Spain, but she lives with her family in the coastal town of Bjärred in southern Sweden. Her father, Asif, is Pakistani and Spanish. Her mother, Monica, is Finnish and Swedish. Yasmin uses both of her parents' last names as a part of her heritage.

Yasmin's father Asif left Spain to work in Sweden in 1995. At that time, Sweden had just become a member of the European Union (EU). EU member countries allow people to move across borders without passports or complicated documents. Asif decided to try life in Sweden where more jobs were available. So, at age six Yasmin, along with her sister Sabina and brother Daniel, moved to frosty Sweden—a completely different world from Spain.

Yasmin remembers that she wasn't ready for the change in cultures. "At first, I was very different from the Swedish girls.

my Story

Europe at Her Doorstep

- **Compare and Contrast** How do Yasmin's thoughts while dancing form a contrast to her environment? (She thinks of the warm Mediterranean, but outside it is cold winter.)

- **Identify Details** What different cultures are part of Yasmin's family background? (Spanish, Pakistani, Finnish, and Swedish)

- **Cause and Effect** Why did Yasmin's family move to Sweden? (Her father thought he would have an easier time finding a job. The EU regulations allowed them to move without documents.)

NOTES

CULTURE

Finland's Languages Although Yasmin's mother is both Finnish and Swedish, she speaks Swedish with her children. Finland is officially a bilingual country with both Finnish and Swedish as official languages. From the 1200s to 1809, Sweden ruled Finland, and its influence is still felt. Ethnic Swedes make up some 5.6 percent of the population today. Approximately the same percentage of people speak Swedish as their first language. In addition to the two official languages, a very small number of people speak either Russian or Sami. Finland borders Russia, which accounts for the presence of Russian speakers. The Sami are the indigenous people of Scandinavia.

GUIDE ON THE SIDE

- **Compare and Contrast** How was Yasmin different from Swedish girls? (She was loud, and she ran around a lot.)

- **Draw Conclusions** Why do you think Yasmin's parents tell her not to mix up her languages? (Sample: They want her to be able to speak and write correctly in each language so she will do well in school.)

- **Compare and Contrast** How are the family's languages similar to the foods they eat? (They come from many sources and are all "mixed up.")

- **Identify Details** What is special about the olive oil the family uses? (It comes from their trees in Spain.)

Yasmin stands in front of Lund's medieval cathedral.

Yasmin with her father and mother

In general, Swedes are much more quiet than Spaniards. I spoke very loud . . . I was a Spanish girl, and I yelled and ran around everywhere. I was more like the Swedish boys."

At home, Yasmin speaks Spanish with her father and Swedish with her mother. Everyone also speaks English. "The language that we speak is similar to the foods we eat. It is very mixed up," laughs Yasmin. She adds, "Sometimes we mix up our languages, even though our parents say we shouldn't. It's just easier to find the word you are looking for in another language. We even mix up languages within one sentence—but we all understand each other."

Even the family meal is a cultural medley. "We make it up as we go," explains Asif as he dices potatoes. He is making a Pakistani dish called alu gosht, a sort of a beef stew. Yasmin explains that this alu gosht includes Spanish olive oil, Swedish potatoes, and Chinese rice. The olive oil comes from the family's own olive trees in Spain!

Yasmin enjoys cooking and shopping at the farmers' market.

QUICK FACTS

Lund, Sweden Founded in about 990, the city of Lund is Sweden's second-oldest city. It has a cathedral that dates back to the 1100s. The university that Yasmin attends was founded in 1666, making it the second-oldest university in the country. The city still has many examples of medieval architecture and streets, which can be seen in the photograph on the opposite page. There are also a number of cultural and art museums. In addition to a historic past, Lund is home to several modern industries, including pharmaceuticals, food processing, and the manufacture of medical equipment. Lund's population is a little more than 100,000.

Yasmin attends classes in linguistics at Lund University.

The strait of Öresund separates Sweden from Denmark.

One of Yasmin's favorite possessions is her video camera. She has made several videos, including many that documented her trip to meet family in Pakistan. Music is also important to Yasmin, and she can play the piano, the flute, and the guitar.

Most days, Yasmin rides the bus to Lund to attend university classes. Lund is a medieval city full of gothic architecture and winding streets. Higher education is free in Sweden, so students from all over the world come to Lund University. Yasmin has many interests such as film and architecture, but she hasn't decided on a major.

One of Yasmin's new hobbies is tae kwon do, a form of martial arts that developed in Korea. At a dojo (a martial arts training school) near the university, she puts on a white uniform and her blue belt. Barefoot, Yasmin and a partner practice a complex routine designed for self-defense.

"Tae kwon do has a philosophy of peace," Yasmin says, "that teaches me to have the right mindset in order to be able to do the sport correctly."

Back in Bjärred, Yasmin walks along the beach. It's cold and windy, but beautiful. Bjärred is famous for its 500-meter pier into the strait of Öresund. It is the longest pier in the country. At the end of the pier is the Bjärred Kallbadhus (bath house). In the winter, people dive from the sauna there into the icy waters of the Öresund. Walking over the snow-covered dunes, Yasmin thinks about how much she cherishes the blazing sun of Spain. At the same time, she looks forward to ice-skating near her home in Sweden. Whether she's ice-skating, studying, or making a video, Yasmin has many choices, since Europe is at her doorstep.

Meet the Journalist

Name Jake Johnson
Favorite Moment Dinner with Yasmin's family

▶ **myStory Video**

Join Yasmin as she shows you about life in her city.

GUIDE ON THE SIDE

- **Summarize** What are Yasmin's interests? (dancing, music, film, architecture, tae kwan do)

- **Identify Evidence** What activities show that Yasmin has been influenced by non-European cultures? (Samples: traveling to Pakistan and making a video there; taking tae kwan do)

- **Build Cultural Awareness** What does Yasmin appreciate about the teachings of tae kwan do? (its philosophy of peace)

- **Categorize** What winter activity is Yasmin able to enjoy in Sweden but not in Spain? (ice skating)

▶ **myStory Video**

Have students watch the video at myworldgeography.com about Yasmin's life and the way it is shaped by diverse cultures. Tell students to use their trackers to take notes on the various influences on Yasmin's life.

Chapter Atlas

OBJECTIVES

Students will know

• climate patterns found in Europe.

• population patterns found in Europe, including the percentage of urban dwellers.

Students will be able to

• label an outline map of Western Europe.

• make a decision about pollution control of the Danube River.

SET EXPECTATIONS

In this section, students will

• read Chapter Atlas.

• decide who should regulate water pollution levels in Europe.

• go On Assignment in Western Europe and interpret maps and charts.

CORE CONCEPTS

You may wish to teach or reteach the following lessons from the Core Concepts Handbook:

• Temperature, pp. 34–35

• Types of Climate, pp. 40–41

• People's Impact on the Environment, pp. 52–53

KEY

Differentiated Instruction

L1 Special Needs **L2** Extra Support

L3 On-Level **L4** Challenge

English Language Instruction

ELL Beginner **ELL** Early Intermediate **ELL** Intermediate

ELL Early Advanced **ELL** Advanced

---

1 Connect
Make learning meaningful

Make Connections Ask students to name the nearest large body of water, such as an ocean or a Great Lake. If your community is inland, ask if any students have lived near such a body of water in the past. Discuss how large bodies of water affect climate.

L2 Extra Support Remind students that ice melts gradually and that very hot soup takes time to cool. Explain that air temperature changes more quickly than water temperature. Ask how that might affect climate.

Activate Prior Knowledge Remind students that in the previous chapter, they learned about the history of modern Europe, including industrialization and wars. Ask how such events might have changed the environment.

L4 Challenge Have students consider the contemporary problem of land mines in former war zones. Ask them to use this knowledge to draw conclusions about how the two world wars might have affected Europe's land.

Prepare Follow the steps in the section **Preview.** Preteach the Key Terms. Then have students complete *Word Wise* in their journals using in-text clues and the glossary for help.

2 Experience
Teach knowledge and skills

Read Use **Background** notes and **Guide on the Side** questions to model active reading. Have students use *Take Notes* in their **Student Journals** to record important places to know in Western Europe on an outline map. Students should use the maps in Section 1 and the Active Atlas at myworldgeography. com for assistance.

ELL Beginner/Early Intermediate Have students make flash cards for Key Terms. On the back, they should write the definition or draw an image to help them remember the term.

L3 On-Level Have students study *Enrichment: Comparing Climatographs* to learn more about how the ocean affects the climates of Europe.

ELL Intermediate/Early Advanced Tell students to use signal words such as *like, alike, also,* and *similar to* when they compare and *unlike, on the other hand,* and *different from* when they contrast.

 Practice: myWorld Activity Students will study a country along the Danube and decide whether it is in that country's national interest to have the European Union regulate water pollution levels. **Step-by-Step Instructions** and **More Activities** follow on p. T88.

SECTION 1 RESOURCE GUIDE

FOR THE STUDENT

my worldgeography.com Student Center
- Active Atlas
- Data Discovery

Student Edition (print and online)
- Chapter Atlas

Student Journal (print and online)
- Section 1 Word Wise
- Section 1 Take Notes

21st Century Learning Online Tutor
- Read Special Purpose Maps
- Make Decisions

FOR THE TEACHER

my worldgeography.com Teacher Center
- Online Lesson Planner
- Presentations for Projection
- SuccessTracker

ProGuide: Europe and Russia
- Section 1 Lesson Plan, pp. T86–T87
- ⃗ myWorld Activity Step-by-Step Instructions, p. T88
- Activity Support: Country Profiles, p. T89
- myWorld Geography Enrichment, p. T90
- Section Quiz, p. T91

Accelerating the Progress of ELLs
- Organizing Information Strategies, p. 48

---

3 Understand
Assess understanding

Review Review *Word Wise* and *Take Notes* in the **Student Journal.**

Assess Knowledge and Skills Use the Section Assessment and the Section Quiz to check students' progress.

Assess Understanding Review students' responses to the Section Assessment Essential Question prompt.

Remediate Use these strategies to review and remediate.

If students struggle to . . .	Try these strategies.
Draw conclusions	Assign additional practice with the **21st Century Online Tutor.**
Make decisions	Give students a pro-and-con chart on which to record information relevant to the decision.
Read the climate or languages maps	Review how to use map keys.

ELL Support

ELL Objective Students will be able to use English to express decisions.

Cultural Connections To give students practice expressing decisions, let them use their native languages to describe a past decision and the reasons for it. Have them share with the class the words from their language that mean *decision* and *reason*.

ELL Advanced Content Tip Introduce the sentence *The Alps stretch from France to Eastern Europe.* Have students look up the word *stretch* in a dictionary and decide which definition applies here. Then have them write a sentence using the word in a similar way.

ELL Activity To start students thinking about the section activity, write the following statements on the board: *Pollution cleanup is cheap. It takes money to start industries. Pollution rarely hurts people.* Have students work in pairs to decide if each statement is generally true or false. **(Interpersonal/Verbal)**

myWorld Activity   **Step-by-Step Instructions**   **30 min**

Danube Cleanup

OBJECTIVES

Students will

• examine data for countries along the Danube River.

• decide whether individual countries are likely to want the EU to regulate water pollution.

LEARNING STYLES

• Verbal

• Visual

• Make Decisions

MATERIALS

• map of Europe showing the Danube River

• Activity Support: Country Profiles, p. T89

Activity Steps

1. Tell students that they are going to represent a European country on a commission to decide whether the EU should regulate water pollution levels in the Danube River. Each student will make a decision for one country and then vote on the question. Make sure students understand that if the proposed EU regulation doesn't pass, regulation will be left up to individual nations.

2. Have students turn to the physical map of Europe in the Chapter Atlas or look at a classroom map. Ask students to name the countries crossed or bordered by the Danube River.

   ELL **Early Intermediate** Write the names of the countries on the board and clearly pronounce each name so students will be able to discuss them with ease.

3. Divide the class into groups of five. Give each student a copy of *Activity Support: Country Profiles.*

Have the groups divide up the countries, one to each member. Tell students to read their country profile and take a few minutes to decide how they will vote on the question *Should the EU regulate water pollution levels?*

   L2 **Extra Support** Help students to understand that the Danube flows east and southeast through many countries to the Black Sea. A country near the river's mouth will receive all the pollution dumped by countries higher up the river.

4. After each student has decided, the group should hold a vote by having each student share his or her decision in turn. When saying yes or no, students should share a reason. After all have shared, the group should tally the votes.

5. The groups should then share their vote tally with the class and discuss their different perspectives.

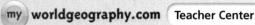

More Activities From myWorld Teachers

Local Connection Have pairs of students examine the climate map in the Chapter Atlas and the description of Europe's climates in Section 1. Have them decide which part of Europe has a similar climate to the climate where they live. **(Visual/Logical)**

Eurasia Have students use an atlas to examine the physical map of Eurasia. Students should trace the border and examine its geographic features. Then they

should write a paragraph stating whether Eurasia should be one continent or two. **(Logical/Verbal)**

Population and Climate Have the class study the climate map in the Chapter Atlas and locate the coldest and warmest climates. Then have them study the population density map in the Chapter Atlas. Discuss whether there is a link between climate and population density. **(Visual/Logical)**

 my worldgeography.com (**Teacher Center**) ⊘   Find additional resources in the online Teacher Center.

Name _____ Class _____ Date _____

myWorld Activity Support   **Country Profiles**

Danube Cleanup

Directions The profiles below give information about five countries found along the Danube River. Each student in your group will represent one country. Use the data in the profile to decide whether your country wants to have the EU regulate water pollution levels in the Danube.

Germany	• source of the Danube River • prosperous economy, many factories • wide support for environmental protection
Slovakia	• a small corner of Slovakia is crossed by Danube • gradually modernizing economy; unemployment the biggest problem • seeking to attract industry with business-friendly policies (low taxes, low regulation)
Hungary	• capital city and center of country are crossed by Danube • in communist past, had very polluted rivers • making the transition to a market economy; has many industries
Croatia	• reached by Danube after it has flowed through many industrial countries • small nation with a struggling economy; many industries controlled by state • in communist past, did not protect the environment
Romania	• one of last two countries reached by Danube • Danube the major source for fishing industry • toxic spills into rivers by Romanian mining industry

Explain Your Decision State whether your country would vote yes on the issue of having the EU regulate water pollution levels. Give at least one reason for your decision.

Should the EU regulate water pollution levels?

_____

Reason:

_____

_____

Name _____ Class _____ Date _____

Enrichment: Comparing Climatographs

Directions Study the climatographs below. Answer the questions that follow and complete the activity.

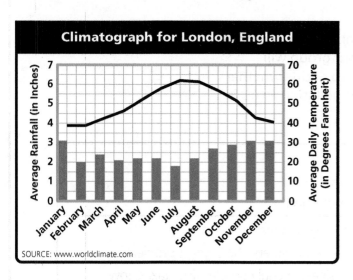

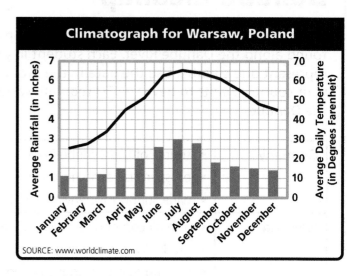

1. London and Warsaw are about the same distance north of the equator. Which city has colder winters? Explain.

_____

_____

2. Which city receives more rainfall overall? Explain.

_____

_____

3. **Activity** Locate the two cities on a map of Europe. What geographic factor explains the difference in temperature and the difference in rainfall between the two cities?

_____

_____

Name _____ Class _____ Date _____

Section Quiz

Directions Answer the following questions using what you learned
in Section 1.

1. _____ Which of the following is an
example of a peninsula?
a. the Alps
b. Eurasia
c. the Great European Plain
d. Scandinavia

2. _____ Which of the following is a landform
that is almost always flat?
a. glacier
b. loess
c. plain
d. peninsula

3. _____ What is the difference between
tundra and taiga?
a. Trees grow in the taiga, not the tundra.
b. The tundra is located south of the taiga.
c. The taiga is a peninsula, and the tundra
is not.
d. Streams provide water to the tundra but
not the taiga.

4. _____ What was the result of a chemical
spill in 1986?
a. pollution in a Norwegian fiord
b. pollution in the Rhine River
c. acid rain falling in the taiga
d. the melting of several glaciers

5. _____ What is loess?
a. a type of fir tree that grows in the
far north
b. a long, narrow, steep inlet
c. a type of soil spread by winds
d. a raised area of rocky land

6. How does the geography of Europe influence where people live?

_____

_____

_____

Chapter Atlas

- Model preparing to read by previewing the Key Ideas, Key Terms, headings, visuals, and captions. Have students make predictions about what they will learn. For ELL support, post the prompt: "I predict I will read about . . ."
- Preview and practice the skill, Read Physical Maps, by looking at the map Western Europe: Physical.

Ask students to identify the mountain system just north of the Adriatic Sea. (the Alps)

- Preteach this section's high-use Academic Vocabulary and Key Terms using the table on the next page and in-text definitions. Have students practice Key Terms by completing the Word Wise page in their journals.

GUIDE ON THE SIDE

Reading Skill

Label an Outline Map While they read, have students identify the Places to Know! on the outline map of the region in the **Student Journal.**

Physical Features

- **Identify Main Ideas** To what continent is Europe attached? (Asia)
- **Categorize** Give examples of a plain and a mountain range in Europe. (North European Plain, Ural Mountains)
- **Identify Details** What lies west of the North European Plain? (Atlantic Ocean)

Section 1

Chapter Atlas

Key Ideas
- The landmass of Eurasia includes the continents of Europe and Asia.
- The climate of Western Europe is primarily temperate, although some areas are near the Arctic Circle.
- Western Europeans are mostly urban dwellers.

Key Terms • peninsula • plain • glacier • loess • tundra • taiga • pollution   ⟩ Visual Glossary

🌐 **Reading Skill: Label an Outline Map** Take notes using the outline map in your journal.

A hillside village on the Greek island of Santorini; below, young women from Mykonos, Greece

Physical Features

The **peninsula** of Europe is attached to Asia, a continent that lies east of the Ural Mountains. A peninsula is land almost surrounded by water but still attached to the mainland. Geographers call this huge landmass composed of Europe and Asia *Eurasia.*

The three main landforms that cover Western Europe are **plains** (flat or gently rolling lands), uplands, and mountains. Most people live on plains. The North European Plain stretches from the Atlantic Ocean to the Urals, making it one of the largest level land areas on earth.

ACADEMIC VOCABULARY

High-Use Word	Definition and Sample Sentences
fertile	*adj.* rich in nutrients; able to grow many plants *Luigi's garden thrived because the soil was fertile.*
dialect	*n.* a regional variety of a language *Giusto spoke a dialect that many other Italians did not understand.*
vast	*adj.* very great in size, number, or quantity *The ocean is a vast body of water.*

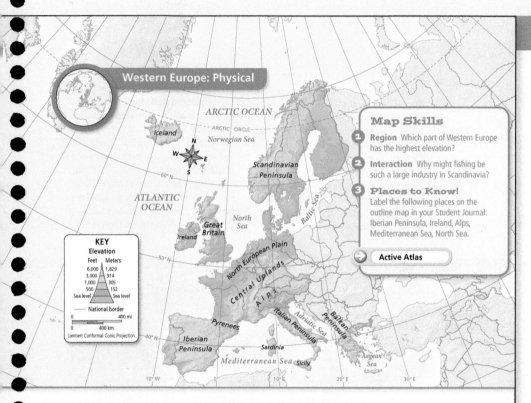

Western Europe: Physical

Map Skills

1. **Region** Which part of Western Europe has the highest elevation?

2. **Interaction** Why might fishing be such a large industry in Scandinavia?

3. **Places to Know!** Label the following places on the outline map in your Student Journal: Iberian Peninsula, Ireland, Alps, Mediterranean Sea, North Sea.

Active Atlas

Most of northern Europe lies on the Scandinavian Peninsula, between the Arctic Ocean, the North Sea, and the Baltic Sea. The west coast of Norway features dramatic fiords, or long, narrow, deep inlets of the sea.

The Central Uplands in the center of southern Europe consist of mountains and plateaus, or raised areas of level land bordered by steep slopes.

The Alps stretch from France to Eastern Europe. Streams formed by **glaciers,** slow-moving masses of ice and snow, flow out of the Alps. These streams feed the Rhine River and the Danube River.

To the south is the warmer Mediterranean region. This region is named for the Mediterranean Sea nearby. Days are sunny and the climate is generally temperate. Here the land is mountainous peninsulas with narrow, <u>fertile</u> plains.

Active volcanoes may be found in Italy, Greece, and Iceland. At times, volcanic activity has led to earthquakes and tsunamis (tidal waves). Since ancient times, earthquakes have been widespread in the Mediterranean countries.

Reading Check **What landform divides Europe from Asia?**

fertile, *adj.,* rich in nutrients; able to grow many plants

MAP SKILLS **1.** the Alpine Mountain System **2.** It has a very long coastline. **3.** Maps should be labeled accurately.

READING CHECK the Ural Mountains

- **Categorize** Which European country has dramatic fiords along its west coast? (Norway)

- **Summarize** What type of landforms are found in the Central Uplands of Western Europe? (mountains and plateaus)

- **Identify Main Ideas** What regions do the Alps separate? (They separate Mediterranean Europe from Northern and Western Europe.)

Analyze Maps Have students look at the physical geography shown on the map.

- What is located to the south of the North European Plain? (Central Uplands)

- What separates the Iberian Peninsula from the rest of Europe? (the Pyrenees)

 Active Atlas

Have students go to myworldgeography.com to explore a physical map of Western Europe.

GEOGRAPHY

Mediterranean Winds Two types of winds influence the climate of the Mediterranean region. The sirocco is a warm wind that blows across the Mediterranean from the south or southeast. As it crosses the sea, it picks up moisture and brings humidity into southern Europe. By contrast, the mistral is a cold, dry wind that blows from the north toward the coast of southern France. The mistral is strongest in winter.

Climate and Ecosystems

- **Cause and Effect** Why does most of Europe have a mild climate? (The Atlantic Ocean carries warm water from the tropics to the western coastline of Europe.)

- **Identify Main Ideas** Which part of Europe has the coldest climate and why? (The northern part; it stretches to the Arctic Circle.)

- **Compare and Contrast** What is one major difference between Europe in ancient times and Europe today? (Europe used to be covered with forests; today most land is clear.)

Analyze Maps Ask students to study the climate map.

- What types of climate does Italy have? (Mediterranean and humid subtropical)

- Which countries have a region of subarctic climate? (Finland, Norway, Sweden, Iceland)

Climate and Ecosystems

Most Western Europeans enjoy a mild climate because the Atlantic Ocean carries warm ocean water from the tropics to Europe's western coast. This water warms the air, bringing mild winters to places as far north as Scandinavia.

Most of Western Europe is located in the temperate zone, although its northern edges reach to the Arctic region. Land close to the Mediterranean Sea has wet winters and dry summers.

In ancient times, forests covered most of Western Europe. Today, people have replanted some forests, but most of the land has been cleared for cities, farms, and industry. One of north central Europe's natural resources is **loess,** a rich soil made of fine sediment deposited by glaciers and spread by centuries of wind.

Northern Scandinavia has few forests because of its Arctic climate. The Arctic **tundra** is a plant community made up of grasses, mosses, herbs, and low shrubs.

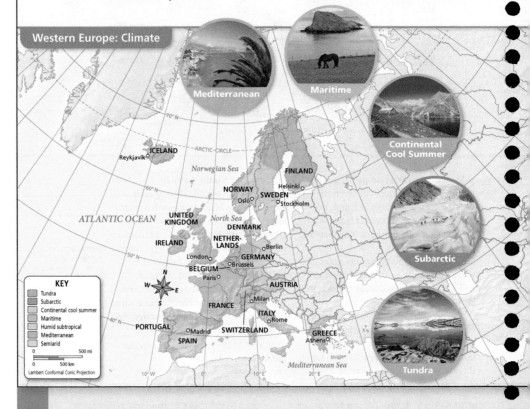

Western Europe: Climate

QUICK FACTS

According to the World Meteorological Organization, Europe has experienced the following weather extremes:

- **Highest temperature:** 118.4°F; Athens, Greece; July 10, 1977
- **Lowest temperature:** −72.6°F; Ust'-Shchugor, Russia; December 31, 1978

- **Greatest average annual rainfall:** 183.0"/year; Crljivica, Bosnia-Herzegovina
- **Least average annual rainfall:** 6.4"/year; Astrakhan, Russia

---

Trees are unable to grow here because it is too cold and dry. The **taiga,** a thick forest of coniferous trees, lies south of this zone. It extends from Scandinavia east across Eurasia for thousands of miles.

Mediterranean vegetation is a mix of small trees, forests, shrubs, and grasses. Trees and shrubs here must be hardy enough to survive the dry summer season.

Reading Check Contrast taiga vegetation with that of the Mediterranean region.

A Diverse Continent

In general, the nations of Western Europe have a high standard of living. Almost all Western Europeans can read and write. This region has strong education systems. There is a direct connection between good education and a high standard of living.

Across Western Europe, people speak a variety of different languages. About half of the people in Europe speak English and their native languages or <u>dialects.</u>

dialect, *n.,* a regional variety of a language

GUIDE ON THE SIDE

- **Compare and Contrast** How are taiga and tundra different? (The tundra is nearly treeless; the taiga is a forest.)

- **Identify Details** Why must Mediterranean shrubs be hardy? (to survive dry summers)

A Diverse Continent

- **Infer** What is the link between literacy and standard of living? (Education helps people get jobs.)

Analyze Maps Ask students to study the natural resources map.

- Which country has all four of the resources shown on this map? (Austria)

- Which countries have only iron as a resource? (Finland, Portugal, Sweden)

- What resource does Greece have? (coal)

Active Atlas

Have students go to myworldgeography.com to explore a natural resources map of Western Europe.

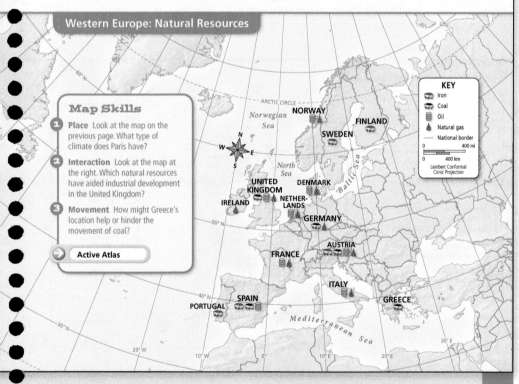

Western Europe: Natural Resources

Map Skills

1. **Place** Look at the map on the previous page. What type of climate does Paris have?

2. **Interaction** Look at the map at the right. Which natural resources have aided industrial development in the United Kingdom?

3. **Movement** How might Greece's location help or hinder the movement of coal?

Active Atlas

KEY
- Iron
- Coal
- Oil
- Natural gas
- National border

0 ___ 400 mi
0 ___ 400 km
Lambert Conformal Conic Projection

MAP SKILLS 1. maritime **2.** coal, oil, natural gas **3.** Its location south of many mountains could hinder the movement of coal, but its long coastline could help such movement by the sea.

READING CHECK Taiga vegetation consists of coniferous trees, while the Mediterranean region has a mix of small trees, forests, shrubs, and grasses.

ANSWERS

HISTORY

The Colonial Past The North African immigrants in France mostly come from Algeria, Tunisia, and Morocco. These three North African countries were once colonies of France. In all three countries, the population consists almost entirely of Muslim Arabs. Morocco and Tunisia gained independence in 1956 after long struggles. Algeria did not gain its independence from France until 1962, after a nearly eight-year war that left a legacy of hostility between the two countries.

- **Problem Solve** How has the European Union solved the problem of conducting business in multiple languages? (Leaders usually conduct their business in English.)

- **Summarize** What have been the effects of immigration on Europe? (Immigrants have changed in some ways and have changed Europeans in some ways.)

Analyze Maps Ask students to study the languages map.

- What language family do French, Italian, and Spanish belong to? (Romance)

- Where are Celtic languages found? (westernmost Europe)

21st Century Learning

Read Special Purpose Maps Have students develop this skill by using the online tutorial and activities. Students will learn how to read special purpose maps and use the information to draw conclusions.

 Activity Atlas

Have students go to myworldgeography.com to explore maps of Western Europe.

Language is part of culture. Sometimes, language unites those from different cultures. For example, when North Africans move to France, they encounter a different culture. But many North Africans speak French. This makes the transition to a new life a little easier.

When European Union (EU) leaders meet to discuss economics or energy policy, they often conduct business in English. This helps make discussion and decision-making easier. The European Union has 27 member nations and 23 official languages, but it is easier if everyone speaks the same language.

Europe is a region of many different cultures. For 2,000 years, Christianity has been the dominant religion. A large Jewish population has also lived there continuously. Since World War II, people from around the world have moved to Europe for jobs and education. They brought different religions, languages, and customs. When people move to a new country, they often take on parts of its cultures. At the same time, newcomers have introduced Western Europeans to new ideas and customs.

Reading Check How many official languages are there in the European Union?

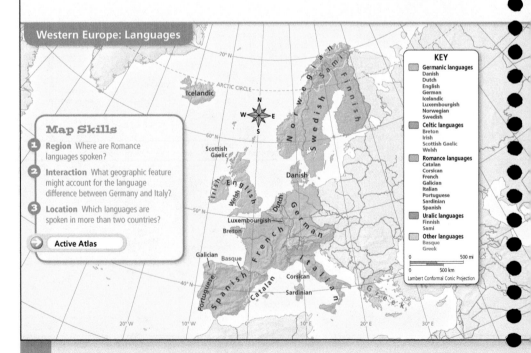

Western Europe: Languages

Map Skills

1. **Region** Where are Romance languages spoken?

2. **Interaction** What geographic feature might account for the language difference between Germany and Italy?

3. **Location** Which languages are spoken in more than two countries?

Active Atlas

KEY

Germanic languages
Danish
Dutch
English
German
Icelandic
Luxembourgish
Norwegian
Swedish

Celtic languages
Breton
Irish
Scottish Gaelic
Welsh

Romance languages
Catalan
Corsican
French
Galician
Italian
Portuguese
Sardinian
Spanish

Uralic languages
Finnish
Sami

Other languages
Basque
Greek

500 mi
500 km
Lambert Conformal Conic Projection

MAP SKILLS 1. France, Italy, Spain, Portugal, Corsica, Sardinia
2. the Alps **3.** German, French, Italian, English, Dutch, Sami.

READING CHECK 23 official languages

PRIMARY SOURCE

Water, a Key Resource "Most people in Europe have access to drinking water of good quality. However, in some parts the quality still frequently does not meet biological and chemical standards. Clean unpolluted water is also essential for our ecosystems. Plants and animals in lakes, rivers, and seas react to changes in their environment caused by changes in chemical water quality and physical disturbance of their habitat. . . . Changes in habitats can result from the physical disturbance through damming, channelisation and dredging of rivers, construction of reservoirs, sand and gravel extraction in coastal waters, bottom trawling by fishing vessels, etc."
—European Environment Agency, "Water pollution—Overview"

Where People Live and Work

Western Europe's geography shapes where and how people live. This region is largely urban and industrialized.

In Western Europe, most of the population lives within 100 miles of the coast. This is because being close to water offers many opportunities for trade. Europe's major rivers, the Danube and the Rhine, carry goods and people. They also carry large quantities of water. Western European highways often follow river routes to connect towns and cities that have grown along these rivers.

In northern Europe, people live near the coast. Even in Arctic climates, being near the ocean offers milder weather. Inland, <u>vast</u> empty areas separate towns and villages. Settlement is sparse because these areas are cold and dry.

In Southern and Central Europe, population is more evenly spaced. In the temperate climate of Italy, population is densest near the coast. People also live in large numbers inland as well.

In general, people do not choose to live in high mountains and marshy wetlands. Instead, they tend to settle in low, sunny, warm places close to water. Natural resources such as water, minerals, and rich farmland also attract people.

A recent report by the European Union addressed climate change trends. This report noted changes such as the melting of glaciers in the Arctic Ocean and drier conditions in the Mediterranean area of Southern Europe. Changes in climate may affect crop yields, water levels in rivers, and human health.

As a highly industrialized region, Western Europe has experienced air and water **pollution.** Pollution is harmful material released into the environment. One result of air pollution is acid rain. This occurs when exhaust from industries mixes with moisture in the air. This precipitation then falls as acid rain. It has damaged historic buildings, bridges, cathedrals, and monuments across Western Europe. Over the years, acid rain has also damaged forests and freshwater lakes.

Water pollution may result from chemical spills. A chemical spill is an accidental release of toxic or dangerous materials.

vast, *adj.,* very great in size, number, or quantity

myWorld Activity
Danube Cleanup

ENVIRONMENTAL CHALLENGES IN WALES Over a period of 30 years, this forest has been destroyed by acid rain, due to the air pollution from nearby industrial plants.

Workers spread chemicals to clean up an oil spill on a Welsh beach. *What might be likely causes for the pollution shown in each photograph?*

CAPTION Industry is the most likely cause.

ANSWERS

CORE CONCEPTS: PEOPLE'S IMPACT ON THE ENVIRONMENT

Review Core Concept 4.3 before discussing climate change and pollution in Europe. Review sustainability and what that means for the use of resources, especially energy resources. Also, discuss the effects of industry and why people have overused or damaged their environment. Then have students look for ways that pollution has affected Europe, both historically and in recent years. Ask, Do you think having a high population density means that Western Europe has more problems with pollution than more sparsely populated regions? Explain.

GUIDE ON THE SIDE

- **Summarize** What caused pollution in the Rhine River? (industrial waste and a chemical factory fire)

The Urban Continent

- **Cause and Effect** Why have European governments limited the expansion of cities? (to preserve land for growing food, forests, and recreation)

Analyze Maps Have students study the population density map.

- Where are the lowest population densities found? (Iceland, Norway, Sweden, Finland)

- Are the central areas of Western Europe densely populated or sparsely populated? (densely)

- What landform explains the band of low population densities running from southern France east through Switzerland and Austria? (the Alps)

 Active Atlas

Have students go to myworldgeography.com to explore a languages map of Western Europe.

One of Western Europe's busiest waterways, the Rhine River, was once one of the region's most polluted. From the 1950s to the 1970s, industrial waste flowed into the river. Fish disappeared from it and swimmers avoided it. A cleanup effort was launched, but in 1986, a chemical spill reversed years of effort. A chemical factory fire in Switzerland led to 30 tons of toxic chemicals being washed into the river as firefighters fought the blaze. Within 10 days, the pollution traveled the length of the Rhine to the North Sea. Today, the Rhine is much cleaner and fish are returning to swim in it again.

Reading Check How have Europe's coasts and waterways affected settlement?

The Urban Continent

Europe has been called the "urban continent" because so many people live in urban areas. An urban area may include a city and its surrounding suburbs. In the United Kingdom, for example, almost nine out of ten people live in cities.

Most countries in Western Europe have dense populations clustered in small land areas. To preserve land for growing food, for forests, and for recreation, most countries set strict limits on the expansion of cities and suburbs. This means that the region's cities tend to be tightly packed with people. Very few Europeans live in single-family houses with yards. Instead, most live in apartment buildings.

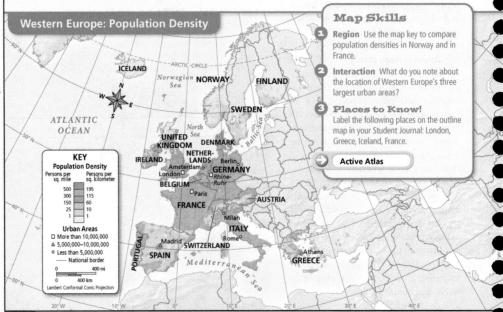

Western Europe: Population Density

Map Skills

1 **Region** Use the map key to compare population densities in Norway and in France.

2 **Interaction** What do you note about the location of Western Europe's three largest urban areas?

3 **Places to Know!** Label the following places on the outline map in your Student Journal: London, Greece, Iceland, France.

Active Atlas

KEY
Population Density

Persons per sq. mile	Persons per sq. kilometer
500	195
300	115
150	60
25	10
1	1

Urban Areas
□ More than 10,000,000
△ 5,000,000–10,000,000
○ Less than 5,000,000
— National border

0   400 mi
0   400 km
Lambert Conformal Conic Projection

READING CHECK They have encouraged settlement as they are easily accessed and offer trade opportunities and areas to live.

MAP SKILLS **1.** Population density is higher in France. **2.** They are in moderate climates near water.
3. Places should be labeled accurately.

MAP SKILLS car, truck, train, boat

READING CHECK Governments have set limits on the expansion of cities.

CULTURE

Café Life In many European cities, such as Paris, cafés are an essential part of urban life. On average, Europeans live in smaller dwellings than Americans, so they often choose to do their socializing in public places such as cafés, where they meet with friends to have coffee and talk. Because European cafés function as gathering places, they have often been the haunt of students, intellectuals, writers, artists, and revolutionaries.

In order to reach their jobs, schools, and other activities, most Europeans use public transportation. Over time, urban areas have built up dense public transportation networks. Train, subway, trolley, and bus services connect neighborhoods and cities all over Europe.

Germany's Rhine-Ruhr region is one of Europe's largest urban areas. Five cities there have more than 500,000 inhabitants. Contrast that with Greenland, a territory of Denmark and the world's largest island. Greenland is six times as large as all of Germany, but has a population of only about 58,000 people.

European governments favor public transportation over driving by setting high taxes on gasoline. Gasoline in Europe can cost twice as much as gasoline in the United States. While most families in Western Europe have a car, they may use it only for occasional trips to the countryside or to a regional shopping center.

Reading Check Why are Europe's cities so crowded?

Germany's Rhine-Ruhr Region

KEY
- Urban area
- Autobahn
- Other highway
- Railway
- River
- ○ City

Cities: Hamm, Gelsenkirchen, Dortmund, Essen, Bochum, Duisburg, Krefeld, Wuppertal, Neuss, Düsseldorf, Solingen, Mönchengladbach, Cologne (Köln), Bonn

Map Skills
The Rhine-Ruhr region is a transportation and industrial hub for the entire continent. What are the different forms of transportation available?

Active Atlas

Section 1 Assessment

Key Terms
1. Use each of the following terms in a sentence: peninsula, loess, tundra, pollution.

Key Ideas
2. What is Eurasia?
3. How does geography affect settlement patterns?
4. Why do some countries restrict urban growth?

Think Critically
5. **Compare and Contrast** Look at the physical map and the climate map in this section. Why is there more farming in France than in Scandinavia?
6. **Draw Conclusions** How does keeping a river like the Rhine clean benefit Western Europe?

Essential Question
Is it better to be independent or interdependent?
7. Look at the languages map in this section. Do you think the number of languages spoken by EU members helps or harms Western Europe? Go to your Student Journal to record your answer.

- **Infer** Why do you think European cities rely so much on public transportation? (Sample: Because cities are very crowded, traffic would be impossible if everyone drove.)
- **Compare Viewpoints** What attitude do European governments have toward driving? (They try to discourage it.)

Analyze Visuals Have students study the chart and the map.
- Why do you think the cities were originally built along rivers? (Before trains and automobiles, boats were the easiest way to travel.)
- What is significant about the location of Duisburg? (It is located near where the two rivers meet.)

Data Discovery

Have students go to myworldgeography.com to explore more data about Western Europe.

SECTION 1 ASSESSMENT 1. Samples: Italy is a peninsula. Loess is very fertile soil. Few plants grow on tundra. Industry can cause pollution. 2. Eurasia is the landmass made of Europe and Asia. 3. People usually settle near water in mild climates. 4. Rural land must be saved for farming. 5. France has more arable land and a moderate climate; Scandinavia is mountainous with a colder climate. 6. Sample: If the river is clean, people can use it for fishing and recreation. 7. Sample: Having so many languages could make it more difficult for people to communicate.

ANSWERS

Energy for the Future

OBJECTIVES

Students will

- identify and define four types of renewable energy.
- **21st Century Learning** analyze a speech delivered by a European commissioner.
- **ELL** learn important terms related to renewable energy.

SET EXPECTATIONS

In this case study, students will

- read Energy for the Future.
- analyze data about energy production.

1 Connect

Ask students if they have ever experienced a power outage because of a storm or some other event outside their control. Ask them to share ways in which they or their families changed their routine because of the power outage. Then explain that nonrenewable sources of energy will run out someday. This case study examines how European countries are switching to renewable energy sources.

L2 Extra Support Write the phrase *power outage* on the board and build a concept web around it during the discussion.

2 Learn

Preview Have students preview pictures and headings. Read the Key Ideas, Key Terms, and definitions. Ask students if they have ever seen wind turbines or solar panels.

Read While students read Energy for the Future, ask the questions found in the **Guide on the Side** to build understanding of Key Ideas and objectives.

ELL Intermediate Have students make word maps of the Key Terms. The word maps should include definitions, related words, and either a sentence or a picture.

 myWorld Activity: Meeting Energy Goals Give students *Activity Support: Analyze Primary Sources.* Suggest that individual students read the excerpt on their own and circle any words **15 min** or phrases they don't understand. Then have pairs of students work together to figure out the meaning from context. Finally, partners should answer the questions.

L1 Special Needs Give students three different colors of highlighters. Allow them to find the answers to the three questions about the primary source, highlight each answer with a different color, and label the answers with the number of the appropriate question.

3 Understand

Review Go back to the Key Ideas. Ask students to give specific examples from the case study that illustrate each of the Key Ideas.

Assess Have students complete **Assessment.** Review their answers to determine if students have met the lesson objectives.

Remediate If students struggle to identify which energy sources are renewable, suggest that they ask the following questions: *Is there an endless supply of this energy source? If not, can it be easily replaced?* If they answer "yes" to either question, the energy source is renewable. Test their knowledge by having them evaluate natural gas, ethanol, diesel fuel, and wind turbines.

Name _____ Class _____ Date _____

myWorld Activity Support   **Analyze Primary Sources**

Meeting Energy Goals

Directions: Read the excerpt below and respond to the questions.

Speech to the UN

"The renewable energies roadmap unveiled earlier this month by the Commission sets a target of 20% for the share of total energy supply to come from renewable sources.

It is not the first time that targets for renewable energy have been fixed. In 1997, the European Union set the objective of achieving a 12% use of renewable energies by 2010. In 2005 the share of renewables was only about 7%.

The reason for the lack of adequate progress has been the absence of legally binding obligations. In many Member States, national policies have been inadequate for achieving the renewables target. The progress across the European Union has generally been patchy and highly uneven. Some Member States have adopted ambitious policies, but overall, national policies have proven vulnerable to the whims of changing governments."

—*Stavros Dimas, EU Commissioner, January 29, 2007*

Analyze Primary Sources

1. What renewable energy goal did the EU set in 1997, and what is its current goal?

   _____

   _____

   _____

2. How well has the EU met its 1997 goal?

   _____

   _____

   _____

3. According to Commissioner Dimas, why is progress toward meeting the renewable energy goal uneven?

   _____

   _____

   _____

ECONOMICS

Overdependence on Fossil Fuels One reason the EU is so eager to develop renewable energy sources is that Europe must import the majority of the fossil fuels it uses. In 2007, the European Union produced 2.676 billion barrels of oil a day. It consumed 14.38 billion barrels of oil a day, or more than five times what it produced. In 2007, it produced 197.8 billion cubic meters of natural gas a day. It consumed 497.3 billion cubic meters, or two-and-a-half times what it produced. Developing renewable sources of energy might help Europe use less fossil fuel and thus make it less dependent on other regions.

Case Study

Energy for the Future

| **Key Ideas** | • Renewable energy sources capture energy from nature using advanced technologies. | • An energy goal for the entire European Union must take into account differences in member nations' economic development. |

| **Key Terms** | • renewable energy | • nonrenewable energy | • fossil fuel |
| | • biofuel | • wind turbine | • hydropower |

Energy and Progress

- **Identify Main Ideas** What is the European Union's goal for renewable energy sources? (to use 20 percent renewable energy by 2020)

- **Identify Details** What might prevent Poland from reaching the EU renewable energy goal? (It has a history of burning coal, and changing all of its equipment will be expensive.)

- **Cause and Effect** How have decades of burning coal affected the environment and human health? (It has caused pollution and lung disease.)

Analyze Visuals Have students look at the photograph.

- If this man were not cooking with solar energy, what forms of energy might he be using? (Samples: electricity or natural gas)

In Italy, a man cooks using a solar reflector. ▼

In a region where 74 percent live in areas of high energy use such as cities, energy consumption is a hot topic. The European Union (EU) has promoted the use of **renewable energy,** or energy sources that can be replaced. Recently, EU member nations decided to boost their use of renewable energy sources by 20 percent by the year 2020.

Energy and Progress

While EU members might agree that it is important to conserve energy and find new sources of energy, changing energy policy raises concerns. The member nations of the EU do not all have the same economic and technological resources. Not every EU member can afford to invest in alternative energy sources.

In some cases, a nation's history affects its energy policy. Poland, for example, has long depended on heavy industry that burns coal as fuel. Changing to technologies that use renewable energy would be expensive for Poland and would take many years to develop. Other EU members such as Sweden and Denmark have long used "green energy" (clean, efficient, renewable energy) and can more easily meet the EU energy goal.

Concerns about energy consumption generally come as a society reaches a certain level of progress. During the Industrial Revolution, for example, Manchester, England, became a center for textile manufacturing. Once a rural market town, Manchester grew quickly as thousands of people moved there for jobs at coal-powered factories. Over the years, coal pollution left a coating of black smoke everywhere. People died from lung diseases after breathing coal smoke all their lives. Eventually, people became more aware of how using pollution-causing fuels affected human health and the environment.

Reading Check **Why might some nations have trouble meeting the European Union's energy goal?**

GEOGRAPHY

Environmental Impact Scientists are divided over the environmental impact of biofuels. Production of biofuels is helping to meet the growing global demand for oil. Burning biofuels instead of gasoline can reduce greenhouse-gas emissions. However, the demand for biofuels is driving up the demand for crops such as corn and sugar cane. In countries such as Brazil, many farmers are clearing away rainforests to plant crops for biofuels. Vegetation converts carbon dioxide into oxygen during photosynthesis. So replacing the densely growing trees and plants of the rainforest with cropland can actually increase the amount of greenhouse gases in the atmosphere. In addition, the loss of rainforest threatens the diversity of plant and animal life on the planet.

Power to the People

Everyday energy comes in many forms: gasoline for cars, natural gas for heating and cooking, or coal for the generation of electric power. Each of these forms of energy is made from fossil fuels and is **nonrenewable energy,** or energy that cannot be replaced. **Fossil fuels** come from carbon-based organic material that took millions of years to form. Nuclear energy, which comes from the metal uranium, is also considered nonrenewable.

Scientists have been able to find new ways to collect energy: wood, crops such as corn, and even weeds for **biofuels** (fuel from organic material), wind and water for electricity, or energy from the sun that solar cells can convert into electricity. These are all forms of renewable energy.

The EU Common Energy Policy seeks ways to bring more energy to its growing population without damaging the environment. Supporters of the policy also want the EU to become less dependent on energy from other parts of the world, such as Russia or Southwest Asia.

Reading Check **Why are fossil fuels considered nonrenewable?**

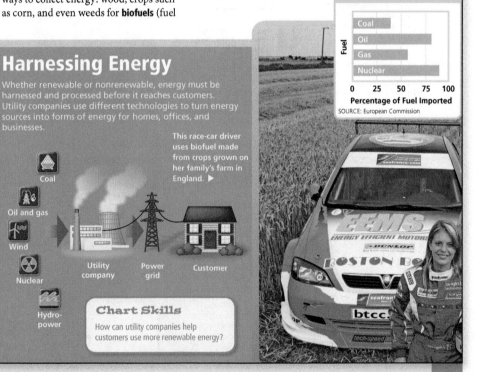

EU Energy Imports

Fuel: Coal, Oil, Gas, Nuclear

0   25   50   75   100
Percentage of Fuel Imported
SOURCE: European Commission

Harnessing Energy

Whether renewable or nonrenewable, energy must be harnessed and processed before it reaches customers. Utility companies use different technologies to turn energy sources into forms of energy for homes, offices, and businesses.

Coal
Oil and gas
Wind
Nuclear
Hydro-power

Utility company Power grid Customer

This race-car driver uses biofuel made from crops grown on her family's farm in England. ▶

Chart Skills
How can utility companies help customers use more renewable energy?

GUIDE ON THE SIDE

Power to the People

- **Summarize** What are the main sources of renewable energy? (biofuels, wind, water, and sun)

- **Draw Conclusions** Why might European leaders want to be less dependent on Russia and Southwest Asia for energy? (Sample: They fear disputes could interrupt their supplies of oil and gas. They do not want to depend on a single energy source in such a circumstance.)

Analyze Charts Have students look at the energy sources graph.

- What source of energy does the EU import the largest percentage of? (nuclear)

ANSWERS

READING CHECK Fossil fuels are nonrenewable because they come from carbon-based organic matter that took millions of years to form.

CHART SKILLS Utility companies can afford to develop more sources of renewable energy.

HISTORY

Windmills and Wind Turbines Windmills, the predecessors to today's wind turbines, have been used for thousands of years for tasks such as grinding and drilling. The earliest-known reference is to a Persian millwright in A.D. 644. Windmill use was widespread from the 12th through the 19th centuries in Europe. With the invention of steam power, their use declined.

With the need for renewable resources, today's wind turbines are becoming much more in demand. Wind energy is the second most rapidly increasing use of energy in the United States. In 2009, President Obama established tax incentives for those wishing to build wind farms in the U.S.

Energy Choices

- **Identify Main Ideas** What is the source of solar energy? (the sun)

- **Draw Conclusions** When people build dams to generate electricity, what type of energy is that? (hydropower)

- **Cause and Effect** Why does the production of biofuels impact food supplies and food costs? (Crops are used to make fuel instead of to feed people. There is less land to grow food.)

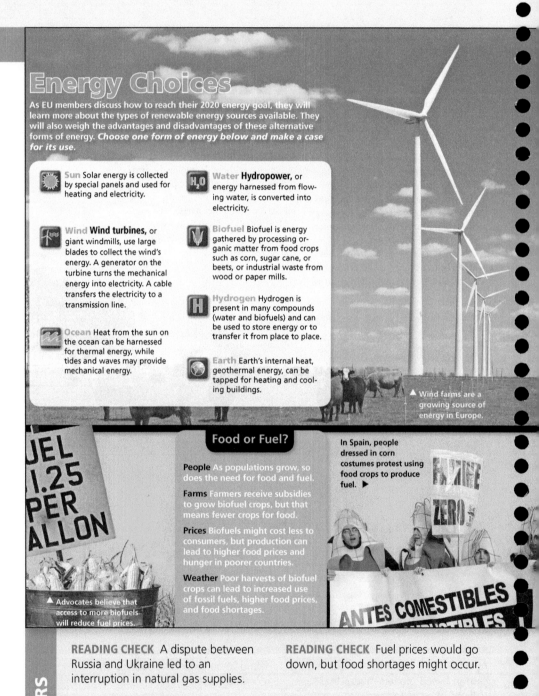

Energy Choices

As EU members discuss how to reach their 2020 energy goal, they will learn more about the types of renewable energy sources available. They will also weigh the advantages and disadvantages of these alternative forms of energy. *Choose one form of energy below and make a case for its use.*

Sun Solar energy is collected by special panels and used for heating and electricity.

Wind **Wind turbines,** or giant windmills, use large blades to collect the wind's energy. A generator on the turbine turns the mechanical energy into electricity. A cable transfers the electricity to a transmission line.

Ocean Heat from the sun on the ocean can be harnessed for thermal energy, while tides and waves may provide mechanical energy.

Water **Hydropower,** or energy harnessed from flowing water, is converted into electricity.

Biofuel Biofuel is energy gathered by processing organic matter from food crops such as corn, sugar cane, or beets, or industrial waste from wood or paper mills.

Hydrogen Hydrogen is present in many compounds (water and biofuels) and can be used to store energy or to transfer it from place to place.

Earth Earth's internal heat, geothermal energy, can be tapped for heating and cooling buildings.

▲ Wind farms are a growing source of energy in Europe.

Food or Fuel?

People As populations grow, so does the need for food and fuel.

Farms Farmers receive subsidies to grow biofuel crops, but that means fewer crops for food.

Prices Biofuels might cost less to consumers, but production can lead to higher food prices and hunger in poorer countries.

Weather Poor harvests of biofuel crops can lead to increased use of fossil fuels, higher food prices, and food shortages.

▲ Advocates believe that access to more biofuels will reduce fuel prices.

In Spain, people dressed in corn costumes protest using food crops to produce fuel. ▶

READING CHECK A dispute between Russia and Ukraine led to an interruption in natural gas supplies.

READING CHECK Fuel prices would go down, but food shortages might occur.

QUICK FACTS

Solar Power Solar cells are devices that absorb and trap sunlight. The energy in the sunlight excites electrons in the absorption layer, causing them to move. By combining two materials that affect electrons differently, the device can cause the electrons to move in one direction, creating an electric current. This transformation is called the photovoltaic effect. A Frenchman, Antoine-César Becquerel, first discovered the effect in 1839. About 50 years later, Charles Fritts made the first solar cell, but the devices were inefficient. At present, solar cells are far more efficient and their cost continues to decline.

GUIDE ON THE SIDE

Learning an Energy Lesson

In 2009, a dispute between Ukraine and Russia led to a three-week interruption of natural gas supplies to Europe. During one of the coldest winters in years, Europeans had to find other ways to stay warm. Schools closed and people used wood fires to heat their homes. Some people froze to death due to lack of heat.

The Russia-Ukraine pipeline supplies 80 percent of the EU's natural gas. Following the 2009 shortage, Europeans realized that they had become too dependent on a single energy source. This event also drew attention to the need to expand renewable energy sources.

Reading Check What event highlighted Europe's energy dependence?

Sharing the Burden

Members of groups like the EU share the benefits as well as the challenges of energy policy. Wealthier nations such as Germany, Denmark, France, and Spain use more renewable energy because they have invested in renewable technologies for many years. France, for example, leads the EU in biofuel production because it has many farms. Spain, with its windy hillsides and plains, is second in wind-energy production.

Some EU members have smaller economies and cannot contribute to the EU energy policy as much as wealthier nations. People in wealthier nations might see the expectation that they spend more on renewable energy as unfair. Some of the newer (and poorer) EU member nations have only recently been able to shift their attention from economic development to energy consumption.

Energy policy must also balance food and energy needs. If European farmers commit too much of their land to crops that will be used for biofuels, there will be less food for people to eat. These crops (corn, soybeans, wheat, and beets) could become scarce and prices could rise.

There is also a concern that land needed for housing or farms might instead be dedicated to energy production. In addition, there could be environmental damage as fossil fuel production expands to forested areas or to ocean drilling sites.

European individuals, companies, and governments are working to resolve these issues. Poorer nations want more economic growth. Europeans must balance that desire with the goals of energy independence and lower pollution.

Reading Check What could happen if more European farmers grew corn for biofuel instead of food?

Assessment

1. Name and define four kinds of renewable energy.
2. In what ways might energy investment differ among EU member nations?
3. How does Spain's geography allow it to be a leader in wind-energy production?
4. What is the primary goal of the EU Common Energy Policy?
5. Write a short paragraph outlining the advantages and disadvantages of growing crops such as corn for biofuel rather than food.

Learning an Energy Lesson

- **Cause and Effect** What caused a shortage of natural gas during the winter of 2009? (A dispute between Ukraine and Russia interrupted supplies.)
- **Compare Viewpoints** How did the natural gas shortage of 2009 change European views? (Leaders realized they had become too dependent on one fuel source.)

Sharing the Burden

- **Summarize** What advantages do France, Germany, Denmark, and Spain have in developing renewable sources of energy? (They have invested in renewable energy for years. France's farms allow it to produce bioethanol. Spain's windy hillsides allow it to use wind turbines.)
- **Identify Main Ideas** Why are poorer nations reluctant to invest in renewable energy? (They prefer to invest in economic growth.)

ASSESSMENT 1. Samples: Solar energy—collected from the sun; wind energy—created by wind turbines; hydropower—created by the power of flowing water; biofuels—made from organic matter; hydrogen—an element that can be burned; ocean—source of thermal and mechanical energy; geothermal energy—created from the internal heat of Earth. **2.** Less-developed nations may not be able to invest as much as other nations. **3.** Spain has windy hillsides. **4.** The goal is to use more renewable energy. **5.** Sample: The advantage is that biofuel burns more cleanly. The disadvantage is that land used for biofuels is not available to grow food.

Northwestern Europe Today

OBJECTIVES

Students will know

- the types of government and government benefits found in Northwestern Europe.
- whether the countries of Northwestern Europe joined the EU and why.

Students will be able to

- compare and contrast countries.
- work in teams to evaluate benefits systems.

SET EXPECTATIONS

In this section, students will

- read Northwestern Europe Today.
- make a political cartoon about cradle-to-grave benefits systems.
- go On Assignment in Western Europe and examine data on charts and graphs.

CORE CONCEPTS

You may wish to teach or reteach the following lessons from the Core Concepts Handbook:

- Trade, pp. 66–67
- Political Systems, pp. 106–107
- Political Structures, pp. 108–109

KEY

Differentiated Instruction

- **L1** Special Needs
- **L2** Extra Support
- **L3** On-Level
- **L4** Challenge

English Language Instruction

- **ELL** Beginner
- **ELL** Early Intermediate
- **ELL** Intermediate
- **ELL** Early Advanced
- **ELL** Advanced

1 Connect
Make learning meaningful

Make Connections Ask students to think about the **myStory Video** of Yasmin's life in Europe. Ask students to list the different cultures that Yasmin draws upon as she lives her daily life. Then ask them ways in which they are influenced by cultures that are different from their family's ethnic background.

L2 Extra Support To help students think of cultures that influence them, give them broad categories to consider, such as music, movies, food, and books.

Activate Prior Knowledge Remind students that in the previous section, they learned that Scandinavia is one of the coldest regions of Europe. Ask them to predict whether Scandinavians will be more independent or interdependent as a result.

ELL Early Intermediate/Intermediate Give definitions for the terms *independent* and *interdependent* using simplified or colloquial language. For example, define independent as "alone" and interdependent as "needs people."

Prepare Follow the steps in the section **Preview.** Preteach the Key Terms. Then have students complete *Word Wise* in their journals using in-text clues and the glossary for help.

2 Experience
Teach knowledge and skills

Read Use **Background** notes and **Guide on the Side** questions to model active reading. Have students use *Take Notes* in their **Student Journal** to record how the United Kingdom and Scandinavia are alike and different. Have students complete **21st Century Online Tutor** *Compare and Contrast*, and apply this skill to reading the section.

L1 Special Needs Have students read the **Online Student Edition** while listening to the accompanying audio.

ELL Intermediate Have students practice comparing and contrasting by completing these sentences: My life is similar to Yasmin's because _____. My life is different from Yasmin's because _____.

L4 Challenge Have students read *Enrichment: Sweden's Ice Hotel* to learn more about life in far northern Scandinavia.

 Practice: myWorld Activity Students will make a political cartoon that expresses support for or criticism of cradle-to-grave benefits systems. **Step-by-Step Instructions** and **More Activities** follow on p. T96.

T94

SECTION 2 RESOURCE GUIDE

FOR THE STUDENT

my worldgeography.com Student Center

- Data Discovery

Student Edition (print and online)
- Northwestern Europe Today

Student Journal (print and online)
- Section 2 Word Wise
- Section 2 Take Notes

21st Century Learning Online Tutor

- Compare and Contrast
- Work in Teams

FOR THE TEACHER

my worldgeography.com Teacher Center

- Online Lesson Planner
- Presentations for Projection
- SuccessTracker

ProGuide: Europe and Russia
- Section 2 Lesson Plan, pp. T94–T95
- myWorld Activity Step-by-Step Instructions, p. T96
- Activity Support: Pros and Cons, p. T97
- myWorld Geography Enrichment, p. T98
- Section Quiz, p. T99

Accelerating the Progress of ELLs
- Comprehension Check Strategies, p. 53

---

3 Understand
Assess understanding

Review Review *Word Wise* and *Take Notes* in the **Student Journals.**

Assess Knowledge and Skills Use the Section Assessment and the Section Quiz to check students' progress.

Assess Understanding Review students' responses to the Section Assessment Essential Question prompt.

Remediate Use these strategies to review and remediate.

If students struggle to . . .	Try these strategies.
Describe the challenges that immigrants face	Replay the **myVideo Story** of Yasmin and her experience as someone who moved from Spain to Sweden.
Understand the link between representative democracy and EU membership	Explain that nations can be voting members of governing bodies just as individuals can.
Work in Teams	Assign additional practice with the **21st Century Online Tutor.**

ELL Support

ELL Objective Students will be able to use English to sequence.

Cultural Connections To connect students to Yasmin's experience of moving back and forth between countries, let students use their native languages to describe visits to their families' homelands or other countries.

ELL Early Beginner/Early Intermediate Content Tip Give students language for sequencing by teaching the terms for ordinal numbers: 1. first; 2. second; 3. third; and so on. Help students sequence the stages of life: baby, child, teenager, adult, etc.

ELL Activity Help students understand cradle-to-grave benefits by giving out cards with these terms and review: *pension, children's day care, healthcare, unemployment benefits, education.* Ask students to place the benefits in order by what age person receives them. If it applies to more than one, place it at the earliest age. **(Visual/Logical)**

my worldgeography.com Lesson Planner

myWorld Activity   **Step-by-Step Instructions**

 25 min

Cradle to Grave?

OBJECTIVES

Students will

- evaluate the pros and cons of a cradle-to-grave system of benefits.
- make a political cartoon expressing support or opposition for such a system.

LEARNING STYLE

- Visual

21st Century Learning

- Work in Teams

MATERIALS

- Markers or colored pencils
- Activity Support: Pros and Cons, p. T97

Activity Steps

1. Divide the class into small groups. Suggest that the group members take on roles, such as researchers, recorder, or artist. Give each student a copy of *Activity Support: Pros and Cons.*

2. Tell the groups to review the material about cradle-to-grave benefits systems in Section 2 of their textbooks. The researchers should call out details about such systems, and the group will decide as a whole whether each one is a pro or con. Then the recorders will list them on the table.

3. After completing the table, the group should decide whether cradle-to-grave systems of benefits are good or bad for society. Then they should think of an example that they can draw to show such benefits systems helping society or hurting society.

L2 Extra Support Remind students that political cartoonists often draw humorous or exaggerated situations to make their point. Many times they label the people and objects in their cartoons so people will know what they represent.

4. The artist will then draw a political cartoon that conveys the group's view of such benefit systems. The completed cartoons should be shown to the class.

L4 Challenge Suggest that students write an editorial about cradle-to-grave systems to support the political cartoon.

More Activities From myWorld Teachers

Local Connection Have groups of students work together to write a list of stories or movies that are set in the United Kingdom and are popular with young people in the United States. **(Verbal)**

Land of the Midnight Sun Have students do research to find out why the lands inside the Arctic Circle have days of 24-hour darkness in winter and days of 24-hour sunlight in summer. They should draw a diagram to explain the scientific reason. **(Visual/Logical)**

United or Not Have students work in pairs to make a chart that lists the ways in which the four countries of the United Kingdom are united under one government and the ways in which they have local self-rule. **(Visual)**

 my worldgeography.com Teacher Center   →   Find additional resources in the online Teacher Center.

Name _____ Class _____ Date _____

myWorld Activity Support **Pros and Cons**

Cradle to Grave?

Directions Working in a small group, review the information in your textbook about the cradle-to-grave system of benefits in Scandinavia. Use the table below to record pros and cons about such systems. Decide as a group whether you are in favor of them. Then on a separate sheet of paper, draw a political cartoon to illustrate your opinion.

Pros of Cradle-to-Grave Systems	Cons of Cradle-to-Grave Systems

Group Decision On the lines below, explain whether or not you are in favor of cradle-to-grave systems and why.

_____

_____

_____

_____

_____

Name _____ Class _____ Date _____

Enrichment: Sweden's Ice Hotel

Directions Read the article below. Answer the questions that follow and complete the activity.

Would you pay money to sleep on a block of solid ice? Tourists who visit the far northern town of Jukkasjärvi (YUK•kas•yair•vey), Sweden do just that. Jukkasjärvi is located 124 miles north of the Arctic Circle. In the winter, darkness lasts around the clock, and at night, the outdoor temperatures can fall to 20°F below zero or colder.

In 1990, an artist used ice from the frozen Torne River to build a large igloo. Some adventurous tourists decided to spend the night inside it. The next day they bragged about what a unique experience it was. Every winter since 1992, artists have built a new ice hotel. They use packed ice from the Torne, which is very clean, and use snow cannons to make snow from the river's water. When spring arrives, the hotel ceiling begins to drip, and the hotel must close. By midsummer, all the ice has melted and flowed back into the river.

During winter when the hotel is open, the stars and the moon are the only source of natural light. The snow on the ground reflects the starlight, making it brighter. The electric lights within the Ice Hotel make the walls glow blue. Inside, the hotel is filled with sculpture, furniture, and even fake fireplaces carved from ice. Tourists who stay there are told to dress warmly. The hotel also loans each one an overall, a hat, mittens, boots, and a thermal sleeping bag. Inside the bedrooms, temperatures hover between 18° and 23°F. Restaurants and bathrooms are located in heated buildings attached to the Ice Hotel.

People who have braved a night in the Ice Hotel say it is the experience of a lifetime. In the short time it has existed, the Ice Hotel has become one of the most popular tourist attractions in Sweden.

1. Why is the area lighted only by starlight and moonlight in the winter?

_____

_____

2. How did the people of Jukkasjärvi turn a harsh climate into an economic advantage?

_____

_____

3. Activity Working with a partner, make a poster to advertise the Ice Hotel. Emphasize what you think are the advantages of staying there.

Name _____ Class _____ Date _____

Section Quiz

Directions Answer the following questions using what you learned
in Section 2.

1. _____ What is a constitutional monarchy?
   a. a government in which a king or queen
      has all the power
   b. a government in which the people elect
      the king or queen
   c. a representative government with a
      mostly ceremonial ruler
   d. a representative government with only
      one set of written laws

2. _____ What is a cradle-to-grave system?
   a. a system of state-run hospitals and
      nursing homes
   b. an association of doctors and nurses
   c. an association of nursery schools and
      public schools
   d. a system of basic services for every stage
      of life

3. _____ Why did Northern Ireland, Scotland,
   and Wales gain their own legislatures?
   a. The EU ordered that change to take
      place.
   b. The UK government is growing more
      regional.
   c. The British Parliament had grown too
      large to be efficient.
   d. The two countries gained independence
      from the UK.

4. _____ What are the two parts of the British
   Parliament?
   a. House of Commons and House of
      Representatives
   b. House of Commons and House of Lords
   c. House of Lords and House of
      Representatives
   d. House of Representatives and Senate

5. _____ What are the white nights of
   Scandinavia?
   a. nights when the sun shines almost all
      night
   b. nights that celebrate a victory over
      Communist invasion
   c. nights when the government provides
      free healthcare
   d. nights of heavy snowfall that covers the
      ground.

6. Complete the chart below with examples of cultural borrowing.

An Example from the United Kingdom	An Example from Scandinavia	An Example from My Life in the United States

Northwestern Europe Today

- Model preparing to read by previewing the Key Ideas, Key Terms, headings, visuals, and captions. Have students make predictions about what they will learn. For ELL support, post the prompt: "I predict I will read about . . ."
- Preview and practice the reading skill, Compare and Contrast, by using examples from your school.

- Preteach this section's high-use Academic Vocabulary and Key Terms using the table on the next page and in-text definitions. Have students practice Key Terms by completing the *Word Wise* page in their journals.

GUIDE ON THE SIDE

Reading Skill

Compare and Contrast While they read, have students practice this skill by completing the *Take Notes* graphic organizer in the **Student Journal.**

The United Kingdom and Ireland

- **Infer** Why do you think Britain is called the United Kingdom? (Sample: It is made of several smaller regions that are united under one monarch.)

- **Identify Main Ideas** What are the characteristics of a constitutional monarchy? (It has a monarch, a constitution, and a representative legislature.)

Section 2

Northwestern Europe Today

Key Ideas
- The United Kingdom has a long history of democracy.
- Scandinavian nations offer a cradle-to-grave system of public services.
- Many people in Northwestern Europe favor limited ties with the European Union.

Key Terms • constitutional monarchy • Parliament • cradle-to-grave system • gross domestic product (GDP) • cultural borrowing

Visual Glossary

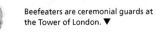
Reading Skill: Sequence Take notes using the graphic organizer in your journal.

Beefeaters are ceremonial guards at the Tower of London. ▼

You might be surprised to learn that England has a queen, yet it also has a long history of democracy. During the summers in northern Scandinavia, there is sunshine at midnight. How can this be? The nations of Northwestern Europe are worth a closer look.

The United Kingdom and Ireland

The United Kingdom, or Britain, is an island nation made up of several regions. England, Wales, and Scotland are located on the largest island, Great Britain. Northern Ireland, on the nearby smaller island of Ireland, is also part of the United Kingdom. Most of this island is the independent nation of Ireland.

British Government You have read about King John signing the Magna Carta in 1215. This document limited the power of the king and gave rights to his people. It was the beginning of democratic government in England. Today, the British government is a **constitutional monarchy.** This means the monarch is the ceremonial leader, but Parliament makes the laws. Unlike the U.S. Constitution, the British constitution is not a single document, but a group of laws and court decisions. The symbolic head is Queen Elizabeth II, who symbolizes Britain's nationhood.

ACADEMIC VOCABULARY

High-Use Word	Definition and Sample Sentences
currency	*n.* a system of money, especially the bills and coins, used in a country *The currency of Norway is the krone.*
heritage	*n.* something possessed as a result of one's natural situation or birth *Individual freedom is a large part of the heritage of West Central Europe.*
transportation	*n.* the means of carrying people or goods from one place to another *During the 1800s, many people used horse-drawn carriages for transportation.*

The British legislature, or **Parliament**, is located in London, England. It is made up of the House of Lords and the House of Commons. At one time, members of the House of Lords inherited their seats. Today, Parliament is moving toward a combination of elected and appointed members in both houses. These members are composed of high-ranking clergy, judges, and national leaders. The head of the majority party in the House of Commons is the prime minister, the true head of the British government.

Since the 1990s, some lawmaking power has moved from a national to a regional level. Scotland has its own Parliament and government that handles laws specific to that country. The Welsh National Assembly can pass laws that directly affect Wales. Northern Ireland also has a separate assembly with its own powers.

The official language of the United Kingdom is English. Some people also speak Welsh, Irish, or Scottish Gaelic. Thousands of immigrants come to Britain every year. Many come from countries that were once part of the British empire.

Prosperity and Partnerships Britain and Ireland both have a high standard of living and strong economies. In the past, Britain owed its wealth to iron and steel, textiles, and shipbuilding. Today, Britain is part of a global economy. The British work with international partners in finance and banking, high-technology fields, and service industries. Entrepreneurs, or people who start businesses, have had much success in Northwestern Europe.

One Nation, Four Countries

Known as the United Kingdom of Great Britain and Northern Ireland, these four countries act together on matters such as foreign policy. However, they act independently with regard to EU involvement and legal issues.

Map Skills

How might giving more power to regional governments strengthen the United Kingdom?

→ **Active Atlas**

SCOTLAND

NORTHERN IRELAND

WALES   ENGLAND

The United Kingdom and Ireland also benefit from being in the European Union. The European Union (EU) is an organization of European nations that promotes free movement of goods and people across borders. Ireland and Britain can trade with other member nations in an open market. There are no tariffs, or taxes, on goods imported from other member nations. Without tariffs, goods and services move freely. The EU has its own <u>currency,</u> the euro. Ireland uses the euro, but Britain does not. The British currency is the pound.

currency, *n.,* a system of money, especially the bills and coins, used in a country

MAP SKILLS It might strengthen the United Kingdom by reducing the desire for independence in the separate countries and by involving more citizens in government.

- **Identify Main Ideas** What is the British legislature called, and what two houses does it contain? (Parliament; it contains the House of Lords and the House of Commons.)

- **Identify Evidence** In what way has the government of the United Kingdom increased self-rule in recent years? (It has transferred some lawmaking control to the regions.)

- **Compare and Contrast** How are the UK and Irish economies similar and different? (Both trade globally and belong to the EU, and both prosper. Only Ireland uses the euro.)

Analyze Charts Have students study the illustration "One Nation, Four Countries."

- What is the largest of the four countries in the United Kingdom? (England)

- Which of the four countries is farthest north? (Scotland)

CORE CONCEPTS: POLITICAL SYSTEMS

Review Core Concept 8.2 before discussing Scandinavia's cradle-to-grave benefits system. Review the concepts of constitutional monarchy and democracy, and explain that in many modern democracies, the people have chosen to have their government provide more social benefits than is typical in the United States. Also explain that the downside of such systems is that they require high taxes.

GUIDE ON THE SIDE

- **Build Cultural Awareness** What are some popular tourists sites in the United Kingdom and Ireland? (Buckingham Palace, Stonehenge, Stratford-upon-Avon, the countryside, and castles)

The Scandinavian Countries

- **Compare and Contrast** Which Scandinavian countries have governments that are similar to the UK? (Denmark, Norway, and Sweden have constitutional monarchies.)

Analyze Charts Have students study the chart about Scandinavian benefits.

- Which benefits are most likely to be used by students? (healthcare and college tuition)

 myWorld Activity

Cradle to Grave? Find Step-by-Step Instructions and an Activity Support on pp. T96–T97. **(Visual)**

 Data Discovery

Have students go to myworldgeography.com to explore more data about Northwestern Europe.

---

heritage, *n.,* something possessed as a result of one's natural situation or birth

A Tourist Destination Britain is the world's sixth most popular travel destination. Many people visit Britain because of their <u>heritage</u>. Americans, for example, often travel to the United Kingdom to revisit the homes of their English, Irish, Scottish, or Welsh ancestors.

Tourists flock to famous places such as London's Buckingham Palace. They also visit ancient and historic sites such as Stonehenge and Shakespeare's hometown, Stratford-upon-Avon. Ireland draws visitors to its prosperous cities and green rural areas. Fishing is popular in Scotland's rivers. History lovers visit Welsh castles and villages.

Reading Check **How has EU membership promoted economic development in Britain and Ireland?**

The Scandinavian Countries
Denmark, Finland, Iceland, Norway, and Sweden make up the area known as Scandinavia. Life near the Arctic Circle is chilly, but full of variety.

Cradle-to-Grave Benefits Sweden, Norway, and Denmark are constitutional monarchies much like the United Kingdom. Each monarch is mainly a symbolic leader. Political decisions are made by an elected parliament. Finland is a democratic republic with a president. All are members of the EU except Norway. Norway has voted to remain outside the EU for several reasons. Some Norwegians feel that the EU's structure is not democratic. They also want to keep Norway's economic and political freedom.

The Cradle-to-Grave System

This system of social services originated after World War II in response to postwar hardships. Funding for the system comes from high taxes, such as payroll taxes and sales tax. These taxes fund benefits such as universal healthcare, education, and pensions.

Chart Skills
How does this diagram show advantages and disadvantages of the cradle-to-grave system?

Data Discovery

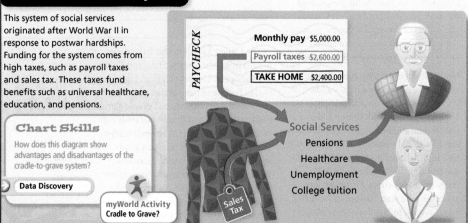

myWorld Activity
Cradle to Grave?

PAYCHECK
Monthly pay $5,000.00
Payroll taxes $2,600.00
TAKE HOME $2,400.00

Sales Tax

Social Services
Pensions
Healthcare
Unemployment
College tuition

CHART SKILLS It shows that citizens pay high taxes but receive many benefits.

READING CHECK Membership has given the UK and Ireland access to more markets with fewer tariffs.

COMMON MISCONCEPTIONS

Blue-Eyed Blonds One of the most common mistakes that Americans make about Scandinavia is that everyone who lives there is a blue-eyed blond. Although Scandinavia does have a higher percentage of light-haired people than other regions of Europe, the population contains people with every hair and eye color. In recent years, immigration has made the population even more diverse in appearance.

The Scandinavian governments have a **cradle-to-grave system,** a system of basic services for citizens at every stage of life. It covers healthcare, education, and retirement. Benefits are funded through taxes. Because people believe this system is important, they are willing to pay high taxes for it. In Sweden, people pay on average almost 60 percent of their income in taxes. Clothing and food are also expensive due to taxes. On the other hand, healthcare costs and rents are low.

Fish, Forests, and Phones In the past, the Scandinavian countries depended on farming. Agriculture and dairy farming are still important in Denmark, where the climate is warmer. Today, the economies of these countries rely on multinational corporations, high-technology industries, and exports. Finland, for example, is a leading manufacturer of mobile telephones.

Scandinavia's geography also affects the economy. Miles of coastline and acres of forests supply the fishing and lumber industries. Oil production in the North Sea also helps this region maintain a high standard of living. Membership in the EU opens Denmark, Finland, and Sweden to free trade and global markets.

Located near the Arctic Circle, the northernmost Scandinavian cities have what are called white nights. From May to July, the sun appears on the horizon for almost 24 hours a day. This is because the northern hemisphere is tilted toward the sun at that time of year.

Reading Check **Why do people in Sweden pay high taxes?**

SCANDINAVIA: LAND OF THE VIKINGS

The gods, giants, and elves of ancient Scandinavian myths remain popular today. The adventures of the Norse warriors known as the Vikings left marks on territory from England to Russia. In modern times, Scandinavia has been known for its famous scientists and artists. These nations also have a long record of gender equality and human rights. *Why might people build replicas of ancient ships today?*

Danish carpenter Ole Kirk Christiansen invented one of the world's most popular children's toys. ▼

The dala horse was once a toy, but has become a symbol of Sweden. ▼

Modern-day replica of a Viking ship ▶

GUIDE ON THE SIDE

- **Compare Viewpoints** Why do Scandinavians believe that it is important to pay high taxes? (They receive many government benefits in return.)

- **Summarize** How have the Scandinavian economies changed? (They used to rely on agriculture; now they rely on multinational corporations, exports, and high-tech industries.)

- **Cause and Effect** What natural resource has recently brought wealth to the region? (oil)

Analyze Visuals Have students look at the photographs in the feature on Scandinavian culture.

- What is one way that Scandinavia has influenced U.S. culture? (Sample: through the invention of toys that many children use)

- How would you describe the carving and decoration on the dala horse? (Sample: The carving is simple, but the decoration is very fancy.)

ANSWERS

Internet Use Countries in Western Europe have a high percentage of Internet users. The figures for 2007 follow:
Denmark: 3.5 million (64%)
Finland: 3.6 million (67%)
Iceland: 0.2 million (67%)
Ireland: 1.7 million (41%)

Norway: 3.8 million (83%)
Sweden: 7 million (78%)
United Kingdom: 40.2 million (66%)
Source: *CIA World Factbook*, 2008

GUIDE ON THE SIDE

Life in Northwestern Europe

- **Cause and Effect** How has technology changed life in Northwestern Europe? (It has linked distant places and made life more fast-paced.)

- **Problem Solve** What has technology helped Danish farmers to do? (produce healthier food)

Analyze Graphs Have students study the graph on GDP per person.

- Approximately how much is Norway's GDP per person? (about $54,000)

- What is the GDP per person of the United Kingdom? (about $36,000)

→ **Data Discovery**

Have students go to myworldgeography.com to explore more data about Northwestern Europe.

Life in Northwestern Europe
Aspects of daily life in northwestern Europe are changing rapidly.

Living With Technology With almost universal access to the Internet, cellphones, and television, faraway places are much nearer. Life has become more fast-paced. Technology has changed how people work in surprising ways. Danish farmers use modern technology to produce healthier food. Scientists in Norway have discovered new ways to preserve water supplies.

Finland uses more than 3 percent of its **gross domestic product** for technology research and development. Gross domestic product (GDP) is the total value of all goods and services produced and sold in a country in a year.

In this region, finding ways to save energy is important. Due to its cold climate, Finland uses a great deal of energy for heating. One way to reduce energy use is driving cars with better gas mileage. Finland has passed a law raising taxes for cars with poor gas mileage. The owners of cars with higher gas mileage pay less in taxes.

Living in Cities Many of the large cities in this region are capital cities: London, Dublin, Copenhagen, Oslo, Stockholm, and Helsinki. These cities are centuries old and rich in history and culture.

London has museums and palaces, and Stockholm has historic city squares. In Dublin, people lunch at pubs, while in Helsinki they relax in saunas. Most people use public transportation rather than their cars for daily travels.

transportation, *n.,* a means of carrying people or goods from one place to another

Chart Skills
Compare Norway's GDP with the world average.

→ **Data Discovery**

GDP per Person, Northwestern Europe

SOURCE: *CIA World Factbook, 2008*

A United Kingdom woman paints figures for a company that exports tableware and gifts. ▼

CHART SKILLS It is more than five times larger.

READING CHECK The Finnish government taxes cars that get poor gas mileage.

CULTURE

Cosmopolitan Cuisine At one time, the British Empire stretched around the globe. A common saying was that "The sun never sets on the British Empire." Immigrants from many former colonies have migrated to the United Kingdom, particularly its capital city of London. As a result, London has a wide variety of ethnic restaurants, including Caribbean, Chinese, Egyptian, Indian, and Lebanese. In fact, Indian curry is one of the most popular dishes in the UK.

Living Together Northwestern Europe is a region of many ethnic groups due to a large immigrant population. Some immigrants have lived there for generations. Others have come more recently.

The EU's open-border policy has also let people move between nations. In this chapter's myStory, you read about how the policy lets Yasmin move easily about Europe for family trips and education.

It is common to see people from the Caribbean, India, Pakistan, Turkey, or Somalia here. These newcomers face many challenges. To find jobs, they must learn how to get around. They may have to learn a language different from their parents' language.

Some immigrants have religious beliefs that <u>conflict</u> with local customs. For example, there is a significant Muslim population in Norway. Muslims have certain religious beliefs about food preparation. These beliefs can lead to higher prices in markets and restaurants—whether or not customers are Muslim.

▲ This London restaurant owner offers food from India, where he grew up.

conflict, v., to clash or to be in opposition

Immigrants may also take part in **cultural borrowing,** an exchange that takes place when groups come into contact and share ideas, language, customs—and even food. Many Londoners enjoy eating at Indian or Ethiopian restaurants. In Copenhagen, people have grown to love Turkish coffee or food that mixes traditional Danish ingredients with those of France or Japan.

Reading Check **What is one way that Finland tries to reduce energy use?**

Section 2 Assessment

Key Terms

1. Use the following terms to describe Northwestern Europe today: constitutional monarchy, cradle-to-grave system, cultural borrowing.

Key Ideas

2. How has a long history of democracy affected Northwestern Europe?

3. Describe how technology has changed daily life for Northwestern Europe.

4. What sorts of challenges do immigrants face in a new country?

Think Critically

5. **Draw Conclusions** How does the EU open market benefit member nations?

6. **Categorize** Name three industries that developed because of Scandinavia's geography.

Essential Question

Is it better to be independent or interdependent?

7. What are the benefits of cultural borrowing? What might be some of the challenges? Go to your Student Journal to record your answer.

SECTION ASSESSMENT **1.** Samples: The United Kingdom is a constitutional monarchy. Scandinavia has a cradle-to-grave system. Immigration has increased cultural borrowing. **2.** Countries with a history of democracy have been open to EU membership because it offers democratic benefits. **3.** Technology has increased production and helped to save energy. **4.** They must find jobs and places to live and learn a new language and customs. **5.** It encourages trade by eliminating regulations. **6.** fishing, forestry, oil production **7.** Cultural borrowing can introduce people to new customs, ideas, or food, but such changes can lead to tensions among people of different backgrounds.

ANSWERS

SECTION 3 LESSON PLAN

West Central Europe Today

OBJECTIVES

Students will know

- characteristics of West Central Europe's rich cultural heritage.
- West Central Europe's ties to international partnerships such as the European Union.

Students will be able to

- identify main ideas and details about life in West Central Europe.
- work as teams on a group project.

SET EXPECTATIONS

In this section, students will

- read West Central Europe Today.
- make a travel poster to persuade tourists to visit West Central Europe.
- go On Assignment in Western Europe and learn about culture and examine data on charts.

CORE CONCEPTS

You may wish to teach or reteach the following lessons from the Core Concepts Handbook:

- Economic Development, pp. 64–65
- Art, pp. 94–95
- Conflict and Cooperation, pp. 110–111

KEY

Differentiated Instruction

L1 Special Needs **L2** Extra Support

L3 On-Level **L4** Challenge

English Language Instruction

ELL Beginner **ELL** Early Intermediate **ELL** Intermediate

ELL Early Advanced **ELL** Advanced

---

1 Connect
Make learning meaningful

Make Connections Ask students to name any French or German foods that they have eaten. Can they name some famous French or German foods that they haven't tried?

L1 **Special Needs** Show pictures of foods such as bratwurst, croissant, sauerkraut, escargot, frog legs. Have students predict if it is French or German.

Activate Prior Knowledge Remind students that in the previous section, they learned about some countries that joined the European Union and some that have remained apart. Ask them to predict which countries of West Central Europe are EU members.

ELL **Beginner/Early Intermediate** Put the names of the countries on separate pieces of paper and allow students to make their predictions by sorting them into *Yes* and *No* stacks.

Prepare Follow the steps in the section **Preview.** Preteach the Key Terms. Then have students complete *Word Wise* in their journals using in-text clues and the glossary for help.

2 Experience
Teach knowledge and skills

Read Use **Background** notes and **Guide on the Side** questions to model active reading. Have students use *Take Notes* in their **Student Journals** to record main ideas and details about culture and international partnerships in the region. Have students complete **21st Century Online Tutor** *Identify Main Ideas and Details*, and apply this skill to reading the section.

ELL **Early Intermediate** Have students study *Enrichment: Technology of the Eiffel Tower*. Ask them to circle the three facts they find most interesting and then repeat the information to a partner.

L2 **Extra Support** Tell students to use a 3-column chart to take notes on each country in West Central Europe's *type of government, economy,* and *culture.*

ELL **Intermediate** Give students this model for how to write persuasive statements for a travel poster: You should visit _____ because it is _____. You can _____ in _____.

 Practice: myWorld Activity Students will identify features of West Central Europe that appeal to tourists and make a travel poster to persuade people to visit the region. **Step-by-Step Instructions** and **More Activities** follow on p. T102.

SECTION 3 RESOURCE GUIDE

FOR THE STUDENT

my worldgeography.com Student Center
- Culture Close-up
- Data Discovery

Student Edition (print and online)
- West Central Europe Today

Student Journal (print and online)
- Section 3 Word Wise
- Section 3 Take Notes

21st Century Learning Online Tutor
- Identify Main Ideas and Details
- Work in Teams

FOR THE TEACHER

my worldgeography.com Teacher Center
- Online Lesson Planner
- Presentations for Projection
- SuccessTracker

ProGuide: Europe and Russia
- Section 3 Lesson Plan, pp. T100–T101
- myWorld Activity Step-by-Step Instructions, p. T102
- Activity Support: Persuasive Details, p. T103
- myWorld Geography Enrichment, p. T104
- Section Quiz, p. T105

Accelerating the Progress of ELLs
- Reading Support Strategies, p. 42

3 Understand
Assess understanding

Review Review *Word Wise* and *Take Notes* in the **Student Journal.**

Assess Knowledge and Skills Use the Section Assessment and the Section Quiz to check students' progress.

Assess Understanding Review students' responses to the Section Assessment Essential Question prompt.

Remediate Use these strategies to review and remediate.

If students struggle to . . .	Try these strategies.
Remember names of international organizations	Have them list the international organizations mentioned in Section 3 and what each one is.
Work in Teams	Assign additional practice with the **21st Century Online Tutor.**
Understand the issues related to German reunification	Have them review the difference between a free market economy and a centrally planned economy.

ELL Support

ELL Objective Students will be able to use English to state main ideas.

Cultural Connections Have students use English to express a main idea about the culture of their family's home country, such as "Music is important in our culture." Allow them to use their native languages to give details that elaborate on the main idea.

ELL Beginner Content Tip Pair students with partners who have more English proficiency. Give each pair a copy of a political map showing Europe, North Africa, and Southwest Asia. Have students find information in the text about where immigrants to Germany and France come from, and use arrows to represent that information on the map.

ELL Activity Give groups of students several magazines. Have them study the advertisements and make a list of persuasive adjectives used in them. Then have students circle the words that might be useful in their travel posters about Europe. **(Visual/Verbal)**

myWorld Activity   Step-by-Step Instructions

 20 min

Make a Travel Poster

OBJECTIVES

Students will

- evaluate why West Central Europe is a popular travel destination.
- make a travel poster featuring some appealing aspect of West Central Europe.

LEARNING STYLE

- Visual
- Interpersonal

21st Century Learning

- Work in teams

MATERIALS

- Poster board
- Colored markers or pencils
- Activity Support: Persuasive Details, p. T103.

Activity Steps

1. Divide the class into pairs. Direct the pairs to decide how they will divide up the tasks of scribe and artist.

2. Remind students of the role that media plays in directing consumer behavior. Advertisers seek to alter consumer behavior by persuading people to buy their products, whether the product is a car, a snack food, or a vacation. For example, grocery store shoppers are looking to supply a need—food with nutritional value—but they may be persuaded by a television commercial to buy a nonnutritious snack food, satisfying a "want," rather than their "need."

3. Then have the students scan Section 3 looking for reasons why West Central Europe is a popular tourist destination. Suggest that they pay close attention to the following categories: Landmarks, Geographic Features, Arts and Culture, and Ways of Life. The scribe should take notes on the Persuasive Details table.

L2 Extra Support To help students understand these broad categories, give examples. For instance, the category *Landmarks* would include cathedrals, palaces, and monuments.

4. After they have completed the table, each pair should pick one detail about life in West Central Europe to feature in their travel poster. Remind students that they want to choose something that will persuade tourists to visit.

L3 On-Level Suggest that before students make their final choice, they review some of the persuasive techniques they have seen used in advertising. For example, many ads stress the uniqueness of what they are selling.

5. Finally, each pair should make a travel poster by having the artist draw an image and having the scribe write a persuasive caption.

More Activities From myWorld Teachers

 Local Connection Have students visit a local grocery store and write down the names of cheeses or cookies that are made in France, Germany, the Netherlands, and Switzerland. **(Verbal)**

Pros and Cons Lead the class in a review of the information in Sections 2 and 3 about those countries that have joined the European Union and those that have not and why. Write a class list of pros and cons about EU membership. **(Logical)**

European Exports Divide the class into groups. Have students search through magazines and cut out clippings of European products exported to America. Then each group will make a collage of the clippings and list the home countries for the products shown. **(Visual)**

 my worldgeography.com (Teacher Center) Find additional resources in the online Teacher Center.

Name _____ Class _____ Date _____

myWorld Activity Support   **Persuasive Details**

Make a Travel Poster

Directions With your partner, discuss the following questions and then follow the instructions for how to complete the table. You will use details from the chart to make a travel poster.

1. Suppose you have outgrown your shoes. You go to the store to buy a new pair. At the same time, you buy a game. Which purchase was a need and which was a want? Explain.

_____

2. Think of advertisements you have seen on television or in magazines. When an ad tells you that you need a product, is it always telling the truth? Explain.

_____

3. In this activity, you will make a travel poster to persuade tourists to visit West Central Europe. Will you be appealing to needs or wants? Explain.

_____

4. Skim Section 3 looking for information about why West Central Europe is so popular with tourists. On the table below, record the things that might persuade tourists to visit this region. Then choose the one you think would be most effective in persuading tourists to travel to West Central Europe. Make a travel poster that features it.

Landmarks	Geographic Features
Arts and Culture	**Ways of Life**

T103

Name _____ Class _____ Date _____

Enrichment: Technology of the Eiffel Tower

Directions Study the diagram below. Answer the questions that follow and complete the activity.

Height: 324 meters (1,063 feet) to the top of antenna

Stairs: 1,665 steps to the top

Weight of iron structure: 7,300 tons

Number of pieces: 18,038

Number of rivets (iron pins): 2.5 million

Construction time: 2 years, 2 months, 5 days

Date opened: March 31, 1889

Visitors through December 31, 2007: 236.4 million

Paint: repainted every 7 years; uses 60 tons of paint

Support: The legs of the tower rest on four underground pillars built on a foundation 15 meters (49 feet) below the surface.

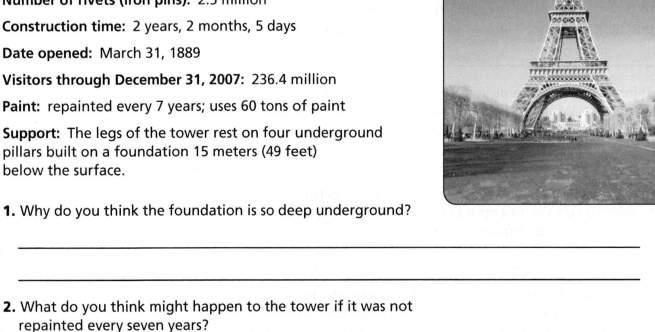

1. Why do you think the foundation is so deep underground?

_____

_____

2. What do you think might happen to the tower if it was not repainted every seven years?

_____

_____

3. Activity Calculate how old the tower was in 2007. Then calculate the average number of visitors per year.

Name _____ Class _____ Date _____

Section Quiz

Directions Answer the following questions using what you learned
in Section 3.

1. _____ What is the statistic gross national
product used to measure?
  a. a country's income
  b. a country's factories
  c. a country's retail stores
  d. a country's taxes

2. _____ What does privatization do?
  a. It makes government wiretapping
    illegal.
  b. It transfers ownership of business from
    government to individuals.
  c. It increases the number of new recruits
    into the national army.
  d. It makes government documents top
    secret.

3. _____ Which West Central European
country recently experienced reunification?
  a. Belgium
  b. France
  c. Germany
  d. Switzerland

4. _____ How did the Dutch make polders?
  a. by dumping fill in low-lying areas
  b. by building levees to collect river
    sediment
  c. by constructing offshore platforms and
    adding soil
  d. by draining land to reclaim it from
    the sea

5. _____ Which of the following countries has
a long history of neutrality in wars?
  a. Austria
  b. Germany
  c. France
  d. Switzerland

6. Complete the table below with details about the culture of several
countries in West Central Europe.

Country	Culture
Belgium	
France	
Germany	
Netherlands	

West Central Europe Today

- Model preparing to read by previewing the Key Ideas, Key Terms, headings, visuals, and captions. Have students make predictions about what they will learn. For ELL support, post the prompt: "I predict I will read about . . ."

- Preview and practice the reading skill, Identify Main Ideas and Details, by using examples from current events.

- Preteach this section's high-use Academic Vocabulary and Key Terms using the chart on the next page and in-text definitions. Have students practice Key Terms by completing the *Word Wise* page in their journals.

Reading Skill

Identify Main Ideas and Details While they read, have students practice this skill by completing the *Take Notes* graphic organizer in the **Student Journal.**

At the Center of the European Union

- **Categorize** Which nations of West Central Europe have chosen not to join the EU? (Switzerland, Liechtenstein, and Monaco)

- **Infer** What do individual EU members need to do to ensure the success of the whole? (cooperate)

- **Identify Details** How much of the European Union's population lives in France and Germany? (about a third)

Section 3

West Central Europe Today

Key Ideas
- The countries of West Central Europe have strong international partnerships.
- The rich cultural heritage of West Central Europe makes tourism one of the region's largest industries.
- People in most of the countries in this region favor strong ties with the European Union.

Key Terms • privatization • gross national product (GNP) • polders • reunification   Visual Glossary

 **Reading Skill: Identify Main Ideas and Details** Take notes using the graphic organizer in your journal.

France's Chartres Cathedral is a masterpiece of medieval Gothic architecture. ▼

Rich in culture, the nations of West Central Europe include some of the largest and most prosperous on the continent. Most are members of the European Union, an organization that plays a major role in life in this region.

At the Center of the European Union

West Central Europe includes Austria, Belgium, France, Germany, Liechtenstein, Luxembourg, Monaco, the Netherlands, and Switzerland. All have joined the European Union (EU) except Switzerland, Liechtenstein, and Monaco. Why have some countries joined the EU while others have not?

EU membership is similar to playing on a school sports team. Each team member has different abilities or strengths, but the team works best when its members work together.

Just as not all students take part in sports, not every country in Europe is a member of the EU. Some countries do not meet certain guidelines. Some want to be members in certain ways, but not in others. Germany and France are the largest EU countries by population. They make up almost one third of the entire EU population. Some critics say that larger countries have more power in the EU government. If a country has more power, it can influence EU laws in its own favor. However, the EU has policies in place so that members work together.

Reading Check How might a larger nation influence laws in an alliance such as the European Union?

Culture Close-up

READING CHECK A larger nation might have more political or economic power and could use that power to encourage lawmakers to make policies for its benefit alone.

ACADEMIC VOCABULARY

High-Use Word	Definition and Sample Sentence
fragile	*adj.* easily broken or destroyed *The ancient pottery is fragile, so it is kept in a locked case.*
recruit	*v.* to increase or maintain the number of *The charity tried to recruit volunteers to build a new playground.*

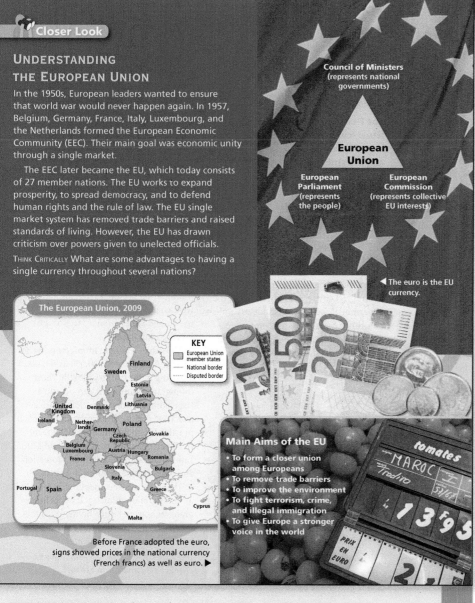

Closer Look

UNDERSTANDING THE EUROPEAN UNION

In the 1950s, European leaders wanted to ensure that world war would never happen again. In 1957, Belgium, Germany, France, Italy, Luxembourg, and the Netherlands formed the European Economic Community (EEC). Their main goal was economic unity through a single market.

The EEC later became the EU, which today consists of 27 member nations. The EU works to expand prosperity, to spread democracy, and to defend human rights and the rule of law. The EU single market system has removed trade barriers and raised standards of living. However, the EU has drawn criticism over powers given to unelected officials.

THINK CRITICALLY What are some advantages to having a single currency throughout several nations?

Council of Ministers (represents national governments)

European Union

European Parliament (represents the people)

European Commission (represents collective EU interests)

◄ The euro is the EU currency.

The European Union, 2009

KEY
- European Union member states
- — National border
- ···· Disputed border

Finland, Sweden, Estonia, Latvia, Lithuania, United Kingdom, Denmark, Ireland, Nether-lands, Germany, Poland, Belgium, Luxembourg, Czech Republic, Slovakia, Austria, Hungary, France, Romania, Slovenia, Italy, Bulgaria, Portugal, Spain, Greece, Cyprus, Malta

Before France adopted the euro, signs showed prices in the national currency (French francs) as well as euro. ▶

Main Aims of the EU
- To form a closer union among Europeans
- To remove trade barriers
- To improve the environment
- To fight terrorism, crime, and illegal immigration
- To give Europe a stronger voice in the world

THINK CRITICALLY It makes trade easier by eliminating the need to exchange currency.

Closer Look

Understanding the European Union

- **Identify Main Ideas** What role did West Central Europe play in the formation of the EU? (The nations that started the EU are in West Central Europe.)

- **Infer** Why do you think the flag shows stars in a circle? (Sample: It symbolizes unity.)

- **Analyze Maps** What region of Europe has the fewest EU members? (Eastern Europe)

- **Categorize** Which aim of the EU is economic? (to remove trade barriers)

myWorld Activity

Norway and the European Union Find Step-by-Step Instructions and an Activity Support on pp. T83–T85. **(Visual/Interpersonal)**

ECONOMICS

High-Speed Trains Starting in 1978, France built a network of high-speed railroad lines that connected Paris to most other major cities in the country. Now the network reaches the borders where it can connect with trains in other countries. The TGV (*train à grande vitesse*, or high-speed train) can travel up to 200 miles per hour, so it cuts travel times significantly. Such an efficient form of transportation helps encourage economic growth.

France: History and Diversity

- **Identify Main Ideas** What are two of the major industries in the French economy? (agriculture and tourism)
- **Identify Details** What attracts tourists to France? (historic sites, scenery, shopping, art, food)
- **Predict** How might continued immigration change France? (Samples: Muslim communities will grow; further conflicts might occur.)

Analyze Visuals Have students examine the photograph of the soccer team.

- How does the soccer team represent the new face of France? (It is mixed, racially and ethnically.)

my World IN NUMBERS

The Nobel Prize for Literature has been awarded to **14** French authors. No other nation has won as many.

Algerian-born Zinédine Zidane (center) played for the French national soccer team, a team known for its ethnic diversity. ▼

France: History and Diversity

Known for its rich heritage, France has taken a leading role in the EU. The changing face of France presents many challenges.

The French Economy France has fertile soil, a mild climate, and large areas of level land. Its farms, dairies, and vineyards produce wines, cheeses, and grains. The EU ensures that these products reach people around the world.

However, France's largest industry is tourism. Around 75 million tourists a year come to see historic sites and scenic landscapes. French cities attract shoppers and art lovers. Some tourists come just to eat French cuisine!

France is a republic with a strong centralized government. In the past, the government owned many industries such as airlines, banks, and telecommunications. Much of that has changed due to **privatization**, or private ownership of businesses.

City of Light Paris, the capital of France, is known as the City of Light. It is the nation's cultural and economic center. Paris straddles the Seine River and is home to more than 2 million people. Its entire urban area covers around 890 square miles (2,300 square km) and is home to 12 million people.

Parisians live among Gothic churches, baroque palaces, elaborate gardens, and modern skyscrapers. Some Parisians work for the EU as their nation helps shape its policies.

The New Face of France In 2005, two North Africans youths were killed after a police chase in a Paris suburb. This event touched off riots all over France. In 2006, some French people held an anti-immigration protest, saying immigrants were changing French culture. Like the United States, France faces tough immigration issues.

More than 5 million immigrants live in France. An estimated 200,000 to 400,000 are living in the country illegally. Most immigrants come from Europe, and a large number come from North Africa and West Africa. Historically, most French practiced Catholicism. Today, 5 percent to 10 percent of the population is Muslim. Immigrants often face job discrimination and poor living conditions in France.

The French government recently added an immigration ministry. It offers immigrants money to return home. With this money, a family may be able to have a better life in its native country.

Reading Check **How have immigrants changed religious life in France?**

ANSWERS

READING CHECK To France's historically Catholic society, immigrants have added a large population who practice Islam.

488   Western Hemisphere
244   Eastern Hemisphere
430   World Geography

COMMON MISCONCEPTIONS

Wooden Shoes Windmills, tulips, and wooden shoes have long been symbols of Dutch culture, but wooden shoes are no longer a regular part of daily life. In past centuries, most Dutch peasants and workmen did wear wooden shoes, called *klompen*, because they protected the feet and kept them dry when walking over muddy fields or lanes. This was an advantage in a country that has so much land below sea level and is prone to flooding. In modern times, very few Dutch people wear *klompen* on a daily basis. Instead, they are used for special occasions and brightly decorated pairs are sold to tourists.

The Low Countries

Belgium, Luxembourg, and the Netherlands form the Low Countries. These countries are small in size, but they are politically and economically powerful.

Belgium: EU Headquarters Belgium serves as the political hub of Europe. Both the EU and NATO have their headquarters in the capital of Brussels. NATO is a military alliance that includes the United States, Canada, and many European nations.

Belgium is a constitutional monarchy. The country has few natural resources, so it relies on trade. It has a high standard of living and a high **gross national product (GNP)**, which is the annual income of a nation's companies and residents. Almost 97 percent of Belgians live in cities.

Belgium is made up of three regions. In Flanders in the north, people speak a form of Dutch called Flemish. In Wallonia in the south, they speak French. In the third region around Brussels, people speak both French and Flemish. Periodically, some Flemish call for independence, but most Belgians prefer a united country.

Landlocked Luxembourg Luxembourg is a tiny landlocked country, one of Europe's oldest and smallest. It is a constitutional monarchy as well as a member of the EU and NATO.

Most of its citizens speak French, German, and Luxembourgish, a German dialect. Its key industries are banking and media. Because of its strict banking laws, people around the world use Luxembourg banks.

The Netherlands: A Fragile Balance The Netherlands is also known as Holland. Its people are Dutch. The Netherlands has a long history as a sea-trading nation.

More than half of the Netherlands is below sea level. For centuries, the Dutch have been working to hold back the sea. One way is to build dikes—levees or long dams—to keep out water. With dikes, the Dutch can live on **polders,** or areas of land reclaimed from lake bottoms or the seabeds. The famous Dutch windmills power pumps to drain water from land.

The Dutch live in a <u>fragile</u> balance with their environment. Industry and consumers produce air pollution. As the Dutch population has grown in urban areas, more rural land is needed for human use. Wildlife habitats may be threatened. Water pollution is also a concern because three of Europe's major rivers flow through the Netherlands.

Reading Check **How do the Dutch use windmills?**

fragile, *adj.,* easily broken or destroyed

The Dutch windmill aids in irrigation for farming. Some farmers also live in windmills. ▶

READING CHECK The Dutch use windmills to power pumps that drain the land.

myWorld Activity
Make a Travel Poster

The Low Countries

- **Identify Main Ideas** What kind of government does Belgium have? (a constitutional monarchy)

- **Cause and Effect** Why do people from around the world use banks in Luxembourg? (It has strict banking laws.)

- **Synthesize** What are the positives and negatives of the Dutch relationship to the sea? (The positive is a history of sea trade; the negative is a fight to protect Dutch land from being flooded.)

Analyze Visuals Have students study the picture of the windmill.

- How might living in a windmill differ from living in a house? (Samples: the noise of the blades, the lack of windows)

myWorld Activity

Make a Travel Poster Find Step-by-Step Instructions and an Activity Support on pp. T102–T103. **(Visual/Interpersonal)**

CULTURE

German Music As early as the 1500s, German music became a powerful influence on European and, later, American music. The leader of the Protestant Reformation, Martin Luther, composed chorales based on Latin hymns. Michael Praetorius and Heinrich Schültz were considered the greatest chorale composers of the 1600s for their blending of German and Italian forms.

In the Baroque period of the 1600s, many German composers rose to greatness, their music becoming the inspiration for composers throughout Europe. This period was dominated by the composer Johann Sebastian Bach, famous for his choral, harpsichord, and organ pieces. Georg Friedrich Handel was most famous for his piece The Messiah.

During the Romantic era, composers Johannes Brahms and Felix Mendelssohn were both very influential. Later composers include Richard Wagner and Richard Strauss.

Germany: Industrial Giant

- **Cause and Effect** What event led to the reunification of East Germany and West Germany? (the fall of the Berlin Wall)

- **Express an Opinion** How do you think West Germans felt about the East Germans who moved west? (Sample: West Germans might have resented them and feared job loss.)

- **Problem Solve** How is Germany trying to prevent intolerance? (through education)

Chart Skills Have students examine the German exports chart.

- What is Germany's top export? (automobiles)

- What is the value of Germany's chemical exports? ($120.7 billion)

Data Discovery

Have students go to myworldgeography.com to learn more about West Central Europe's economy.

Germany: Industrial Giant

Germany has the largest population in the EU and Western Europe. Its economy is one of the world's largest.

A United Germany When the Berlin Wall came down in 1989, it marked the end of the split between East Germany and West Germany. **Reunification,** or the process of becoming unified again, brought many changes. Many East Germans "voted with their feet." They left the east and went west for a better life.

Germany is a member of international organizations such as the EU and NATO. Germany also joins other nations for international meetings about global economic issues. Through its membership in the Organization for Security and Co-operation in Europe (OSCE), Germany helps keep the region safe.

A Rich Culture German culture includes some of the world's finest music, art, poetry, films, and literature. Germans have also been leaders in the study of botany, mathematics, and military technology.

Modern German culture remains colored by the painful memories of World War II and the Holocaust, in which Nazis murdered six million European Jews and other innocent people. That troubled period partly resulted from excessive nationalism.

While many Germans feel proud of their nation, they want to avoid the mistakes of the past. They believe that one way to ensure a better future is through education. The country ranks high in the number of university professors, published book titles, and Nobel laureates.

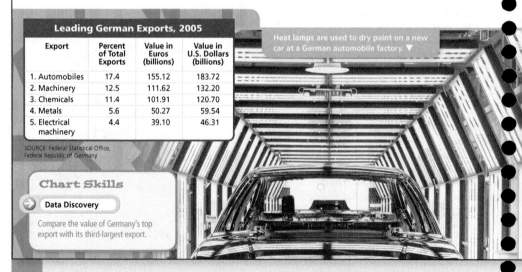

Leading German Exports, 2005			
Export	Percent of Total Exports	Value in Euros (billions)	Value in U.S. Dollars (billions)
1. Automobiles	17.4	155.12	183.72
2. Machinery	12.5	111.62	132.20
3. Chemicals	11.4	101.91	120.70
4. Metals	5.6	50.27	59.54
5. Electrical machinery	4.4	39.10	46.31

SOURCE: Federal Statistical Office, Federal Republic of Germany

Chart Skills

Data Discovery

Compare the value of Germany's top export with its third-largest export.

Heat lamps are used to dry paint on a new car at a German automobile factory. ▼

CHART SKILLS Its top export earns 50 percent more.

READING CHECK for work or to return to their family's homeland

READING CHECK tourism

SECTION 3 ASSESSMENT 1. Samples: The gross national product is the annual income of a nation's businesses and residents. Privatization is the process of moving

GOVERNMENT

Swiss Democracy Switzerland is considered one of the most democratic countries in the world. It is a confederation of 26 states called cantons. (Six of these are officially called demicantons, but they have all the powers of full cantons.) Switzerland has many features of direct democracy in its political process. Citizens are involved in every level of government—local, cantonal, and national. For example, they review and approve many government expenditures, and they have the power to launch initiatives and referenda. Because of this, political decision making can be slow, but once decisions are made, they generally have wide popular support.

Building Tolerance Like the rest of Europe, West Germany <u>recruited</u> guest workers from nearby poorer countries to address the postwar labor shortages of the 1950s. Today, immigrants still come to Germany from these same regions: Turkey, the Middle East, and Eastern Europe. Other immigrants are of German descent and are returning to Germany after generations of living in Poland or Romania.

Because of its past and its diverse population, modern Germany encourages tolerance. However, conflict still occurs. Anti-immigrant and anti-Semitic groups such as the neo-Nazis have staged violent marches. Many Turks, Germany's largest immigrant group, claim that they often encounter racism and prejudice. Even popular Turkish soccer players say they have been taunted because they are not "real Germans." German leaders continue to encourage open-mindedness.

Reading Check What are some reasons that immigrants have moved to Germany?

Austria and Switzerland

Austria shares a language as well as economic and cultural ties with Germany. Austria was once the center of the Austro-Hungarian empire. Its size was dramatically reduced during the two world wars. When Soviet occupation ended in 1955, Austria has become a prosperous democracy. Tourism is a top industry in this country, famous for its Alpine scenery and ski resorts.

Switzerland is one of the world's oldest democracies. It has a long history of neutrality, or not taking sides in wars. This neutrality has led to Switzerland's uneasy relationship with international organizations such as the United Nations. Switzerland did not formally join the UN until 2002. Some people believe joining the UN will help the nation to grow. Other worry that membership will damage Switzerland's neutrality.

Reading Check What industry contributes to the economies of both Alpine nations?

recruit, *v.,* to increase or maintain the number of

Winter sports enthusiasts keep tourism a top industry in both Austria and Switzerland. ▼

- **Cause and Effect** Why did West Germany recruit guest workers after World War II? (It had a labor shortage.)

Austria and Switzerland

- **Build Cultural Awareness** To which neighboring country does Austria have strong linguistic and cultural ties? (Germany)

- **Compare and Contrast** How is Switzerland different from most other countries? (It is neutral.)

Section **3** Assessment

Key Terms

1. Write a one-sentence definition of each of the following terms: gross national product, privatization, polders.

Key Ideas

2. Most of the immigrants in France and Germany come from which regions?

3. Give some examples of the cultural heritage in West Central Europe.

Think Critically

4. **Identify Evidence** What actions of the Dutch suggest that the country has a high population density?

5. **Draw Inferences** How might Switzerland's history of neutrality have affected its history?

Essential Question

Is it better to be independent or interdependent?

6. Why might EU membership appeal to smaller countries? Go to your Student Journal to record your answer.

businesses to private ownership. Polders are areas of land reclaimed from seas and lakes. **2.** France: Europe, north and west Africa; Germany: Turkey, the Middle East, and Eastern Europe **3.** Its culture includes imposing architecture, great literature and music, and scientific advances. **4.** The Netherlands has worked to reclaim land from the sea. **5.** Sample: Neutrality might have helped it prosper by avoiding the expense and damage of war. **6.** Smaller countries believe that as EU members they can compete better in global markets.

A Sense of Identity

OBJECTIVES
Students will
- make connections between important documents and the subject of European identity.
- **21st Century Learning** identify bias in statements.
- **ELL** learn to recognize and use the prefix *inter-*.

SET EXPECTATIONS
In this case study, students will
- read and analyze two documents on the topic of European identity.
- write a definition of citizenship.

1 Connect

Write the word *citizenship* on the board. Ask students to name all the different political entities of which they are citizens. Encourage them to think of some of the less obvious answers, such as county, township, school district. Then ask, What do citizens do? Record the answers in a concept web around the word *citizenship*. Finally, explain that students are about to read two documents that touch on the question of whether the people in EU nations should consider themselves primarily European citizens or citizens of nations.

2 Learn

Preview Have students preview the two pages and identify the background of each person who is quoted. Read the Key Ideas, glossary terms, and definitions. Clarify any questions about the meaning of these words by providing examples.

Read Slowly read aloud the excerpt "Sharing a European Identity" without stopping. Read the document again, this time stopping to read the questions at the left, and prompt students to rethink and analyze the meaning of the words. Have students answer the questions using the location of the letters to provide clues. Do the same for the excerpt "Is a European Identity Possible?" Lead a discussion starting with students' responses to the questions. Ask, What do you identify with most, your community, state, country, or continent? Why?

ELL Advanced Explain that the word *inter-national* is formed from three word parts: the prefix *inter-*, which means "between," the root *nation*, and the suffix *-al*, which means "relating to." Ask students to suggest meanings for several words that use the prefix *inter-*: *interact*, *interstate*, and *interpersonal*. Have them check their definitions in a dictionary.

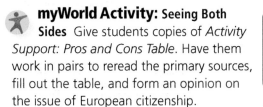 **myWorld Activity: Seeing Both Sides** Give students copies of *Activity Support: Pros and Cons Table*. Have them work in pairs to reread the primary sources, fill out the table, and form an opinion on the issue of European citizenship.

20 min

3 Understand

Review Go back to the Key Idea. Discuss with students how each writer views the question of European identity.

Assess Have students complete **Analyze the Documents.** Review their answers to determine if students have met the lesson objectives.

Remediate If students struggle to understand the concept of shared European and national citizenship, have the class discuss which of the following are aspects of state citizenship, which are aspects of U.S. citizenship, and which are both: voting, paying taxes, getting a passport, getting a driver's license, getting a marriage license, serving in the army.

Name _____ Class _____ Date _____

myWorld Activity Support   **Pros and Cons Table**

Seeing Both Sides

Directions When you are trying to decide whether or not you agree with an idea, it is important to try to see both sides first. One way to do that is to fill out a pros and cons table. *Pros* are arguments in favor of something. *Cons* are arguments against it. As you read the quotations by Nicole Fontaine and Leszek Kolakowski, consider the issue listed below. Fill out the Pros and Cons Table beneath the issue to help you form your own opinion. Then answer the questions at the bottom.

Issue: Should Europeans think of themselves as EU citizens rather than citizens of individual countries?

Pros (reasons to think of themselves as European citizens)	Cons (reasons to think of themselves as national citizens)

1. Which of the two excerpts offered the most pros?
   Which one offered the most cons?

   _____

   _____

2. Now that you have considered both sides, what is your opinion about the issue?

   _____

   _____

CULTURE

The Myth of Europa The continent of Europe was named for Europa, who in Greek mythology was a beautiful princess from Phoenicia. One morning as she was out picking spring flowers with her friends, Zeus looked down from Mount Olympus and fell in love with her. He transformed himself into a handsome bull and approached Europa. Intrigued by his gentle nature, she climbed unto his back when he lowered himself to the ground. Immediately, Zeus carried her across the Mediterranean to Crete, where she remained and had three sons by Zeus.

Identify Bias Use the introduction to help the students understand the authors' backgrounds. Before they read, ask them to predict which author is more likely to be in favor of having a European identity because of his or her job. Then use the lettered prompts to help students analyze each author's opinions.

ANSWERS

Ⓐ EU law is the basis for national law.

Ⓑ the flag and the anthem

Ⓒ Sample: She defines it as sharing a flag, an anthem, laws, currency, the right to vote, and the right to run for office.

Primary Source

A Sense of Identity

| Key Idea | • The European Union promotes the idea of a common European identity, but deeply rooted nationalism causes many people to continue to identify with their nations more strongly. |

▲ Yasmin is a European of Spanish, Pakistani, and Finnish heritage.

Nationalism has played a major role in European history. While national pride can be positive, it has also caused destructive wars that tore Europe apart. After World War II, European leaders founded the European Union (EU) to promote political and economic cooperation. Anyone who is a citizen of an EU nation also has European citizenship. But what is European citizenship? Will it ever replace national identity? In these passages, Nicole Fontaine, former President of the European Parliament, and Leszek Kolakowski, a Polish historian, express different views.

A girl draws the EU flag with chalk. ▶

Stop at each letter on the right to think about the text. Then answer the question with the same letter on the left.

Ⓐ **Draw Conclusions** What is the relationship between Community, or EU, law and the laws of the separate nations?

Ⓑ **Categorize** Which of these trappings of citizenship are mostly symbolic?

Ⓒ **Summarize** How does Fontaine define European citizenship?

institutional, *adj.,* related to institutions, or established organizations

trapping, *n.,* a thing usually associated with something

underpin, *v.,* to act as a foundation for

bulk, *n.,* a large part, or the largest part

Sharing a European Identity

❝ Not only do Europeans enjoy the **institutional** **trappings** of citizenship such as a common flag, a common anthem, Community law **underpinning**
Ⓐ and directing the vast **bulk** of national legislation, a form of common government, . . . and of course,
Ⓑ a common currency which in less than two years' time will be the only currency to be found in our wallet:
Ⓒ we share something else as citizens, namely the right to vote and to stand for election. ❞

—Nicole Fontaine,
President of the European Parliament,
speech of January 29, 2000

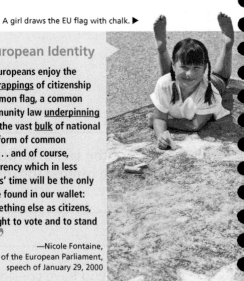

21st Century Learning — IDENTIFY BIAS

To assist your students in identifying bias, explain that *bias* is a preference or dislike that is not based on evidence. A person who is biased will sometimes approach an issue with his or her mind already made up. Often, people do not intend to be biased. Rather bias can occur if someone has an emotional reason for wanting something to succeed or fail. For example, a company that hopes to gain millions of dollars from a new experimental product might have the bias of expecting tests of the product to show positive results. Suggest that as students read the two quotations, they ask themselves, Why does EU citizenship or European identity matter to this person? Will this person be hurt or helped if the EU fails?

Stop at each letter on the right to think about the text. Then answer the question with the same letter on the left.

D Identify Main Ideas and Details What two forces does Kolakowski think stand in the way of unification?

E Analyze Cause and Effect Why does he think many people distrust attempts to unify Europe?

F Summarize How does Kolakowski think that European identity could relate to national identity?

complex, *adj.,* having many different pieces
separatist, *adj.,* in favor of remaining apart
xenophobic, *adj.,* afraid of foreigners
wary, *adj.,* cautious, suspicious

Is a European Identity Possible?

❝ The question of national identity is endlessly <u>complex</u>. Given the extent to which progress towards unification has been accompanied by a rise in <u>separatist</u> and <u>xenophobic</u> tendencies, **D** it is too soon to talk about the end of the nation state. And modern attempts—made by Napoleon, by Hitler, by Moscow—to unify Europe **E** by force have made the various peoples of the continent <u>wary</u>. But assuming that national identities will persist, can a European identity be built alongside them or over **F** them? Is there such an identity, and if not, is it desirable? Is there, or can there be, such a thing as European patriotism? ❞

—Leszek Kolakowski, "Can Europe Happen?" *The New Criterion,* May 2003

▲ Dairy farmers drove their tractors in the streets during a 2009 protest against EU milk pricing policies.

ANSWERS

D separatism and xenophobia

E They remember previous military attempts to unify the continent by conquest.

F They can coexist or European identity can replace national identity.

Analyze the Documents

1. **Identify Bias** Is Fontaine or Kolakowski more likely to have a biased view of European identity? Explain.
2. **Writing Task** Write your own definition of national identity. Name the qualities that define your own national identity.

◀ Flags at the European Parliament in Strasbourg, France

ANALYZE THE DOCUMENTS 1. Samples: Fontaine is more likely to be biased because she is an EU politician so her job is to promote European identity. Kolakowski is more likely to be biased because he is looking at historical examples and does not believe that the present can turn out differently.
2. Sample: It is a feeling of belonging to a country. Trappings include the flag, the dollar, "The Star Spangled Banner," the U.S. Constitution, and freedoms such as freedom of speech.

Southern Europe Today

OBJECTIVES

Students will know

- the traditional heritage of the countries of Southern Europe.
- economic changes in Southern Europe brought about by EU membership and globalization.

Students will be able to

- analyze cause and effect in discussing recent events.
- read a map scale and measure distances.

SET EXPECTATIONS

In this section, students will

- read Southern Europe Today.
- locate neighboring continents and countries.
- go On Assignment in Western Europe and learn more about myStory and examine data in charts.

CORE CONCEPTS

You may wish to teach or reteach the following lessons from the Core Concepts Handbook:

- Migration, pp. 78–79
- Language, pp. 90–92
- Foundations of Government, pp. 104–105

KEY

Differentiated Instruction

L1 Special Needs **L2** Extra Support
L3 On-Level **L4** Challenge

English Language Instruction

ELL Beginner **ELL** Early Intermediate **ELL** Intermediate
ELL Early Advanced **ELL** Advanced

1 Connect
Make learning meaningful

Make Connections Ask students to share examples in which they, their relatives, or their friends have started using a more modern technology. Ask them what improvements and problems the change caused.

L2 **Extra Support** To help students think of examples of technology, give them specific categories such as *telephone, computer, home appliances, automobiles,* and *entertainment.*

Activate Prior Knowledge Ask students what they know about the climate and physical geography of Southern Europe. Have them discuss how those features might affect agriculture and other parts of the economy.

ELL **Early Intermediate** Give students the words *Greek, Italian, Spanish,* and *Portuguese.* Explain that these words are used as nouns to name the languages of Greece, Italy, Spain, and Portugal, and also as adjectives to describe people or things related to those countries.

Prepare Follow the steps in the section **Preview.** Preteach the Key Terms. Then have students complete *Word Wise* in their journals using in-text clues and the glossary for help.

2 Experience
Teach knowledge and skills

Read Use **Background** notes and **Guide on the Side** questions to model active reading. Have students use *Take Notes* in their **Student Journals** to record the causes and effects of economic change and immigration in Southern Europe. Have students complete **21st Century Online Tutor** *Analyze Cause and Effect,* and apply this skill to reading the section.

L1 **Special Needs** Have students read the **Online Student Edition** while listening to the accompanying audio.

ELL **Intermediate/Early Advanced** Give students a list of words and phrases that are used to signal writing about cause and effect, such as *because, as a result, affected,* and *due to.*

L4 **Challenge** Have students read *Enrichment: Pablo Picasso* to learn more about this important Spanish artist.

Practice: myWorld Activity Students will identify the closest neighboring continents to the countries of Southern Europe and measure the distances between them. **Step-by-Step Instructions** and **More Activities** follow on p. T110.

SECTION 4 RESOURCE GUIDE

FOR THE STUDENT

my worldgeography.com **Student Center**

- myStory Video
- Data Discovery

Student Edition (print and online)
- Southern Europe Today

Student Journal (print and online)
- Section 4 Word Wise
- Section 4 Take Notes

21st Century Learning **Online Tutor**

- Analyze Cause and Effect
- Read Physical Maps

FOR THE TEACHER

my worldgeography.com **Teacher Center**

- Online Lesson Planner
- Presentations for Projection
- SuccessTracker

ProGuide: Europe and Russia

- Section 4 Lesson Plan, pp. T108–T109
- myWorld Activity Step-by-Step Instructions, p. T110
- Activity Support: Measuring Distances, p. T111
- myWorld Geography Enrichment, p. T112
- Section Quiz, p. T113

Accelerating the Progress of ELLs

- Peer Learning Strategies, p. 46

---

3 Understand
Assess understanding

Review Review *Word Wise* and *Take Notes* in the **Student Journal.**

Assess Knowledge and Skills Use the Section Assessment and the Section Quiz to check students' progress.

Assess Understanding Review students' responses to the Section Assessment Essential Question prompt.

Remediate Use these strategies to review and remediate.

If students struggle to . . .	Try these strategies.
Understand cultural diffusion	Replay the **myStory Video** about Yasmin and the cultural influences in her life.
Analyze cause and effect	Assign additional practice with the **21st Century Online Tutor.**
Describe the economic changes in Southern Europe	Review important concepts such as *privatizing, diversification,* and *open markets*.

ELL Support

ELL **Objective** Students will be able to use English to analyze cause and effect.

Cultural Connections To help students practice describing cause and effect, let them use their own languages to tell the reason that they or someone they know moved to the United States.

ELL **Advanced Content Tip** Draw two cause-and-effect charts on the board. In the first, write the word *immigration,* linked by lines to three blank boxes in a row below it. The second chart will be similar but use the term *financial crisis.* Review the meaning of the terms. Tell students to use information from the text to fill in the boxes with effects.

ELL **Activity** Distribute photocopies of a political map of Southern Europe. Have students identify which islands are part of Italy and which are part of Greece. Tell them to draw a circle around each of those countries and their islands. Explain that while working on the section activity, students should consider both the mainland and islands. **(Visual)**

 **myWorld Activity** | **Step-by-Step Instructions**

 15 min

Southern Europe's Neighbors

OBJECTIVES

Students will

- determine which other continents are located nearest to countries of Southern Europe.
- measure distances between Southern Europe and those continents.

LEARNING STYLE

- Visual
- Logical

21st Century Learning

- Read Physical Maps

MATERIALS

- Physical maps of the world
- Rulers
- Activity Support: Measuring Distances, p. T111

Activity Steps

1. Divide students into pairs. Make sure that each pair has a physical map of the world and a ruler.

2. Review with the class that Spain, Italy, and Greece are all located on peninsulas that extend south of the main landmass of Europe. Point out that because of this, these three countries are closer to other continents than the countries of Northwest Europe or West Central Europe are.

> **ELL Intermediate** Remind students that the definition of a peninsula is a landform with water on three sides. Suggest that they trace the outline of the Iberian and Italian peninsulas to help them remember the definition.

3. Explain to students that their task is to determine whether Spain, Italy, and Greece are closer to Africa or Asia, to find the nearest African or Asian country for each, and to measure the distances to those neighboring countries. They are to record their information on the table on *Activity Support: Measuring Distances,* page T111.

> **L2 Extra Support** Remind students that Africa lies south of Europe across the Mediterranean Sea, while Asia lies to the east and is part of the same landmass as Europe.

4. Point out the question at the bottom of the table, and ask students to answer it once they have finished their map work.

More Activities From myWorld Teachers

Local Connection Remind students that Spain once owned a large part of North America. Have small groups look at a U.S. map and make a list of at least ten place names of Spanish origin. Ask the groups to share their lists with the class. **(Visual/Verbal)**

Romance Languages Have students research Romance languages. Tell them to find out what language Romance languages are descended from, and which Romance languages are spoken in Southern Europe. **(Verbal)**

Travel Routes Have pairs of students study Italy and Greece on the physical map of Europe. Tell them to study coastlines and mountains, and decide whether it is easier to travel between the two countries by land or by sea. Have them explain why. **(Visual/Logical)**

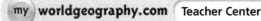 **my worldgeography.com** | **Teacher Center** Find additional resources in the online Teacher Center.

Name _____ Class _____ Date _____

myWorld Activity Support   **Measuring Distances**

Southern Europe's Neighbors

Directions With a partner, examine a physical map of the world. Find out whether Spain, Italy, and Greece are each closer to Africa or Asia. Also find the nearest African or Asian country for each of the three Southern European countries and measure the distance between them. Record your findings on the table below.

Country of Southern Europe	Is it closer to Africa or Asia?	Which African or Asian country is closest?	About how many miles apart are they at the nearest point?
Spain			
Italy			
Greece			

Draw Conclusions How do you think location might affect immigration to Spain, Italy, and Greece? Explain.

_____

_____

_____

_____

Name _____ Class _____ Date _____

Enrichment: Pablo Picasso

Directions Read the biography below. Answer the questions that follow.

Pablo Picasso (1881–1973) was born in Malaga, Spain. He was the son of a drawing teacher. By the age of 13, the young Picasso was already showing his talent as an artist. In 1900, he traveled to Paris, France, which was then the center of the art world.

Picasso is famous for experimenting with many artistic styles. First, he went through a Blue Period, in which the color blue dominated many of his paintings. A well-known painting from this time shows an old man and his guitar. Later Picasso went through his Rose Period. In 1907, Picasso stopped painting realistic-looking pictures. Instead, he painted figures that were influenced by African sculptures and masks. Next, Picasso began to experiment with breaking up figures into geometric shapes. This style was called Cubism.

His experiments with artistic styles had a strong influence on other artists. As a result, Picasso is considered one of the most important modern painters. Picasso also used his art to record the culture and history of his native Spain. Some of his works are black-and-white prints that celebrate bullfighting. Perhaps his most famous painting is a huge black-and-white painting of animals and people in distress called *Guernica* (1937). It shows the terrible destruction of the town of Guernica during the Spanish Civil War. This event marked the first time in the history of war that airplanes had dropped bombs on a town of people.

After World War II, Picasso often painted works that were inspired by artists from the past. He died in 1973.

1. How does Picasso's work show the influence of his native culture?

_____

_____

2. How does Picasso's work show cultural diffusion?

_____

_____

3. Activity Write a brief report that argues why Picasso was one of the most important modern artists.

Name _____ Class _____ Date _____

Section Quiz

Directions Answer the following questions using what you learned
in Section 4.

1. _____ What does the EU goal of solidarity
mean?
   a. expansion
   b. modernization
   c. unity
   d. wealth

2. _____ Which two countries are on the
Iberian Peninsula?
   a. Italy and Greece
   b. Italy and Spain
   c. Portugal and Greece
   d. Portugal and Spain

3. _____ What is an example of cultural
diffusion?
   a. Greek music in Athens
   b. Islamic architecture in Spain
   c. Portuguese restaurants in Lisbon
   d. Roman roads in Italy

4. _____ What is deportation?
   a. convincing an immigrant to apply for
   citizenship
   b. charging an immigrant a fee to stay in
   a country
   c. sending an immigrant back to his or her
   homeland
   d. teaching an immigrant the country's
   language and customs

5. _____ What is one of the biggest threats to
the economies of Southern Europe?
   a. regulation from the EU
   b. a decline in education
   c. a withdrawal of U.S. aid
   d. competition from Asia

6. How is Southern Europe still affected by the legacies of ancient
Greece and ancient Rome?

_____

_____

_____

Southern Europe Today

- Model preparing to read by previewing the Key Ideas, Key Terms, headings, visuals, and captions. Have students make predictions about what they will learn. For ELL support, post the prompt: "I predict I will read about . . ."

- Preview and practice the reading skill, Cause and Effect, by using examples from a book popular with your students.

- Preteach this section's high-use Academic Vocabulary and Key Terms using the table on the next page and in-text definitions. Have students practice Key Terms by completing the *Word Wise* page in their journals.

GUIDE ON THE SIDE

Reading Skill

Analyze Cause and Effect
While they read, have students practice this skill by completing the *Take Notes* graphic organizer in the **Student Journal.**

A Region of Tradition

- **Identify Main Ideas** What ancient civilizations were located in Southern Europe? (ancient Greece and ancient Rome)

- **Synthesize** How does the European Union draw upon the political heritage of Greece and Rome? (It is committed to the ideals of democracy and the protection of people's rights regardless of wealth or status.)

- **Identify Evidence** What physical evidence of the medieval and Renaissance periods does this region have? (cathedrals and palaces)

Section 4

Southern Europe Today

Key Ideas
- An ancient and rich history lives on in Southern Europe today.
- The nations of Southern Europe have enjoyed strong growth as members of the European Union.
- Contemporary issues facing the region include immigration and globalization.

Key Terms
- Iberian Peninsula
- cultural diffusion
- diversify
- deportation

Visual Glossary

 Reading Skill: Analyze Cause and Effect Take notes using the graphic organizer in your journal.

The nations of Southern Europe have enjoyed especially strong growth as members of the European Union. Today, these nations face some of the region's greatest challenges.

A Region of Tradition
Spain, Portugal, Italy, and Greece have an ancient history of civilization. This rich past lives on in traditions that still shape the region today.

The Legacy of Empire Although the ancient Greeks and Romans lived thousands of years ago, their legacies remain. The idea of democracy—that citizens should have a voice in government—began in ancient Greece. The protection of people's rights regardless of wealth or class began in ancient Rome. Today, the European Union (EU) assures members of its commitment to these same ideas. The 12 stars on the EU flag and the EU motto, "United in diversity," tell of the goals of fairness and solidarity, or an attitude shared by a group.

Most of the languages spoken in Southern Europe originated in ancient Greek or Latin. The **Iberian Peninsula** (Spain, Andorra, and Portugal) remains a center of culture and commerce as it has since the Age of Exploration. Farmers and shepherds here live as they have for centuries. The cities of Southern Europe have cathedrals and palaces, many of which date back to the Middles Ages or the Renaissance.

◀ The Leaning Tower of Pisa, in Italy

ACADEMIC VOCABULARY

High-Use Word	Definition and Sample Sentence
confidence	*n.* the quality or state of being certain *Voters liked the candidate who showed confidence but not too much pride.*
crisis	*n.* an uncertain or difficult situation, possibly heading toward disaster *The engineer said that the cracks in the dam were definitely a crisis.*

GUIDE ON THE SIDE

Centuries of trade have influenced the artistic traditions of Southern Europe. Pablo Picasso, a famous Spanish artist, invented a new style of painting after he saw African art for the first time. Asian music influenced Italian opera composers in the 1800s. In Spain, the beautiful Alhambra Palace is a remnant of Islamic culture in Europe.

Religious Heritage Throughout history, armies, traders, and missionaries have passed through Southern Europe. This activity resulted in religious and cultural exchanges. Historians continue to study these events, as they still have a great effect on modern society.

In Rome, Italy, the tiny country of Vatican City serves as the worldwide center of the Roman Catholic Church. Saint Peter's Basilica, one of the holiest sites for Roman Catholics, was built near the site of an ancient Roman racetrack. Athens, Greece, a center of the Greek Orthodox Church, is also home to the Parthenon, an ancient Greek temple of the goddess Athena. Granada, Spain, blends Christian, Jewish, and Muslim influences. This is an example of **cultural diffusion,** or the spread of culture, and it is visible in Granada's colorful neighborhoods and restaurants and in local customs.

Artistic Richness Many famous artists, musicians, novelists, poets, and architects have come from the nations of Southern Europe. Italian architect Renzo Piano has designed buildings in cities around the world. Maria Callas, a famous soprano from Greece, sang many memorable roles for the opera stage.

Mediterranean Culture Mix

Along the Mediterranean, the nations of Southern Europe blend cultural influences that come from centuries of immigration, trade, art, and tradition. *What different cultural influences do you see below?*

For generations, Italians have celebrated religious holidays with city-wide processions that include holy statues. ▶

The Barcelos cockerel is a symbol of Portugal. ▶

◀ Dancing the flamenco, Yasmin keeps alive art from Spanish, Roma, Arabic, Jewish, and African cultures.

CAPTION Italian, Portuguese, Spanish, Roma, Arabic, Jewish, and African

- **Build Cultural Awareness** Where are the centers of the Roman Catholic Church and the Greek Orthodox Church found? (The center of the Roman Catholic Church is in Vatican City, located within Rome, and the Greek Orthodox Church is in Athens.)

- **Identify Details** What is an example of cultural diffusion in Spain? (the city of Granada, which blends Christian, Jewish, and Muslim influences)

- **Draw Conclusions** Why might Southern Europe have such a rich artistic tradition? (Sample: the heritage of Greece and Rome)

Analyze Visuals Have students examine the photographs on this page.

- Which photograph shows a religious tradition? (the procession in Italy)

- Which photograph shows an example of cultural diffusion? (Yasmin dancing the flamenco)

HISTORY

General Franco In 1931, the Spanish king was deposed and a republican form of government was established. In 1936, a leftist political party won the election, and political instability followed. In July of that year, General Francisco Franco declared that a military uprising was about to begin. Franco led the Falangista forces in the Spanish Civil War that followed. When he achieved victory in 1939, Franco began to rule Spain as a dictator allied with other fascists like Mussolini. He ruled until 1975, and over time his rule became less authoritarian. Unlike most dictators, he planned for a peaceful transition of power to take place after him. He chose Juan Carlos, a grandson of the last Spanish monarch, to become king after his death. Spain is now a constitutional monarchy similar to many other nations of Western Europe.

GUIDE ON THE SIDE

Modern, Prosperous Cities

- **Infer** How might dictatorships hinder economic growth? (by interfering with economic decisions, by not allowing people to control their own money)
- **Cause and Effect** How does modernizing help create economic growth? (Modern factories can produce better quality goods; modern transportation systems can ship materials more quickly.)
- **Identify Main Ideas** What region is competing economically with Southern Europe? (Asia)

Analyze Visuals Have students examine the photograph of the cheese-making factory.

- Why do you think the cheesemaker wears something to cover his hair? (Sample: for cleanliness)

Southern Europe is rich in both classical and modern music. Spain's many classical composers include the pianist Isaac Albéniz who first performed at age four. Rock is popular everywhere, but world music has become a new favorite. Some of this music retains ethnic or folk traditions. Fado (FAH doo), sad songs about fate or destiny, is popular in Portugal, as is the music from African nations that were once Portuguese colonies. Flamenco, a Spanish dance, incorporates Arab music and African rhythms. The largest world music festival in the world is in Ariano Irpino, Italy.

Cheese-making is one of Italy's oldest industries. ▼

Reading Check How has cultural diffusion influenced life in Spain?

Modern, Prosperous Cities

Economic growth has been strong in this region, especially from 1980 to the early 2000s. Along with this growth, there has been a rise in living standards.

Economic Changes Many of the countries of Southern Europe lived under dictatorships until relatively recently. With the end of these regimes, these nations entered a new period of freedom and prosperity. In Spain, for example, the death of Francisco Franco in 1975 allowed a peaceful transition to democracy after decades of dictatorship.

As governments became more democratic, leaders liberalized, or made less strict, the laws for running businesses. This encouraged entrepreneurs to open new businesses. Jobs increased at both large and small companies. In addition, increasing privatization made businesses stronger and lowered prices.

Modernization has also boosted economic growth in the region. In Spain, for example, factories bought new, improved machinery. Modern factories can produce better goods for less money. Modern shipping companies then make sure that these goods reach buyers more quickly.

One challenge to Southern Europe's economy has been an increase in Asian imports. These imports are often some of the same goods made in Southern Europe. Because Asian manufacturers can make these goods in larger quantities and their workers earn less, their prices are lower. As a result, many countries in this region have had to work hard to compete.

ANSWERS

READING CHECK It has shaped Spanish art, architecture, music, and dance.

ECONOMICS

Modernizing for the Olympics In preparation for hosting the 2004 Olympic games, Athens went through a period of modernization. Among the projects the city completed were new roads and bridges and additional subway, train, and tramlines. Such improvements to its transportation system would continue to help the Athenian economy after the Games by providing faster transportation for both goods and people. In addition, by decreasing the need for commuting by car, public transportation would help reduce air pollution in the city.

Focus on Portugal Since joining the European Union in 1986, Portugal has experienced impressive economic growth. Much of this growth is due to Portugal's efforts to **diversify,** or add variety to, its types of industries. Many service-based industries, such as telecommunications, are now centered in Portugal.

Portugal's industries had once been limited to traditional products such as textiles, footwear, cork and wood products, and porcelain. Increasingly, a large service sector has developed. This sector includes telecommunications, financial services, healthcare, and tourism. Tourism is also a major industry for Portugal, bringing in almost $10 billion per year.

Privatization has also helped Portugal's economy. Moving businesses from government control to private control has helped business owners gain <u>confidence</u> in their nation's economy. This leads to growth in trade and and more jobs.

Portugal has also benefited from joining the EU single market. Soon after Portugal adopted the euro in 2002, the nation enjoyed a spike in economic growth that has since leveled off.

Still, Portugal has not escaped economic trouble. During the years of growth, debt increased. Repaying this debt will probably slow economic growth.

Effects of EU Membership Membership in the EU made this region better off. With access to open markets and funding from richer members, EU nations generally gain stronger economies and higher living standards.

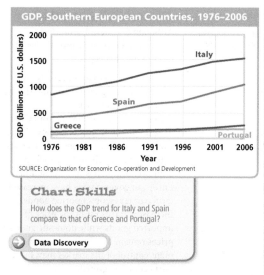

GDP, Southern European Countries, 1976–2006

SOURCE: Organization for Economic Co-operation and Development

Chart Skills

How does the GDP trend for Italy and Spain compare to that of Greece and Portugal?

➜ **Data Discovery**

Italy has long been an EU leader. Italy adopted the euro as its currency in 1999. Spain, Portugal, and Greece also experienced economic growth as EU members. This growth has slowed due to competition from Asia.

EU members sometimes find economic growth indirectly affected by the addition of new members. For example, Portugal has historically supplied Europe with low-cost labor. Recently, Portugal had its EU development funding cut by several billion euros. This happened with the entrance of new member nations such as Romania and Slovakia. Workers from these nations have begun to move to other EU countries like Portugal and are willing to work for lower wages.

Reading Check Describe one economic change in Southern Europe.

confidence, *n.,* the quality or state of being certain

- **Identify Main Ideas** What step did Portugal take to improve its economy? (It diversified or added variety to its economic activities.)

- **Cause and Effect** How did EU membership affect the economies of Southern European nations? (Each nation experienced economic growth.)

Chart Skills Have students examine the graph on GDP in Southern European Countries.

- About how much did Italy's GDP grow? (It approximately doubled.)

- How would you describe the change in GDP for Portugal? (It has changed very little; the line is almost flat.)

CHART SKILLS GDP has risen more sharply for Italy and Spain than for Greece and Portugal.

READING CHECK Modernization has enabled factories to produce better-quality goods faster and to reach international markets, making this region more competitive.

ANSWERS

GEOGRAPHY

Energy Poor One geographic factor that hampers the economies of Southern Europe is a lack of energy resources. Not one of the countries has significant oil or natural gas supplies, and few mineral resources exist in the region. Portugal used to mine coal but stopped producing it in 1994. Hydroelectric plants supply some of the region's power needs, but in general, the four countries are heavily dependent on imported oil. Such a dependency makes the economies of Southern Europe vulnerable to the erratic fluctuations of petroleum prices. To counteract this economic weakness, Spain has taken the lead in developing solar and wind power.

GUIDE ON THE SIDE

Challenges for the Region

- **Identify Main Ideas** How is China competing with Southern Europe? (by producing goods for less and selling them for lower prices)

- **Cause and Effect** What are the positive and negative effects of tariffs? (Positive: protect industry from competition by imports; Negative: slow economic growth)

- **Cause and Effect** Why did the village of Badolato welcome Kurd immigrants? (It needed workers to continue to exist.)

Analyze Visuals Have students look at the paired photographs on this page.

- Which one of these photographs might show the result of economic competition? (the woman going to the unemployment office)

 myWorld Activity

Southern Europe's Neighbors Find Step-by-Step Instructions and an Activity Support on pp. T110–T111.

---

crisis, *n.,* an uncertain or difficult situation, possibly heading toward disaster

 myWorld Activity
Southern Europe's Neighbors

Challenges for the Region

Although Southern Europe has experienced economic growth, it still faces many challenges.

Maintaining Growth Europe is now part of a larger, global economy. This has benefits and drawbacks.

In recent years, products from China have flooded European markets. Chinese workers earn lower wages, so the products they make sell for less. To help domestic companies survive, Southern European governments have increased tariffs, or taxes, on imported goods. Increasing tariffs raises the price of imported goods while domestic goods' prices remain low. Increasing government control of the market may, however, hurt economic growth.

The worldwide financial crisis of 2008 also posed serious economic challenges.

The economies of Spain, Portugal, Italy, and Greece have all experienced slowdowns. Industrial production fell, leading to a decrease in GDP. Some experts think that Southern Europe's years of rapid economic growth may be at an end.

Regional Newcomers Badolato, a village in Italy, had almost disappeared when a group of Turkish Kurds arrived. The Italians welcomed these refugees, who gave new life to the village. Because Italians are no longer having large families, the population is decreasing. With fewer people to fill open jobs, many employers now rely on immigrants such as those that have come to Badolato and other cities in Southern Europe.

However, Southern Europeans don't want so much immigration that it threatens their jobs or culture. Their governments have tried to control immigration.

Facing Regional Challenges
Muslim families in Rome (left) protest against anti-immigrant violence. At right, a woman enters an employment office in Spain, where unemployment has risen dramatically. *How does each photograph show challenges faced in Southern Europe?*

NO ALL A VIOLENZA
NO A TERROR
NO A
Comunidad de Madrid
SERVICIO REGIONAL DE EMPLEO
CONSEJERÍA DE EMPLEO Y MUJER

READING CHECK competition from Asian manufacturers and the worldwide financial crisis

CAPTION One shows a protest against violence; the other shows a job seeker.

SECTION 4 ASSESSMENT 1. Cultural diffusion affected architectural styles in Spain. Spain and Portugal are on the Iberian Peninsula. Immigration is increasing

CAPTION Greece has a long coastline giving it access to the sea.

CORE CONCEPTS: MIGRATION

Review Core Concept 6.3 before discussing the challenge of immigrants in Southern Europe. Review the difference between voluntary and involuntary migration and the push and pull factors that motivate people to migrate. Have students look for information in the section that will help them understand the reasons that people migrate to Southern Europe. Also, ask them to look for an example of involuntary migration in the section.

▲ Colorful shipping containers fill the busy port at Piraeus in Greece. *How does the geography of Greece contribute to its shipping industry?*

In Italy, the government uses fingerprinting to monitor immigrants. Some ethnic groups, such as the Roma (formerly known as Gypsies), believe these methods lead to discrimination.

The fear of **deportation**, or being sent back to one's home country, leads many immigrants to hide from officials in their new country. Any immigrant who does not follow a country's laws may be deported. As elsewhere in Europe, immigration shows the benefits and the challenges of living in an interconnected world.

Focus on Greece Since ancient times, Greek trading ships have brought back exotic goods from foreign lands. These same traders also introduced the world to Greek art and culture and important ideas such as democracy.

Shipping is still important in Greece, and China is a major trading partner. In 2007, Greek ships carried about 60 percent of China's imports of raw materials. These commodities included coal, oil, and iron ore. In China, those products fueled the nation's explosive growth. This trade agreement benefited both Greece and China as well as other global trading partners. Yet, when global trade began to shrink in 2008, everyone involved in this trade experienced setbacks.

Reading Check **What has caused Southern Europe's economic slowdown?**

Section 4 Assessment

Key Terms

1. Use each of the following terms in a complete sentence: Iberian Peninsula, cultural diffusion, diversity, deportation.

Key Ideas

2. Describe three ways in which the past still affects Southern Europe.

3. What economic advantages did EU membership bring to Southern Europe?

4. What other cultures have spread ideas to Southern Europe through cultural diffusion?

Think Critically

5. **Identify Evidence** How has Southern Europe responded to immigration?

6. **Draw Inferences** Why are countries generally more open to immigrants during economic boom times?

? Essential Question

Is it better to be independent or interdependent?

7. Has the European Union helped Southern Europe? Explain why or why not. Go to your Student Journal to record your answers.

European diversity. Some immigrants fear deportation. **2.** Influences include art, language, religion, and democracy. **3.** EU membership gave access to open markets and business development funds. **4.** Muslim and African cultures have had an influence. **5.** They sometimes welcome immigrants but fear that too many will threaten jobs and culture. **6.** When a country's economy is growing, it needs more workers; when it is experiencing hard times, it wants to reduce immigration to make sure its native-born citizens can find work. **7.** Samples: Yes because it has helped boost their economies; no, because it has allowed workers from other countries to compete for jobs.

ANSWERS

KEY TERMS AND IDEAS

1. Most of Western Europe is located in temperate regions, and tropical currents in the Atlantic warm the winds that blow over Western Europe.

2. Most Western Europeans live on plains within 100 miles of the coast or near rivers. Such locations make agriculture, transportation, and trade easier.

3. A constitutional monarchy is a government with a representative legislature and a symbolic king or queen as head of state. Belgium, Denmark, Luxembourg, the Netherlands, Norway, Sweden, and the UK have this form of government.

4. The cradle-to-grave system provides government services for all stages of life.

5. When people migrate from one country to another, different cultures come into contact with each other. This leads to cultural borrowing and cultural diffusion.

6. The countries of West Central Europe tend to have more diverse, modern economies than those of Southern Europe. However, Southern Europe is modernizing, and all countries there are pursuing free trade and market economies.

7. The former East Germany had many economic problems caused by its inefficient command economy, so unified Germany has had to try to create jobs and improve the standard of living in the East.

8. Ancient Greek, Ancient Roman, African, Asian, and Arab-Muslim cultures have all influenced the artistic traditions of Southern Europe.

THINK CRITICALLY

9. The British viewpoint is against adopting the euro, largely because they want to retain more control over their economy. France and Germany promoted the euro and were among the first nations to adopt it.

10. Sample: Western Europe is becoming more diverse as people from Eastern Europe and former European colonies move there.

11. Some students will say that nationalism will decrease as people begin to see themselves as belonging to the continent or the EU as a whole. Other students will say that fears of losing national identity to the EU might cause a resurgence of nationalism.

12. A main cause of pollution is industrial waste. Pollution has caused acid rain and toxic chemical spills in Europe.

Western Europe

Chapter Assessment

Key Terms and Ideas

1. **Discuss** Why does most of Western Europe have a mild climate?

2. **Describe** Where do most Western Europeans live, and why?

3. **Recall** What is a **constitutional monarchy,** and which nations have this form of government?

4. **Summarize** What does the **cradle-to-grave system** provide for citizens of Scandinavian countries?

5. **Explain** How does migration help cause **cultural borrowing** and **cultural diffusion**?

6. **Compare and Contrast** How are West Central Europe and Southern Europe similar? How are they different?

7. **Explain** What problems has Germany had to overcome since **reunification**?

8. **Recall** What cultures have influenced the artistic traditions of Southern Europe?

Think Critically

9. **Compare Viewpoints** How does the British viewpoint toward the EU compare to the viewpoint of France and Germany? Support your answer with details from the chapter.

10. **Draw Conclusions** How has immigration affected Western Europe? Explain.

11. **Predict** What long-term effect do you think EU membership will have on nationalism in Europe? Explain.

12. **Core Concepts: People's Impact on the Environment** What are some of the main causes of pollution? How has pollution affected Europe?

Places to Know

For each place, write the letter from the map that shows its location.

13. Scandinavian Peninsula
14. Italy
15. Iceland
16. France
17. Iberian Peninsula
18. Mediterranean Sea
19. Greece
20. **Estimate** Using the scale, estimate how far Iceland is from France.

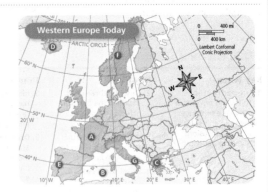

Western Europe Today

PLACES TO KNOW

13. F
14. G
15. D
16. A

17. E
18. B
19. C
20. about 1,200 miles

myWorld Chapter Activity

Norway and the European Union Find Step-by-Step Instructions, Student Instructions and Rubric, and an Activity Support on pp. T84–T85.
(Visual/Verbal/Interpersonal)

21st Century Learning

Develop Cultural Awareness Remind students that they should research and present cultural diffusion without making a judgment about which cultures are better than others.

 Online Assessment

Tailor review and assessment to each student's needs with an array of online assessments.
- Self-Test
- On Assignment Article or Slideshow
- Success Tracker

? Essential Question
myWorld Chapter Activity

Norway and the European Union Follow your teacher's instructions to study data on whether or not Norway should join the European Union. Read and analyze graphs, photographs, and information about the advantages and disadvantages of EU membership for Norway. Take a stand based on your conclusions in support of your position on EU membership for Norway.

21st Century Learning

Develop Cultural Awareness

Western Europe's contact with other nations has added much to life on the continent. Make a small poster on each of the topics below to focus on cultural diffusion in Western Europe.
- Art and architecture
- Music
- Language
- Food

Document-Based Questions

Success ⭐ Tracker™
Online at myworldgeography.com

Use your knowledge of Western Europe and Documents A and B to answer Questions 1–3.

Document A

Joining the Eurozone	
EU Member	Year Euro Adopted
Austria	1999
Belgium	1999
Finland	1999
France	1999
Germany	1999
Greece	2001
Ireland	1999
Netherlands	1999
Slovakia	2009
Spain	1999

1. Which Southern European country was last to adopt the euro?
   A Greece
   B Ireland
   C Slovakia
   D Spain

Document B

" The people of Denmark have voted to reject membership of the single European currency. . . . The leader of the far-right, anti-Euro Danish People's Party, Pia Kjaersgaard, described the outcome as a great victory. 'This victory is a victory for Danes' wish to defend democracy, self-determination and the country's sovereignty,' she said."

—"Danes Say No to Euro,"
BBC News Online, September 28, 2000

2. According to Kjaersgaard, why did the Danish people reject the euro?
   A They don't trust other EU members.
   B They are waiting to see if it succeeds.
   C They want to control their economy.
   D They have too much debt to switch.

3. Writing Task Explain why some Western European countries may want to have some independence from the EU.

DOCUMENT-BASED QUESTIONS

1. A

2. C

3. Sample: Some Western Europeans want to stay independent from the European Union because, as Kjaersgaard said, they want to keep their country's self-determination and sovereignty. They believe that they will have more democracy if they control their national affairs instead of being under the EU's control. Some also want to keep their national currency.

CHAPTER RESOURCE GUIDE

Plan With Understanding by Design*

Chapter Objectives
Begin With the End in Mind

Students will demonstrate the following enduring understandings:
- Foreign investment and foreign trade are important for economic growth.
- Governments need to invest in human and physical capital to achieve economic growth.
- Cultural or ethnic differences can cause conflict, but these conflicts can also be resolved peacefully.

Connect
Make Learning Meaningful

Student Edition
- **Essential Question** How can you measure success?
- **myStory** Serhiy describes his life in rural Ukraine and anticipates the ways it will change when he finishes high school and joins the military.

my worldgeography.com
myStory Video Get to know Serhiy through a video of his life and home.

Experience
Teach Knowledge and Skills

Student Edition
- Read Sections 1 and 2.
- Answer Reading Checks and Section Assessment questions.

my worldgeography.com
On Assignment Visual Glossary, Active Atlas, Data Discovery, Language Lesson, and Culture Close-up

Student Journal
- Sections 1 and 2 Word Wise
- Sections 1 and 2 Outline Map and Take Notes

Teacher's Edition
myWorld Activities
- Section 1: Hailstorm, p. T122
- Section 2: Press Conference, p. T130

21st Century Learning Online Tutor
- Synthesize
- Read Physical Maps
- Compare and Contrast
- Ask Questions

Understand
Assess Understanding

Assessment Booklet
- Chapter Tests • Benchmark Tests

Teacher's Edition
myWorld Chapter Activity Students role-play business people considering locating a business in Eastern Europe. Groups will research countries and create a proposal explaining their choice.

Student Journal
Essential Question Writer's Workshop

my worldgeography.com
On Assignment Students will write and submit an online article or multimedia slideshow about Eastern Europe.

Success Tracker™
Online at myworldgeography.com
Administer chapter tests and remediate understanding.

Student Edition
Chapter Assessment

---

* *"Understanding by Design" is registered as a trademark with the Patent and Trademark Office by the Association for Supervision of Curriculum Development (ASCD). ASCD has not authorized, approved or sponsored this work and is in no way affiliated with Pearson or its products.*

Connect to the Essential Question

 Essential Question

How can you measure success?

Use the Essential Question poster and follow these steps to help students understand the Essential Question.

Connect to Their Lives

1. Have students explain what success means to them. (If students have already studied this Essential Question, encourage them to note changes in the way they define success now.) As students respond, emphasize the diversity of ways success can be measured, such as grades, sports, drama, or relationships with peers or teachers. Ask, Should there be common measures for success such as grades?

2. Have students identify evidence for these measures of personal success. Post the following table for them to complete or have students turn to the *Essential Question Preview* page in their **Student Journal:**

Measures of Personal Success			
Family	Friends	School	Other (Sports, Arts, Chores)

3. Discuss students' responses. Ask, Why might different people measure success differently?

Connect to the Content

4. Now have students brainstorm ways to measure a country's success. Students might say to look at violence or poverty levels.

5. Ask students to identify evidence for these measures of national success. Post the following table for them to complete: (Help them to understand what might be included in each category, e.g. education under Social Services.)

Measures of National Success			
Economy	Politics	Social Services	Environment

6. After previewing the chapter, have students make chapter-related predictions on the *Essential Question Preview* page in the **Student Journal.**

7. Remind students that they will answer a prompt related to the Essential Question on each section's *Take Notes* page in the **Student Journal.**

Explore 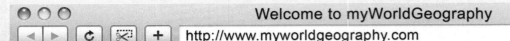 my worldgeography.com

○ ○ ○   Welcome to myWorldGeography

◀ ▶ | c | ⌕ | + | http://www.myworldgeography.com

ON ASSIGNMENT: Eastern Europe

For this chapter's assignment, students will
- take a digital trip to Eastern Europe.
- take on the role of a journalist.
- gather notes, images, and data throughout their journey.
- write an article or create a multimedia slideshow connecting the information and images gathered during their trip and this chapter's Essential Question: *How can you measure success?*

ITINERARY

During their trip, students will make the following stops:

 myStory Video

Learn more about Serhiy's life in rural Ukraine.

 Active Atlas

Read physical, religious, political, and climate maps of Eastern Europe.

Data Discovery

Gather data from graphs about the economic situation of countries in Eastern Europe.

 Culture Close-up

Explore the architecture of Budapest.

 Language Lesson

Hear phrases in Ukrainian.

 Self-Test

Assess their own knowledge of chapter content.

While on their trip, students will practice the following skills:

- **Interpret** maps of Eastern Europe
- **Evaluate** factors that determine a country's success or failure
- **Synthesize** evidence into an article

TIGed
TakingITGlobal for Educators

Extend the reach of every lesson by helping students connect to a global community of young people with common interests and concerns. Visit myworldgeography.com to
- explore Country Pages relating to Eastern Europe.
- delve deeper into this chapter's Essential Question, *How can you measure success?*
- find online alternatives to and solutions for the Unit Closer 21st Century Learning Activity.

my worldgeography.com

TEACHER CENTER

Preview and assign student materials, enrich your teaching, and track student progress with the following resources:
- Online Lesson Planning and Resource Library
- Presentations for Projection
- Online Teacher's Edition and Ancillaries
- Google Earth Links

Assess Enduring Understandings

myWorld Chapter Activity **Step-by-Step Instructions** 2 hr

Open for Business

Teach this activity at the end of the chapter to assess enduring understandings.

OBJECTIVES

Students will demonstrate the following enduring understandings:
- Foreign investment and foreign trade are important for economic growth.
- Governments need to invest in human and physical capital to achieve economic growth.
- Cultural and ethnic differences can cause conflict, but these differences can also be resolved peacefully.

Students will provide the following evidence of understanding:
- Business Environment Analysis
- Business Proposal Presentation

LEARNING STYLES
- Verbal
- Interpersonal
- Verbal

MATERIALS
- Activity Support: Student Instructions and Rubric, p. T118
- Activity Support: Investigation Notes, p. T119
- Large paper
- Activity Cards: #61–66
    - 61. Czech Republic
    - 62. Ukraine
    - 63. Bosnia
    - 64. Slovenia
    - 65. Poland
    - 66. Hungary

Activity Steps

1. Set Expectations Tell students they will take the role of entrepreneurs looking to establish a business in Eastern Europe. Using the Activity Cards, the chapter text, and myworldgeography.com, students will evaluate six countries in the region as possible locations for their business and create a proposal to introduce their business. Review *Student Instructions and Rubric* on the following page.

2. Start-up Meetings Organize groups of six. Distribute *Activity Support: Investigation Notes* and assign each group a business from the table and each member a country from the list on this page. As a class, review needs of each business.

   L2 Extra Support Discuss why each listed business needs the items listed. For example, a café needs access to fresh foods in order to attract customers.

3. Jigsaw Research Convene jigsaw groups by country. As needed, duplicate Activity Cards and then distribute by country to the groups. Have students use the Activity Cards to learn about the

business environment in their assigned country. Tell students to record ways that this country would, or would not, fill the needs of their assigned business, ending with a concluding reason for or against locating in that country.

   ELL Intermediate Have students review photos and visuals from the chapter in order to support their understanding of a country's business environment.

4. Analysis Reconvene business groups to exchange information and reasons and then vote to choose a country for the group's business.

5. Oral Presentation Have students draft and, if time allows, orally present a proposal to their boss at their company. Proposals should identify the business's needs and describe why the target country is a good fit.

   L4 Challenge Invite students to create a computer slideshow to accompany their proposal presentation.

KEY **Time** **Individual** **Pairs** **Small Group** 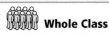 **Whole Class**

Name _____ Class _____ Date _____

myWorld Chapter Activity Support **Student Instructions and Rubric**

Open for Business

Activity Instructions Read the following summary of your myWorld Chapter Activity. Follow your teacher's directions for more information.

1. Work with your classmates to identify the needs of one type of business that might locate in an Eastern European nation.

2. Use the Activity Cards, the chapter text, and myworldgeography.com to learn about the business environment in one Eastern European nation. Record pros and cons of that country as a location for your business. Prepare to argue for or against choosing this country for your business.

3. Meet with your business group to exchange information and ideas and to vote for the country best suited to the group's assigned business.

4. Create a proposal explaining to your boss at your company why that country is a good fit for your business. If time allows, present that proposal orally to the class.

myWorld Chapter Activity Rubric	3 Exceeds Understanding	2 Reaches Understanding	1 Approaches Understanding
Discussion and Analysis	Participates with enthusiasm; shares more than one pro or con per category	Participates with some enthusiasm; shares one pro or con per category	Participates inconsistently; is missing some pros or cons in each category
Proposal	Description is vivid, needs are complete, and reasons are clearly explained	Description is clear but lacks detail, needs are complete, reasons are briefly explained	Description is sometimes clear, needs are sometimes incomplete, and reasons are confusing

Name _____ Class _____ Date _____

Open for Business

Directions Circle your group's assigned business and list your assigned country. Then read about your business's needs. Record information about the country's business environment and identify one important reason for or against locating your specific business there.

Business 1: Customer Service Call Center	Business 2: Chain of Café/ Gourmet Markets	Business 3: Manufacture of Farm Equipment
Needs educated workers who speak many languages; stable political situation for training	**Needs** one large or many urban centers; educated and financially secure customers; culture that cares about food; access to local fresh foods	**Needs** heavy machinery factory; skilled industrial workers; nearby markets for farm equipment; resources such as steel; good energy/ transportation grid

Your country_____

1. Is the location of this country good for your business? Explain.

   _____

2. How high are the taxes in this country?

   _____

3. Will your business find what it needs, such as workers, raw materials, customers, or infrastructure (communication, transportation) in this country?

   _____

   _____

4. Is corruption a problem in this country? Are there other political problems?

   _____

   _____

Recommendation Return to your business group and share one main reason for or against choosing this country for your business.

Eastern Europe

- Introduce the Essential Question so that students will be able to understand the big ideas of this chapter (see earlier page, Connect to the Essential Question).
- Help students prepare to learn about Eastern Europe by looking at the chapter's maps, charts, and photos.

- Have students make and record chapter predictions with the *Essential Question Preview* in the **Student Journal.**
- Ask them to analyze maps on this page.

GUIDE ON THE SIDE

Explore the Essential Question . . .

Have students complete the Essential Question Writer's Workshop in their **Student Journal** to demonstrate in-depth understanding of the question in the context of this chapter.

Analyze Maps Point out the political map.

- Which country is the largest? (Ukraine)
- In which part of the region do many small countries border one another? (the southwestern part, along the Adriatic Sea)
- What advantages might countries in this part of the region have? What problems might they face? (They might gain from being on the Adriatic Sea and its ports, which offer access to the Mediterranean. They might face problems from having to get along with so many different neighbors.)

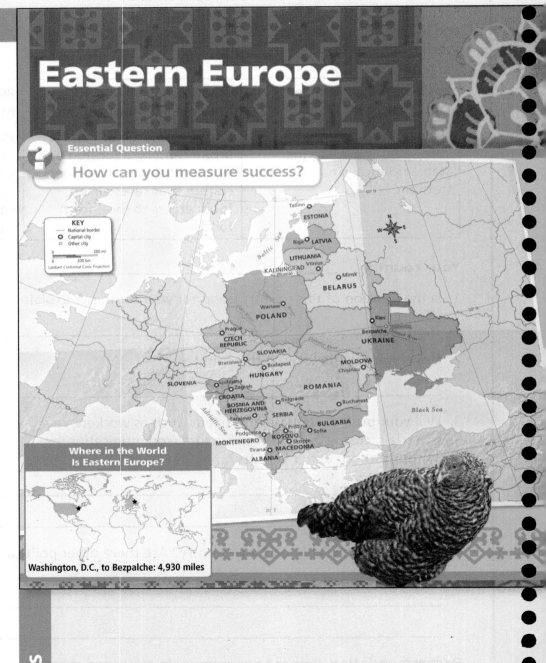

Eastern Europe

Essential Question

How can you measure success?

KEY
— National border
◎ Capital city
○ Other city

200 mi
200 km
Lambert Conformal Conic Projection

Where in the World Is Eastern Europe?

Washington, D.C., to Bezpalche: 4,930 miles

INTRODUCE 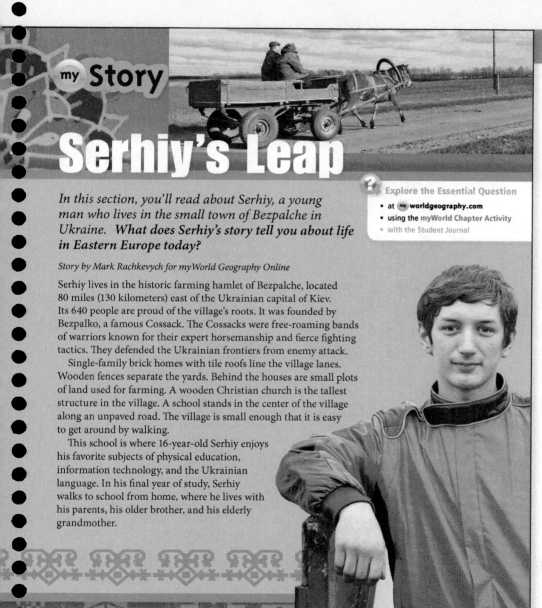my Story

Get students excited to learn about Eastern Europe by first experiencing the region through the eyes of Serhiy, a young man living in rural Ukraine.

- Read myStory and watch the myStory Video about Serhiy's life.

- Have students complete *Serhiy's Leap* in the **Student Journal** to prepare to learn about Serhiy's life in his village and his decision to leave after graduating from high school.

my Story

Serhiy's Leap

In this section, you'll read about Serhiy, a young man who lives in the small town of Bezpalche in Ukraine. What does Serhiy's story tell you about life in Eastern Europe today?

? Explore the Essential Question
- at **my worldgeography.com**
- using the **myWorld Chapter Activity**
- with the Student Journal

Story by Mark Rachkevych for myWorld Geography Online

Serhiy lives in the historic farming hamlet of Bezpalche, located 80 miles (130 kilometers) east of the Ukrainian capital of Kiev. Its 640 people are proud of the village's roots. It was founded by Bezpalko, a famous Cossack. The Cossacks were free-roaming bands of warriors known for their expert horsemanship and fierce fighting tactics. They defended the Ukrainian frontiers from enemy attack.

Single-family brick homes with tile roofs line the village lanes. Wooden fences separate the yards. Behind the houses are small plots of land used for farming. A wooden Christian church is the tallest structure in the village. A school stands in the center of the village along an unpaved road. The village is small enough that it is easy to get around by walking.

This school is where 16-year-old Serhiy enjoys his favorite subjects of physical education, information technology, and the Ukrainian language. In his final year of study, Serhiy walks to school from home, where he lives with his parents, his older brother, and his elderly grandmother.

GUIDE ON THE SIDE

my Story

Serhiy's Leap

- **Summarize** What is Serhiy's community like? (It is a small village with brick homes and small farming plots.)

- **Infer** What religion do you think most people practice in Serhiy's village? How do you know? (Most people practice Christianity. The Christian Church is the tallest structure in town.)

→ On Assignment

Have students to go myworldgeography.com to receive their assignments from a virtual newspaper editor. Students will explore Eastern Europe and beyond in order to better understand Serhiy's story and the key ideas of the chapter.

ECONOMICS

Privatization Ukrainian privatization distributed land from large government farms to individuals and families. Unlike some other parts of Eastern Europe, people got land based on the jobs they had worked in the government farm system. Those who worked in non-agricultural jobs, such as at schools, received less land than those who worked in the actual farm system. In the village of Nagorna, each family ended up with about .5 hectares (2.4 acres).

- **Identify Details** How does Serhiy's family make a living? (His mother delivers mail. The rest of the family farms.)

- **Compare and Contrast** How has land ownership in Serhiy's community changed since Ukraine became an independent country? (Land used to be owned by the government, but after independence, it was distributed to individual families.)

- **Identify Details** What kinds of tasks does Serhiy do in his life? (He does farm chores, he studies for school, and he rides motorbikes and builds computers.)

- **Infer** Which of these tasks are most interesting to him? (He likes the technical tasks, like building a computer.)

Serhiy buys bread at the only shop in Bezpalche.

Scattering corn for the chickens is one of Serhiy's regular afternoon chores. He also must feed the family's pigs (below).

His mother works a postal route three hours a day. On their small farm, his family grows beets, onions, cabbage, corn, and potatoes, and tends four pigs and three milking cows. Serhiy is personally responsible for caring for more than 40 rabbits. Small farms like this are common in Ukraine.

Ukraine used to be part of the Soviet Union. The Soviet government managed all the land in the country. Now Ukraine is an independent country. The new leadership broke up the large government farms, giving each family a small plot of land.

In villages like these, nature doesn't allow for breaks or long vacations. Serhiy rises at 6:00, feeds the livestock, and does other chores around the pens. Then he eats breakfast and heads to school for his first class, which begins at 8:30. He returns home at 2:30 and eats lunch. His favorite lunch is potatoes fried in lard and onions. His next chore is to take care of the rabbits. His grandmother pays him a small weekly allowance for this task. Then, at sunset, Serhiy starts his homework.

Short and broad-shouldered, Serhiy enjoys physical activity. He loves motorbikes and anything technical. "I even assembled a computer from scratch with a friend of mine," Serhiy says proudly, pointing at his PC, which he knows inside and out.

NOTES

QUICK FACTS

Employment Only about 25 percent of Ukraine's workforce remains in the agricultural sector. Most Ukrainians work in service jobs. This means that young people like Serhiy have the most opportunity when they learn a service skill, such as computer programming, and move to cities and towns.

Serhiy plays games on a computer that he assembled himself, but he has no Internet connection.

The city of Kiev is about 80 miles from Serhiy's village.

But Serhiy can enjoy these hobbies only when time permits. On the weekends, his brother drives him 25 miles (40 kilometers) to the regional capital to take preparatory classes. Serhiy wants to go to the military academy in Kharkiv in eastern Ukraine. He hopes to become a pilot. But to do so, he will need to do well on the entrance exam. The prestigious and highly competitive academy accepts only one out of every four applicants.

Serhiy knows his small world and way of life will come to an end next summer when he graduates. Even if he is not accepted to the military academy, he will leave his village. The grocery store is the only real business in Bezpalche, so most young people must go elsewhere to make a living. Once his studies begin, he will not be able to take trips into the woods or drive his motorbike on country roads.

Still, Serhiy looks forward to military life. After all, could it be tougher than life in Bezpalche? Yet he worries, "Cities have wide boulevards, and I'll be a stranger among impersonal strangers."

He's willing to make the transition since he is drawn to the physical rigor of military exercises, the technical hardware and weaponry, and the challenges the regimen brings. "My family supports my decision, and my mother just worries like any other mother does," Serhiy says half-jokingly.

And if he doesn't get accepted when he applies in Kharkiv next summer, what is his backup plan? "Then I'll probably study computer programming in Cherkassy, the neighboring regional capital," Serhiy says.

How does he feel about leaving an environment where everything is familiar, where there are no surprises, and where everybody knows his name? "Well, I'm not just going to stay here," he says. "No one from my graduating class plans to remain in the village next summer, nobody."

Meet the Journalist

Name Mark Rachkevych
Favorite Moment Eating in a market and chatting with villagers in Bezpalche

 myStory Video

Join Serhiy as he shows you more about his life in Ukraine.

GUIDE ON THE SIDE

- **Identify Details** What two options is Serhiy considering for after high school? (the military or further study of computer programming)

- **Compare and Contrast** How will his life after high school be different from his life now? (He will almost certainly leave his village.)

- **Infer** How will Serhiy's life in his village prepare him for the possibilities after high school? (He is prepared for hard work and has experience with technical tasks. These experiences will help him be a soldier or a computer programmer.)

myStory Video

Have students watch the video at myworldgeography.com about Serhiy's life in his village.

NOTES

Chapter Atlas

OBJECTIVES

Students will know

- physical geography and environmental challenges in Eastern Europe.
- major religious groups in Eastern Europe.

Students will be able to

- label an outline map of Eastern Europe.
- synthesize information about the region's climate, environmental challenges, and religions.

SET EXPECTATIONS

In this section, students will

- read Chapter Atlas.
- answer and discuss questions about the region in a hailstorm activity.
- go On Assignment in Eastern Europe and complete the chapter assignment.

CORE CONCEPTS

You may wish to teach or reteach the following lessons from the Core Concepts Handbook:

- Types of Climate, pp. 40–41
- People's Impact on the Environment, pp. 52–53
- Religion, pp. 92–93

KEY

Differentiated Instruction

L1 Special Needs **L2** Extra Support
L3 On-Level **L4** Challenge

English Language Instruction

ELL Beginner **ELL** Early Intermediate **ELL** Intermediate
ELL Early Advanced **ELL** Advanced

1 Connect
Make learning meaningful

Make Connections Have students think about the **myStory Video** of *Serhiy's Leap*. Ask, What did the land look like around Serhiy's home? (Flat? Mountainous?) What kinds of crops did his family and neighbors grow? Have students think about the land around their city or community. Ask, Could farmers grow the same kinds of crops? Why or why not?

L2 Extra Support Show a photo of a wheat or corn farm from the American Midwest and compare it to the area where Serhiy lives. Ask students to suggest reasons why this flat land is easier for growing crops than hilly land.

Activate Prior Knowledge Remind students that in the chapter Europe in Modern Times they learned about the history of religion in Europe. Ask students to predict which religious groups are probably important in Eastern Europe.

ELL Early Intermediate Use visuals from Europe in Modern Times to remind students of major religious changes in Europe, such as the Protestant Reformation.

Prepare Follow the steps in the section **Preview.** Preteach the Key Terms. Then have students complete *Word Wise* in their journals using in-text clues and the glossary for help.

2 Experience
Teach knowledge and skills

Read Use **Background** notes and **Guide on the Side** questions to model active reading. Have students use *Take Notes* in their **Student Journal** to record important places to know in Eastern Europe on an outline map. Students should use the maps in the Chapter Atlas and the Active Atlas at myworldgeography.com for assistance.

L2 Extra Support Use a sequence flow chart to help students track the changes created by glaciers, such as pits dug by ice, then filled with melted ice to form lakes.

ELL Intermediate Review the English words *plain* and *plane,* as well as multiple meanings of each. Use visuals to clarify the geographic meaning of *plain*.

 Practice: myWorld Activity Students will answer questions about Eastern Europe and contribute their responses to a "hailstorm" of crumpled paper. They will then choose and discuss responses from a pile to share and increase perspective on key regional issues. **Step-by-Step Instructions** and **More Activities** follow on pp. T122–T123. Have students complete **21st Century Online Tutor** *Synthesize* as and apply this skill to the activity.

SECTION 1 RESOURCE GUIDE

FOR THE STUDENT

my worldgeography.com Student Center
- Active Atlas

Student Edition (print and online)
- Chapter Atlas

Student Journal (print and online)
- Section 1 Word Wise
- Section 1 Take Notes

21st Century Learning Online Tutor
- Synthesize
- Read Physical Maps

FOR THE TEACHER

my worldgeography.com Teacher Center
- Online Lesson Planner
- Presentations for Projection
- SuccessTracker

ProGuide: Europe and Russia
- Lesson Plan, pp. T120–T121
- ✦ myWorld Activity Step-by-Step Instructions, p. T122
- Activity Support: Hailstone Strips, p. T123
- myWorld Geography Enrichment, p. T124
- Section Quiz, p. T125

Accelerating the Progress of ELLs
- Comprehension Check Strategies, p. 53

---

3 Understand
Assess understanding

Review Review *Word Wise* and *Take Notes* in the **Student Journal**.

Assess Knowledge and Skills Use the Section Assessment and Section Quiz to check students' progress.

Assess Understanding Review students' responses to the Section Assessment Essential Question prompt.

Remediate Use these strategies to review and remediate.

If students struggle to . . .	Try these strategies.
Describe variations in the region's climate	Provide index cards for each climate zone, with features and countries on opposite sides.
Contrast land use patterns	Use visuals to help students link mechanized and non-mechanized agriculture to the most suitable geography.
Read elevations in the region on a physical map	Assign additional practice with the **21st Century Online Tutor**.

ELL Support

ELL Objective Students will be able to describe key geographic features and locations in the region in English.

Cultural Connections Invite students to use English or home languages to describe a feature of physical geography that has an impact on daily life in their families' home countries.

ELL Early Advanced Content Tip Pronounce proper names on the section maps and have students repeat. Point out pronunciations that are unusual for English, such as Czech (CHEK). Repeat with additional place names from the text, such as Dnieper (NEE-per).

ELL Activity Scaffold the Hailstorm activity by prereading the questions on *Activity Support: Hailstone Strips*. Post a word bank of physical and climate features, such as *plains, mountains, rivers, wet, and rainy*. Then model responses with sentence frames, such as: Christians in the region may be (religion), (religion), or (religion). **(Verbal)**

myWorld Activity **Step-by-Step Instructions**

⏱ 20 min 👥

Hailstorm

OBJECTIVES

Students will

- respond to questions about climate, religion, and environment in Eastern Europe.
- identify and share new perspectives on the issues raised by the questions.

LEARNING STYLE

- Kinesthetic
- Verbal

21st Century Learning

- Synthesize

MATERIALS

- Scissors
- Activity Support: Hailstone Strips, p. T123

Activity Steps

1. Tell students they will be asked to respond in writing to questions about Eastern Europe's physical and cultural geography. They will contribute their responses to a pile. Students will then take turns retrieving random responses and reading these aloud for group discussion.

2. Distribute scissors and *Activity Support: Hailstone Strips* and then review directions. Give students time to write their responses.

   L1 **Special Needs** Have students take each written answer and look for proof in the text and visuals that the answer is correct.

   ELL **Beginning** Transcribe responses for students not ready for the sentence frames in the ELL Activity on the previous page.

3. Tell students to cut out their answer strips and crumple each into a piece of "hail." Organize

students in a circle and provide a target area for students to throw their "hailstones."

4. Invite volunteers, or draw names from a hat, to select students to retrieve and read aloud a response.

   L4 **Challenge** Prewrite several follow-up questions related to those on the Activity Support. When these students read a response, ask additional questions on the response topic.

5. Give each student an opportunity to share a new perspective he or she has gained about the section content.

More Activities From myWorld Teachers

Local Connections Have students make awareness posters about environmental challenges in their area. Discuss whether they are similar to or different from those facing countries in Eastern Europe. **(Visual/Verbal)**

 Chain Mail Start a chain letter with a key feature of physical or human geography from Chapter Atlas. "Deliver" it to a student. Each student must add

a feature and explain how it relates to those already listed and then "deliver" the letter to a different classmate. **(Kinesthetic/Verbal)**

 Board Game Have students design the board and game pieces for a geography game about Eastern Europe. Have students explain the main goal and basic rules of the game. They should include key geographic features on the board. **(Visual)**

my worldgeography.com **Teacher Center** ⊙ Find additional resources in the online Teacher Center.

Name _____ Class _____ Date _____

myWorld Activity Support   **Hailstone Strips**

Hailstorm

Directions Read and answer the questions below. Then cut out the strips on the dotted lines. As your teacher asks each question, crumple up your response and throw it as directed by your teacher.

✂ -

Question 1 What is one effect that a glacier has on the land?

_____

_____

- -

Question 2 How does the climate vary from the south to the north of Eastern Europe?

_____

_____

- -

Question 3 What are some environmental challenges that countries in Eastern Europe face?

_____

_____

- -

Question 4 What are the three major groups of Christians in Eastern Europe?

_____

_____

- -

Question 5 Which area of Eastern Europe has been most strongly influenced by Islam?

_____

_____

- -

Question 6 What is one thing you will remember for the rest of your life about Eastern Europe?

_____

_____

Name _____ Class _____ Date _____

Enrichment: Geographic Contrasts

Directions Study the table. Then answer the questions that follow and complete the activity.

Cities and Climate	Bucharest, Romania	Prague, Czech Republic	Sofia, Bulgaria	Tirana, Albania
Latitude/ Longitude	44.25° N 26.06° E	50.05° N 14.25° E	42.42° N 23.20° E	41.20° N 19.48° E
Altitude	301 ft	1,198 ft	1,804 ft	292 ft
January Temperature	27°F	28°F	30.5°F	45°F
January Precipitation	1.8 inches	0.7 inches	1.3 inches	5.3 inches
July Temperature	73°F	64°F	68°F	75°F
July Precipitation	2.1 inches	2.6 inches	2.2 inches	1.2 inches

1. Look at data for January precipitation. Which city is the driest in winter?

_____

2. How do the latitudes and altitudes of Sofia and Tirana compare? Is the climate in these cities similar?

_____

_____

3. Activity Use latitude and longitude to locate each city on the climate map in your chapter. What is the climate zone for each city?

_____

_____

Name _____ Class _____ Date _____

Section Quiz

Directions Answer the following questions using what you learned
in Section 1.

1. _____ What is the climate like during an
ice age?
  a. cold rain for many days
  b. suddenly very cold
  c. cold but no snow
  d. very cold for a long time

2. _____ What kind of land is most suited for
mechanized farming?
  a. hilly land
  b. steep mountains
  c. flat plains
  d. rocky coasts

3. _____ What causes acid rain?
  a. burning coal and other fossil fuels
  b. slow movement of glaciers
  c. shortage of oil and gas supply
  d. factory's overusing rivers

4. _____ Many people are emigrating from
Ukraine. What does this mean?
  a. Many people are moving to Ukraine
  from other countries.
  b. Many people are leaving cities in
  Ukraine to move to rural areas.
  c. Many people are leaving Ukraine to
  settle in other countries.
  d. Many people from Ukraine are taking
  trips to other countries.

5. _____ In which country do many Muslims
live today?
  a. Poland
  b. Latvia
  c. Ukraine
  d. Bosnia

6. Complete the table below to list important ideas about the physical
and human geography of Eastern Europe.

Landforms and Bodies of Water	Climate
Religious Groups	Resources and Environmental Challenges

Chapter Atlas

SECTION PREVIEW

- Model preparing to read by previewing the Key Ideas, Key Terms, headings, visuals, and captions. Have students make predictions about what they will learn. For ELL support, post the prompt, "I predict I will read about . . ."
- Preview and practice reading physical maps by looking at the physical map of the region. Help students make predictions from the map. Ask,

Which area has more mountains and which area is more flat? How might the way people use the land in these areas differ?

- Preteach this section's high-use Academic Vocabulary and Key Terms using the table on the next page and in-text definitions. Have students practice Key Terms by completing the *Word Wise* page in their journals.

GUIDE ON THE SIDE

Physical Features

- **Identify Main Ideas** What are the two main landforms in Eastern Europe? (mountains, broad plains)

Identify Details

- Which part of Eastern Europe is most mountainous? (the Balkan Peninsula)
- Which mountains meet in the south of the region? (the Carpathian Mountains and the Transylvanian Alps)

Reading Skill

Label an Outline Map While they read, have students identify the Places to Know! on the outline map of the region in the **Student Journal.**

Section 1

Chapter Atlas

Key Ideas
- Glaciers have shaped the physical features of this region.
- Climate varies from the south to the north of the region.
- Eastern European countries face many environmental challenges.
- Eastern Europe has a varied religious background.

Key Terms • ice age • mechanized farming • acid rain • emigrate

Visual Glossary

Reading Skill: Label an Outline Map Take notes using the outline map in your journal.

▲ The "Iron Gates" of the Danube River separate Romania from Serbia and the Carpathian Mountains from the Balkans.

◀ A young woman from Estonia

Physical Features

Eastern Europe is a region with both broad plains and high mountains. The most mountainous part of the region is the Balkan Peninsula, which juts into the Mediterranean Sea to the south. Two ranges, the Dinaric Alps and the Balkan Mountains, cover much of the peninsula.

Mountain ranges also stretch through the middle of Eastern Europe. The Carpathian Mountains begin close to the Danube River in Slovakia. They arch northeast and then bend back toward the Danube River, joining the Transylvanian Alps to the south.

ACADEMIC VOCABULARY

High-Use Word	Definition and Sample Sentence
accumulate	*v.* to build up over time *With five people in the family, a lot of laundry accumulates each week.*
dominant	*adj.* having the most power or influence *The dominant color in a forest is green.*

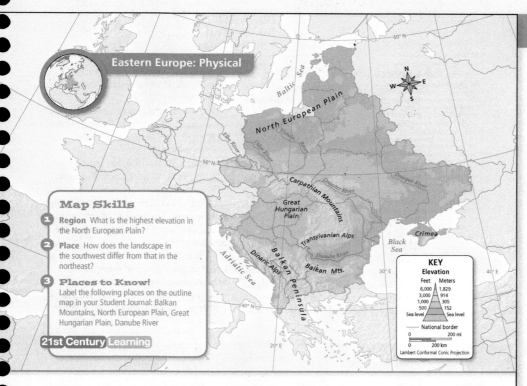

Eastern Europe: Physical

North European Plain

Baltic Sea

Carpathian Mountains

Great Hungarian Plain

Transylvanian Alps

Balkan Mts.

Dinaric Alps

Balkan Peninsula

Adriatic Sea

Black Sea

Crimea

Danube River

Dniester River

Dnieper River

Elbe River

Oder River

Vistula River

KEY
Elevation

Feet	Meters
6,000	1,829
3,000	914
1,000	305
500	152
Sea level	Sea level

—— National border

0 ____ 200 mi

0 ____ 200 km

Lambert Conformal Conic Projection

Map Skills

1. **Region** What is the highest elevation in the North European Plain?

2. **Place** How does the landscape in the southwest differ from that in the northeast?

3. **Places to Know!**
Label the following places on the outline map in your Student Journal: Balkan Mountains, North European Plain, Great Hungarian Plain, Danube River

21st Century Learning

Between these two groups of mountains lies the Great Hungarian Plain. Another large plain, the North European Plain, stretches from the Baltic Sea to the Black Sea. Most of the farms and cities of this region are in these broad flatlands.

The physical features of the northern part of this region were shaped by an **ice age,** or time of lower temperatures when much of the land is covered in ice. Ice piled up as deep as two miles thick. Heavy sheets of ice, called glaciers, moved slowly across the land. Glaciers scraped up rocks and soil as they moved. They then dropped these materials when they melted. This process created ridges of hills that extend for hundreds of miles across the region.

Glaciers also formed lakes and rivers. The pressure of the glacier dug pits into the land. When the ice melted, pits became lakes. Most lakes in Europe are located in glaciated areas.

In the southern part of this region, deep valleys crisscross steep mountains. The Danube river flows through the Iron Gates, one of these deep valleys.

Reading Check What effects have glaciers had on the physical features of Eastern Europe?

MAP SKILLS 1. about 1000 feet (305 meters) above sea level **2.** In the southwest, the landscape is mountainous, while in the northeast it is flat. **3.** Students should correctly locate and label each place on the outline map in their **Student Journal.**

READING CHECK Glaciers have created ridges of hills, dug out land for lakes, and deposited material that blocked the flow of rivers.

ANSWERS

- **Summarize** Where are most farms and cities in Eastern Europe? (in the broad flatlands of the Great Hungarian Plain and the North European Plain)

- **Draw Conclusions** Why do you think farms and cities are located where they are? (The flatness of the plains makes it easy to build on; and it has good soil for farming.)

- **Cause and Effect** How did an ice age shape the land of Eastern Europe? (Ice ages allowed glaciers to form, which in turn shaped the land.)

Map Skills Have students locate physical features on the map.

- Into what bodies of water do the region's rivers flow? (Baltic Sea, Black Sea)

- Which rivers flow through the North European Plain? (Vistula, Oder)

21st Century Learning

Read Physical Maps Have students develop this skill by using this interactive online tutorial and activities. Students will learn how to read physical maps and will apply the skill to new situations.

HISTORY

Weather Eastern Europe's weather has played a role in past events and continues to do so in the present. For example, in 1806, French Emperor Napoleon invaded Poland on his way to attacking Russia. He met the Polish winter and his invasion failed. It was simply impossible to move equipment, supplies, and men through the harsh conditions. More recently, in 1999, a huge blizzard in Hungary completely shut down 400 villages. Some villages were unreachable until the four days of heavy snow ended.

Climate and Agriculture

- **Identify Main Ideas** What is the main factor affecting climate in Eastern Europe? (latitude)

- **Summarize** How does that important factor affect the climate in different parts of the region? (In the southern latitudes, summers are dry and winters are rainy. In the more northern latitudes, winters are very cold and summers are generally mild.)

Map Skills Have students examine the map and locate the climate zones.

- Which is the largest climate zone in the region? (continental, cool summer)

→ **Active Atlas**

Point out the map of Eastern Europe's climate zones
- Have students go to myworldgeography.com to learn more about the climate of Eastern Europe.

Climate and Agriculture

The climate varies across Eastern Europe. In particular, the climate of the northern part of the region is very different from the climate of the southern part. As a result, farmers in the north face different challenges than farmers in the south. In the north, the winters can be very harsh. In the south, the mountains make cultivating the land difficult.

Latitude is the most important factor that influences climate in Eastern Europe. In the south, a band of Mediterranean and subtropical climate extends across much of the Balkan Peninsula. Summers here are dry, while winters are rainy. The rain and snow that <u>accumulate</u> in the mountains in wet winter months are very important for agriculture. During the hot, dry months of spring and summer, melting snow flows downhill to the crops in the parched valleys below.

The continental cool summer climate covers much of the rest of Eastern Europe. In this area, winters are cold, and summers are generally mild.

Patterns of rainfall across the region vary from east to west. Each year, most of Eastern Europe receives between 20 and 40 inches of precipitation, or falling rain or snow. The amount of precipitation in the west is generally greater than the amount in the east.

Hills and mountains also have a major effect on the amount of precipitation an area receives. In general, warm air can hold more moisture than cool air. The higher air goes, the cooler it gets. When

accumulate, *v.,* to build up over time

Eastern Europe: Climate

Continental, cool summer

Mediterranean

ESTONIA
LATVIA
LITHUANIA
BELARUS
POLAND
CZECH REPUBLIC
SLOVAKIA
UKRAINE
HUNGARY
MOLDOVA
SLOVENIA
ROMANIA
CROATIA
BOSNIA AND HERZEGOVINA
SERBIA
MONTENEGRO
BULGARIA
KOSOVO
ALBANIA
MACEDONIA
Baltic Sea
Black Sea

KEY
Continental cool summer
Continental warm summer
Humid subtropical
Mediterranean
— National border
0   300 mi
0   300 km
Lambert Conformal Conic Projection

Map Skills
1. **Place** Identify one country in Eastern Europe with a mostly Mediterranean climate.
2. **Region** What is the relationship between climate and latitude?

→ **Active Atlas**

MAP SKILLS **1.** Albania **2.** Climate changes as latitude changes.

ECONOMICS

Olive Oil in Montenegro The Balkan nation of Montenegro once had a thriving olive oil industry supplied by more than 450,000 olive oil trees. That industry fell on hard times during the late years of the 1900s. In 2002, American aid organizations began to help the Montenegrins bring their olive oil industry back to life. These organizations supplied money for harvesting machines, education for olive oil growers, and training for workers. Since that time, some areas have seen production increase three times over. In the area called Bar, an important Montenegrin olive oil area, people once again express their pride with the local saying, "Be as proud as Bar is of its olive orchards."

air cannot hold as much water, the water falls back to the earth as rain or as snow.

It is easy to see, then, how mountains affect precipitation. When wind blows against a range of mountains, the air rises and cools. Then it drops its moisture and continues over the mountains. Therefore, the side of the mountains facing the wind receives much more rain than the other side. The result is big differences in climate over small distances. Areas along the Adriatic coast, for example, receive as much as 200 inches of rainfall a year. The dry valleys on the other side of the Dinaric Alps may receive only 30 inches of rainfall during the same period of time.

The growing season on the North European Plain is shorter than the growing season farther south in the region.

Still, many people farm in this region. **Mechanized farming,** or farming with machines, is easy on the large expanses of flat land. Wheat and rye are common crops in this region. They are well suited to the cooler climate and easy to harvest with machines.

Because machines are important for agriculture here, many farms in northeastern Europe are large. Large farms are not as common in the southern part of this region. Because of the mountains, mechanized farming is more difficult. Also, more people are available to work the land. Many crops such as citrus fruits, olives, and grapes grow well in the warm climate.

Reading Check **How is agriculture in the north of Eastern Europe different from that in the south?**

my World IN NUMBERS

In Albania, **58%** of the labor force work on farms. Most work on small family farms.

- **Compare and Contrast** How is rainfall on the Adriatic Coast different from east of the Dinaric Alps? (On the coast, 200 inches of rain may fall in a year. Inland areas may get only 30 inches.)

- **Cause and Effect** What causes the difference in climate between coastal and inland areas? (Air rising over the mountains cools and drops its moisture as rain on the coastal side of the mountains. Air that reaches the inland side of the mountains is quite dry so brings little rain.)

Analyze Visuals Have students compare the photographs.

- How does geography contribute to the different farming methods in these photographs? (The north has flat land where machine farming is easy. In the south, the land is too mountainous for machine farming.)

Harvesting Wheat in the North
Wheat grows best in areas without extremes of temperature. So wheat is a good crop for countries with cool summers and flat land.

Growing Olives in the South
Olive trees do well with warm, dry summers and cannot survive very cold winters. For that reason, olive growing is best suited to countries with a Mediterranean climate.

READING CHECK In the north, agriculture is mostly mechanized. In the south it mostly uses human labor instead of machines.

ANSWERS

CORE CONCEPTS: PEOPLE'S IMPACT ON THE ENVIRONMENT

Review Core Concepts 4.3 before discussing Eastern Europe's energy choices and environmental challenges. Discuss effects of different industries on the environment and ways that deforestation from any cause can in turn create additional negative outcomes.

Review reasons that countries need energy resources in order to thrive, and ask students to suggest ways that they think countries could manage those resources responsibly in order to protect the environment.

GUIDE ON THE SIDE

Closer Look

Coal or Nuclear: Difficult Energy Choices

- **Cause and Effect** Why does Eastern Europe need energy? (to fuel economic growth)

- **Ask Questions** What questions would you ask to help you choose an energy source for the region? (Sample: Which is less expensive? Which creates more jobs?)

- **Express Opinions** Which energy source do you think is better for Eastern Europe? (Sample: Nuclear energy makes more sense in the long run. It is cleaner and can be safer.)

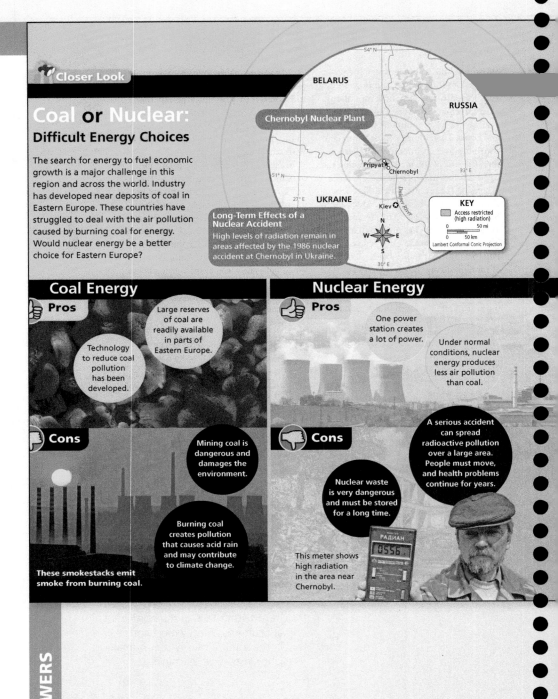

Closer Look

Coal or Nuclear: Difficult Energy Choices

The search for energy to fuel economic growth is a major challenge in this region and across the world. Industry has developed near deposits of coal in Eastern Europe. These countries have struggled to deal with the air pollution caused by burning coal for energy. Would nuclear energy be a better choice for Eastern Europe?

Long-Term Effects of a Nuclear Accident
High levels of radiation remain in areas affected by the 1986 nuclear accident at Chernobyl in Ukraine.

BELARUS
RUSSIA
Chernobyl Nuclear Plant
Pripyat
Chernobyl
UKRAINE
Kiev
Dnieper River

KEY
Access restricted (high radiation)
0   50 mi
0   50 km
Lambert Conformal Conic Projection

Coal Energy

Pros

Large reserves of coal are readily available in parts of Eastern Europe.

Technology to reduce coal pollution has been developed.

Cons

Mining coal is dangerous and damages the environment.

Burning coal creates pollution that causes acid rain and may contribute to climate change.

These smokestacks emit smoke from burning coal.

Nuclear Energy

Pros

One power station creates a lot of power.

Under normal conditions, nuclear energy produces less air pollution than coal.

A serious accident can spread radioactive pollution over a large area. People must move, and health problems continue for years.

Cons

Nuclear waste is very dangerous and must be stored for a long time.

This meter shows high radiation in the area near Chernobyl.

PRIMARY SOURCE

Chernobyl Share these comments from Ukrainians 20 years after the Chernobyl accident:

"Today is probably the first time that we can openly look into the eyes of the national and international community and say that a solution to the . . . Chernobyl problem was formally found."

—2007, President Viktor Yushchenko about hiring a firm to improve the cover on Chernobyl's ruins

"We started an organization for youth who wanted to change their future. [It gives] young people information about the ecological situation in our country, and in our city. We try to make children think about these problems and do something to protect our environment."

—2006, Chernobyl survivor and student activist interviewed for *bbc.com* in "Chernobyl Voices: Viktoria Bormotova"

Natural Resources and the Environment

Physical geography influences industry as well as agriculture. The location of Eastern Europe's factories depends on the location of natural resources. For example, industry has grown in areas of Poland where coal is available. Both iron ore and coal are found in one region of Ukraine. As a result, steel is an important industrial product there.

Oil and gas are in very short supply in Eastern Europe. Many countries must import the oil and gas they need to develop industry. For example, countries such as Ukraine, Moldova, and Belarus have become dependent on oil and gas imports from Russia.

The need for energy to fuel industry has created serious environmental problems. In 1986, an explosion occurred at one of the towers at the Chernobyl nuclear power plant in Ukraine. Winds spread radioactive pollution over a huge area in Europe. Many people became sick and died from the radiation. Farmland was contaminated, so that the food grown there was no longer safe to eat. More than

20 years later, the area around the power plant was still contaminated. A reporter described one city in Ukraine that had been evacuated shortly after the accident:

66 A dead city. Homes, schoolrooms, playgrounds, and other places are crumbling as wild nature reclaims the land. Pripyat once had some 50,000 residents. Now they are gone, perhaps forever. Only the artifacts of their lives remain behind, rotting to dust. 99

—Jeffrey Young, Voice of America, June 10, 2009

Other Eastern European countries have drawn on their coal reserves. Burning coal and other fossil fuels sends chemicals into the air that cause **acid rain**, that is, precipitation that is acidic. Forests have been damaged by acid rain and other pollution. In parts of Poland and the Czech Republic, forests have been destroyed by acid rain, and soils are too contaminated for crops. Worse, polluted water and soil have caused higher rates of birth defects, cancer, and other diseases.

Today, many countries have begun to address environmental problems. To join the European Union, countries must install equipment to make power plants cleaner. Now the problem of acid rain is much less serious in Eastern Europe, and the forests are starting to recover.

Reading Check What has caused damage to the forests of Eastern Europe?

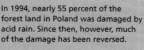
In 1994, nearly 55 percent of the forest land in Poland was damaged by acid rain. Since then, however, much of the damage has been reversed.

READING CHECK acid rain

Natural Resources and the Environment

- **Categorize** What resources are readily available to industries in Eastern Europe? (coal, iron ore) What resources are less available? (oil, gas)

- **Cause and Effect** How does the availability of resources affect the type of industry in Ukraine? (Availability of coal and iron makes steel an important industry.)

- **Summarize** How has industry in Eastern Europe affected the region's environment? (Industry has harmed the region's environment through nuclear accidents and acid rain from coal burning.)

- **Compare and Contrast** How has the problem of acid rain in Eastern Europe changed in recent years? (It is much less serious.)

- **Cause and Effect** What explains the change? (Countries have made changes, such as having industry install equipment that make power plants cleaner.)

CULTURE

Orthodox Churches Like the Protestant faith, the Orthodox faith has many divisions within it. The divisions are organized mostly around geography, yielding for example, the Church of Serbia, the Church of Albania, and the Church of Bulgaria. Each division has its own leader. The differences between the divisions often reflect the cultural traditions of members. Like other Christians, Orthodox Christians believe that Jesus Christ was God in human form. They differ from other Christians in giving the Holy Spirit a particularly important role in parts of the religious service. A few Orthodox divisions, such as the Church of Ukraine and the Church of Estonia, are not recognized by all the other divisions.

GUIDE ON THE SIDE

Religious Diversity in Eastern Europe

- **Identify Details** What is the dominant religion in Eastern Europe? (Christianity)

- **Summarize** How was Christianity first divided? (It split into the Catholic Church and the Eastern Orthodox Church.)

- **Compare and Contrast** How are Christians in Estonia likely to be different than Christians in Poland? (Mostly Protestants live in Estonia, while mostly Catholics live in Poland.)

Map Skills Point out and discuss the map of religions.

- In which part of Eastern Europe is Eastern Orthodoxy most common? (the eastern part)

→ **Active Atlas**

Point out the map of Eastern Europe's religions.

- Have students go to myworldgeography.com to learn more about religious diversity in Eastern Europe.

512   Western Hemisphere
268   Eastern Hemisphere
452   World Geography

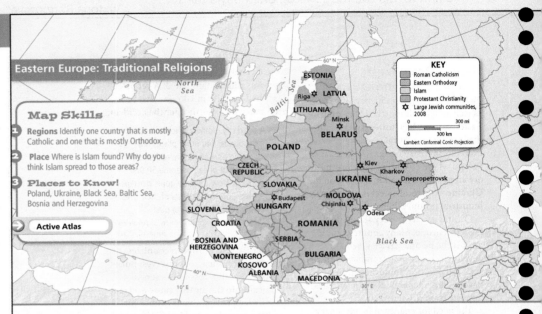

Eastern Europe: Traditional Religions

Map Skills

1. **Regions** Identify one country that is mostly Catholic and one that is mostly Orthodox.

2. **Place** Where is Islam found? Why do you think Islam spread to those areas?

3. **Places to Know!** Poland, Ukraine, Black Sea, Baltic Sea, Bosnia and Herzegovina

→ **Active Atlas**

KEY
- Roman Catholicism
- Eastern Orthodoxy
- Islam
- Protestant Christianity
- ☆ Large Jewish communities, 2008

0 ___ 300 mi
0 ___ 300 km
Lambert Conformal Conic Projection

Religious Diversity in Eastern Europe

Eastern Europe is a region with a diverse religious history. Christianity is the <u>dominant</u> religion. In addition, many Jewish people and Muslims call this region home.

dominant, *adj.,* having the most power or influence

The first major division in the Christian religion occurred with the split between the Catholic Church and the Eastern Orthodox Church in the year 1054. The pope in Rome led the Catholic Church, while the patriarch of Constantinople was the leading figure for Eastern Orthodoxy. Constantinople is now Istanbul, in Turkey. From these centers, both churches sent missionaries into Eastern Europe. Eastern Orthodoxy became dominant in much of the Balkan Peninsula, as well as in Ukraine and Belarus.

With the Reformation in the 1500s, Protestant groups broke off from the Catholic Church. The Reformation began in Germany, and Protestantism spread to countries in northeastern Europe, including Estonia and Latvia. The Roman Catholic Church remained stronger in most of Central Europe, including Poland, the Czech Republic, Slovakia, and Hungary.

Christianity is not the only religion in Europe. Today, Muslims are the largest group of non-Christians. Many Muslims live in Bosnia, Albania, Kosovo, and the Crimean Peninsula in Ukraine. In fact, the southern part of Eastern Europe has long been a borderland where the Christian and Muslim worlds meet. This boundary has shifted over time as control of the region passed between Christian and Islamic states.

MAP SKILLS 1. Sample: Christian: Hungary; Orthodox: Romania
2. Bosnia and Herzegovina, Kosovo, Albania, Serbia, and Bulgaria. These areas are close to the Mediterranean, which offers access to nearby Muslim regions. **3.** Students should correctly locate and label each place on the outline map in their **Student Journal.**

READING CHECK Bosnia and Herzegovina, Kosovo, Albania, Serbia, and Bulgaria

SECTION 1 ASSESSMENT 1. Burning coal and fossil fuels causes acid rain.
2. Mechanized farming is used widely in northern parts of Eastern Europe where

HISTORY

Soviet Restrictions The Eastern European countries of Belarus, Estonia, Moldova, Latvia, Lithuania, and Ukraine were once part of the Soviet Union (USSR). These countries were controlled by the main Soviet government. Other countries in the region were technically independent, but were heavily influenced by the USSR. That government opposed religion, believing that it was used to keep working people from questioning authority. In 1991, the Soviet Union came apart and the nations in Eastern Europe soon achieved full independence.

A Catholic bishop from the Czech Republic

A Muslim imam from Bosnia

An Eastern Orthodox priest from Ukraine

A Jewish rabbi from Poland

Judaism also has a long history in Eastern Europe. Europe was once home to most of the world's Jewish people. But during the Holocaust of the 1940s, two thirds of the Jews in Europe were murdered. Many others later left the region. Since then, there has been a revival of Jewish communities in some areas. In others, Jewish people continue to **emigrate**, or leave one area to move to another. About 30,000 Jews leave Ukraine each year for the United States, Israel, and other places.

The laws of the Soviet Union restricted religion. For many years, Eastern European governments discouraged religion.

Today, many people in Eastern Europe do not belong to any religion. More than half of the people in the Czech Republic and 40 percent of those in Estonia claim no religious faith.

Still, religious life has become more active since the end of communism. Now people have more opportunities to start and join religious organizations. With the fall of communist governments, people in this region have had the chance not only to return to traditional religious practices, but also to live more freely in other areas of their lives.

Reading Check Where are many Muslims found in this region?

myWorld Activity
Hailstorm

Section **1** Assessment

Key Terms

1. What causes acid rain?

2. Use the term *mechanized farming* to describe agriculture in Eastern Europe.

Key Ideas

3. Where are the major groups of mountains located in Eastern Europe?

4. How does the climate of Eastern Europe change from the north to the south?

5. What are some of the important resources of Eastern Europe?

Think Critically

6. **Identify Cause and Effect** Why are crops grown in the north different from those grown in the south of this region?

7. **Draw Inferences** What might influence whether people in a region practice one religion or another?

? Essential Question

How can you measure success?

To join the European Union, countries must meet certain environmental standards. Do you think protecting the environment should be one measure of a country's success? Explain why or why not. Go to your Student Journal to record your answer.

the land is flat and open. **3.** Mountains are located on the Balkan Peninsula and through the middle of the region. **4.** The north has harsh winters and mild summers while the south has rainy winters and dry summers. **5.** Important resources include coal and iron ore. **6.** The north supports grain crops on its flat plains. The south supports tree crops on its mountains. **7.** Sample: migration, conquest, politics, location, missionary work. **8.** Yes. Successful countries can afford to care for their environments. They also take responsibility for their actions.

GUIDE ON THE SIDE

- **Summarize** How has the Jewish community in Eastern Europe changed since 1940? Explain. (It is much, much smaller. Many Jews were killed during the Holocaust, and many others left.)

- **Identify Details** How did governments in the region treat religion under Soviet laws? (It was discouraged.)

- **Draw Conclusions** Do you think people in Eastern Europe want religion in their lives now? Explain. (Yes; religious life has become more active since the end of Communism.)

Analyze Visuals Have students compare the photographs.

- How are all these religious leaders the same? (They are all men.)

myWorld Activity

Hailstorm Find Step-by-Step Instructions and an Activity Support on pp. T122–T123. **(Kinesthetic/ Verbal)**

Influence of Religion on Cultures of Eastern Europe

OBJECTIVES

Students will

- understand the influence of Christianity, Islam, and Judaism on the cultures of Eastern Europe.
- **21st Century Learning** compare views and traditions among different faiths from the region.
- **ELL** be able to read, write, and speak English words for major world religions and their followers.

SET EXPECTATIONS

In this case study, students will

- read Influence of Religion on Cultures of Eastern Europe.
- write statements and develop a festival to appreciate regional religions.

1 Connect

Have students share information about religions practiced in your community. Post two real examples of houses of worship and invite volunteers to add more. As needed, display pictures of churches, temples, or mosques. Ask students to share examples of religious festivals or traditions. Help them link each to the faiths represented by the houses of worship.

ELL Beginner Provide labeled visuals for use in answering the question: *What religions do you know about?* Have students draw their own pictures of familiar religious traditions and match these to the appropriate faith.

2 Learn

Preview Have students preview Key Ideas, Key Terms, visuals, and headings. Ask them to predict differences they expect to learn about roles of religion in different Eastern European countries. Ask students to identify religions discussed in Connect in the Case Study visuals.

L2 Extra Support Review that Protestants, Catholics, and Eastern Orthodox Christians share many basic Christian beliefs.

Read While students read Influence of Religion on Cultures of Eastern Europe, ask questions found in **Guide on the Side** to build understanding of Key Ideas and lesson objectives.

ELL Intermediate Review that Orthodox Christianity is the same as Eastern Orthodoxy, and that Muslims practice Islam.

myWorld Activity: Interfaith Celebration Distribute *Activity Support: Holidays* and have students learn about holidays celebrated by religions in Eastern Europe. Ask students to identify similarities and differences, then write statements of appreciation for two traditions unfamiliar to them. Students representing each religion will then exchange information and develop a festival to celebrate shared aspects of all the religions. **(Verbal/Interpersonal)**

25 min

L3 On-Level Review that Judaism was once widespread in the region.

ELL Early Advanced Explain that *interfaith* means "between faiths" just as "international" means "between nations."

3 Understand

Review Diagram each religion in the Case Study, linking it to countries in the region. Ask students to describe how each religion contributes to the unique culture of the countries.

Assess Check students' answers to the Assessment questions for completeness and accuracy. Evaluate participation in the role-play for accuracy and enthusiasm, and concluding statements for a clearly stated comparison.

Remediate If students are struggling to understand the Key Ideas, post a four-column table labeled with red subheadings from the Case Study. Have students copy the table on blank paper. Invite a volunteer to read each text section aloud, then help students identify key points to list about the country and religion in that section.

Name _____ Class _____ Date _____

myWorld Activity Support   **Holidays**

Interfaith Celebration

Directions Read about religious rituals in Eastern Europe. Circle similarities and underline differences. Then write a statement of appreciation for two faiths that are unfamiliar to you. A statement of appreciation can express something about a different faith that is interesting or appealing to you. Bring your statements to a planning session for a festival that celebrates all the religions and what they have in common. With your group, identify shared features to include in that festival.

Protestants in Estonia	Christmas celebration begins December 1 with candles in the window. On December 21, people decorate trees. Christmas night, the more you eat, the stronger you will be in the coming year. A traditional dessert is marzipan, a candy made from almonds.
Jews in Eastern Europe	The Sabbath, or day of rest, runs from sundown Friday to sundown Saturday, and includes a special meal Friday night with prayer, candles, challah (egg bread), and chopped fish. The focus is on spiritual thoughts instead of everyway work or tasks.
Muslims in Bosnia	Eid-ul-Adha is celebrated on a different winter day each year. The "festival of sacrifice" includes giving lamb to families and friends. People pray in the morning, then gather for a special lunch. Each family member has a favorite dish.
Catholics in Poland	Large pilgrimages happen in August in Poland. Many people walk for weeks, and on August 15 they arrive at the Sanctuary of the Black Madonna, where they have a feast. Pilgrims give thanks and also pray for health and happiness.
Orthodox Christians in Serbia	Christmas is celebrated on January 7. On the morning before, people buy or cut down a tree. People prepare bread called cesnica, which has a coin hidden in it. The person who finds the coin will be fortunate in the new year.

Statement of Appreciation _____

_____

Statement of Appreciation _____

_____

QUICK FACTS

Lutherans in Estonia Teutonic (German) knights brought Christianity to the region of Estonia in the 1200s. In 1524, the Lutheran Church was established. Perhaps because Lutheranism spread from other nations, some of which at times controlled Estonia, many Estonians have often associated religion with foreign rule. Today, few Estonians claim any religion at all. Those that do overwhelming associate themselves with the Lutheran church.

Protestants in Estonia

- **Cause and Effect** What event led to the rise of Lutheranism in Estonia? (the Protestant Reformation)

- **Compare and Contrast** How did religious services in Estonia change under Lutheranism? (Services were held with Bibles written in Estonian.)

- **Build Cultural Awareness** How did changes in religious practices affect Estonian literature? (Because the Bible was written in Estonian, many people learned to read. This led to the development of stories and folk tales that celebrated Estonian culture.)

Case Study

Influence of Religion on Cultures of Eastern Europe

Key Ideas
- Christianity, Islam, and Judaism have all influenced the cultures of countries in Eastern Europe.
- The role of religion is different in each country in Eastern Europe.

Key Terms • secular • nationalism • pilgrimage • fasting

Religion has shaped the traditions and cultures of the countries in Eastern Europe. Most of the region is Christian, but different forms of Christianity dominate in different countries. In other areas, Islam is the majority religion. And, while Judaism has never been the dominant religion in any country in Europe, Jewish communities have also influenced Eastern European culture. The examples below show some ways that religion has shaped the countries of this region.

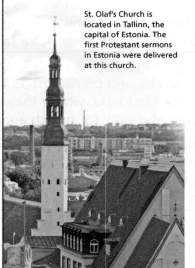

St. Olaf's Church is located in Tallinn, the capital of Estonia. The first Protestant sermons in Estonia were delivered at this church.

Protestants in Estonia

Protestant Christianity is the main faith in Estonia. Roman Catholicism was long ago the chief religion. But after the Protestant Reformation, the country turned to Lutheranism, a form of Protestant Christianity.

Lutheranism brought many changes to Estonian culture. Previously, religious services had been held in Latin, the language of the Catholic Church. The Bible was in Latin, too. But Lutherans performed church services in the Estonian language. They translated the Bible into Estonian. As a result, many Estonians learned to read and write. Estonian literature began to develop. Pastors and teachers wrote children's stories based on traditional folk tales. These stories helped spread cultural and religious values.

The Estonian people today are mostly **secular,** that is, they are not very religious. But Lutheran beliefs still lie at the heart of Estonian culture.

Reading Check **What is the main religion in Estonia?**

READING CHECK Lutheranism

HISTORY

Pilgrimages Poles have completed religious pilgrimages in good times and bad. Historians think the practice began as early as the Middle Ages. It continued during World War II, though pilgrims usually had to travel in secret. Under communism, pilgrims had to avoid being poisoned or chased by special government agents. Today, Catholics around the world can make virtual pilgrimages. People partner with a pilgrim on the ground, offering prayer and encouragement to the traveler in exchange for the traveler's prayers at the pilgrimage destination. One popular destination is Poland's major Marian Shrine—the Sanctuary of the Black Madonna of Czestochowa.

Catholicism in Poland

The Roman Catholic Church plays a major role in a number of Eastern Europe countries. It is especially important in Poland. Most Poles belong to the Catholic Church. Catholicism is integral to Polish life. It is a key part of Poland's national identity.

For centuries Poland was occupied by its powerful neighbors, Russia and Germany. The Catholic Church in Poland opposed foreign rule. It helped unify Poles and promote Polish **nationalism**. Nationalism is a strong devotion to one's nation. The role of the Church as defender of Polish culture continued even under communist rule. The communists tried to stamp out religion. But they could not end Polish loyalty to the Catholic Church.

Today Catholicism continues to influence daily life in Poland. Most Poles go to church. They take part in religious holidays and parades. They also make **pilgrimages,** or religious journeys, to Catholic shrines. In many ways, Catholic values still guide Polish culture.

Reading Check How did the Catholic Church help unify Poland?

Map of the Jewish quarter of Kraków, Poland.

The Jewish Heritage of Eastern Europe

During the 1900s, the Jewish population of Eastern Europe endured great suffering. Millions were killed during the Holocaust. When the region was under communist control, many of the remaining Jews left the region because of prejudice and restrictions on practicing their religion. The Jewish population remains small, but many people now celebrate the contribution of Jews to the culture of Eastern Europe.

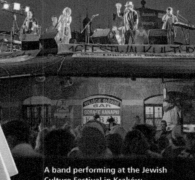

A band performing at the Jewish Culture Festival in Kraków

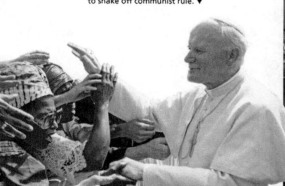

Pope John Paul II, below, was the first Polish pope. He supported Polish efforts to shake off communist rule. ▼

READING CHECK It brought Poles together to defend their nation against foreign rule.

Catholicism in Poland

Build Cultural Awareness

- To what religion do most Poles belong? (Roman Catholicism)
- What was the Catholic Church's position toward foreign rule? (It opposed it.)

Summarize

- What are some ways that religion protected Polish culture? (The Church kept Polish culture alive even under communism.)
- What are some ways that Poles observe their religion? (They go to church, celebrate religious holidays and parades, and make pilgrimages to holy sites.)

The Jewish Heritage of Eastern Europe

- **Cause and Effect** Why did many Jewish people continue to leave Eastern Europe even after the Holocaust? (prejudice and discrimination)

COMMON MISCONCEPTIONS

Bosnians and Serbs While Bosnians and Serbs identify many differences between their two cultures, ethnically or physically, they share a common heritage. Their languages are also very much the same. The main difference between these two groups is that of religious affiliation. Most Bosnians identify themselves as Muslim, even if they are unobservant. On the other hand, most Serbs identify themselves as Orthodox Christians. Because of this, a Bosnian Serb is someone who lives in Bosnia but feels linked culturally to Serbia due to his or her religious affiliation.

Orthodox Religion in Serbia

- **Summarize** What role does Orthodox Christianity play in Serbian culture? (It is the main religion.)

- **Infer** How do most Serbians feel about their religion? (It is an important part of their national identity.)

- **Compare and Contrast** What are some ways that Orthodox Christianity is different than Western forms of Christianity? (Sample: The Orthodox church has nine patriarchs instead of one authority figure. Holidays are celebrated on different days.)

Orthodox Religion in Serbia

Eastern Orthodox Christianity is the main religion in Serbia and many other Balkan states. Orthodox Christianity shares ancient roots with Catholicism. In the Middle Ages, however, disagreements over beliefs and practices led Christians to split into separate Catholic and Orthodox churches.

Instead of a single authority, the Orthodox church has nine patriarchs, or high-ranking bishops. The Serbian Orthodox Church has its own partriach.

In Serbia, Christian holidays are celebrated according to the Orthodox calendar. For example, Christmas is celebrated on January 7 rather than December 25. The Christmas feast includes roast pork and special bread with a coin baked inside. Whoever gets the piece with the coin is said to have good luck for the coming year. Orthodox families in Serbia also have a patron saint whom they honor on a particular day.

Serbia is home to other religions, too, including Islam. But many Serbians believe that Orthodox Christianity is a key part of their national identity.

Reading Check What is the main religion in Serbia?

An Orthodox priest leads a religious procession in Serbia.

READING CHECK Orthodox Christianity

READING CHECK The Ottoman Turks brought Islam to Bosnia when they conquered the region in the late 1300s.

CULTURE

Bosnian Religious Tolerance The tradition of religious tolerance in Bosnia helped preserve a valuable Jewish text. The Sarajevo Haggadah was created around 1350 in Spain, and was sold to the Bosnian National Museum in 1894. It was twice saved from destruction by librarians at the museum, both of whom were Bosnian Muslims.

The first was Dervis Korkut, who in 1941, refused to give the book to German Nazis and instead gave it to a Muslim imam (clergy) to protect during World War II. The second was Enver Imamovic, who hid the book during the Bosnian War of 1992–1995, saving it from the bombs that destroyed Sarajevo.

Muslim Culture in Bosnia

Islam is the chief religion in Bosnia. Muslim influence there dates to the Ottoman conquest of the Balkans in the late 1300s. The Ottoman Turks ruled the region for 500 years. Many Bosnians converted to Islam during this time.

Bosnian Muslims tend to be less strict in their religious practices than Muslims in Southwest Asia. Some consume alcohol, pork, and other foods seen as forbidden by Islam. More women work outside the home. In addition, Bosnian Muslim women do not generally cover their heads, as do many Muslim women in Southwest Asia.

Still, Islam is important in the lives of many Bosnians. They read the Quran, the Muslim holy book. They celebrate the key Muslim holidays, known as the Eids. They also observe Ramadan, a month of **fasting**, or limits on eating. During this period, Muslims avoid eating between sunrise and sunset every day.

Bosnia has a long history of religious tolerance. The Ottomans allowed non-Muslims to practice their own faiths. Bosnia has suffered ethnic conflict in recent years. But most Bosnians continue to maintain a tradition of tolerance.

Reading Check How did Islam enter Bosnia?

Like all Muslims, these Bosnian men are expected to pray five times each day.

Assessment

1. How did Lutheranism promote literacy in Estonia?
2. How are religion and national identity linked in Poland and Serbia?
3. How is Bosnia different from many Muslim countries?
4. Why do you think Eastern Europe became home to many religions?
5. How does religion in Eastern Europe reflect divisions within Christianity?

ASSESSMENT 1. Lutheran beliefs led to Bibles in Estonian, which gave many people the opportunity and reason to learn to read. **2.** In both countries, people identify strongly with their religion as individuals and as national citizens. **3.** Bosnians practice a more secular form of Islam than many Muslims elsewhere. **4.** Sample: Many different people have conquered or settled the region, bringing their different religions with them. **5.** Some parts of Eastern Europe are dominated by Catholicism, others by Protestantism (Lutheranism), and yet others by Orthodox Christianity.

Eastern Europe Today

OBJECTIVES

Students will know

- ways regional countries are improving governments and economies.
- political problems and ethnic conflicts that have led some countries to fail.

Students will be able to

- compare and contrast political and economic changes in Eastern Europe.
- ask questions about economic and political change in the region today.

SET EXPECTATIONS

In this section, students will

- read Eastern Europe Today.
- participate in a press conference about economic and political changes in Eastern Europe today.
- learn about Budapest and complete the Chapter Assignment online.

CORE CONCEPTS

You may wish to teach or reteach the following lessons from the Core Concepts Handbook:

- Economic Systems, pp. 62–63
- Art, pp. 94–95
- Political Systems, pp. 106–107

KEY

Differentiated Instruction

- **L1** Special Needs
- **L2** Extra Support
- **L3** On-Level
- **L4** Challenge

English Language Instruction

- **ELL** Beginner
- **ELL** Early Intermediate
- **ELL** Intermediate
- **ELL** Early Advanced
- **ELL** Advanced

1 Connect
Make learning meaningful

Make Connections Ask students to think about the **myStory Video** about Serhiy's daily life. Ask them to recall economic conditions in Serhiy's community and country. Discuss how these conditions have influenced Serhiy's life today and his hopes for the future. Ask students to predict how these changes might influence the long-term future of Ukraine and other Eastern European nations.

L2 Extra Support Ask students what most young people in your community do after high school and link this to the choices Serhiy has.

Activate Prior Knowledge Remind students that in the chapter Europe in Modern Times they learned about the rise and fall of the Soviet Union. Help students to review the political and economic results of the Soviet collapse. Ask them to predict how these changes might affect people living in the nations of Eastern Europe.

L3 On-Level Discuss Core Concepts 4.5 Economic Systems. Post a two-column table for key features of command and market economies.

Prepare Follow the steps in the section **Preview.** Preteach the Key Terms. Then have students complete *Word Wise* in their journals using in-text clues and the glossary for help.

2 Experience
Teach knowledge and skills

Read Use **Background** notes and **Guide on the Side** questions to model active reading. Have students use *Take Notes* in their **Student Journal** to compare and contrast successful and less successful countries in Eastern Europe. Have students complete **21st Century Online Tutor** *Compare and Contrast* and apply this skill to reading the section.

L1 Special Needs Have students listen to the audio **Online Student Edition** and list questions, then read online for answers.

ELL Intermediate/Early Advanced Preteach compare and contrast terms, such as *also, in addition, like, unlike, instead,* and model sample sentences.

L3 On-Level Have students read *Enrichment:* The *Jewish People of Eastern Europe* to learn more about this important group in the region's history.

Practice: myWorld Activity Students will prepare for and participate in a press conference held by representatives of Eastern European nations. **Step-by-Step Instructions** and **More Activities** follow on pp. T130–T131.

SECTION 2 RESOURCE GUIDE

FOR THE STUDENT

my worldgeography.com Student Center
- Culture Close-up
- Data Discovery

Student Edition (print and online)
- Eastern Europe Today

Student Journal (print and online)
- Section 2 Word Wise
- Section 2 Take Notes

21st Century Learning Online Tutor
- Compare and Contrast
- Ask Questions

FOR THE TEACHER

my worldgeography.com Teacher Center
- Online Lesson Planner
- Presentations for Projection
- SuccessTracker

ProGuide: Europe and Russia
- Lesson Plan, pp. T128–T129
- myWorld Activity Step-by-Step Instructions, p. T130
- Activity Support: Q & A Plan, p. T131
- myWorld Geography Enrichment, p. T132
- Section Quiz, p. T133

Accelerating the Progress of ELLs
- Reading Support Strategies, p. 42

3 Understand
Assess understanding

Review Review *Word Wise* and *Take Notes* in the **Student Journal.**

Assess Knowledge and Skills Use the Section Assessment and Section Quiz to check students' progress.

Assess Understanding Review students' responses to the Section Assessment Essential Question prompt.

Remediate Use these strategies to review and remediate.

If students struggle to . . .	Try these strategies.
Compare and contrast economic or political progress of nations in the region	Have them use one word to describe each country's progress, then contrast the words.
Describe conflicts in the region	Have students recall a recent argument. Ask, Could such an argument occur between countries or ethnic groups?
Understand the impact of economic change on population distribution	Replay the **myStory Video.** Review reasons for urbanization in the region.

ELL Support

ELL Objective Students will be able to use five *Ws* and *H* questions to construct answers in English.

Cultural Connections Ask students to use their home languages to contrast political or economic systems in their families' home countries and the United States.

ELL Early Intermediate Content Tip Post English question words: *who, what, why, where, when,* and *how.* Read text chorally and post sample Big and Little Questions. Circle terms that link Little Questions to Big Questions. Model how to construct answers from questions.

ELL Activity Display a current map of Eastern Europe. Using sticky notes, help students create symbols for each country's economic and political progress: ↑℞ for thriving democracy (Ukraine); ↑$ for thriving economy (Slovakia), ↓℞ for failing governments (Moldova) or economies ↓$; and ↗↘ for intermediate or unstable results. Have volunteers place notes on the map. **(Visual)**

my worldgeography.com Lesson Planner

20 min

myWorld Activity   **Step-by-Step Instructions**

Press Conference

OBJECTIVES

Students will

- develop questions about economic, political, and cultural changes in Eastern Europe.
- participate in a press conference about economic, political, and cultural changes in Eastern Europe.

LEARNING STYLE

- Verbal
- Logical

21st Century Learning

- Ask Questions

MATERIALS

- Two paper cups
- Activity Support: Q & A Plan, p. T131

Activity Steps

1. Tell students that they will participate in a press conference about economic, political, and cultural changes in Eastern Europe today. Students will ask or answer questions in assigned roles as journalists or national representatives. After the press conference, journalists will write a brief news article and national representatives will write a brief memo to their nation's leader.

2. Distribute *Activity Support: Q & A Plan* and review directions. Assign students as journalists or national representatives, and divide section content.

   ELL **Early Intermediate** Designate students as journalists, where they will present prepared questions.

3. Allow 5 minutes for students to review their section and write questions and likely answers on their Activity Supports.

   L2 **Extra Support** Clarify Big Questions (multiple correct answers) and Little Questions (related to Big Questions; one correct answer).

4. Stage a mock press conference with national representatives at the head of the class, taking turns at a lectern, and journalists gathered in a group. Give each group an upside-down paper cup punctured with holes to use as a microphone.

   L4 **Challenge** Encourage students to ask additional follow-up questions or provide answers that include significant detail.

5. Have students complete the Activity Support to prepare for follow-up writing. Journalists will write a brief news story about the information they learned at the press conference. National representatives should write a brief memo to their nation's leader describing the positions or information they distributed to the press.

More Activities From myWorld Teachers

Local Connections Have students create a Big Question and Little Question about your community's economic, political, or cultural situation. Urge them to draft it as a blog posting for a political web site in the community. **(Verbal)**

 Skit Have groups role-play returning members of a tour to an Eastern European nation. Groups should present what they learned on their trip, using found or created visuals for detail. **(Kinesthetic/Visual)**

 Chopin Festival Have pairs find, share, and discuss examples of music by Polish composer Frederic Chopin. **(Rhythmic/Verbal)**

my worldgeography.com   **Teacher Center** → Find additional resources in the online Teacher Center.

Name _____ Class _____ Date _____

 myWorld Activity Support   **Q & A Plan**

Press Conference

Directions Prepare for a press conference about Eastern Europe's
recent history. List likely questions from journalists and responses
from national representatives. Bring your list to the press conference.

Big Questions (about important changes or events)	Little Questions (follow-ups to clarify or add detail)
Sample How did the fall of the Soviet Union affect Poland and the Baltic States?	**Sample** What kind of government followed in Poland and the Baltic States?
Question 1 _____ _____ General Answer _____ _____	Question 1 _____ _____ Exact Answer _____ _____
Question 2 _____ _____ General Answer _____ _____	Question 2 _____ _____ Exact Answer _____ _____
Question 3 _____ _____ General Answer _____ _____	Question 3 _____ _____ Exact Answer _____ _____

Write It Up If you are a journalist, write the lead paragraph for a
news article. If you are a national representative, write the opening
paragraph for a memo to your nation's leader about the concerns
reporters expressed at the news conference.

Name _____ Class _____ Date _____

Enrichment: The Jewish People of Eastern Europe

Directions Read the selection below. Then answer the questions that follow and complete the activity.

About 80 percent of the Jewish people alive today have roots in Eastern Europe, yet many cities in the region currently have very small Jewish populations. One important reason for this is the Holocaust of World War II, in which Nazi Germans murdered millions of Jews. Another important reason is emigration, which means leaving your home to live in another country.

Millions of Eastern European Jews emigrated during the 1800s and early 1900s. They left for many reasons. One important reason was to escape economic problems in Eastern Europe, much of which was part of Russia at that time. Growth in industry pushed some Jewish artisans out of work. Jewish people also left to escape discrimination and anger. They had a different culture, religion, and language from others in the region. In 1881, the Russian government led organized killings called pogroms. Many fled Eastern Europe to escape these pogroms.

Jewish people went many places in the world, including to Canada, South Africa, Argentina, Palestine (today Israel), and, overwhelmingly, to America. By 1924, some three million Eastern European Jews had come to America. Most arrived through New York City, where they established a long-lasting community.

Some Jewish communities in Eastern Europe are beginning to grow again. Many nations in the region are beginning to recognize ways that Jewish culture is important in their history.

1. What is emigration?

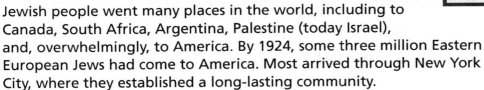

_____

2. What are the two main reasons that Jewish people emigrated from Eastern Europe?

_____

_____

3. Activity Using information from this page and the chapter text, write a letter from an emigrant to his or her family back in Eastern Europe. Tell why you left and what you hope to find in your new life.

Name _____ Class _____ Date _____

Section Quiz

Directions Answer the following questions using what you learned in Section 2.

1. _____ Why do businesses need capital?
   a. to buy supplies and equipment
   b. to join the European Union
   c. to export their goods
   d. to find employees

2. _____ Which describes the work of an entrepreneur?
   a. organizing and managing your own business
   b. growing food for your family's own use
   c. working in a factory to make machines
   d. joining an office in your country's government

3. _____ Why did the republics of Yugoslavia secede?
   a. They wanted to change the name of the country to Slovenia.
   b. They were unhappy with Serbia's rule of the national government.
   c. They wanted to add more republics to make Yugoslavia stronger.
   d. They were unhappy with the leadership of President Tito.

4. _____ Which describes the policy of *ethnic cleansing*?
   a. holding meetings to resolve ethnic conflict
   b. getting rid of all ethnic titles to make all citizens equal
   c. removing everyone not part of one ethnic group
   d. inviting people of one ethnic group to work as cleaners

5. _____ Which country is known for its peppery cuisine?
   a. Poland
   b. Hungary
   c. Latvia
   d. Ukraine

6. Choose one country in each group below. Briefly describe political and economic change in that country. Then draw a conclusion about how political change affects business.

Country Groups	Changes in Government	Changes in Business
Poland/Baltic Nations		
Central Europe		
Balkan Nations		
Ukraine, Belarus, Moldova		
How government affects business		

- Model preparing to read by previewing the Key Ideas, Key Terms, headings, visuals, and captions. Have students make predictions about what they will learn. For ELL support, post the prompt, "I predict I will read about . . ."

- Preview and practice comparing and contrasting with examples from the classroom.

- Preteach this section's high-use Academic Vocabulary and Key Terms using the table on the next page and in-text definitions. Have students practice Key Terms by completing the *Word Wise* page in their journals.

GUIDE ON THE SIDE

Poland and the Baltic Nations

- **Sequence** What happened to Poland's government after the Soviet era ended? (Poland became a democracy.)

- **Cause and Effect** What effect did Solidarity have on Poland's new government? (The group opposed communism and led the first democratic government.)

- **Compare and Contrast** In what ways did Poland's economy change after the Soviet era ended? (It became a market economy, with more private business.)

Reading Skill

Compare and Contrast While they read, have students practice this skill by completing the *Take Notes* graphic organizer in the **Student Journal.**

Section 2

Eastern Europe Today

Key Ideas
- Some countries of this region have had great success building new governments and economies.
- Other countries have broken apart or have failed to form strong, democratic governments.
- Ethnic conflict has troubled some countries.

Key Terms • entrepreneur • capital • cuisine • secede • ethnic cleansing

 Visual Glossary

Reading Skill: Compare and Contrast Take notes using the graphic organizer in your journal.

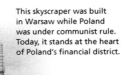

This skyscraper was built in Warsaw while Poland was under communist rule. Today, it stands at the heart of Poland's financial district.

Each country in Eastern Europe has taken a different path since the end of communism. Some countries have built strong economies. Some countries are successful democracies. Other countries have broken apart, divided by ethnic conflict.

Poland and the Baltic Nations

Poland and the Baltic nations of Lithuania, Latvia, and Estonia have been among the most economically successful countries in Eastern Europe. They have also created democratic governments. Still, this change has not been easy. The people of these countries faced challenges and uncertainty after the fall of the Soviet Union.

Poland's Quick Reforms Poland was the first nation in Eastern Europe to make the transition to democracy at the end of the communist era. In the 1980s, a Polish labor union called Solidarity opposed the communist party, which controlled the government. After the fall of communism, the popular leader of Solidarity, Lech Walesa (lek vah WEH suh), was elected president.

Poland's leaders then took on the challenge of creating a market economy. In the communist system, the government controlled prices and planned production for the economy. In the early 1990s, the government stopped controlling prices, cut support for old state-owned factories, and encouraged new private businesses. After a slow start, the Polish economy recovered and grew throughout the 1990s.

ANSWERS

ACADEMIC VOCABULARY

High-Use Word	Definition and Sample Sentence
ethnic	*adj.* defined by a shared nationality, identity, or heritage *In my neighborhood, most people have an Italian ethnic background.*
potential	*n.* ability, possibility *Jim can spell any word and has the potential to win the National Spelling Bee.*

Many citizens became **entrepreneurs**, people who organize and manage their own businesses. This Polish entrepreneur comments on starting a new business:

> ❝ I truly never would have thought my idea of opening a high-end art supply store would work out when my country became independent from the Soviet Union. But because the arts are so important here in Poland, and the government helped me all along the way, it's been a very exciting time. ❞
>
> —Entrepreneur from Bialystok, Poland

The Transition in the Baltic States The Baltic nations of Lithuania, Latvia, and Estonia were once republics of the Soviet Union. All three nations left behind the communist economic system and moved to a market economy during the 1990s. They now have democratic governments.

Estonia's economy has been especially successful. Industries in Estonia have **capital**, money or wealth used to invest in a business. Capital allows businesses to obtain more modern equipment to make high-quality goods. They can export these goods to other countries. Today, Estonia's main trading partners are Finland, Germany, and Sweden. Latvia and Lithuania have also experienced growth. Although Russia is still Lithuania's main trading partner, Lithuania now trades with Germany and Poland as well.

All of the Baltic nations as well as Poland have been accepted into the European Union. Membership in the EU has helped these nations to find new trading partners and improve their economies.

Cultural Life in Poland and the Baltic States Poland and the Baltic nations are well known for their rich cultural heritage. Poles have worked hard to preserve their history and culture. Many Polish cities have art and history museums. Poles also celebrate their cultural heritage at festivals. For example, music festivals highlighting the music of the famous Polish composer Frederic Chopin are popular.

In recent years, people in the Baltic States have revived traditions and religious practices that the Soviets banned. For example, Latvians now celebrate the summer festival of Jani (YAH nee) with traditional songs and dances.

Reading Check What is one reason Estonia has had economic success in recent years?

Each June, Latvians celebrate the Jani festival. Women and men—even cattle—wear wreaths of flowers or leaves.

- **Identify Details** How did entrepreneurs contribute to Poland's new economy? (They started many new businesses.)
- **Identify Main Ideas** What kind of governments did the Baltic nations have after the Soviet era? (democratic)
- **Compare and Contrast** How were the economies of Estonia, Latvia, and Lithuania the same after the Soviet era? How was Estonia's economy different? (They all moved to market economies. Estonia's economy was especially successful.)
- **Infer** Why is expanding trade beyond Russia important for Lithuania? (It provides other customers if Russia can't or won't buy a product.)
- **Build Cultural Awareness** How has culture in the Baltic states changed since the end of the Soviet era? (Traditions and religious practice have been revived.)

READING CHECK Estonian industry has used capital to invest in modern equipment, and thus increased exports.

ANSWERS

HISTORY

Velvet Revolution Czechoslovakia's transition from Soviet-style communism to democracy happened so smoothly that it is known as the Velvet Revolution. The Revolution took place in November 1989, when huge numbers of Czechs and Slovaks took to the streets to protest communist rule. The communist government stepped down and former playwright Vaclav Havel was elected to run the new democracy. He resigned in protest over the split into Slovakia and the Czech Republic.

Central Europe

- **Sequence** How did Czechoslovakia change politically after the Soviet era ended? (It became a democracy, later splitting into two democratic nations, Slovakia and the Czech Republic.)

- **Compare and Contrast** How has economic change since the end of the Soviet era been the same for Slovakia and the Czech Republic? How has it been different? (Both are market economies. Slovakia's growth was slow at first because of a less diverse economy, but the government took action and the economy improved.)

Chart Skills Have students compare economic output on the graphs.

- How have the economies of both countries changed? (Both have grown.)

Data Discovery

Have students go to myworldgeography.com to learn more about economic output in Eastern Europe.

ethnic, *adj.,* defined by a shared nationality, identity, or heritage

Central Europe

The countries of Central Europe include the Czech Republic, Slovakia, Hungary, and Slovenia. Like other countries of Eastern Europe, these nations needed to build new governments and strengthen their economies.

Slovakia and the Czech Republic In 1989, communism gave way to democracy in Czechoslovakia. Soon, representatives of the Czechs and Slovaks disagreed about how to run the country. They divided peacefully in 1993 into two nations: the Czech Republic and Slovakia. Most people in the Czech Republic are of the Czech ethnic group. The majority of people in Slovakia are ethnic Slovaks.

Both nations have built democratic governments and experienced economic growth. The change to a market economy was easier for the Czech Republic. This nation had a strong economy with many different industries. It was able to modernize many of its factories fairly quickly.

Under Soviet control, Slovakia's economy was less diverse. Because building new industries takes time, economic growth was slow at first. However, Slovakia's government took action. In 1998, it lowered taxes for any foreign companies that created new businesses and jobs. Foreign investment increased rapidly, bringing more money to help improve Slovakia's economy. Both Slovakia and the Czech Republic have joined the European Union and expanded trade with the nations of Western Europe.

Chart Skills

To figure out each nation's growth rate as a percentage, subtract the 1993 number from the 2008 number. Then, divide this number by the 1993 number. Which nation had a higher growth rate during this time period, Slovakia or the Czech Republic?

Data Discovery

Industrial Growth in the Former Czechoslovakia

Since they separated in 1993, both Slovakia and the Czech Republic have enjoyed economic growth. These figures represent economic output per person in each nation.

Czech Republic

1993	$12,774
2008	$26,000

Slovakia

1993	$8,371
2008	$21,900

SOURCE: *CIA World Factbook*

Workers in a Czech car factory ▼

CHART SKILLS Slovakia

CULTURE

Hungarian Food Popular Hungarian foods include

- strudels (layered pastry with sweet filling) and pastries.
- Hungarian-style coffee (served strong as kávé or with milk as tejeskávé).
- fish soup (Halászlé) and other local fish dishes.

- goulash (stew or soup with beef and vegetables, spiced with paprika).
- Hortobágyi palacsinta (meat filled pancakes).
- paprikás süllőszelet (fish with paprika sauce).

Hungary Hungary has had some economic and political success since the fall of communism. It now has a stable, democratic government and a market economy. Debt has been a challenge, however. Hungary borrowed from other countries to modernize its economy. The resulting heavy debt has slowed economic growth. The government must deal with this problem for Hungary's economy to develop successfully.

Hungarians have also been returning to many traditions since the end of communism. Most Hungarians are Roman Catholic. Traditional Christian holidays are celebrated again as national holidays. The Hungarian language is different from other languages spoken in Europe. Hungarians also cook a unique **cuisine**, that is, style of food. Many Hungarian dishes use

the spice paprika, which is made from bell or chili peppers. Hungarians take great pride in their distinct cultural heritage.

Slovenia In 1918, Slovenia became part of the new country of Yugoslavia. There was tension between the different republics of Yugoslavia. Many Slovenians came to believe that their homeland would be better off if they split from Yugoslavia. The leaders of Slovenia had managed their economy more successfully than some other republics in Yugoslavia.

In 1990, fully 90 percent of Slovenia's citizens voted for independence. Slovenia fought the short Ten-Day War to separate from the rest of Yugoslavia. Slovenia then began to build a democratic government and a free market economy. Despite many challenges, Slovenia has improved its economy. It became the first Balkan country to join the EU and the North Atlantic Treaty Organization (NATO) in 2004.

Reading Check How has Hungary changed since the end of communism?

my World IN NUMBERS

If there were **100** people in the world, about **34** would live in a democracy.

The Danube River flows through Budapest, the capital of Hungary. Budapest is a major center of business, transportation, and culture. ▼

Culture Close-Up

READING CHECK It has a democratic government and a market economy. Religious traditions are celebrated again.

GUIDE ON THE SIDE

- **Cause and Effect** What factors have affected economic growth in Hungary? (High levels of debt have slowed growth.)
- **Compare and Contrast** How was Slovenia different from the other republics of Yugoslavia? (It had a more successful economy.)
- **Infer** Why do you think Slovenians voted for independence from Yugoslavia? (People felt that their nation could succeed better independently.)

 Culture Close-up

Have students go to myworldgeography.com to learn more about the architecture of Budapest.

COMMON MISCONCEPTIONS

Ethnic Cleansing In fact, much of the Balkan violence in the 1990s labeled as "ethnic" cleansing centered on religious differences. Point out that most people in the region considered their ethnicity to be determined by their religion. This is not true in all communities or cultures. For example, many Americans link their ethnicity to the culture or nationality of their ancestors, even if they are not religiously observant.

The Balkan Nations

- **Summarize** How was Yugoslavia formed? (Each of the six territories became a republic in the new nation.)

- **Identify Details** How was each republic different? (Each had a main ethnic group that was the majority.)

- **Sequence** What happened after Tito died? (The union weakened and republics seceded.)

- **Analyze Text** How does the term *ethnic cleansing* show anger between ethnic groups? (The word *cleansing* suggests an ethnic group is polluting the area.)

Map Skills Have students locate divisions of Yugoslavia on the map.

- Why do you think Bosnia and Herzegovina, Croatia, and Serbia have populations of mixed ethnic groups? (They share borders and populations likely overflow.)

 Active Atlas

Have students go to myworldgeography.com to learn more about the division of Yugoslavia.

The Balkan Nations

All the former communist nations of the Balkan Peninsula have gone through major political changes since 1990. At times, these changes involved warfare and the breakup of nations along ethnic or religious lines. Conflicts and political problems have disrupted the economies of the region.

Yugoslavia Splits After World War I, the country of Yugoslavia was created from six different territories—Serbia, Croatia, Slovenia, Macedonia, Montenegro, and Bosnia (formally known as Bosnia and Herzegovina). Each of these territories formed a republic within Yugoslavia. In each republic, a different ethnic group formed the majority.

After World War II, Yugoslavia's strong leader, Josip Broz Tito, kept the country united. But after Tito died in 1980, the union began to weaken.

Serbia was the largest republic and dominated the national government. Other republics resented Serbia's power. They began to **secede**, or break away, from the union. In 1991, Slovenia and Croatia declared independence. Macedonia broke away later that year, followed by Bosnia a year later.

The new countries combined different ethnic groups. For example, most people in Croatia are Croats, but many Serbs also live there. Conflicts broke out among the different ethnic groups. Some groups tried to gain complete control of an area by attacking and forcing out the other ethnic groups. This policy is called **ethnic cleansing**. Serbs in some areas of Bosnia, for example, killed Muslims or forced them from their homes. Serbs then took control of those areas. Ethnic cleansing is a violation of international law.

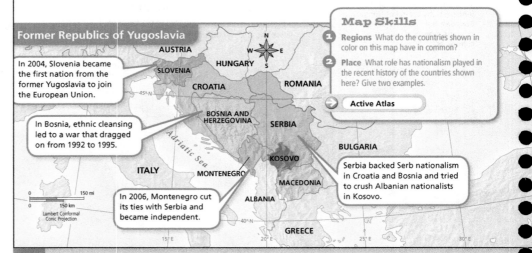

Former Republics of Yugoslavia

In 2004, Slovenia became the first nation from the former Yugoslavia to join the European Union.

In Bosnia, ethnic cleansing led to a war that dragged on from 1992 to 1995.

In 2006, Montenegro cut its ties with Serbia and became independent.

Map Skills
1. **Regions** What do the countries shown in color on this map have in common?
2. **Place** What role has nationalism played in the recent history of the countries shown here? Give two examples.

Active Atlas

Serbia backed Serb nationalism in Croatia and Bosnia and tried to crush Albanian nationalists in Kosovo.

AUSTRIA · HUNGARY · SLOVENIA · CROATIA · ROMANIA · BOSNIA AND HERZEGOVINA · SERBIA · ITALY · MONTENEGRO · KOSOVO · BULGARIA · MACEDONIA · ALBANIA · GREECE · Adriatic Sea

0 150 mi
0 150 km
Lambert Conformal Conic Projection

MAP SKILLS 1. They were all part of Yugoslavia. **2.** Ethnic conflict has led to many problems for the region, such as ethnic cleansing, war in Bosnia, and Serbian efforts against Albanians in Kosovo.

GOVERNMENT

European Union Membership According to European Union diplomat Dimitris Koukoulas, it is up to the government in Bosnia and Herzegovina to make changes for EU membership. He cites political instability as a big obstacle to EU membership for the country:

"I wouldn't say there is no movement forward, but it is very slow, and what is still missing is a consensus among all political forces to keep . . . away from political infighting . . . . There [must be] an agreement between all political forces to have their differences, but to agree on European integration."

Still, in 2008, Bosnia did sign a preliminary agreement with the EU as a first step toward gaining membership.

— from "EU Diplomat: Western Balkans Still Burdened by Legacy of War" from EuroActiv.com

Ethnic Conflict Continues As conflicts arose in the 1990s, the United Nations, the United States, and other European countries worked to negotiate peace between warring groups. The United Nations and NATO sent troops to enforce peace treaties. These efforts have brought an end to large-scale warfare in the region. Still, ethnic violence continues in some areas.

These conflicts disrupted economies in the region. Unstable conditions made trade difficult. In addition, many people were forced from their homes and had to start new lives in different countries.

Some governments in this region are trying to make reforms in order to join the European Union. In general, the governments of the former Yugoslavia have been slow to shift from government control to private enterprise. The standard of living in these countries is low compared to that of many other nations of Eastern Europe.

Other Balkan Nations Yugoslavia was not the only communist nation on the Balkan Peninsula. Romania, Albania, and Bulgaria also became communist after World War II. Unlike Yugoslavia, Romania and Bulgaria were dominated by the Soviet Union. When communism ended in the late 1980s, these countries also shifted to market economies.

Political corruption was a problem in all three countries. Bulgaria and Romania have been accepted as members of the European Union after dealing with many political and economic problems. Albania, by contrast, has not been accepted into the European Union. This country remains poorer and less developed. Still, Albanians continue to work to improve their economy and control crime. Albania also hopes to be accepted into the European Union.

Reading Check Why did some republics secede from Yugoslavia?

Albania was the last country in Eastern Europe to give up communism. It is still one of the poorest nations in Europe.

- **Express Opinions** What should the international community do about ethnic conflict, especially if ethnic cleansing is happening? (Sample: They should try to bring the groups together. They should try to stop ethnic cleansing, using force if necessary.)

- **Cause and Effect** How did ethnic conflict affect the economy in the former Yugoslavia? (It slowed economies and made growth difficult.)

- **Identify Main Ideas** What main problem faced Romania, Albania, and Bulgaria after the Soviet era? (political corruption)

- **Compare and Contrast** How does the progress of each country compare? (Bulgaria and Romania have made more progress than Albania.)

READING CHECK They resented Serbia's power and domination of national government.

ANSWERS

PRIMARY SOURCE

Russians in Ukraine Like many former Soviet republics, Ukraine has a large ethnic Russian population. In addition, speaking Russian has been a necessary tool for success. These university students disagree about whether to make Russian a second official language:

Zoya Pavlovska says, "I do not think it's a good idea to introduce Russian as a second official language in Ukraine. . . . Language is part of national culture, and knowing your native tongue gives you an access to the treasures and values of [that] culture."

Olena Samolyst disagrees: "The histories of Russia and Ukraine were too closely intertwined . . . for the accumulated cultural and historical legacy to be ignored. . . . I think that Russian should be given the status of the second official language."

GUIDE ON THE SIDE

Ukraine, Belarus, and Moldova

Compare and Contrast

- How has Ukraine changed since independence? (It has a democratic government and more press freedom.)

- What problems does it still have? Explain. (Political corruption and complicated business laws have limited foreign investment; Agricultural expansion has been difficult.)

- How are the goals of the constitution in Belarus different from the way the government runs the country? (The constitution lists freedoms but the government does not allow them to citizens.)

- **Cause and Effect** What problems does Belarus have because of its trading relationship with Russia? Explain. (Because Russia is its main trading partner, Belarus's economy suffers if Russia's economy suffers.)

potential, *n.,* ability, possibility

Ukraine, Belarus, and Moldova

Ukraine, Moldova, and Belarus all gained independence from the Soviet Union in 1991. Since then, all have changed in different ways. Ukraine is a democracy. Belarus is the only example of a dictatorship in Europe today. Moldova is a small country with a very weak government that cannot control all of its territory or provide many basic services.

Ukraine Ukraine is the second-largest country in Europe in land area and the sixth largest in population. Since gaining independence, Ukraine has created a democratic system of government. Freedom of the press has increased since independence. Ukraine still faces serious political problems such as corruption. However, Ukraine's democracy has also survived some serious conflicts. For example, disputes over the results of the 2004 presidential elections led to widespread protests, but the different parties worked out a peaceful resolution.

Still, Ukraine's economy has not grown rapidly. Corruption and complicated business laws have discouraged foreign companies from investing. Russia is still the largest trading partner for Ukraine.

In addition, efforts to expand agriculture have been difficult. The Soviets had set up collective farms, where land and equipment were shared among many farmers. The Ukrainian government divided this land among the families who lived on each farm. However, small farms without advanced equipment are not profitable. Many people, like Serhiy, are leav-

Ukraine has become a working democracy. Traveling ballot boxes allow people in remote villages, like this woman, to vote in their own homes.

ing rural areas because they cannot make a living on their small family farm. Still, Ukraine has rich soil. Many believe that this country has the <u>potential</u> to improve its agriculture and achieve more economic success.

Belarus Since 1994, Belarus has been ruled by President Lukashenko. The country's constitution lists many freedoms. In reality, the government limits liberties such as freedom of the press and freedom of religion. People who have opposed Lukashenko have been punished.

Belarus must import many of the raw materials and energy resources that it needs from other countries. The country's main trading partner has been Russia. These close ties create another risk. When Russia's economy has difficulties, the economy of Belarus also suffers. Economic growth has been slow. Almost half of the population lives in poverty.

Moldova Moldova is a tiny country with ties to its neighbor Romania and also to Russia. Many of its people speak Romanian, but there are also large numbers of Ukrainians and Russians.

ANSWERS

READING CHECK Sample: improve the economy, resolve political turmoil

SECTION 2 ASSESSMENT 1. Some republics did not like Serbia's leadership of the Yugoslav union, so they seceded. Ethnic groups wanted their own areas, and some tried to create these with ethnic cleansing of other groups. **2.** Capital is money or wealth used to invest in businesses. **3.** Nations have become democracies with

524 Western Hemisphere
280 Eastern Hemisphere
460 World Geography

QUICK FACTS

Press Freedom in Belarus The international organization Reporters Without Borders has repeatedly condemned Belarus for its limits on press freedom. In 2008, RWB ranked Belarus 154th out of 173 countries in its press freedom index. One way that Belarus limits press freedom is by refusing foreign journalists permission to work there. In 2009, the government began requiring foreign journalists to get permission from the government, permission that is almost universally denied.

This protest sign compares President Alexander Lukashenko of Belarus to two notorious dictators of the past: Joseph Stalin of the Soviet Union and Adolf Hitler of Nazi Germany.

About 80 percent of the people of Moldova live below the poverty line. Many poor peasants in rural villages, like this boy, have barely enough to survive.

GUIDE ON THE SIDE

- **Identify Details** What is the issue in Moldova's civil war? (People in the region called Transdniestria claim independence from Moldova, but the Moldovan government wants to keep the region from seceding.)

- **Identify Evidence** Some people describe Moldova as "a failed state." What evidence supports this description? (Civil war continues without end and the economy is so poor that many people live off money sent from relatives in other countries.)

Moldova continues to face political turmoil, economic challenges, and corruption.

Most of the Russians and Ukrainians live in a region called Transdniestria. This region declared its independence in 1990. Moldova fought a war to keep the region from seceding. The leaders of Transdniestria and Moldova agreed to stop fighting, but they could not find a solution. Moldova still claims the territory, but it does not control the area. Transdniestria still claims independence. Other governments have accused Transdniestria of being a center for smuggling, or illegal trade.

Moldova has also had slow economic growth. Thousands of people have left the country to look for jobs in Romania. Many Moldovans must live on the money that their relatives abroad send back to them. Like Belarus, Moldova is one of the poorest countries in Europe. The government faces many serious political and economic challenges.

Reading Check What is one challenge faced by Moldova?

myWorld Activity Press Conference.

Section 2 Assessment

Key Terms

1. Use the terms *secede* and *ethnic cleansing* to describe the breakup of Yugoslavia.
2. What is capital?

Key Ideas

3. What political and economic changes have taken place in Poland and the Baltic nations since the end of communism?
4. What is one reason that conflict broke out in the Balkans in the 1990s?
5. Which country is more democratic, Ukraine or Belarus? Explain your answer.

Think Critically

6. **Identify Cause and Effect** How could joining the European Union improve a country's economy?
7. **Draw Inferences** Why were many Polish citizens able to become entrepreneurs in the 1990s?

Essential Question

How can you measure success?

Give an example of one country in Eastern Europe that has been successful in recent years. Why do you think this country has been successful? Go to your Student Journal to record your answer.

myWorld Activity

Press Conference Find Step-by-Step Instructions and an Activity Support on pp. T130–T131. **(Verbal/Logical)**

Ethnic Conflict in Bosnia

OBJECTIVES

Students will

- use primary sources to identify arguments for a diverse Bosnia or unified Serbia.
- **21st Century Learning** compare different viewpoints on ethnic conflict in Bosnia and Serbia.
- **ELL** use English proper nouns and adjectives to describe nationality, ethnicity, and religious affiliation.

SET EXPECTATIONS

In this lesson, students will

- read and analyze two documents arguing for a unified Serbia and a diverse Bosnia.
- write a paragraph exploring the positive and negative influence of pride in ethnic identity.

1 Connect

Have students complete the following statements orally or in private writing: *I am* (nationality). *I am* (religion). *I am* (ethnic group). Clarify that nationality is a political designation, such as American. Religion is a designation of faith, such as Muslim. Ethnicity is a designation related to heritage, such as Latino. Explain that in Bosnia these designations often overlap.

ELL **Intermediate/Early Advanced** Help students identify English nouns and adjectives for nationalities, ethnicities, and religions.

L1 **Special Needs** Clarify how categories overlap: A shirt can be blue. A jacket can also be blue.

2 Learn

Preview Have students preview images and documents. Using a Section 2 map, ask students why a unified Serbia might be impossible. Read the Key Idea, glossary terms, and definitions, using examples to clarify meaning. Read the introduction.

Read Slowly read the excerpt of Milosevic's comments without stopping. Read the document again, this time stopping to read the questions at the left and prompt students to analyze the meaning of his words. Have students answer the questions using the location of the letters as clues. Repeat for Emir Tica's comments. Start a discussion with students' responses. Ask, In what ways does Milosovic believe Serbians are unique? In what ways does Tica believe that Bosnians can be varied?

ELL **Intermediate** Clarify *hand in hand* as "attached to" and *mad* as "crazy."

myWorld Activity: **Identity Twister**
Distribute *Activity Support: Categories* and review directions. Have students list categories. Choose 3–5 appropriate categories, such as language or religion, and label a Twister board. As you call out categories, have students try to touch all areas that apply. If they get twisted up, start over. Then discuss why conflict may result when people identify with one category—religion—over another—nationality.

20 min

L3 **On-Level** Let students submit anonymously. Choose appropriate categories.

L2 **Extra Support** Allow students to complete the activity on paper by drawing lines to connect circles.

3 Understand

Review Go back to the Key Idea. Discuss with students how Bosnian Serbs and Bosnian Muslims pursued their separate ideas of the best future.

Assess Have each student complete **Analyze the Documents.** Review their answers to determine if students have met the lesson objectives.

Remediate If students struggle to discuss pride in one's ethnic identity, review the phrase's meaning. Clarify that *ethnic identity* can be defined in many different ways. Explain that many Bosnian Serbs believed that ethnic identity was closely tied to religious affiliation.

Name _____   Class _____   Date _____

myWorld Activity Support   Categories

Identity Twister

Directions During the Bosnian War, people in the area chose a group to join. Some chose by religion, others by ethnic background, and others by nationality. Explore this process in your classroom. List categories you think apply to you and classmates, such as "home language" if students speak many different languages. Circle three important categories. Follow your teacher's instructions to explore the categories, then answer the questions to connect your experience to the reading.

Possible Categories

_____ _____ _____ _____

_____ _____ _____ _____

1. Which categories did you fit into? Explain which you didn't fit into.

   _____

2. What happened when you fit into more than one category?

   _____

3. What categories have people in Eastern Europe used to organize in groups?

   _____

4. Which categories contributed to the conflicts of the Bosnian War?

   _____

5. Why might some categories feel more important than others?

   _____

6. Have you ever decided to ignore a category or group that is important to you in order to avoid a conflict? Describe the situation and what happened.

   _____

   _____

CORE CONCEPTS: WHAT IS CULTURE?

Review Core Concepts 7.1 before students read the primary sources about ethnic conflict in Bosnia. Discuss elements of culture, such as language, religion, ethnic heritage, common institutions, and shared values. Explain that a culture may define itself by some or all of the elements. Point out the phrase "challenge of disunity" in the excerpt by Slobodan Milosevic. Ask, What challenges might leaders face in creating cultural unity when culture can be defined in so many different ways?

GUIDE ON THE SIDE

Compare Viewpoints Use the lettered prompts to help students analyze the documents and compare viewpoints.

ANSWERS

Ⓐ He is talking about disunity and internal conflict.

Ⓑ Muslims who might try to control how Serbs live.

Ⓒ He wanted them to fight for a unified Serbia.

Primary Source

Ethnic Conflict in Bosnia

Key Idea
• Although Bosnia has long been home to diverse ethnic groups, some Serbians in the 1990s attacked Bosnian Muslims, hoping to establish a purely Serbian state.

▲ This newspaper was found in the streets of war-torn Bosnia.

Bosnian Muslims, Serbs, and Croats had lived in peace for years. But when Bosnia declared independence in 1992, many Bosnian Serbs felt threatened. They did not want to live in a Muslim-led country. In fact, some Serbs had long resented their Muslim neighbors. This distrust went back to Muslim Turks' conquest of Serbia in the late 1300s. Determined to create a unified Serbian nation, Bosnian Serbs went to war. In the following sources, the former president of Serbia calls for ethnic unity, and a Bosnian Muslim soldier explains his views on Bosnia and why he chose to fight.

Slobodan Milosevic (mee LOH sheh vich), leader of Serbia, 1989–1997, and leader of Yugoslavia, 1997–2000 ▼

Stop at each circled letter on the right to think about the text. Then answer the question with the same letter on the left.

Ⓐ **Identify Main Ideas** What "greatest evil" is Milosevic talking about?

Ⓑ **Draw Inferences** Who might Milosevic be referring to here as "those who would take away our dignity"?

Ⓒ **Draw Conclusions** What do you think Milosevic wanted Serbs to do?

sap, *v.,* to drain, reduce

coalition, *n.,* alliance, groups working together

For a Unified Serbian People

❝ Serbia and the Serbian people are faced with one of the
Ⓐ greatest evils of their history: the challenge of disunity and internal conflict. This evil, which has more than once caused so much damage and claimed so many victims, more than once <u>sapped</u> our strength, has always come hand in hand with
Ⓑ those who would take away our dignity. . . . All who love Serbia
Ⓒ dare not ignore this fact, especially at a time when we are confronted by the . . . forces in the anti-Serbian <u>coalition</u> which threaten the people's rights and freedoms. ❞

Slobodan Milosevic, quoted in "The Fall of Yugoslavia"

ANALYZE THE DOCUMENTS

1. Milosovec believes that Serbians are mistreated or harmed in a mixed ethnic society. He wants Serbians to live with and be ruled by other Serbians. Tica believes that a diverse culture is good, and that people in Bosnia can be defined by their shared nationality instead of by religion or ethnicity. **2.** Sample: In Bosnia, ethnic pride was a negative force. It drove the Serbians to try to separate themselves from other groups in the region. They decided that these other groups were

21st Century Learning — COMPARE VIEWPOINTS

To assist your students in comparing viewpoints, use the scaffolded questions to the left of each excerpt. Encourage students to consider primary source writings as artifacts that have to be investigated with the close attention an archaeologist would use to examine an object. Repeated readings and breaking sentences into smaller parts are important strategies for identifying, and then comparing, viewpoints. Once students can identify and restate the views expressed by each man, help them to highlight statements that relate to the same topic or issue as they look for contrast. For example, Milosovec speaks of "disunity" as an evil. Tica describes Bosnia as a "mixed country" and presents that as a positive result. For additional help, refer students to the **21st Century Learning Online Tutor** *Compare Viewpoints*.

Stop at each circled letter on the right to think about the text. Then answer the question with the same letter on the left.

D Identify Evidence Why did Tica (TEE tsuh) think there was a "terrible misunderstanding"?

E Summarize Why did Tica decide to fight?

F Compare and Contrast How does Tica compare Serbian plans for Bosnia with life in the United States?

For a Diverse Bosnia

66 Bosnia is a mixed country. There has always been some kind of tolerance, in this town anyway. In the first days of this war, I thought there was some **D** terrible misunderstanding. When they started <u>shelling</u> my city, I understood only one thing: someone wants to destroy my life, take my job, kill my parents, wreck my apartment. When I started **E** fighting, it was just to defend my family. . . . My country is Bosnia, with all three peoples in it. I call myself a Bosnian, and I know what that means. But the Serbs and Croats want ethnic <u>cantons</u>, racially pure. Who . . . wants to live in an ethnic canton? **F** I don't. It would be like having California for the whites and Chicago for the blacks, instead of America. It's completely mad. 99

shell, *v.,* to bomb, fire upon
canton, *n.,* small territory

Emir Tica, quoted in *Seasons in Hell: Understanding Bosnia's War*

ANSWERS

D He could not believe that people had gone to war over ethnic differences.

E He started fighting to defend his family.

F He compares Serbian plans with putting only white Americans in California and only black Americans in Chicago.

During the ethnic conflict in Bosnia, heavy shelling left many people homeless. ▼

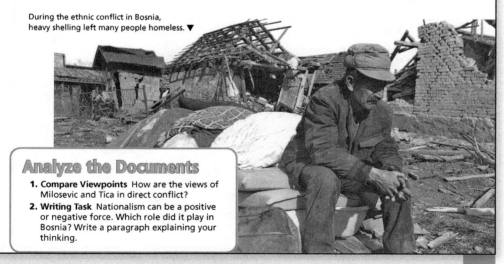

Analyze the Documents

1. **Compare Viewpoints** How are the views of Milosevic and Tica in direct conflict?
2. **Writing Task** Nationalism can be a positive or negative force. Which role did it play in Bosnia? Write a paragraph explaining your thinking.

inferior to them and should be avoided. These beliefs led the Serbians to hatred and war.

1. Mechanized farming is easy on the large, flat areas of land on the North European Plain.

2. Climate on the inland side of a mountain range is often dryer than on the coastal side. Air drops its moisture as it rises over the mountains and cools. It has very little left when it reaches the inland side of the mountains.

THINK CRITICALLY

8. Both areas are broad flatlands where similar crops can be grown with mechanized farming.

9. Communist restrictions on religion probably reduced the number of people practicing religion. Reversing those restrictions has probably encouraged expansion of religious practices.

10. It lowered taxes on foreign companies that created businesses with new jobs for Slovakians.

11. Sample: The need for fuel has led to environmental damage. Countries cannot expand their economies without fuel for their businesses and industries, however in Eastern Europe this fuel has often been dirty coal. Coal burning has caused acid rain and other pollution.

---

3. Resources have influenced the type of industries in the region and where those industries are located.

4. Major religious groups are Muslims, Orthodox Christians, Catholics, and Protestants. Jews also once had an important presence.

5. Poland now has many entrepreneurs and a growing economy.

---

6. The Czech Republic has had faster economic growth than Slovakia since independence because of a more diverse economy.

7. Balkan states seceded because they did not like Serbia's control of the national government.

Eastern Europe

Chapter Assessment

Key Terms and Ideas

1. **Recall** Why is **mechanized farming** common on the North European Plain?

2. **Compare and Contrast** Why can the climate differ on different sides of a mountain range?

3. **Explain** How have resources influenced industry in Eastern Europe?

4. **Recall** What are the main traditional religions in Eastern Europe?

5. **Explain** How has Poland's economy been successful since the breakup of the Soviet Union?

6. **Compare and Contrast** Did the Czech Republic or Slovakia have faster economic growth after the breakup of the Soviet Union and the end of communism? Why?

7. **Explain** Why did many Balkan states **secede** from Yugoslavia?

Think Critically

8. **Make Inferences** Why might agriculture on the Hungarian Plain and the North European Plain be similar? Use the maps in this section to answer the question.

9. **Draw Conclusions** What long-term effect might the end of communist policies toward religion have on religious practices in Eastern Europe?

10. **Solve Problems** What action did the government of Slovakia take to improve its economy?

11. **Core Concepts: People's Impact on the Environment** What is one economic activity that has resulted in damage to the environment in this region?

Places to Know

For each place, write the letter from the map that shows its location.

12. **Bosnia and Herzegovina**

13. **Poland**

14. **Ukraine**

15. **Balkan Mountains**

16. **Baltic Sea**

17. **Black Sea**

18. **Estimate** Using the scale bar, estimate the distance from the Black Sea to the Baltic Sea.

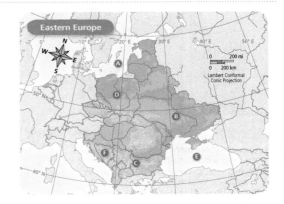

PLACES TO KNOW

12. F

13. D

14. B

15. C

16. A

17. E

18. about 1000 miles, or 1600 km

myWorld Chapter Activity

Open for Business Find Step-by-Step Instructions, Student Instructions and Rubric, and an Activity Support on pp. T117–T119. **(Verbal/Interpersonal/Visual)**

 21st Century Learning

Evaluate Web Sites Students' evaluations should show a successful search and thoughtful consideration of the site and its goals. If students need help with this skill, direct them to the online tutorial *Evaluate Web Sites.*

→ **Online Assessment**

Tailor review and assessment to each student's needs with an array of online assessments.
- Self-Test
- On Assignment Article or Slideshow
- Success Tracker

? Essential Question

 **myWorld Chapter Activity**

Open for Business You work at a business that is hoping to open a new branch in Eastern Europe. Evaluate information about different countries, and choose the country that would offer the best location for your business.

21st Century Learning

Evaluating Web Sites

Search for three different Web sites that provide information on nuclear energy. What benefits and drawbacks does each site give for nuclear energy? Find the name of the organization that created each site. Can you find the goals of this organization? Do the goals of the organization influence the information that is presented on the site?

Document-Based Questions

Success ★ Tracker™
Online at myworldgeography.com

Use your knowledge of Eastern Europe and Documents A and B to answer Questions 1–3 below.

Document A

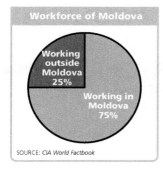

Workforce of Moldova

Working outside Moldova 25%

Working in Moldova 75%

SOURCE: *CIA World Factbook*

1. According to the graph, what percentage of Moldovan workers had jobs in other countries?

   A 15 percent
   B 20 percent
   C 25 percent
   D 30 percent

Document B

" Many specialists, doctors, go to work abroad. They go where they are paid better, but for the country, this is not a solution."

—Grigore, a student in Moldova

2. According to Document B, why do some people go abroad to work?

   A They do not like Moldova's government.
   B They cannot find jobs in Moldova.
   C They think the weather in Moldova is too cold.
   D They earn more money if they work abroad.

3. **Writing Task** What do you think the speaker in Document B meant when he said "for the country, this is not a solution"? Write a paragraph explaining both the benefits and drawbacks to Moldova of so many people leaving the country to find jobs.

WRITING TASK TIP

Paraphrase Demonstrate how to paraphrase a quotation in order to discuss it in writing. Post an example, paraphrasing "for the country, this is not a solution" as *This hurts the country.* Point out the simple language that can help students to focus narrowly on the quotation's meaning. Direct students then to link the paraphrased statement to their reading about Moldova and its economy.

DOCUMENT-BASED QUESTIONS

1. C

2. D

3. Sample: The speaker meant that when highly educated people leave a country, those people can't help the country progress and improve. This is a drawback for the country. One benefit of people leaving might be that there are more jobs available for those who stay.

Plan With Understanding by Design*

Chapter Objectives
Begin With the End in Mind

Students will demonstrate the following enduring understandings:
- In countries with much ethnic diversity, nationalism can lead to separatism and conflict.

- A history of autocracy can make it more difficult to establish democracy.
- Transportation networks are necessary to connect isolated regions.

Connect
Make Learning Meaningful

Student Edition
- **Essential Question** What should governments do?
- **myStory** Boris rides his skateboard around Moscow and competes on it internationally.

my worldgeography.com
myStory Online Get to know Boris through a video about his life and family.

Student Journal
Essential Question Preview

Experience
Teach Knowledge and Skills

Student Edition
- Read Sections 1, 2, and 3.
- Answer Reading Checks and Section Assessment questions.

my worldgeography.com
On Assignment myStory Video, Active Atlas, Data Discovery, Language Lesson, Culture Close-up, and Self-Test

Student Journal
- Sections 1, 2, and 3 Word Wise
- Sections 1, 2, and 3 Take Notes

Teacher's Edition
myWorld Activities
- Section 1: Roam Across Russia, p. T144
- Section 2: Make a Living Timeline, p. T150
- Section 3: Quiz Yourself, p. T158

21st Century Learning Online Tutor
- Read Physical Maps
- Analyze Cause and Effect
- Sequence
- Identify Main Ideas and Details

Understand
Assess Understanding

Assessment Booklet
- Chapter Tests
- Benchmark Tests

Teacher's Edition
myWorld Chapter Activity
Students will analyze information about challenges facing Russia and then write a memo prioritizing those challenges.

Student Edition
Chapter Assessment

my worldgeography.com
On Assignment Students post an online article or slideshow about what governments should do.

Success Tracker™
Online at myworldgeography.com
Administer chapter tests and remediate understanding.

Student Journal
Essential Question Writer's Workshop

Connect to the Essential Question

 Essential Question

What should governments do?

Use the Essential Question poster and follow these steps to help students understand the Essential Question.

Connect to Their Lives

1. Have students think of different ways that the U.S. government affects their lives. (If students have already studied this Essential Question, encourage them to note changes to their opinions.) Tell them to consider areas such as law, taxes, the military, the environment, and transportation. Post the following chart for them to complete or have students turn to the *Essential Question Preview* page in their **Student Journal.**

How the U.S. Government Affects My Life				
Laws	**Taxes**	**Military**	**Environment**	**Transportation**

2. Encourage students to consider conversations about government that they may have heard on television, at school, or at home. Then ask the following two questions: Do you think the government should be doing everything you listed on the chart? Is there something that you think the government should do that it isn't doing?

Connect to the Content

3. Remind students that nations sometimes go through hard times, such as wars or economic slowdowns. Ask whether students think a government should take different actions during bad times than it does during good times. Have students record their ideas on the Venn diagram below.

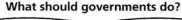
What should governments do?

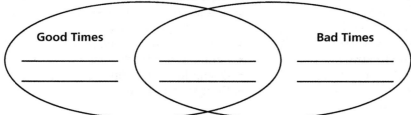
Good Times   Bad Times

4. After previewing the chapter, have students make chapter-related predictions on the *Essential Question Preview* page in the **Student Journal.**

5. Remind students that they will answer a prompt related to the Essential Question on each section's *Take Notes* page in the **Student Journal.**

Explore my worldgeography.com

○ ○ ○   Welcome to myWorldGeography

◀ ▶ ⟳ ✂ +   http://www.myworldgeography.com

ON ASSIGNMENT: Russia

For this chapter's assignment, students will

- take a digital trip to Russia.
- take on the role of a journalist.
- gather notes, images, and data throughout their journey for their story.
- write an article or make a multimedia slideshow connecting the information and images gathered during their trip and this chapter's Essential Question: *What should governments do?*

ITINERARY

During their trip, students will make the following stops:

→ **myStory Video**

Learn about Boris, a competitive skateboarder who lives in Moscow.

→ **Active Atlas**

Study physical, political, and special-purpose maps of Russia.

→ **Data Discovery**

Gather data from charts and graphs about Russia.

→ **Language Lesson**

Learn some Russian words.

→ **Culture Close-up**

Explore Red Square in Moscow.

→ **Self-Test**

Assess their own knowledge of chapter content.

While on their trip, students will practice the following skills:

- **Interpret** graphic representations of data.
- **Synthesize** information into an interesting article.
- **Evaluate** the roles of government.

TIGed
TakingITGlobal for Educators

Extend the reach of every lesson by helping students connect to a global community of young people with common interests and concerns. Visit myworldgeography.com to

- explore Country Pages relating to Russia.
- delve deeper into this chapter's Essential Question, *What should governments do?*
- find online alternatives to and solutions for the Unit Closer 21st Century Learning Activity.

my worldgeography.com

TEACHER CENTER

Preview and assign student materials, enrich your teaching, and track student progress with the following resources:

- Online Lesson Planning and Resource Library
- Presentations for Projection
- Online Teacher's Edition and Ancillaries
- Google Earth Links

Assess Enduring Understandings

myWorld Chapter Activity   **Step-by-Step Instructions**   2 hr

Memo to Russia

Teach this activity at the end of the chapter to assess enduring understandings.

OBJECTIVES

Students will demonstrate the following enduring understandings:
- In countries with much ethnic diversity, nationalism can lead to separatism and conflict.
- A history of autocracy can make it more difficult to establish democracy.
- Transportation networks are necessary to connect isolated regions.

Students will provide the following evidence of understanding:
- Analysis Table
- Memo

LEARNING STYLES
- Visual
- Verbal
- Interpersonal

MATERIALS
- Activity Support: Student Instructions and Rubric, p. T140
- Activity Support: Analysis Table, p. T141
- Activity Cards: #67–72
  - 67. Pollution Data
  - 68. Poverty Data
  - 69. Health Data
  - 70. International Partnerships
  - 71. Conflicts at Home and Abroad
  - 72. Crime Data

Activity Steps

1. **Set Expectations** Tell students that they will use six activity cards to evaluate the urgency of Russia's current challenges. They will first study one challenge, then hear about other challenges, and complete an Analysis Table. Finally, they will write a memo to the Russian government explaining how they would prioritize efforts to deal with the challenges. Review *Activity Support: Student Instructions and Rubric* on the next page.

2. **Analysis Table Jigsaw**
   - Divide the class into six groups to analyze data about these challenges: pollution, poverty, health, international partnerships, conflicts, and crime. Distribute one activity card to each group and give each student a copy of the *Analysis Table*.
   - In the first group, students discuss the information on the card and record their conclusions on the appropriate line of the *Analysis Table*. Each student should rate how urgent they think the challenge is on a scale of 1 to 10, with 10 being the most urgent.

   ELL **Early Intermediate/Intermediate** Give students these definitions: **challenge** something that is difficult; **urgent** needing to be done right away; **priority** something that should be done first.

   - Using a jigsaw, put students in new groups. Students share their earlier conclusions. Each one completes the *Analysis Table,* using his or her judgment to rate how urgent each challenge is.

   L2 **Extra Support** Let students practice evaluating urgency by having the class rate the following challenges: repainting a city hall, putting out a fire, strengthening a dam, building a new stadium.

3. **Rank the Challenges** Students should list Russia's challenges by their urgency ratings with the most urgent challenges at the top. If students gave some challenges the same rating, they should review the conclusions to decide which one is more urgent.

4. **Memo** Each student writes a memo to the Russian government explaining the top three challenges they think the government should address and why.

  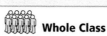

Name _____ Class _____ Date _____

myWorld Chapter Activity Support   **Student Instructions and Rubric**

Memo to Russia

Activity Instructions Read the following summary of your myWorld Chapter Activity. Follow your teacher's directions for more information.

1. You and your fellow group members are advisors to the Russian government. You will be given a card with information about one of the challenges facing Russia today.

2. In your group, study the card and answer the questions on it. Write your conclusions on the correct line of *Activity Support: Analysis Table.* Rate how urgent this challenge is on a scale of 1 to 10, with 10 being most urgent. Record your rating on the table. Your rating may differ from the ratings of other people.

3. The teacher will then rearrange the groups and you will hear about the other five challenges. Record the conclusions of the other groups on the remaining lines on your Analysis Table. Finally, rate how urgent each challenge is in your opinion.

4. Below the table, list Russia's challenges according to your ratings. Put the most urgent challenges at the top.

5. Write a memo to the Russian government. Tell the government which three challenges are most urgent, the order in which they should be addressed, and why.

myWorld Chapter Activity Rubric	3 Exceeds Understanding	2 Reaches Understanding	1 Approaches Understanding
Group participation	Participates fully in analyzing the data, listens to others, contributes to the group conclusion based on the data	Helps analyze the data and participates in the discussion	Able to describe the general opinion of the group
Memo: Organization	Recommends the order in which all six challenges should be tackled; explains reasons for rankings with many details	Recommends the order of the top three challenges; clearly explains reasons for rankings	Recommends only the top one or two priorities; vaguely explains rankings
Memo: Grammar & Spelling	Makes recommendations with correct grammar and no spelling errors	Makes recommendations with few grammar and spelling errors that do not interrupt understanding	Makes recommendations with several spelling and grammar errors that interrupt understanding

Name _____ Class _____ Date _____

myWorld Chapter Activity Support   Analysis Table

Memo to Russia

Directions Fill out the Analysis Table using the activity cards and information from classmates. Then rate the urgency of each challenge on a scale of 1 to 10. Rank the challenges from first (most important) to sixth at the bottom of the page. On a separate sheet of paper, write your memo to the government about the three most important challenges.

Challenge Card	Notes About the Activity Card	Conclusion About this Challenge	Urgency 1 to 10
Pollution			
Poverty			
Health			
International Partnerships			
Conflicts at Home and Abroad			
Crime			

Set Priorities Reorder the challenges so that the most urgent is first and the least urgent is sixth. Use the ratings and conclusions on your chart to create your list.

1. _____   4. _____

2. _____   5. _____

3. _____   6. _____

Memo to Russia Write a clear memo that states the order of your top <u>three</u> priorities and explain why you think the government should deal with these challenges first.

Russia

- Introduce the Essential Question so that students will be able to understand the big ideas of this chapter. (See earlier page, **Connect to the Essential Question.**)
- Help students prepare to learn about Russia by looking at the chapter's maps, charts, and photos.

- Have students make and record chapter predictions with the *Essential Question Preview* in the **Student Journal.**
- Ask them to analyze maps on this page.

GUIDE ON THE SIDE

Explore the Essential Question . . .

Have students complete the Essential Question Writer's Workshop in their **Student Journal** to demonstrate their in-depth understanding of the question in the context of this chapter.

Analyze Maps Point out the map of Russia.

- Which of the cities shown on this map is closest to Russia's European neighbors? (St. Petersburg)
- What body of water is the city of Magadan near? (Sea of Okhotsk)
- What city is located near Lake Baikal? (Irkutsk)
- Which city is farthest north and which city is farthest south? (Murmansk and Vladivostok)

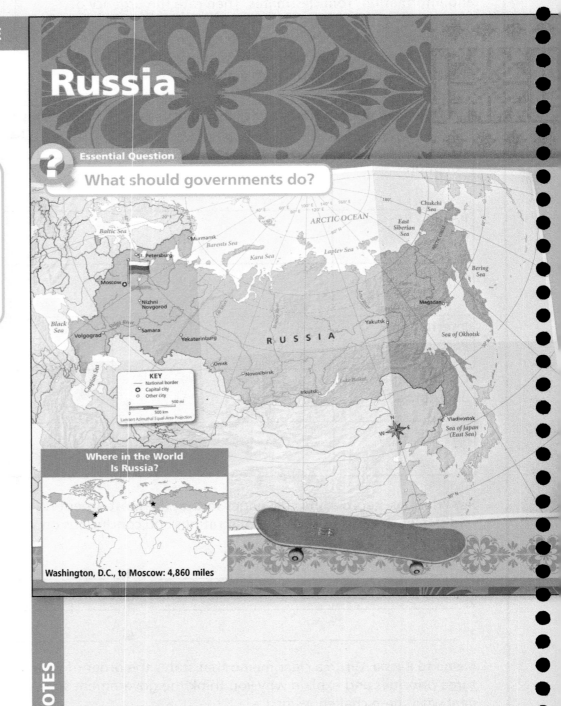

Russia

Essential Question

What should governments do?

KEY
— National border
✪ Capital city
○ Other city
0 ___ 500 mi
0 ___ 500 km
Lambert Azimuthal Equal-Area Projection

Where in the World Is Russia?

Washington, D.C., to Moscow: 4,860 miles

INTRODUCE Story

Get students excited to learn about Russia by first experiencing the region through the eyes of Boris, a teenage boy who rides his skateboard around Moscow and takes part in skateboarding competitions in other countries.

- Read myStory and watch the myStory Video about his life.
- Have students complete *Boris's Bigspin* in the **Student Journal** to prepare to learn how recent changes in Russia have affected Russian citizens.

my Story

Boris's Bigspin

In this section, you'll read about Boris, a young skateboarder living in Moscow. What does Boris's story tell you about life in Russia today?

Explore the Essential Question
- at **worldgeography.com**
- using the **myWorld Chapter Activity**
- with the **Student Journal**

Story by Dmitry Saltykovskiy for myWorld Online

It's a sunny day in Moscow, and people hurry past a huge monument to the German philosopher Karl Marx. The 200-ton block of stone bears the inscription "Workers of the world, unite," a quote from Marx that became famous among communist workers. When the statue was unveiled in 1961, Russia was a communist nation, and Marx was an honored figure. Today, Russia is a very different place, and the monument to Marx is better known as a fun place for skateboarders to try tricks like the ollie or the bigspin.

Boris, a 15-year-old Russian skateboarder, loves to try jumps off of the step at the base of the monument. When the Soviet Union collapsed in 1991, Boris had not yet been born. He has never lived under communism, but he still has clear memories of hard times in Russia.

"I was born in troubled times," Boris says. "After the Soviet Union fell, people were trying to make money. It was a dangerous period with lots of crime and fighting between businesses. My father disappeared around that time. I was just four years old. He owned his own business, and he was kidnapped. We never saw him again. I am sad that I can't really remember what he looked like now."

GUIDE ON THE SIDE

my Story

Boris's Bigspin

- **Identify Details** Why doesn't Boris remember what it was like to live in the Soviet Union? (He was born after it collapsed.)

- **Infer** What do you think might have happened if someone did a skateboard trick on the Marx monument during communist rule? (Sample: He or she would get in trouble.)

- **Identify Main Ideas** What happened to Boris's father? (He was kidnapped during a difficult time in Russian history.)

→ **On Assignment**

Have students go to myworldgeography.com to receive their assignments from a virtual newspaper editor. Students will explore Russia in order to better understand Boris's story and the key ideas of the chapter.

GEOGRAPHY

Moscow's Green Spaces Moscow, the city where Boris lives, has devoted a high percentage of its land to parks and green spaces. About 290 square feet of parkland exists for every Muscovite. This is a higher ratio than can be found in most major world cities. Not only does Moscow have a large amount of preserved land, but it also has many different types of parks, providing a variety of experiences.

- Historic parks include museums, gardens, historic villages, former churches, and aristocratic estates.
- Wildlife and nature parks include the Moscow Zoo, a forest, and a national nature reserve.
- Leisure and memorial parks include the world-famous Gorky Park, with its amusement park, and Victory Park, which has memorials to the military.

GUIDE ON THE SIDE

- **Identify Evidence** How do you know that Boris is successful as a skateboarder? (He has won prize money, and he is sponsored by a sports brand.)
- **Compare and Contrast** According to Boris, how is life in Russia now different from life in Soviet times? (There was no skateboarding, and Soviet people couldn't travel the way he does.)
- **Identify Details** How did Boris use his prize money to help his family? (He was able to use it to make his mother's birthday special.)

Analyze Visuals Point out that in some photographs, Boris is wearing some safety equipment but no helmet. Explain that safety standards vary from country to country.

- Why might different countries have different safety standards? (Samples: different forms of government, more willingness as a culture to take risk)

Boris talks with friends after school.

Boris on a Moscow city street

Boris in front of a monument to Karl Marx

Boris goes everywhere by skateboard, including the skate park. At the indoor skate park, skaters ride curved ramps, and the clatter of decks hitting the floor fills the air.

During the Soviet era, the sport of skateboarding did not exist. Boris is one of the first young Russians to take part in paid skateboard competitions. He even has a sponsorship by a major sports brand—something else that's new in Russia.

"There was no skateboarding during Soviet times—things have changed so much since then. In those days, people couldn't travel at all outside the Soviet Union. Today, I am able to travel all over the world to participate in competitions."

"My mom was really proud when I started winning competitions," Boris recalls. "She was amazed when I managed to get a sponsorship deal. It was a really nice moment for me when I could use some of my prize money to make her birthday special."

Boris says that his mother and stepfather are proud of his skateboarding, although they worry about him being injured. They also hope that he will consider a professional career someday. "Moscow is growing so quickly that I've become interested in real estate!" Boris laughs.

CULTURE

Russian Versus Georgian Surnames Boris recently changed his last name to a more Russian-sounding name. The characteristic surnames of Russia and Georgia are very distinctive, so people in the region can often infer someone's ethnic background solely by the way their name ends. In both countries, the majority of surnames originated as patronymics, names that identify a person by their father. An English example is *Johnson*, meaning "son of John." In Russian surnames, common endings include *-ov* (for example, former leader Yuri Andropov), *-ev* (Mikhail Gorbachev), or *-in* (Vladimir Putin). In western Georgia, most surnames end with *-dze* (for example, former president Eduard Shevardnadze). In eastern Georgia, the more common ending is *-shvili* (for example, Stalin's original last name, Dzhugashvili).

Boris at the skate park in Moscow

Boris shoots basketball at the park.

Working on the computer at home

Following the 2008 Russian invasion of Georgia, Boris decided to change his last name. Georgia had once been part of the Soviet Union, but it declared its independence in 1991. Since then, relations have been tense between Russia and Georgia.

"My father was half Georgian, and he had a very un-Russian sounding last name. With all the problems between our two countries, my mom decided that we should change our name. I was really sad because I felt like I was giving away a piece of my father, but really we had no choice. Russians have become quite anti-Georgian and my name marked me as different."

The tension between Russia and Georgia also means that Boris has been unable to visit family in Georgia. "I used to go there every summer. It was really nice to get out of Moscow when the weather was hot. Now there are no airplane flights."

The wheels of Boris's deck leave the ground, and then he rolls off to the park for a game of basketball. For Boris, his skateboard is not only the best way to get around Moscow, but also a ticket to a promising future in the new Russia.

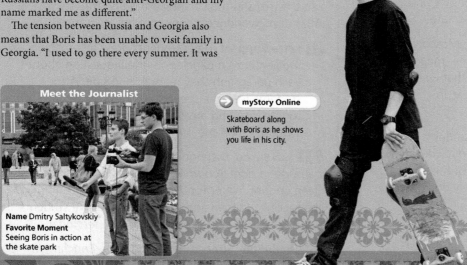

Meet the Journalist

Name Dmitry Saltykovskiy
Favorite Moment Seeing Boris in action at the skate park

 myStory Online

Skateboard along with Boris as he shows you life in his city.

GUIDE ON THE SIDE

- **Cause and Effect** Why did Boris change his surname? (It was a Georgian surname, and many Russians are anti-Georgian because of a recent war between Georgia and Russia.)

- **Compare Viewpoints** Why was Boris sad about changing his name? (He felt that he was giving away a piece of his father.)

- **Cause and Effect** What other effect has the conflict between Russia and Georgia had on Boris's life? (He can no longer fly to Georgia to visit the family he has there.)

myStory Video

Have students watch the video at myworldgeography.com about Boris's life and the way it has been shaped by recent changes in Russia. Tell students to use their trackers to take notes about Boris's story.

NOTES

Chapter Atlas

OBJECTIVES

Students will know

- the landforms, climates, and natural resources of Russia.
- the patterns of Russian population distribution.

Students will be able to

- identify and describe important places in Russia.
- label an outline map of important places in Russia.

SET EXPECTATIONS

In this section, students will

- read Chapter Atlas.
- plan a trip across Russia.
- go On Assignment in Russia and explore maps and charts.

CORE CONCEPTS

You may wish to teach or reteach the following lessons from the Core Concepts Handbook:

- Types of Climate, pp. 40–41
- Ecosystems, pp. 42–43
- Population Distribution, pp. 76–77

KEY

Differentiated Instruction

L1 Special Needs **L2** Extra Support
L3 On-Level **L4** Challenge

English Language Instruction

ELL Beginner **ELL** Early Intermediate **ELL** Intermediate
ELL Early Advanced **ELL** Advanced

---

1 Connect
Make learning meaningful

Make Connections Review the four continental U.S. time zones. Ask, How do the time zones affect U.S. life? For example, how do they affect making business calls between New York and California? Tell students that Russia is so large that it has 11 time zones. Ask what difficulties that might create.

L2 Extra Support Have students locate Moscow and Vladivostok on the chapter opener map of Russia in their textbooks. Explain that when it is 9:00 A.M. in Moscow, it is 4:00 P.M. in Vladivostok.

Activate Prior Knowledge Ask students what they learned about the climate of Scandinavia earlier in this unit. Explain that a large region of Russia has an equally cold climate. Ask how densely populated they think that region of Russia is.

ELL Intermediate Explain that the term *permafrost* was formed from the words *permanent* and *frost*. Ask students what they think it means.

Prepare Follow the steps in the section **Preview.** Preteach the Key Terms. Then have students complete *Word Wise* in their journals using in-text clues and the glossary for help.

2 Experience
Teach knowledge and skills

Read Use **Background** notes and **Guide on the Side** questions to model active reading. Have students use *Take Notes* in their **Student Journal** to put places to know in Russia on an outline map. Students should use the maps in the Chapter Atlas and the Active Atlas at myworldgeography.com for assistance.

L2 Extra Support Have students draw a line down the center of a page and write a question about each paragraph they read on one side. After students read the section, partners can work together to find answers to the questions and write them on the other side of the page.

ELL Advanced Distinguish between the synonyms *harbor* and *port*. A *harbor* is a protected inlet with deep enough water for ships. A *port* is a harbor with the facilities to load and unload cargo. Have students write sentences or make drawings as a reminder.

L4 Challenge After students complete *Enrichment: Climates Across Russia,* have them write and deliver a mock-televised weather forecast for all three cities during a particular month.

 **Practice: myWorld Activity** Students will learn about Russian places by planning a trip. **Step-by-Step Instructions** and **More Activities** follow on p. T144.

SECTION 1 RESOURCE GUIDE

FOR THE STUDENT

my worldgeography.com Student Center
- Active Atlas
- Data Discovery

Student Edition (print and online)
- Chapter Atlas

Student Journal (print and online)
- Section 1 Word Wise
- Section 1 Take Notes

21st Century Learning Online Tutor
- Read Physical Maps
- Ask Questions

FOR THE TEACHER

my worldgeography.com Teacher Center
- Online Lesson Planner
- Presentations for Projection
- SuccessTracker

ProGuide: Europe and Russia
- Section 1 Lesson Plan, pp. T142–T143
- ⟨⟩ myWorld Activity Step-by-Step Instructions, p. T144
- Activity Support: Trip Planner, p. T145
- myWorld Geography Enrichment, p. T146
- Section Quiz, p. T147

Guide to ELL Success
- Peer Learning Strategies, p. 46

---

3 Understand
Assess understanding

Review Review *Word Wise* and *Take Notes* in the **Student Journal.**

Assess Knowledge and Skills Use the Section Assessment and Section Quiz to check students' progress.

Assess Understanding Review students' responses to the Section Assessment Essential Question prompt.

Remediate Use these strategies to review and remediate.

If students struggle to . . .	Try these strategies.
Distinguish between European Russia and Asiatic Russia	Have them turn a sheet of paper sideways and draw a vertical line four inches from the left edge. They can record facts about European Russia on the left and Asiatic on the right.
Ask questions	Assign additional practice with the **21st Century Online Tutor.**
Determine elevation on a physical map	Review the colors in the elevation key.

ELL Support

ELL Objective Students will understand and use English words relating to climate.

Cultural Connections Allow students to use their native languages to describe the coldest weather they have ever experienced. Ask them to complete the following sentence in English: "I was so cold that I felt _____."

ELL Early Intermediate/Intermediate Content Tip Explain to students the difference between the terms *melt* and *thaw* by using the following examples: An ice cube melts by turning into water. A frozen loaf of bread thaws by reaching room temperature and becoming softer. Ask, Does frozen ground melt or thaw?

ELL Activity Have pairs of students take each other on a visualization journey to a place they once visited. If students are comfortable, have the listeners close their eyes to help them picture what the describers are saying. Suggest that students describe the arrival, an adventure while there, and the departure. **(Verbal)**

myWorld Activity   **Step-by-Step Instructions**

 15 min

Roam Across Russia

OBJECTIVES

Students will
- plan the itinerary of a trip to Russia.
- write questions about the places they will visit.

LEARNING STYLE
- Visual
- Verbal

21st Century Learning
- Ask Questions

MATERIALS
- Activity Support: Trip Planner, p. T145

Activity Steps

1. Divide the class into pairs. Tell students that they are going to plan a trip to five places in Russia. Then they will brainstorm questions to help them plan what to pack and know what to expect from the trip.

2. Students should scan Section 1 for place names and then read surrounding text to review why those places are important. After identifying possible destinations, the pair should decide on the five places they most want to visit.

   L2 Extra Support Suggest that one partner act as the scanner and reader, while the other takes notes. Students should jot down several place names and their significance before deciding on the final five.

3. After students have decided on five places to visit, they should locate them on a map of Russia. Have partners work together to decide the order of their

itinerary. Encourage them to choose the most logical route with the least amount of backtracking.

   ELL Beginner Give students these model sentences to use in discussing the itinerary: "First, I will go to _____." "Next, I will go to _____." "Last, I will go to _____."

4. Finally, tell partners to suppose they will chat online with a young person living in Russia. Have them work together to write four questions they would ask the person to help them plan their trip.

   L3 On Level Remind students that when people travel, they encounter many things that are different, such as food, clothing, customs, money, and transportation systems. Suggest that they write questions about those differences.

 More Activities From myWorld Teachers

Local Connection Hold a class discussion about population distribution in your state. Ask if the state has any sparsely populated areas, like Siberia, or whether it is densely populated throughout the state, like European Russia. **(Verbal/Logical)**

Transcontinental Railroad Have pairs of students measure the length of the Trans-Siberian Railroad on a map. Then have them calculate the average number of

miles of track that were laid each year during the 16 years it took to build. **(Logical/Visual)**

Take a Stand on Siberia Post signs with these statements on opposite walls: "Siberia's resources must be developed" and "Developing Siberia poses too many challenges." Let students put themselves between the two extremes in a spot that best shows their position and then explain their reasons. **(Kinesthetic/Logical)**

my worldgeography.com   Teacher Center   ➜   Find additional resources in the online Teacher Center.

Name _____ Class _____ Date _____

myWorld Activity Support   **Trip Planner**

Roam Across Russia

Directions Working with a partner, review Section 1. Scan the text for place names, choose five places you would like to visit, and list them in the table below. Then write the reason why you want to visit each one. Next, look at a map of Russia to figure out the order in which to visit the five places. Number them in the column on the right. After you have finished the table, write four questions that would help you research information you would need to travel to Russia. A sample question has been written for you.

Place to Visit in Russia	Why I Want to Go There	Order in Trip

Questions to Help Me Plan My Trip

Sample Question *What will the weather be like there?*

1. _____

2. _____

3. _____

4. _____

Name _____ Class _____ Date _____

Enrichment: Climates Across Russia

Directions Study the graph below. Answer the questions that follow.

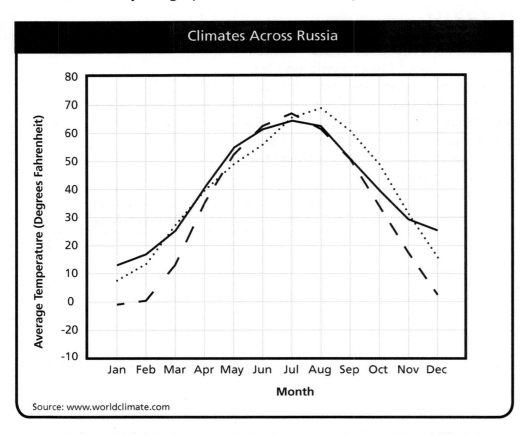

Source: www.worldclimate.com

1. Which city has the coldest winters?

_____

2. In which months are temperatures in all three cities most alike?

_____

3. Which city has the smallest difference between its warmest and
coldest temperatures?

_____

Name _____ Class _____ Date _____

Section Quiz

Directions Answer the following questions using what you learned in Section 1.

1. _____ Why is Lake Baikal significant?
   a. It is shrinking because of too much irrigation.
   b. It is frozen 12 months of the year.
   c. It is the starting point of the Trans-Siberia Railway.
   d. It holds 20 percent of Earth's fresh water.

2. _____ What is European Russia's longest river?
   a. Dvina
   b. Lena
   c. Volga
   d. Yenisey

3. _____ Which of the following is true of the Russian Far East?
   a. It is the coldest region in Russia.
   b. It lies just east of the Ural Mountains.
   c. It has many active volcanoes.
   d. It is home to the city of St. Petersburg.

4. _____ Which of the following does Russia lack?
   a. petroleum reserves
   b. many usable harbors
   c. coniferous forests
   d. continuous, long coastlines

5. _____ What group makes up 80 percent of Russian citizens?
   a. Armenians
   b. Mongols
   c. Slavs
   d. Turks

6. Complete the table below. For each geographic feature listed on the left, write down whether it is found in European Russia or Asiatic Russia.

a. Lake Baikal	
b. Higher population density	
c. Capital city of Moscow	
d. Mineral resources	
e. Good farmland	
f. Vast stretches of permafrost	

T147

Chapter Atlas

- Model preparing to read by previewing the Key Ideas, Key Terms, headings, visuals, and captions. Have students make predictions about what they will learn. For ELL support, post the prompt, "I predict I will read about . . ."

- Preview and practice the skill, Read a Physical Map, by looking at the map *Russia: Physical*. Ask, What is the name of the peninsula in the Russian Far East?

- Preteach this section's high-use Academic Vocabulary and Key Terms using the table on the next page and in-text definitions. Have students practice Key Terms by completing the *Word Wise* page in their journals.

GUIDE ON THE SIDE

 Reading Skill

Label an Outline Map While they read, have students identify the Places to Know! on the outline map of the region in the **Student Journal.**

Physical Features

- **Identify Main Ideas** What is Siberia? (the Asian part of Russia)

- **Identify Evidence** What evidence shows that Russia stretches almost halfway around the world? (It has 11 time zones out of the world's 24; it takes 11 hours to fly the full east-to-west length of the country.)

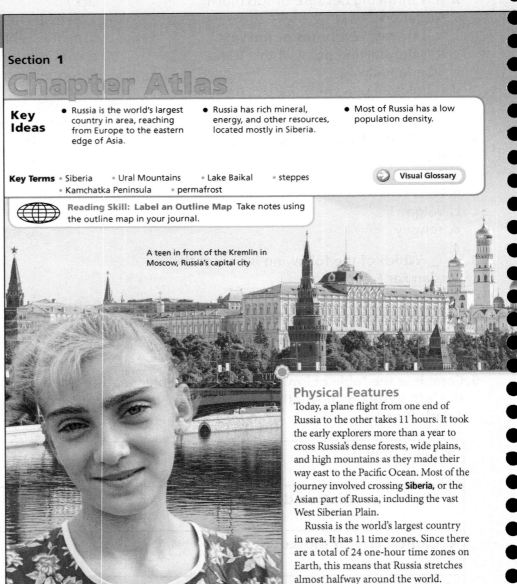

Section 1

Chapter Atlas

Key Ideas
- Russia is the world's largest country in area, reaching from Europe to the eastern edge of Asia.
- Russia has rich mineral, energy, and other resources, located mostly in Siberia.
- Most of Russia has a low population density.

Key Terms • Siberia • Ural Mountains • Lake Baikal • steppes • Kamchatka Peninsula • permafrost

Visual Glossary

 Reading Skill: Label an Outline Map Take notes using the outline map in your journal.

A teen in front of the Kremlin in Moscow, Russia's capital city

Physical Features

Today, a plane flight from one end of Russia to the other takes 11 hours. It took the early explorers more than a year to cross Russia's dense forests, wide plains, and high mountains as they made their way east to the Pacific Ocean. Most of the journey involved crossing **Siberia,** or the Asian part of Russia, including the vast West Siberian Plain.

Russia is the world's largest country in area. It has 11 time zones. Since there are a total of 24 one-hour time zones on Earth, this means that Russia stretches almost halfway around the world.

ACADEMIC VOCABULARY

High-Use Word	Definition and Sample Sentence
spectacular	*adj.* striking or excellent *The sunset over the ocean was spectacular.*
maintain	*v.* to keep in good condition *Javier maintains his house because he is proud of it.*
pursue	*v.* to follow *The teacher pursued a policy of assigning daily homework.*

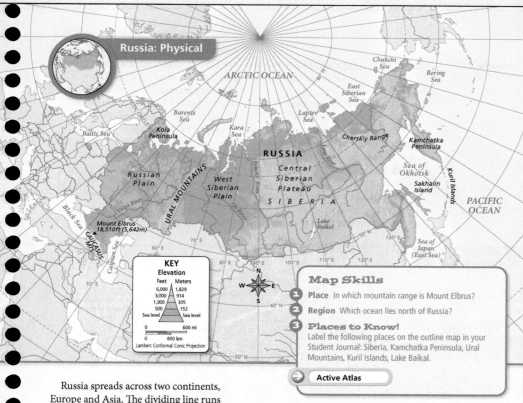

Russia: Physical

KEY
Elevation
Feet	Meters
6,000	1,829
3,000	914
1,000	305
500	152
Sea level	Sea level

0   600 mi
0   600 km
Lambert Conformal Conic Projection

Map Skills

1. **Place** In which mountain range is Mount Elbrus?
2. **Region** Which ocean lies north of Russia?
3. **Places to Know!**
Label the following places on the outline map in your Student Journal: Siberia, Kamchatka Peninsula, Ural Mountains, Kuril Islands, Lake Baikal.

 Active Atlas

Russia spreads across two continents, Europe and Asia. The dividing line runs along the low peaks of the **Ural Mountains,** a range that separates European Russia from Asian Russia. European Russia is located east of Latvia, Lithuania, Estonia, Belarus, and Ukraine. Asian Russia lies immediately north of China, Mongolia, and Kazakhstan.

A Vast Land
Russia has many different kinds of landforms and waterways. The Russian Plain covers much of European Russia.

It stretches east to the Ural Mountains. South of the Russian Plain are the Caucasus Mountains. These mountains run east-west between the Caspian Sea and the Black Sea. They form the southern border between European Russia and Asia.

East of the Urals is the broad West Siberian Plain. Farther east are central and eastern Siberia. This huge area consists of rugged plateaus framed by high mountains on the east and south.

MAP SKILLS 1. Caucasus Mountains **2.** Arctic Ocean **3.** Places should be labeled accurately.

GUIDE ON THE SIDE

- **Identify Main Ideas** On what two continents is Russia located? (Europe and Asia)

- **Connect** What countries lie to the south of Asiatic Russia? (China, Mongolia, and Kazakhstan)

A Vast Land

- **Compare and Contrast** How are the Ural and Caucasus mountains alike? (Both ranges serve as boundaries between Europe and Asia.)

- **Identify Details** What large plain lies east of the Ural Mountains? (West Siberian Plain)

Analyze Maps Have students look at the physical map of Russia.

- What mountain range is in northeast Russia? (the Cherskiy)

- What large island lies off Russia's east coast? (Sakhalin Island)

 Active Atlas

Have students go online to learn more about the physical geography of Russia.

QUICK FACTS

Lake Baikal Located in southeastern Siberia, Lake Baikal is the oldest freshwater lake on Earth. Its age is estimated to be 20 to 25 million years old. It is 395 miles long and almost 50 miles across at its widest point. Its surface area is about 12,200 square miles. More than 330 rivers and streams flow into it. Among them are the Selenga, Barguzin, Upper Angara, Chikoy, and Uda rivers. Lake Baikal is located in a hollow surrounded by mountains, and the region experiences tectonic activity. An earthquake in 1862 flooded part of the Selenga delta and created a new bay in Lake Baikal.

GUIDE ON THE SIDE

- **Summarize** What is European Russia's longest river, and where does it end? (the Volga, the Caspian Sea)
- **Compare and Contrast** What do the Dvina, Ob, Yenisey, and Lena rivers all have in common? (They flow north.)
- **Infer** Why do you think that rivers, such as the Amur, are often used as national boundaries? (Sample: They make clear dividing lines, and they slow down invaders, so they can be used for defense.)
- **Draw Conclusions** What geographic reason explains why Russia would not have many usable harbors on its long northern coastline? (Sample: Because of the cold climate, the harbors are often blocked by ice.)

Analyze Maps Have students look at the climate map of Russia.

- Where is the tundra climate found? (on the northern coastline)
- Why are there no areas of humid subtropical climate? (Russia is too far north.)

 Active Atlas

Have students go online to learn more about the climates of Russia.

spectacular, *adj.,* striking or excellent

Many of these <u>spectacular</u> mountains are volcanic in origin. Some are covered by glaciers year-round.

European Russia's longest river, the Volga, flows into the Caspian Sea. This river is famous in the songs and stories of the Russian people. Russia's European rivers also include the Don, which flows into the Black Sea, and the Dvina, which flows north to an arm of the Arctic Ocean.

In Siberia, there are many other large rivers that flow north to the Arctic Ocean. These include Russia's longest, the Yenisey, as well as the Ob and Lena. Another important Siberian river is called the Ankara. Far to the east is the mighty Amur River, which forms the border between Russia and China.

Despite its many rivers, canals, and long coastlines, Russia lacks many good harbors and ports. In European Russia, usable ports include St. Petersburg, Kaliningrad, Novorossiysk, and Sochi. In addition, there are ports in Murmansk in the far north on the Arctic Ocean and Vladivostok on the Pacific coast.

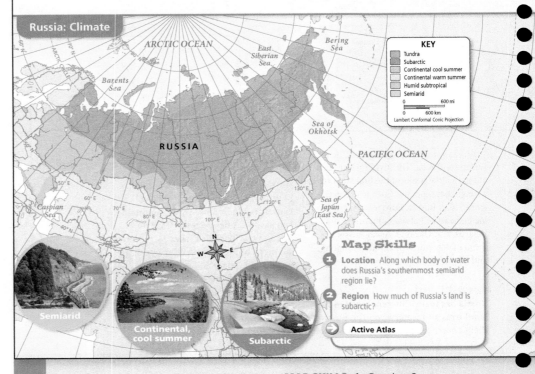

Russia: Climate

Map Skills

1. **Location** Along which body of water does Russia's southernmost semiarid region lie?
2. **Region** How much of Russia's land is subarctic?

→ **Active Atlas**

MAP SKILLS 1. Caspian Sea
2. more than half

GEOGRAPHY

The Kamchatka Peninsula The Kamchatka Peninsula lies between the Sea of Okhotsk to the west and the Pacific Ocean and the Bering Sea to the east. The peninsula is about 750 miles long and 300 miles wide at its broadest point. It has very rugged terrain. Two mountain ranges extend down the peninsula: the Sredinny Mountains extend down the center, and the Vostochny Mountains extend down the eastern side. Located in the Vostochny is the Klyuchevskaya Volcano, which is one of the highest volcanoes in the world. It rises to an elevation of 15,584 feet. It has erupted more than 50 times in the last three centuries.

Russia, however, does have many large lakes and seas. Perhaps the most famous is **Lake Baikal** in the heart of Siberia. More than one mile deep, Lake Baikal holds about 20 percent of Earth's fresh water— more than all of the North American Great Lakes combined. Baikal is also home to plants and animals found nowhere else. Due to the threat of pollution from factories located along its shores, Lake Baikal was the birthplace of Russia's environmental movement.

Reading Check Which landform separates European Russia from Asian Russia?

Climate and Vegetation

Vast stretches of Russian lands have a subarctic climate because they lie near the Arctic Circle. North of this area is the tundra climate region, a cold, dry, treeless area covered in snow for most of the year. European Russia in the southwest has a continental climate. In cities such as Moscow and St. Petersburg, people experience long, cold winters and warm summers. Parts of southern Russia have a semiarid, or moderately dry, climate.

Russia's natural vegetation is closely tied to its climate. In the cool continental climate north of Moscow, thick coniferous forests grow. South of Moscow are temperate forests. To the east, vast areas of grasslands called **steppes** cover the land. Here, mild, moist summers and rich soils make good farmland.

In Siberia, weather and climate are more extreme than in European Russia. Here, winters are long and cold. Cold, dry conditions in parts of Siberia account for a type of low-lying vegetation called tundra. Tundra covers about one tenth of Russia and stretches all the way from the Finnish border east to the **Kamchatka Peninsula.** This peninsula in the Russian Far East is famous for its 160 volcanoes, 29 of which are active.

Near Yakutsk, Siberia, a family hauls water that they took from a hole in the ice on a local lake.

READING CHECK the Ural Mountains

QUICK FACTS

The Amur Tiger The largest living cat in the world is the Amur tiger, also called the Siberian tiger (although it is found in Russia's Far East not Siberia). Adult males can weigh 800 pounds and be up to 10 feet long. By the mid-1900s century, there were only 50 Amur tigers alive in Russia. Today, there are about 450 Amur tigers in the wild, but the species is still considered endangered. The Amur tiger faces threats such as poaching, impoverished local hunters, practitioners of traditional Chinese medicine, and loss of habitat due to fire or logging. Protecting and preserving the Russian cat population is an ongoing joint effort of Russian conservationists, various NGOs, and other international wildlife conservation groups.

GUIDE ON THE SIDE

- **Problem Solve** What problem does permafrost cause? (It is permanently frozen soil that is difficult to build on.)
- **Cause and Effect** Why does the Far East region have different vegetation than the rest of Russia? (It is warmer.)

Russia's Resources

- **Draw Conclusions** What industries would you expect to find in Siberia? (fishing, logging, mining)
- **Identify Evidence** What details show that Siberia has many energy resources? (It provides hydroelectric power, coal, oil, and gas.)

Analyze Charts Have students look at the graph about railroads.

- About how many more miles of railroad does Russia have than Germany? (almost twice as many)

 myWorld Activity

Roam Across Russia Find Step-by-Step Instructions and an Activity Support on pp. T144–T145. **(Visual/Verbal)**

 Data Discovery

Have students go online for more about the Trans-Siberian Railroad.

South of the tundra is the Russian taiga, a land of dense coniferous forests. The Russian taiga covers more than four million square miles (10 million square kilometers). One of the many challenges for human settlement in northern Russia is **permafrost.** This is permanently frozen soil that often lies beneath the tundra and the taiga. It makes construction of roads, railroads, and housing difficult.

Vegetation in Russia's Far East region differs from that of the rest of the country. Because this area is close to the ocean and is located farther to the south, it is warmer and has vegetation similar to the nearby Koreas. Its animals include the Amur tiger, the world's largest cat. The eastern edge of Russia features the Kuril Islands and the Kamchatka Peninsula.

Reading Check Where in Russia are there active volcanoes?

 myWorld Activity
Roam Across Russia

Russia's Resources

Russia has rich mineral and energy resources, especially in Siberia. Its resources include timber, fish, and hydroelectric power. About one third of all of Earth's coal is located in Siberia. In spite of extremes of climate and the country's massive size, vast reserves of oil and gas in West Siberia have made Russia wealthy in recent years.

Russia also has metal ores such as iron, gold, cobalt, nickel, and platinum ore. It sells these valuable minerals to many different buyers around the world for industrial use.

It can be difficult to mine Russia's rich natural resources because they are so hard to reach. Long distances and harsh climates separate resources from processing plants and markets.

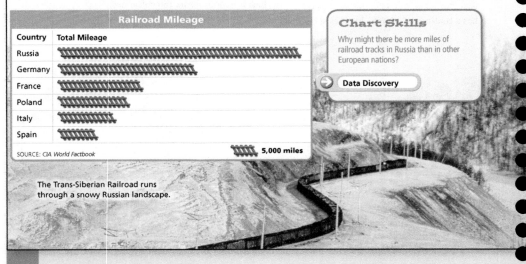

Railroad Mileage

Country	Total Mileage
Russia	
Germany	
France	
Poland	
Italy	
Spain	

SOURCE: CIA World Factbook

5,000 miles

Chart Skills

Why might there be more miles of railroad tracks in Russia than in other European nations?

Data Discovery

The Trans-Siberian Railroad runs through a snowy Russian landscape.

READING CHECK the Kamchatka Peninsula

CHART SKILLS It has more territory that needs to be linked by railroad than other nations do.

ECONOMICS

Mineral Exports Russia is among the world's top producers of the metals tungsten and cobalt. Both metals occur in small quantities in Earth's crust and require extensive processing to extract. Tungsten is an extremely strong metal that is resistant to many acids. It is used to create stronger steels and other alloys, and tungsten wire is used in light bulb filaments. Cobalt is one of only three metals that are magnetic at room temperature, and it remains stable under very high temperatures. It is used to create heat-resistant and magnetic alloys. It also goes into alloys used to make tools.

This makes it important for Russia to build and <u>maintain</u> an extensive transportation system to move products to markets. The poor quality of roads can make transport difficult. Truck drivers often find it easier to drive on frozen rivers and lakes than on Russian roads.

Many of Russia's great rivers are navigable, or passable, for only a few months of the year because they are usually blocked by ice. Underground pipelines generally transport Russia's huge reserves of oil and natural gas. An extensive railroad network moves goods to consumers.

Large-scale economic development in Siberia began only after the Trans-Siberian Railroad was completed in 1905. This famous railroad connects the city of Moscow in the west with Vladivostok on the Pacific. It also connects with rail lines running to Mongolia and China. It was built to help Russians settle the open lands of Siberia, to develop industrial centers, and to transport troops to the Pacific to protect Russia against threats of invasion by Japan and China.

maintain, *v.*, to keep in good condition

Reading Check Name two challenges Russia faces in developing its economy.

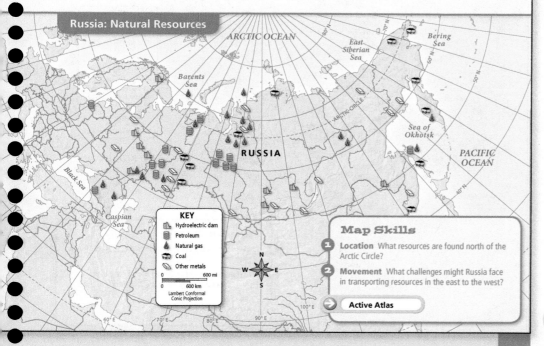

Russia: Natural Resources

ARCTIC OCEAN
Bering Sea
East Siberian Sea
Barents Sea
ARCTIC CIRCLE
Sea of Okhotsk
RUSSIA
PACIFIC OCEAN
Black Sea
Caspian Sea

KEY
- Hydroelectric dam
- Petroleum
- Natural gas
- Coal
- Other metals

0   600 mi
0   600 km
Lambert Conformal Conic Projection

Map Skills

1 **Location** What resources are found north of the Arctic Circle?

2 **Movement** What challenges might Russia face in transporting resources in the east to the west?

 Active Atlas

MAP SKILLS 1. coal, metals, petroleum, natural gas **2.** great distances, building roads and railroads over permafrost

READING CHECK Great distances separate the resources from processing plants; the roads are generally poor.

GUIDE ON THE SIDE

- **Problem Solve** How do Russian truck drivers avoid bad roads? (They drive on frozen rivers.)
- **Synthesize** What geographic feature of Siberia makes it difficult to build roads? (the permafrost)
- **Cause and Effect** Why was the Trans-Siberian Railroad built? (to encourage settlement of open spaces, spur development of industry, and ease transport of troops)

Analyze Maps Have students examine the natural resources map.

- What mineral is found in far northeastern Russia? (coal)
- Would you expect to find more industry in the east or west? (west)

 Active Atlas

Have students go online to learn more about Russia's resources.

CORE CONCEPTS: POPULATION DISTRIBUTION

Review Core Concept 6.2 before discussing the population patterns in Russia. Remind students of the difference between population distribution and population density. Review that population densities are an average and that the actual number of people living in a place might vary across the region being described. Finally, ask students the following questions: When you studied Western Europe, what did you learn about how climate affects population distribution? How did the availability of resources affect population? What other factors affected where people live? Encourage students to note whether similar patterns are true of Russia.

GUIDE ON THE SIDE

The People of Russia

- **Draw Conclusions** Why does the majority of the Russian population live in European Russia? (That is the region with the mildest climates and best soils.)

- **Identify Details** What are the two largest cities in Russia? (Moscow and St. Petersburg)

- **Infer** St. Petersburg is often called Russia's "window to Europe." What reason can you give to explain this name? (Sample: It was built to be a city that would rival the capitals of Europe, and it is located in Europe.)

Analyze Maps Have students look at the population map.

- Around what city is the region of greatest population density? (Moscow)

- Would you characterize Russia as having an overall low or high population density? (low)

The People of Russia

Russia has a population of about 140 million people. Most live in the European part of the country. Russia's most densely settled areas also have the best climates and soils for agriculture. In contrast, the huge landmass of Siberia is sparsely populated, with around 20 people per square mile.

The largest cities are also located in the west, in European Russia. Moscow, the capital, is the largest metropolitan area in Russia, with more than 10 million people.

St. Petersburg, Russia's second largest city, is located on the Baltic Sea. It was called Leningrad during the Soviet era. St. Petersburg was founded by Russia's tsar, or emperor, Peter the Great, to rival the capitals of Europe.

Russia's huge population consists of many diverse ethnic groups with many languages and customs. The first Russians were East Slavs, who migrated into the area from east-central Europe. Today, about 80 percent of the population are Russian-speaking Slavs.

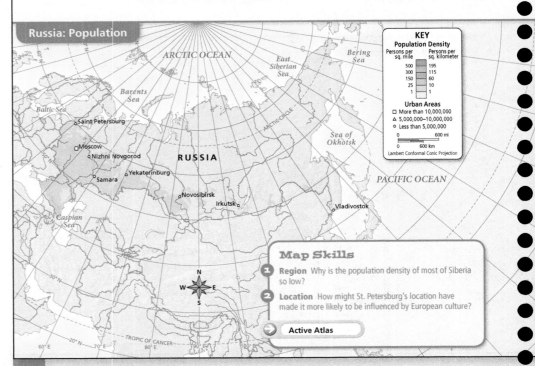

Russia: Population

KEY

Population Density

Persons per sq. mile	Persons per sq. kilometer
500	195
300	115
150	60
25	10
1	1

Urban Areas
- ☐ More than 10,000,000
- △ 5,000,000–10,000,000
- ○ Less than 5,000,000

0 ——— 600 mi
0 ——— 600 km
Lambert Conformal Conic Projection

Map Skills

1. **Region** Why is the population density of most of Siberia so low?

2. **Location** How might St. Petersburg's location have made it more likely to be influenced by European culture?

Active Atlas

ANSWERS

MAP SKILLS 1. cold climate **2.** It is near other European nations.

READING CHECK East Slavs

SECTION 1 ASSESSMENT 1. Samples: Siberia is a vast region. The Ural Mountains divide Europe from Asia. Lake Baikal has 20 percent of Earth's fresh water. The steppes are grasslands. The Kamchatka Peninsula has volcanoes. Permafrost makes construction difficult. **2.** The climate is very cold, so people must dress warmly and build on permafrost. **3.** Most mineral resources are in Siberia. **4.** It lies farther

CULTURE

Ethnic Groups of Russia Of the more than 100 ethnic groups in Russia, only five are large enough to constitute one percent or more of the population. Russians make up 79.8 percent of Russia's population. The second-largest group is the Tatars, which is a group of related Turkic-speaking peoples. They make up 3.8 percent of the population. The Tatars were originally nomadic tribes who lived in northeastern Mongolia and the area around Lake Baikal. The third-largest ethnic group in Russia is the Ukrainians, who make up 2 percent of the population. Like Russians, Ukrainians are a Slavic people, and their language is closely related to Russian. The next two ethnic groups are both Turkic peoples: the Bashkir make up 1.2 percent of the population, and the Chuvash make up 1.1 percent of the population.

In Moscow, Boris (right) joins his friends to talk about sports and school. Boris participates in skateboarding competitions all over the world.

Language Lesson

This family lives in a village near Siberia's Lake Baikal. They belong to the minority Buryat nationality but also speak Russian.

Traditionally, the Slavic people who form most of the population were Russian Orthodox Christians. However, the communist rulers of the Soviet Union <u>pursued</u> a policy of discouraging religion. Today, after the collapse of the Soviet Union, more and more Russians attend Orthodox churches. Religious observance has also increased for Russia's many Muslims, Protestants, Jews, and Buddhists.

Along with Slavic Russians, there are at least 100 other ethnic and nationality groups in Russia. Each has a distinctive culture, language, and religion. Since Russian-speaking Slavs have dominated the nation for such a long time, many of these minority groups struggle to maintain their unique identities.

pursue, *v.,* to follow

Reading Check Who were the first Russians?

Section 1 Assessment

Key Terms

1. Use each of the following key terms in a complete sentence: Siberia, Ural Mountains, Lake Baikal, steppes, Kamchatka Peninsula, permafrost

Key Ideas

2. What challenges does climate present for human settlement in Russia?

3. Where are most of Russia's mineral resources found?

4. Why does the Far East region of Russia have a milder climate than most of the rest of the country?

Think Critically

5. **Identify Evidence** What facts could you use to explain why Siberia has a low population density?

6. **Solve Problems** What might minority groups do to preserve their identity in a country whose population is mostly ethnic Russian?

? Essential Question

What should governments do?

7. Look at the railroad mileage chart in this section. The Russian government paid the cost of building the Trans-Siberian Railroad. Why might governments invest in transportation systems? Go to your Student Journal to record your answer.

south, closer to the moderating influence of the ocean. **5.** Samples: Data could include temperatures to show the harsh climate, vegetation maps to show that it has shrubby plants, and data about permafrost to explain why construction is difficult **6.** Samples: They can teach their languages, beliefs, and customs to their children; they can write books and make films to preserve their culture. **7.** Sample: Transportation systems are needed for economic growth. In Russia's case, the country needed a way to reach the resources in Siberia.

ANSWERS

GUIDE ON THE SIDE

- **Summarize** What changes has religion undergone in Russia in the last century? (Traditionally, people were Russian Orthodox. Under communism, the government discouraged religion. Since the communist government fell, church attendance has increased.)

- **Identify Details** What other religions are practiced in Russia besides Russian Orthodox Christianity? (Protestant Christianity, Judaism, Islam, Buddhism)

- **Identify Main Ideas** How many ethnic groups are in Russia? (more than 100)

Language Lesson

Have students go online to learn more about the languages of Russia.

SECTION 2 LESSON PLAN

History of Russia

OBJECTIVES

Students will know

- important events and people from the history of tsarist Russia.
- reasons for the rise and fall of the Soviet Union.

Students will be able to

- explain the causes and effects of the Russian Revolution.
- sequence events from Russian history.

SET EXPECTATIONS

In this section, students will

- read History of Russia.
- participate in Making a Living Timeline.
- go On Assignment in Russia, explore a timeline, and visit Red Square.

CORE CONCEPTS

You may wish to teach or reteach the following lessons from the Core Concepts Handbook:

- Economic Systems, pp. 62–63
- Political Systems, pp. 106–107
- Cultural Diffusion and Change, pp. 96–97

KEY

Differentiated Instruction

L1 Special Needs   **L2** Extra Support

L3 On-Level   **L4** Challenge

English Language Instruction

ELL Beginner   **ELL** Early Intermediate   **ELL** Intermediate

ELL Early Advanced   **ELL** Advanced

---

1 Connect
Make learning meaningful

Make Connections Discuss what it is like to be in a group where one person insists on always getting his or her own way. Ask, How might other members respond? Explain that Russia has a long history of autocratic rulers who had unlimited power. Ask, How might people respond to such rulers?

ELL Early Intermediate Introduce the term *tsar*, pronounce it, and define it as a Russian emperor. Explain that it comes from the Roman title *Caesar*.

Activate Prior Knowledge Remind students that they studied the French Revolution in the chapter *Europe in Modern Times*. Explain they will read about another revolution in this chapter. Post a class definition of revolution that you will return to once you read about the Russian Revolution. Ask them to predict how a revolution might affect Russia.

L2 Extra Support Give students this list of events. Ask them to predict the order: rule by radicals; revolution overthrows government; rule by absolute monarch; radical government kills thousands. Correct the sequence after reading.

Prepare Follow the steps in the section **Preview.** Preteach the Key Terms. Then have students complete *Word Wise* in their journals using in-text clues and the glossary for help.

2 Experience
Teach knowledge and skills

Read Use **Background** notes and **Guide on the Side** questions to model active reading. Have students use *Take Notes* in their **Student Journal** to list causes and effects of the Russian Revolution and the fall of the Soviet Union. Have students complete **21st Century Online Tutor** *Analyze Cause and Effect*, and apply this skill to reading the section.

L3 On Level Have students read *Enrichment: Josef Stalin* and then create a timeline of his life.

ELL Advanced Point out that the terms *socialism* and *communism* contain the suffix -*ism*, which often stands for a set of beliefs or practices. Ask students to think of other words using -*ism*.

L4 Challenge Have pairs of students research the 15 republics of the Soviet Union, which are now independent nations. Create a class poster gallery or Web site with links about each nation, highlighting its capital, whether it is in Europe or Asia, its population, its form of government, and a unique cultural feature.

 Practice: myWorld Activity Students work in groups to make a living timeline in which each student presents one event in chronological order. **Step-by-Step Instructions** and **More Activities** follow on p. T150.

SECTION 2 RESOURCE GUIDE

FOR THE STUDENT

my worldgeography.com Student Center

- Timeline
- Culture Close-up
- Active Atlas

Student Edition (print and online)

- History of Russia

Student Journal (print and online)

- Section 2 Word Wise
- Section 2 Take Notes

21st Century Learning Online Tutor

- Analyze Cause and Effect
- Sequence

FOR THE TEACHER

my worldgeography.com Teacher Center

- Online Lesson Planner
- Presentations for Projection
- SuccessTracker

ProGuide: Europe and Russia

- Section 2 Lesson Plan, pp. T148–T149
- myWorld Activity Step-by-Step Instructions, p. T150
- Activity Support: Events Table, p. T151
- myWorld Geography Enrichment, p. T152
- Section Quiz, p. T153

Accelerating the Progress of ELLs

- Reading Support Strategies, p. 42

---

3 Understand
Assess understanding

Review Review *Word Wise* and *Take Notes* in the **Student Journal.**

Assess Knowledge and Skills Use the Section Assessment and Section Quiz to check students' progress.

Assess Understanding Review students' responses to the Section Assessment Essential Question prompt.

Remediate Use these strategies to review and remediate.

If students struggle to . . .	Try these strategies.
Identify effects of the Russian Revolution	Give them a two-column table for note taking with the heads *Political Effects* and *Economic Effects*.
Analyze causes of the fall of the Soviet Union	As a class, create a mural-size cause-and-effect diagram on which to record details from the section.
Sequence events	Assign additional practice with the **21st Century Online Tutor.**

ELL Support

ELL Objective Students will use English to describe important historic events.

Cultural Connections Let students use their native languages to describe a historic event from their family's country of origin. Then have them use English to try to explain when it happened.

ELL Intermediate Content Tip Explain the term *collectivization* by saying that the government "collected" land from many farms and joined it into one large farm that the government owned and operated.

ELL Activity Have students work with a partner to practice describing events. Each student should choose a recent current event. Then they should answer the following questions by completing the sentence models.
Who was involved? _____ was involved.
What did they do? They _____.
When did this event happen?
It happened on _____. **(Verbal)**

 20 min

myWorld Activity   **Step-by-Step Instructions**

Make a Living Timeline

OBJECTIVES

Students will
- identify a sequence of events in Russian history.
- create a human timeline in which each student represents an event.

LEARNING STYLE
- Verbal
- Kinesthetic

21st Century Learning
- Sequence

MATERIALS
- Activity Support: Events Table, p. T151

Activity Steps

1. Tell the class that they are going to work in groups to create a living timeline of Russian history in which each student will represent an event.

2. Divide the class into five groups, each with an assigned time period: Group A, up to 1400; Group B, 1480–1681; Group C, 1682–1905; Group D, from World War I to Stalin's death; and Group E, from after Stalin to the present.

3. Give each student a copy of *Activity Support: Events Table*. Working as a team and using their texts, students should fill out the table with the name of each event, a brief summary of what happened, and any clues as to when it took place. Tell groups to make sure they have one event per group member.

L2 **Extra Support** Remind students that even if no date is given, they can often figure out approximately when an event took place. Tell them to look for clues such as "after a year."

4. After the table is done, groups should assign each member an event. Using the time clues in the table, the group should determine the sequence of events.

5. Students should work individually to write a brief description of their event. They should write the name of their event in large print on the front of a sheet of paper with the description on the back.

6. When the groups are ready, form a living timeline of Russian history by putting the whole class in line, with Group A first, then Group B, etc. Within each group, students should line up in the sequence of their events. Students should take turns holding up their paper, naming their event, and reading the description aloud. After the presentation, ask the class if any events need to be moved.

ELL **Intermediate** Give students the option of acting out part of their event instead of writing about it.

More Activities From myWorld Teachers

Local Connection Ask students to brainstorm the problems or areas for improvement that they see in their communities. Have groups of students work to write Five-Year Plans outlining what should be done to fix those problems. **(Interpersonal)**

Window to Europe Have students work with a partner to locate St. Petersburg on a map. They should write an illustrated letter to Peter the Great

explaining the geographic reasons why he should build a city there. **(Visual/Verbal)**

Free the Serfs! Have students write a poem or a rap song calling for the tsar to free the serfs. Play other protest music in class to give them examples from real life. Let them present their work in class. **(Rhythmic/Verbal)**

 my worldgeography.com   **Teacher Center** ⟶   Find additional resources in the online Teacher Center.

Name _____ Class _____ Date _____

myWorld Activity Support   **Events Table**

Make a Living Timeline

Directions You and the members of your group are going to
become experts on one period of Russian history. Working in your
group, review the part of Section 2 that covers your assigned period
and identify events. Pick as many events as there are people in your
group. On the table below, record the name of each event, what
happened, and the date or information about when it happened.
Then assign one event to each member of your group. Each person
should write 3–4 sentences describing his or her assigned event.

Event	What Happened	When It Happened

My Event _____

My Description of the Event _____

_____

_____

_____

Make the Timeline Write the name of your event in large letters on
a sheet of paper. On the back of the paper, write a description of the
event and when it happened. Then stand in line with the rest of your
group, so that the events are in sequence. In chronological order, first
to last, name your events and read the descriptions to the class.

Name _____ Class _____ Date _____

Enrichment: Josef Stalin

Directions Read the biography below. Answer the questions and complete the activity that follows.

Josef Stalin was born in 1879 in Georgia. His father was a shoemaker and his mother was a clothes washer. His name was originally Iosif Vissarionovich Dzhugashvili. As an adult he took the name *Stalin*, meaning "man of steel." Stalin became interested in revolutionary ideas as a young man. He took part in many strikes and demonstrations. As a result, he was arrested seven times. Stalin joined the Bolsheviks, and in 1912 Lenin gave him a place on the Central Committee. During the Russian Revolution, Stalin played an important role and gained high office in the revolutionary government.

After Lenin died in 1924, Stalin gradually wiped out his rivals. He ordered them killed or forced them to leave. Stalin increased his control over the Soviet government until he was acting as a dictator. In 1928, he put his first Five-Year Plan into place. The policy of collectivizing, or combining, farms proved to be a disaster. It caused the deaths of as many as ten million people. Stalin also forced people to build factories and industrialize, which created problems such as pollution. In addition, during the 1930s, Stalin persecuted educated people. He was afraid that they would challenge his authority.

At the start of World War II, Stalin was an ally of Hitler. After Germany invaded the Soviet Union, Stalin joined the Allies. After the war ended in 1945, he forced the nations of Eastern Europe to set up communist governments friendly to the Soviet Union. These actions caused the Cold War with the West. By the time Stalin died in 1953, he had left behind economic and political disasters that would last for decades.

1. In what ways did Stalin affect the Soviet Union?

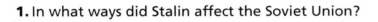

_____

2. Why do you think he chose the name Stalin? What did he want it to convey?

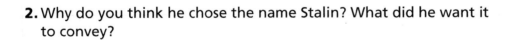

_____

3. Activity Create a timeline of Stalin's life.

T152

Name _____ Class _____ Date _____

Section Quiz

Directions Answer the following questions using what you learned in Section 2.

1. _____ Which communist leader was known for brutal policies that led to the death of millions of Russians?
   a. Nikita Khrushchev
   b. Vladimir Lenin
   c. Josef Stalin
   d. Boris Yeltsin

2. _____ Which empire influenced the religion, architecture, and art of Kievan Rus?
   a. Byzantine empire
   b. Han China
   c. Mongol empire
   d. Ottoman empire

3. _____ Which event caused so much unrest that it helped bring about the Russian Revolution?
   a. Crimean War
   b. October Manifesto
   c. Russo-Japanese War
   d. World War I

4. _____ During the 1700s and 1800s, how did Russia differ from Western Europe?
   a. It was the first country to build a railway across its nation.
   b. It established the first communist government in the world.
   c. It freed its serfs, while other nations kept them bound to the land.
   d. It did not develop industry or representative government.

5. _____ What was the unexpected result of Mikhail Gorbachev's reforms?
   a. The tsar was killed.
   b. The Soviet Union fell apart.
   c. Stalin came to power.
   d. Voters elected Vladimir Putin.

6. Complete the table below by writing one reason why each person was significant.

Peter the Great	
Nicholas II	
Vladimir Lenin	
Boris Yeltsin	

History of Russia

- Model preparing to read by previewing the Key Ideas, Key Terms, headings, visuals, and captions. Have students make predictions about what they will learn. For ELL support, post the prompt, "I predict I will read about . . ."

- Preview and practice the reading skill, Cause and Effect, by using examples from a book or movie.

- Preteach this section's high-use Academic Vocabulary and Key Terms using the table on the next page and in-text definitions. Have students practice Key Terms by completing the *Word Wise* page in their journals.

GUIDE ON THE SIDE

Reading Skill

Cause and Effect While they read, have students practice this skill by completing the *Take Notes* graphic organizer in the **Student Journal.**

Russia Emerges

- **Identify Main Ideas** From what ethnic group are most Russians descended? (East Slavs)

- **Identify Details** Who were some of the groups that invaded Russia? (Goths, Huns, Avars, Magyars, Khazars)

- **Categorize** What did the cities of Kiev and Novgorod begin as? (trading posts)

 Timeline

Have students go online to learn more about events in the history of Russia.

Section 2

History of Russia

Key Ideas
- Following centuries of invasion, Russia became an empire under the tsars.
- The Russian Revolution introduced communism and led to the establishment of the Soviet Union.
- Communism's flaws caused the Soviet Union to collapse, leading to its breakup into Russia and other republics.

Key Terms • tsar • Kremlin • serf • Bolsheviks • soviet • collectivization

 Visual Glossary

Reading Skill: Cause and Effect Take notes using the graphic organizer in your journal.

Russia's history spans many centuries. It is a rich story of invaders, ruthless leaders, and dramatic change that continues today.

Russia Emerges

Modern Russians are descended from East Slavs who migrated from Poland and Ukraine into western Russia in the 400s and 500s. They encountered invading Goths from Germany, along with Huns, Avars, Magyars, and Khazars from Asia.

The East Slavs The East Slavs were energetic traders. They founded trading posts along rivers that became the cities of Kiev and Novgorod. By the 800s, Scandinavian raiders and merchants, called Vikings, dominated Novgorod, Kiev, and other trading centers. They soon merged with the Slavic population.

Early Russia The Scythians, who arrived on the steppes before the East Slavs, were skilled goldsmiths. ▼

Kievan Rus Period The Viking prince Rurik and his allies invade Kiev in this medieval Russian drawing. ▶

East Slav

| 200 | 300 | 400 | 500 | 600 | 700 | 800 |

ACADEMIC VOCABULARY

High-Use Word	Definition and Sample Sentence
servitude	*n.* a legal requirement to work for another *The peasants lived in servitude and worked for nobles.*
denounce	*v.* to reject publicly *The rebels denounced the king for his harsh rule.*

The role of Vikings in Russian history remains uncertain. Russia's *Primary Chronicle* claims that Slav and Finnish tribes invited a Viking of the Rus tribe to rule them. Some later scholars claimed that "Rus" refers to a Slav, not Viking, tribe. In any case, it was the Rus who gave their name to the first known East Slavic state: the Kievan Rus.

The Kievan Rus Forms Located in present-day Ukraine, Kiev became the region's economic and cultural center. Kiev's early rulers grew rich from trade and united the Slavic tribes. Under Vladimir, the Kievan Rus formed close ties with the Byzantine empire around the year 1000.

Vladimir adopted the Byzantines' Eastern Orthodox Christianity. He converted all of Kiev in a mass ceremony. Byzantine culture influenced Russian language, art, and music as well as the architectural style of Russian churches.

Gradually, many tribal leaders became princes. Princes were granted large areas of land, or appanages. They ruled these appanages and passed them on to family members. Competition between princes in the Kievan Rus was fierce. Some historians believe this rivalry weakened the state and invited a Mongol invasion.

In 1240, Mongol armies from Central Asia, known as the Golden Horde, took Kiev. The Kievan Rus collapsed. Russian princes now had to accept the authority of Mongol khans, or rulers.

As Kiev declined, the city of Moscow began to grow in importance. Its princes ruled an area known as Muscovy. It was a key trading center, and the Mongol khans favored its rulers. In 1328, the head of the Eastern Orthodox Church moved to Moscow, making the city even more important.

Reading Check **What caused the fall of the Kievan Rus?**

Mongol Period Tamerlane, a Turkic chief, challenged Mongol rule in Russia in the 1300s. ▼

Muscovy Period Ivan IV, or Ivan the Terrible, was the first Russian ruler to be crowned tsar. ▶

1156 Building begins at the Kremlin.

Kievan Rus			Mongol Rule		Muscovy
900	1000	1100	1200	1300	1400	1500

988 Prince Vladimir converts to Christianity.

1147 Moscow is founded.

Timeline

READING CHECK Rivalry among princes weakened the state, and Mongol armies captured Kiev.

ANSWERS

CORE CONCEPTS: POLITICAL SYSTEMS

Review Core Concept 8.2 before reading Section 2 on the history of Russia. Remind students of the difference between nation-states and empires. Also review the differences among the following forms of government: monarchy, communist dictatorship, and democracy. Explain that students will be reading about two different kinds of changes. First, they will learn about Russia's growth from a small state to a conquered region to a large empire. Second, they will learn how Russia went through two major changes in its form of government during the last century.

Imperial Russia

- **Summarize** What were the accomplishments of Ivan III? (He overthrew the Golden Horde, established a Russian state, and started the construction of the Kremlin.)

- **Problem Solve** What problem did Boris Godunov try to solve by creating serfdom? (food shortages)

- **Identify Details** How did Peter the Great try to modernize Russia? (He imported Western ideas and technologies.)

- **Identify Evidence** What evidence shows that Catherine the Great wanted to make Russia stronger? (Sample: She added extensive territory, including much of Ukraine and Poland, to Russia.)

Closer Look

Westernization of Russia

- **Draw Conclusions** Why did Peter the Great want men to shave off their beards? (to look more modern and Western)

- **Infer** Why do you think Peter the Great decided to start the new city of St. Petersburg rather than modernize Moscow? (Sample: He thought it would be easier to build a modern city from scratch.)

Imperial Russia

Prince Ivan III of Muscovy overthrew the Golden Horde by 1480. He set about establishing a Russian state to rival those of Europe. He began by calling himself **tsar,** or emperor, a term derived from *Caesar,* the title of the Roman emperors.

The Rise of the Tsars Ivan III was eager to show Russia's greatness to the world. He invited European architects to design the **Kremlin,** a grand complex of palaces, state offices, and churches in Moscow.

The reign of tsar Boris Godunov was a time of political unrest and lawlessness. People left the farms for cities. Food shortages resulted. Godunov forced people to work the land by beginning the practice of serfdom. A **serf** is a peasant who is legally bound to live and work on land owned by his or her lord.

The Romanov Dynasty In 1613, an assembly elected a new tsar, Michael Romanov, the 16-year-old son of an influential noble. The Romanovs ruled Russia for the next 300 years.

The first great Romanov tsar, Peter the Great, dreamed of a Russia to rival European nations. As an absolute monarch, he modernized and westernized Russia, importing western ideas and technologies.

Catherine II, known as Catherine the Great, took power in 1762. She ruled as an "enlightened despot," or wise ruler. Catherine transformed the new capital, St. Petersburg, into a cultural center. By the end of her rule in 1796, Catherine had greatly expanded Russia. She added some 200,000 square miles through wars, including much of Ukraine and parts of Poland.

Closer Look

Westernization of Russia

Peter the Great used force in his efforts to westernize Russia. His reforms called for changes to very old customs. Many Russians resented the tsar's autocratic, or unlimited, power. Still, his reforms improved life in Russia greatly. Peter set up academies of science, mathematics, and engineering. He also increased trade with Europe. This brought new technologies to Russia.

Why might Russians have resented westernization by force?

Peter insisted that Russian nobles shave their beards to follow the European custom of being clean-shaven. ▶

THINK CRITICALLY Sample: They might have valued their own culture and resented being made to give it up.

HISTORY

Ivan the Terrible Born in 1530, Ivan IV became grand prince of Moscow when he was only three years old. In January 1547, at the age of 16, Ivan was crowned tsar of all Russia. During the early part of his reign, Ivan embarked on many reforms. He reorganized government, strengthened the Russian Orthodox Church, and limited the powers of hereditary princes and nobles. After one of his wars went badly, Ivan began a reign of terror, attacking and executing many nobles whom he suspected of disloyalty. Violence also destroyed Ivan's chance to establish a lasting dynasty. In 1581, he became so enraged that he murdered his only healthy son. Ivan himself died three years later. Fyodor I, the sickly son who ruled after Ivan, died without an heir in 1598. Boris Godunov then became tsar.

In spite of their reforms, neither Peter the Great nor Catherine the Great helped the serfs, who made up most of the population. To maintain power, the tsars needed the support of nobles. Nobles lived off of the work of the serfs, so they preferred to keep them in <u>servitude.</u>

The Imperial Age Ends In spite of westernization, Russia lagged behind Western Europe in many ways. While many European nations moved toward democracy in the 1800s, Russia's tsars clung to absolute monarchy. Where much of Europe began to industrialize, Russia's economy remained dependent on agriculture and serf labor.

Russia lost the Crimean War to Britain, Turkey, and France in 1856. This loss shocked the nation. In addition to the loss of life and land, the war revealed the poor state of the Russian army. Soldiers used outdated equipment, and most marched in their own ragged clothing. Many were escaped serfs who had joined the army hoping for liberty.

Russia's leaders aimed to modernize. Support grew for emancipation, or freeing, of the serfs. Tsar Alexander II freed them in 1861, but made them pay nobles for land. Peasants did not gain economic freedom and remained desperately poor.

Some Russian reformers pushed for greater democracy. Meanwhile, in 1905, violent worker unrest scared Russia's leaders. Tsar Nicholas II responded with the October Manifesto. This charter granted civil rights and limited democracy. Russian troops crushed the worker revolts, but the peace was short-lived.

servitude, *n.,* a legal requirement to work for another

Reading Check **Why didn't early Russian tsars free the serfs?**

GUIDE ON THE SIDE

- **Compare and Contrast** How did Russia differ from Western Europe? (It did not industrialize but remained dependent on agriculture.)

- **Identify Evidence** What did losing the Crimean War show about Russia? (Its army was in a poor state.)

- **Cause and Effect** Why didn't emancipation improve the lives of serfs? (The tsar made them pay nobles for land, so they remained in poverty.)

Peter hired Italian architects to design his new capital, St. Petersburg, in a European style. ▼

Russian artists used European techniques to make fine decorative objects such as this china vase. ▼

READING CHECK They wanted to please the nobles, who depended on serfs to work their land.

ANSWERS

COMMON MISCONCEPTIONS

Communist Party Members It is common to speak as though all citizens of the Soviet Union were members of the Communist Party. In reality, Communist Party members made up a very small proportion of the population. In the late 1980s, at the very end of the Soviet Union, party members accounted for only about 9.7 percent of the Soviet population. This was

4 percentage points higher than in 1956. Another common misconception is to think of the Communist Party as a workers' party. The proportion of Soviet citizens who were peasants or members of the working class was 72.2 percent. However, those two classes made up only 56.9 percent of party membership.

Communist Russia

- **Express an Opinion** Do you think Nicholas II did the right thing by increasing his autocratic powers? (Sample: No, it created resentment and led to his forced abdication.)

- **Cause and Effect** How did the Russian Revolution change Russian government? (Rule by tsars ended. A communist government took over.)

- **Compare and Contrast** How did Lenin's view of communism differ from Marxism? (Lenin put the government and economy under the control of the Communist Party.)

Analyze Visuals Have students look at the photograph of Lenin.

- How would you describe the expression on Lenin's face? (Samples: intense, angry)

 Culture Close-up

Have students go online to learn more about Red Square.

myWorld Activity
Making a Living Timeline

Communist Russia

Russia's monarchy collapsed during World War I. The war put a huge burden on Russia. Because peasants had to leave farms to fight in the army, food production fell dangerously. Inflation pushed prices out of reach of workers. Nicholas II increased his powers and tried to prevent unrest.

However, Russia's parliament forced Nicholas II to give up the throne in March, 1917. In October of 1917, Vladimir Lenin and the Bolsheviks took power. The **Bolsheviks** were a Russian political group that called for worker control. The Bolsheviks killed Nicholas and his family in 1918. After 300 years, the Romanov dynasty had come to an end.

The Bolshevik takeover is known as the Russian Revolution. The Bolksheviks put in place a new political and social system called communism.

◀ Lenin gained support for communism by speaking publicly. *How might public speeches influence people's opinions?*

Culture Close-Up

What Is Communism? Lenin based the Bolshevik government on his understanding of the works of Karl Marx, a German philosopher from the 1800s. Marx wrote during the Industrial Revolution. He wanted to ease the widespread poverty that had developed among workers.

Marx thought that the people as a whole, not individuals, should own workplaces. In this way, everyone would share the goods and services produced. Marx believed that the working class, or people who work for a living, should control both the government and the economy as a group. The working class would in time no longer be a group separate from the owners. Instead, a classless, or communist, society would develop.

Lenin and the Bolsheviks used Marx's arguments before the revolution to try to gain support in **soviets,** or workers' councils. Lenin claimed that the Bolsheviks spoke for the working class.

After the revolution, the Bolsheviks renamed themselves the Communist Party. Lenin put the government and the economy under Communist Party control. The Communists fought a civil war in Russia. They crushed their opponents.

Repression and Domination In 1922, Russia united with other parts of the former Russian Empire to form the Soviet Union.

After Lenin died in 1924, Josef Stalin took control of the party and government. He issued Five-Year Plans pushing for the development of heavy industry and rapid collectivization of agriculture.

CAPTION Sample: A persuasive speaker might convince people to adopt his or her opinions.

PRIMARY SOURCE

Applause for Stalin "A tribute to Comrade Stalin was called for. Of course, everyone stood up. . . . For three minutes, four minutes, five minutes, the 'stormy applause, rising to an ovation,' continued. But palms were getting sore and raised arms were already aching. And the older people were panting from exhaustion. It was becoming insufferably silly even to those who really adored Stalin. However, who would dare be the *first* to stop? . . . NKVD men were standing in the hall applauding and watching to see *who* quit first! . . . Then, after eleven minutes, the director of the paper factory assumed a businesslike expression and sat down in his seat. . . . That, however, was how they discovered who the independent people were. And that was how they went about eliminating them. That same night the factory director was arrested."
—Alexander Solzhenitsyn, *The Gulag Archipelago*

Collectivization is a shift of control from an individual or company to a group called a collective.

These policies forced many peasants to become tenants on their land, with the state acting as landlord. Stalin used brutal tactics to enforce his policies and maintain power. He crushed all opposition and sent millions into prisons and labor camps. Millions died there.

The horrible famine of 1932–1933 showed how disastrous collectivization could be. Collectives in Ukraine and the Caucasus region were forced to send all their grain to Russia. This left none for the Ukrainians. More than six million people died. Still, one of Stalin's officers called the famine a great success. He said it showed the peasants "who is the master. It cost millions of lives, but the collective farm system is here to stay."

Cold War Russia The Soviet Union worked with Western powers to defeat Germany during World War II. After the war, however, relations with the West, particularly the United States, chilled.

Soviet troops had occupied Eastern Europe. They opposed democracy and set up pro-Soviet communist governments. This brought tension with the United States and other Western nations.

The West aimed for containment, an effort to contain, or to stop the spread of, communism throughout the world. The United States and the Soviet Union vied for economic, political, and cultural power around the world. This rivalry, which stopped short of direct, armed conflict, was called the Cold War.

Reading Check How did Stalin deal with opposition?

Understanding Communism

The two basic elements of communism are a centralized, one-party government and government economic control. The government made all decisions about where people should live and work. People had to obey the government completely. *Does government control ensure the loyalty of the people? Explain why or why not.*

The figures in this Soviet monument carry a hammer and a sickle, the symbols of the Soviet Union. ▶

SOVIET GOVERNMENT
- Controlled by the Communist Party
- Centrally-planned economy
- The state owns all land, businesses, and housing.
- The state provides healthcare, childcare, and education.

COMMUNIST PARTY

Central Committee Top members of the Communist Party who elect the Politburo and general secretary

Politburo The "Political Bureau" of the Communist Party, it set government policies.

General Secretary The leader of the Communist Party and Politburo and head of the government

CAPTION Sample: No, if government maintains harsh control, it will make people angry.

READING CHECK He crushed it by killing or imprisoning opponents.

ANSWERS

GUIDE ON THE SIDE

- **Express an Opinion** How do you think individual farmers felt about collectivization? (Sample: They resented losing their farms.)
- **Synthesize** Why didn't the Soviet Union stop collectivization once it became clear that the policy was a failure? (Stalin favored the policy, and he used brutal tactics to maintain control.)
- **Infer** Why did the government force Ukrainians to send their grain to Russia? (Sample: Russians dominated the Soviet Union.)
- **Cause and Effect** Why did Western countries oppose the Soviet Union during the Cold War? (They wanted to stop the spread of communism.)

Analyze Charts Direct students to examine the Understanding Communism chart.

- What was the title of the leader of the Communist Party? (General Secretary)

QUICK FACTS

Chernobyl The nuclear power station at Chernobyl was 65 miles north of Kiev, Ukraine. The plant came into operation in stages between 1977 and 1983. It had four reactors; each one could produce 1,000 megawatts of electricity. The accident happened on April 25–26, 1986. Technicians working at reactor unit 4 conducted an experiment, during which they shut down the safety systems. The experiment went wrong, causing the chain reaction to go out of control. Several explosions took place, which created a fireball and blew off the reactor lid. High levels of radioactivity escaped, and 32 people died. Among the long-term effects were thousands of cases of cancer and other diseases caused by radiation.

GUIDE ON THE SIDE

Communism to Nationalism

- **Compare and Contrast** How were Khrushchev and Gorbachev different? (Khrushchev maintained tight control, while Gorbachev advocated openness.)

- **Identify Evidence** What evidence, uncovered by the policy of glasnost, weakened faith in the government? (evidence of low standards of living, the failure in Afghanistan, and the health problems and environmental damage caused by the Chernobyl accident)

- **Infer** What do you think was the goal of perestroika? (Sample: Its goal was to revive the economy by reducing government control and creating freer markets.)

Analyze Visuals Have students look at the paired photographs.

- Which of the two leaders seems to convey that he is willing to fight? How? (Yeltsin; he is holding up a fist.)

 myWorld Activity

Make a Living Timeline Find Step-by-Step Instructions and an Activity Support on pp. T150–T151. **(Verbal/Kinesthetic)**

548 Western Hemisphere
304 Eastern Hemisphere
482 World Geography

Communism to Nationalism

Stalin's successor, Nikita Khrushchev, **denounced** Stalin's brutal tactics. Still, the Communist Party kept tight control.

denounce, *v.,* to reject publicly

The Communist System Weakens The communist system slowly weakened. To compete in the Cold War, the government focused on building weapons and military vehicles. The government failed to invest in new technologies.

Meanwhile, state ownership gave farmers little reason to grow more food. As a result, the Soviet Union went into debt to import food and high-technology goods. The Soviet economy could not meet its people's wish for better living standards.

During the 1980s, the Soviet Union fought a failed war to support a communist government in Afghanistan. As with the Crimean War, the lost war in Afghanistan brought calls for reform.

Openness and Restructuring Real reform in the Soviet Union began with Mikhail Gorbachev. After he came to power in 1985, he introduced two new policies, glasnost and perestroika. Glasnost, or "openness," meant greater freedom of speech and media freedom.

Glasnost destroyed the myth that people were living well under communism. It highlighted failures in the country's long war in Afghanistan. Glasnost also forced the government to reveal details about the 1986 Chernobyl nuclear accident. This accident caused serious health problems and environmental damage.

Perestroika, or "restructuring," reduced government control over the economy and created freer markets. Also, for the first time, the government allowed non-communist parties to form.

The Collapse Comes The Soviet Union eased its control over Eastern Europe. People in non-Russian parts of the Soviet Union began to seek independence.

Some top Communist Party officials resisted these changes. In August 1991, Soviet security officials seized power.

Hardline communists disliked Mikhail Gorbachev. They saw him as a leader who wanted to reduce the power of the Soviet government.

Boris Yeltsin raises his fist in triumph after the 1991 coup. Yeltsin's actions broke the power of the Communists and led to the fall of the Soviet Union.

READING CHECK glasnost (openness) and perestroika (restructuring)

SECTION 2 ASSESSMENT **1.** The tsar was Russia's authoritarian ruler. A serf was a peasant who was forced to farm a noble's lands. Bolshevik revolutionaries challenged the authority of the old system. **2.** Peter modernized and westernized it. **3.** Lenin centralized control of both. **4.** The country experienced a terrible famine in 1922–1923, and millions died. **5.** Sample: Stalin used brutal tactics

ECONOMICS

Shock Therapy When Boris Yeltsin became president of Russia, the economy was about to collapse. Goods were so scarce that the country had only two days' reserve of grain and flour. Yeltsin took radical steps known as "shock therapy" to jump start a free-market economy. His government eliminated price controls and began to privatize industry by selling off state property. The immediate effect was rampant inflation that ate up personal savings. People who were able to quickly adopt capitalistic methods grew rich. Others, especially those who worked for set government salaries, were suddenly poor. In the new economic freedom, corruption and organized crime took hold, creating problems that Vladimir Putin later had to fight. When Yeltsin died in 2007, it was still unclear whether his shock therapy had created chaos or paved the way for future growth.

Within three days, supporters of democracy forced the Soviet officials to back down. At the end of 1991, the Soviet Union officially broke apart, and the Cold War came to an end. All of the former Soviet republics gained independence. The largest of these was Russia.

The Russian Federation As the first president of a new Russia, Boris Yeltsin was head of a nation on the verge of economic collapse. The sudden shift to a free-market economy brought great hardship. Inflation and unemployment soared. A very few individuals gained control of state-owned property. These well-connected individuals, known as oligarchs, held great influence over the politics and economy of Russia.

The Russian Federation, as the country was now called, also had to deal with unrest in its non-Russian regions. From 1994 to 2005, Russia fought a war against rebels in Chechnya who wanted independence. Both sides brutally mistreated

The Soviet Union and Present-Day Russia

KEY
Soviet Union, 1991
Russia, 1992

people. The region was left in ruins by the time Russia regained control.

Yeltsin resigned in 1999, naming Vladimir Putin as acting president. Putin then won an election in 2000. Putin reduced the power of the oligarchy and increased the power of the government.

Reading Check What new policies did Gorbachev set?

Section 2 Assessment

Key Terms
1. Explain how the following key terms describe power relations in Russian history: tsar, serf, Bolshevik

Key Ideas
2. What changes did Peter the Great make to Russia?
3. What changes did Lenin make to the economy and government of Russia?
4. What were some results of collectivizing agriculture?

Think Critically
5. **Compare Viewpoints** How were Stalin's and Gorbachev's ideas about government different?
6. **Synthesize** What caused the Soviet Union to collapse?

Essential Question
What should governments do?
7. Think about the famines that have occurred throughout Russian history. What actions might a government take during disasters such as famines? Go to your Student Journal to record your answer.

to maintain control and killed millions; Gorbachev introduced openness and restructuring. **6.** Sample: Gorbachev's reforms let nationalistic feelings emerge; conservatives tried to halt reform; the people rebelled and the government fell; the Soviet Union dissolved. **7.** Sample: It should distribute food as fairly as possible.

GUIDE ON THE SIDE

- **Cause and Effect** How did the changes to the economy affect Russia? (inflation, unemployment, the rise of oligarchs)
- **Identify Main Ideas** What region tried to break away from Russia, leading to a long war? (Chechnya)
- **Summarize** What was the outcome of the war in Chechnya? (Russia regained control, but the region was left in ruins.)

Analyze Maps Have students look at the map comparing the Soviet Union to the Russian Federation.

- How would you describe the location of the lands that the Soviet Union had but Russia does not? (They were to the east and southeast of Russia.)

ANSWERS

The Russian Revolution

OBJECTIVES

Students will

- make connections between important documents and revolutionary language.
- **21st Century Learning** draw conclusions about the effects of documents.
- **ELL** understand the meaning of and difference between the terms *peasant* and *wage worker.*

SET EXPECTATIONS

In this lesson, students will

- read and analyze two documents about the Russian Revolution.
- write a letter to a historical figure.

1 Connect

On the board, create a concept web around the word *revolution.* Ask students to name revolutions that they have studied and to list types of revolutions, such as political and technological.

Have students contribute words they associate with revolutions, such as *violence* or *change.* Then ask, How do revolutions begin? What role do speeches and writings play in sparking revolutions?

2 Learn

Preview Tell students that they are going to read two documents—one of which helped cause a political revolution and one of which was a reaction to a revolutionary leader. Have students preview the two pages and identify the image of Vladimir Lenin and the dates of the two documents. Read the Key Idea, glossary terms, and definitions. Clarify any questions about the meaning of these words by providing examples.

Read Slowly read aloud the excerpt from "A Call to Power" without stopping. Read the document again, this time stopping to read the questions at the left, and prompt students to rethink and analyze the meaning of the words. Have students answer the questions using the location of the letters to provide clues. Do the same for the excerpt from "Letter to Lenin." Lead a discussion starting

with students' responses to the questions. Ask, What general impression do these documents give you of the Russian Revolution? Did the revolution accomplish what its leaders said it would?

ELL Intermediate Explain that revolutionaries often claim to fight for those who do not have property or wealth. Give students the following definitions: **peasant** a farm worker; **wage worker** one who works for hourly pay. Ask students to write a sentence using each term.

myWorld Activity: Revolutionary Language Distribute copies of *Activity Support: Language Analysis,* and have pairs of students analyze the persuasive techniques used in the excerpts from "A Call to Power" and "Letter to Lenin."

20 min

3 Understand

Review Go back to the Key Idea. Discuss with students how each writer interpreted the revolutionary events happening around him. List their observations so all students can see the differences between the two.

Assess Have students complete **Analyze the Documents.** Review their answers to determine if students have met the lesson objectives.

Remediate If students struggle to identify emotional language, ask the class to identify which is the more emotional term in the each of the following pairs: ruler and dictator; slaughter and death; starvation and hunger; brutality and harshness. Ask students if they think this distinction is personal or if it would be true for all people.

Name _____ Class _____ Date _____

myWorld Activity Support   Language Analysis

Revolutionary Language

Directions During political revolutions, leaders use fiery language to try to win people to their side. Read the descriptions below of techniques that writers and speakers use to draw people to their cause during revolutionary periods. Below each description, write down examples of each type of language found in *Primary Source: The Russian Revolution.*

Emotional Language
Revolutions are periods when people feel strongly about events. Speakers and writers try to stir up emotions to convince others of their points of view. One way they do this is by calling their opponents names. For example, during the American Revolution, colonists called King George III a tyrant.

Examples of Emotional Language

_____

_____

Idealistic Language
Revolutions are usually violent. As a result, the leaders want to prove that they are doing the right thing. One way to do this is to call on ideals, or high standards. For example, leaders of the French Revolution claimed to act for equality. Revolutionary leaders also often claim to help people who are suffering. A world in which people help those who suffer or a world in which people are treated equally is an ideal. When people talk about making these ideals a reality, the way they speak is considered "idealistic."

Examples of Idealistic Language

_____

_____

HISTORY

Vladimir Lenin Born in Russia in 1870, Vladimir Ilich Ulyanov (who later took the name Lenin) was one of six children. His family was happy, loving, and well-educated. In spite of this stable beginning, Lenin and all his siblings took part in revolutionary activities. As a law student, Lenin was expelled and exiled for attending an illegal meeting. He earned his degree in 1891 and began to practice law, defending workers and peasants.

This deepened his hatred of the class system. He moved to St. Petersburg in 1893 and became a Marxist. Many Russian intellectuals believed that Russia was safe from revolution because its population was mostly peasant, not working class. But Lenin came up with the new idea that revolution should be led by a strong party of professional revolutionaries instead of by workers. His doctrine became the force behind Soviet communism.

GUIDE ON THE SIDE

Draw Conclusions Use the lettered prompts to help students understand the text and draw conclusions about Lenin's intentions.

ANSWERS

Ⓐ They have disarmed the officer cadets, so they want to overthrow the government before the cadets get new weapons.

Ⓑ To the question *Who must take power?* Lenin answered evasively saying, "That is not important at present" and "some other institution" would do it.

Ⓒ Lenin claimed to be acting for the army, the peasants, and the starving.

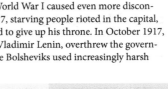

Primary Source

The Russian Revolution

Key Idea
- During the Russian Revolution, Bolsheviks promised the people a better life, but soon turned to brutal methods to keep power.

▲ A Russian serf weaves cloth on a loom, about 1910.

For centuries, tsars ruled Russia with absolute power. Under their rule, a huge gap existed between wealthy landowners and poor workers. In 1905, a revolution led to the creation of a parliament, but it was ineffective. The suffering caused by World War I caused even more discontent among Russians. In early 1917, starving people rioted in the capital, St. Petersburg. The tsar was forced to give up his throne. In October 1917, revolutionary Bolsheviks, led by Vladimir Lenin, overthrew the government. Civil war broke out, and the Bolsheviks used increasingly harsh measures to maintain control.

Lenin addresses a political meeting in 1917. ▼

Stop at each letter on the right to think about the text. Then answer the question with the same letter on the left.

Ⓐ Analyze Cause and Effect What have the revolutionaries already done, and why does that make it important to act quickly?

Ⓑ Identify Evidence How does Lenin try to cover up his intention to take power? Explain.

Ⓒ Identify Main Ideas and Details For whom does Lenin claim the revolutionaries are acting?

disarm, *v.*, to force a person or country to give up a supply of weapons

cadet, *n.*, a person who is training to become a military officer

relinquish, *v.*, to give up or surrender

A Call to Power

❝ We must at all costs, this very evening, this very night, arrest the **Ⓐ** government, having first <u>disarmed</u> the officer <u>cadets</u>, and so on. We must not wait! We may lose everything! Who must take power? **Ⓑ** That is not important at present. Let the Revolutionary Military Committee do it, or "some other institution" which will declare that it will <u>relinquish</u> power only to the **Ⓒ** true representatives of the interests of the people, the interests of the army, the interests of the peasants, the interests of the starving. ❞
—Vladimir Lenin, "A Call to Power," October 24, 1917

21st Century Learning DRAW CONCLUSIONS

Remind students that conclusions can be based not just on information in the text but also on their own knowledge. Encourage students to view the task as having two steps. First, they should understand the main ideas and details expressed by each writer. To assist your students in reaching that understanding, use the scaffolded questions at the left of each excerpt. Then students should use their own knowledge about the Russian Revolution to

conclude what happened to the writer of the letter. Ask, According to Section 2, what happened to people who opposed Josef Stalin? Judging from the events that the soldier described in his letter, do you think Lenin's reaction to opposition was similar to or different from Stalin's reaction? Based on these various pieces of information, what do you think Lenin did after he read this letter?

GUIDE ON THE SIDE

Stop at each letter on the right to think about the text. Then answer the question with the same letter on the left.

D **Identify Bias** What attitude toward Lenin is conveyed by the words "bloodthirsty beast"?

E **Draw Conclusions** In the beginning, how did ordinary people feel about the revolution?

F **Compare and Contrast** According to the Russian Red Army soldier, what did the revolution bring about? Is that similar to or different from what he expected?

intrude, *v.*, to force oneself into a situation where one isn't wanted

ranks, *n.*, a body of people grouped together as members of an organization

Constituent Assembly, *n.*, an elected legislature that the Bolsheviks disbanded

existence, *n.*, standard of living

Letter to Lenin

D 66 My words to you, you bloodthirsty beast. You intruded into the ranks of the revolution and did not allow the Constituent Assembly to meet. You said: 'Down with prisons, Down with shootings, Down with soldiering. Let wage workers be secure.' In a word you promised heaps of gold and a heavenly existence. The people **E** felt the revolution, began to breathe easily. We were allowed to meet, to say what we liked, fearing nothing. And then you, Bloodsucker, appeared and took **F** away freedom from the people. . . . You've organized a terror and thousands of the people are shot mercilessly every day; . . . workers are starving, the people are without shoes or clothes. 99
—a Red Army soldier, "Letter to Lenin," December 25, 1918

▲ This military cap and the seal above it bear the hammer and sickle, symbols of the Soviet Union.

Red Army soldiers, 1932 ▼

Analyze the Documents

1. **Draw Inferences** What do you think happened to the soldier who wrote the letter to Lenin? Explain.
2. **Writing Task** Write your own letter to Lenin in which you tell him what, if anything, you think he should have done differently.

ANSWERS

D Anger, fear, hatred

E They breathed easily and thought they would have a heavenly existence.

F Many have been shot, and many are starving. This is the exact opposite of what he expected.

21st Century Learning

Draw Conclusions Use the lettered prompts to help students identify the main point made by each writer. Then explain that students should use their own knowledge to draw conclusions about the events.

ANALYZE THE DOCUMENTS 1. He was probably shot or imprisoned because his letter mentions shootings and loss of freedom. **2.** Letters will vary but should be addressed to Lenin and contain accurate historic details to portray his rule or the fate of the Soviet Union. Sample:

Dear Lenin, I think you were wrong. Your revolution harmed more people than it helped. The man who ruled after you, Stalin, killed millions and millions of people.

SECTION 3 LESSON PLAN

Russia Today

OBJECTIVES

Students will know

- the reasons the Russian economy improved after 1991.
- how increased government controls have set back democratic reform in Russia.

Students will be able to

- identify main ideas and details about current issues in Russia.
- categorize quiz questions by whether they test main ideas or details.

SET EXPECTATIONS

In this section, students will

- read Russia Today.
- create and play a trivia game to quiz themselves.
- go On Assignment in Russia and explore charts and maps.

CORE CONCEPTS

You may wish to teach or reteach the following lessons from the Core Concepts Handbook:

- People's Impact on the Environment, pp. 53–63
- Trade, pp. 66–67
- Conflict and Cooperation, pp. 110–111

KEY

Differentiated Instruction
- **L1** Special Needs
- **L2** Extra Support
- **L3** On-Level
- **L4** Challenge

English Language Instruction
- **ELL** Beginner
- **ELL** Early Intermediate
- **ELL** Intermediate
- **ELL** Early Advanced
- **ELL** Advanced

---

1 Connect
Make learning meaningful

Make Connections Ask students how they identify themselves when they meet someone new. What descriptions do they use to explain who they are? Then ask, How do you think your identity might change as you get older? Tell students that they are about to study how Russia's identity has changed in recent decades.

L2 Extra Support To help students answer the question about their identity, suggest that they consider hobbies, sports, talents, and ethnic background.

Activate Prior Knowledge Review how Gorbachev's reforms led to the breakup of the Soviet Union and the end of communist rule. Ask students to predict how those changes have affected Russia.

ELL Early Intermediate Introduce the term *superpower;* show that it is a compound of *super* and *power*. Explain that during the Cold War, the United States and the Soviet Union were the world's two superpowers. Allow students to list words or draw pictures of things they associate with superpowers.

Prepare Follow the steps in the section **Preview.** Preteach the Key Terms. Then have students complete *Word Wise* in their journals using in-text clues and the glossary for help.

2 Experience
Teach knowledge and skills

Read Use **Background** notes and **Guide on the Side** questions to model active reading. Have students use *Take Notes* in their **Student Journal** to record main ideas and details about challenges facing Russia. Have students complete **21st Century Online Tutor** *Identify Main Ideas and Details*, and apply this skill to reading the section.

ELL Early Advanced In the section *Human Rights and the Law*, point out the sentence "Russia's record on human rights remains uneven." Explain that in this sentence, the word *uneven* does not mean "unlevel." It means "varying in quality."

L4 Challenge Have students complete *Enrichment: Russian Oil Exports*. Then have them calculate the percentage that exports changed for each year shown on the graph.

L1 Special Needs Have students read the **Online Student Edition** while listening to the accompanying audio.

 Practice: myWorld Activity Students will quiz each other on the section by making and playing a trivia game. **Step-by-Step Instructions** and **More Activities** follow on pp. T158–159.

SECTION 3 RESOURCE GUIDE

FOR THE STUDENT

my worldgeography.com Student Center

- Data Discovery
- Active Atlas

Student Edition (print and online)

- Russia Today

Student Journal (print and online)

- Section 3 Word Wise
- Section 3 Take Notes

21st Century Learning Online Tutor

- Identify Main Ideas and Details
- Categorize

FOR THE TEACHER

my worldgeography.com Teacher Center

- Online Lesson Planner
- Presentations for Projection
- SuccessTracker

ProGuide: Europe and Russia

- Section 3 Lesson Plan, pp. T156–T157
- 🏃 myWorld Activity Step-by-Step Instructions, p. T158
- Activity Support: Russia Trivia Game, p. T159
- myWorld Geography Enrichment, p. T160
- Section Quiz, p. T161

Accelerating the Progress of ELLs

- Organizing Information Strategies, p. 48

3 Understand
Assess understanding

Review Review *Word Wise* and *Take Notes* in the **Student Journal.**

Assess Knowledge and Skills Use Section Assessment and Section Quiz to check students' progress.

Assess Understanding Review students' responses to the Section Assessment Essential Question prompt.

Remediate Use these strategies to review and remediate.

If students struggle to . . .	Try these strategies.
Understand Russia's economic recovery	Have them record details in a three-column table with the heads *Income, Exports,* and *Poverty.*
Identify main ideas and details about Russia	Demonstrate how to make concept webs with main ideas in the center based upon red headings in the chapter.
Categorize quiz questions	Assign additional practice with the **21st Century Online Tutor.**

ELL Support

ELL Objective Students will be able to use English to ask questions.

Cultural Connections To give students practice in asking questions, allow them to use their native languages to compose five questions they could use for a trivia game about their family's homeland. Have them translate one question into English.

ELL Advanced Content Tip Provide a list of international organizations mentioned in the section and their purpose, such as the G-8, NATO, the European Union, and the Shanghai Cooperative Organization. Have students circle the organizations that Russia belongs to.

ELL Activity On the board write, "Putin was elected president in 2000." Model how to write questions about that fact by having students complete the following sentences with *who, what,* or *when:*

"_____ office was Putin elected to?"

"_____ did the election take place?"

"_____ was elected president?"

(Verbal/Logical)

 **myWorld Activity**   **Step-by-Step Instructions**

 30 min

Quiz Yourself

OBJECTIVES

Students will

• write and categorize review questions about the section.

• quiz themselves by playing a trivia game.

LEARNING STYLE

• Verbal

• Kinesthetic

21st Century Learning

• Categorize

MATERIALS

• Activity Support: Russia Trivia Game, p. T159

• Index cards

• Sets of different colored buttons or small objects to use as tokens

Activity Steps

1. Explain to the class that they are going to work in groups to create and play a trivia game about recent events in Russia.

2. Divide the class into groups of five or six. Give each group a copy of *Activity Support: Russia Trivia Game*, a stack of index cards, and a set of game tokens, so that each group member will be able to use a different color or shape.

3. Have each student write five questions about Section 3. They should write each question on the front of a single index card with the answer on the back. Encourage students to write both obvious and difficult-to-answer questions.

   ELL **Intermediate** Give students these question models: When did _____ take place? Who was _____? What was the cause of _____? What was the effect of _____? Why did _____?

4. When students are done, the groups should collect the questions and discard any duplicates. If they end up with fewer than 20 questions, have them write replacements as a group. Then the group should work together to categorize the questions as either Main Ideas or Details, and label each card just below the question.

   L2 **Extra Support** Remind students that a main idea is a general statement about a topic. It usually must be stated in a sentence. Details are the facts, statistics, and quotations that support the main idea.

5. Have groups exchange their sets of questions. Then go over the rules listed in *Activity Support: Russia Trivia Game*. Finally, allow groups to play the game.

 More Activities From myWorld Teachers

Local Connection Have students find editorials that criticize state or local government and bring them to share in class. Ask the class, How does freedom of the press help democracy? Why do you think the Russian government suppresses criticism? **(Verbal/Logical)**

Russia and the World Divide the class into teams of three or four. Pair teams to debate the question "Is Russia a superpower?" Assign teams the "yes" and "no" positions. Give the teams time to find evidence in the chapter to support their position before holding the debate. **(Verbal/Logical)**

Political Cartoon Have pairs of students review Section 3 and choose an action by the Russian government that they have a strong opinion about. They should then work together to make a political cartoon that expresses their opinion about the action. **(Visual)**

 my worldgeography.com | **Teacher Center** ➔   Find additional resources in the online Teacher Center.

Name _____ Class _____ Date _____

myWorld Activity Support   **Russia Trivia Game**

Quiz Yourself

Directions Work in a group to create a Russia trivia game. Each person should write five questions about Section 3. Put each question on a separate card with the answer on the back. Then as a group, evaluate the questions. Throw out any duplicates. Label the rest of the questions as Main Idea or Detail questions. Exchange your set of questions with another group, and play the game according to the rules below.

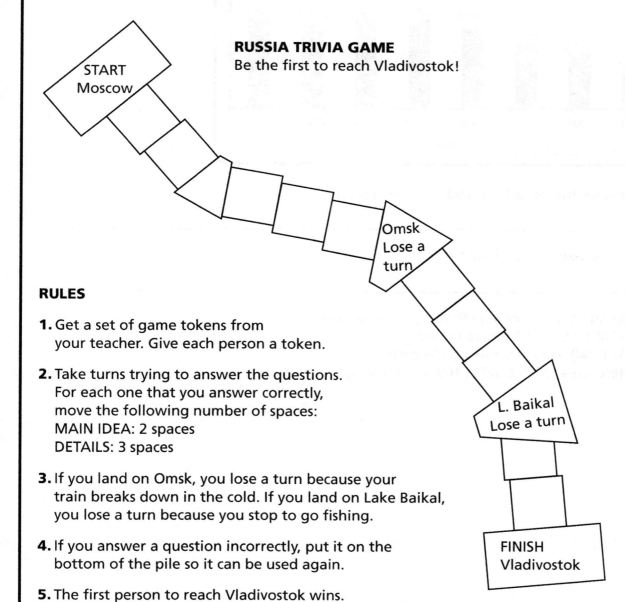

RUSSIA TRIVIA GAME
Be the first to reach Vladivostok!

START
Moscow

Omsk
Lose a turn

L. Baikal
Lose a turn

FINISH
Vladivostok

RULES

1. Get a set of game tokens from your teacher. Give each person a token.

2. Take turns trying to answer the questions. For each one that you answer correctly, move the following number of spaces:
MAIN IDEA: 2 spaces
DETAILS: 3 spaces

3. If you land on Omsk, you lose a turn because your train breaks down in the cold. If you land on Lake Baikal, you lose a turn because you stop to go fishing.

4. If you answer a question incorrectly, put it on the bottom of the pile so it can be used again.

5. The first person to reach Vladivostok wins.

T159

Name _____ Class _____ Date _____

Enrichment: Russian Oil Exports

Directions Study the graph below. Answer the questions that follow and complete the activity.

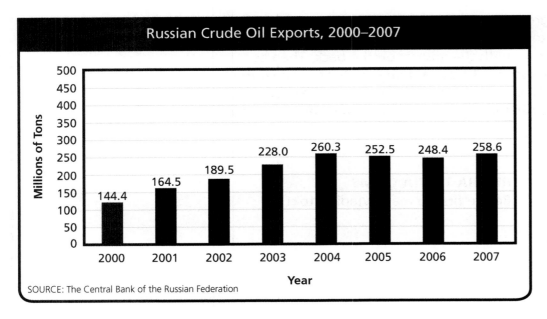

Russian Crude Oil Exports, 2000–2007

SOURCE: The Central Bank of the Russian Federation

1. In which year were the exports of crude oil the highest?

_____

2. In which years did exports decrease?

_____

3. Activity Calculate the percentage that exports changed
from 2000 to 2001. Use the formula below:
1st step: (2001 total) – (2000 total) = difference
2nd step: difference ÷ (2000 total) x 100% = % change

Name _____ Class _____ Date _____

Section Quiz

Directions Answer the following questions using what you learned
in Section 3.

1. _____ How did Vladimir Putin try to
strengthen Russia?
   a. by becoming friendlier to the United
   States
   b. by increasing the central government's
   power
   c. by forming a military alliance with Japan
   d. by increasing freedoms of the press and
   speech

2. _____ How does the Russian government
usually react to critical news stories?
   a. It explains its actions to the public in a
   press conference.
   b. It tries to reform its procedures to end
   the problem being discussed.
   c. It censors the press and tries to stop the
   stories from being published.
   d. It blames the old communist rulers for
   any difficulties.

3. _____ Which of the following remains a
serious problem in Russia?
   a. few energy resources
   b. low life expectancy
   c. serfs who lack skills
   d. war with the United States

4. _____ How did the Russian economy
change from 1999 to 2007?
   a. Personal incomes increased and poverty
   decreased.
   b. It switched from reliance on petroleum
   to high-technology industries.
   c. It withdrew from trading in the global
   economy.
   d. Prices fell, causing deflation and loss
   of GDP.

5. _____ Which of the following international
partnerships does Russia belong to?
   a. the European Union
   b. the Group of 8
   c. NATO
   d. Human Rights Watch

6. In the boxes below, write brief descriptions of Russia's current
relationship with two other powerful nations.

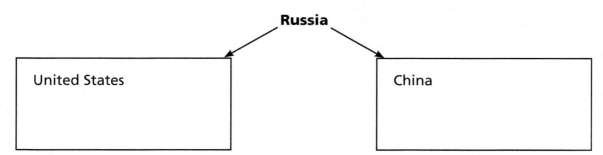

Russia

United States   China

Russia Today

- Model preparing to read by previewing the Key Ideas, Key Terms, headings, visuals, and captions. Have students make predictions about what they will learn. For ELL support, post the prompt, "I predict I will read about . . ."

- Preview and practice the reading skill, Identify Main Ideas and Details, by using examples from a previous chapter.

- Preteach this section's high-use Academic Vocabulary and Key Terms using the table on the next page and in-text definitions. Have students practice Key Terms by completing the *Word Wise* page in their journals.

GUIDE ON THE SIDE

 Reading Skill

Identify Main Ideas and Details While they read, have students practice this skill by completing the *Take Notes* graphic organizer in the **Student Journal.**

Russia Recovers

- **Analyze Sources** According to James Billington, what challenge do Russians face? (They must find a new national identity that does not involve being hostile to others.)

- **Categorize** What problems did Russia experience after the Soviet Union ended? (depression, alcoholism, violence, crime, and corruption)

- **Infer** Why do you think Russians turned to a strong leader like Putin? (Sample: Because of all the problems, they wanted someone who would take charge and act decisively.)

Section 3

Russia Today

Key Ideas
- Russia had a strong economic recovery in the early 2000s.
- Many of Russia's democratic reforms have disappeared as government control has grown.
- Russia uses its energy resources as a source of international power.

Key Terms • KGB • disposable income • censor • superpower

 Visual Glossary

Reading Skill: Identify Main Ideas and Details Take notes using the graphic organizer in your journal.

Shoppers walk through a new public plaza in Moscow. ▼

Few nations have experienced as much upheaval as Russia did in the 1900s. Since 2000, the country has continued to change at a remarkable pace.

Russia Recovers

Gorbachev's policies of glasnost and perestroika opened a new era of social and political change in Russia. One of the biggest changes has been Russia's increasing self-confidence.

Finding a New Identity At the end of the Soviet period, Russians discovered that communism was more than a political system—it was also a cultural identity. If Russia was no longer a communist nation, then what should it be? In 1990, historian James Billington said:

❝ It boils down to whether [Russians] can find an…identity for themselves as a way of feeling good about themselves without feeling hostile to others. ❞

The hardships that occurred in the shift to a market economy brought a rise in depression and alcoholism. The country also faced violence, crime, and corruption. Although there had been corruption during the Soviet era, it increased greatly in the years that followed.

Restoring Confidence Elected president in 2000, Vladimir Putin acted quickly to rebuild the country. He did this through strong leadership and by increasing government control. Since then, some have charged that Putin's policies undermine human rights, democracy, and peaceful relations with Russia's neighbors and the United States.

ACADEMIC VOCABULARY

High-Use Word	Definition and Sample Sentence
demonstrate	*v.* to show the workings of *The general demonstrated how the new weapon worked.*
cooperate	*v.* to work together toward an agreed goal *The rival teams decided to cooperate to raise money for park improvements.*

Some scholars point to Putin's background as a member of the **KGB**, the Soviet secret police. His past may have led him to favor strong government control. Supporters argue that his policies reduced political corruption, crime, and terrorism. His reforms to banking, private property, and labor law helped Russia's economy grow. Under Putin, some Russians began to believe that state-controlled capitalism might work better than a free-market economy.

However, many Russians preferred the Soviet era, when the government was in charge of pensions, healthcare, and wages. Many feel that under communism they faced less uncertainty.

Putin strengthened the Russian military. He <u>demonstrated</u> Russia's renewed military might by crushing unrest in regions on Russia's borders, such as Chechnya, where rebels had fought Russian control since 1994.

Putin's two terms as president also brought real improvements in daily life. His economic reforms reduced poverty and led to the emergence of a new middle class. Many in this new middle class are professionals who work in fields related to the global economy. The middle class now makes up about one fifth to one third of the population. Since 1999, Russians on average have doubled their **disposable income,** or the amount of money left after taxes are paid. By the end of 2007, fewer than 15 percent of all Russians lived below the poverty level. Just ten years earlier, 38 percent lived in poverty.

Putin also oversaw dramatic growth in Russia's energy industry. This industry took advantage of Russia's vast oil and natural gas reserves. Russia became one of the world's leading producers of oil and gas.

demonstrate, *v,* to show the workings of

Reading Check How did Putin change the role of Russia's government?

Contrasting Systems

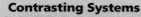

Under the communist Soviet Union, Russians, such as the woman at the left, faced empty shelves in stores. American shoppers, such as the woman at the right, seldom encounter such shortages. *How might communism affect the supply of items such as food and clothing?*

Communism	Democratic Capitalism
• The Communist Party makes all political decisions. • Command economy (The government makes most economic decisions and owns most property.) • The political leadership values obedience, discipline, and economic security.	• The people and their elected representatives make decisions. • Market economy (Private consumers and producers make most economic decisions and own most property.) • The political leadership values freedom and prosperity.

READING CHECK Putin strengthened the military and the government's control of the economy.

CAPTION Communism might create shortages because the government cares more for the needs of the state than those of individuals.

GUIDE ON THE SIDE

- **Problem Solve** What actions did Putin take to help the Russian economy? (reforms to banking, private property, and labor law)
- **Compare Viewpoints** Why do you think many Russians preferred the old system in which the government controlled pensions, healthcare, and wages? (Sample: They felt that someone was taking care of their needs.)
- **Cause and Effect** What improvements have economic changes brought to Russians? (a reduction in poverty, an increase in disposable income, and growth of the middle class)
- **Identify Main Ideas** In what industry did Russia become one of the world's leaders? (production of oil and gas)

Analyze Charts Have students look at the chart on contrasting systems.

- In which system do the people have more power? (democratic capitalism)
- Which system puts more stress on obedience? (communism)

CORE CONCEPTS: TRADE

Review Core Concept 5.5 before reading Section 3. Review the difference between domestic trade and foreign trade, and remind students of the existence of world trade patterns. Remind students of comparative advantage. Ask, Based on what you know about Russia's resources, what might be Russia's major exports? Discuss how the balance of imports and exports can effect a nation's economy. Ask, How do you predict the fall of communism might affect Russia's ability to take part in global trade? Do you think Russia's economy has most likely grown or declined in recent years?

GUIDE ON THE SIDE

Russia Faces Challenges

- **Cause and Effect** What is the main cause of low life expectancy for men in Russia? (alcoholism)

- **Categorize** What types of migration have been occurring in Russia? (Some people have left the cities for the country so they can grow their own food; at the same time, some people have moved to the cities looking for work. In addition, many skilled Russians have left the country to seek work in other lands.)

Analyze Charts Have students look at the chart comparing quality of life in the United States and Russia.

- Which country has a longer overall life expectancy? How much longer is it? (the United States; 12.2 years)

- Which country has a lower infant mortality? (the United States)

⊘ **Data Discovery**

Have students go online to learn more about quality of life.

Comparing Standards of Living

Life Expectancy

	United States	Russia
Overall	78.1 years	65.9 years
Male	75.3 years	59.1 years
Female	81.1 years	73.1 years

Infant Mortality (per 1,000 births)

	United States	Russia
Total	6.3 deaths	10.8 deaths
Male	7.0 deaths	12.3 deaths
Female	5.6 deaths	9.2 deaths

SOURCE: *CIA World Factbook*

Chart Skills

How does life expectancy for men in Russia compare with that for men in the United States? How does it compare for women in these two nations?

⊘ **Data Discovery**

◀ Two Russian women haul coal to heat their homes and to cook food.

Russia Faces Challenges

Russia's new wealth and stability brought newfound confidence. However, Russians have also been facing some serious challenges.

Social and Economic Woes With change came new health concerns. Russia's birth rates and life expectancy are low. Life expectancy is the number of years a person can expect to live. Male life expectancy is the lowest of all industrialized nations in the world. Alcoholism is a major problem in Russia. Half of working-age men die due to excessive drinking. Rates of infectious disease are also high. These include HIV/AIDS and tuberculosis, a lung disease.

Social and economic changes since the 1990s have led to an increase in migration. After the fall of the Soviet Union, civil unrest and unemployment forced thousands of people to leave their homes. Many left polluted cities with high unemployment. Some returned to former lives in the countryside. There, they could raise some of their own food. At the same time, others migrated from rural areas to more thriving cities to try to find work. Large numbers of Russians, many of them skilled workers, have left their homeland to seek better lives in North America, Israel, and Western Europe.

Putin Draws Criticism Putin's efforts to solve some of Russia's major problems have had mixed results. He remains popular among Russians, but criticism continues in spite of the government's efforts to silence it.

CHART SKILLS 1. It is 16.2 years less.
2. In Russia, it is 8 years less.

PRIMARY SOURCE

Radio Censorship "At their first meeting with journalists since taking over Russia's largest independent radio news network, the managers had startling news of their own: from now on, they said, at least 50 percent of the reports about Russia must be 'positive.' In addition, opposition leaders could not be mentioned on the air and the United States was to be portrayed as an enemy, journalists employed by the network, Russian News Service, say they were told by the new managers, who are allies of the Kremlin. . . . The implementation of the '50 percent positive' rule at the Russian News Service leaves an increasingly small number of news outlets that are not managed by the Kremlin."

—Andrew Kramer, "50% Good News Is the Bad News in Russian Radio," *New York Times*, April 22, 2007

The Russian constitution calls for freedom of speech and of the press. However, the government continues to control the media. The government owns most of the large radio and television stations. This means that if the government doesn't want the general public to know about a news story, they can **censor** it, or keep it from being reported.

One of Putin's most controversial actions was to put Russia's energy industry under government control. Private energy companies suddenly lost all that they owned to the government. Putin argued Russia needed control of its energy industry to regain its status as a global superpower. A **superpower** is an extremely powerful nation.

Human Rights and the Law Russia's record on human rights remains uneven. Ethnic and religious tensions continue, especially with Muslims and others from the Caucasus region. A few Russian journalists who have criticized the government have died under suspicious circumstances. Some have accused the Russian government of killing them.

Corruption in business practices and politics is common in Russia. In 2008, Dmitry Medvedev won election to follow Putin as president. Medvedev promised to fight corruption, although critics questioned his commitment. Medvedev said,

> ❝ [Corruption] must receive our sustained attention because this problem is a profound and important one. ❞

Reading Check How does the Russian government control the media?

Russia and the World

Russia remains one of the world's leading powers. It has the world's largest stockpile of nuclear weapons. It is also one of the world's top energy producers.

A World Partner Russia is a member of the Group of 8 industrialized nations, or G-8. As a member of the G-8, Russia joined the United States in 2006 to announce shared anti-terror initiatives. Russia has worked with the G-8 on other issues. These include climate change, energy, and economic development.

Russia has also taken part in other international efforts. One of these was the North Korean Six-Party Talks, aimed at convincing North Korea to give up nuclear weapons.

Russia has strongly opposed efforts by the former Soviet republics of Ukraine and Georgia to join NATO. Both countries border on Russia.

my World IN NUMBERS

In 2008, the economic output per person for Russia was **$15,800**. For the United States, it was **$47,000**.

◄ A protester holds a photograph of Russian journalist Anastasia Baburova, who was killed in 2009.

READING CHECK The government owns most radio and televisions stations, so it can censor stories.

- **Synthesize** Are the Russian government's actions in censoring media legal under Russia's constitution? Explain. (Sample: No, the constitution promises freedoms of speech and of the press, but the government suppresses them.)

- **Cause and Effect** What happened to the Russian energy industry? (Putin put it under government control.)

- **Infer** Why do you think President Medvedev identified corruption as a problem? (Sample: Foreign businesses might not invest in Russia if they have to pay bribes.)

Russia and the World

- **Synthesize** How does Russia's G-8 membership relate to its goal of being a superpower? (The G-8 is a group of powerful nations that addresses major issues.)

- **Draw Conclusions** Why do you think Russia does not want North Korea to have nuclear weapons? (Sample: It is nearby, so its weapons endanger Russia.)

ANSWERS

ECONOMICS

Group of Eight The Group of Eight is an organization of governments whose leaders meet to discuss economic issues annually. Begun in 1975, the group was originally known as the Group of 7. It included the United States, the United Kingdom, France, West Germany, Italy, Canada, and Japan. West Germany became Germany after reunification. Russia joined the group officially in 1997, although it had informally participated in talks since 1994. The Group of Eight does not have a formal charter or a permanent secretariat. Before each annual meeting, representatives of the national leaders do the advance preparation for the upcoming discussions. The location of the meetings rotates among the eight countries.

GUIDE ON THE SIDE

myWorld Activity
Russia Trivia Game

- **Summarize** What happened when Russia supported independence movements in regions of Georgia? (Georgia tried to regain control, and then Russia invaded Georgia. This action damaged Russia's international relationships.)

- **Identify Details** To where does Russia export oil? (Europe and Asia)

- **Categorize** What western alliance have many former Soviet republics joined? (the European Union)

Analyze Maps Have students look at the Russian energy map.

- What countries labeled on this map do not receive Russian oil by pipeline? (Austria, Italy, Romania, Bulgaria, Turkey, Moldova)

 myWorld Activity

Quiz Yourself Find Step-by-Step Instructions and an Activity Support on pp. T158–T159. **(Verbal/Kinesthetic)**

→ **Active Atlas**

Have students go online to learn more about Russian oil exports.

Russia has supported independence movements in the Georgian regions of Abkhazia and South Ossetia. Georgian troops entered South Ossetia in 2008 to try to regain control of the region. Russian troops responded by driving Georgian troops out of South Ossetia. Russian forces also bombed and invaded other parts of Georgia. Russia's invasion of Georgia damaged its relations with the United States and other Western nations.

Russian Energy Russia has also flexed its muscles in global energy markets. Russia is the second largest oil-exporting nation in the world. Russia is also the world's largest exporter of natural gas. Oil and gas pipelines from Russia reach far into Europe and Asia. In the past, Russia has halted the flow of natural gas to Western Europe through Ukraine. It has done this in response to disagreements with the government of Ukraine. Russia has signed exclusive agreements to supply gas to Germany and other European nations to try to win their backing for Russian policies. Western Europeans have criticized Russia for using energy to increase its power.

Cooperation and Conflict Russia controls much of the energy supply for the European Union (EU). Russia has opposed the EU membership of former Soviet republics such as Estonia, Latvia, and Lithuania.

Transporting Russian Energy

Map Skills
1. **Region** According to the map, Russian oil pipelines extend to which European nations to the west?
2. **Movement** Through which nations must Russian gas travel to reach Italy?

→ **Active Atlas**

KEY
— Oil pipeline
— Gas pipeline
Lambert Azimuthal Equal-Area Projection

MAP SKILLS 1. Germany, Poland, Latvia, Lithuania, Slovakia, Croatia, Hungary, Czech Republic, Ukraine, Belarus **2.** Ukraine, Slovakia; Austria

READING CHECK The Shanghai Cooperative Organization is a loose alliance that includes China, Russia, and several Central Asian countries.

SECTION 3 ASSESSMENT 1. Samples: The KGB was the Soviet secret police. Disposable income is income after tax. To censor is to restrict what can be published. A superpower is one of the strongest nations in the world. **2.** It took

ANSWERS

HISTORY

Sino-Soviet Relations When China first became communist, it formed an alliance with the Soviet Union. By the 1960s, Chinese leader Mao Zedong believed the Soviet Union had drifted away from pure communism. China and the Soviet Union began to compete over which country would have the most influence in the developing world. In 1962, Mao criticized the Soviet Union for backing down from the Cuban missile crisis with the United States, and the Soviet Union backed India in a brief war against China. In addition, the Soviet Union signed a Nuclear Test-Ban Treaty with the United States and Britain in 1963. The Chinese government viewed that as an anti-Chinese plot. In 1969, clashes took place on the Sino-Soviet border, but the two countries managed to avoid war. They did not become allies again until the 2001 Sino-Russian treaty.

However, Russia has <u>cooperated</u> with the EU on matters such as energy and climate change. These agreements include other former Soviet republics such as Ukraine, Belarus, and Kazakhstan.

Russia is a trading partner with Iran, which has poor relations with the United States. Russia has also loaned money to Iran to build nuclear reactors.

The United States has objected to this project. It is concerned that Iran will use the reactors to develop nuclear weapons. Russia's relationship with the United States has remained calm but cool.

Another foreign policy issue is Russia's relationship with China, the world's largest country in population. The Soviet Union and China had been competitors and enemies. This changed when Russia and China formed the Shanghai Cooperation Organization with several Central Asian countries in 2001. This organization has become a loose alliance. Joint military practices between Russia and China have worried Western nations.

The Future of Russia Strong post-Soviet leadership has reshaped Russia's politics and economy. Rich natural resources and continued superpower status make Russia an important player on the global stage. Whether it works together with the United States and other Western powers or takes a more hostile attitude, Russia has the world's full attention.

Reading Check What is the Shanghai Cooperation Organization?

cooperate, *v.,* to work together toward an agreed goal

Georgian soldiers run past a building bombed by Russian warplanes during the 2008 conflict. ▼

Section 3 Assessment

Key Terms
1. Define each key term using a complete sentence: KGB, disposable income, censor, superpower.

Key Ideas
2. In what ways did the Russian government under Vladimir Putin halt democratic reform?
3. How did Russia's petroleum industry change under Putin?
4. What are some of the major health problems in Russia?

Think Critically
5. Draw Conclusions Why do you think Russia has opposed membership in the European Union for former Soviet republics?
6. Draw Inferences Why might Russia want closer relations with China?

Essential Question
What should governments do?
7. Think about the life expectancy and infant mortality graphs in this section. What do you think the government can do about the health problems in Russia? Go to your Student Journal to record your answer.

CASE STUDY LESSON PLAN

The Soviet Industrial Legacy

OBJECTIVES
Students will
- know how Stalin's Five-Year Plans transformed the Soviet economy.
- identify positive and negative effects of forced industrialization.
- **ELL** learn English words related to the term *industrialization.*

SET EXPECTATIONS
In this case study, students will
- read The Soviet Industrial Legacy.
- identify evidence of the effects of pollution.

---

1 Connect

Have the class discuss the sacrifices they would make to get ahead. Ask, Would you be willing to give up free time? Would you work in a place that damages your health? Then ask, What sacrifices does a government have the right to ask people to make for progress? Discuss students' responses. Tell them that many Russians today must deal with poor health and pollution because of past government decisions to industrialize.

L2 Extra Support Help students make connections by reminding them that Stalin put people he considered political enemies in labor camps. Such prisoners could not choose whether to work in dangerous conditions.

---

2 Learn

Preview Have students preview pictures, headings, and Key Terms. Review what Josef Stalin's Five-Year Plans were, and remind them that Stalin ruled as a dictator with almost total control over the Soviet government. Ask, Did Stalin successfully modernize the Soviet economy? Tell them they will return to this question after reading.

Read While the students read "The Soviet Industrial Legacy," ask questions found in the **Guide on the Side** to build understanding of Key Ideas and objectives.

🏃 **myWorld Activity: City in a Dead Zone** Give students *Activity Support: Identify Evidence* and ask them to read the article excerpt and answer the questions. Then ask them to form small groups and work together to decide what they think the

⏱ **30 min** 👥👥

Russian government should do about the situation in Norilsk. They can write an editorial or write and perform a mock-televised political ad. Remind them to use evidence from the article to show why the government should take their proposed action. **(Verbal/Kinesthetic)**

ELL Intermediate Give groups of students the following list of words related to *industrialization: industry, industrial, industrious, industrialism.* Have them work together to write down what they think each word means. Provide a dictionary so they can check their definitions.

L2 Extra Support If students have difficulty answering the activity questions, have them practice Identifying Evidence on the **21st Century Online Tutor.**

---

3 Understand

Review Discuss students' responses to the questions, probing for understanding of key issues.

Assess Ask students to recall whether they believed that Stalin successfully modernized the Soviet economy. Have them list both a positive and negative effect of Stalin's industrialization program. (Positive: education, more industry; negative: pollution, too much emphasis on heavy industry)

Remediate If students are struggling to understand the Key Ideas, have them create a flowchart with three boxes. The heads for the boxes should be *Stalin's Economic Plans, The Effects of Stalin's Plans,* and *The Economy After Stalin.* Have students skim the text and fill in the flowchart with important details.

Name _____   Class _____   Date _____

myWorld Activity Support   **Identify Evidence**

City in a Dead Zone

Directions Read the primary source below about the pollution caused by mining operations in Norilsk. Answer the questions that follow.

Excerpt from "Toxic Truth of a Secretive Siberian City"

Twenty-four hours a day, seven days a week, the chimneys pump out a toxic cocktail of pollutants which the company responsible openly admits is mostly sulphur dioxide.

Once in the atmosphere this gas turns into acid rain. . . . We drove to one of the woods just outside Norilsk to see for ourselves what has happened.

We soon found many trees which were either dead or dying. According to local residents the evidence is even easier to see later in the year. "Things start to grow green then," Doctor Svetlana Golubkova told us. "But the gas cloud goes over and they die."

Even more worrying for her is the impact on the health of the population, particularly children.

She says she has detected a clear trend. "In the 1960s a lot of people came here and they were all healthy. But now there are very, very few healthy children being born here and that is all because of the environment."

—BBC online, April 5, 2007

When answering the questions, use textual evidence, words from the article, to support each answer.

1. What evidence shows that acid rain kills forests?

   _____

2. How does acid rain affect human health? What evidence shows that?

   _____

   _____

3. What evidence shows that the mining operations cause pollution?

   _____

   _____

CULTURE

Five-Year Plans for Chess In its desire to prove the superiority of the communist way of life, the Soviet government extended central planning into cultural areas. For example, Moscow decided that the Soviet Union must dominate the world of chess. Stalin's commissar of war Nikolai Krylenko declared, "We must organize shock brigades of chess players and begin immediately a Five-Year Plans for chess."

The government invested money in training chess players; at its peak, the Soviet system boasted five million players. Soviet chess players rose to become some of the most accomplished grand masters in the world. They competed against U.S. players in international tournaments, and if they won, received unparalleled privileges for what was perceived as a Cold War victory.

Build for the Motherland

- **Compare Viewpoints** According to Stalin, what belief was supposed to make Soviet citizens willing to endure hardship? (the belief that they were making honorable sacrifices for the motherland)

- **Infer** Why do you think the Soviet plan concentrated on heavy industry? (Sample: They needed such industry to produce weapons and other military equipment.)

- **Cause and Effect** What probably happened to people who spoke out against the Five-Year Plans? (Sample: They were put in gulags and forced to work on industrialization projects.)

Case Study

The Soviet Industrial Legacy

Key Ideas	• Stalin's Five-Year Plans boosted the development of industry in the Soviet Union. • Stalin used force to increase the pace of industrial development.	• Free-market reforms have reduced government control of the modern Russian economy.
Key Terms	• Five-Year Plan • industrialization • command economy	• heavy industry • gulag

These days, most adults in the village of Muslumovo on the Techa River have health problems. "What can we do?" says a local man. "We need water. Cows drink it, birds drink it, we drink it. And by the time we're forty, we're all ill." Recently, scientists discovered the cause of this widespread sickness. In 1957, there was an explosion at the nearby Mayak nuclear plant. The radiation that is making everyone ill dates back even further to the Soviet industrial push of the 1930s.

Both men and women worked on Soviet industrialization projects. ▼

Build for the Motherland

Following Lenin's unexpected death in 1924, a new Soviet leader emerged. Josef Stalin wanted to transform the Soviet Union with a series of **Five-Year Plans.** These were government plans for the economy that made basic decisions and set priorities for five years. Each Five-Year Plan pushed for the collectivization of farms and rapid **industrialization,** or development of industry. These government plans concentrated on building **heavy industry,** or the manufacture of steel, equipment, or weapons. Stalin's plans indeed transformed the Soviet Union, but at a terrible cost.

Stalin believed that for communism to survive, the Soviet Union would have to become a world industrial leader. He imposed a full-scale **command economy,** or one in which the government makes all basic economic decisions. He expected citizens to accept all economic hardships as honorable sacrifices for the Soviet motherland.

By the 1930s, millions of workers were working on the nation's construction projects as inmates of forced-labor camps. Later known as **gulags,** these camps housed political prisoners charged with crimes such as private ownership of land or criticism of the government.

CORE CONCEPTS: ECONOMIC SYSTEMS

Review Core Concept 5.3 before reading the case study. Remind students of the differences between command economies and market economies. Ask, In which type of economic system does the government play a larger role? Explain to students, that under Stalin, the Soviet government developed Five-Year Plans that directed what the economy was supposed to produce. Ask, Judging from that information, what type of economy did the Soviet Union have—command or market? Then ask students to suppose that they work as farmers or factory owners. How would they feel if the government controlled what they could produce?

Industrialization and the Gulags

Millions of gulag prisoners built Stalin's factories, dams, and canals. Perhaps as many as 20 million people passed through the gulags from 1928 to 1939. Conditions in the camps were horrible. Prisoners lived in fear and exhaustion. Food was poor and medical care almost nonexistent. Millions died as a result.

THINK CRITICALLY How did Stalin use the gulags for industrialization?

▲ Gulag laborers were treated like beasts of burden.

Soviet Industrial Growth

SOURCE: European Historical Statistics, 1750–1993

Soviet Industrial Centers

KEY
— 1939 border
○ Industrial center

ARCTIC OCEAN
SOVIET UNION
Leningrad, Moscow, Perm, Donbas, Sverdlovsk, Chelyabinsk, Kuzbas

Stalin believed that the success of the Five-Year Plans depended on education. Before the Revolution, 65 percent of the population was illiterate. The government taught millions to read and write. Worker training programs also prepared men and women for Five-Year-Plan projects.

Stalin expanded universities so that students could learn math, science and engineering. Even there, Stalin attempted to dictate the behavior and thinking of professors and students.

At first, people were eager to work on Stalin's projects. They believed that if they worked hard, they would live well. However, workers soon discovered that they were expected to produce a great deal for low wages. In addition, they paid heavy fines if they were late or absent.

Many Soviets expected that the Five-Year Plans would raise standards of living, but Stalin pushed only heavy industry. This led to widespread shortages in clothing, housing, and food.

Reading Check **Why did Stalin want to transform the Soviet economy?**

THINK CRITICALLY He forced prisoners to work on his construction projects.

READING CHECK He wanted the Soviet Union to be a global industrial leader.

HISTORY

The Gulag System One way that Josef Stalin kept his grip on power was to send his enemies to the prison system in Siberia called the gulag. The word *gulag* is an acronym made from the Russian words for "chief administration of corrective labor camps." Hundreds of camps existed, each one holding 2,000–10,000 people. Prisoners included intellectuals, the wealthy, political opponents, peasants who resisted collectivization, disloyal military officers, ordinary criminals, and prisoners of war. Millions of gulag prisoners were employed in forced labor camps doing construction or mining. About ten percent of all prisoners died each year from starvation, overwork, the harsh climate, or summary executions. Western scholars estimate that between 15 and 30 million people died in the gulag.

Stalin's Industrial Legacy

- **Express an Opinion** Do you think Stalin would have agreed with the statement "The ends justify the means"? Explain. (Sample: He would have agreed because he ignored damage in order to industrialize faster.)

- **Cause and Effect** How did waterways become damaged? (from the construction of dams)

Analyze Visuals Have students look at the photographs of the three industrial cities.

- Why do you think people continue to live in these cities? (Samples: for jobs, because they cannot afford to leave)

Stalin's Industrial Legacy

Industrialization left its mark on all of modern Russia. Factories, mines and industrial cities cover what had been Siberian wilderness. Universities expanded by Stalin educate today's scientists and business people.

The rush to industrialize also meant that the Soviet government ignored pollution, health issues, and environmental concerns in favor of economic progress.

Acid rain has damaged thousands of acres of woodlands. Vast areas of what was once good farmland are now unusable due to soil contamination. Waterways and habitats remain damaged from dams built to generate hydroelectric power. Perhaps the most serious threat is radioactive pollution such as that found in Muslumovo.

Reading Check What have been some of the negative effects of industrilization?

The Legacy Remains

Muslumovo

In the 1930s, the region around Muslumovo supplied copper for industry and the military. People began to become ill in the 1950s, but they kept quiet. They feared the government's reaction if they complained. The modern Russian government has been more sympathetic, offering villagers new homes in another town.

▲ A sign in Muslumovo forbids villagers from fishing in the area due to high levels of radiation.

Kuzbass

Kuzbass, or the Kuznetsk Basin, holds some of the largest coal deposits in the world. This coal fueled new factories in the basin and elsewhere along the Trans-Siberian Railroad. The basin also supplied iron, steel, zinc, and aluminum. Today, the Kuznetsk Basin remains an important industrial center in Russia.

▲ A woman walks through snow covered with soot released by the factories in the Kuzbass region.

Norilsk

During the Soviet era, foreigners were not allowed to visit Norilsk. The Soviets did not want outsiders to know about the missiles kept there. This secrecy also hid the city's pollution. Norilsk processes nickel, copper, platinum, gold, and silver, and almost half of the world's supply of palladium, a metal used in automobile exhaust systems.

▲ A copper worker in Norilsk breathes through a filter to keep contaminants out of his lungs.

READING CHECK pollution, radiation exposure, neglect of healthcare

READING CHECK They might believe that he did what was necessary to move the country ahead.

CHART SKILLS It increased by about seven times.

PRIMARY SOURCE

No Return to Central Planning In 2009, Vladimir Putin declared that the world economic crisis should not be an excuse to return to a command economy: "True, the state's increased role in times of crisis is a natural reaction to market setbacks. Instead of streamlining market mechanisms, some are tempted to expand state economic intervention to the greatest possible extent. The concentration of surplus assets in the hands of the state is a negative aspect of anticrisis measures in virtually every nation. In the 20th century, the Soviet Union made the state's role absolute. In the long run, this made the Soviet economy totally uncompetitive. This lesson cost us dearly. I am sure nobody wants to see it repeated."

—Vladimir Putin, speech at the World Economic Forum, January 28, 2009

The New Russian Economy

After the fall of the Soviet Union, the Russian economy collapsed. The recovery and boom of the early 2000s came mainly from earnings from Russia's massive energy resources. Wages rose, and Russians could afford to purchase consumer goods they had never before owned.

Russia: Average Monthly Wage, 2001–2008

SOURCE: Goskomstat

Chart Skills

In modern Russia, stores selling electronic goods (such as the one above in Moscow) are relatively new. Compare the average monthly wage in 2001 with the wage in 2008. How much did the average monthly wage change during these years?

The New Russian Economy

Industrialization left another kind of legacy in Russia. A recent survey showed that many Russians have a favorable view of Stalin's dictatorship. They believe that Stalin did much for Russia. They, too, see themselves working to make Russia great.

Many of the more successful Russians in today's economy are under age 35. One young company executive recently exclaimed, "Is there anything better that can be offered to me than creating the new Russian economy?"

This younger generation has grown up since the collapse of communism, and many accept the uncertainties of a market economy. They use computers, cellphones, and the Internet—all of which are fairly new to Russia. Many are optimistic about being able to earn good wages and about starting new businesses.

The push to industrialize had both positive and negative results for Russia. Stalin's vision for Russia continues to influence life today.

Reading Check Why might modern Russians have a positive view of Stalin?

Assessment

1. Summarize the main purpose of Stalin's Five-Year Plans.

2. How did Stalin use education to promote industrialization?

3. State one way in which each city on the previous page shows evidence of the Soviet push to industrialize.

4. How might more economic freedom change Russia?

5. What types of technology can modern Russians use that were not available during the Soviet period?

GUIDE ON THE SIDE

The New Russian Economy

- **Identify Bias** Why might older Russians have a more difficult time with the new economy? (Sample: They might still be influenced by communist beliefs.)

- **Summarize** What do young Russians hope for the future? (They want to be able to earn good wages and start up new businesses.)

Analyze Charts Have students look at the bar graph of monthly wages.

- In which two years did wages increase the most? (2007 and 2008)

1. Siberia presents Russia with advantages because of its wealth in mineral resources. It presents challenges because of its climate, the presence of permafrost, and its inaccessibility.

2. The tunda has a cold, dry climate and low-lying vegetation. Steppe vegetation is mostly grasses.

THINK CRITICALLY

9. Sample: Stalin's main motive was to stay in power, no matter how many other people died.

10. Sample: Yes, Stalin did not care about the loss of human life; he cared only about getting his own way.

11. Sample: The rule of the Mongols, the tsars, and the Communist Party during the Soviet era; and the more recent moves by Putin to crush criticism are all examples of autocratic government.

12. Sample: They are used to having strong central government, and the turmoil that occurred after the Soviet Union collapsed frightened them.

3. The tsars were autocratic rulers; some westernized Russia but did not free the serfs.

4. They were impressive buildings that were used for government functions.

5. Under communism, the control of the government and economy was centralized in the Communist Party.

6. Collectivization was the policy of combining smaller farms into large state-controlled farms. The end result was poor yields and mass starvation.

7. Sample: It might make him more secretive and authoritarian.

8. Sample: The government might fear that negative news stories would motivate people to rise against the government again.

Russia

Chapter Assessment

Key Terms and Ideas

1. **Recall** In what ways does **Siberia** present Russia with great advantages and great challenges?

2. **Compare and Contrast** Describe the climate and vegetation on the tundra and the **steppes.**

3. **Explain** What sort of rulers were the Russian **tsars?**

4. **Recall** How did the buildings of the **Kremlin** demonstrate power in imperial Russia?

5. **Discuss** How did communism shape the Soviet government and economy?

6. **Summarize** What was **collectivization** and how did affect the Soviet Union?

7. **Discuss** How might Putin's **KGB** background affect his beliefs about the role of government?

8. **Explain** What might prompt the Russian government to **censor** a news story?

Think Critically

9. **Draw Conclusions** Why do you think Josef Stalin took actions such as collectivization and the jailing of opponents? Explain.

10. **Compare Viewpoints** One of Stalin's officers said the Great Famine would show the peasants "who is the master. It cost millions of lives, but the collective farm system is here to stay." Do you think Stalin agreed with him? Why?

11. **Identify Evidence** What historical evidence would support the statement "Russia has a long history of autocratic government"?

12. **Drawing Inferences** Why do you think many Russians want the government to be in control of wages, pensions, and healthcare?

Places to Know

For each place, write the letter from the map that shows its location.

13. **Kamchatka Peninsula**
14. **Yakutsk**
15. **Lake Baikal**
16. **Moscow**
17. **St. Petersburg**
18. **Ural Mountains**
19. **Estimate** Using the scale, estimate the distance from Moscow to Lake Baikal.

PLACES TO KNOW

13. B
14. F
15. E
16. A

17. D
18. C
19. about 3,200 miles

myWorld Chapter Activity

Memo to Russia Find Step-by-Step Instructions, Student Instructions and Rubric, and an Activity Support on pp. T139–T141. **(Visual/Verbal/Interpersonal)**

21st Century Learning

Search for Information on the Internet Remind students to look for information about who runs and maintains the Web sites they use. Many Web sites have a page called "About Us" that will describe the organization that runs the Web site. The types of Web sites listed in the activity are usually reliable.

 Online Assessment

Tailor review and assessment to each student's needs with an array of online assessments.
- Self-Test
- On Assignment Article or Slideshow
- Success Tracker

? Essential Question
myWorld Chapter Activity

 Memo to Russia Follow your teacher's instructions to examine information on some of the challenges facing Russia today. Consider environmental data, Russian health and crime figures, as well as the nation's international partnerships and other information as you set priorities. After your review, prepare an official government memo detailing which problem Russia should address first and why.

21st Century Learning
Search for Information on the Internet

Search for three different Web sites for additional information about the political, economic, and social challenges facing Russia. The following types of Web sites might prove helpful:
- encyclopedias or museums
- international organizations, such as the UN or World Trade Organization
- U.S. sites such as *CIA World Factbook*

Document-Based Questions

Success Tracker™
Online at myworldgeography.com

Use your knowledge of Russia and Documents A and B to answer questions 1–3.

Document A

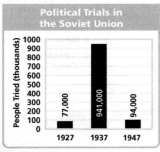

Political Trials in the Soviet Union

Year	People Tried (thousands)
1927	77,000
1937	941,000
1947	94,000

SOURCE: Open Society Archives

Document B

" You might well ask why a prisoner worked so hard for ten years in a camp. . . . In the camps they had these gangs to make the prisoners keep each other on their toes. . . . It was like this—either you all got something extra or you all starved."

—Alexander Solzhenitsyn, *One Day in the Life of Ivan Denisovich* (a book about life in a Soviet prison camp)

1. How did the number of people brought to trial change from 1927 to 1937?
   A It decreased.
   B It increased by half.
   C It increased by more than 10 times.
   D It increased by 100 times.

2. What would be the punishment if a prisoner stopped working hard?
   A The guards would whip him in front of his gang.
   B The guards would take food away from his gang.
   C He would be put into a new labor camp.
   D He would have to give his food to his gang.

3. **Writing Task** What do you think the gang would say to a prisoner who stopped working hard? Write a dialogue.

WRITING TASK TIP

Dialogue Demonstrate on the board how to write dialogue by listing a character's name followed by a colon and then the lines that are to be spoken. Brainstorm a class list of Russian names that students can use for the characters in their dialogue.

DOCUMENT-BASED QUESTIONS

1. C
2. B
3. Sample:
   SERGEI: Pavel, keep working. We'll all be in trouble if the guard sees you.
   PAVEL: I'm so tired. My feet are frozen.
   SERGEI: If you stop working, none of us will get any food tonight. I will beat you myself if you cause the whole gang to be punished.

BACKGROUND

Media Bias Two famous cases of biased media occurred in the late 1800s. In 1894 in France, an army officer named Alfred Dreyfus was convicted of being a spy for Germany. The charges were false; another man who really was a spy forged the evidence. Dreyfus was Jewish, and the newspaper coverage of the case was strongly anti-Semitic. This bias stirred public opinion against Dreyfus, making it difficult for him to get a fair trial. He was imprisoned for four years. At about the same time, Cuba began fighting for independence from Spain. In 1898, the United States sent the battleship *Maine* to Havana to guard U.S. lives and property there. The ship sank after an explosion of unknown origin. Some U.S. papers were quick to blame Spain and demand that the United States intervene in Cuba. This campaign helped ignite the Spanish-American War.

GUIDE ON THE SIDE

21st Century Learning

Analyze Media Content Give students the following definition of *bias*: "an unfair liking for or dislike of something." Ask students to name examples of bias that they have encountered. Post their responses on the board. They might mention things like racial prejudice, bias against children in public places, or hostility toward poor, handicapped, or overweight people. Remind the class that media include newspapers, television, radio, magazines, and other means of mass communication. Explain that students will be analyzing two examples of media content to see if they contain bias.

21st Century Learning ✦ Analyze Media Content

Media Watchdog

Your Mission Use the Media Analysis Checklist to study the poster on the facing page. Examine how the poster conveys its message. Then go online and evaluate an article or opinion piece.

Media messages are everywhere in modern society. Can you believe everything you see, hear, and read on television, in print, or on the Internet? Who keeps track of the media's honesty and objectivity? When a member of the media is accused of bias, how can you know who is right?

By understanding how to analyze media content, you can spot bias and persuasive messages. Practicing this skill will help you to evaluate whether or not public officials and news sources are telling you the truth. You can also apply these techniques to advertising, which will help you decide how to spend your money more wisely.

Media Analysis Checklist

1. Author
2. Intended audience
3. Words or phrases
4. Images and other design elements
5. Overall message
6. Persuasive techniques
7. Examples of bias, if any

ANSWERS

MEDIA WATCHDOG RUBRIC
3. Students complete each line of the Media Analysis Checklist with specific details about the poster. Students find an appropriate article or opinion piece about Europe or Russia. Students complete a second Media Analysis Checklist with specific details about the article or opinion piece.

CULTURE

Retouched Photos One way in which bias is introduced into media is through the process of altering photographs. In the former Soviet Union, this practice was widespread. Often, when a Communist Party leader fell into disfavor, technicians altered historical photographs to eliminate the disgraced person from the record. For example, in several instances the figure of exiled leader Leon Trotsky was removed from photographs where he appeared with Vladimir Lenin. Computer programs make it even easier to alter photographs today, and the practice still continues. In April 2009, two conservative newspapers in Israel removed two women officials from a photograph of the Israeli cabinet. They did so because of their cultural belief that it is improper for women to have their photographs made public.

Go to myWorldGeography.com for help with this activity.

STEP 1

Determine the Message.

Copy the Media Analysis Checklist at the left onto your own paper. Use it to record your observations about the poster at the right. Who published the poster, and who is its intended audience? (Hint: Look at the flag at the bottom of the poster.) Read the poster and study its visual elements, such as the use of colors or photographs. Considering the words and visuals together, what is the poster's message?

STEP 2

Check for Bias.

Next, evaluate how the poster uses persuasive techniques such as bright colors or a photograph with children. Note how the poster uses words that are short, simple, and to the point. Do these words encourage you to feel a certain way? Consider whether or not your reaction is based on facts or on opinions and feelings. Record your observations on your Media Analysis Checklist.

STEP 3

Analyze Online Media.

Make a second, blank copy of the Media Analysis Checklist. Now go online to sources suggested by your teacher. Find an article or opinion piece about Europe or Russia, and analyze it as you did the poster. Once you have completed your Media Analysis Checklist, use your findings in a class discussion.

It's not them and us, it's you and me

2008 European Year of Intercultural Dialogue

9 May – Europe Day

GUIDE ON THE SIDE

TIGed
TakingITGlobal for Educators

Have your students go to myworldgeography.com to find solutions to this 21st Century Learning Activity, *Media Watchdog*.

 21c Online Tutor

Using the 21st Century Online Tutor, students can get more tips on how to analyze media content for bias. Students respond onscreen to successfully learn and apply analysis and evaluation skills.

Ancient and Medieval Europe

See rubric on p. T6.

myWorld Chapter Activity: Piecing Together the Past

Sample Field Report:

	Artifact
Describe the artifact.	It is a mosaic that is a portrait of an empress.
What is the artifact's date?	A.D. 500s
What was it made of?	Chips of stone
What was its purpose?	Decoration, honor

Artifacts on the timeline should be sequenced correctly.

Section 1
Ancient and Medieval Europe

myWorld Activity: Let's Make a Trade

1. grain, livestock, lumber	2. Sample: grain
3. fish, olive oil, gold, silver, iron	4. Sample: olive oil
5. Asia Minor, Egypt, Mesopotamia	6. Sample: Egypt

Maps should show Greece and a trading partner, arrows with symbols for trade goods, and a map key.

Enrichment: Greek Gods and Goddesses

1. Sample: Poseidon; he controlled the seas.

2. Sample: Hades because he was the god of the dead and Ares because he was the god of war

3. Family trees should show Poseidon and Hades as Zeus's brothers, Hera as Zeus's wife, and Athena, Apollo, Artemis, Ares, and Hermes as Zeus's children.

Section 1 Quiz

1. b   2. c   3. a   4. b   5. d
6. **Athens** democratic; interested in philosophy, culture, and learning **Sparta** Ruled by an oligarchy, pursued war, women had more rights **Similar** Both were Greek city-states, and both fought against Persia.

Primary Source: Ancient Greek Literature

myWorld Activity: Planning an Odyssey

Sample:
I. A. Captain Terrific

   B. a remote island

   C. to find lost treasure

II. St. Louis

   A. A terrible storm threatens Captain Terrific's plane.
   B. Captain Terrific flies the plane to safety.

III. San Francisco

   A. a villain who sabotages the ship

   B. Captain Terrific repairs the ship and stops it from sinking.

IV. Hawaii

   A. a beautiful woman who wants Captain Terrific to stay and marry her after he finds treasure

   B. Captain Terrific talks her into going away with him.

V. Conclusion

   A. They reach the remote island

   B. They find a chest full of gold coins.

Section 2
Ancient and Medieval Europe

myWorld Activity: What's the News in Rome
Fact Gathering

Sample:
Event from Roman History: the assassination of Caesar
Who: Julius Caesar, aristocrats
What: an assassination
Where: the Forum in Rome
When: March 15, 44 B.C.
Why: to end tyranny and restore the republic
How: several men using knives

Enrichment: Biography of Julius Caesar

1. Caesar provided recreation, made reforms that helped the poor, and won battles.

2. Samples: He was a good ruler because he made reforms and won wars. He was a poor ruler because his ambitions caused civil war that tore Rome apart.

Section 2 Quiz

1. b **2.** d **3.** c **4.** a **5.** c

6. Literature the poetry of Virgil and Horace, and the essays of Cicero **Building** arches, concrete, and aqueducts **Art** realistic statues

Primary Source: The Fall of the Roman Empire

myWorld Activity: Act Before It's Too Late!

Samples:
Name the danger: using lead
Category: cultural
What will happen if Romans ignore the danger: widespread sickness, weakness, early death
What Romans can do to end the danger: switch to copper or another metal
What visual image you want to use: a skull and crossbones
A quotation from one of the excerpts to use on mural: "Lead is one of the most poisonous metals a person can ingest."

Section 3 Ancient and Medieval Europe

myWorld Activity: Write in Cyrillic

1. A, E, K, M, O, T

2. B, H, P, C, Y, X

My first name: Samples: Capa (Sara), Ebah (Evan)
Sentence: Sentences will vary; students should try to transliterate their partners' sentences back into English, but they may have difficulty because the languages use different sounds.

Enrichment: Feudalism Social Pyramid

1. the king

2. Nobles were vassals to the king but lords to the knights.

3. The peasants did; they had to farm the lands of the lords.

Section 3 Quiz

1. c **2.** c **3.** a **4.** a **5.** b
6.

A lord owed his vassals	A vassal owed his lord
land and protection	military service and economic support

Primary Source: Learned Women of the Middle Ages

myWorld Activity: A Capable Wife

1. seeks wool and flax, works with willing hands, provides food, buys a field, plants a vineyard

2. Sample: She is honest and hard-working.

3. Sample: She seems similar to Christine de Pisan, who told wives to give food to the poor.

Section 4 Ancient and Medieval Europe

myWorld Activity: Trade Spices up Life

Sample Result:
The Arab trader will have 500 wooden logs, 500 porcelain dishes, and 2 tons of cinnamon.
The Italian trader will have 100 bolts of silk, 4 tons of coffee, and 300 pounds of pepper.
The Chinese trader will have 6 tons of wheat, 450 bolts of cotton, and 400 casks of wine.

Enrichment: Descriptions of the Black Death

1. Sample: It killed people very quickly, and it had horrible symptoms, such as vomiting blood.

2. People were so scared of the disease that they wouldn't help people who were sick, even if they were relatives.

3. Sample public service announcement: The fleas on rats cause this disease. Keep your homes free of garbage and get a cat.

Section 4 Quiz

1. b **2.** c **3.** c **4.** b **5.** d
6. Cause infected fleas **Effects** huge population loss, anti-Semitism, decline of feudalism

Europe in Modern Times

See rubric on p. T42.

myWorld Chapter Activity: Technology: Then and Now

Sample Analysis Table:
Answers in order of Card Number, Inventions, Who Used Them, Positive Effects, Negative Effects, and Recent Invention:

49. map, compass, astrolabe; sailors; safer journeys; aided colonial conquest; GPS

50. printing press, movable type; printers; spread ideas and literacy; conflict from spread of new ideas; Internet

51. telescope, anatomy drawing; scientists and doctors; more knowledge; imprisoned for denying church teachings; CAT scan

52. spinning jenny, flying spinning frame; textile industry; more cloth, produced more cheaply; loss of home textile industry; robots in textile factories

53. cannons, machine guns, rifles, airplanes; army, navy; better national defense; higher death tolls in war; stealth planes, drones

54. steam locomotive and engine; travelers, merchants; faster transportation; pollution; bullet train

Section 1
Europe in Modern Times

myWorld Activity: A Life-Changing Product

Sample:

Trade Item	How It Changed Life in Europe	Advertising Slogan
Magnetic compass	It made long voyages safer.	It will help you find your way.
Porcelain	It made beautiful dishes.	Add beauty to every meal.
Silk cloth	It was a bright, beautiful cloth.	Dress like a queen.
Gunpowder	It made more powerful, destructive weapons.	Conquer the world with gunpowder!
Spices	They masked the taste of spoiled food.	Waste less, enjoy more!
Tea	It provided energy.	Get more done by drinking tea.

Enrichment: Biography of Leonardo da Vinci

1. Sample: He could create art for them, design buildings, and help with mechanical things.

2. Sample: Yes, he was good at art, science, mathematics, and technical subjects.

3. Sample: Dear Leonardo, Please come live and work at my court. I want you to paint my portrait and invent weapons to help me defeat my enemies. I will pay you gold and let you live in my palace.

Section 1 Quiz

1. d   2. a   3. a   4. c   5. a
6. This invention made it possible to create multiple copies of books more quickly than before, so more people were able to buy books and acquire knowledge.

Primary Source: Renaissance Views of Rulers

myWorld Activity: A Queen's Opinion

1. It is more glorious to see a crown. She meant that rulers must overcome many problems within their kingdom, so it is more work that one would think to be a ruler.

2. She believed God wanted her to maintain truth and glory and defend his kingdom.

3. Sample: She cared about her people.

4. They were more like the ideas of More, who wanted his rulers to provide for their people.

Section 2
Europe in Modern Times

myWorld Activity: Sailing for Riches

Sample:
Costs of the Voyage

Equipment to Buy: sails, guns, swords, compass, astrolabe
Supplies to Buy: hardtack, dried food, barrels for water
People to Hire: sailors, navigators, soldiers

Benefits of the Voyage

Possible Economic Gains: gold, silver, resources
Possible Political Gains: a colony to rule
Other Possible Gains: the favor of the pope for converting people in other lands

Enrichment: The Columbian Exchange

1. Sample: wheat bread, oatmeal, and canned peaches

2. Sample: peanut butter, potato chips, and guacamole

3. Sample Menu for the Americas: baked sweet potatoes, corn chips and guacamole, fruit salad with pineapple and papaya, potato chips and peanuts

Section 2 Quiz

1. b   2. d   3. b   4. b   5. c
6.

England	North America or the Atlantic coast, India, Australia
France	North America or Canada, India
Netherlands	North America, East Indies
Portugal	India, Southeast Asia, China
Spain	North and South America, the Caribbean

Section 3
Europe in Modern Times

myWorld Activity: Long Live the Revolution

1. Sample: It will sound as though it was written during the revolution.

2. Sample: It will feature diary-type entries.

3. Sample: Revolutionary Thoughts

4. Sample: blue for background, red for headlines

5. Students should create banner artwork that includes the blog title and a picture that relates to the Revolution.

6. Each blog post should have a title, a date, the author's name, and subject tags. Its text should focus on students' chosen subjects.

Enrichment: Important Inventions

1. thermometer, barometer

2. telescope, microscope

3. Sample: Scientists base their initial question or problem on their observations. Later, after they form a hypothesis, they must gather evidence to support or disprove it. Observation and measurement help them gather evidence.

Section 3 Quiz

1. a   2. b   3. d   4. a   5. b
6. Locke wrote that people are born with the right to life, liberty, and property. Montesquieu recommended dividing governments into branches. Rousseau wrote that government depends on the people's consent.

Section 4
Europe in Modern Times

myWorld Activity: Runaway Prices

Sample answers for discussion questions:
During times of runaway prices, people have to choose which necessities they can afford and which they cannot. They might have to go without food to buy medicine.
People would be likely to vote for a leader who promises to restore prosperity and not be concerned about what other opinions or positions he or she has.

Enrichment: Military Deaths of World War II

1. 5,216,900

2. Germany

3. Soviet Union, 11,000,000

4. the United Kingdom

Section 4 Quiz

1. c   2. a   3. b   4. d   5. a
6. The characteristics of fascism were extreme nationalism, military might, propaganda, the importance of the state, and rule by dictators.

Primary Source: The World Wars in Art

myWorld Activity: Vivid Writing

	From "In Flanders Fields"	From *Survival in Auschwitz*
Sight	Poppies, crosses, larks in flight, sunset, torch	Pile of mixed-up shoes, naked people, German's interested expression
Sound	Larks singing, guns	German spoken, sweeping, door slamming
Smell		
Taste		
Touch	"Felt dawn," holding torch	Freezing wind

1. Sample: I feel sad for the people who died.

2. Sample: the words *We are the Dead. Short days ago/We lived, felt dawn, saw sunset glow.*

3. Sample: I feel horrified by what's happening to the people.

4. Sample: the words *freezing wind, naked, writhe*

Section 5
Europe in Modern Times

myWorld Activity: Tear Down This Wall

1. Sample: The poster will criticize the division of Germany.

2. Sample: Put our country back together!

3. Sample: It could show a map of Germany with a crack splitting it in two and people building a bridge across the crack.

Enrichment: The Berlin Wall

1. The loss of skilled and educated workers hurt the economy.

2. Life was not as enjoyable as in the West.

3. Sample: They had been separated from family members and couldn't wait to see them again.

Section 5 Quiz

1. b   **2.** a   **3.** b   **4.** c   **5.** b

6. Answers should include several of the following events in order: Poland held free elections; other Eastern European countries overthrew communism in 1989; East Germans began to protest openly; border guards opened the Berlin Wall; East Germany ousted its communist government; the two Germanys were reunified.

Primary Source: Democracy in Eastern Europe

myWorld Activity: Outline an Introductory Paragraph

1. In both cases, they were controlled by large empires that had ruled the regions for centuries.

2. Eastern Europe struggled for more than a hundred years to gain democracy.

Sample Outline:

A. **Hook** Did you know people have died for democracy?

B. **Thesis Statement** People must make sacrifices in order to gain democracy.

C. 1. Eastern Europe fought for democracy for at least 140 years.

   2. People who fought for democracy were jailed.

   3. People who fought for democracy were executed.

Western Europe

See rubric on p. T84.

myWorld Chapter Activity: Norway and the EU

Sample Analysis Table:

Control of Revenue	Less trade restriction	3	Less oil control	9
Cultural Identity	Ease of travel	5	Immigrants change culture.	4
Sovereignty	United Europe	7	Less democracy	5
Protectionism	Lower prices on imports	4	Farmers must compete.	6
Sustainable Resources	More help protecting fishing areas	4	Less influence over fishing quotas	7
Independence	Strong allies	4	Fear of rule by others	8
		27		39

Sample:
My final vote: I vote no, because Norway will lose too much control if it joins the EU.

Section 1
Western Europe

myWorld Activity: Danube Cleanup

Samples: Germany: yes, has worked to protect the environment in the past; Slovakia: no, may affect businesses along the Danube; Hungary: no, may affect industrial growth; Croatia: yes, polluted water could affect the population; Romania: yes, polluted water will hurt the fishing industry

Enrichment: Comparing Climatographs

1. Warsaw has colder winters. Its January average temperature is about 25° F, while the average January temperature in London is about 39° F.

2. In most months, London recieves more rain.

3. London is closer to the ocean. The influence of the ocean would make the temperatures milder and cause more rain to fall on London.

Section 1 Quiz

1. d **2.** c **3.** a **4.** b **5.** c

6. People tend to live in low, flat plains with fertile soil. They often choose to live near rivers or coastlines. They are more likely to live in sunny, warm places such as Southern Europe. Finally, they also live near natural resources such as minerals.

Case Study: Energy for the Future

myWorld Activity: Meeting Energy Goals

1. The goal in 1997 was 12 percent renewable energy; the current goal is 20 percent.

2. As of 2005, it had reached only 7 percent.

3. Progress is uneven due to the whims of changing governments.

Section 2
Western Europe

myWorld Activity: Cradle to Grave?

Samples:

Pros of Cradle-to-Grave Systems

universal healthcare
free education
income for senior citizens

Cons of Cradle-to-Grave Systems

high taxes
people too dependent on government

Group Decision

Sample: We don't think cradle-to-grave systems are a good idea because the taxes to pay for such a system are too high and citizens don't take responsibility for themselves.

Enrichment: Sweden's Ice Hotel

1. Within the Arctic Circle, the sun does not rise for much of the winter.

2. By building a unique hotel and appealing to adventure-seekers, they convinced tourists to visit Sweden.

3. Posters should highlight the advantages of the Ice Hotel, and of visiting Sweden.

Section 2 Quiz

1. c   **2.** d   **3.** b   **4.** b   **5.** a

6. Samples:

An Example from the United Kingdom	An Example from Scandinavia	An Example From My Life in the United States
Indian food in restaurants	Turkish coffee in Copenhagen	Samples: Mexican and Chinese food; international music

Section 3
Western Europe

myWorld Activity: Make a Travel Poster

1. The shoes were a need; the game was a want. It is easier to live without games than without shoes.

2. Sample: No, ads often say we need something that is an extra. They are just trying to convince us to buy it.

3. Sample: The poster will appeal mostly to wants, although it might appeal to the need for relaxation or educational experiences.

4. Samples:

Landmarks churches, palaces, castles	Geographic Features mountains, beaches
Arts and Culture museums, concerts	Ways of Life good food, high fashion, soccer games

Enrichment: Technology of the Eiffel Tower

1. Huge pillars are needed to hold the weight of the enormous tower.

2. It would probably rust and fall apart.

3. 108 years; 2.189 million per year

Section 3 Quiz

1. a   **2.** b   **3.** c   **4.** d   **5.** d

6. Sample:

Country	Culture
Belgium	Divided into French-speaking and Dutch-speaking regions
France	Famous for its cuisine; Catholic but some Muslim immigrants; art museums
Germany	Music, art, poetry, films, literature
Netherlands	Much sea trade

Primary Source: A Sense of Identity

myWorld Activity: Seeing Both Sides

Pros common anthem, flag, laws, currency; right to vote and to stand for election

Cons too soon to think of Europe as a nation-state; too much history of conquest

1. Fontaine offers more pros and Kolakowski offers more cons.

2. Sample: Europeans should consider themselves as citizens of their own countries, because that is where their history lies.

Section 4
Western Europe

myWorld Activity: Southern Europe's Neighbors

Country of Southern Europe	Is it closer to Africa or Asia?	To which African or Asian country is it closest?	About how many miles apart are they at the nearest point?
Spain	Africa	Morocco	8
Italy	Africa	Tunisia	90
Greece	Asia	Turkey (part in Europe; part in Asia)	0; they share a border.

Draw Conclusions

Sample: Southern Europe might be more likely to have African or Asian immigrants than other regions of Europe.

Enrichment: Pablo Picasso

1. Some of his paintings depict Spanish culture and history.

2. Some of his art was influenced by African sculpture and masks.

3. Reports should state an opinion and give reasons. Sample reason: He experimented with many styles and influenced many other artists.

Section 4 Quiz

1. c **2.** d **3.** b **4.** c **5.** d

6. Modern democratic and republican governments and the ideal of protecting individual rights have their origins in ancient Greece and Rome. The languages of southern Europe are descended from ancient Latin and Greece. Architecture and art still remain from the classical civilizations.

Eastern Europe

See rubric on p. T118.

myWorld Chapter Activity: Open for Business

Students should use the Activity Cards, chapter text, and online information to support arguments for a particular country as the best location for their assigned business. Sample answers for café and gourmet market in Bosnia: **1.** Yes, Bosnia is a good location for a café and gourmet market. **2.** 30 percent **3.** My business can find very good produce and meat, which are important for a successful food business. It will also find customers in urban areas and near tourist attractions. **4.** There is some, but not much, corruption in Bosnia. Recent years of ethnic conflict have created some problems in the economy, but this is mostly improving. **Recommendation** I recommend Bosnia for the location of our café and gourmet market. After years of war, there is great demand for new businesses and places to gather.

Section 1
Eastern Europe

myWorld Activity: Hailstorm

Sample:

1. Glaciers carve out new landforms, such as ridges and hollows that become lakes.

2. In the south, summers are dry and hot while winters are mild. In the north, winters are very cold and summers are mild. In both parts of the region, mountains create extreme climates.

3. Environmental challenges include acid rain, pollution from coal burning, and problems linked to nuclear energy.

4. Protestants, Roman Catholics, Eastern Orthodox Christians

5. The southern part of the region, such as Bosnia, Albania, and parts of Ukraine, has been most influenced by Islam.

6. Sample: It is a region of great cultural diversity.

Enrichment: Geographic Contrasts

1. Prague

2. The latitudes are quite similar, but Sofia is at a much higher altitude. Tirana gets much more rain in winter and experiences warmer temperatures all year. Sofia gets more rain in summer and is cooler throughout.

3. Sofia: humid subtropical; Prague: continental cool summer; Tirana: Mediterranean; Bucharest: continental warm summer

Section 1 Quiz

1. d **2.** c **3.** a **4.** c **5.** d
6.

Landforms and Bodies of Water Landforms include Balkan Mountains, Balkan Peninsula, Carpathian Mountains, Dinaric Alps, Transylvanian Alps, Great Hungarian Plain, and Northern European Plain. Bodies of water include the Baltic Sea, Black Sea, Adriatic Sea, Dnieper River, Dneister River, Danube River, Oder River, and Vistula River.

Climate Mediterranean climate in south with dry, hot summers and rainy, cool winters; humid continental climate in center and north with very cold winters and mild summers; precipitation decreases from east to west.

Religious Groups Eastern Orthodox is dominant in Balkans, Ukraine, and Belarus. Catholicism is dominant in the center: Poland, Czech Republic, Slovakia, and Hungary. Protestantism is dominant in Estonia and Latvia. Islam is dominant in Bosnia, Albania, and Ukraine. Judaism has diminished since the Holocaust and WWII.

Resources and Environmental Challenges Crops: wheat, barley, citrus fruits, olives, grapes. Fossil fuels and metals: coal, iron ore. Challenges: limited oil and gas; water pollution and acid rain from industry

Case Study: Influence of Religion on Eastern European Cultures

myWorld Activity: Interfaith Celebration

Students' statements of appreciation should recognize positive qualities in the traditions of a particular faith. Sample statements:

Judaism I appreciate that Jewish people set aside everyday cares to gather one night a week for a special meal that celebrates spiritual matters.

Catholicism I appreciate that so many Polish Catholics devote time and energy to travel for religious reasons.

Festival Ideas Students' ideas should focus on the fact that all religions share a commitment to faith and ritual, even though specifics of both may vary. Ideas might include opportunities to educate others about these faiths and opportunities to exchange ideas and seek common ground about global issues.

Section 2
Eastern Europe

myWorld Activity: Press Conference

Questions and answers will vary but should reflect students' understanding of the major events and changes in Eastern Europe's history. Follow-up questions should show thoughtful analysis of how small details could affect a larger issue or policy. Sample response: **Big Question** How did the fall of the Soviet Union affect Ukraine, Belarus, and Moldova? **Answer** Since the fall of the Soviet Union, Ukraine has generally prospered politically and economically. Both Belarus and Moldova have struggled more since the end of Soviet rule. **Little Question** What kind of government followed in each country? **Answer** Ukraine has a stable and relatively strong democracy. Belarus has limited democracy. Moldova has a corrupt government that is struggling with civil conflict. **Paragraph** The news lead or memo opening should clearly state a main idea about conditions or events in Eastern Europe and then provide facts to support those conditions or events.

Enrichment: Jewish People of Eastern Europe

1. leaving home to live in another country
2. Jewish people left Eastern Europe to escape economic problems, discrimination, and death.
3. Letters will vary but should include factual reasons for emigrating, as well as hopes for economic prosperity and freedom from prejudice.

Section 2 Quiz

1. a **2.** a **3.** b **4.** c **5.** b
6. Answers in order of Country Groups, Changes in Government, and Changes for Business. Students choose one country.

Poland and the Baltic Nations

Poland quick transition to democracy and market economy under popular leader as first president **Baltic Nations** democratic governments and market economies

Poland increase in entrepreneurs and economic growth **Estonia** light industry helps economic growth **Latvia or Lithuania** cost of upgrading factories burdens economies.

Central Europe

Czechoslovakia divides peacefully into Czech Republic and Slovakia, both democratic **Hungary** strong democracy, market economy **Slovenia** democracy, market economy

Czech Republic modernizes quickly **Slovakia** struggles to expand industry **Hungary** economic burdens of debt from modernization **Slovenia** strong economy

Balkan Nations

Bulgaria, Romania, and Albania corrupt democracies, developing market economies **Former Yugoslavia** democratic; ethnic conflict led to ethnic cleansing, ethnic separation, and political instability

Bulgaria, Romania, and Albania poverty **Former Yugoslavia** slow privatization and lower standard of living

Ukraine, Belarus, Moldova

Ukraine sometimes corrupt government, market economy, complex business laws **Belarus** government control on market economy **Moldova** ongoing civil war

Ukraine slow business growth **Belarus** market economy limited **Moldova** slow economic progress

Conclusion Sample: Successful democracy supports greater economic growth

Primary Source: Ethnic Conflict in Bosnia

myWorld Activity: Identity Twister

Categories Sample answers: language, ethnicity, favorite activity, age, national citizenship, gender, religion **1.** I fit into all the categories except for ethnicity. I don't strongly identify with any ethnic group. **2.** When I fit into more than one group, I had to stretch into positions that twisted me around. **3.** In Eastern Europe, people have mostly used religion to organize categories. **4.** Tension between religious and national citizenship categories contributed to the Bosnian War. **5.** People want to find ways to distinguish themselves from others, so they choose to make some categories very important. Religion is very personal, so perhaps it feels especially important. **6.** Sample: Sometimes when I want to participate in a team or group that meets on my day of worship, I set aside my religious commitment in order to participate. I don't feel comfortable with this, but I don't see another practical solution. People have different days of worship and there is no way to avoid them all.

Russia

See rubric on p. T140.

myWorld Chapter Activity: Memo to Russia

Sample Analysis Table:

Challenge Card	Notes	Conclusion	Urgency 1 to 10
Pollution	Both air and water pollution	Risk to health	7
Poverty	Declining in recent years	Not as serious	2
Health	Poor life expectancy, much heart disease	Many Russians at risk	8
Int'l Partnerships	Sees NATO as threat	Could lead to conflict	6
Conflicts at Home and Abroad	Several conflicts inside and outside borders	Could start a war	10
Crime	Very high murder rate	High risk to Russian people	9

Set Priorities

Samples:
1. Conflicts at home and abroad
2. Crime
3. Health
4. Pollution
5. International partnerships
6. Poverty

Memo to Russia Student memos should list three priorites in order of urgency and give clear reasons for the ranking.

Section 1
Russia

myWorld Activity: Roam Across Russia

Samples:

Place to Visit in Russia	Why I Want to Go There	Order in Trip
Moscow	It is the capital.	1
St. Petersburg	It has beautiful buildings.	2
Vladivostok	It is a port in the Far East.	5
Lake Baikal	It is beautiful.	4
Murmansk	I want to see what it's like in the Arctic Circle.	3

Questions to Help Me Plan My Trip

Samples:
1. What do Russians in different regions eat?
2. What is the currency?
3. Do many people speak English?
4. Do cities have public transportation?

Enrichment: Climates Across Russia

1. Omsk
2. April and July
3. Moscow

Section 1 Quiz

1. d   **2.** c   **3.** c   **4.** b   **5.** c
6.

a. Lake Baikal	Asiatic
b. Higher population density	European
c. Capital city of Moscow	European
d. Mineral resources	Asiatic
e. Good farmland	European
f. Vast stretches of permafrost	Asiatic

Section 2
Russia

myWorld Activity: Make a Living Timeline

Samples:

Event	What Happened	When It Happened
Conversion to Eastern Orthodox Christianity	Vladimir converted all of Kiev.	Between 980 and 1015
Conquest by Golden Horde	The Mongols took Kiev.	1240
Michael Romanov became tsar.	Beginning of new dynasty that would last 300 years	1613
Worker unrest in 1905	An uprising that brought about limited democracy	1905

Enrichment: Josef Stalin

1. Sample: He caused starvation and pollution. He persecuted millions of people to keep control of power. He made enemies of other countries.

2. Sample: He wanted to convey how strong he was.

3. 1879 Born in Georgia
   1912 Joins Central Committee
   1924 Lenin dies; Stalin eliminates rivals.
   1928 Starts first Five-Year Plan
   1930s Persecutes opponents
   After 1945 Sets up communist governments in Eastern Europe
   1953 Dies

Section 2 Quiz

1. c   **2.** a   **3.** d   **4.** d   **5.** b
6.

Peter the Great	A tsar who tried to westernize Russia
Nicholas II	The tsar who was overthrown and killed in the revolution
Vladimir Lenin	The Bolshevik leader during the revolution
Boris Yeltsin	The first president of Russia after the Soviet Union dissolved

Primary Source:
The Russian Revolution

myWorld Activity: Revolutionary Language

Samples:

Examples of Emotional Language We may lose everything; you bloodthirsty beast; bloodsucker; you organized a terror.

Examples of Idealistic Language the true representatives of the interests of the people; the interests of the peasants, the interests of the starving; heaps of gold; a heavenly existence

Section 3
Russia

myWorld Activity: Quiz Yourself

Sample Questions:

1. Who became the leader of Russia after Yeltsin? (main idea) Vladimir Putin

2. What is the main cause of Russia's low life expectancy? (details) alcoholism

Enrichment: Russian Oil Exports

1. 2004

2. 2005, 2006

3. 13.9 percent

Section 3 Quiz

1. b   2. c   3. b   4. a   5. b

6. United States: The two countries are no longer enemies but do not trust each other. China: After decades of competition, the two countries recently signed a treaty of friendship.

Case Study:
The Soviet Industrial Legacy

myWorld Activity: City in a Dead Zone

1. The gas cloud passes over and trees die.

2. It damages human health. Healthy people who moved there eventually became sick.

3. The company admits that the plants emit sulfur dioxide.

Acknowledgments

The people who made up the **myWorld Geography** team—representing composition services; core design, digital, and multimedia production services; digital product development; editorial; editorial services; materials management; and production management—are listed below.

Leann Davis Alspaugh, Sarah Aubry, Deanna Babikian, Paul Blankman, Alyssa Boehm, Peter Brooks, Susan Brorein, Megan Burnett, Todd Christy, Neville Cole, Bob Craton, Michael Di Maria, Glenn Diedrich, Frederick Fellows, Jorgensen Fernandez, Thomas Ferreira, Patricia Fromkin, Andrea Golden, Mary Ann Gundersen, Christopher Harris, Susan Hersch, Paul Hughes, Judie Jozokos, John Kingston, Kate Koch, Stephanie Krol, Karen Lepri, Ann-Michelle Levangie, Salena LiBritz, Courtney Markham, Constance J. McCarty, Laurie McKenna, Anne McLaughlin, Rich McMahon, Mark O'Malley, Alison Muff, Jen Paley, Gabriela Perez Fiato, Judith Pinkham, Paul Ramos, Charlene Rimsa, Marcy Rose, Rashid Ross, Alexandra Sherman, Owen Shows, Melissa Shustyk, Jewel Simmons, Ted Smykal, Emily Soltanoff, Frank Tangredi, Simon Tuchman, Elizabeth Tustian, Merle Uuesoo, Alwyn Velasquez, Andrew White, Heather Wright

Maps

XNR Productions, Inc.

Illustration

Kerry Cashman, Marcos Chin, Dave Cockburn, Jeremy Mohler

Note: T page numbers below refer to teacher resource pages. Other page numbers refer to Western Hemisphere Student Edition pages.

Photography

TABLE OF CONTENTS: Pages vi–ix, **All,** Pearson Education, Inc.

EUROPE AND RUSSIA: Pages 372–377, **bkgrnd sky,** ImageSource/Getty Images; **373, All,** Pearson Education, Inc.; **Bkgrnd,** Vidler Vidler/Photolibrary; **374, TM,** Robert Zywucki/Shutterstock; **LT,** Roy Rainford/Robert Harding World Imagery; **375, M,** Pichugin Dmitry/Shutterstock; **376, T,** Hulton Archive/Getty Images; **B,** Jose Fuste Raga/Photolibrary; **377, All,** Pearson Education, Inc.

ANCIENT AND MEDIEVAL EUROPE: Pages 378–381, **All,** Pearson Education, Inc.; **382, LB,** HO/AFP/Getty Images/Newscom; **384–385, RB,** Jonothan Potter/Dorling Kindersley; **385, RB,** Peter Hayman/The British Museum/Dorling Kindersley; **RB,** Paul Harris/Dorling Kindersley; **386, M,** DEA/G. DAGLI ORTI/Getty; **RT,** Gianni Dagli Orti/Corbis; **387, RT,** Nick Nicholls/The British Museum/Dorling Kindersley; **388, LM,** Hoberman Collection/Corbis; **390, T,** Art Resource, NY; **B,** Picture Desk, Inc./Kobal Collection; **391, T,** The Trustees of The British Museum/Art Resource, NY; **B,** Alessandro Saffo/Grand Tour/Corbis; **T20,** Bettmann/Corbis; **392, L,** Réunion des Musées Nationaux/Art Resource, NY; **394, LT,** John Heseltine/Dorling Kindersley; **395, B,** Franck Guiziou/Hemis/Corbis; **397, RT,** PoodlesRock/Corbis; **398, T,** Bildarchiv Preussischer Kulturbesitz/Art Resource, NY; **B,** The Art Archive/Musée du Louvre Paris/Gianni Dagli Orti; **399,** Erich Lessing/Art Resource, NY; **400, LB,** Cameraphoto Arte, Venice/Art Resource, NY; **401, RB,** Museum of History of Sofia, Sofia, Bulgaria/Archives Charmet/Bridgeman Art Library; **403, RT,** Gianni Dagli Orti/Corbis All Rights Reserved; **405, RT,** Réunion des Musées Nationaux/Art Resource, NY; **406, T,** Art Resource, NY; **B,** Erich Lessing/Art Resource, NY; **407,** HIP/Art Resource, NY; **408, LB,** Geoff Dann/Dorling Kindersley; **409, RT,** Werner Forman/Art Resource, NY; **411, RB,** SIME s.a.s/eStock Photo; **412, L,** Bridgeman Art Library; **LB,** Bettmann/Corbis; **413, RB,** Snark/Art Resource, NY; **414, M,** Bettmann/Corbis; **LB,** *The Dance Macabre* (detail, 1485), Artist unknown. Fresco. L'Oratorio dei Disciplini/Superstock; **LT,** Frank Greenaway/Dorling Kindersley; **L,** maxstockphoto/Shutterstock.

EUROPE IN MODERN TIMES: Pages 418–421, **All,** Pearson Education, Inc.; **T48,** Alinari Archives/Corbis; **422,** Philip Gatward/Dorling Kindersley; **423, RM,** *The Last Supper* (1495–1498), Leonardo da Vinci. Fresco. Santa Maria della Grazie, Milan/A.K.G., Berlin/SuperStock; **RB,** Dorling Kindersley; **424, LT,** Ellen Howdon/Dorling Kindersley, Courtesy of Glasgow Museum; **T,** FPG/Getty Images; **RT,** Pearson Education, Inc.; **425, M,** Dorling Kindersley; **RB,** Adrea Pistolesi/Getty Images; **428, BM,** *Portrait of Henry VIII* (16th century), Hans Holbein the Younger, Oil on canvas. Belvoir Castle, Leicestershire. The Bridgeman Art Library Ltd.; **LB,** *Portrait of Catherine of Aragon (1485–1536), 1st Queen of Henry VIII* (1825), from "Memoirs of the Court of Queen Elizabeth," Watercolor and gouache on paper. Private Collection/The Bridgeman Art Library; **430, RB,** Scala/Art Resource, NY; **430, RT,** The Granger Collection, New York; **431, RT,** Scala/Art Resource, NY; **431, RB,** Alinari Archives/Corbis; **432, Bkgrnd,** Joel W. Rogers/Corbis; **433, RT,** Reuters New Media Inc./Corbis; **BM,** James Stevenson/Dorling Kindersley, Courtesy of the National Maritime Museum, London; **RB,** Clive Streeter/Dorling Kindersley, Courtesy of The Science Museum, London;

LT, Dorling Kindersley; **434, LB,** *Padshahnama: Europeans Bring Gifts to the Shah Jahan.* The Royal Collection, Her Majesty Queen Elizabeth II; **435, RT,** Chas Howson/The British Museum/Dorling Kindersley; **436, LB,** Erich Lessing/Art Resource, NY; **437, RM,** *Louis XIV, King of France (1701),* Hyacinthe Rigaud. Oil on canvas, 277 x 194 cm. Louvre, Paris, France. Photo: Herve Lewandowski. Louvre, Paris, France. Réunion des Musées Nationaux/Art Resource, NY; **438, LB,** Martin Jones/Corbis; **439, LT,** The Granger Collection, New York; **T,** Shutterstock; **441, RB,** Reduced model of a guillotine (18th century), French School, Wood & metal. Musée de la Ville de Paris, Musée Carnavalet, Paris, France, Giraudon/Bridgeman Art Library; **RT,** Getty Images/De Agostini Editore Picture Library; **BM,** Musée de la Révolution Française, Vizille, France/The Bridgeman Art Library; **442, TM,** Lebrecht Music & Arts Photo Library; **RT,** The Francis Frith Collection/Corbis; **443, RT,** Underwood & Underwood/Corbis; **LT,** Musée National de l'Education, Rouen, France/The Bridgeman Art Library; **444, B,** Bettmann/Corbis; **446, LB,** Hulton-Deutsch Collection/Corbis; **447, RB,** Dorling Kindersley; **448, LT,** Andy Crawford/Dorling Kindersley/Imperial War Museum, London; **449,** PhotoDisc/Getty Images; **450, RT,** PhotoDisc/Getty Images; **450, RB,** Hulton Deutsch Collection/Corbis; **451, B,** Bernard Bisson/Sygma/Corbis; **452, B,** Bettmann/Corbis; **453, RT,** U.S. Navy/Photo Researchers, Inc.; **454, RB,** AP Images; **B,** Bettmann/Corbis; **456, BM,** Bettmann/Corbis; **LB,** Bettmann/Corbis; **457, L,** The Punch Cartoon Library; **R,** Str Old/Reuters; **458, T,** Peter Dejong/AP Images; **LT,** Peter Dench/Corbis; **459, T,** Dorling Kindersley; **460, RT,** Popperfoto/Getty Images; **RB,** *Portrait of Lajos Kossuth (1802–1894) at the Chain Bridge in Budapest, 1849* (19th century), Hungarian School, Coloured engraving. Hadtörténeti Muzeum, Budapest, Hungary, Archives Charmet/The Bridgeman Art Library; **461, RT,** Liba Taylor/Corbis; **461, B,** Peter Turnley/Corbis.

WESTERN EUROPE: Pages 464–467, **All,** Pearson Education, Inc.; **468, Bkgrnd,** Sylvain Grandadam/age Fotostock; **B,** J. D. Heaton/age Fotostock; **470, RM,** iStockphoto.com; **M,** Dhoxax/Shutterstock; **T,** Pierre Jacques/Hemis/Corbis; **M,** Bo Zaunders/Corbis; **RB,** Rick Price/Corbis; **RB,** Gavin Hellier/Robert Harding World; **473, B,** Lawson Wood/Corbis; **RM,** Simon Fraser/Photo Researchers, Inc.; **476,** Davide Erbetta/Grand Tour/Corbis; **477, T,** Aneese/Dreamstime.com; British Touring Car, Eleanor Bentall/Corbis; **479,** Ethanol Fuel, Car Culture/Corbis; **480,** Dallas and John Heaton/Stock Connection; **483, M,** Pearson Education, Inc.; **RB,** Erik Svensson and Jeppe Wikstrom/Dorling Kindersley; **R,** David Lomax/Robert Harding/Getty Images; **484,** Annie Griffiths Belt/Corbis; **485,** Ken Straiton/Corbis; **T104,** Alija /istockphoto.com; **486, LB,** Patrick Müller © Centre des monuments nationaux, Paris; **487, T,** Britta Jaschinski/Dorling Kindersley; **B,** Prentice Hall School; **RB,** Le Segretain Pascal/Corbis Sygma; **RM,** Perrush/Shutterstock; **488,** Cristophe Ena/AP Photo; **489,** Bjorn Svensson/Photolibrary; **490,** George Hammerstein/Solus-Veer/Corbis; **491,** Fancy/Veer/Corbis; **492, T,** Pearson Education, Inc.; **B,** LWA-Dann Tardif/Corbis; **493, T,** Ean Christophe Verhaegan/AFI images; **B,** Ullstein-CARO/Peter Arnold Inc.; **494,** Dorling Kindersley; **495,** Pearson Education, Inc.; **RM,** Bob Sacha/Corbis; **RB,** iStockphoto.com; **496,** Massimo Borchi/Corbis; **498, RB,** Reuters/Susana Vera (SPAIN); **499,** George Christakis/epa/Corbis.

EASTERN EUROPE: Pages 502–505, **All,** Pearson Education, Inc.; **506, Bkgrnd,** Erich Lessing/Magnum Photos, Inc.; **LB,** Stefano Pensotti/age Fotostock; **508, LB,** Per Karlsson-BKWine.com/Alamy; **LB,** Jaroslaw Grudzinski/Shutterstock; **509, M,** Dean Conger/Corbis; **B,** AFP/Getty Images; **510, RB,** Zaichiki/Alamy; **RB,** Reuters/Vasily Fedosenko; **RM,** David Veis/AP Photo/CTK; **LM,** iStockphoto.com; **LB,** Photoshot Holdings Ltd./Alamy; **511,** Stan Kujawa/Alamy; **513, TM,** Idealink Photography/Alamy; **RT,** ziontek/Dabrowski-KPA/Zuma Press, © 2004 by Wziontek/Dabrowski-KPA (Newscom TagID: zumaphotos661194) [Photo via Newscom]; **LT,** Hidajet Delic/AP Photo; **LT,** Martin Bureau/AFP/Getty Images; **515, RT,** Wojtek Buss/age Fotostock; **RB,** Pegaz/Alamy; **L,** James L. Stanfield/National Geographic/Getty Images; **516,** Reuters Photographer/Reuters; **517,** AFP photo/Milan/Radulovic; **T132,** Library of Congress; **518, LB,** Steven May/Alamy; **519, RB,** imagebroker/Alamy; **520, B,** Petr Josek Snr/Reuters; **521, B,** Carlos Nieto/age Fotostock; **523, B,** Getty Images/De Agostini Editore Picture Library; **524, RT,** Viktor Drachev/AFP/Getty Images; **525, LT,** East News/Getty Images; **RT,** AFP Photo/Daniel Mihailescu/Newscom; **526, RB,** Frederic Hugon/AFP/Getty Images/Newscom; **RT,** Antoine Gyori/Corbis Sygma; **527, B,** Brauchli David/Corbis Sygma.

RUSSIA: Pages 530–533, **All,** Pearson Education, Inc.; **534, Bkgrnd,** Sergey Yakovlev/Shutterstock; **LB,** David Turnley/Corbis; **536, R,** isoft/iStockphoto.com; **M,** Dean Conger/Corbis; **L,** Superstock; **537,** Gerd Ludwig/Corbis; **538,** Sovfoto/Eastfoto; **541, R,** Gideon Mendel/Corbis; **L,** Pearson Education, Inc.; **T152,** Bettmann/Corbis; **542, L,** Werner Forman/Art Resource, NY; **R,** Erich Lessing/Art Resource, NY; **543, L,** Jeremy Horner/Corbis; **R,** *Ivan the Terrible* (20th century), English School, Gouache on paper. Private Collection/© Look and Learn/The

Bridgeman Art Library; **544, L,** The Art Gallery Collection/Alamy; **R,** The Granger Collection, New York; **545, LB,** David South/Alamy; **LT,** The Gallery Collection/Corbis; **RB,** Réunion des Musées Nationaux/Art Resource, NY; **546,** Photos 12/Alamy; **547,** Charles & Josette Lenars/Corbis; **548, L,** Gianni Giansanti/Sygma/Corbis; **R,** Peter Turnley/Corbis; **550 RB,** Hulton-Deutsch Collection/Corbis; **RT,** Scheufler Collection/Corbis; **551, RB,** Fabian Cevallos/Corbis Sygma; **RM,** Darryl Sleath/Shutterstock; **RT,** Krasowit/Shutterstock; **552,** Iain Masterton/Alamy Images; **553, L,** Peter Turnley/Corbis; **R,** AntonioDiaz/Shutterstock; **554,** Vasily Fedosenko/Reuters/Corbis; **555,** Lystseva Marina/ITAR-TASS Photo/Corbis; **557,** Gleb Garanich/Reuters/Corbis; **558, RB,** Bettmann/Corbis; **559, RT,** The Art Archive/Private Collection/Marc Charmet; **560, LB,** Sergei Karpukhin/Reuters; **ML,** Gerd Ludwig/Reuters; **RB,** David Tunley/Corbis; **561,** Sysoyev Grigory/ITAR-TASS/Corbis.

EUROPE AND RUSSIA UNIT CLOSER: Page 564, B, Shutterstock; **LB,** Shutterstock; **RT,** Shutterstock; **RT,** Shutterstock; **564–565, Bkgrnd,** Shutterstock; **565, R,** European Communities, 1995–2009; **R,** Shutterstock.

Text

Grateful acknowledgment is made to the following for copyrighted material:

Page 396 National Council of Churches of Christ in America "Acts 16:4-10" from *The New Revised Standard Version of the Bible.* Copyright © 1989 the National Council of Churches of Christ in the USA. All rights reserved. Used by permission.

Page T31 National Council of Churches of Christ in America "Proverbs 31—Ode to a Capable Wife" from *The New Revised Standard Version of the Bible.* Copyright © 1989 the National Council of Churches of Christ in the USA. All rights reserved. Used by permission.

Page 406 "Hildegard to Odo Soissons" from *Selected Writings* by Hildegard of Bingen, translated with an introduction and notes by Mark Atherton (Penguin Classics, 2001). Translation and editorial matter copyright © Mark Atherton 2001. Used by permission.

Page 456 Address at the Institute of Contemporary Arts, London; quoted in *The Independent, March 22, 1990.*

Page 524 "What Language is Spoken in Ukraine?" from *http://www.wumag. kiev.ua/index2.php?param=pgs20032l72.*

Page 558 Excerpt from "Russia Close-Up: Overcoming Soviet Industrial Legacy," from *Russia Today, July 29, 2007.*

Page 561 Excerpt from "Russia Rising," by Fen Montaigne, from *National Geographic, November 2001.* Copyright © National Geographic Society.

Note: Every effort has been made to locate the copyright owner of material reproduced in this publication. Omissions brought to our attention will be corrected in subsequent editions.